Pro Visual Studio LightSwitch 2011 Development

Tim Leung and Yann Duran

Apress®

Pro Visual Studio LightSwitch 2011 Development

ISBN-13 (pbk): 978-1-4302-4008-2

ISBN-13 (electronic): 978-1-4302-4009-9

President and Publisher: Paul Manning
Lead Editor: Tom Welsh
Technical Reviewer: John Rivard and Jeff Sanders
Editorial Board: Steve Anglin, Mark Beckner, Ewan Buckingham, Gary Cornell, Louise Corrigan, Morgan Ertel, Jonathan Gennick, Jonathan Hassell, Robert Hutchinson, Michelle Lowman, James Markham, Matthew Moodie, Jeff Olson, Jeffrey Pepper, Douglas Pundick, Ben Renow-Clarke, Dominic Shakeshaft, Gwenan Spearing, Matt Wade, Tom Welsh
Coordinating Editor: Tracy Brown
Copy Editors: Sharon Wilkey and Mary Bearden
Compositor: Bytheway Publishing Services
Indexer: SPI Global
Artist: SPI Global
Cover Designer: Anna Ishchenko

Distributed to the book trade worldwide by Springer Scie nce+Business Media New York, 233 Spring Street, 6th Floor, New York, NY 10013. Phone 1-800-SPRINGER, fax (201) 348-4505, email orders-ny@springer-sbm.com, or visit www.springeronline.com.

For information on translations, please email rights@apress.com, or visit www.apress.com.

Apress and friends of ED book s may be purchased in bulk f or academic, corporate, or promo tional use. eBoo k versions and licenses are also available for most title s. For more information, reference our Special Bulk Sales and eBook Licensing web page at www.apress.com/bulk-sales.

Any source code or other supplementary materials referenced by the author i n this text is av ailable to re aders at www.apress.com. For detailed inf ormation about how to lo cate your book's source code, go to www.apress.com/source-code/.

Contents at a Glance

Contents

About the Authors

 **Tim Leung** is a professional software developer based in England. For the past 12 years, he has specialized in enterprise application development using products from the Microsoft technology stack. In particular, he possesses deep knowledge of the Microsoft .NET Framework and SQL Server. He is an active member of the UK developer community and often delivers presentations on technical topics. He is also a chartered member of the British Computer Society. Tim is passionate about the concept of rapid application development and was awarded the Microsoft Community Contributor Award in 2011 for contributions to the LightSwitch community.

 **Yann Duran** is a self-employed, self-taught software developer, based in Australia, who has been involved in writing software, in one form or another, for over 25 years. He started with hand-assembling Z80 assembly code on his Tandy Model 16 computer (dual 8-inch disk drives, 64KB RAM) in the early 80s, and then taught himself a raft of software technologies in the following years. These included Turbo Pascal, MS Access (VBA), SQL Server (T-SQL), VB.NET, WinForms, Entity Framework (EF), Windows Presentation Foundation (WPF), and finally LightSwitch. Yann has been passionate about programming since he was in high school, in the days before the PC arrived, when "computers" were actually programmable calculators with punch cards and magnetic strips, and huge mainframes. He has also worked in computer sales, delivering software seminars and IT support, but programming has always remained his passion. Yann has been active in the LightSwitch community since Beta 1, and was awarded the Microsoft Community Contributor Award in 2011 for his contributions to that community.

About the Technical Reviewers

■ **John Rivard** is a software design engineer for Microsoft Visual Studio. Over his career, he has worked on a variety of developer tools including Visual FoxPro, Visual Basic .NET, the .NET Framework, and Silverlight. John is the architect for Visual Studio LightSwitch, a model-based development tool for creating business applications quickly and easily for the desktop and the cloud. John started at Microsoft Corporation in 1991 and is a graduate of the University of Washington in computer engineering.

■ **Jeff Sanders** is a published author, technical editor, and accomplished technologist. He is currently a group manager/senior architect at Avanade.

Jeff has years of professional experience in the field of IT and strategic business consulting, leading both sales and delivery efforts. He regularly contributes to certification and product roadmap development with Microsoft, and speaks publicly on Microsoft enterprise technologies. With his roots in software development, Jeff's areas of expertise include collaboration and content management solutions, operational intelligence, digital marketing, distributed component-based application architectures, object-oriented analysis and design, and enterprise integration patterns and designs.

Jeff is also the CTO of DynamicShift, a client-focused organization specializing in Microsoft technologies, specifically Office365/BPOS, SharePoint Server, StreamInsight, Windows Azure, AppFabric, Business Activity Monitoring, BizTalk Server, and .NET. He is a Microsoft Certified Trainer and leads DynamicShift in both training and consulting efforts.

He enjoys non-work-related travel, spending time with his wife and daughter, and wishes he had more time for both. He may be reached at jeff.sanders@dynamicshift.com.

Acknowledgments

Writing a book is an enormous task. It can easily take over your whole life and suck up every waking minute of your time. It really ought to come with a health warning! Putting this book together wouldn't have been possible without the help of many people, to whom we are very grateful.

First, we'd like to thank everyone who has helped or supported us throughout this process. It's impossible to name everyone, because we've been in touch with so many people. If we've left you out, it's not because we're not grateful!

At Apress, we'd like to say a special thanks to Tom Welsh, our development editor. Tom has been the first port of call for any issues that we've had and has done a fantastic job in looking after us. We're also grateful to our coordinating editors Annie Beck and Tracy Brown for all the assistance that they've given us. Last but not least, our acquisitions editor Jonathan Hassell deserves a special mention because this book would not have been possible without him.

In writing this book, we've had the privilege of working with some of the greatest minds at Microsoft. In particular, our technical reviewer John Rivard has been a real inspiration and has given us valuable insight into the product. We also want to thank Beth Massi and Doug Rosen for all the help and assistance that they've given us. We'd like to acknowledge everyone in the LightSwitch team, particularly those who have contributed articles to the LightSwitch community. These include (but are not limited to) Sheel Shah, Andy Kung, and Eric Erhardt.

Finally, we'd like to thank friends and family for all their patience and for putting up with us during the project.

Foreword

All businesses use software to automate their business functions. At their heart, such applications are about gathering, storing, and processing data, and so could perform tasks that we typically consider under the rubric of *business applications*—for example, tracking finances or assets (as in ERP software). But it also includes the process of software development, systems management, or anything else involving data. There is a lot of this business software out there, a lot more being written, and even more that people wish they had the time, budget, and skill to write.

Building such software involves two concerns: the business problem to be solved (the domain) and the technology into which a solution is rendered. First you have to have one person who understands both the domain and the technology necessary to render it into software, or you have to have a team with a mix of skills. That's enough to kill many small projects.

Assuming you can get the right people together, the technologist then spends a great deal of time on issues that have nothing to do with the business problem being solved, including UI, protocols, business logic mechanisms, security, integration with Microsoft Office, and much, much more. One needs a good deal of skill, time, inclination, and budget to get a project accomplished.

To help people write business applications faster, we wrote Microsoft Visual Studio LightSwitch, the simplest way for developers of all skill levels to develop business applications for the desktop and cloud. Using LightSwitch, the core technical problems are solved, and a lot of projects—which without LightSwitch would have never seen the light of day—are now in production.

Pro Visual Studio LightSwitch 2011 Development provides a conceptual and practical introduction to many core LightSwitch building blocks, including importing and defining data schema, designing queries and screens, validating data, authenticating and authorizing application users, and deploying the final product.

However, the challenge with rapid application development environments is that they're great at solving the problems they anticipated, but what if you need to do more? Happily, LightSwitch was designed without the glass ceiling that constrains the tools of the 4GL generation, so the full power of Visual Studio is available to you if you want it—the limit is your imagination.

Tim and Yann have a lot of imagination, and they have explored many ways to supplement LightSwitch in this book. They offer solutions for a number of problems that LightSwitch does not address but that you may encounter as you write your applications. Theirs is a cookbook. Some recipes won't have ingredients you like, some you'll season to fit your taste, some will open possibilities you hadn't even considered, and some you'll use as is. A sampling includes sending email, creating reports, and implementing auditing.

They share a passion with the LightSwitch team and with their readers: to build great business applications, fast. Together we can make businesses more successful through software.

Steve Anonsen, Distinguished Engineer, Microsoft Visual Studio
John Rivard, Partner Software Design Engineer, Microsoft Visual Studio

Introduction

We've designed this book to show you how to write professional applications using Microsoft LightSwitch.

As software developers, we understand how difficult it is to develop software in real life. End users expect their applications to be reliable, functional, and polished. They'll also have preferences in terms of how they want their application to look and feel.

To help you meet these real-life expectations, we've focused this book on many of the typical scenarios that customers or clients will ask of you. For example, we'll show you how to perform various tasks that are not natively supported. These include creating reports, sending email, and working with data in nonstandard ways.

To make life easy for you, LightSwitch hides away much of what it does. This is great when you're a beginner. But if you need to create some advanced applications or if you just happen to be curious, this can soon become a hindrance. To help you as much as possible, we've tried to focus on the following:

- Describing what LightSwitch does beneath the surface

- Showing you where and how to write code in LightSwitch

If you come from the following background, you'll be sure to get the most out of this book:

- You have some programming experience, either with .NET or some other programming language environment.

- You have a basic understanding of database concepts such as tables, columns, and data types.

- You've installed LightSwitch and have spent some time familiarizing yourself with the development environment.

However, don't worry if you don't meet the exact profile that we've just described. We'll now guide you through a few of the basics to get you started.

Understanding the Basics

Although we've targeted this book at those with some development experience, don't worry if you're only just starting out. The book explains everything that you need to know.

But if you want to ground yourself a bit more in the basics, we recommend that you visit the LightSwitch Developer Center at the following URL:

```
http://msdn.microsoft.com/en-us/lightswitch/ff796201
```

Through the developer center, you'll find the latest news on LightSwitch as well as links to the MSDN help and forums. You'll also find links to a series of *how to* videos that we highly recommend. The star behind these videos is Beth Massi, and she has kindly spoken to us about her role as the LightSwitch community manager.

A Word from the LightSwitch Community Manager

My name is Beth Massi and I'm currently the community manager for the Visual Studio LightSwitch Team at Microsoft. My professional programming career started in the 1990s using Clipper and FoxPro to build information systems for the health-care industry. I remember back then, just out of college, how these rapid application development (RAD) languages and tools made it so much easier to build database applications for businesses, especially over the alternatives at the time. I also remember how helpful the community was for newbies like me. There was always a feeling of "no question is a stupid question" on the forums, and almost everyone was excited and welcoming to me. Because of my passion for these RAD tools and the closeness of that community, I built many valuable relationships that took my career to the next level. I started to give back by writing and building free application frameworks and then eventually speaking at user groups and conferences. As the years flew by, I moved to VB.NET and Visual Studio and brought the same passion for the developer community with me, which helped me get my first Solutions Architect MVP award in 2005.

After being an MVP for a few years, Microsoft approached me to help them with the Visual Basic developer community. I couldn't pass up the opportunity to be a part of the community as an official Microsoft employee. I produced hundreds of articles and videos and delivered presentations all over the world. I've met many types of developers doing many interesting things and have helped people troubleshoot many interesting problems. Microsoft has given me the ability to reach the entire world, and I will always appreciate that.

Even before the first beta of Visual Studio LightSwitch was available, internally I was begging to be part of the LightSwitch team. I wanted to use the successes I had with the Visual Basic community to help kick-start a new community on one of the most RAD development environments I had seen come from Microsoft in a very long time—especially one that focused on building business applications. I felt the nostalgia of the old dBase community I started from and wanted to foster a similar vibe. So when the first beta for Visual Studio LightSwitch was released at the end of 2010, I had the opportunity to become the community manager for the team and I jumped on it.

First order of business was to create a slew of training content and erect a web site on MSDN called the LightSwitch Developer Center (`http://msdn.com/LightSwitch`). This is your one-stop-shop for videos, articles, samples, starter kits, and much more to get you productive quickly. The site continues to grow as we build more content every week. If you are new to LightSwitch, I encourage you to visit the learning center Getting Started section (`http://bit.ly/LearnLightSwitch`) as well as the How Do I videos (`http://bit.ly/LightSwitchVideos`). From the LightSwitch Developer Center, you can easily get to our forums (`http://bit.ly/LightSwitchForums`), where we have an active community helping answer questions with LightSwitch team members. You can also see the latest blogs on the home page from our LightSwitch bloggers, including the LightSwitch Team (`http://blogs.msdn.com/LightSwitch`) and myself (`www.BethMassi.com`). Finally, I encourage you to join the conversation on Twitter (`@VSLightSwitch`) as well as our Facebook page (`facebook.com/VSLightSwitch`) and let us know what you think!

I am confident that the LightSwitch community will continue to grow and that I will see newbies become MVPs just as I did so many years ago. I couldn't be happier to help nurture the community in the goodness that is Visual Studio LightSwitch. Enjoy!

Where to Download LightSwitch

To get started, you'll need to download and install LightSwitch. You can download a free 90-day trial by following the link at the developer center. On the download page, you'll have a choice of downloading a web installer (3.7MB) or the full LightSwitch CD in ISO format (577MB). The web installer detects the components that are installed on your machine and installs only the additional components that are needed.

The full ISO download is ideal if you want to install LightSwitch on multiple machines, or if you suspect that you'll need to reinstall LightSwitch at some point in the future.

If Visual Studio 2010 is already installed on your computer, LightSwitch integrates itself into your existing Visual Studio 2010 installation. If not, LightSwitch installs itself as a stand-alone product.

When you're ready to purchase LightSwitch, you can do so by clicking Help ä Register Visual Studio 2011 from within LightSwitch. This opens a dialog box displaying a button that takes you to the Microsoft Store, enabling you to purchase LightSwitch. You'll receive a product key at the end of the process.

You can then convert your trial version into the full version by entering your product key.

System Requirements

To create applications by using LightSwitch, your development computer needs to meet the following specifications.

The operating system requirements are as follows:

- Windows 7 (x86 and x64)
- Windows Vista (x86 and x64) with Service Pack 2—all editions except Starter Edition
- Windows XP (x86) with Service Pack 3—all editions except Starter Edition
- Windows Server 2008 R2 (x64)—all editions
- Windows Server 2008 (x86 and x64) with Service Pack 2—all editions
- Windows Server 2003 R2 (x86 and x64)—all editions
- Windows Server 2003 (x86 and x64) with Service Pack 2 (Users will need to install MSXML 6, if it is not already present.)

The hardware requirements are as follows:

- Computer with a 1.6GHz or faster processor
- 1024MB RAM (1.5GB if running in a virtual machine)
- 3GB of available hard-disk space
- 5400RPM hard drive
- DirectX 9–capable video card running at 1024×768 or higher-resolution display

How This Book Is Structured

The book is divided into six main parts:

- Part 1: LightSwitch Concepts
- Part 2: Working with Data
- Part 3: Interacting with Data
- Part 4: Getting Data Out
- Part 5: Securing Your Application
- Part 6: Deployment

In the first part, we describe the architecture behind LightSwitch and explain the parts that make up a LightSwitch application.

Part 2 focuses on data. We show you how to design tables, write queries, access data via code, and how to validate your data.

Part 3 shows you how to use RIA Services to perform more-sophisticated tasks using data. It also introduces the screen designer and explains that you're not just limited to the controls that LightSwitch provides. The custom controls chapter shows you how to go beyond the controls that are natively provided. We also show you how to reuse code by creating extensions.

In part 4, we show you how to create reports and how to send emails.

Part 5 explains how to restrict what your users can or can't do in your application. We also show you how to audit the activity that takes place in your application.

Part 6 shows you how to deploy your application. It also includes a troubleshooting section that shows you what to do when things go wrong.

Conventions

The following sections describe conventions used throughout this book.

Examples

To give this book a bit of real-life feel, we've based many of our examples on a fictional company. This company specializes in selling healthy organic snacks through the Web.

The snacks are delivered by mail, and the business model works by means of subscription. There are three types of subscription (bronze, silver, gold), and these are priced on a monthly basis. Each subscription type entitles you to a number of free snacks per month, and higher-level subscriptions entitle you to receive more food packages and a greater variety of food.

The company has embraced LightSwitch and has started using it throughout all parts of the business.

The office workers use an application called *OfficeCentral*. This application supports the activities that take place in the office and includes features such as the following:

- Timesheet

- Expenses

- Project codes

- Holiday request tracking

- Purchase order tracking

- Invoice tracking

- Asset tracking

- Accident report book

- Staff home contact details

The staff responsible for shipping the deliveries works from a warehouse and uses an application called *ShipperCentral*. This application enables workers to view and amend orders, delivery details, and customer details.

The management uses an application called *AdminCentral*. This application supports the managerial side of the business and allows managers to keep an eye on *churn* rates, subscription cancellations, and revenues. One of the business objectives is to encourage bronze customers to upgrade to silver or gold packages, and the application helps management meet this objective. It contains features for generating mailshots to lapsed subscribers and for generating a targeted email marketing campaign.

As you might appreciate, LightSwitch is a perfect tool for handling most of these scenarios. In fact, the preceding ideas might also give you some inspiration as to how you could incorporate LightSwitch in your own organization.

In many of the examples, we've used tables such as Employee, Customer, and Orders. We've chosen these types of tables because such data structures are fairly self-explanatory. For example, each customer is associated with one or more orders, and the typical data that you'd store for a customer would include first name, surname, and address details.

Code

C# and VB.NET are the languages that are supported by LightSwitch. Throughout this book, you'll find code samples in both languages.

LightSwitch tries to remove much of the complexity that goes with writing an application. In the LightSwitch designer (in the screen and query designers, for example), you'll find a Write Code button that allows you to handle various LightSwitch events. When you click this button, LightSwitch opens the code editor window and allows you to start writing code.

Because LightSwitch tries to make this as simple as possible, the location of the file that you're working on isn't always obvious. To clarify the code that we're describing, we've added a file location at the start of most code listings. Listing 1 shows a typical code listing.

Listing 1. *Hello World Example*

```
VB:
```

```
File: ShipperCentral\Server\UserCode\ApplicationData.vb
```

```
'REM VB Code appears here
```

```
C#:
```

```
File: ShipperCentral\Server\UserCode\ApplicationData.cs
```

```
//REM C# Code appears here
```

For both the VB and C# examples, the File heading specifies the file name and path. In this example, ShipperCentral refers to the project name. This would relate to the name of your LightSwitch project. The name Server refers to a subfolder called Server. This folder contains the contents of the Server project. You'll find out what this project does in Chapter 2, and learn more about the other projects that you'll find, such as Client and Common. Finally, UserCode is a subfolder, and ApplicationData.vb/ApplicationData.cs refers to the name of the VB or C# file inside the folder.

Terminology

If you're a database professional, you'll be familiar with the terms *table*, *row*, and *column*. SharePoint developers work with lists and list items. The LightSwitch IDE refers to *tables* for SQL data sources, and *lists* for SharePoint data sources. But when you're working in code, LightSwitch refers to both of these objects *as entity sets*.

There are several ways that you can express the same thing in LightSwitch. In most cases, we've tried to use the names that are exposed by the LightSwitch API. However, the context of a sentence sometimes makes it confusing to adhere to a single naming convention. For example, LightSwitch uses the word *property* to refer to the *fields* that are added to a table (a customer surname property, for example). When you're working in code, it's often hard to distinguish between a user-defined property and a property that's generated by LightSwitch. It can also become confusing once you begin talking about properties of properties.

Therefore, we've occasionally used these terms interchangeably. To avoid any confusion, Table 1 provides a translation of words that are used to refer to the same thing.

Table 1. Translation of Terms Used to Describe Data

LightSwitch	SQL Server	SharePoint
Entity set	Table	List
Entity type	Column data type	Field type
Entity object	Row	List item
Property	Field	Field

Tips/Notes/Cautions

Throughout this book, we've included various tips and notes to help you along your way. If there's anything important that might cause damage, we've added the details into a caution section to help you.

Comments and Errata

Although we've tried hard to be accurate, mistakes do sometimes happen, particularly with a book of this size. If you have any feedback or want to report any bugs, please visit the official page for this book on the Apress web site:

http://www.apress.com/microsoft/net-framework/9781430240082

This page will also show you any errata, mistakes that have been discovered after publication.

PART 1

LightSwitch Concepts

CHAPTER 1

Forms Over Data and Beyond

If you've ever gone skydiving, you'll recognize that using Microsoft Visual Studio LightSwitch is much like a skydiving experience.

As you jump from the airplane at 10,000 feet, you'd see a magnificent view of countryside, cities, and towns linked together by roads, railways, and other pieces of infrastructure. A high-level view of LightSwitch is rather like that. It consists of several large pieces that are all interconnected and synchronized together.

Of course, jumping from an airplane can be scary and so too can using LightSwitch, particularly if you start to push toward the technical limitations of the product. Although this book doesn't provide a cure for vertigo, we hope that the contents will at least alleviate any fears of LightSwitch that you may have and help you get the most out of your development experience.

As we descend from that 10,000-foot view, we can see some more ways in which LightSwitch is like skydiving. Writing LightSwitch applications can be very fast. It can also be a lot of fun because you don't have to worry about writing the boring, repetitive boilerplate code you seem to have to write in other applications.

When we finally hit the ground (we hope, as lightly as a feather), you can look back on the experience and appreciate the thrill of what has just happened. We hope that with the help of this book, your journey into the advanced LightSwitch development adventure will be just as exciting.

Who Is LightSwitch For?

According to Microsoft, LightSwitch provides the "easiest way to build data centric applications for the desktop or cloud." This focus on ease of use means that LightSwitch is often labeled as a tool for nondevelopers. But according to the architects behind the product, LightSwitch was never designed as a tool for nondevelopers. It was designed for an audience that Microsoft calls "breadth professional developers." This group describes practical people with wide technical skills who look to technology to solve specific problems.

Since LightSwitch's release, it's attracted a wide audience of people from many different backgrounds and varying abilities.

During the early beta-1 days, LightSwitch was initially thought of as a natural successor to Access, kind of "Access.NET," or even a "Microsoft Access for the web" as it were. Grouping LightSwitch and Access together was a natural association for many developers, because both products are data-centric rapid application development (RAD) tools. Because of these similarities, many Access developers are converting to LightSwitch. Many developers with experience in FoxPro and Excel/VBA are also using LightSwitch for the same reason.

Meanwhile, information technology (IT) departments and decision makers have found that LightSwitch provides the perfect tool for *power users*, and they have encouraged this group of users to turn to LightSwitch. Power users are highly intelligent individuals who've not selected IT as their chosen career path but are experts in some other business domain. However, they've found themselves developing applications to help perform their main job function.

Because these individuals haven't been trained to program computers, they might cobble together an application (perhaps using Access and Excel) to solve a specific business problem. But if the individual leaves or if the application needs to scale, it becomes notoriously hard for IT departments to support such solutions. LightSwitch applications are easier for IT departments to maintain because they can leverage their existing .NET and SQL Server skills. Because LightSwitch uses a three-tier architecture and actively guides the developer toward writing code in the right place, it's more difficult to write applications badly in the first place.

Farther up the scale, LightSwitch attracts many professional developers who have come from .NET, ASP.NET, and Silverlight backgrounds. These professional developers realize how much time LightSwitch can save them, so they have embraced the product. They understand how useful LightSwitch can be for developing *forms over data* applications and how easy it is to write web-based applications with it.

We've therefore seen that LightSwitch attracts a wide audience, but all of these groups share one thing in common. They see LightSwitch as a serious tool for solving business problems and understand how powerful it can be.

The rest of this chapter shows you how LightSwitch stands out from the crowd and discusses some of the key technologies that have gone into the product. We'll start by giving you a high level overview and then cover the following topics:

- The model centric architecture of LightSwitch.

- The data, logic, and presentation tiers.

- How the Model-View-ViewModel pattern applies to LightSwitch.

- How a LightSwitch application actually works.

The 10,000-Foot View

LightSwitch applications conform to a traditional three-tier architecture, containing presentation, application (business logic), and data tiers. This has many advantages and benefits. In addition to being modular (a good practice), the three-tier design provides a scalability that was sorely missing from Access applications and enables tiers to be replaced or modified without affecting others. To give an example, Microsoft may choose to replace the current Silverlight client with an HTML/JavaScript client or some other emerging technology in a future version. The three-tier architecture makes this possible without the whole application needing to be rewritten. In fact, active members of the LightSwitch community have already written several articles about creating HTML frontends to LightSwitch.

At the presentation level, the client is a Silverlight 4.0 application, running either inside a browser or as an OOB (out-of-browser) desktop application. The client connects to middle tier logic using WCF-RIA (Windows Communication Foundation–Rich Internet Applications) services. The middle tier itself also consists of a set of WCF-RIA domain services running under ASP.NET 4.0.

If you're unfamiliar with RIA services, this technology was introduced in 2009 and is used to marshal data between a database and the LightSwitch application. Specifically, RIA services coordinate the application logic between the middle and presentation tiers. The biggest benefit it provides is that it significantly simplifies the development of n-tier solutions in a RIA web environment such as Silverlight.

At the data tier level, Microsoft SQL Server is the database of choice. You can also attach to other data sources, including SQL Azure, SharePoint 2010, and custom adapters written using RIA domain services. Connections to SharePoint technically take place using an OData (Open Data Protocol) endpoint exposed by the SharePoint API (Application Programming Interface).

LightSwitch utilizes the power of the Microsoft ADO.NET Entity Framework 4.0. This is an ORM (Object Relational Mapping) system, which was first introduced in .NET 3.5. One of the key benefits of using an ORM is that it abstracts away the schema of the database from the conceptual view that is visible in code. It eliminates the problem of what is commonly known as the *object relational impedance mismatch* that is often experienced in database-oriented applications. In simple terms, an ORM allows you to refactor database tables without affecting the view of the data in code.

To query data from LightSwitch, you can use LINQ (Language INtegrated Query). This was also introduced in .NET 3.5 along with Entity Framework V1. LINQ provides a set of common query operators, the biggest advantage being that you can use the same syntax for querying various different data sources. For example, you can just use LINQ rather than having to learn the individual, and very different, syntaxes of query technologies like T-SQL, XPath, LDAP, and the various other query languages that would otherwise be necessary to query different types of data. If you're using LINQ for the first time, a tool called LinqPad (`www.linqpad.net/`) provides a greatly simplified and easy-to-use learning environment.

Architecturally, LightSwitch is based on a model-centric architecture. Applications are authored in terms of building blocks such as entities, screens, and data services that are animated by the LightSwitch runtime (using Silverlight and .NET technology stacks). Having these building blocks means that the LightSwitch business logic doesn't have a specific technology dependency. LightSwitch incorporates all of these proven .NET technologies along with best practices for their use. Any application you create using LightSwitch will therefore also be based on this solid foundation.

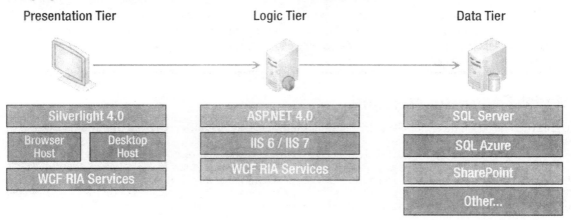

Figure 1-1. LightSwitch components

Figure 1-1 shows the three tiers that make up a LightSwitch application and identifies the main components that belong to each tier. We'll now explain each tier in more detail.

```
WHY THE NAME LIGHTSWITCH?
```

LightSwitch is certainly an unusual name, so where did it come from?

During the writing of this book, we spoke to a product manager at Microsoft who was involved in the naming of LightSwitch. Unfortunately, Microsoft's public relations department has prevented us from disclosing any details about product naming. The process that they use is secretive.

During the early life of a Microsoft product, internal code names are used for identification. In the case of LightSwitch, the code name was Kitty Hawk. These code names often relate to towns and places and in the case of LightSwitch, Kitty Hawk most likely refers to a town in North Carolina. At some point afterward, the actual name is determined through a formalized process, which might include a focus group.

Because we can't publish any details about the naming of the product, we'll share some of the rumors that exist instead. LightSwitch uses Silverlight, which might explain the *light* part of the name. It's also been noted that the first characters of each word in both product names are swapped around (i.e., **Light**Switch vs. **S**ilverlight).

Interestingly, we spoke to a very senior member of the LightSwitch team who didn't know the history behind the name. In his opinion, however, this was something that was better left unknown. He believes that the product naming might be based on something quite mundane; if we don't know the story, we can allow our imagination to supply a better one.

Model-Centric Architecture

LightSwitch is based on a model-centric architecture. What exactly do we mean by this and why is it important?

When you're writing a LightSwitch application, imagine that you're a bricklayer rather than a programmer. The raw materials at your disposal include entity, query, screen, and control building blocks. To build an application, you simply put these building blocks together in the appropriate way. The important analogy here is that building blocks are the main construct used for building applications, not code. Figure 1-2 shows the building blocks that are defined by LightSwitch.

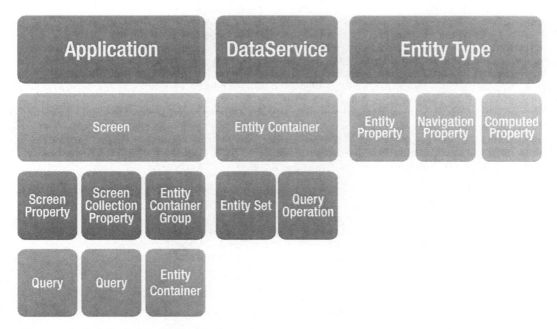

Figure 1-2. LightSwitch building blocks

When you create a new project, LightSwitch creates a new empty model (which we'll refer to as the LSML model). This model takes the form of an XML file called `ApplicationData.lsml`. When you create a new screen in your application, LightSwitch adds the XML markup that represents a screen building block into your `ApplicationData.lsml` file. The same thing happens when you add data sources, tables, and queries. At the end of the design process, your application is expressed entirely in XML.

On its own, XML isn't capable of doing very much—after all, it's just data. Something needs to turn these data into a functioning application, and this role is carried out by the LightSwitch runtime.

The LightSwitch runtime comes into action when a user actually runs your application. It reads the model and performs many other functions such as loading the application, authorizing access, and retrieving data. The LightSwitch runtime consists of the many technologies that were mentioned earlier, such as Silverlight, WCF, Entity Framework, and the DLLs that belong in the `Microsoft.LightSwitch` namespace. The runtime runs on both the client and logic tiers.

The beauty of this architecture is that it abstracts the definition of your application away from the actual implementation. Hypothetically speaking, some other runtime could be written and used instead. This new runtime might target different devices or operating systems. The benefit of the architecture is that it doesn't impose any solid dependency on any specific technology. The model-driven design therefore makes LightSwitch more extensible and more future proof.

The Data Tier

As mentioned earlier, LightSwitch provides first-class support for reading and writing to SQL Server, SQL Azure, and SharePoint 2010 data sources. You can very easily create screens to display data, and you can even display data from multiple data sources on a single screen.

LightSwitch also depends on a special SQL Server database called the intrinsic or ApplicationData database. Any users and tables that you create in LightSwitch are added to this database.

When you run or debug a LightSwitch application at design time, LightSwitch hosts your intrinsic database using a local instance of Microsoft SQL Server Express. At design time, a local instance of SQL Server Express must be used and other editions of SQL Server are not supported. In production, however, this restriction doesn't apply, and the intrinsic database can be hosted using any version of Microsoft SQL Server 2005 or above, as well as Microsoft SQL Azure.

When you run an application at design time, an intrinsic database is created and any data you enter are persisted between debug iterations.

However, you should treat these data as temporary because any major changes made to your data schema can force the intrinsic database to be deleted and re-created. (LightSwitch will warn you before it does this to prevent data loss.) Another important point is that any data entered during design time won't be retained when you deploy your application.

For security, LightSwitch uses the ASP.NET SQL membership provider, and if you take a peek inside the intrinsic database, you'll see the tables that are used. Examples include the `dbo.aspnet_Membership`, `dbo.aspnet_Roles`, and `dbo.aspnet_Users` tables.

At design time, the intrinsic database is created, re-created, and updated dynamically by LightSwitch using the table definitions you've specified in the designer. Specifically, it generates the intrinsic database schema using the modeled `EntityContainer` building block.

The Logic Tier

The logic tier can also be known as the middle tier, business layer, or business logic layer. Its main task is data access and processing.

For each data source you add to your application, LightSwitch creates a corresponding *data service* in the logic tier. A data service encapsulates the data access operations on a data source and is exposed as a public service endpoint at the logic tier boundary. The Silverlight client uses this data service to carry out data access that is needed for a given data source.

Data services expose *entity sets*, which contain operations for retrieving, updating, and saving data. An entity set is a container for items of the same entity, and all data access is carried out through an entity set.

By default, each entity set contains `all` and `single` queries, which return all records and single records by primary key. The queries you create yourself are also exposed as an entity set operation. Figure 1-3 illustrates the relation between data services, entity sets, and operations.

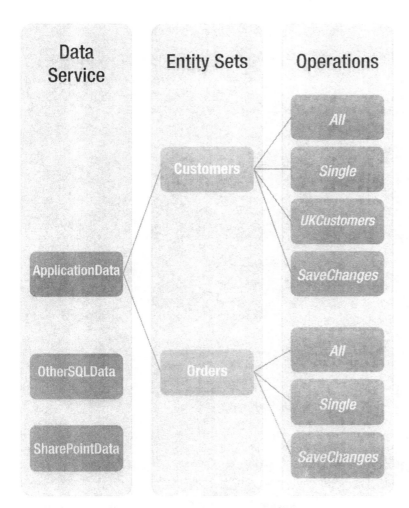

Figure 1-3. Data service, entity sets, and operations

When a query is executed, it passes through the *query pipeline*. The query pipeline exposes various points in the lifecycle of a query that you as a developer can intercept and inject with custom code. During the preprocessing phase, for example, you can tailor the results of a query by appending additional query operators using LINQ.

Each entity set also includes a single built-in operation called SaveChanges. When working with a LightSwitch application, the client maintains a set of all the added, updated, and deleted records in an object called a *change set*. When the user clicks the save button on a screen, the change set is passed to the logic tier and the SaveChanges operation is called. At this point, the processing enters the *save pipeline* and, just as with the query pipeline, the save pipeline can be intercepted with custom code. Figure 1-4 shows the phases in the save and query pipelines and highlights some of the points where you can write your own code.

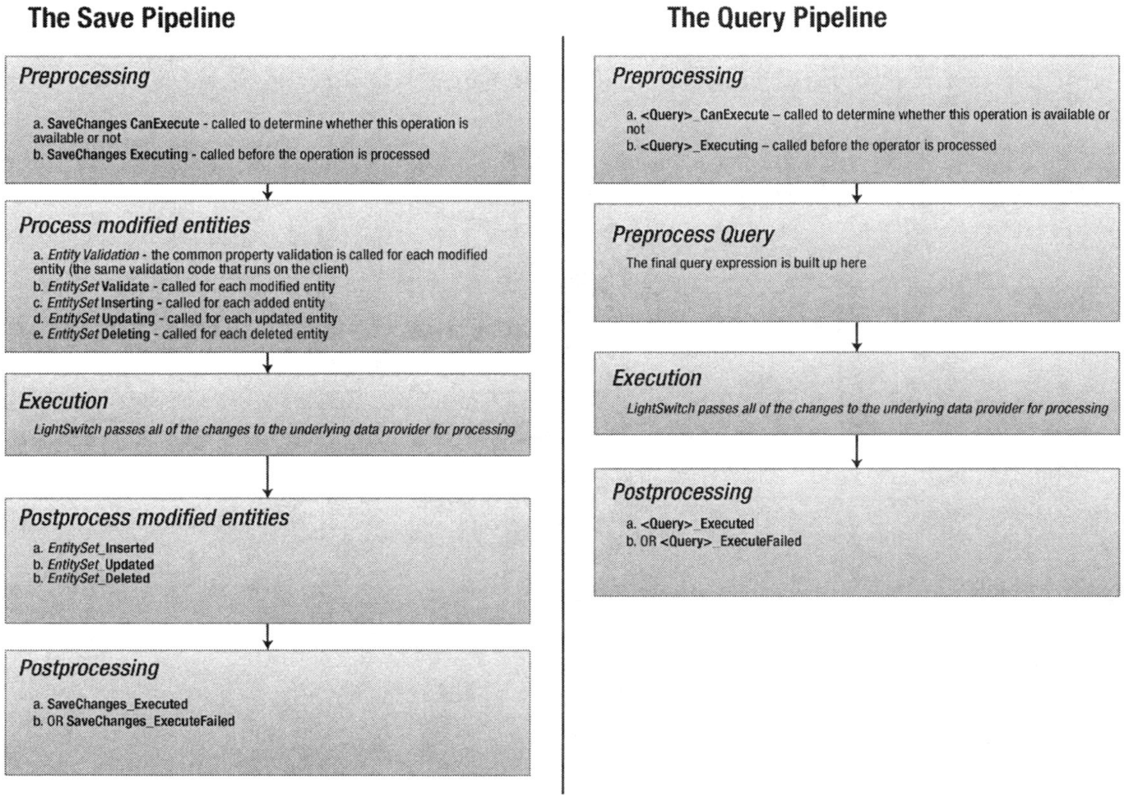

The Save Pipeline

Preprocessing

a. **SaveChanges CanExecute** - called to determine whether this operation is available or not
b. **SaveChanges Executing** - called before the operation is processed

Process modified entities

a. *Entity Validation* - the common property validation is called for each modified entity (the same validation code that runs on the client)
b. *EntitySet* **Validate** - called for each modified entity
c. *EntitySet* **Inserting** - called for each added entity
d. *EntitySet* **Updating** - called for each updated entity
e. *EntitySet* **Deleting** - called for each deleted entity

Execution

LightSwitch passes all of the changes to the underlying data provider for processing

Postprocess modified entities

a. *EntitySet*_**Inserted**
b. *EntitySet*_**Updated**
b. *EntitySet*_**Deleted**

Postprocessing

a. **SaveChanges_Executed**
b. OR **SaveChanges_ExecuteFailed**

The Query Pipeline

Preprocessing

a. **<Query>_CanExecute** – called to determine whether this operation is available or not
b. **<Query>_Executing** – called before the operator is processed

Preprocess Query

The final query expression is built up here

Execution

LightSwitch passes all of the changes to the underlying data provider for processing

Postprocessing

a. **<Query>_Executed**
b. OR **<Query>_ExecuteFailed**

Figure 1-4. *The Save Pipeline and Query Pipeline*

When updates are applied at the database, LightSwitch uses optimistic concurrency and doesn't apply any locks to the database. If concurrency violations are encountered, it alerts the user and displays a dialog with the proposed, current, and server values. The **SaveChanges** operation also takes place inside a transaction, and all data changes are committed atomically. Either all changes are saved successfully or no changes will be saved at all.

■ **Note** Unlike Microsoft Access and other DBMSs (database management systems), if you create a query in LightSwitch, you cannot modify the columns that are returned in the query. This behavior is explained by the way data access must occur through entity sets that are fixed in their structure.

Data Providers

When LightSwitch creates a data service, it configures the data service to work with a *data provider* that corresponds with the data storage service that's used (e.g., the database). The data provider offers a set of libraries that enables the logic tier to communicate with the storage service. Table 1-1 shows the data providers that LightSwitch uses.

Table 1-1. *Data Providers Used by Data Storage Service Type*

Data Storage Service	Data Provider
Microsoft SQL Server	SqlClient for the Entity Framework
Microsoft SQL Azure	SqlClient for the Entity Framework
Microsoft SharePoint	OData client
Custom RIA services	Requires a WCF-RIA domain service

Although LightSwitch uses the Entity Framework to connect to the SQL Server, you don't need to understand how this works, nor do you need to learn how to use the Entity Framework API. When you're writing code, LightSwitch produces entity classes that allow you to get to your data easily and naturally. For instance, you can use the following code to retrieve a customer surname:
`ApplicationData.Customer.Surname`. LightSwitch makes it really simple and intuitive for you to work with data.

The Presentation Tier

The presentation tier controls what the user sees and does. It's responsible for showing data to the user, allowing data entry to happen, and all other tasks that relate to human interaction. Importantly, it also performs operations such as data validation and it keeps track of data changes and interacts with the *data services* in the logic tier.

The activities of the LightSwitch client can be summarized into the following three categories:

- User interface (UI),
- Client business logic,
- Data service access.

Everything that happens on the client is encapsulated inside the LightSwitch *shell.* From a top level, the *hosting, shell UI,* and *theming* services are the parts that make up the shell, and this is shown in Figure 1-5. We'll now describe the parts that make up the client in more detail.

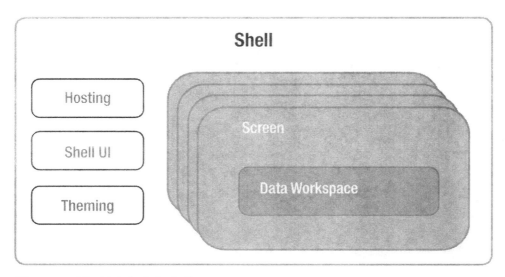

Figure 1-5. The LightSwitch shell

Screens

A screen represents a piece of user interface that is used to view or enter data, just like a form in an Access application. Multiple screens can be opened in a LightSwitch application, but there can only be one single active screen at any time.

Each screen contains a *data workspace* that is used for fetching and managing data. The data workspace manages the state of the data in a *change set*, and this is submitted to the *data service* on the logic tier when the user initiates a save.

Because each screen contains its own data workspace, data changes made in one screen are not reflected in other screens. Data cannot be shared between screens, and each screen retains an independent view of the data.

Other important concepts include the *screen object*, *screen layout*, and *visual tree*.

You can think of the screen object as a business object that contains no UI. When designing a screen, you can access data in code and add items such as properties or screen parameters. All of these objects are exposed in code through the screen object.

The screen layout and visual tree are concepts that emerge at runtime. We'll describe both of these in the "MVVM Applied to LightSwitch" section later in this chapter.

Hosting Process

LightSwitch applications are hosted using the Silverlight runtime. One of LightSwitch's most useful features is that an application can be configured to run either *out of browser*, as a desktop application, or inside a browser, without having to be rewritten. You can switch an application from one mode to the other by simply setting a radio button option in the properties of your LightSwitch project.

Browser applications are hosted by the Silverlight runtime inside the browser. Users install the Silverlight runtime as a browser plug-in, and supported web browsers include Internet Explorer, Firefox,

Safari, and Chrome. Browser applications execute inside a sandbox, and access to features such as Export to Excel is prohibited. Access to certain parts of the file system is also restricted.

Desktop applications are hosted by the Silverlight out-of-browser host service (`sllauncher.exe`). LightSwitch configures your application to require elevated permissions, which give access to features such as Export to Excel, and COM-based automation.

When you're writing LightSwitch applications, it's useful to know if your application is running as a browser or a desktop application. Before you perform any COM-based operation such as automating Outlook, it's a good idea to check where your application is running by writing some code. Chapter 11 includes code that shows you how to do this.

WILL LIGHTSWITCH RUN ON MACS, LINUX, OR MOBILES?

A question that people regularly ask is whether LightSwitch will run on Macs, iPads, Linux, and various brands of cell phones. The simple answer is that as long the platform supports a Silverlight 4.0 client, LightSwitch will run. The mobile story is not as promising. It's worth noting that Windows Mobile doesn't currently support LightSwitch because it uses a derivation of Silverlight 3.0.

All server side components must be deployed onto Windows servers.

The Shell UI

The shell UI is a key part of the LightSwitch presentation layer, and it controls what's visible to the end user. It provides the user interface logic that performs tasks such as logging in, generating, and activating screens.

You can change various aspects of the shell's behavior for each LightSwitch application using the properties pane of your project (Figure 1-6).

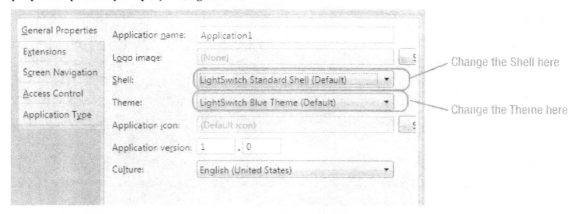

Figure 1-6. Changing the shell and the theme settings in the project's property tabs

LightSwitch ships with one standard default shell, which will be familiar to any LightSwitch developer. As the LightSwitch market matures, additional shells from third party vendors and members of the community will become available (either free or for sale).

Figure 1-7 illustrates the standard screen sections you'll see using the default LightSwitch shell. These include:

- *The screen region.* The central area where screens are displayed.

- *The navigation region.* Used for launching and activating screens.

- *The command region* Displays command buttons such as Save and Refresh.

- *The validation region.* Used for displaying any validation errors.

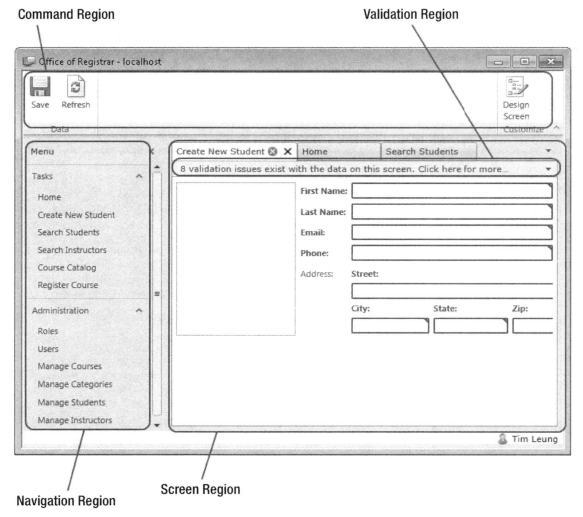

Figure 1-7. Default screen regions

Figure 1-8 shows the *Outlook shell* that was developed by Infragistics. It highlights just how radically the look and feel of an application can be modified.

As shown in the illustration, this shell allows screens to be tiled rather than tabbed, it displays a screen command bar section for each screen instead of showing a ribbon bar, and includes a slider control on the right-hand side that lets you increase or decrease the number of screens shown in the middle pane.

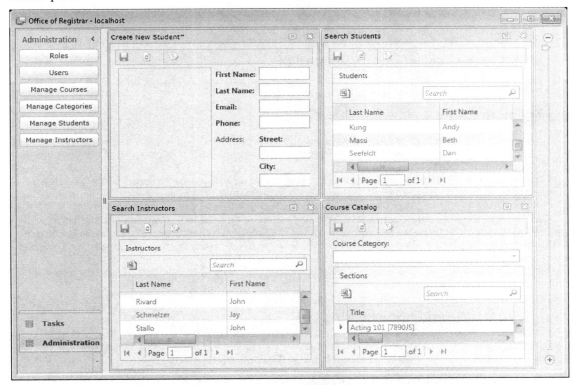

Figure 1-8. Infragistics's Outlook style shell

If you choose to do so, you can also write your own custom shell extension, and Chapter 10 shows you how to do this. When writing your own shell extensions, LightSwitch exposes various views models that you can consume. The types of data that you can bind to in a custom shell include:

- Current user,
- Application logo,
- Screen activation and navigation,
- Active screens,
- Screen commands,

- Screen validation errors.

It's worth pointing out that the four screen regions in the default shell that were mentioned earlier (see Figure 1-7) are not concepts that are strictly defined in LightSwitch. The shell implements the layout using the view models mentioned above, and you could, for example, choose to create a shell that doesn't include any of the elements in the navigation region.

■ **Tip** It is even possible to create an entirely empty shell. This will allow you to construct a LightSwitch application's UI based entirely on custom Silverlight controls.

The Theming Service

The theming service makes up the final part of the presentation layer. You'd use a theme to apply a set of presentation preferences, such as fonts and colors. Unlike changing the shell, the visual changes applied by a theme are more subtle.

Like shells, themes are also applied using the properties pane for your project. Themes are often designed to work with a specified shell, but it is entirely possible for shells and themes to be *mixed and matched*.

Themes and shells enable a consistent *look and feel* to be applied to the various parts of your application. It can often be a struggle for those new to LightSwitch when they try to set various control attributes (such as its font and its color) at a screen level, because many of these attributes are designed to be controlled by a theme, rather than set for each individual control.

Themes are also one of several LightSwitch extension points, and Chapter 10 shows you how you can create your own custom theme.

Model-View-ViewModel (MVVM)

Applications that you create in LightSwitch are based on the M-V-VM pattern (also known simply as MVVM). Like many other software patterns, MVVM is designed to:

- Ensure a clean separation of concerns.

- Make applications more maintainable and more testable.

- Simplify UI design.

You don't need to do anything extra in your code for MVVM to work. LightSwitch automatically takes care of this for you. In this section, we'll show you the advantages that it offers, and we'll begin by explaining the history behind this pattern.

Software design is complex by nature, and programmers have always searched for ways to make things easier. Just the UI layer alone is responsible for user interaction, validation, data access, and client-side business logic. Without any real pattern in place, applications can easily get out of hand.

To add structure and simplify the job of software design, a pattern called Model View Presenter (MVP) has gained much popularity in developer circles. This is a variation of the Model View Controller (MVC) pattern, which has existed since 1979.

The *Model* part of MVP refers to data, *Views* are what you seen on the screen, and the *Presenter* element hooks the two together. A key characteristic of this pattern is the role that's played by the presenter. The presenter populates the view with data, carries out validation, and reacts to user input.

Like all things in life, patterns evolve, and in 2004, Martin Fowler published his Presenter Model (PM) pattern. You can find further details about this pattern on his web site: `http://martinfowler.com/eaaDev/PresentationModel.html`.

Just like the earlier patterns, the PM pattern features views that are separated from their state and behaviors. However, this pattern also includes an abstraction of view called a Presentation Model. The view becomes a rendering of the Presentation Model, which contains little or no code and is frequently updated by the Presentation Model. Both the Presentation and View Models are therefore closely synchronized.

In 2005, John Gossman (a technical architect at Microsoft for the Silverlight and WPF (Windows Presentation Foundation) products) unveiled the MVVM pattern. In simple terms, MVVM is a tailor-made version of the Presenter Model that targets the WPF and Silverlight platforms. In fact, the only real difference between the PM and MVVM patterns is the explicit use of the WPF and Silverlight data-binding capabilities.

The MVVM pattern is highly characterized by the role of the View Model. The responsibilities of the View Model include:

- *UI logic*. For example, data validation.

- *Data conversion*. If you want to display integer data using a *slider* control that renders decimal data, the View Model does the necessary conversion and coercion.

- *Storing the state of the UI*. If you're showing a collection of data through a data grid and the user selects a record, the View Model can keep track of the currently selected record.

According to the MVVM pattern, the view should only concern itself with the presentation of data and could be virtually code free. Views should only really display the data from the View Model and do no more than absolutely necessary.

An application designed around MVVM allows you to easily switch controls in and out. You'll see this when you start working with LightSwitch. For example, the data item that represents a surname can be easily changed to use a label, textbox, or any other control that supports the underlying data type (in this example, `string`).

The View Model communicates with the view through data binding. The View Model exposes properties that the view can bind to. Therefore, the view doesn't need to know anything about the View Model and means that the two are loosely coupled.

This helps to establish a *clear separation of concerns*, the aim of which is to separate the parts that make up a system into logically distinct pieces. By splitting out functionality in this way, it enables applications to be created that are cleaner, more maintainable, and more testable. Because LightSwitch is based on MVVM, your applications will benefit from the advantages that it brings.

Understanding the role of the view and the View Model is extremely important when writing Custom Controls, because it is easy to include logic in the control that really belongs in either the model or the View Model. You can find out more about Custom Controls in Chapter 9.

MVVM Applied to LightSwitch

Due to the model-based architecture of LightSwitch, the MVVM pattern only emerges at runtime. This can make it a bit tricky to understand at first. The following list shows the parts that make up the MVVM pattern and how they relate to LightSwitch:

- Model = entity and screen data objects

- View Model = screen `ContentItems` (these are generated at runtime)

- View = Silverlight controls.

The Model part of MVVM is the conceptual representation of the data. It consists of the entities and queries that are defined in your application.

At runtime, LightSwitch constructs the screen layout dynamically by interpreting your LSML model. The screen layout contains a tree of *content items,* which could represent data items, lists, commands, or parent items. A content item at runtime represents the View-Model element of MVVM.

Finally, the runtime builds the Silverlight visual tree. This object contains the actual tree of Silverlight controls, which is shown to the user. These Silverlight controls make up the View part of MVVM.

Figure 1-9 shows how the elements of MVVM map to the items on the screen designer. These types of illustrations are difficult because the screen designer is an expression of the LSML data model, whereas MVVM pattern is something that only emerges at runtime. However, this is still useful to help illustrate how the MVVM pattern fits in.

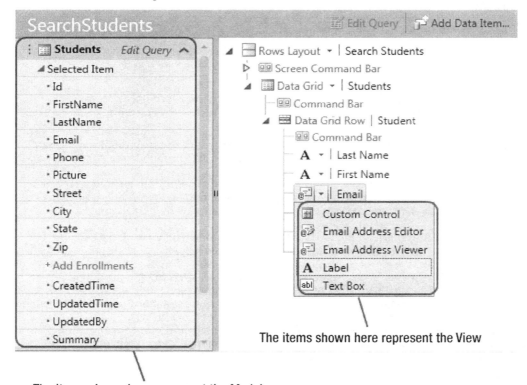

Figure 1-9. View and View-Model illustrated through a screen

As shown in Figure 1-9, the items that appear on the left-hand side of the screen designer (entities and screen data objects) are the Model part. Similar illustrations have been published that label the items on the left-hand side as the View Model. But just to avoid any confusion, the entities and screen data objects actually represent the Model part of MVVM.

When you run your application, the LightSwitch runtime generates content items for each data item on your screen. The content item makes up the View-Model part of MVVM.

The screen designer allows you to change the control for each data item in your screen. The control that you select is the view.

■ **Note** While debugging, LightSwitch lets you design the layout of a screen while the application is actually running. This is possible because the screen layout is determined dynamically at runtime. The runtime editor modifies the Content Items inside the screen layout and a new Visual Tree can be built up. Your visual changes can then be seen immediately.

The LightSwitch Application Lifecycle

If you've worked with .NET in the past, you may be curious as to how everything ties together in LightSwitch. This section describes the lifecycle of a LightSwitch application. Specifically, it explains what happens during the design, build, and runtime stages.

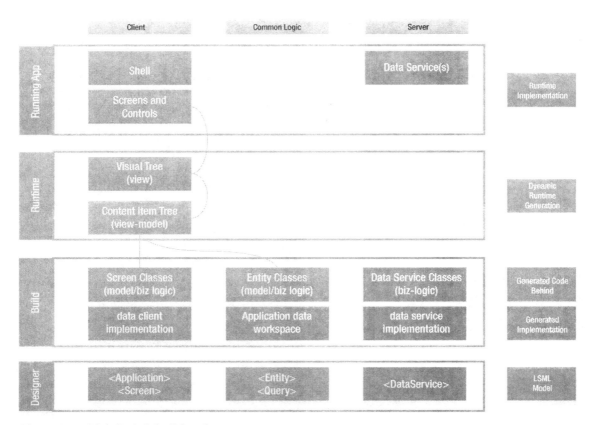

Figure 1-10. *LightSwitch build and run process*

Figure 1-10 illustrates the LightSwitch development process in the form of a diagram. The columns in the diagram show the client, server, and common logic parts of your application. The common logic is executed on both the client and server. You'll see in Chapter 2 how LightSwitch creates a .NET project called `Common` that contains this logic

To make sense of this diagram, we'll start off at the bottom. This section represents the tasks that are carried out in the LightSwitch designer. As mentioned earlier, LightSwitch applications are constructed using building blocks. When you add screens, tables, or data sources using the designer, the XML mark-up that represents these building blocks are added to your `ApplicationData.lsml` file. The bottom section of Figure 1-10 highlights how:

- The `Application` and `Screen` building blocks are used to build the client.

- The `Entity` and `Query` building blocks are built into the common project.

- The `DataService` building block is used to build the code that runs on the server.

When you build your LightSwitch solution (or press the F5 key), LightSwitch compiles the client, server, and common code. During this stage, it compiles (and autogenerates where necessary) the following types of code:

- *The user code and business logic that you've written.* This includes the VB or C# code that you've written to handle the click of a button, or any user code that customizes the results of a query.

- *Screen and entity classes.* If you've created a table called customers, for example, LightSwitch generates a corresponding entity class called customers that you can call in your code.

- *The "framework" that supports your LightSwitch application.* For example, this includes the data access classes that are used in each tier and items such as the `Application` and `DataWorkspace` objects, which we'll refer to in later chapters.

An important point to remember is that UI elements are not compiled into your Silverlight client. When a user runs your application, the client carries out a process called *dynamic runtime generation*. This is the process that generates the user interface for your application.

So how exactly does the LightSwitch client render a screen? At compile time, LightSwitch embeds a copy of your LSML file inside the Silverlight XAP file (think of the XAP file as your compiled Silverlight application). This allows the LightSwitch client to access the contents of your LSML file. When a user opens a screen, LightSwitch searches for the corresponding screen building block in the LSML file. When it finds the screen, it builds the screen layout by constructing a tree of `ContentItem`s. As you'll recall, content items make up the View-Model part of MVVM.

After building the content item tree, LightSwitch creates the Silverlight visual tree. It works out the Silverlight control to use by reading the Control setting that's stored against each `ContentItem` building block. The Silverlight control makes up the View part of MVVM.

If you're familiar with Silverlight, you might wonder if XAML (Extensible Application Markup Language) comes into play during this process. LightSwitch generates the Silverlight controls dynamically when the visual tree is built and, therefore, there isn't any XAML involved in the process. However, you can design your own custom controls using XAML, and Chapter 9 shows you how.

After dynamic runtime generation, the screens and controls are composed using MEF (Managed Extensibility Framework) and data templates.

LightSwitch also composes the shell at runtime using MEF. It works out the shell to use by reading the details held against the `Application` building block in the LSML file.

■ **Note** LightSwitch projects can be created in C# or VB.NET. However, a project cannot be changed from one language to the other after it has been created.

Summary

This chapter introduced you to Microsoft LightSwitch. LightSwitch is a tool that allows you to quickly develop data-centric applications for the desktop or web. In this chapter, we've shown you:

- The technologies that LightSwitch uses.

- The role of client and server tiers.

- How LightSwitch uses a built in intrinsic database.

- How the MVVM pattern applies in LightSwitch.

LightSwitch applications are built using well-known patterns and best practices such as n-tier application layering and MVVM, as well as technologies such as Entity Framework and RIA services.

LightSwitch uses a model-driven architecture. The definition of your application is saved in an XML file called `ApplicationData.lsml`. When a user runs your application, the LightSwitch runtime turns this XML model into a fully functioning application.

LightSwitch relies on a special database called the intrinsic database. This database stores the tables you create within LightSwitch, as well as security details such as login names and security roles. If you want to connect to external data, the data sources you can use include SQL Server, SharePoint 2010, and custom RIA services.

The logic tier (or middle tier) is responsible for performing data access and processing. LightSwitch creates a data service for each data source in your application. The LightSwitch client calls data service operations to insert, update, or retrieve data. All data operations pass through either the save or query pipeline. These pipelines expose points where you can inject your own custom code.

On the client, LightSwitch applications are based on Silverlight 4.0. Web applications are hosted using the Silverlight runtime inside your browser. If you choose to create a desktop application, LightSwitch generates a Silverlight out-of-browser application.

Within your application, screens are used for data entry and retrieval. Each screen maintains an independent view of your data using a data workspace.

You can easily alter the appearance of your application by changing the shell and theme settings. Changing the shell allows you to radically change the appearance of your application. More subtle changes (such as changes to font colors and sizes) can be made by changing the theme.

The MVVM pattern helps to enforce a clean separation of concerns. This means that LightSwitch applications are broken down into distinct features with minimal overlap. A feature of the MVVM pattern is that the view is as dumb as possible and contains minimal code. This makes it very easy in LightSwitch to change the controls that are used to render your data.

CHAPTER 2

Working in Visual Studio

If you've ever had to replace your smart phone with a different make and model, it can be a real struggle getting to grips with something that you're unfamiliar with. For example, installing apps might be simple, but understanding how everything works beneath the surface could be quite obscure. Likewise, you might also choose to switch off Wi-Fi (or some other operation) by navigating through several levels of menus, because a more direct route isn't apparent.

In many ways, learning LightSwitch is a similar experience. Behind the *point and click* facade of the GUI, what actually happens behind the scenes? Are there easier ways to perform tasks that you can already achieve?

In this chapter, we'll *unwrap* LightSwitch and expose the inner workings of the product. You'll learn about the constituent projects that make up a LightSwitch solution and find out more about the role that SQL Server Express plays.

Switching to File View

The default view that's shown to you when working with LightSwitch is called *Logical view*. This basic view organizes a project into various folders such as Data Sources, Entities, and Screens. The Logical view enables you to add and edit items such as screens, queries, and data sources.

In addition to the Logical view, there is a second view called the *File view*. Knowing how to switch to this view is important if you want to undertake any serious LightSwitch development. This view allows you to see the various parts that make up a LightSwitch solution and enables you to work on individual projects. In addition, it allows you to add references to external DLLs in individual projects.

To switch to File view, use the drop-down in Solution Explorer and select the File View option, as shown in Figure 2-1.

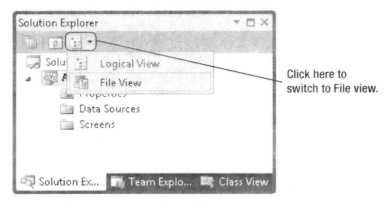

Click here to
switch to File view.

Figure 2-1. *Switching between Logical and File views*

After switching to File view, you'll see a project listing. The toolbar within Solution Explorer includes a Show All Files button, as illustrated in Figure 2-2. Clicking this button displays all files that exist on the file system and reveals two additional projects, which are the `ClientGenerated` and `ServerGenerated` projects. With this option turned off, these projects are hidden along with a few other files, which include `default.htm` and `Silverlight.js` files.

Click here to
Show All Files

Figure 2-2. *Solution Explorer in File view*

Figure 2-2 illustrates the projects that make up a LightSwitch solution. These include the following:

- `Client`
- `ClientGenerated`
- `Common`
- `Server`
- `ServerGenerated`

In the following section, you'll discover what these projects actually do.

Root Folder Contents

If you examine the root folder of a LightSwitch project in Windows Explorer, you'll find subfolders that correspond to the projects that have been mentioned. You'll also find several other files that are needed to support your LightSwitch application.

_pvt_extensions Folder

A `_pvt_extensions` folder is created if any custom extensions are used in your project. This folder contains a subfolder for each extension that's used. For example, a `LightSwitchFilter` folder will be created if the LightSwitch filter extension is used in your project.

Silverlight.js

The `Silverlight.js` file is a JavaScript file that is automatically added to all Silverlight web applications. It contains various helper functions that support the use of Silverlight within the browser.

Default.htm

`Default.htm` is the web page that's used for hosting the Silverlight LightSwitch client. This file is used when an application is set to run as a web application. It's also used to load an out-of-browser (desktop) application. After the out-of-browser application is installed, this file is no longer needed for the application to run.

If you examine the contents of this file, you'll find JavaScript functions for performing various tasks. These include generating JavaScript alerts in case of errors, and pop-up alerts if the user attempts to navigate away from the web page without saving their changes.

ServiceConfiguration.cscfg

`ServiceConfiguration.cscfg` is an Azure configuration file, in XML format. This file is used for storing settings when applications are deployed to Windows Azure. If you're familiar with web development but unfamiliar with Azure, `ServiceConfiguration.cscfg` is analogous to the `web.config` file in an ASP.NET application. This file is important because it enables post deployment modification of settings through the Windows Azure portal. LightSwitch has added these because `web.config` cannot be edited in Azure without redeploying the whole application.

Listing 2-1 shows the default contents of the file. You'll find various settings here for configuring the tracing feature that is built into LightSwitch.

Listing 2-1. The Default Contents of the ServiceConfiguration.cscfg File

```
<ServiceConfiguration
    serviceName="Application1"
    xmlns="http://schemas.microsoft.com/ServiceHosting/2008/10/ServiceConfiguration">
    <Role name="LightSwitchWebRole">
        <Instances count="1" />
        <ConfigurationSettings>
            <!-- A value of true will enable diagnostic logging on the server -->
            <Setting name="Microsoft.LightSwitch.Trace.Enabled" value="false" />

            <!-- A value of true only lets local access to Trace.axd -->
            <Setting name="Microsoft.LightSwitch.Trace.LocalOnly" value="true" />

            <!-- The valid values for the trace level are:
                None, Error, Warning, Information, Verbose -->
            <Setting name="Microsoft.LightSwitch.Trace.Level" value="Information" />

            <!-- True indicates that logging sensitive information is OK -->
            <Setting name="Microsoft.LightSwitch.Trace.Sensitive" value="false" />

            <!--This contains a semi-colon separated list
                of categories that will be enabled at the specifed trace level -->
            <Setting name="Microsoft.LightSwitch.Trace.Categories"
                value="Microsoft.LightSwitch" />

            <!-- True indicates http requests should be redirected to https -->
            <Setting name="Microsoft.LightSwitch.RequireEncryption" value="true" />
        </ConfigurationSettings>
        <Certificates>
        </Certificates>
    </Role>
</ServiceConfiguration>
```

ServiceDefinition.csdef

ServiceDefinition.csdef is an Azure configuration file. It contains the metadata used by the Windows Azure fabric and includes settings such as roles, service endpoints, and configuration settings.

A notable setting here is the vmsize attribute. This is used to control the size of the virtual machine when deployed to Azure. The price that you'll pay for hosting is directly related to this setting. By default, this is set to Small but can be manually changed to ExtraSmall if you want cheaper hosting. Table 2-1 illustrates the virtual machine options at the time of this writing.

Table 2-1. Azure Virtual Machine Options

Virtual Machine Size	Cost	CPU Cores	Memory	Disk Space
ExtraSmall	$	Shared	768MB	20GB
Small	$$	1	1.75GB	225GB

Virtual Machine Size	Cost	CPU Cores	Memory	Disk Space
Medium	$$$	2	3.5GB	490GB
Large	$$$$	4	7GB	1,000GB
ExtraLarge	$$$$$	8	14GB	2,040GB

Listing 2-2 shows the default contents of the ServiceDefinition.csdef file. You'll see the elements that relate to configuration settings, bindings, endpoints, and certificates.

Listing 2-2. ServiceDefinition.cscfg File

```
<ServiceDefinition
    name="Application1"
    xmlns="http://schemas.microsoft.com/ServiceHosting/2008/10/ServiceDefinition">
    <WebRole name="LightSwitchWebRole"
            vmsize="Small"
            enableNativeCodeExecution="true">
        <ConfigurationSettings>
            <Setting name="Microsoft.LightSwitch.Trace.Enabled" />
            <Setting name="Microsoft.LightSwitch.Trace.LocalOnly" />
            <Setting name="Microsoft.LightSwitch.Trace.Level" />
            <Setting name="Microsoft.LightSwitch.Trace.Sensitive" />
            <Setting name="Microsoft.LightSwitch.Trace.Categories" />
            <Setting name="Microsoft.LightSwitch.RequireEncryption" />
        </ConfigurationSettings>
        <Sites>
            <Site name="Web">
                <Bindings>
                    <Binding name="HttpIn" endpointName="HttpIn" />
                    <Binding name="HttpsIn" endpointName="HttpsIn" />
                </Bindings>
            </Site>
        </Sites>
        <Endpoints>
            <InputEndpoint name="HttpIn" protocol="http" port="80" />
            <InputEndpoint name="HttpsIn" protocol="https" port="443"
                certificate="SSLCertificate" />
        </Endpoints>
        <Certificates>
            <Certificate name="SSLCertificate" storeLocation="LocalMachine"
                storeName="My" />
        </Certificates>
    </WebRole>
</ServiceDefinition>
```

GeneratedArtifacts Folder

In several of the LightSwitch projects, you'll find folders called **GeneratedArtifacts**. These folders contain code that is autogenerated by LightSwitch.

ApplicationDefinition.lsml File

The **ApplicationDefinition.lsml** (LightSwitch Markup Language) file (mentioned in Chapter 1) is the most important file in LightSwitch. The definition and details of screens and queries are defined in this file. You'll find this file in the **Data** folder.

All other projects in the solution reference this file. Figure 2-3 shows the **ApplicationDefinition.lsml** file in the **Data** folder, and a reference to it in the **Server** project.

Figure 2-3. *References to* ApplicationDefinition.lsml *in other projects*

Because the **ApplicationDefinition.lsml** file contains so much content, it often causes contention when multiple developers are working together on a project through source control.

Although the official recommendation is not to manually edit this file, there are some features and fixes that can be performed only through a manual edit. Cloning a LightSwitch screen is one example requiring you to manually edit the LSML. *We strongly recommend that you close out of LightSwitch and back up the LSML file before editing.*

To illustrate the LSML, we'll create an application that contains a **Customers** table and three screens based on the search, create, and detail templates. Listing 2-3 shows an outline of the LSML file that is generated.

Listing 2-3. Contents of ApplicationDefinition.lsml File

```xml
<?xml version="1.0" encoding="utf-8" ?>
<ModelFragment xmlns="http://schemas.microsoft.com/LightSwitch/2010/xaml/model"
               xmlns:x="http://schemas.microsoft.com/winfx/2006/xaml">
  <Application Name="LightSwitchApplication"
               Version="1.0.0.0"
               DefaultNavigationItem="!module/NavigationItems[Tasks]"
               Shell=":Standard"
               Theme=":Blue">
  </Application>

  <EntityContainerGroup Name="DataWorkspace">
  </EntityContainerGroup>

  <EntityContainer Name="ApplicationData" IsIntrinsic="True">

    <SubmitOperation Name="SaveChanges" />

    <EntitySet CanDelete="True"
               CanInsert="True"
               CanUpdate="True"
               EntityType="Customer"
               Name=" Customers" />

    <QueryOperation Name=" Customers_Single"
                    ReturnType=" Customer">
    </QueryOperation>

    <QueryOperation Name=" Customers_SingleOrDefault"
                    ReturnType="Customer">
    </QueryOperation>

    <QueryOperation Name="Customers_All"
                    ReturnType="Customer*">
    </QueryOperation>
  </EntityContainer>

  <DataService DataProvider="EntityFrameworkDataProvider"
               EntityContainer="ApplicationData"
               Name="ApplicationDataMapping" />

  <EntityType Name="Customer">
….
</EntityType>

  <Screen Name="CustomerDetail">
….
</Screen>

  <Screen LaunchMode="Multiple" Name="CreateNewCustomer">
```

```
....
</Screen>

  <Screen Name="SearchCustomers">
....
</Screen>

</ModelFragment
```

In Chapter 1, you learned about the model-based architecture behind LightSwitch. You may recognize that the XML elements in this file correspond to the LightSwitch building blocks that were described in that chapter.

The `Application` element contains the details that relate to the client application such as shell, theme, and menu navigation contents.

You'll find an `EntityContainer` element for each of the data sources in your application. The `IsIntrinsic` attribute indicates to LightSwitch that the specified database is the intrinsic database. This is the database that is defined by, and deployed with, your LightSwitch application.

Within this element, you'll find `EntitySet` elements for each table. `QueryOperation` elements define the operations for retrieving records from a given entity set.

An `EntityType` element exists for each table, and child elements define the columns and data types within the table.

Finally, the contents of screens are saved in `Screen` elements. If you've ever closed out of the screen designer without saving changes, you would have been prompted to save your changes to the `ApplicationDefinition.lsml` file. The reason you receive this dialog box is that the screen details are contained in the `screen` elements of the LSML.

Creating Nested Navigation Groups

Here's an example of where you might want to manually modify the LSML file. Out of the box, LightSwitch doesn't support the notion of nested *navigation groups*. Navigation groups are used by LightSwitch shells to present the UI for launching screens. To overcome this limitation, you can manually modify the LSML to create a nested navigation menu.

The navigation hierarchy is defined in the `Application` section of the LSML. Listing 2-4 shows an outline of this section.

Listing 2-4. Outline of the LSML Application Section

```
<Application Name="LightSwitchApplication"
             Version="1.0.0.0"
             DefaultNavigationItem="!module/NavigationItems[Tasks]"
             Shell=":Standard"
             Theme=":Blue">
  <Application.Methods>
    <ApplicationMethod Name="ShowCustomerDetail">
      <ApplicationMethod.Attributes>
        <ShowScreenMethod TargetScreen="CustomerDetail" />
      </ApplicationMethod.Attributes>
      <ApplicationMethodParameter Name="CustomerId"
                                  ParameterType=":Int32" />
    </ApplicationMethod>
```

```
<!--Comment - Additional <Application.Methods> elements
          appear here for each screen-->

<Application.NavigationItems>
        <!--Comment - Navigation items appear here  - further details in Listing 2-5-->

</Application.NavigationItems>

<!--Comment - ApplicationCommand elelments are the 'links' for opening new screens→

<ApplicationCommand Name="ScreenCommandShowCreateNewCustomer"
                    Target="!module/Methods[ShowCreateNewCustomer]" />
<ApplicationCommand Name="ScreenCommandShowSearchCustomer"
                    Target="!module/Methods[ShowSearchCustomer]" />
</Application>
```

You'll find multiple `<Application.Method>` elements for each screen in your application. Toward the end of the `<Application>` element, the `ApplicationCommand` elements point to the methods that are defined earlier.

The important part that defines the navigation hierarchy belongs inside the `<Application.NavigationItems>` element. Listing 2-5 shows the snippet LSML that you would use to create a nested hierarchy. In this example, `Group1` and `Group3` are top-level groups. `Group2` is a child of `Group1`.

Listing 2-5. LSML Fragment for Creating Nested Navigation Groups

```
<Application.NavigationItems>
  <ApplicationNavigationGroup Name="Group1">
    <ApplicationNavigationGroup.Attributes>
      <DisplayName Value="Main Group 1" />
    </ApplicationNavigationGroup.Attributes>

    <ApplicationNavigationGroup Name="Group2">
      <ApplicationNavigationGroup.Attributes>
        <DisplayName Value=" Group 1 SubMenu" />
      </ApplicationNavigationGroup.Attributes>
      <ApplicationNavigationLink
          Command="!module/Commands[ScreenCommandShowCreateNewCustomer]"
          Name="link2" />
    </ApplicationNavigationGroup>
  </ApplicationNavigationGroup>

  <ApplicationNavigationGroup Name="Group3">
    <ApplicationNavigationGroup.Attributes>
      <DisplayName Value="Main Group 2" />
    </ApplicationNavigationGroup.Attributes>
    <ApplicationNavigationLink
        Command="!module/Commands[ScreenCommandShowSearchCustomer]"
        Name="link3" />
  </ApplicationNavigationGroup>

</Application.NavigationItems>
```

The <ApplicationNavigationGroup> element defines a navigation group. *Tasks* and *Administration* are groups that appear by default in a LightSwitch application. These <ApplicationNavigationGroup> elements can be nested inside each other to create a nested hierarchy. Figure 2-4 shows a more realistic example of what a nested navigation group would look like.

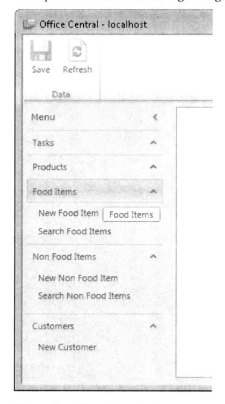

Figure 2-4. Nested navigation group

In this illustration, Products and Customers are children of the Tasks group. The Products group contains the child groups Food Items and Non Food Items. If you collapse a parent group, all child groups are collapsed at the same time. For example, collapsing Products hides both the Food Items and Non Food Items groups.

Although this technique works against the standard LightSwitch shell, it isn't guaranteed to work against other third-party shells.

The important point about this demonstration is that it introduces you to the contents of the LSML file and provides an example of why you might want to manually edit it.

Server Project

The **Server** project is a full .NET 4.0 class library and contains the logic that is executed on the server. Any code that you've written to handle data source events and validation logic is added to this project.

As soon as you write some code that handles a data source event against a table in your intrinsic database, a `UserCode` folder is created. Your code is then placed inside a file called `ApplicationDataService.vb` or `ApplicationDataService.cs,` depending on your chosen language.

If you were to attach to an external database called Northwind and write some code to handle a data source event for a table in the Northwind database, this code would be created in a file called `NorthwindDataService.vb` or `NorthwindDataService.cs`. As you saw in Chapter 1, a *data service* is created for each data source in your application. This explains why the term `DataService` in used in the file names. The event-handling code that you write for any entity in a data source is saved in a single data service file.

Examples of data source events are the events that make up the save pipeline. These are shown in the following list.

- `Deleted`
- `Deleting`
- `Inserted`
- `Inserting`
- `Updated`
- `Updating`
- `Validating`

Server access control events such as `CanDelete`, `CanInsert`, and `CanRead` are also saved in the `DataService` file. The query method code that you write to handle events in the query pipeline such as `PreprocessQuery` will also find itself in the file.

You can also use the `ServerGenerated` project to store various application settings. In Chapter 14, you'll learn how to send emails from the server. Rather than hard-coding the SMTP server address into your code, the address can be stored in a settings file, which makes it possible to change this setting after deployment.

ServerGenerated Project

The `ServerGenerated` project is an ASP.NET 4.0 that's executed on the server. You'll find a `web.config` file in this project that contains the connection string to your intrinsic database.

The files that support the Entity Framework model are also autogenerated into this folder. These include the files `ApplicationData.ssdl`, `ApplicationData.csdl`, and `ApplicationData.msl`. You'll also find .MSL, .CSDL, and .SSDL files for each additional data source that is defined in your application.

SSDL stands for *Store Schema Definition Language* and defines the schema of the tables at a SQL Server level. CSDL stands for *Conceptual Schema Definition Language,* and this defines the entities and relationships that are visible to LightSwitch.

In LightSwitch, there is always a one-to-one relationship between entities and tables. However, the Entity Framework allows for more-complex mappings, and a mapping layer defines the relationship between the conceptual and logical store layers. These mappings are stored in an MSL file, which stands for *Mapping Schema Language*. Figure 2-5 illustrates the relationships between CSDL, MSL, and SSDL files.

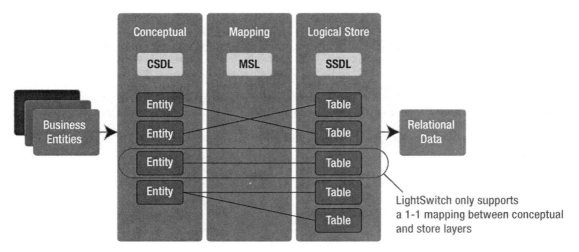

Figure 2-5. *The relationships between conceptual, mapping, and store layers*

Client Project

The client project is a Silverlight 4.0 class library project. It contains the client-side business logic that's executed on the client. For example, if you write some code to handle a button click, the code ends up in this project. Because this is a Silverlight project, only references to Silverlight DLLs can be added to this project.

As soon as you write any screen-related code, a `UserCode` folder is created and the code's file is placed inside this folder. If you create a Customer Detail screen, for example, any code that you write is added into a file called `CustomerDetail.vb` (or `CustomerDetail.cs`). Separate screen code files are generated for each screen, with file names that match the name of the screen. If a screen is renamed, LightSwitch automatically renames the underlying screen code file. The screen code file contains the user code that you write to handle the following screen events:

- `Activated`
- `Closing`
- `Created`
- `InitializeDataWorkspace`
- `Run`
- `SaveError`
- `Saved`
- `Saving`

The `Client` project also contains a file called `Application.vb` (or `Application.cs`). This `Application` file contains the user code that you would write to control security. For example, if a

CustomerDetail_CanRun method is created to control who can access the screen, this method is saved into the Application code file.

ClientGenerated Project

The ClientGenerated project is a Silverlight 4.0 application project. The main purpose of this project is to create a Silverlight XAP file.

An XAP file is a *Silverlight Application Package* and contains a compiled Silverlight application. Just like the Microsoft Office DOCX and XLSX files, XAP files are zip files that contain the files that are needed for the LightSwitch application to run. Renaming a XAP file to ZIP and opening it reveals the content.

After building a LightSwitch application, you can find the XAP file in the \bin\Release\Web or \bin\Debug\Web directory, depending on the build type. Assuming that you've called your LightSwitch application OfficeCentral, the file will be named OfficeCentral.Client.Xap. The XAP file contains the DLLs that are built from the Client and ClientGenerated projects, dependent DLLs, the LSML file, and an XAML file containing the shell definition.

Another important file that you'll find inside the XAP file is the AppManifest.xaml file. This file defines the DLLs that are included in the XAP. Listing 2-6 illustrates an example AppManifest file. The EntryPointAssembly attribute indicates that Microsoft.LightSwitch.Client.Internal.dll is the main assembly for the application. An instance of the Microsoft.LightSwitch.Runtime.Shell.Implementation.App class is instantiated when your LightSwitch application starts. The RuntimeVersion attribute defines the Silverlight version the application is built for, and the remainder of the file defines associated DLL files.

Listing 2-6. Contents of AppManifest.xaml

```
<Deployment
    xmlns="http://schemas.microsoft.com/client/2007/deployment"
    xmlns:x=http://schemas.microsoft.com/winfx/2006/xaml
    EntryPointAssembly="Microsoft.LightSwitch.Client.Internal"
    EntryPointType="Microsoft.LightSwitch.Runtime.Shell.Implementation.App"
  RuntimeVersion="4.0.50826.0">
  <Deployment.Parts>
    <AssemblyPart x:Name=" OfficeCentral.ClientGenerated"
        Source=" OfficeCentral.ClientGenerated.dll" />
    <AssemblyPart x:Name="Application.Common" Source="Application.Common.dll" />
    <AssemblyPart x:Name=" OfficeCentral.Client" Source=" OfficeCentral.Client.dll" />
    <AssemblyPart x:Name="Microsoft.LightSwitch.Base.Client"
        Source="Microsoft.LightSwitch.Base.Client.dll" />
    <AssemblyPart x:Name="Microsoft.LightSwitch.Client"
        Source="Microsoft.LightSwitch.Client.dll" />
.........
  </Deployment.Parts>
</Deployment>
```

The ClientGenerated project can be used to make resources available to the client. In Chapter 11, you'll learn how to create reports by using Microsoft Word automation. A DOT Word template file provides the template on which the report is based. The ClientGenerated project is the mechanism that enables the DOT file to be distributed to the client.

Common Project

The Common project contains code that's executed on both the client and server. This project is a plain Silverlight 4.0 class library project. However, the initial assembly references are set to those belonging in the *portable class library* subset.

Portable class libraries were introduced in .NET 4.0. These types of libraries can run on multiple .NET Framework platforms. In LightSwitch, the assembly built from the Common project is called from both the Silverlight client and ASP.NET server applications.

You'll find a UserCode folder in the Common project. This folder contains the user code that you write for each entity. For example, the Created, Changed, and Compute methods are saved here. The GeneratedArtifacts folder contains a series of autogenerated code for each entity.

SQL Server

SQL Server plays a major role in LightSwitch. This section shows you where your data is saved and why SQL Server Express is required, examines some of the inner workings of user instances, and describes how you can diagnose issues by using SQL Profiler.

Where Is the Intrinsic Database?

When you create a new LightSwitch project, an *intrinsic* database called ApplicationData is created in the project folder. This data source is the default place where user tables are created. The LightSwitch security tables containing users and roles are also created here. You'll find the database file at bin\data\ApplicationData.mdf.

If you're not too familiar with SQL Server, the MDF file is the primary file that is used for storing the data and database objects. Tables, views, indexes, constraints, and stored procedures are examples of the types of objects that are stored in the MDF file. When debugging applications, an ApplicationData.ldf file is created in the same directory as the MDF file. The LDF file contains the contents of the SQL Server transaction log.

■ **Caution** This intrinsic database is designed to store temporary data for use during debugging time. This data is not deployed with the application, and there may be times when the LightSwitch IDE has to delete the data in order to achieve a schema change.

Why Do I Need SQL Express?

Some users may prefer to host the intrinsic database by using a non-Express version of SQL Server, particularly if a full version of SQL Server is available on the local development machine. This scenario is not supported, and errors will occur if you modify the database connection string in the web.config file to point to a non–SQL Express instance. SQL Express is required so that LightSwitch projects can be shared between users. By using the Auto Attach feature of SQL Express, both the database and LightSwitch project files are self-contained in a single folder. This allows you to easily back up and share your LightSwitch project.

Note that the SQL Server Express requirement does not apply to deployed applications. During deployment, you can choose to host the intrinsic database in a full version of SQL Server, SQL Express, or even SQL Server Azure if you wish.

What Is a SQL Server User Instance?

Unfortunately, many LightSwitch developers first encounter the term *SQL user instance* following a failure to connect to the intrinsic database. In order to explain what this is, we'll describe the problems that user instances were designed to solve.

In simple terms, an *instance* is a copy of SQL Server that runs on a machine. Each instance has its own settings and logins, and listens on a distinct port number.

The usual way of accessing the contents of a SQL Server database file is to first attach it in SQL Server. If you're using an edition of SQL Server other than SQL Server Express, this step must be carried out. After you do this, a security login must be created, and that login added to the user list for the database. For developers, this is a cumbersome process. To make life easier, SQL Server Express includes an Auto Attach feature. This allows you to use a SQL Express database, just by specifying a database file name in the connection string. There's no need for you to do anything else in SQL Server Management Studio, or to carry out any additional setup tasks. This feature makes it really easy for you to use databases and share them with others.

The traditional way of attaching a database can present a second challenge. This is because you must have SQL Server administrative privileges to attach a database. The exact problem is that you might not be an administrator, or you might work in a corporate environment where you've been denied the necessary permissions. User instances provide the solution to these problems. They allow you to auto-attach a database without needing any administrative permissions. This feature is found *only* in the Express version and isn't available in any other edition of SQL Server.

A user instance is like a normal instance, but is created on demand when a connection to the database is first made. The user instance runs under the security context of the user who initiates the connection. This therefore gives the user full administrative control over the instance, even if the user doesn't have administrative privileges on the machine.

User instances are hosted by a *parent* SQL Server Express instance. If you want to use a user instance, you'd create a connection to the parent SQL Server Express instance and specify the user instance flag in the connection string.

Tip Chapter 17 contains various tips to help you diagnose and solve SQL Server problems.

Attaching the SQL Server Intrinsic Database by Using Server Explorer

In this section, we'll show you how to use Server Explorer to connect to your intrinsic database. By connecting to the database in this way, you can work with data inside of Visual Studio without having to run your application.

You can also create database diagrams that enable you to view multiple tables and relationships in your database. This allows you to see the bigger picture, because the LightSwitch designer lets you view only one table at a time.

In order to view the intrinsic database in Server Explorer, open Server Explorer by clicking View ➤ Server Explorer, or click Ctrl+Alt+S. After Server Explorer appears, right-click the Data Connections icon and select the Add Connection option, as shown in Figure 2-6. The Add Connection dialog box appears (see Figure 2-7).

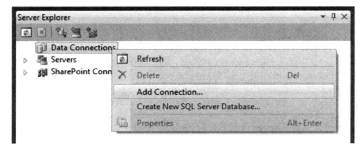

Figure 2-6. In the Server Explorer window, choose the Add Connection option

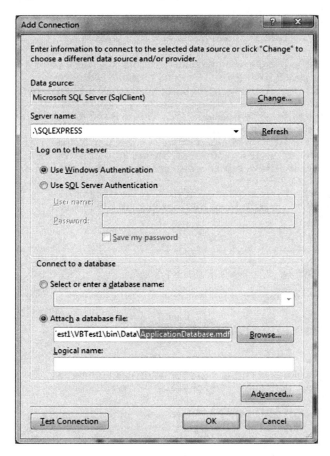

Figure 2-7. The Add Connection dialog box

In the Add Connection dialog box, enter the SQL Server Express instance name into the Server Name text box. Select the option to Attach a Database File and provide the path to your `ApplicationDatabase.mdf` file. Now click the Advanced button, and in the Advanced Properties dialog box, set the User Instance option to True, as shown in Figure 2-8.

Figure 2-8. Set the User Instance option to True.

Complete the steps in the Add Connection dialog box. When you are finished, the connection to your intrinsic database will be shown in Server Explorer, as you can see in Figure 2-9.

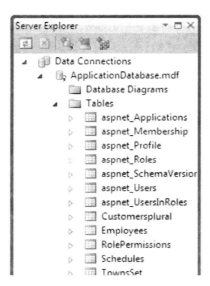

Figure 2-9. *The ApplicationDatabase file now appears in Server Explorer.*

Notice how all of the database objects are visible beneath the Tables node. You'll also see a set of aspnet_* tables. These tables are used by LightSwitch to manage security, users, and roles.

By using the options that appear in the Database Diagrams node, you can create and manage your own database diagrams.

It's important to bear in mind that additional tables or columns added through Server Manager will not be reflected in your LightSwitch model. Therefore, you should continue to design your tables by using the LightSwitch table designer.

■ **Note** When the time comes to deploy your application, you might want to include the data that you've entered at debugging time. For example, you might want to script out the data that you've entered so that you can add it to your deployment package. Attaching the database allows you to get to your data and to carry out this task..

Profiling the Intrinsic Database by Using SQL Server Profiler

SQL Server Profiler is a very useful debugging tool. It allows you to see the exact SQL that LightSwitch generates and submits to SQL Server. You'll find it included in some of the paid-for versions of SQL Server. If you don't have access to SQL Server Profiler, a free alternative is AnjLab SQLExpressProfiler. This product is open source, and you can download it from http://sites.google.com/site/sqlprofiler/.

SQL Server Profiler can help you uncover some of the inner workings of LightSwitch. We'll show you how to use Profiler now because we'll refer to the traces that it creates later in the book.

During debugging time, LightSwitch hosts the intrinsic database by using a user instance of SQL Server Express. If you want to start a trace in Profiler, you can't connect to a SQL Server user instance by using TCP/IP and a server name. Instead, you have to use named pipes. To find out the address to use, connect to SQL Server Express by using Management Studio, or by using Server Explorer as described earlier.

If you're using Server Explorer, create a new connection to the master database of your SQLEXPRESS instance. Now start your LightSwitch application. Next, create a new query by choosing Data ➤ New Query. Execute the SQL command shown in Listing 2-7 to return the pipe name, as shown in Figure 2-10.

Listing 2-7. *SQL to Find Out the Pipe Name*

```
SELECT owning_principal_name,instance_pipe_name FROM sys.dm_os_child_instances
```

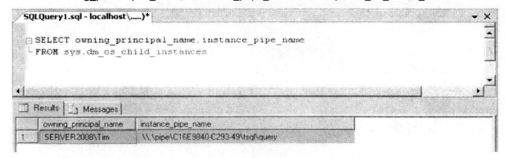

Figure 2-10. *The pipe name is shown in the results.*

Now that you know the pipe name, you can use SQL Server Profiler to trace your intrinsic database. Connect to the server by using the pipe name (shown in Figure 2-11) and begin a trace. Perform some actions in your LightSwitch application, and the results will be shown in the trace (see Figure 2-12).

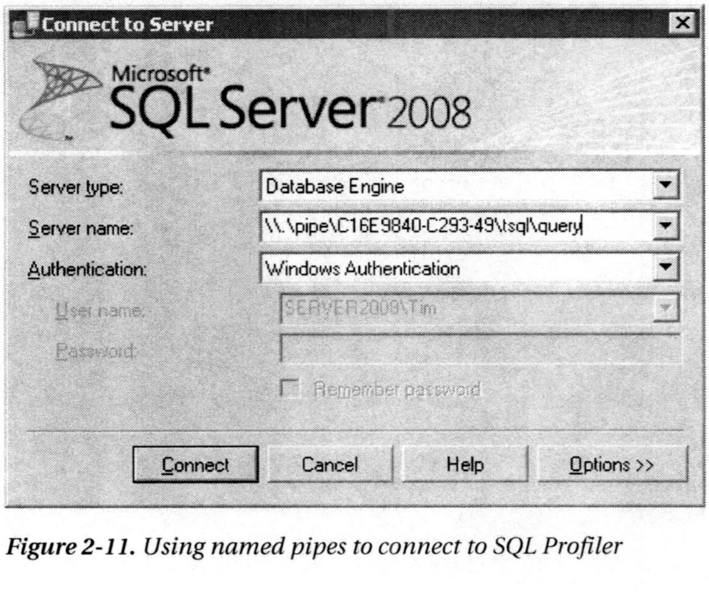

Figure 2-11. *Using named pipes to connect to SQL Profiler*

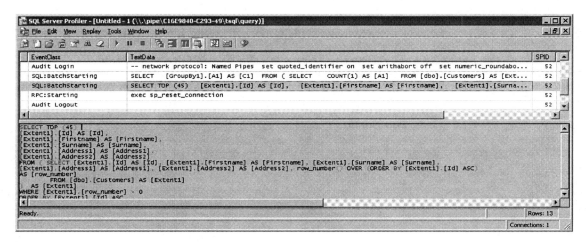

Figure 2-12. *Illustration of trace results*

Debugging LightSwitch Code

Even the best programmers will make mistakes when writing applications. Fortunately, the Visual Studio IDE contains some powerful tools that will help you detect and correct problems.

You may have some familiarity using the debugger. If not, this section will help you understand some of the basics before moving on further into this book.

Debugging Concepts

Breakpoints are a key part of debugging. You can insert these into your code by clicking on the left margin of the code window. When the code execution reaches the breakpoint, the program stops executing temporarily. You can then step through the remaining code one line at a time by pressing F10, or by clicking the Step Over button. If you want to dive into functions or subprocedures that are being called in the current line, pressing F11 allows you to Step Into the child procedures.

If you want to skip over several lines of code without having to step over each line individually, you can place the cursor on a line beneath and select the Run to Cursor option, as shown in Figure 2-13.

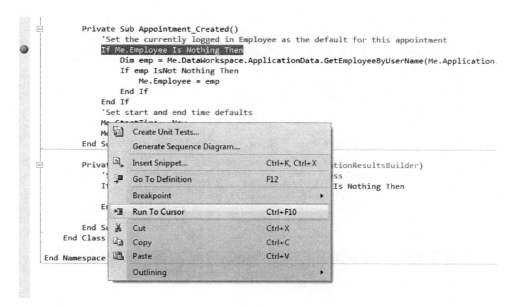

```
Private Sub Appointment_Created()
    'Set the currently logged in Employee as the default for this appointment
    If Me.Employee Is Nothing Then
        Dim emp = Me.DataWorkspace.ApplicationData.GetEmployeeByUserName(Me.Application
        If emp IsNot Nothing Then
            Me.Employee = emp
        End If
    End If
    'Set start and end time defaults
    Me
    Me
End Su
```

	Create Unit Tests...	
	Generate Sequence Diagram...	
	Insert Snippet...	Ctrl+K, Ctrl+X
	Go To Definition	F12
	Breakpoint	▶
	Run To Cursor	Ctrl+F10
	Cut	Ctrl+X
	Copy	Ctrl+C
	Paste	Ctrl+V
	Outlining	▶

Figure 2-13. Using the Run to Cursor option

If during a session you want to run your application for a while without stopping at breakpoints, you can select the Disable All Breakpoints option under the Debug menu. When you're ready to break into breakpoints again, you can select the Enable All Breakpoints option to continue.

Locals Window

The Locals window, shown in Figure 2-14, allows you to keep track of local variables. These variables appear beneath the Name column, and additional attributes can be shown by expanding the tree nodes.

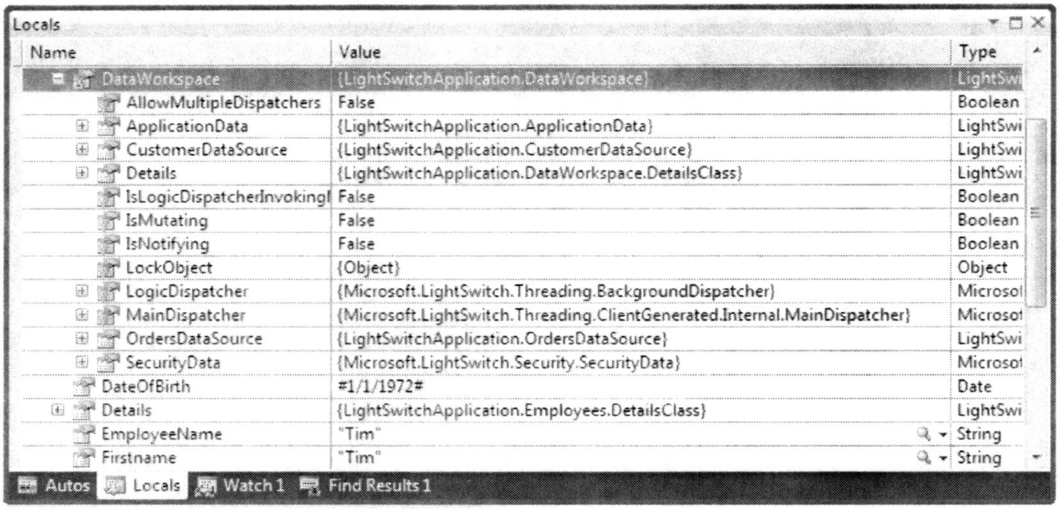

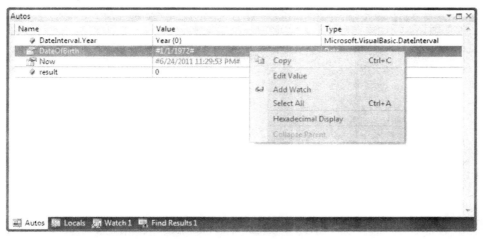

Figure 2-14. Local variables shown in the Locals window

Autos and Watch Windows

The Autos window is one of the main windows used during debugging. This window displays the values of variables and properties as they are evaluated by the compiler. These values disappear when the objects fall out of scope.

Unlike the Autos window, the Watch window allows you to view values throughout the execution of a program. Figure 2-15 illustrates how a watch can be added through the Autos window by selecting the Add Watch option.

Figure 2-15. Adding a watch via the Autos window

Immediate and Command Windows

The Immediate window, shown in Figure 2-16, is a very versatile tool. It allows you to easily interrogate variable values by using the ? operator. The Immediate window provides IntelliSense assistance to help you construct the correct syntax. Unlike the other debugging windows, the Immediate window allows you to change the values of properties and variables while debugging.

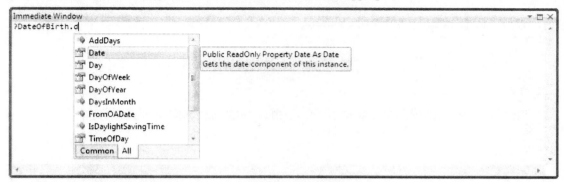

Figure 2-16. Using the ? command in the Immediate window

The Command window, shown in Figure 2-17, allows you to run Visual Studio commands such as File.SaveAll. You don't need to be in debug mode to run commands in the Command window. As in the Immediate window, the commands in the Command window also support IntelliSense.

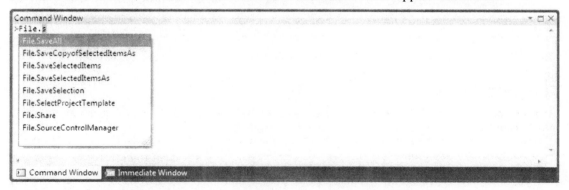

Figure 2-17. Command window

While in the Command window, you can switch to the Immediate window by typing immed. Conversely, you can switch to the Command window from the Immediate window by typing cmd.

Attaching to the Debugger

The Debug ➤ Attach to Process menu option allows you to attach processes to the debugger. For example, if you want to debug using the Firefox browser instead of Internet Explorer, you can attach the

Firefox Silverlight client to the debugger by attaching to the `plugin-container.exe` (type `Silverlight`) process. This is shown in Figure 2-18.

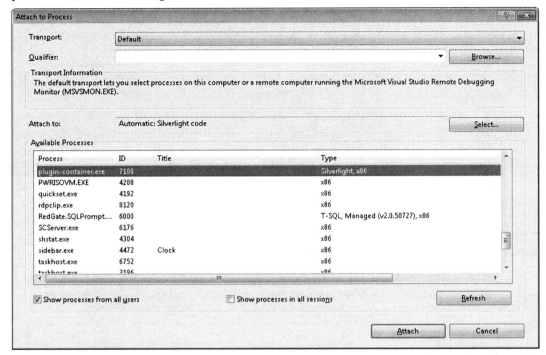

Figure 2-18. *Attaching processes to the debugger*

Debugging Queries

Experienced developers will often extend queries by using the `_PreProcessQuery` or `_Executed` methods. When LINQ or other coding errors are encountered, these exceptions will be *swallowed* by LightSwitch. A red cross appears against any grids that are bound to the query, and no indication is given as to what the exact cause of the error might be.

To help diagnose such errors, failed queries raise the `_ExecuteFailed` event, giving access to the underlying exception. Handling this event and placing a breakpoint on the method (Figure 2-19) allows you to interrogate the exception by using tools such as the Immediate or Autos windows.

```vb
Namespace LightSwitchApplication

    Public Class ApplicationDataService

        Private Sub Teenagers_PreprocessQuery(ByRef query As System.Linq.IQueryable(Of LightSwitc
            'the query below contains an error
            query = query.Where(Function(a) a.Age = 18)
        End Sub

        Private Sub Teenagers_ExecuteFailed(exception As Exception)
            'create an empty event handler to allow you to place a breakpoint above
        End Sub

    End Class

End Namespace
```

Figure 2-19. Handling_ExecuteFailed

Debugging Threading Issues

Let's imagine that you've written a complex piece of screen code. This code performs an operation that takes a long time to complete. When your code runs, your application still remains responsive. In other words, it can still respond to mouse clicks and keystrokes, and provides a positive experience for the user. Your application can do this because LightSwitch uses two threads.

In LightSwitch, all UI tasks and user interaction is carried out by a UI thread (also known as the *main dispatcher*). Each screen gets its own thread for carrying out tasks that are not UI related. This thread is called the *screen thread*, or *logic thread*. Whenever you write any user code on a screen, the operation is executed on the screen thread by default.

Let's say that you want to perform a task that requires some user intervention. For example, imagine that you want to show a File Open dialog box. You must write code to specifically carry out this task on the UI thread. If you fail to do this, LightSwitch throws an exception.

If you're debugging a piece of code, it's really useful to be able to identify what thread you're running on. To find this out, place a breakpoint in your code. You can then use the Immediate window and call the `CheckAccess` method, as shown in Listing 2-8. If the result is **true**, your code is running on the UI thread. If **false**, it's running on the logic thread.

Listing 2-8. CheckAccess Method

```
Microsoft.LightSwitch.Threading.Dispatchers.Main.CheckAccess()
```

There are three *dispatchers* that you can use in LightSwitch. These allow you to execute code on a different thread. The following list summarizes the LightSwitch object that you can use to reference the dispatcher.

- Main dispatcher (UI thread)—`Dispatchers.Main`

- Screen dispatcher (logic thread)—`Screen.Details.Dispatcher`

- Application dispatcher—`Application.Details.Dispatcher`

In addition to the UI and logic dispatchers, the application dispatcher is responsible for running global application code that isn't associated with any specific screen.

■ **Note** If you need to diagnose problems after deployment, the tracing feature in LightSwitch can help you to do that. You can find out more about this in Chapter 17.

Compacting LS Solutions for Backup

You may have discovered that LightSwitch projects take up a lot of space on the file system. The size taken up by an empty project is around 89MB. After building the project for the first time, the size increases to around 132MB , even though there are still no tables or screens in the project.

The size of LightSwitch projects can present a problem when trying to back up or share your work with others. Because the bin and obj folders are regenerated following each build, these folders can be deleted prior to backing up. If you choose to do this, however, make sure not to delete the file bin\data\ApplicationData.mdf, because this contains your design-time intrinsic database.

You can simplify this task by creating a batch file to automate the process. The content of such a script is shown in Listing 2-9.

Listing 2-9. *Batch File to Compact Solution*

```
rd /q /s Bin\Debug
rd /q /s Bin\Release

rd /q /s Client\Bin\Debug
rd /q /s Client\Bin\Release

rd /q /s Client\obj\Debug
rd /q /s Client\obj\Release

rd /q /s ClientGenerated\Bin\Debug
rd /q /s ClientGenerated\Bin\Release

rd /q /s ClientGenerated\obj\Debug
rd /q /s ClientGenerated\obj\Release

rd /q /s Common\Bin\Debug
rd /q /s Common\Bin\Release

rd /q /s Common\obj\Debug
rd /q /s Common\obj\Release

rd /q /s Server\Bin\Debug
rd /q /s Server\Bin\Release

rd /q /s Server\obj\Debug
rd /q /s Server\obj\Release

rd /q /s ServerGenerated\bin\Debug
rd /q /s ServerGenerated\bin\Release
rd /q /s ServerGenerated\bin
```

```
rd /q /s ServerGenerated\obj\Debug
rd /q /s ServerGenerated\obj\Release
```

Create this file in the root folder of your project and execute it in order to delete all extraneous files. The remaining files and folders can be *zipped* into a compressed file to further reduce file size.

Summary

This chapter has covered the following topics:

- How LightSwitch projects are organized on the file system
- The purpose of the LSML file
- The role that SQL Server Express plays in LightSwitch
- How to debug LightSwitch code

You can switch your LightSwitch project into File view by clicking a button in Solution Explorer. This reveals the projects that make up a LightSwitch solution. The projects that you'll find are as follows:

- `Client` contains the client-side business logic.
- `ClientGenerated` builds the Silverlight XAP file.
- `Server` contains server-side business logic.
- `ServerGenerated` contains the ASP.NET server project.
- `Common` contains the common business logic used on the client and server.

`ApplicationDefinition.lsml` is a very important file and contains the definitions of all screens and entities in your application. In some advanced scenarios, you'll need to manually modify this file by using a text editor. The example that we've given in this chapter shows you how to create nested navigation groups. Whenever you modify this file outside of LightSwitch, we strongly recommend that you back up the file.

The intrinsic database stores the tables that you create in LightSwitch. During design time, a temporary database is created in the location `bin\data\ApplicationData.mdf`. This temporary database is used to store your data between debugging sessions. The data that you enter at design time won't be deployed with your final application. If you need to get to this data, you can connect to the `ApplicationData.mdf` file by using Server Explorer or SQL Server Management Studio.

The intrinsic database must be hosted by SQL Server Express at development time (although there isn't any limitation for deployed applications). The SQL Server Express requirement makes it easy for you to share LightSwitch projects. If someone else opens a project that you've created, there isn't any need for them to create or attach a corresponding database. The auto-attach, and user instance features of SQL Server Express make this possible.

Finally, you've seen how to debug LightSwitch applications by using the debugger. When you're debugging problems with queries, it's a good idea to place a breakpoint in the `ExecuteFailed` method. This allows you to get to the actual exception. When debugging threading issues, you can call the `CheckAccess` method on the main dispatcher to work out what thread you're running on.

PART 2

Working With Data

CHAPTER 3

Working with Data

Data is the core feature that makes LightSwitch what it is. Data is the heart and soul of the product, and without it, LightSwitch would not be capable of doing very much. To illustrate the prominence of data, the very first screen that you see when creating a LightSwitch application prompts you to either create a new table or attach to existing data.

In this chapter, you will learn how to use data in LightSwitch. This includes creating tables and fields, attaching to existing data, setting up relationships, and programming computed properties.

Understanding Entities and Properties

We begin this chapter by explaining a couple of fundamental items. An *entity* is the basic unit of data that is used within LightSwitch. Database developers are familiar with tables and rows. An entity can be thought of as a single row from a database table. A database row contains one or more fields, and LightSwitch *properties* are analogous to the fields or columns from a table.

To give a second example, LightSwitch can be used to connect to a Microsoft SharePoint 2010 list. A SharePoint list item will map to a LightSwitch entity, and a list column will be exposed as a LightSwitch property.

Screens in LightSwitch are based on entities (or *entity collections* in the case of list or grid-type screens). Entities can also be programmatically accessed through code, and Chapter 4 provides many coding examples.

Note To clarify the correct technical terminology, *entity collections* are not the same as *entity sets*. A list or grid binds to an entity collection, which is the result of querying an entity set. An entity set represents the table or list on the server where the entities come from and return to.

Attaching to Existing Data

LightSwitch allows you to connect to a wide range of data sources. If you select the option to attach to existing data, LightSwitch provides you with three default choices. You can attach to any of the following:

- A database
- A SharePoint list

- A Windows Communication Foundation Rich Internet Application (WCF RIA) service

The list doesn't end there, however. As long as a compatible entity framework provider is available for your data source, LightSwitch can consume the data. This enables you to connect to data sources such as Oracle and MySQL (as shown in Figure 3-1). To clarify what we mean by a compatible entity framework provider, not all providers are created equal. LightSwitch requires specific features to be supported by the entity framework provider, so the compatibility is worth checking before you attempt to use a provider in LightSwitch.

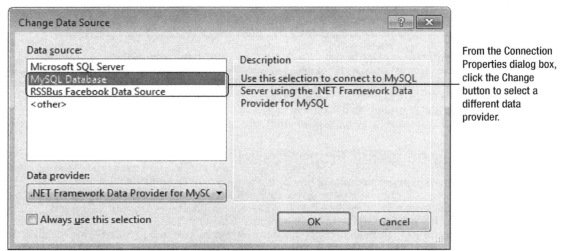

From the Connection Properties dialog box, click the Change button to select a different data provider.

Figure 3-1. Connecting to a MySQL data source

If an entity framework provider is unavailable, you can write your own RIA service or even your own custom data source extension. Both options provide you with much flexibility in terms of connecting to the data of your choice.

When using an external data source, you can't add new tables or modify the schema of an existing table. For example, you can't add new database fields or modify the names of existing fields.

However, it is possible to change the data type of a LightSwitch property to another compatible business type. For example, a property that LightSwitch has imported as a string can be changed to the LightSwitch Phone Number type.

Attaching to an Existing Database

To attach to an existing SQL Server database, right-click the Data node in Solution Explorer and select the Add a Datasource option. Choose the SQL Server option and follow the steps until you reach the Connection Properties dialog box.

This standard dialog box enables you to enter the details of your SQL Server. If you want to connect to a SQL Server instance running on your local machine, you can specify localhost or type the full-stop character (a period) as the server name.

The next dialog box, shown in Figure 3-2, enables you to choose the tables and views to use in your LightSwitch application.

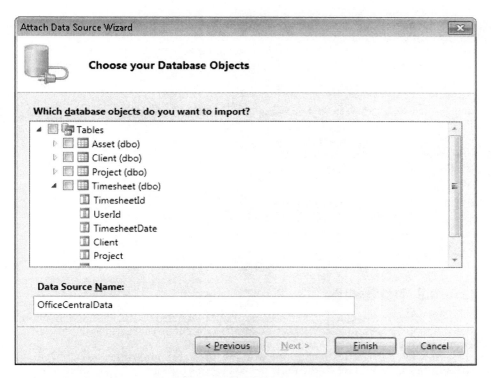

Figure 3-2. *Choose your Database Objects dialog box*

Stored procedures, user-defined functions, and other SQL objects are not supported and do not appear in this dialog box. If you want to use stored procedures, you can do so by writing a custom RIA service.

▪ **Note** After attaching to an external table, you can use the table designer to reorder the columns. Although this won't affect the underlying SQL table, any new screens that you create will have their data entry controls ordered in the sequence that you have specified.

Finding Missing Tables

Some users often report that tables appear to be missing from the Choose Your Database Objects dialog box. This problem is caused by primary keys not being defined on the missing tables. After primary keys have been set up, the tables will appear correctly in the Data Source Wizard.

If an identity column has been specified without a primary key defined, the table appears in read-only mode. Figure 3-3 illustrates the alert that LightSwitch shows you when it encounters such a table.

For those unfamiliar with SQL Server, *identity columns* are auto-incrementing fields similar to sequences in Oracle or autonumbers in Microsoft Access.

Likewise, any views that you want to add must contain a derivable primary-key column and can be attached only in read-only mode.

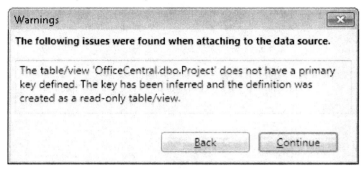

Figure 3-3. *Table attached in read-only mode*

Refreshing an External Data Source

After adding an external data source, two things could change about that data source. First, the location of the data source could change. For example, a SQL Server database might be moved to a different server. Second, tables and fields can be added, edited, or deleted.

In order for your LightSwitch application to continue working, the data source must be refreshed. To do this, right-click the data source and select the Refresh Data Source option. The first dialog box that appears is the Choose Your Database Objects dialog box, illustrated earlier in Figure 3-2.

If the location of the data source has changed, click the Previous button to return to the Connection Properties dialog box. This will enable you to update the connection details. If tables or fields have been added, edited, or deleted, click the Next button to progress through the Data Source Wizard. If any changes are found, these will be indicated by icons with a red x or exclamation point, as shown in Figure 3-4.

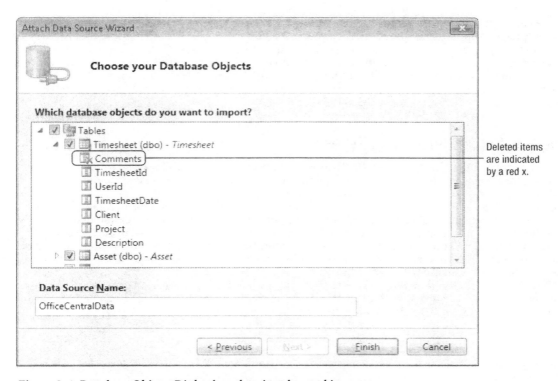

Figure 3-4. Database Objects Dialog box showing changed items

Clicking the Finish button will update all screens and remove controls that are bound to the deleted fields. Any references made to those fields in code will not be updated. If references exist in code, they will become invalid and show up in the Error List window as errors. At this point, you can work your way through the error list and resolve any remaining errors.

☰ **Note** Although the Refresh Data Source option allows you to change the connection string from one SQL Server to another, you can't change the underlying data provider. For example, you can't change from SQL Server to MySQL without deleting the tables in the LightSwitch model and reimporting.

Working with *Datetimeoffset* and Other Unsupported Data Types

When connecting to an existing database, there are five SQL column types that are currently unsupported. These are the spacial types geography and geometry, hierarchyid, sql_variant, and datetimeoffset. If you have an existing database that uses any of these data types, LightSwitch will be unable to read or write to any of these fields.

The data type datetimeoffset is the one that causes the most concern with developers. It is commonly used in applications that span multiple time zones.

If you want to create an application that supports multiple time zones, the simplest solution is to save all datetime values in UTC (Coordinated Universal Time). Server-side code related to entities can be used to ensure that all dates are saved in this format. The .NET datetime class contains a DateTime.ToUniversalTime method that can be used to convert times. A custom control can then be written to display the UTC value in the local time zone.

Using SQL Server Binary Data Types

A useful feature included in SQL Server 2008 is the FileStream feature. This allows you to save varbinary(max) data such as images and documents into the file system instead of inside the database. T-SQL can still be used to insert, update, and read the binary data.

One advantage of using FileStream is that it makes it easier to access your data, particularly if you integrate your LightSwitch solution with other systems (such as an ASP.NET web site) that need to access the data. If you're using SQL Server 2008 Express, the database size is limited to 4GB. FileStream data does not count toward this 4GB limit, so a second advantage is that it allows you to store more data. A third benefit is that FileStream provides better performance over database storage if the average size of the files that are stored is larger than 1MB.

Note that the FileStream data type is supported only in external SQL Server 2008 and is not directly supported in the intrinsic LightSwitch database. If you're wondering how FileStream-enabled databases are backed up, the standard SQL backup will include the FileStream data.

■ **Note** If you attach a table that contains an image column, LightSwitch will set the data type for that column to Binary by default. If you want the column to behave as an image column and to use the built-in LightSwitch image controls, be sure to open the table in the LightSwitch designer and change the data type from Binary to Image.

Attaching to SharePoint Data

LightSwitch can connect to a SharePoint 2010 server and attach to list data. LightSwitch uses a custom OData provider, and therefore versions prior to SharePoint 2010 are not supported. At the time of this writing, SharePoint Online is also unsupported. You can attach to SharePoint lists by using the Data Source Wizard in a similar fashion to connecting to SQL Server data.

Various limitations exist when using SharePoint data, however. First, LightSwitch cannot be used to manage SharePoint attachments or documents. Second, there is limited support for the SharePoint column types of Picture and Hyperlink. This is because no native controls exist for formatting these data items. Formatted text is also not fully supported, because there is no native HTML control built in to edit the content.

Attaching to WCF RIA Services Data

If a data provider doesn't exist for your chosen data source, you can write your own RIA service to make a data connection. Because this involves writing your own entity classes, it is best done for in-house solutions or for connecting to services with data schemas that rarely change. Chapter 7 describes how to do this in more detail.

Deleting a Data Source

If you delete a data source, LightSwitch will remove all entities that relate to the data source from all screens in your application. The screens themselves will not be deleted, but only the instances of the entities and related controls.

Creating a Table in the Intrinsic Database

When tables are created in LightSwitch, they are created in the intrinsic database. As mentioned earlier, the LightSwitch designer cannot be used to add or modify tables in an external SQL database or other attached data source. To create a table, right-click the ApplicationData node in Solution Explorer and select the option to create a new table.

Modifying Table Properties

Figure 3-5 illustrates the properties that can be modified after you've created a table.

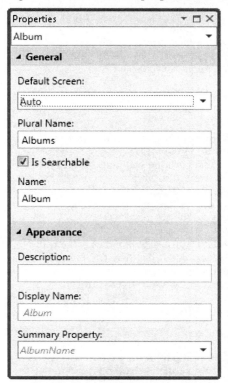

Figure 3-5. The properties of a table

The properties are as follows:

- *Name*: The name is used to identify the table. The name must begin with an alphabetic character and can contain only alphanumeric characters and the underscore character. Other special characters such as spaces or periods (the full-stop character) are not permitted.

- *Display Name*: The display name is shown by default in the navigation pane.

- *Description*: This field is used to provide a longer description of the table.

- *Plural Name*: This field indicates the default name used when the table collection is added onto a screen. It's also used to refer to the collection when writing code.

- *Summary Property*: If a summary control is added onto a screen, the text displayed on the summary control uses the field specified here. Also, LightSwitch creates an entity object that allows you to refer to a record in code. This object includes a ToString method that returns the value of the summary property.

- *Default Screen*: The summary control renders itself as a link. Clicking the link opens the screen specified here. The drop-down list includes an Auto option. If Auto is selected, LightSwitch will automatically generate a screen based on the table.

- *Is Searchable*: If this option is selected, the contents of the table are searchable. However, autosearching is supported only for string data types. If you create a screen by using the search screen template, the search results do not include data that is saved in numeric and datetime columns, even if the Is Searchable check box is selected.

Moving Intrinsic Tables to an External Data Source

After creating a table in the intrinsic database, you might want to move it to an external database without deleting or creating any screens that are based on that entity. There is no native way to do this. Instead, you must create a connection to your database by using the technique outlined in Chapter 2: script your table and re-create it in your new database. Unless you want to re-create all screens that use the table, you will need to manually modify your ApplicationData.lsml file and change all references to the table to point to the new data source. If there is any possibility that you may want to move your tables to an external database, the best advice we can give you is to create the tables externally in the first place.

There are some advantages to be gained from using external data sources. SQL gurus can easily control other database objects such as stored procedures, triggers, and custom views. You could then use Visual Studio Professional (or above) or SQL Server Management Studio to create and edit the database and attach to it using LightSwitch. LightSwitch will subsequently not manage publishing or updating the schema.

Working with LightSwitch Data Types

When tables are created in the LightSwitch entity designer, corresponding tables are created in the intrinsic SQL Server database. These fields will also be exposed through code and are mapped to .NET data types. Table 3-1 illustrates the relationship between the LightSwitch, .NET, and SQL Server types. For example, a Boolean field created in LightSwitch will be created as a bit field in the SQL Server database. Working in the other direction, a float field in an external data source will be exposed as a Double when attached to LightSwitch.

Table 3-1 also highlights the Email Address, Money, and Phone Number business types and how these map to the SQL nvarchar data type. Business types are custom data types provided by LightSwitch. These extend the native data types that are provided by .NET. For example, the Phone Number business type is an extension of the String type.

Table 3-1. Mappings between LightSwitch, .NET, and SQL Data Types

LightSwitch Type	VB.NET Type	C# Type	SQL Type
Binary	Byte()	byte[]	varbinary (max)
Boolean	Boolean	Bool	bit
Date	DateTime	DateTime	datetime
DateTime	DateTime	DateTime	datetime
Decimal	Decimal	Decimal	decimal
Double	Double	Double	float
Email Address	String	String	nvarchar
Image	Byte()	byte()	varbinary (max)
Short Integer	Short	Short	smallint
Integer	Integer	Int	int
Long Integer	Long	Long	bigint
Money	Decimal	Decimal	decimal (18,2)
Phone Number	String	String	nvarchar
String	String	String	nvarchar

■ **Note** If the table designer fails to list any of the business types, make sure that the Microsoft LightSwitch Extensions option has not been inadvertently deselected in the Extensions section of the properties pane for your project.

String Data Type

The underlying SQL data type used for storing string data is nvarchar. This data type provides storage for variable-length Unicode data and supports international character types.

When a new string field is created, the maximum field size is set to 255 characters. As a matter of good practice, this should be modified as appropriate for the data to be stored. It is unlikely that a Surname field would require 255 characters, for example. Setting the maximum field to something more appropriate will help improve performance.

Behind the scenes, LightSwitch creates an nvarchar column that corresponds to the required field length. For example, setting the maximum field length to 25 creates an nvarchar(25) field within the SQL Server table.

If you need to create an unlimited-length string, or a field of data type nvarchar(max) in SQL Server terms, it may not be clear how to do this through the entity designer. The way to do this is to clear the contents of the Maximum Length text box and leave it blank, as shown in Figure 3-6.

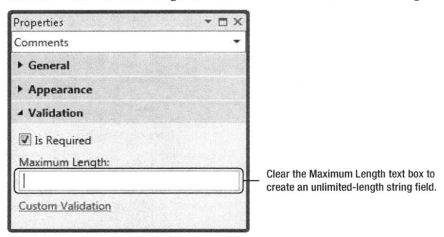

Clear the Maximum Length text box to create an unlimited-length string field.

Figure 3-6. Properties of a string field

Double and *Decimal* Numeric Types

If you want to store numbers with decimal places, LightSwitch provides a choice of either the double or decimal data types.

The practical difference between the two types is that doubles can store a wide range of numbers in a smaller amount of memory. However, doubles are less precise and are subject to rounding errors when calculations are performed with them.

Decimals do not suffer from such rounding errors but take up more space and are slower to compute. Sums of money should always be based on the decimal data type. Therefore, notice how the LightSwitch Money business type is mapped to the SQL decimal type.

Other important attributes that relate to decimals are precision and scale. *Precision* is the total number of digits in a number. *Scale* is the number of digits after the decimal place. Figure 3-7 illustrates this using the example number 123456.789.

The precision is 9.
The scale is 3.

Figure 3-7. Identifying precision and scale

Decimal fields in LightSwitch are created with a default precision of 18 and scale of 2. In keeping with good practice, the precision and scale should be set to values appropriate for the data being stored. As shown in Figure 3-8, these settings are entered in the Validation section of the Properties window.

Figure 3-8. Setting the precision and scale

Phone Number Business Type

Phone Number is one of three business types included in LightSwitch. As its name indicates, this type is designed for entering phone numbers. Any data entered into this field is saved as nvarchar string data in the database.

After selecting the Phone Number type for a property, the Phone Number Formats dialog box, shown in Figure 3-9, enables you to input a list of valid formats.

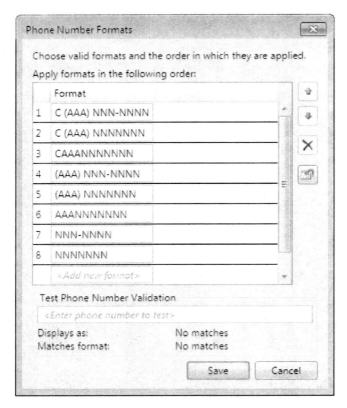

Figure 3-9. Phone Number Formats dialog box

The symbols that you can use to specify formats are as follows:

- *C*: Country code

- *A*: Area or city code

- *N*: Local number

- +, -, (,), . : Additional symbols that are also supported

When a Phone Number property is added onto a screen, the phone number control is the default control used to display the data. When a phone number is entered, this control attempts to validate the phone number against the first format in the list. If the digits match the format, the phone number appears in that format. Otherwise, an attempt is made to validate the phone number against all remaining formats in the list until a match is made.

When a phone number is saved in the database, the string data is saved without any formatting. If you want to create your own reports or to use the phone number data outside of LightSwitch, you'll need to write your own procedures to format the data.

The US phone number formats are added by default. For those living in the United Kingdom, here is list of formats valid for that country:

- (AAA) NNNNNNNN

- (AAAAA) NNNNN

- +CC (AA) NNNNNNNN

- +CC (AAAA) NNNNN

- +CCC (AA) NNNNNN

- +CCC (A) NNNNNN

Unfortunately, it's not possible to specify formats on a global or application basis. They must be specified each time a phone number field is used in a table.

Email Business Type

Email is another business type included in LightSwitch. Just like the Phone Number business type, the underlying database storage type is nvarchar.

After adding an Email property to a table, you'll find two extra settings in addition to the settings that are available for the string type (shown in Figure 3-10). These are as follows:

- *Default Email Domain*: If an email domain is omitted, the email domain will be appended to the end of the email address. This setting is ideal when creating an *internal* system that is used by a single company. This setting applies only when entering data by using the built-in email control, and does not apply when the property is programmatically set.

- *Require Email Domain*: If this option is selected, the user must enter an email domain when entering an email address. This setting applies to LightSwitch's data validation functionality, which operates independently of data entry.

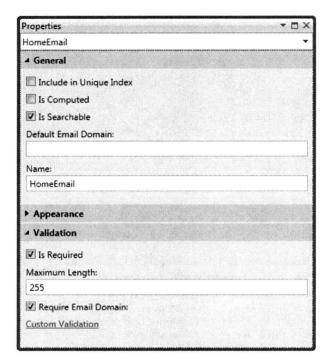

Figure 3-10. Email business type properties

Money Business Type

Money is the third business type that is provided by LightSwitch.

After adding a Money field to a table, the additional properties that you can set are shown in Figure 3-11. These are as follows:

- *Currency Code*: Use this field to specify the locale for the currency. For example, if you wish to use US dollars, specify en-US. The most common language codes are listed in Appendix 1.

- *Is Formatted*: If this option is selected, the currency symbol, grouping separator, and custom decimal digits are displayed.

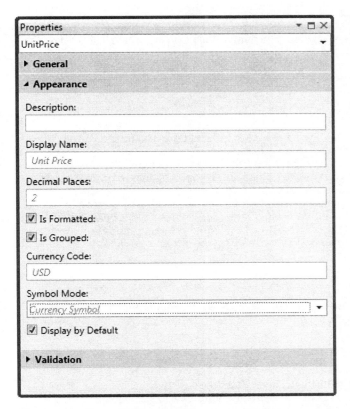

Figure 3-11. Money field properties

The following options become relevant only if the Is Formatted check box is selected:

- *Is Grouped*: If this option is selected, digit grouping separators will be shown. For example, 1,234,567.89 will be displayed rather than 1234567.89.

- *Symbol Mode*: You can choose from Currency Symbol, ISO Currency Symbol, or No Currency Symbol. Here are some examples of how the currencies would be formatted:

  - *Currency Symbol*: $123.45

  - *ISO Currency Symbol*: 123.45 USD

  - *No Currency Symbol*: 123.45

- *Decimal Places*: Currency values will be formatted to the number of decimal places indicated here.

■ **Note** If the currency code is not explicitly set, it defaults to US format rather than the culture that is set on your machine.

Image Data Type

The image type is designed to store images. LightSwitch includes Image Editor and Image Viewer controls that enable you to select and view images, respectively.

Note that these controls support images in only JPG and PNG format (other common image types such as BMP and GIF are not supported). If you wish to upload and view image files in other formats, you will need to purchase a third-party custom control or write your own.

Also, LightSwitch doesn't perform any image compression on upload, and big images can bloat your database. When editing or saving a record that contains an image, LightSwitch carries out a concurrency check by sending the original image back to the server. This can slow the process of updating records, and if this becomes a problem, you can improve performance by saving images to a separate table.

Binary Data Type

The binary data type can be used to store binary large objects such as documents, videos, or other file types. Chapter 8 explains how you can design a screen to upload and download files.

DateTime Data Type

The LightSwitch DateTime type corresponds to the SQL Server datetime data type.

When working in code, it's important to realize that there is a difference in size between the .NET and SQL Server datetime fields. Table 3-2 illustrates the differences.

Table 3-2. Minimum and Maximum datetime Values

	Minimum Value	Maximum Value
.NET	0001-01-01 00:00:00.000	9999-12-31 23:59:59.999
SQL Server	1753-01-01 00:00:00.000	9999-12-31 23:59:59.997

This difference might present a problem if, for example, code is written to set a date variable to the maximum value by using the .NET DateTime.Max method. Some developers choose to do this in order to prevent null values from being saved into the database. On saving the record, LightSwitch will report that the date is too big for the SQL type. Additional code must therefore be written in order to perform this translation if you wish to use the DateTime.Min and DateTime.Max functions in LightSwitch.

If you are using an attached SQL 2008 database, an alternative suggestion is to utilize the datetime2 data type. This data type offers more precision and a greater range of date values, and corresponds more closely with the .NET DateTime type. LightSwitch chose to use datetime rather than datetime2 for compatibility with SQL 2005.

Changing Data Types

When developing an application, any data entered in LightSwitch is persisted between debug sessions in a temporary local database. Changing data types in a table can result in the entire contents of the table being deleted.

The LightSwitch designer will generally warn you before any data is deleted (shown in Figure 3-12), but you should take care if you have spent a lot of time entering data. If design time data is important to you, you should consider using an external SQL Server database rather than the intrinsic database.

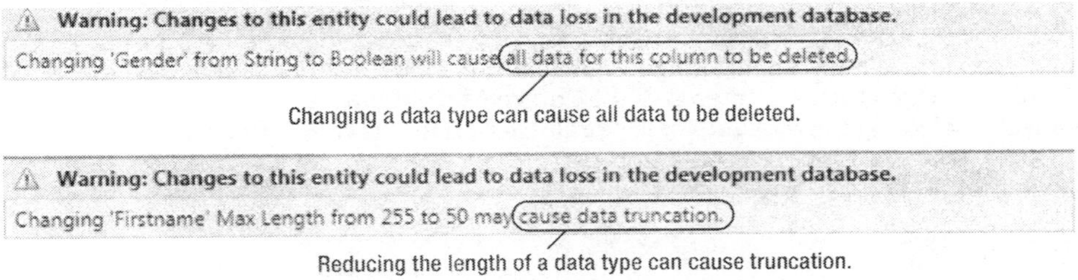

Figure 3-12. Warnings that appear when changing types

Choosing Field Names

It is always a good idea to avoid using *reserved* names when naming fields. Although such naming can be valid, it could cause you problems later.

A naming rule that you may have encountered is that field names cannot be the same as table names. If you create a field that matches the table name, the LightSwitch designer reports that *FieldName* has already been used by the entity type and cannot be used.

If you attach to a SQL table that contains a field name matching the table name, LightSwitch renames the field name in the model. For example, if you attach a table named Customer that also contains a Customer field, this field will be named Customer1 by LightSwitch. If the field name matches a data type (if you have a field named date for example), LightSwitch prefixes c to the start of the name so that it becomes c_Date.

Naming a field with the prefix Entity (for example, EntityKey) has been known to cause problems and is therefore not recommended. This is likely due to a conflict caused by objects in the entity framework. In addition, there are also other entity and entity set names that can conflict with the built-in tables added by LightSwitch or ASP.NET.

Ensuring Unique Values

Each field contains an Include in Unique Index check box. Selecting this check box includes the field in a combination index.

It is not possible to create individual unique fields (that is, multiple unique indexes) by using the designer. If this is required, validation can be written to enforce uniqueness. Chapter 5 contains some example code that shows how to do this.

If an attached SQL database is used, this could also be enforced by creating unique indexes at the SQL Server level.

Creating Choice Lists

Creating a choice list enables you to use the AutoCompleteBox or modal window picker controls when creating screens. You can create these on fields from external data sources as well as the tables that you create yourself in the intrinsic database.

A *choice list* is a set of name-value pairs and can be created for most data types including fields that are based on Boolean and numeric types. To give you an example, a choice list could be created for a Boolean field with the choice values of Yes and No. The data types that do not support choice lists include Image and Binary types.

To create a choice list, click the Choice List link from the properties pane for your field and enter a list of Value and Display Name pairs. When the autocomplete box is rendered on a screen, the items will be displayed in the order in which they are entered in the Choice List window. Items can be reordered by right-clicking an item and selecting the Move Up or Move Down options, as shown in Figure 3-13.

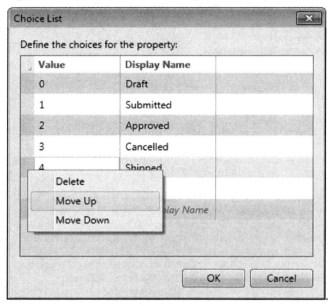

Figure 3-13. Reordering items by using the right-click option

The designer prevents you from entering multiple-choice list items by using copy and paste. If you need to rapidly enter multiple-choice list items, you can manually edit the ApplicationDefinition.lsml file, as described in Chapter 2. Open the LSML file in Notepad and find the XML that relates to the choice list. The choice items can be added manually in XML format, as illustrated in Listing 3-1.

Hand-editing the LSML file carries risk, and the usual warnings that apply to editing this file should be heeded.

Listing 3-1. Choice List Excerpt from the LSML File

```
<EntityProperty Name="OrderStatus" PropertyType=":Int32">
    <EntityProperty.Attributes>
        <Required />
        <NotSearchable />
        <SupportedValue DisplayName="Draft" Value="0" />
        <SupportedValue DisplayName="Submitted" Value="1" />
        <SupportedValue DisplayName="Approved" Value="2" />
        <SupportedValue DisplayName="Cancelled" Value="3" />
        <SupportedValue DisplayName="Shipped" Value="4" />
        <SupportedValue DisplayName="Fulfilled" Value="5" />
    </EntityProperty.Attributes>
</EntityProperty>
```

Choice List vs. Related Tables

When creating AutoCompleteBoxes, a common question is whether the items should be based on a choice list or a related table.

In summary, a choice list is ideal for data items that are relatively static. Creating choice lists with integer/name mappings also helps ensure the proper normalization of a database. The disadvantage of using a choice list is that adding or deleting items requires that the application be recompiled and redeployed, which can be cumbersome. Table 3-3 summarizes the pros and cons of using a choice list as compared to a related table.

Table 3-3. Choice List and Related Table Pros and Cons

Choice List	Related Table
✓ Very simple to create.	✗ More-complex setup. The choice tables need to be created and relationships set up.
✓ Choice list values are deployed with the application.	✗ An extra step is required to populate the database table with values after deployment.
✗ Adding or deleting a choice value requires a rebuild and redeployment of the application, as opposed to just adding a row to a table.	✓ List items can be maintained through the application.
✗ Choice list items must be duplicated if you want to use them in more than one field.	✓ List items can be entered once into a table and used in multiple fields.

Setting Relationships

It's important that correct data relationships are set up in LightSwitch Doing this makes setting up parent-child grids, or drop-down boxes, very easy. This section describes the various types of relationships that are available in LightSwitch.

One-to-Many Relationships

One-to-many relationships are the most basic type of relationship that can be created in LightSwitch. The following example illustrates the Client and Project tables in the OfficeCentral application. Each client can have one or more projects associated with it.

To demonstrate the creation of the relationship, create the Client and Project tables as illustrated in Figure 3-14. At this point, no relationship has been set up.

Figure 3-14. Client and Project tables without a relationship

To create the relationship, click the Relationships button in the designer and create the relationship as shown in Figure 3-15.

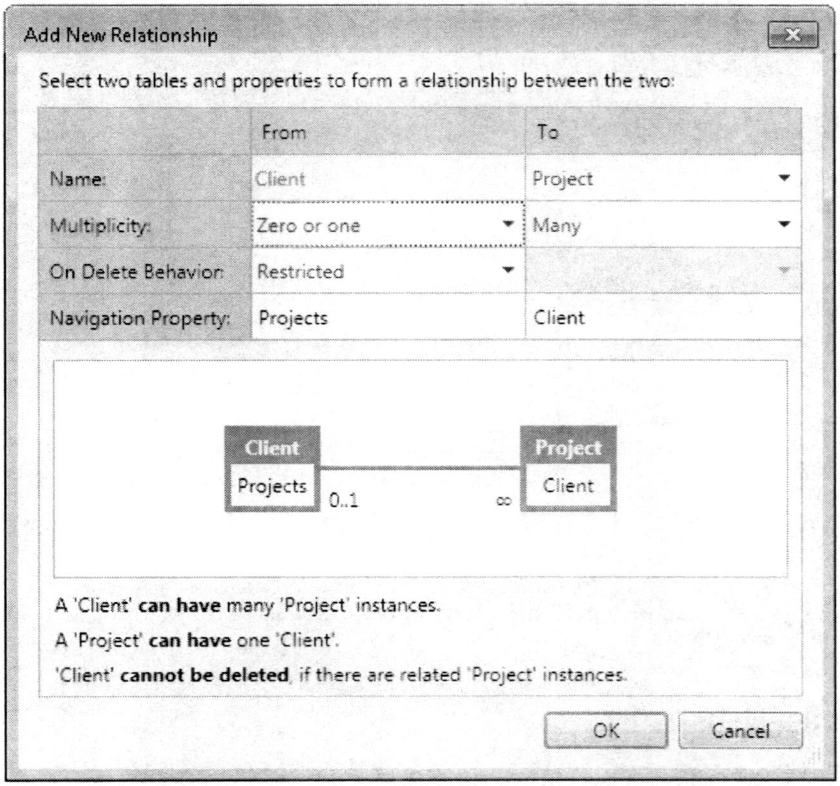

Figure 3-15. *Add New Relationship dialog box*

The Multiplicity row enables you to define the type of relationship between the two tables. In this case, we have selected a zero- or one-to-many relationship. When multiplicities are selected by using these drop-down boxes, a description of the relationship is given in plain, simple English at the bottom of the dialog box.

The final section of the dialog box enables you to set the name of the Navigation Property for each table. Navigation properties provide the mechanism that enables you to navigate related entities. When writing code, they appear as objects in IntelliSense and can also be used to construct LINQ expressions in code.

What Happens in SQL Server?

Figure 3-15 illustrates how LightSwitch guides you through creating relationships by using simple language and how relationships are exposed through navigation properties. Although this simplifies the process for beginners, this simplicity may feel a little alien to more-experienced database developers. What actually happens at the SQL Server level when these relationships are created through LightSwitch? Figure 3-16 shows the answer to this question.

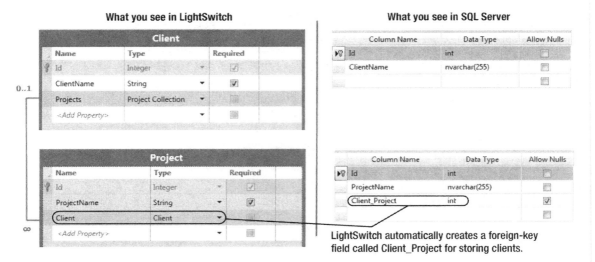

Figure 3-16. *Illustration of SQL schema*

Notice how LightSwitch creates a column in the project table named `Client_Project` and also creates the corresponding foreign-key relationship. LightSwitch therefore creates the foreign key in the same way as if you were creating it manually.

Self-Referencing Relationships

Self-referencing, or recursive, relationships are relationships in which entities reference themselves. They are often found when modeling hierarchies. An example of a self-referencing relationship is an `Employee` table that contains a `Manager` field. The `Manager` field will refer to a related row in the same table.

In order to create a self-join, open the Add New Relationship dialog box and select the same table in the To side of the relationship, as illustrated in Figure 3-17. Then rename the navigation properties to `Manager` and `StaffMembers`. This will result in two navigation properties in the same entity, each representing one end of the relationship (Figure 3-18).

Figure 3-17. Setting up a self-join in the Add New Relationship dialog box

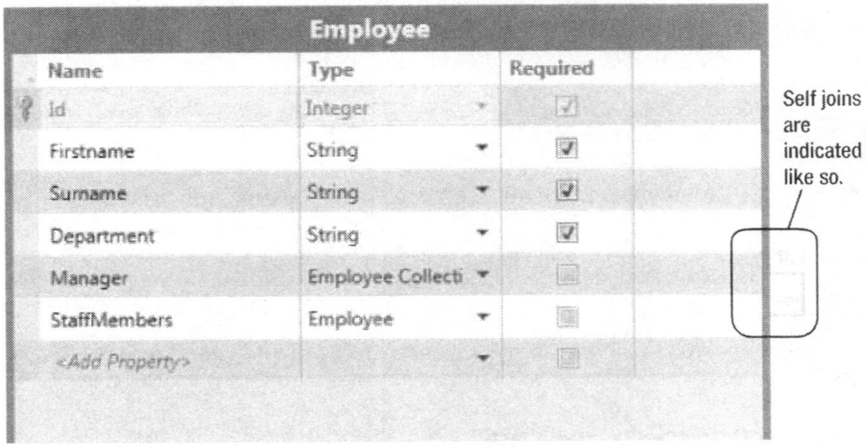

Employee			
Name	Type	Required	
◊ Id	Integer ▼	☑	
Firstname	String ▼	☑	
Surname	String ▼	☑	
Department	String ▼	☑	
Manager	Employee Collecti ▼	☐	
StaffMembers	Employee ▼	☐	
<Add Property>	▼	☐	

Self joins are indicated like so.

Figure 3-18. An example of a self-join

Many-to-Many Relationships

In the relationship designer, *many-to-many relationships* are not natively supported. Many-to-many relationships are therefore implemented in LightSwitch through the use of a *junction table*. In other words, an intermediary table must be created that contains two one-to-many relationships.

In the OfficeCentral application, the details of products and product attributes are stored. In our example business, the Product table contains food items. The Attribute table is used to store characteristics about the product, such as contains nuts, suitable for vegetarians, or high in protein. A product can contain many attributes, and an attribute can be referenced by many products.

After creating the Product and Attribute tables, create a ProductAttribute table to store the many-to-many relationship. In the table designer for the ProductAttribute table, create a one-to-many relationship between the Product and ProductAttribute table. Next, create a one-to-many relationship between the Attribute and ProductAttribute table.

Figure 3-19 illustrates the table structure that we've created.

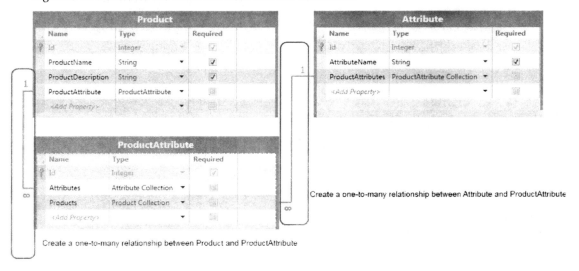

Figure 3-19. How to create a many to many relationship

This completes the table design. Chapter 8 demonstrates how to create a screen for entering data into these tables.

One-to-One Relationships

One-to-one relationships are not supported in LightSwitch. However, there are often good reasons for having one-to-one relationships, which are often created following normalization or performance tuning.

An example of a one-to-one relationship is a database with the tables Person and EmployeeDetail. When recording information about a person, employee details are split off into a separate table. This means that the Person table isn't littered with lots of empty fields when entering a person that isn't an employee.

There is no easy workaround to implement one-to-one relationships in the entity designer. The following chapter on Screen Design provides some strategies on how to construct screens based on tables with one-to-one relationships.

Cannot Create Relationships in Attached SQL Databases

If you connect to an existing SQL Server database and attempt to set up a relationship in LightSwitch that does not exist in SQL Server, you will receive the error *Cannot add a relationship between tables because they are in the same container.* The inability to create a relationship makes it very difficult to use controls such as modal window pickers and AutoCompleteBoxes to select related data when creating screens. Figure 3-20 illustrates this exact error when attempting to set up a relationship between the Client and Project tables.

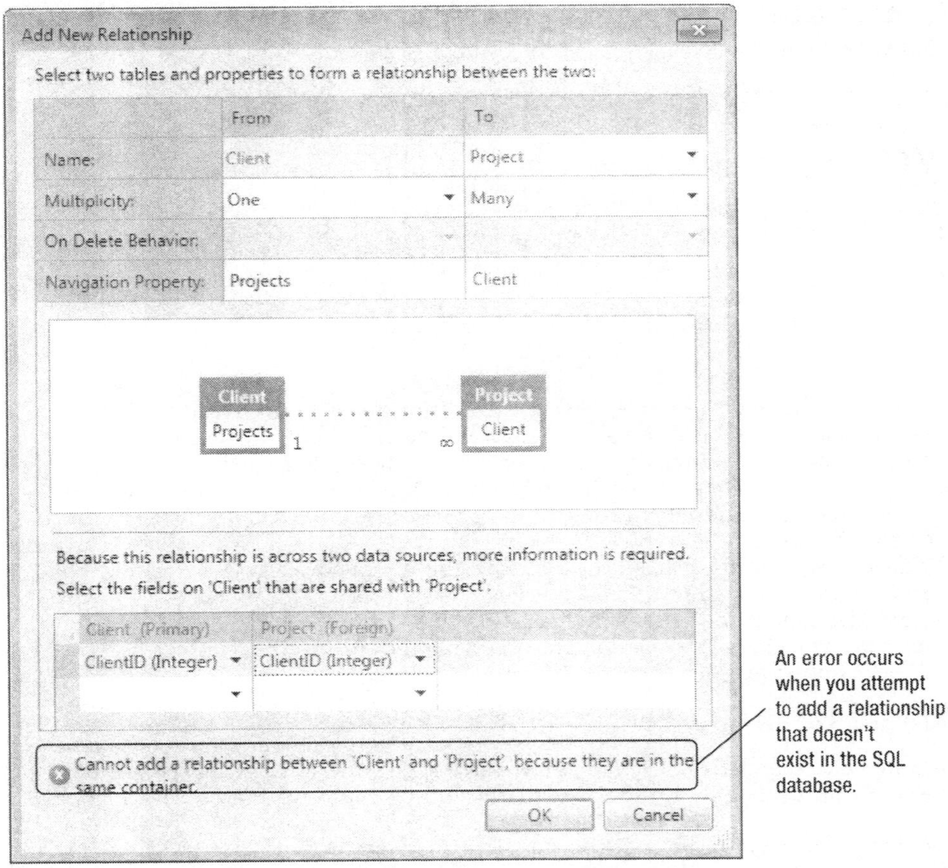

Figure 3-20. Cannot add a relationship error

The obvious fix is to create the correct relationships in the underlying SQL Server database. In many cases, however, this is not possible—for instance, if the database is owned by someone else or if you have insufficient privileges. The workaround for this problem is to place both tables in separate data sources. Assuming that the Client table is in the same database, right-click the Data Sources option in Solution Explorer and select the option to Add Data Source. Set the connection details of the new data source to be the same as your initial data source and add the Project table into the new data source.

The relationship can now be successfully set up between the two tables. The technical name for such a relationship is a *virtual relationship*. This indicates a relationship that exists in the LightSwitch model, but not in the actual underlying data store.

■ **Note** When using this workaround, LightSwitch sees the two data sources as totally different and does not permit updates (in the default case) to both simultaneously. This means you cannot easily update the relationship in some cases, and this technique is therefore more suited for read-only screens.

Deletion Behavior

When creating a relationship, the On Delete Behavior setting can be used to determine what happens when a record is deleted. There are three possible settings:

- Cascade Delete
- Restricted
- Disassociate

Returning to our client and project example, setting the deletion behavior to Cascade Delete will delete all related projects when a client is deleted. This ensures that you don't end up with orphan records that are not associated with a parent. If the behavior is set to Restricted, clients cannot be deleted until all related projects have first been deleted. The final Disassociate option will set all project references to null on related projects prior to the deletion of a client. The Disassociate option is valid on only zero- or one-to-many relationships.

The deletion behavior option is not available and is grayed out if you have created a relationship between two separate data sources. When working between data sources, LightSwitch makes no guarantees about referential integrity or multiplicity on *virtual* relationships. The deletion options are available only for tables designed in the intrinsic database and not for external data sources.

Using Computed Properties

Computed properties are fields that derive their values through calculations and typically from other properties. They are read-only by definition and appear in the entity designer with a calculator icon next to the field.

These properties are very versatile. The code that you write for computed properties is contained in the Common folder and calculated on both the client and server tiers. From a practical point of view, this means that computed properties shown on a screen can be recalculated immediately without requiring interaction that triggers a server event, such as clicking the Save button on the screen.

In the compute method where you write the code for your computed properties, LightSwitch exposes properties that relate to the fields in your table. These are accessible through the this variable in C# or the me variable in VB.NET. All of the autogenerated properties (and any child properties that are generated) are automatically tracked by LightSwitch. If a tracked property changes, it forces a recalculation of the computed property. The important point is that computed properties are recalculated only when changes are made to properties that are autogenerated by LightSwitch.

The following section illustrates several examples of computed properties. This should give you a flavor of the type of code that is involved in constructing a computed property.

■ **Note** Computed properties are fully supported in attached tables and are not just limited to tables that you create in the intrinsic database.

Summary Properties with Computed Fields

Each table allows you to specify a designated summary property. LightSwitch shows the summary property though the summary control. By default, this control is automatically added to data grids and AutoCompleteBoxes. By setting the summary to a computed property, display items can be formatted much more tidily.

In this first example, a computed property is created in the Project table. Each project is associated with a client. The client details are saved in a separate table, and a one-to-many relationship exists between the Client and Project tables.

The following example concatenates the client name from the client table along with the project name. Because Client is a related table, this example also highlights how you can reference related tables in a computed property.

Open the Project table and create a new property called ProjectDescription. In the General section of the properties pane for the new field, select the Is Computed check box. Click the Edit Method hyperlink that appears, and the code window opens. Now enter the code as shown in Listing 3-2.

Listing 3-2. Formatting Strings in a Computed Field

VB:
```
File : OfficeCentral\Common\UserCode\Project.vb

Private Sub ProjectDescription_Compute(ByRef result As String)
    result = String.Format("{0} - {1}", Me.Client.ClientName, Me.ProjectName)
End Sub
```

C#:
```
File : OfficeCentral\Common\UserCode\Project.cs

partial void ProjectDescription_Compute(ref string result)
{
    result = string.Format("{0} - {1}", this.Client.ClientName , this.ProjectName);
}
```

The Summary Property setting on the table can be set to ProjectDescription (as shown in Figure 3-21), and the ProjectDescription field will now be shown in the summary control.

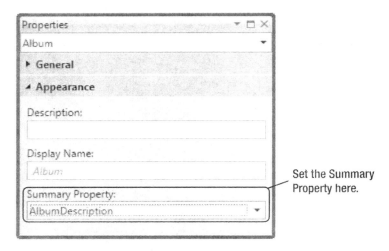

Set the Summary Property here.

Figure 3-21. Summary Property set to a computed field

.NET String Formatting Tips

Listing 3-2 illustrates a common pattern for building strings using the .NET `String.Format` method. This method accepts two parameters. The first parameter contains the string to be displayed. This display string contains placeholders for data in the format `{0},{1}` and so on. The second parameter accepts a comma-separated list of data items that will be substituted into the display string.

The data placeholders can be further formatted by passing in length and format string arguments in the format `{index[,length][:formatString]}`. The length parameter controls the minimum length that is displayed. The parameter is left-aligned if length is positive, and right-aligned if length is negative. If the data to be displayed is smaller than the length argument, the data item is padded out with spaces until the minimum length is reached.

An additional format string can be passed in with a colon. To demonstrate this concept, the computed property code is modified as shown in Listing 3-3.

Listing 3-3. Left- and Right-Aligning Strings by Using the Length Parameter

```
'This is the syntax that we use {index[,length][:formatString]}

result = String.Format("{0, 15} - {1}", "FrescoFoods", "Walnuts")
'This is the result:  "FrescoFoods    -  Walnuts"

result = String.Format("{0, -15} - {1}", "FrescoFoods", "Walnuts")
'This is the result:  "    FrescoFoods -  Walnuts"
```

Numeric values in .NET can be formatted by constructing a format string that begins with a format specifier followed by a number that indicates the desired number of decimal places. These format specifiers are summarized in Table 3-4.

Table 3-4. .NET Format Specifiers

Format Specifier	Description
C or c	Currency
D or d	Decimal
E or e	Scientific (exponential)
F or f	Fixed-point
G or g	General
N or n	Number
P or p	Percent
R or r	Round-trip
X or x	Hexadecimal

Listing 3-4 shows some examples of numeric format strings and the results that are returned.

Listing 3-4. Numeric Formatting Examples

```
'This is the syntax that we use {index[,length][:formatString]}
Dim dbl As Double = 87654.321
result = dbl.ToString("N2") ' - 87,654.3
result = dbl.ToString("P2") ' - 8765432.10%
result = dbl.ToString("C0") ' - $87,654

result = String.Format("{0, 15} - {1} (Sales {3: N0}) ", " FrescoFoods ", "Walnuts", dbl)
'This is the result:  "FrescoFoods     -  Walnuts (Sales 87,654) "
```

Formatting Data with Computed Properties

Creating a computed property is a simple way to format the numeric data that appears on screens, and the following example illustrates how to do this using the formatting code from Listing 3-4.

Let's imagine a Product table with a weight field of data type decimal that is used to store the weight of a product in grams. In order to display this field to two decimal places, a computed field called WeightFormatted is created by using the code in Listing 3-5.

Listing 3-5. Formatting Data to Two Decimal Places by Using a Computed Property

VB:
File : ShipperCentral\Common\UserCode\Product.vb

```
Private Sub WeightFormatted_Compute(ByRef result As String)
    result = Weight.ToString("N2")
End Sub
```

C#:
File : ShipperCentral\Common\UserCode\Product.cs

```
partial void WeightFormatted_Compute(ref string result)
{
    result = Weight.ToString("N2");
}
```

The WeightFormatted computed field can now be used on screens to display the weight to two decimal places.

■ **Note** In Listing 3-5, Weight is assumed to be a required field. When referring to nonrequired fields, properties are exposed as nullable objects. In this case, if the entity is not null, the value can be obtained by using the value or GetValueOrDefault property. More details on nullable fields can be found in Chapter 4.

Arithmetic Calculations Using Computed Properties

Computed properties are often used to perform arithmetic calculations. In this example, two computed properties are created in the Order entity. The first one calculates the total weight of the order. The second one calculates the average weight of each line item. This example also highlights how you can reference related items through a navigation property.

Create two computed string fields called TotalWeight and AverageWeight. Then enter the code as shown in Listing 3-6.

Listing 3-6. Arithmetic Calculations Using Computed Properties

VB:
File : \ShipperCentral\ShipperCentral\Common\UserCode\Order.vb

```
Private Sub TotalWeight_Compute(ByRef result As Integer)
    result = Me.OrderItems.Sum(Function(item) item.Product.Weight))
End Sub

Private Sub AverageWeight_Compute(ByRef result As Integer)
    result = Me.OrderItems.Average(Function(item) item.Product.Weight))
End Sub
```

C#:
File : \ShipperCentral\ShipperCentral\Common\UserCode\Order.cs

```csharp
partial void TotalWeight_Compute(ref int result)
{
    result = this.OrderItems.Sum (item => item.Product.Weight);
}

partial void AverageWeight_Compute(ref int result)
{
    result = this.OrderItems.Average(item => item.Product.Weight);
}
```

The code in Listing 3-6 demonstrates how aggregate functions such as sum and average are carried out on related child items. These aggregate functions are performed using .NET lambda expressions. Don't worry if you don't fully understand the syntax that is shown. All will become clear in Chapter 6.

Date Calculations Using Computed Properties

The next example illustrates how to calculate time differences. The Order table contains OrderDate and ShippingDate columns. The order processing time can be calculated by working out the difference between the two dates and times.

Create a string computed property called ProcessingTime and enter the code as shown in Listing 3-7.

Listing 3-7. Calculating Date and Time Differences

VB.NET:
File : \ShipperCentral\Common\UserCode\Order.vb

```vbnet
Private Sub ProcessingTime_Compute(ByRef result As String)
    If ShippedDate.HasValue AndAlso OrderDate.HasValue Then
        Dim span = ShippedDate - OrderDate
        result = String.Format("{0} days{1} hrs {2} mins", span.Days, span.Hours,
span.Minutes)
    Else
        result = "0"
    End If
End Sub
```

C#:
File : \ShipperCentral\Common\UserCode\Order.cs

```csharp
partial void ProcessingTime_Compute (ref string result)
{
    if (ShippedDate.HasValue && OrderDate.HasValue)
    {
        TimeSpan span = ShippedDate.Value.Subtract(OrderDate.Value);
        result = String.Format("{0} days{1} hrs {2} mins", span.Days, span.Hours,
span.Minutes);
    }
```

```
        else
        {
            result = "0";
        }
}
```

Listing 3-7 illustrates the use of the .NET TimeSpan object, which can be useful for converting time durations into the corresponding string representations of days, hours, minutes, and seconds.

■ **Caution** Computed properties that include the DateTime.Now function (a function that returns the current time) can be dangerous. This is because LightSwitch doesn't know when to recompute the value, and this could lead to subtle errors in your program. This problem isn't limited to just DateTime.Now, but any external value not managed by LightSwitch.

Rounding and Truncating Numbers

When working with numbers, it's important to understand the impact that rounding and truncation might have. Let's return to the earlier example of displaying product weights that are rounded to two decimal places. Each order contains one or more order items. Each order item has an associated product.

Next, a computed property is created on the Order entity to calculate the total weight of the products that are contained in the order. If the computed property is written to sum up the nonrounded product weight (Listing 3-8), a discrepancy can occur (as shown in Figure 3-22).

Listing 3-8. Summing Nonrounded Values

VB:
```
File : \ShipperCentral\Common\UserCode\Orders.vb

Private Sub OrderWeight_Compute(ByRef result As Decimal)
    result = Decimal.Round(Me.OrderItems.Sum(Function(item) item.ProductWeight), 2)
End Sub
```

C#:
```
File : \ShipperCentral\Common\UserCode\Orders.cs

partial void OrderWeight_Compute(ref decimal result)
{
    result = decimal.Round (this.OrderItems.Sum(item => item.ProductWeight), 2);
}
```

Figure 3-22. Rounding errors

To resolve these kinds of problems, the computed property code should be amended to apply a sum on the rounded values (Listing 3-9).

Listing 3-9. Summing Up Rounded Values

VB:
File : \ShipperCentral\Common\UserCode\Orders.vb

```
Private Sub OrderWeight_Compute(ByRef result As Decimal)
    result = Decimal.Round(Me.OrderItems.Sum(Function(item)
Decimal.Round(item.ProductWeight,2)), 2)
End Sub
```

C#:
File : \ShipperCentral\Common\UserCode\Orders.cs

```
partial void OrderWeight_Compute(ref decimal result)
{
    result = decimal.Round (this.OrderItems.Sum(item => Decimal.Round(item.ProductWeight,2)),
2);
}
```

By default, the Round method in .NET applies *bankers' rounding*. If numbers are always rounded up when the fractional unit is 0.5, the results are unevenly skewed upward. Bankers' rounding prevents this problem from happening by rounding toward the even number. There's no need to worry too much about the LINQ syntax that is used here. The important point is to be cautious when applying calculations based on rounded or truncated values. Although users may not be too concerned with product weights adding up correctly, it would definitely be more of a problem if this were a financial report that contained money values.

Returning Images with Computed Properties

It's not just string and numeric data that can be returned in a computed property. The following example demonstrates how to create a computed property that returns an image. To give an example of where this might be useful, imagine visualizing order details on a data grid. A computed image property could be used to display a small icon against each row to illustrate the order status.

Create an image field called Icon and enter the code as shown in Listing 3-10.

Listing 3-10. Returning an Image in a Computed Property

VB.NET:
File : \ShipperCentral\Common\UserCode\Product.vb

```
Private Sub Icon_Compute(ByRef result As Byte())
    'The string beneath represents a base64Encoded image. It has been truncated to save space
in this book.
    Dim base64EncodedImage As String = "/9j/4AAQSkZJRgABAQEAYABgAAD"
    result = Convert.FromBase64String(base64EncodedImage)
End Sub
```

C#:
File : \ShipperCentral\Common\UserCode\Product.cs

```
partial void Icon_Compute(ref byte[] result)
{
    //The string beneath represents a base64Encoded image. It has been truncated to save space
in this book.
    string base64EncodedImage = "/9j/4AAQSkZJRgABAQEAYABgAAD";
    result = Convert.FromBase64String(base64EncodedImage);
}
```

The computed property returns a hard-coded, base-64 encoded image. You can find various web sites that will convert image files into their base-64 encodings. An example can be found at http://www.dailycoding.com/Utils/Converter/ImageToBase64.aspx.

Alternatively, the images can be retrieved from a table. Chapter 4 describes in further detail the code that would be used to do this.

Sorting and Filtering on Computed Properties

A slight limitation of computed properties is that you cannot sort or filter by these properties. If you create a query based on a table with computed properties, these properties will not appear in the drop-down list of available items when creating a filter or sort.

To work around this problem, the first option is not to use a computed property but to use a normal property instead. Code can be written in the inserting and updating events (explained in Chapter 4) on your entity to permanently store the data in a normal, persisted property. You can then sort and filter your data using this property.

If you are using an external SQL data source, a second workaround is to use a SQL Server computed column rather than a LightSwitch computed property. A limitation on SQL Server computed columns, however, is that they can refer to only the data in the same table and are less powerful than their LightSwitch equivalent. The earlier example of creating a TotalWeight computed property in the Product table cannot be re-created in a SQL Server computed column.

The following example demonstrates how to create a computed column that calculates the total price in a Product table. Computed columns can be created by using the table designer in SQL Server Management Studio. After opening the product table in Management Studio, create a TotalPrice column and view the properties of the column. In the Computed Column Specification text box that appears, enter T-SQL CAST(Quantity AS decimal(18,2)) * UnitPrice, as illustrated in Figure 3-23.

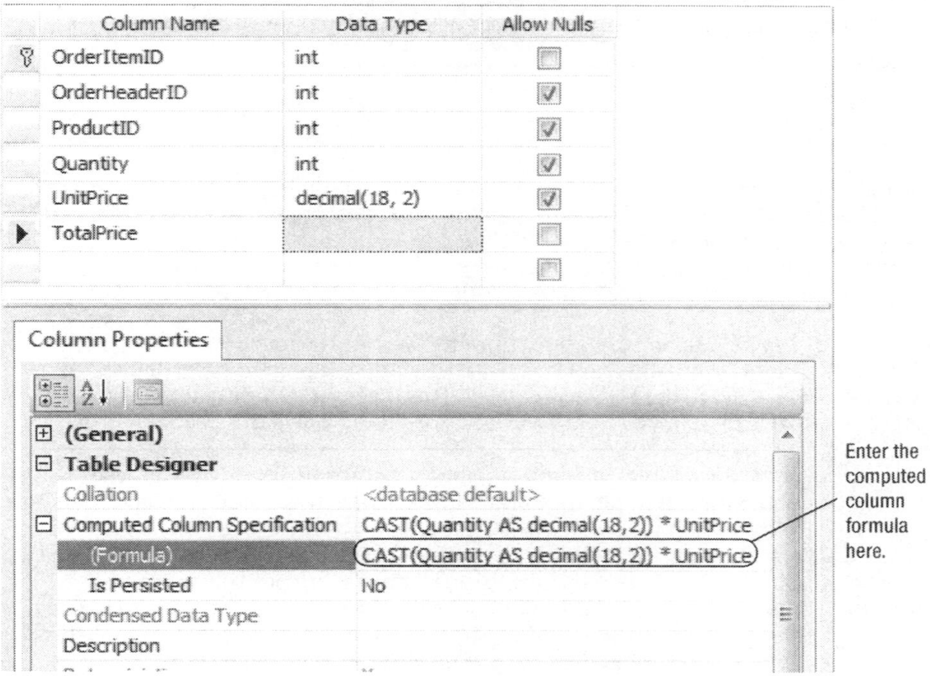

Figure 3-23. Creating computed columns in SQL Server

In the example T-SQL, UnitPrice is an integer field and Quantity a decimal field. The CAST command is used to convert the quantity field into a decimal value to enable the multiplication to take place.

SQL computed columns are calculated each time the field is queried. Setting the Is Persisted value to true will improve performance by saving the calculated values into the table. These persisted values will be updated each time the underlying data changes.

If a column is set to Is Persisted, Deterministic or Imprecise, an index can be created on the column. Creating an index on a computed column will further improve performance when performing searches in LightSwitch.

Deterministic columns will always return the same value for any given set of inputs. A computed column that calculates someone's age is an example of something that is nondeterministic.

A disadvantage of using SQL computed columns is that computed values will be updated only when the data is refreshed from the server. For example, if a LightSwitch screen is created based on the Product table, updating a quantity text box will not automatically update the computed TotalPrice value until the record is saved. LightSwitch computed columns will update immediately because the computed field logic exists in the common project and executes on both the client and the server.

■ **Note** Chapter 6 introduces writing queries and explains how custom sorting can be implemented through the PreProcessQuery method. This provides another technique for solving this particular problem and unlike SQL computed columns, this method can be easily applied to tables belonging in the intrinsic database.

Summary

This chapter has covered many data-related topics. You have learned that entities and properties are the core units of data used in LightSwitch. Entities are synonymous with rows from a database table, and properties can be thought of as fields or columns from a table.

By default, you can use LightSwitch to attach to SQL Server, SharePoint, or RIA service data sources. You can attach to any data source as long as a compatible entity framework provider for that data source is available.

If using SQL Server, try to ensure that all tables have primary keys and correct relationships set up. Tables without primary keys cannot be attached to LightSwitch. Relationships cannot be defined in LightSwitch if they haven't been set up at the SQL Server level. This makes it very difficult to use the AutoCompleteBox on screens to select related records. A workaround to resolve this problem is to use two separate data sources.

All of the standard data types are available. In addition, there are three business types: Phone Number, Email Address, and Money. These business types map to standard SQL data types, and you have seen how all of the other LightSwitch data types map to underlying SQL types.

If you want to create a screen that contains an autocomplete box, you can choose to use a related table or create a choice list. Choice lists are ideal for short lists of data that are unlikely to change.

Various types of relationships can be set up, and cascade delete options can be set up to delete all related child records when a parent record is deleted. Many-to-many relationships can be established through the use of a junction table, and self-referencing relationships can also be created.

Finally, you have seen various examples of writing computed properties to perform string formatting, date arithmetic, and calculations that involve related child records.

CHAPTER 4

Accessing Data from Code

Sooner or later, you will reach the limits of what you can achieve by using the graphical designers. To progress further, you will need to write code. LightSwitch provides a strong set of APIs to help you out in this task. There are many things that you can achieve through code, one of which is accessing data.

In this chapter, you will learn how to access your data by using code. This not only includes the data that you have defined through your data sources, but also security details such as the currently logged-on user. When data is committed to the database (or underlying data store), it passes through the save pipeline, and LightSwitch automatically manages the issues that relate to transactions and concurrency. This chapter shows you how all of this works and more.

Introducing Data Access

In Chapter 1, you learned about the architecture that sits behind a LightSwitch application. This is summarized in Figure 4-1, which illustrates the interaction between client and server.

Each screen in an application maintains an independent view of the data by using a DataWorkspace object. The main role of this object is to fetch and manage data. The data workspace contains a *change set* for each data source that is used to track all of the data changes that relate to that data source.

When the time comes to save, the SaveChanges operation that corresponds to the data source on the server is invoked by the client. When the call is made, the change set is serialized and passed into the SaveChanges method. When the change set is received by the server, it is deserialized into a server data workspace, and the save pipeline operates on those changes.

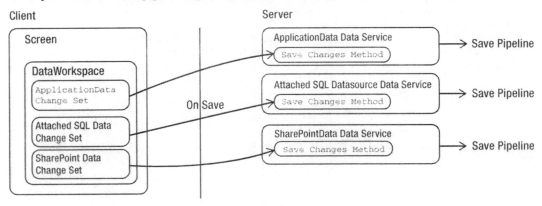

Figure 4-1. Client and server interaction during a save

LightSwitch allows you to programmatically access most of the data objects that have been mentioned. For example, you can use code to access the data workspace, change sets, entities, and entity properties. On the server, you can inject code into the save pipeline and write additional logic.

Using LightSwitch Data Access Objects

Figure 4-2 illustrates the data access objects that LightSwitch exposes to you.

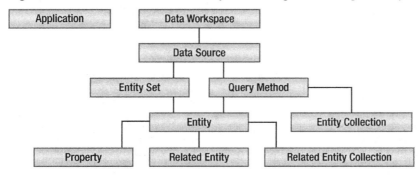

Figure 4-2. Data access objects

LightSwitch does a very good job of automatically generating objects that are used for accessing data. The object names match the names of the items in your solution, which makes it intuitive for you to write code. For example, if you create a table called Customers in your project, you can programmatically access the details of your customer through an object called Customer. The inner workings of all of these objects are described in the following sections in greater detail.

Application Object

The Application object is a top-level object that allows you to access details such as the current user. The properties and methods that are available to you will depend on where that object is used. Figure 4-3 illustrates the IntelliSense options that are visible when writing code on a screen, as compared to writing code in the common or server projects.

When writing screen code, methods that relate to managing screens are available. Because there isn't any notion of a screen when writing code on the server, these screen methods are not available. In both instances, a User property is exposed (which is explained later in this chapter).

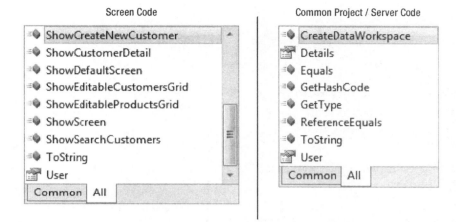

Figure 4-3. The Application object properties and methods

Using the Application Object in Screen Code

LightSwitch includes various methods for managing screens when using the application object to write client-side code. LightSwitch automatically generates a Show method for each screen in your application, which you can use to open screens. For example, Figure 4-3 illustrates a method called ShowCreateNewCustomer. In this example, CreateNewCustomer is the name of a screen in the application.

The ShowScreen method allows you to write code that navigates to another open screen in your application. Listing 4-1 shows how you would use this method to open a screen called CustomerSearchScreen, along with a few of the other screen methods that are available to you.

Listing 4-1. Navigating to a Different Open Screen

VB:
```
File: ShipperCentral\Client\UserCode\HomeScreen.vb

'Activating the customer search screen if it is already open
Application.ActiveScreens.First(↩
    Function(screen) screen.GetName() = "CustomerSearchScreen"↩
    ).Activate()


'Opening a screen called CreateNewCustomer
Application.ShowCreateNewCustomer()

'Opening the CustomerDetail  screen for customer ID 8
Application.ShowCustomerDetail(8)

'Opening the CustomerDetail  screen for customer ID 8 using the ShowDefaultScreen method
Dim cust = DataWorkspace.ApplicationData.Customers_Single(8)
Application.ShowDefaultScreen(cust)
```

C#:
File: ShipperCentral\Client\UserCode\HomeScreen.cs

```
//Activating the customer search screen if it is already open
Application.ActiveScreens.First(⏎
    screen => screen.GetName() == "CustomerSearchScreen"⏎
    ).Activate();

//Opening a screen called CreateNewCustomer
Application.ShowCreateNewCustomer();

//Opening the CustomerDetail  screen for customer ID 8
Application.ShowCustomerDetail(8);

//Opening the CustomerDetail  screen for customer ID 8 using the ShowDefaultScreen method
Customer cust = DataWorkspace.ApplicationData.Customers_Single(8);
Application.ShowDefaultScreen(cust);
```

The ShowDefaultScreen method allows you to pass in any entity and opens the entity in the default screen.

The application object also exposes a collection called ActiveScreens. This collection contains a reference to each screen that is currently open in your application. As an example of how you would use this collection, you could create a button on your screen to refresh all other screens that are currently open. The code in Listing 4-2 shows you how to do this.

Listing 4-2. Refreshing All Open Screens in Your Application

VB:
File: ShipperCentral\Client\UserCode\HomeScreen.vb

```
Dim screens = Me.Application.ActiveScreens()
For Each s In screens
    Dim screen = s.Screen
    screen.Details.Dispatcher.BeginInvoke(
        Sub()
            screen.Refresh()
        End Sub
Next
```

C#:

File: ShipperCentral\Client\UserCode\HomeScreen.cs

```
var screens = this.Application.ActiveScreens;
foreach (var s in screens)
{
    var screen = s.Screen;
    screen.Details.Dispatcher.BeginInvoke(() => {
        screen.Refresh();
    });
}
```

Data Workspace

The DataWorkspace object is the top-level data access object and provides access to your data sources. LightSwitch exposes a data source object for each data source in your application. The programmatic object name will be identical to the name of your data source. Figure 4-4 illustrates the data source objects that are visible through IntelliSense and how these relate to the data sources that you see in Solution Explorer.

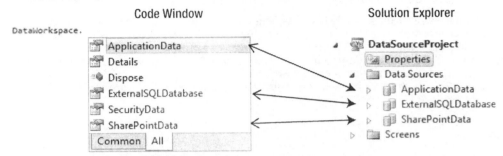

Figure 4-4. The DataWorkspace object

Data Source Object

Data source objects allow you to access query methods and entity collections. Figure 4-5 illustrates the IntelliSense options that are visible at a data source level. The data source object provides access to *entity sets* such as Orders, OrderStatus, and Products. These entity sets relate to the entities that you have added into your data source and allow you to access collections of data.

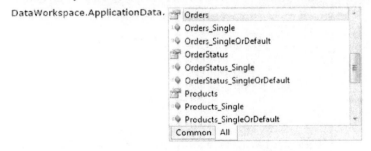

Figure 4-5. Data source methods shown in IntelliSense

LightSwitch generates two *query methods* called _Single and _SingleOrDefault for each entity in the data source. The examples shown in Figure 4-5 illustrate query methods called Orders_Single and Orders_SingleOrDefault. These methods would allow you to retrieve a single record by the ID property or primary key. The difference between Single and SingleOrDefault is that Single throws an exception if the record is not found. SingleOrDefault returns null rather than throwing an exception.

Listing 4-3 illustrates the code that you would use to retrieve the order record with an OrderID of 8. This code can be used on both the client and server.

Listing 4-3. Retrieving a Single Record

VB:
```
Dim orderRecord as Order = Me.DataWorkspace.ApplicationData.Orders_Single(8)
```

C#:
```
Order orderRecord = this.DataWorkspace.ApplicationData.Orders_Single(8);
```

Data source properties also expose a details class. This can be used to access details that relate to the change set and to access the original value of any modified data. The details class is described further in the "Working with Change Sets" section.

An important method found in the data source object is the SaveChanges method. This method saves the changes that you have made to the data store. However, you typically don't call this directly, but rather call the screen's Save method, which delegates the save operation to the appropriate data source object.

Entity Sets

Entity sets allow you to programmatically access sets of data. Figure 4-6 illustrates the methods and properties that you can access.

```
Dim customers = DataWorkspace.ShipperCentralData.Customers
customers.|
```

Figure 4-6. Methods and properties of entity sets

Entity sets contain methods that allow you to check whether the current user has permission to read, update, or delete entities in the collection. Chapter 14 covers security and authorization in further detail.

Entity collections contain an extension method called Search. This enables you to programmatically perform a search by passing a parameter array of search terms.

Entity collections also contain a method called Add, which allows you to add a new record. Listing 4-4 illustrates the code that you would use to do this. The Add method returns an instance of an entity object (which will be described in the next section).

There is no method at the entity-set level to delete entities. Deleting entities is carried out through the actual entity object.

Listing 4-4. Adding a New Record

VB:
```
Dim OrderRecord = New Order()
```

C#:
```
Order OrderRecord = new Order();
```

■ **Note** Entity sets and entity collections are not the same, as you might recall from Chapter 3. Entity sets represent tables and lists in the store. The term *collection* is often used to refer to something cached locally. Within LightSwitch, entity collections are used for navigation properties.

Entities

An *entity object* represents a single instance of an entity. In LightSwitch terms, an entity represents a single row in a table or a list in the data source. Figure 4-7 illustrates the IntelliSense options for an entity object that relates to a customer entity.

```
Dim CustomerEntity As Customer = DataWorkspace.ShipperCentralData.Customers_Single(0)
CustomerEntity.|
```

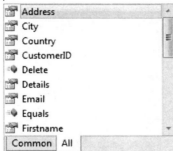

Figure 4-7. Customer entity methods and properties

An entity object contains methods that you can use to delete an entity, or to read or update the properties in your entity. An entity object also allows you to retrieve the details of related entities. For the preceding customer entity, LightSwitch exposes an entity navigation property called Orders that allows you to programmatically work with the related orders.

To delete an entity, you would call the Delete method. Listing 4-5 demonstrates the code that you would use to delete an order record with an ID of 8. Calling the Save method on the data source object commits the deletion in the data store.

Listing 4-5. Deleting an Entity

VB:
```
Dim OrderRecord as Order = Me.DataWorkspace.ApplicationData.Orders_Single(8)
orderRecord.Delete()
```

C#:
```
Order OrderRecord = this.DataWorkspace.ApplicationData.Orders_Single(8);
orderRecord.Delete();
```

Entities also contain a Details object that you can use to obtain further details about the entity. In particular, this object includes a DiscardsChanges method that you can use to undo any changes. An example of calling this method is explained in upcoming "Working with Change Sets" section.

Properties and Nullable Data Types

LightSwitch programmatically exposes the properties that belong to an entity. You can use these to get or set the corresponding values.

The data type of the property corresponds to the data type defined in the table. If a field is not defined as *required*, LightSwitch exposes the property by using a nullable data type (except for String and Binary, which are reference types). Nullable data types were introduced in .NET 2.0, and this can sometimes cause confusion for users who have not seen this feature before. Figure 4-8 illustrates a Product table that contains two fields called Price and Discount. Price is a required field, whereas Discount is a field that is *not required*. Discount is therefore exposed as a nullable double. Figure 4-8 illustrates the difference that is shown through the code window.

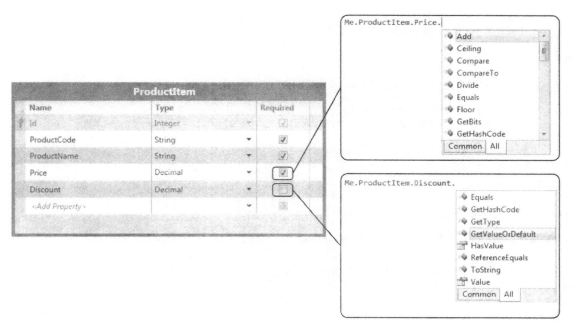

Figure 4-8. Nullable data types in IntelliSense

These nullable types include additional properties and methods, which are shown in Table 4-1.

Table 4-1. Properties and Methods of Nullable Data Types

Property/Method	Description
HasValue property	Returns a Boolean value indicating whether the property contains a value.
Value property	Returns the current value of the property.
GetValueOrDefault(T) method	Returns the value of the property if it is not null. Otherwise, T is returned.

You can always assign a value or null (Nothing in VB) directly to a nullable property. But getting the value requires care. Accessing the Value property will throw an exception if it is null. Using GetValueOrDefault is often safer.

In the example that follows, a screen button is created that multiplies the discount by the price and shows this to the user through a message box.

When writing this type of code, the price cannot be directly multiplied by the discount because discount is a nullable double and price is not. Listing 4-6 shows how you would carry out this multiplication by calling the GetValueOrDefault method of the discount property.

Listing 4-6. *Using the GetValueOrDefault Method*

VB:

File: ShipperCentral\Client\UserCode\ProductDetail.vb

```
Private Sub ShowDiscountedPrice_Execute()
    ShowMessageBox(ProductProperty.Discount.GetValueOrDefault(0) * ProductProperty.Price)
End Sub
```

C#:

File: ShipperCentral\Client\UserCode\ProductDetail.cs

```
private void ShowDiscountedPrice_Execute()
{
    ShowMessageBox(ProductProperty.Discount.GetValueOrDefault(0) * ProductProperty.Price) ;
}
```

If you choose not to use the GetValueOrDefault method, you could achieve the same thing by writing logic that uses the HasValue or Value properties.

■ **Note** If you receive a compilation error along the lines of *Cannot implicitly convert type decimal to decimal*, it is likely to be caused by nullable variables. The GetValueOrDefault method can help you resolve such errors.

Working with Screen Data

Many developers want to programmatically access the data items that are shown on a screen. For example, you might want to loop through all orders shown on a data grid and set the shipped date to today's date. Alternatively, you might want to create a button that changes a surname field to uppercase when clicked. These examples may appear fairly unrealistic, but the purpose of this exercise is to illustrate how you can programmatically access these screen properties.

Developers new to Silverlight or WPF (Windows Presentation Foundation) may approach this task by attempting to access the surname text box control directly or by looping through the data in the data grid control. Such developers might be accustomed to accessing grid data by ordinal row and column numbers, looping through row objects in the grid, or using ItemDataBound or ItemCommand type events that are exposed by the control. LightSwitch doesn't work like this, and this shift in thinking may be difficult for some developers at first.

The controls that you see on screens such as text boxes, lists, and grids are purely views and exist only to display data, nothing else. Therefore, getting and setting the data shown on controls is not done through the controls themselves. Instead, the correct way to do this is to work with the actual underlying screen data (the model). Because the controls are data bound to the model through the view model, the screen data will automatically refresh itself as soon as the model data changes.

Setting Text Box Values

Let's begin with a text box illustration. In this example, a screen is created based on a customer table using the New Data Screen template. After creating the screen, we'll create a new method called MakeUpperCase by using the Add Data Item dialog box. A button is created on the screen by dragging the method onto the Command Bar area.

The screen template automatically creates a customer property for you called CustomerProperty. This name is used in code to access all of the fields that relate to a customer. Figure 4-9 illustrates how this appears in the screen designer.

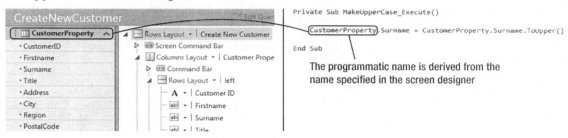

Figure 4-9. Accessing screen properties in code

When the screen is run and the button clicked, the Surname property is changed to uppercase, and LightSwitch automatically updates the text box to reflect the change.

Accessing Grid and List Values

You can access the data in a data grid in a similar fashion to the preceding text box example. In the following example, a screen is created based on the Orders table by using the editable screen template. After creating the screen, create a new method called SetShippingDate by using the Add Data Item dialog box. Figure 4-10 shows the screen in the designer.

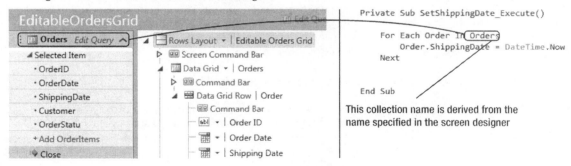

Figure 4-10. Accessing a screen collection property in code

Listing 4-7 shows the code that is used to loop through the Orders collection on the screen.

When the screen is run and the button clicked, the shipping dates on all orders in the grid are set to today's date by using the underlying order collection. Once again, LightSwitch automatically updates the grid to reflect the change.

Listing 4-7. Accessing Grid Values

VB:
```
File : ShipperCentral\Common\UserCode\OrderDetailGrid.vb

Private Sub SetShippingDate_Execute()
    For Each order In Me.Orders
        order.ShippingDate = DateTime.Now
    Next
End Sub
```

C#:
```
File : ShipperCentral\Common\UserCode\OrderDetailGrid.cs
private void SetShippingDate_Execute()
{
    foreach (Order order in this.Orders) {
        order.ShippingDate = DateTime.Now;
    }
}
```

In grid- and list-type screens, LightSwitch exposes the data as a *visual collection* (of type Microsoft.LightSwitch.Framework.Client.VisualCollection). A visual collection contains the records that are currently shown in the grid or list. In this example, the visual collection is called Orders. Visual collections include some useful methods that you can use. These are shown in Table 4-2.

Table 4-2. Visual Collection Methods

Method	Description
SelectedItem	Gets or sets the record that is currently selected in the visual collection.
AddAndEditNew	Adds a new record to the visual collection and opens a modal window to edit it. You can optionally supply a completeAction argument. This specifies a method to be run when the modal window is closed.
AddNew	Adds a new record to the visual collection.
EditSelected	Opens a modal window for the currently selected item.
DeleteSelected	Marks the currently selected record for deletion and removes it from the visual collection. The actual deletion happens when the data workspace is saved.

Note Visual collections contain only the page of data that is currently visible to the end user. If the collection supports paging (the default) or if the end user has filtered the list, any code that references it (such as that shown in Listing 4-7) will operate only on the records that are currently visible.

Setting AutoCompleteBox Values

Setting AutoCompleteBox values can be difficult at first. New users to LightSwitch often search for SelectedItem or SelectedValue properties in an attempt to set an AutoCompleteBox value.

Like all controls, AutoCompleteBox values are set by setting the underlying data value. In this example, an order detail screen is created that contains an AutoCompleteBox showing order status values. The order statuses are stored in a related table with the relationships properly set up (rather than defined in a choice list). A button is created that sets the status to *shipped* and also changes the shipped date to today's date. Figure 4-11 illustrates how the screen appears in the designer. Listing 4-8 shows the code that is used to set the value of the AutoCompleteBox.

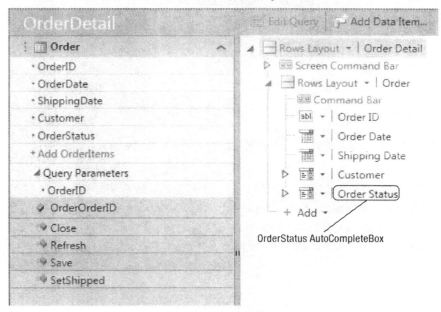

Figure 4-11. *Accessing an AutoCompleteBox in code*

To set the AutoCompleteBox value, the OrderStatus property on the Order property must be set. The OrderStatus must be set to an object of type OrderStatus. Listing 4-8 shows the code that is used to do this. A lambda expression is used to search for the status by name. More details on this type of syntax can be found in Chapter 6.

If you wanted to set the AutoCompleteBox value by ID rather than the string value of Shipped, you could use the OrderStatus_SingleOrDefault method on the data source object that was mentioned earlier.

Listing 4-8. Setting an AutoCompleteBox Value in Code

VB:

```
File: ShipperCentral\Client\UserCode\OrderDetailGrid.vb

Private Sub SetShipped_Execute()
    Order.ShippingDate = DateTime.Now
    Order.OrderStatus = Me.DataWorkspace.ApplicationData.OrderStatusSet.Where(
        Function(status) status.StatusDescription = "Shipped").FirstOrDefault()
End Sub
```

C#:

```
File: ShipperCentral\Client\UserCode\OrderDetailGrid.cs

private void SetShipped_Execute()
{
    Order.ShippingDate = DateTime.Now;
    Order.OrderStatus = this.DataWorkspace.ApplicationData.OrderStatusSet.Where
        (status => status.StatusDescription == "Shipped").FirstOrDefault();
}
```

■ **Note** The code that is used to look up the status requires a round-trip to the server. If this code is going to be called several times, caching the lookup entity in the screen object will help performance. This is most easily done by creating a private field yourself and initializing it in the _Loaded method.

Working with Change Sets

Change sets are used to get the data items that have changed, retrieve the original values prior to you changing them, and to discard any changes that you may have made. You can access change set properties and methods by using the details member of a data source. For example, the code snippet that you would use to access the change set details relating to the intrinsic database would be DataWorkspace.ApplicationData.Details. For other data sources, you would replace ApplicationData with the name of the data service object. Change sets are available when writing client, server, or common code.

Table 4-3 summarizes the change set properties and methods that are available through the details object.

Table 4-3. Methods and Properties Relating to Change Sets

Method/Property	Description
DiscardChanges method	Discards all changes that have been made in the change set.
GetChanges property	Gets all changes that have been made in the change set. Returns an object of type Microsoft.LightSwitch.EntityChangeSet.
HasChanges property	Returns a Boolean value indicating whether changes have been made.

The HasChanges property returns a Boolean value indicating whether any changes have been made. When changes are made on a LightSwitch screen, an asterisk symbol appears next to the title that is shown in the screen tab. The HasChanges method returns the same information.

The DiscardChanges method restores any changes that have been made to properties back to their original values, removes any records that have been added, and undeletes any records that may have been deleted.

The GetChanges method returns an object of type Microsoft.LightSwitch.EntityChangeSet. You can use this collection to inspect the changes that have occurred.

Discarding Changes

To demonstrate the use of DiscardChanges, a screen is created by using the Orders table, based on the editable screen template. After creating the screen, a new method is created called DiscardScreenChanges by using the Add Data Item dialog box. Listing 4-9 illustrates the code that is called in this method.

Listing 4-9. Code to Discard All Screen Changes

VB:

File: ShipperCentral\Client\UserCode\OrderDetailGrid.vb

```
Private Sub DiscardScreenChanges_Execute()
    Me.DataWorkspace.ApplicationData.Details.DiscardChanges()
End Sub
```

C#:

File: ShipperCentral\Client\UserCode\OrderDetailGrid.cs

```
partial void DiscardScreenChanges_Execute()
{
    this.DataWorkspace.ApplicationData.Details.DiscardChanges();
}
```

Getting Items That Have Changed

The GetChanges method returns a collection of entities that have been modified. You can loop through these items and do whatever you want to do with them.

As an example, Listing 4-10 illustrates a piece of code that handles the saving event on an editable grid screen that displays orders. The code loops over the orders that have been modified. If the order status is 4 (indicating a shipped order), the change is discarded. This is done by calling the DiscardChanges method of the details object that relates to the order entity.

At the end of the process, a message showing the modified order numbers is displayed to the user.

Listing 4-10. Code to Discard Screen Changes

VB:

```
File: ShipperCentral\Client\UserCode\OrdersGrid.vb

Imports System.Text
Private Sub OrderGrid_Saving(ByRef handled As Boolean)

    Dim message As StringBuilder = New StringBuilder("Modified Orders:")
    For Each order As Order In _
        DataWorkspace.ApplicationData.Details.GetChanges().OfType(Of Order)()
        If order.OrderStatus.OrderStatusID  = 4 Then
            order.Details.DiscardChanges()
        Else
            message.AppendLine(order.OrderID.ToString())
        End If
    Next
    ShowMessageBox(message.ToString())

End Sub
```

C#:

```
File: ShipperCentral\Client\UserCode\OrdersGrid.cs

using System.Text;
private void OrderGrid_Saving(ref bool handled)
{
    StringBuilder message = new StringBuilder("Modified Orders:");

    foreach (Order order in
        DataWorkspace.ApplicationData.Details.GetChanges().OfType<Order>())
    {
        if (order.OrderStatus.OrderStatusID == 4)
        {
            order.Details.DiscardChanges();
        }
        message.AppendLine(order.OrderID.ToString());
    }
```

```
    this.ShowMessageBox(message.ToString());
}
```

Retrieving Original Values

The details object of an entity contains a properties collection. This collection contains a reference to all of the properties (fields) in an entity. You can retrieve the original value of a property by calling the OriginalValue property.

Listing 4-11 demonstrates some validation code on the surname field of a customer table. If the surname value changes from the original value, the comment field on the table must also be modified. If not, a message is shown to the user. The IsChanged property can be used to return a value indicating whether a field has been modified.

Listing 4-11. Code to Retrieve Orginal Values

VB:

```
File: ShipperCentral\Client\UserCode\CustomersDetail.vb

Private Sub Customer_Validate(results As ScreenValidationResultsBuilder)
    If Customer.Details.Properties.Surname.IsChanged
        AndAlso  Customer.Details.Properties.Surname.IsChanged = False  Then
        results.AddScreenError("Surname has changed from " &
                Customer.Details.Properties.Surname.OriginalValue & "To" &
                Customer.Surname &
                ". Comment must be updated when surname changes"
        )
    End If
End Sub
```

C#:

```
File: ShipperCentral\Client\UserCode\CustomersDetail.cs

partial void Customer_Validate(ScreenValidationResultsBuilder results)
{
    if (Customer.Details.Properties.Surname.IsChanged &&
        (Customer.Details.Properties.Surname.IsChanged == false)) {
            results.AddScreenError(
                Customer.Details.Properties.Surname.OriginalValue + "To" +
                Customer.Surname +
                ". Comment must be updated when surname changes");
    }
}
```

Working with the Save Pipeline

So far, you have seen how to access data objects in code. You will now see what happens when you perform a save. After the client serializes the change set and passes it to the save pipeline on the server, the code passes through several phases, which are shown in Figure 4-12. At each phase, there are interception points that allow you to inject your own custom code.

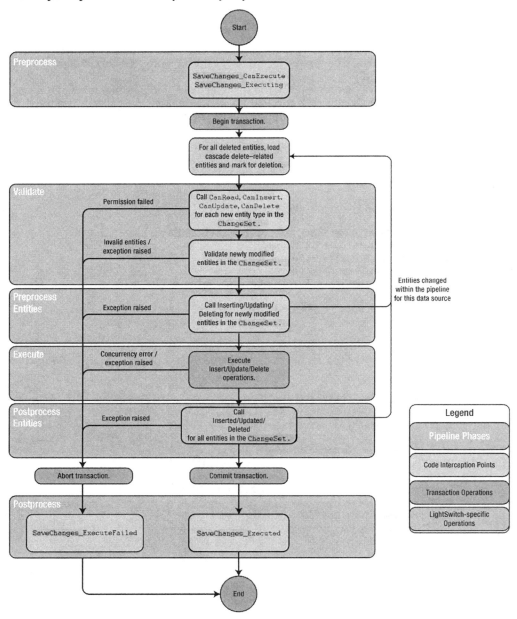

Figure 4-12. The phases in the save pipeline

The table designer gives you access to the methods in the save pipeline. When you open a table and select the Write Code option, the save pipeline methods appear as shown in Figure 4-13. All of these are listed in Table 4-4.

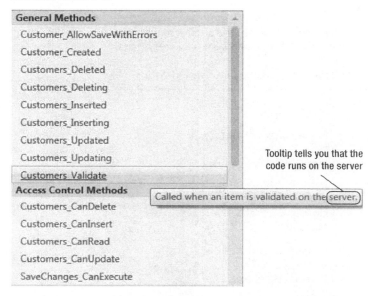

Figure 4-13. Writing code in the save pipeline

The General Methods section contains events that relate to the save pipeline. These events are prefixed with the entity set name (in this example, Customers). If you hover the mouse over the events that are shown, the tooltip shows you where the code is run. Those events that run on the server are associated with the save pipeline.

This section also contains entity-specific methods that belong in the common project. These methods are prefixed with the entity name (in this example, Customer).

The Access Control Methods section contains the methods that are called to carry out security checks. You can find out more about this topic in Chapter 14.

The remaining methods in the save pipeline are listed under the Data Source Methods section. This section includes the SaveChanges_Executed and the SaveChanges_ExecutedFailed methods.

Table 4-4. Events in the Save Pipeline

Event	Description
Preprocessing	
SaveChanges_CanExecute	Called to determine whether SaveChanges can be executed
SaveChanges_Executing	Called before the operation is processed

Event	Description
Validation	
EntitySet_CanRead, CanInsert, CanUpdate, CanDelete	Called for each entity in the change set, to check permissions to see whether the requested changes can be performed
EntitySet_Validate	Called for each modified or inserted entity
Preprocess Entities	
EntitySet_Inserting	Called for each inserted entity
EntitySet_Updating	Called for each updated entity
EntitySet_Deleting	Called for each deleted entity
Postprocess Entities	
EntitySet_Inserted	Called for each inserted entity
EntitySet_Updated	Called for each updated entity
EntitySet_Deleted	Called for each deleted entity
Postprocessing	
SaveChanges_Executed	Called after a successful processing of SaveChanges
SaveChanges_ExecuteFailed	Called after a failure in processing

At the very start of the pipeline, the Preprocess, Validate, and Preprocess Entity phases occur. These phases allow you to perform security checks and validation.

If any errors occur during the save operation, an exception is raised and the SaveChanges_ExecuteFailed event is raised. This exception can be captured and handled on the client if necessary. If any entities are changed, execution returns to the start of the pipeline, and the validation methods are carried out again. If the processing succeeds, any changes made to entities in the original change set are serialized and returned to the client. This allows the client to get the ID values or any other changes that have been made during processing.

It is important to note that any entities that you have added via the save pipeline will not be returned to the client. To retrieve items that have been added, you would need to handle the Screen_Saved event and manually call code to refresh the data. The refresh method on the screen visual collection can be called to do this (for example, Customers.Refresh() on a customer grid screen). Alternatively, you can call the screen methods Me.Refresh() in VB.NET or this.Refresh() in C# (although this would completely restart the screen and reload all of the screen's data).

To give an example of why you might want to intercept the save pipeline, the entity set inserted, updated, or deleted methods could be used to create audit records whenever entities are modified. Chapter 15 explains this in more detail.

Calling Server-Side Code from the Client

You have seen how server-side code can be initiated only through a save operation on an entity. However, at times you might want to trigger a server-side operation from the client. For example, you might want to create a screen button that backs up a database, calls a web service to perform validation, or sends an email.

One technique for triggering server-side code is to create a *dummy table* that exists purely for the purpose of running server code. Chapter 12 demonstrates how this technique can be used for sending SMTP (Simple Mail Transfer Protocol) email from the server.

Using the *EntityFunctions* Class

The System.Data.Objects namespace contains a useful class called EntityFunctions. This class contains simple, *canonical* methods that can assist when writing server code. It contains functions for working with aggregate, math, string, and date data. For example, there are aggregate functions to help calculate average, minimum, maximum, standard deviation, and variance results.

The math type functions include a power function for calculating exponents, and other functions such as ceiling, round, and floor.

When working with dates, various methods are included for performing date calculations. These are ideal for C# developers who do not have access to functions, such as DateDiff, that are available in VB.NET. These date functions are summarized in Table 4-5.

To use this class, you will need to add a reference to System.Data.Entity in the server project.

Table 4-5. Date Methods in the EntityFunctions Class

Method Name	Description
DiffDays	Gets the difference in days
DiffHours	Gets the difference in hours
DiffMicroseconds	Gets the difference in microseconds
DiffMilliseconds	Gets the difference in milliseconds
DiffMinutes	Gets the difference in minutes
DiffMonths	Gets the difference in months
DiffNanoseconds	Gets the difference in nanoseconds
DiffSeconds	Gets the difference in seconds
DiffYears	Gets the difference in years

Method Name	Description
GetTotalOffsetMinutes	Gets the difference in offset minutes
TruncateTime	Truncates the time element

Managing Transactions in LightSwitch

LightSwitch includes built-in support for transactions for data in the intrinsic, or attached, SQL Server data sources. In this section, we'll define what a transaction is and show you how they are managed in LightSwitch.

■ **Note** Data operations performed against a SharePoint data source are not transactional.

Understanding Transactions

You probably know what a transaction is already, but just in case, we'll start off with a brief explanation. A banking system is the traditional example that is given when describing transactions. Let's suppose that Tim attempts to make a payment of $100 to Yann. Behind the scenes, two things happen. First, $100 is deducted from Tim's account. Second, that $100 is added into Yann's account. Either both of these operations must succeed, or both must fail. The outcome that should never happen is for one operation to succeed and the other to fail. For example, $100 should never be added into Yann's account if the amount fails to be deducted from Tim's account.

Understanding ACID Principles

Many computer science students have encountered the acronym ACID during their studies. This term is used to define the properties of a transaction and consists of the following:

- *Atomicity.* As illustrated in the preceding example, atomicity is the all-or-nothing rule. Operations in a transaction must either all succeed or all fail.

- *Consistency.* This states that the data affected by the transaction must be consistent. For example, if database rules and operations exist such as constraints, triggers, and cascade deletes, these must all be correctly applied within a transaction.

- *Isolation.* Separate transactions should each maintain an independent view of the data, and operations that take place in one transaction should not interfere with those from another transaction.

- *Durability.* This guarantees that after a transaction is committed, it survives permanently. In the event of a system failure or power loss, uncommitted transactions should be rolled back.

Reading Data in LightSwitch

Let's return to our banking example. Once again, Tim makes a payment of $100 to Yann. A transaction begins, and $100 is deducted from Tim's account. At this precise moment, the bank manager Annie views Tim's balance. What does Annie see? Does she see the $100 deduction or not?

In LightSwitch, the answer to this question is no. When reading data, LightSwitch uses the transaction isolation level of *Read Committed,* which is inherited from the default transaction isolation level of SQL Server. In other words, Annie will see the $100 deduction only when this amount has been added into Yann's account and the transaction has been committed.

When reading data from a SQL Server data source, LightSwitch never shows uncommitted changes. This behavior cannot be changed.

Implementing Transactions in .NET

This section offers you some insight into how transactions are implemented in .NET. There are two main kinds of transactions: connection transactions and ambient transactions.

Connection transactions are tied to a database connection. In traditional ADO.NET code, you would connect to a SQL Server database by creating a SqlConnection object. A transaction would be started by calling the BeginTransaction method, and either the Commit or Rollback method would be called at the end of the process. Connection transactions can be difficult to work with if data access code is contained in different methods or classes. For example, if the SQL commands that you want to execute are contained in several different methods, you would need to write code that passes the SqlConnection object into each separate method.

Ambient transactions were introduced in .NET 2.0 to help overcome this problem and to simplify the task of working with transactions. You use a TransactionScope object, which is found in the SystemTransactions namespace. To begin a transaction, you would create a new TransactionScope object. Any database code that is subsequently called will enlist in the ambient transaction. Every database call can use its own connection and can even close and dispose of its connection before the ambient transaction is committed. This enlistment process happens automatically. There isn't any additional code that you need to write to include a command into a transaction. At the end of the process, you would call the Complete and Dispose methods on the TransactionScope object to commit the transaction. Calling Dispose without Complete would roll back the transaction.

Ambient transactions are also not just limited to database calls. Operations based on transaction-aware providers can also enlist in a transaction. Therefore, any changes made to data from a transaction-aware RIA service can also be included inside a transaction.

Implementing Transactions in the Save Pipeline

When the SaveChanges operation is called, a data workspace is created and the change set that was passed to the method from the client is loaded into that workspace. Each data workspace owns its own SqlConnection and creates a connection transaction at the start of the save pipeline process.

By default, ambient transactions are not used. However, you could create your own transaction scope, and the save pipeline would use this. This would allow you to enroll in a distributed transaction (DTC is not used by default) or to modify the default isolation level.

During a save, the default transaction isolation level is RepeatableRead. This means that other transactions cannot modify data that is read by the current transaction until the current transaction completes.

Because the save pipeline works against a single data source, transactions do not happen across data sources. To create transactions across data sources during the current save operation, you would need to create a transaction scope and make changes to your second data source within a new data workspace. This is explained in more detail later in this chapter.

Because there is scope for data inconsistency to arise when working against multiple data sources, LightSwitch protects novice developers by making screen sections based on other data sources read-only. This behavior is shown in Figure 4-14.

Figure 4-14. Screen sections are read-only when multiple data sources are used

Creating an Ambient Transaction

If you wanted to create your own transaction scope, you would do this in the Executing phase of the pipeline and commit it in the Executed phase. Listing 4-12 shows an example of saving data changes in the intrinsic database. If the changes succeed, an audit record is created in a second data source called AuditDataSource. If the changes to the intrinsic database fail, an audit record must not be created.

To use this code, you will need to add a reference to the System.Transactions.dll file in the server project.

Listing 4-12. Creating Your Own Transaction Scope

VB:

```
File: ShipperCentral\Server\UserCode\ApplicationDataService.vb

Imports System.Transactions

Namespace LightSwitchApplication

    Public Class ApplicationDataService

        Dim transaction As TransactionScope

        Private Sub SaveChanges_Executing()

            Dim transactionOptions = New TransactionOptions()
            transactionOptions.IsolationLevel = IsolationLevel.ReadCommitted
```

```vb
            'Create an audit record as part of the transaction
            Me.transaction = New TransactionScope(
                TransactionScopeOption.Required, transactionOptions)
                Using dataworkspace2 = this.Application.CreateDataWorkspace()
                Dim auditRecord = dataworkspace2.AuditDataSource.Audits.AddNew
                auditRecord.AuditDesc = "Data change made " & DateTime.Now.ToString()
                dataworkspace2.AuditDataSource.SaveChanges()
                End Using

        End Sub

        Private Sub SaveChanges_Executed()
            'Commit the transaction
            Me.transaction.Complete()
            Me.transaction.Dispose()
        End Sub

        Private Sub SaveChanges_ExecuteFailed(exception As System.Exception)
            'Rollback the transaction on a error
            Me.transaction.Dispose()
        End Sub

    End Class

End Namespace
```

C#:
File: **ShipperCentral\Server\UserCode\ApplicationDataService.cs**

```csharp
using System.Transactions;

namespace LightSwitchApplication
{
    public class ApplicationDataService
    {
        TransactionScope transaction;

        private void SaveChanges_Executing()
        {
            TransactionOptions transactionOptions = new TransactionOptions();
            transactionOptions.IsolationLevel = IsolationLevel.ReadCommitted;

            //Create an audit record as part of the transaction
            this.transaction = new TransactionScope(
                TransactionScopeOption.Required, transactionOptions);
            using (var dataworkspace2 = this.Application.CreateDataWorkspace()) {
            Audit auditRecord = dataworkspace2.AuditDataSource.Audits.AddNew();
            auditRecord.AuditDesc = "Data change made "
                + DateTime.Now.ToString();
            dataworkspace2. AuditDataSource.SaveChanges();
            }
        }
```

```
    private void SaveChanges_Executed()
    {
        //Commit the transaction
        this.transaction.Complete();
        this.transaction.Dispose();
    }

    private void SaveChanges_ExecuteFailed(System.Exception exception)
    {
        //Rollback the transaction on an error
        this.transaction.Dispose();
    }
}
}
```

In the preceding code, an ambient transaction is created in the executing method. The constructor allows you to pass in a TransactionOption object, and this can be used to set the transaction isolation level. A new instance of a data workspace is created, and this is used to create an entry in an audit table.

If the data changes in the data service are saved successfully, the transaction scope is *completed* in the SaveChanges_Executed method, and this commits the transaction. Otherwise, the transaction scope is disposed in the SaveChanges_ExecuteFailed method, and the transaction is rolled back. This means that the audit record that was created in the SaveChanges_Executing method will not be persisted to the data store, along with any other data changes that were attempted in the save pipeline.

Rolling Back Transactions—A Demonstration

To summarize what has been said in simple terms, LightSwitch automatically provides transactions for data operations at a data source level without you having to write any additional code. To prove that this actually works (when working against a single data source), a data entry screen is created that allows customers and orders to be created.

To mimic a data store failure at the SQL Server level, we'll create a database trigger on the order table to raise an error during an insert. This code is shown in Listing 4-13.

Listing 4-13. Database Trigger to Mimic a Data Insert Failure

```
CREATE TRIGGER [dbo].[OrderFailureTrigger]
   ON  [dbo].[Order]
AFTER INSERT
AS
BEGIN
    RAISERROR('Order Insert Failure Demonstration',16,1)
END
```

Both a customer and order record are now created by using our LightSwitch screen. When the Save button is clicked, the order record insertion fails, and both operations are rolled back. Figure 4-15 illustrates the error that the user sees.

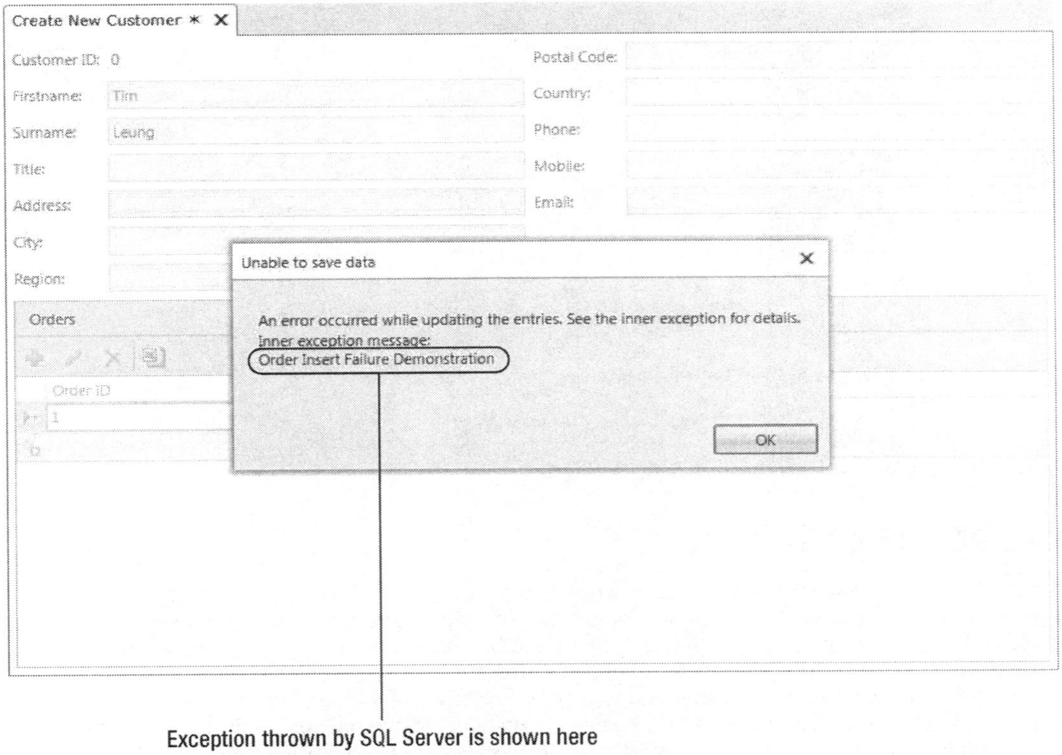

Exception thrown by SQL Server is shown here

Figure 4-15. Error dialog box that is shown to the user

By using SQL Server Profiler to trace the activity that is carried out by LightSwitch (as explained in Chapter 2), we can confirm that LightSwitch starts a transaction and rolls it back when the failure occurs during the insert of the order record. The rollback operation is confirmed in the screenshot shown in Figure 4-16.

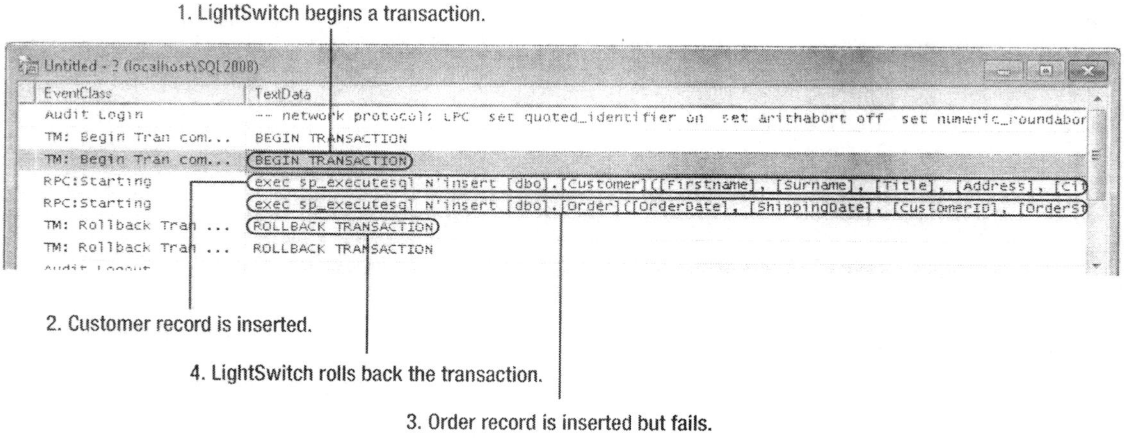

1. LightSwitch begins a transaction.

2. Customer record is inserted.

4. LightSwitch rolls back the transaction.

3. Order record is inserted but fails.

Figure 4-16. Transactions as seen through SQL Profiler

Understanding Concurrency

Concurrency is yet another important aspect that needs to be understood when writing applications. Let's suppose that Tim and Yann both edit a product record at the same time. Tim increases the price of the product and modifies the comment field of the record. Seconds later, Yann also changes the price, updates the product photo, and attempts to save the record.

What happens at this moment in time, and what data exactly will the database contain? In this particular example, LightSwitch prevents Yann from saving his changes because that would overwrite the changes that have been made by Tim. LightSwitch prevents data from being saved if modifications have been made since the record was first opened.

LightSwitch uses optimistic concurrency control and works without locking any of the underlying records. LightSwitch handles concurrency issues by automatically displaying a *data conflict screen* to the end user. For more-complex scenarios, you can even write your own code to handle concurrency issues.

Displaying a Data Conflict Screen

The neat thing about LightSwitch is that you don't need to worry about data conflicts. By default, LightSwitch handles all of this for you through a data conflict screen. This is automatically created and shown to the user when a conflict occurs. Figure 4-17 illustrates the screen that Yann would see.

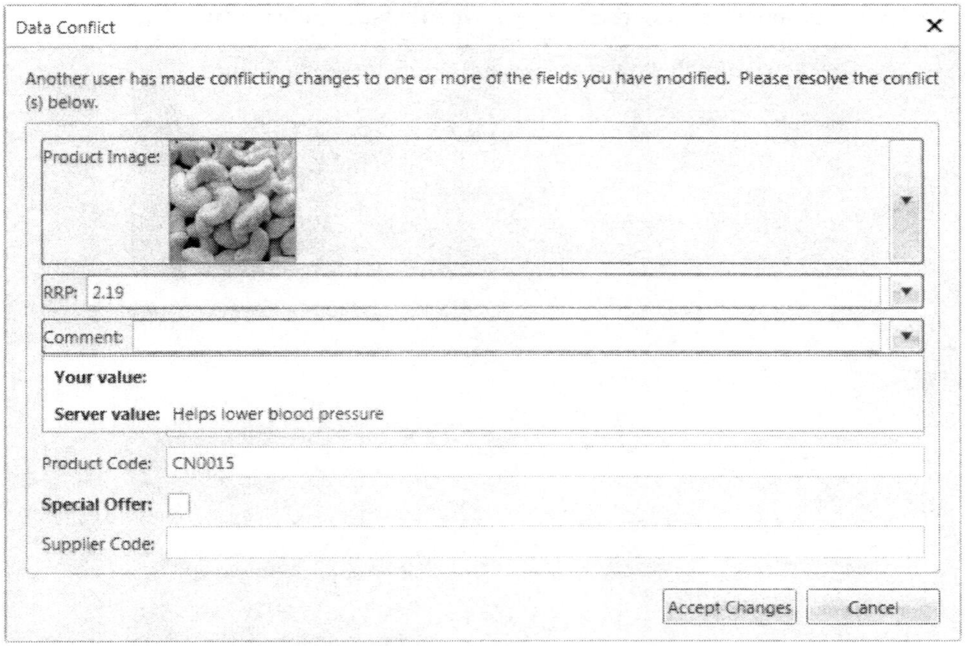

Figure 4-17. *Autogenerated data conflict screen*

The data conflict screen allows Yann to see the state of the data when the record was first opened, the current data, and the proposed changes. This allows him to review the changes before committing his changes.

But how does LightSwitch detect that a conflict has occurred? We can find out by profiling the database. Figure 4-18 shows the result. LightSwitch constructs a WHERE clause that includes all of the fields.

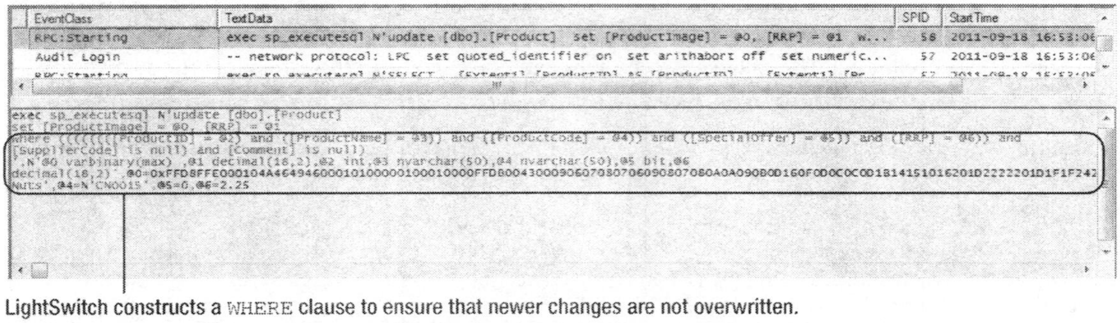

LightSwitch constructs a WHERE clause to ensure that newer changes are not overwritten.

Figure 4-18. *WHERE clause that is generated for conflict detection*

In the preceding example, you have seen what happens when a data conflict occurs. The other possible scenario is that Tim deletes the product record. In this instance, there is nothing that Yann can do to recover the record. The dialog box illustrated in Figure 4-19 will be shown to him.

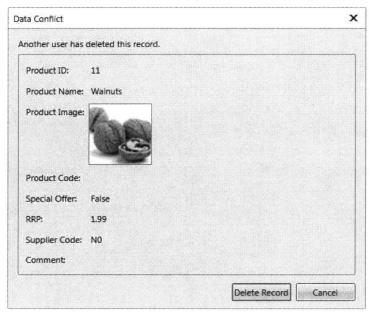

Figure 4-19. Dialog box shown to the user when a record is deleted

Handling Conflicts in Code

If you prefer not to display the data conflict screen to the user, you can perform the data conflict resolution manually in code. When a data conflict occurs, a ConcurrencyException is thrown by the data service. This exception can be handled by using client-side code at the screen level.

It isn't possible to handle concurrency exceptions at the server level by using a method such as SaveChanges_ExecuteFailed. This is because changes can't be resaved in the save pipeline, so even if you corrected any data conflicts in the SaveChanges_ExecuteFailed method, there wouldn't be any way for you to save those changes.

Listing 4-14 shows how conflicts can be resolved in code. If an attempt is made to alter the price of a product, the user will be allowed to make this change even if it overwrites changes that have been made by another user.

In this example, error-handling code is attached to the Saving method of a product screen. If a ConcurrencyException is raised by the data service, an EntitiesWithConflicts collection is returned with the exception. This contains a collection of entities. The exact properties that are causing the conflict can be found by inspecting the entity's Details.EntityConflict.ConflictingProperties object.

If a conflict in price is detected, you can call the ResolveConflicts method to resolve the conflict. This method accepts the argument ConflictResolution.ClientWins or ConflictResolution.ServerWins. ClientWins means that the server copy will be overwritten by the out-of-date client version. ServerWins means that the up-to-date server version will replace the client version.

The Saving method on the client includes a handled parameter. By setting this to true, LightSwitch does not automatically save data changes, and this is what enables us to manually call the SaveChanges method on the data source object.

Listing 4-14. Resolving Conflicts in Code

VB:

File: ShipperCentral\Client\UserCode\ProductDetail.vb

```vb
Private Sub ProductDetail_Saving(ByRef handled As Boolean)

    handled = True

    Try
        Me.DataWorkspace.ApplicationData.SaveChanges()
    Catch ex As ConcurrencyException

        For Each entityConflict In ex.EntitiesWithConflicts.OfType(Of Product)()

            Dim conflictingPrice = ↩
        entityConflict.Details.EntityConflict.ConflictingProperties.Where(
                Function(x) x.Property.Name = "Price").SingleOrDefault

            If conflictingPrice IsNot Nothing Then
                ' There is a conflict with the price
                conflictingPrice.EntityConflict.ResolveConflicts(
                    Microsoft.LightSwitch.Details.ConflictResolution.ClientWins)
                Try
                    Me.DataWorkspace.ApplicationData.SaveChanges()
                Catch ex2 As Exception
                    ' An exception has occurred with the second save
                    ShowMessageBox(ex2.Message.ToString())
                End Try
            Else
                ' There is a conflict with some other property
                ShowMessageBox("Error - data has been modified by another user")
            End If
        Next

    End Try

End Sub
```

C#:

File: ShipperCentral\Client\UserCode\ProductDetail.cs

```csharp
partial void ProductDetail_Saving(ref bool handled)
{
    handled = true;
```

```
try
{
    DataWorkspace.ApplicationData.SaveChanges();
}
catch (ConcurrencyException ex)
{

    foreach (var entityConflict in ex.EntitiesWithConflicts.OfType<Product>())
    {
        var conflictingPrice = ⬑
    entityConflict.Details.EntityConflict.ConflictingProperties.Where
            (x => x.Property.Name == "Price").SingleOrDefault();

        if ((conflictingPrice != null))
        {
            // There is a conflict with the price
            conflictingPrice.EntityConflict.ResolveConflicts(
                Microsoft.LightSwitch.Details.ConflictResolution.ClientWins);
            try
            {
                this.DataWorkspace.ApplicationData.SaveChanges();
            }
            catch (Exception ex2)
            {
                this.ShowMessageBox(ex2.Message.ToString());
            }

        }
        else
        {
            // There is a conflict with some other property
            this.ShowMessageBox("Error - data has been modified by another user");
        }
    }

}
}
```

⬛ **Caution** Calling ResolveConflicts(ConflictResolution.ClientWins) will overwrite the server record in its entirety, rather than just the properties that are in conflict. For example, if user A modifies the price and description, and user B subsequently modifies just the price, ResolveConflicts(ConflictResolution. ClientWins) also overwrites the description even though the description property was not in conflict.

Working with User Data

There are a couple of places where you can access user-related details in LightSwitch. As mentioned earlier, the application object provides access to the currently logged-on user. The code in Listing 4-15 shows you the code to retrieve the username.

Listing 4-15. Accessing the Currently Logged-on User

VB:
```
Me.Application.User
```
C#:
```
this.Application.User;
```

LightSwitch manages membership and permissions in a built-in data source called `SecurityData`. This data source is backed by an ASP.NET membership provider. The membership provider allows you to access membership and security features such as the `ChangePassword` and `IsValidPassword` methods. The `ChangePassword` method allows you to change the password for a user by passing in username, old password, and new password arguments. The `IsValidPassword` method accepts a password string and returns a Boolean result that indicates whether the password adheres to the rules relating to password strength.

You can also access role and permission details by using the `Role`, `Permission` and `RolePermission` collections. Figure 4-20 illustrates some of the methods that are shown to you through the IntelliSense window.

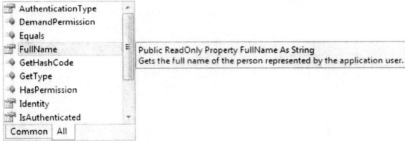

Figure 4-20. IntelliSense options that relate to the user

Summary

In this chapter, you have learned how to access data in code. This chapter has:

- described the data access objects that are generated by LightSwitch
- showed you how to work with data on screens
- illustrated the stages in the save pipeline
- explained the purpose of change sets
- described how transactions and concurrency are handled

LightSwitch generates data access objects with names that match the tables and fields that you have defined in your project. This makes it intuitive for you to write code that accesses data.

When writing client-side screen code, the Application object allows you to access the logged-on user and provides methods for accessing and opening screens.

When creating screens, the user interface elements are bound to screen properties that appear on the left side of the screen designer. You can programmatically access these properties in code by using the name of the property. Because UI elements are bound to screen properties, you can change the values that are shown in controls by modifying the screen property values in code.

Each screen contains an independent view of the data in a data workspace. The data workspace contains a change set for each data source. When a save is performed, the change set is passed to the server and is processed through the save pipeline.

There are various phases in the save pipeline that allow you to inject your own custom code. You can access these events by opening a table in the table designer and clicking the Write Code button. The tooltip that appears for the events will show you where the code is executed. Events that execute on the server relate to the events in the save pipeline.

The events in the save pipeline occur within a transaction (except when working against SharePoint data sources). All data changes that you attempt to save on a screen will happen atomically (per data source). In other words, either all or nothing will be saved for each data source. If an error occurs when saving a data item, any other changes that may have already been made in that data source will be rolled back.

If you attempt to make a change that overwrites a change that someone else has made, LightSwitch automatically detects this and displays a data conflict screen to the user. This allows the user to correct the data conflict and to resubmit the change.

CHAPTER 5

Validating Data

There's an old saying in IT: *garbage in, garbage out.* You may have heard this saying or perhaps even a stronger variation of the same adage. In essence, it means that if you enter nonsense data into a computer system, the results of any processing will also be rubbish. Any robust computer system needs to ensure that quality data is entered into the system.

Fortunately, LightSwitch allows you to apply validation and business rules in several places throughout your application. First, you can easily apply validation declaratively by using the table designer. Any screens that you create in LightSwitch will then automatically validate the data type and length of the data that you have defined. If the data length of a property is subsequently changed, LightSwitch handles all of this automatically for you without you having to do a thing. For more-complex scenarios, you can write your own custom validation rules. These rules can be applied at a property or entity level.

When designing screens, validation can be performed at a screen level. This allows you to perform validation that is specific to the function of a particular screen. Finally, any validation that is present at the storage level will also be applied. An example of this is a database constraint defined at the SQL Server level.

Where Is Validation Performed?

Validation is performed both on the client and server. Figure 5-1 illustrates the workflow.

On the client, screen and entity validation is carried out. All predefined entity rules are performed on the client as soon as data changes occur, and this means that validation errors are shown immediately to the user. For example, if text is entered that exceeds the maximum length, the user is alerted to this error as soon as the focus leaves the text box.

Validation errors must be corrected before the data can be submitted to the server for a save. After the server receives the data, the same entity validation is repeated. The screen validation will not be carried out again because the screen object does not exist on the server. From a practical point of view, this means that any local screen properties that you define will not be revalidated on the server.

After the data is validated on the server, it is submitted to the data-storage layer (which typically is SQL Server). If any validation errors are detected here, they are returned to the server, which ultimately returns the error to the user in the form of an error message.

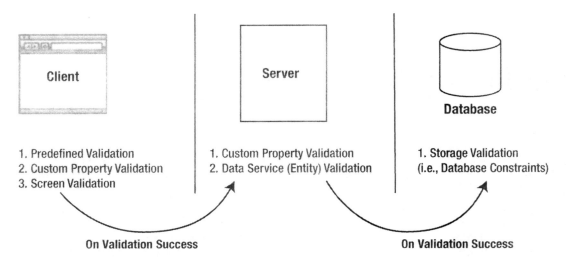

Figure 5-1. *Validation workflow*

Predefined Validation

LightSwitch does much of the work for you by allowing you to specify validation rules declaratively through the table designer. Figure 5-2 shows how various aspects of validation can be applied by using the properties pane for a field in a table.

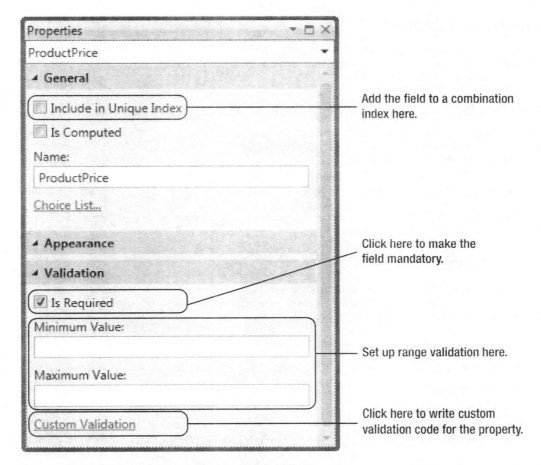

Figure 5-2. Setting validation properties at a field level

Because the field is of data type `Double`, LightSwitch automatically ensures that only numeric data can be entered. Data type validation will also occur for all other data types that are available in LightSwitch.

▪ **Note** LightSwitch creates storage constraints for many of these settings. This ensures that validation is also carried out at the server. For example, if the Include in Unique Index check box is selected, a unique index is created in the SQL Server database.

Data Length Validation

The String data type allows you to specify a maximum length. As mentioned in Chapter 3, the default maximum field size is set to 255 characters. If you want to allow the user to enter unlimited text, you can simply clear the maximum field size text box.

Range Validation

The Numeric and Date data types allow you to perform range validation by specifying the Minimum Value and Maximum Value properties. This type of range validation applies to the data types Date, DateTime, Decimal, Double, Money, and all Integer types.

Required Field Validation

Selecting the Is Required check box makes a property mandatory. Behind the scenes, LightSwitch creates a NOT NULL constraint on the database column.

Custom Validation

Although predefined validation is fine for simple validation scenarios, you likely will want to enforce more-complex validation rules. This is achieved by writing custom validation, which you can apply at a property or entity level (as part of the save pipeline).

░ **Note** Some of the code samples here contain LINQ (Language Integrated Query) syntax that may be unfamiliar to you. Don't worry if you struggle to understand this code. All of this is described in more detail in Chapter 6.

How to Write Client/Server/Common Validation Code

In LightSwitch, validation can run on the client, on the server, or on both the client and server. It is important to target the validation at the right tier. For example if you want to write validation that relies heavily on data, you don't want to download lots of data onto the client just to perform this task. This is likely to impede performance and is better done server side.

To further help you understand where validation is performed, Figure 5-3 illustrates the LightSwitch IDE and shows you where the validation is carried out.

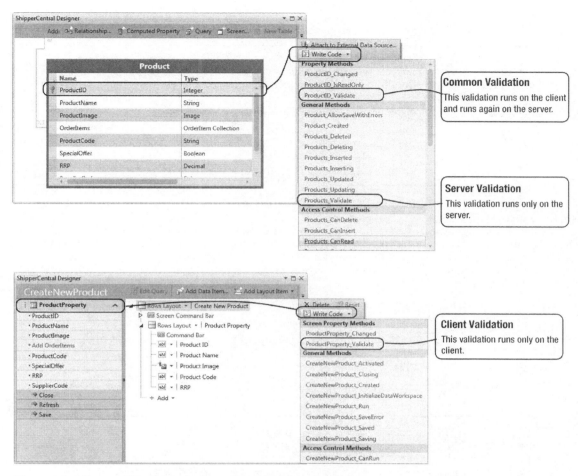

Figure 5-3. Where validation is performed in relation to the designer

Creating Validation Rules and Warnings

After clicking the Custom Validation link, the code window opens. A method stub is automatically created that contains the commented-out line `results.AddPropertyError("<Error-Message>")`. Uncommenting this line generates a property validation error. You can construct validation rules by writing conditional logic around this line of code.

The `results` parameter is of type `EntityValidationResultsBuilder`. Table 5-1 summarizes the methods that are available to you.

Table 5-1. EntityValidationResultsBuilder Methods

Method	Description
AddPropertyError	Generates a validation error at a property level
AddPropertyResult	Produces a validation warning at a property level
AddEntityError	Generates a validation error at an entity level
AddEntityResult	Produces a validation warning at an entity level

If the AddPropertyError or AddEntityError methods are used, records cannot be saved to the data source until the validation conditions are met.

At times you might want to display a validation warning but still allow the user to save the record. In this situation, you can use the AddPropertyResult and AddEntityResult methods. The second parameter of these methods accepts a severity level that can be either ValidationSeverity.Informational or ValidationSeverity.Warning. A different icon is shown on the screen depending on the severity level, as illustrated in Figure 5-4.

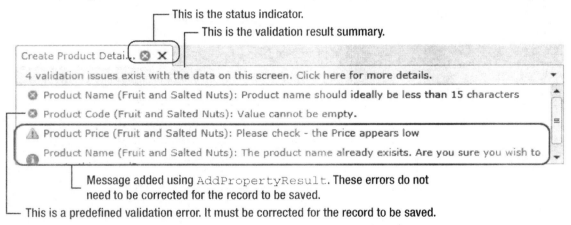

Figure 5-4. Severity icons that are shown

> ■ **Note** At a screen level, you have seen how entity validation occurs immediately, as soon a user leaves a text box or control. Some LightSwitch developers have taken an imaginative approach to this and have written logic in the validate method in scenarios where an immediate response is required. For example, logic might be written in the Surname_Validate method to change the surname characters to uppercase, and this logic will run as soon the user leaves the surname text box. In Chapter 8, you'll learn how to use INotifyPropertyChanged. When the value of a property changes, this provides a better way to control the values of other properties in your application.

The Validation Engine

This section briefly explains how client-side validation works in LightSwitch. LightSwitch includes an efficient client-side validation engine. In particular, validation results are cached after they are first derived. This avoids having to rerun *all* validation rules when just one single rule fails validation. Behind the scenes, LightSwitch uses a system of dependency tracking. This is illustrated in Figure 5-5.

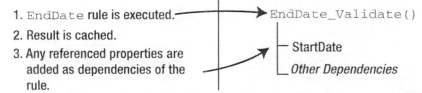

1. EndDate rule is executed. ──────────► EndDate_Validate()
2. Result is cached.
3. Any referenced properties are added as dependencies of the rule. ──── ┌─ StartDate
　　　　　　　　　　　　　　　　　　　　　　　　　　　　　　　　　　　└─ *Other Dependencies*

Figure 5-5. Validation dependency applied in client-side validation

Let's suppose you create a validation rule on a field/property called EndDate. The rule specifies that EndDate must be greater than StartDate. When the validation rule is first executed, LightSwitch registers StartDate as a *validation dependency* of the EndDate validation rule. If the StartDate property changes afterward, LightSwitch schedules the validation rule for reevaluation.

The validation engine can track most properties that are exposed by the LightSwitch API. In addition to entity and screen properties, the engine also tracks details properties such as IsReadOnly, SelectedItem, and ValidationResults.

To further reduce overhead, the validation engine does not compute results for unmodified properties. For example, say you've created a customer entity and the surname property is set to Is Required. If you open a new data screen based on this customer entity, the screen does not report the surname as missing, even though it is. This is because the rule is evaluated only when the surname property is modified. You need to type something into the surname text box and modify the value before the rule is executed.

Properties Tracked by the Dependency Engine

We've mentioned that most properties are tracked by the LightSwitch dependency engine. These include most of the properties that you can access using the details API. The entity properties that are tracked are shown in Table 5-2.

Table 5-2. Entity Properties That Are Tracked

Object	Property That Is Tracked
DataService	HasChanges
Entity	AllowSaveWithErrors, EntityState, IsValidated, ValidationResults
EntityStorageProperty	IsReadOnly, IsValidated, IsChanged, Value, ValidationResults
EntityReferenceProperty	IsReadOnly, IsValidated, IsChanged, IsLoaded, Value, ValidationResults
EntityCollectionProperty	IsReadOnly, IsValidated, IsLoaded, Value (for example, contained entities), ValidationResults
EntityComputedProperty	IsReadOnly, IsValidated, IsChanged, Value, ValidationResults
ValidationResults	HasError, Values
ExecutableObject	CanExecute, CanExecuteAsync, CanExecuteAsyncCancel, ExecutionState, ExecutionError

Examples of properties that are not tracked include the OriginalValue property on the EntityStorageProperty and EntityReferenceProperty objects. Regular .NET properties are also not tracked by the dependency engine. If you create your own .NET objects, for example, these will not be tracked.

Silverlight Implementation

When validation fails, the corresponding control is surrounded with a red border to indicate this failure to the user. But how exactly does this work?

In Chapter 1, you learned how the MVVM pattern is implemented within LightSwitch. The red highlighting is a function of the View part of MVVM, and this is presented to the user as a Silverlight control.

During runtime, a screen layout is created that contains a tree of content items. A content item forms the View-Model part of MVVM. At compile time, .NET classes are generated for each content item. The Silverlight controls are then data bound to the content items.

The generated .NET class for each content item implements the INotifyDataErrorInfo interface. This enables the content item (the View-Model model) to expose the error to the Silverlight control (the View). The Silverlight control can then act accordingly and perform the presentational tasks needed to alert the user to the validation error.

Accessing Validation Results in Code

When writing code, you may want to access the validation results programmatically. You can do this at the screen or entity level by using the details API. Listing 5-1 provides some example syntax.

Listing 5-1. Programatically Accessing Validation Results

VB:
File: ShipperCentral\Common\UserCode\ProductDetail.vb

```
' Examples of calling the IsValidated and HasErrors properties
Dim firstnameValid As Boolean = Me.Details.Properties.Firstname.IsValidated
Dim firstnameHasErrors As Boolean =
    Me.Details.Properties.Firstname.ValidationResults.HasErrors

' Get a count of all results with a severity of 'Error'.
Dim errorCount As Integer = Me.Details.ValidationResults.Errors.Count

' Concatenate the error messages into a single string.
Dim allErrors As String = ""
For Each result In Me.Details.ValidationResults
    allErrors += result.Message + " "
Next
```

C#:
File: ShipperCentral\Common\UserCode\ProductDetail.cs

```
// Examples of calling the IsValidated and HasErrors properties
bool firstnameValid = this.Details.Properties.Firstname.IsValidated;
bool firstnameHasErrors = this.Details.Properties.Firstname.ValidationResults.HasErrors;

// Get a count of all results with a severity of 'Error'.
int errorCount = this.Details.ValidationResults.Errors.Count();

// Concatenate the error messages into a single string.
string allErrors="";
foreach (ValidationResult result in  this.Details.ValidationResults ){
    allErrors += result.Message  + " ";
}
```

You can use the Properties object to return only those errors for a specific property (for example, Details.Properties.Firstname). The IsValidated property indicates whether a property has been validated. As mentioned earlier, properties are validated only when they are modified. The HasErrors property indicates whether there are any errors with a severity level of Error.

Finally, the validation results are exposed through a ValidationResults collection that you can loop through. Accessing ValidationResults causes validation to be carried out on objects that have not already been validated.

Custom Validation Examples

This section presents various code examples to help you get a feel for the type of validation that you can write.

We'll show you how to apply validation based on the values of other fields in the same record, and show you how to prevent the entry of duplicate records. We'll also show you how to use regular expressions, validate file sizes, and show you how to validate a property based on related data.

Required Validation Based on Other Conditions

Making fields mandatory is simple: just select the Is Required check box for the property in the entity designer. You may want to make some fields mandatory based on some other condition, and custom validation can be written to achieve this.

For example, imagine an Employee table that contains a Country of Residence field and a Social Security Number field. If the Country of Residence field is set to US, the Social Security Number field becomes mandatory. Otherwise, that field is optional. Listing 5-2 shows the property validation code that would be written for the Social Security Number field to apply this validation.

To do this, open the table in the entity designer and select the property that you wish to base your validation on. Click the Write Code button and select the validate method that is shown in the Property Methods group.

Listing 5-2. *Making Fields Required Based on Some Condition*

VB:
File: ShipperCentral\Common\UserCode\EmployeeDetail.vb

```
Private Sub SocialSecurityNumber_Validate(results As EntityValidationResultsBuilder)
    If CountryOfResidence = "US" AndAlso Len(SocialSecurityNumber) = 0 Then
        results.AddPropertyError ("Social Security Number must be entered")
    End If
End Sub
```

C#:
File: ShipperCentral\Common\UserCode\EmployeeDetail.cs

```
partial void SocialSecurityNumber_Validate(EntityValidationResultsBuilder results)
{
    if (CountryOfResidence == "US" && string.IsNullOrEmpty(SocialSecurityNumber) ) {
        results.AddPropertyError("Social Security Number must be entered");
    }
}
```

■ **Note** You must select the property (for example, SocialSecurityNumber) before clicking the Write Code button. If you don't, the property's validate method (SocialSecurityNumber_Validate) will not appear in the drop-down of available options. Developers new to LightSwitch are sometimes surprised by this and struggle to find the validate method after clicking the Write Code button.

Enforcing Uniqueness and Preventing Duplicates

LightSwitch allows you to specify uniqueness by selecting the Is Unique check box in the fields in the entity designer. If the Is Unique check box is selected for more than one field in a table, a combination index is created for the set of fields that have been selected.

You may want to enforce uniqueness on two or more fields independently within a table. Listing 5-3 shows how this can be done. In this example, the product table contains a product code and a supplier code. For each row that is entered, both of these fields must be unique.

To use this code, open the table in the entity designer and select the property that you want to base your validation on. In this example, we have chosen the ProductCode property. Click the Write Code button and select the validate method that is shown in the Property Methods group.

Listing 5-3. Enforcing Unique Records

VB:

```
File : ShipperCentral\Common\UserCode\Product.vb

Private Sub ProductName_Validate(results As EntityValidationResultsBuilder)

    If Len(Me.ProductName) > 0 Then
        Dim duplicateOnServer = (
            From prod In Me.DataWorkspace.ApplicationData.Products.Cast(Of Product)()
            Where
            prod.ProductID <> Me.ProductID AndAlso
            prod.ProductName.Equals(Me.ProductName,
                StringComparison.CurrentCultureIgnoreCase)
            ).ToArray()

        Dim duplicateOnClients = (
            From prod In Me.DataWorkspace.ApplicationData.Details.GetChanges().
                OfType(Of Product)()
            Where
            prod IsNot Me AndAlso
            prod.ProductName.Equals(Me.ProductName,
                StringComparison.CurrentCultureIgnoreCase)
            ).ToArray()

        Dim deleltedOnClient = Me.DataWorkspace.ApplicationData.Details.GetChanges().
            DeletedEntities.OfType(Of Product)().ToArray()

        Dim anyDuplicates = duplicateOnServer.Union(duplicateOnClients).Distinct().
            Except(deleltedOnClient).Any()

        If anyDuplicates Then
            results.AddPropertyError("The product name already exists")
        End If

    End If

End Sub
```

C#:

File : ShipperCentral\Common\UserCode\Product.cs

```csharp
partial void ProductName_Validate(EntityValidationResultsBuilder results)
{
    if (this.ProductName.Length > 0)
    {
        var duplicatesOnServer = (
            from prod in this.DataWorkspace.ApplicationData.Products.Cast<Product>()
            where (prod.ProductID != this.ProductID) &&
            prod.ProductName.Equals(this.ProductName,
                StringComparison.CurrentCultureIgnoreCase)
            select prod
                ).ToArray();

        var duplicatesOnClient = (
            from prod in this.DataWorkspace.ApplicationData.Details.GetChanges().
                OfType<Product>()
            where (prod != this) &&
            prod.ProductName.Equals(this.ProductName,
                StringComparison.CurrentCultureIgnoreCase)
            select prod
                ).ToArray();

        var deleltedOnClient =
            this.DataWorkspace.ApplicationData.Details.GetChanges().
                DeletedEntities.OfType<Product>().ToArray();

        var anyDuplicates =
            duplicatesOnServer.Union(duplicatesOnClient).
                Distinct().Except(deleltedOnClient).Any();

        if (anyDuplicates)
        {
            results.AddPropertyError("The product name already exists");

        }

    }
}
```

This code checks both the client and server for duplicates. It excludes any deletions that have been made on the client. If any duplicates are found, a property error is raised.

Compare Validation

We've chosen the term *compare validation* for this section because it matches the name of a control that is used in ASP.NET. In essence, this type of validation works by checking the value of a property against that of another property. The following example illustrates a holiday request system. The holiday end date entered by the user cannot be earlier than the start date. Listing 5-4 shows the sample code.

Listing 5-4. Compare Validation

VB:
File : ShipperCentral\Common\UserCode\HolidayRequest.vb

```
Private Sub StartDate_Validate(results As EntityValidationResultsBuilder)
    If Me.StartDate > Me.EndDate Then
        results.AddPropertyError ("Start Date cannot be later than End Date")
    End If
End Sub
```

C#:
File : ShipperCentral\Common\UserCode\HolidayRequest.cs

```
partial void StartDate_Validate(EntityValidationResultsBuilder results)
{
    if (this.StartDate > this.EndDate) {
        results.AddPropertyError("Start Date cannot be later than End Date");
    }
}
```

Regular Expression Validation

Regular expressions (regexes) are a powerful and efficient tool for carrying out pattern matching. They can be used in LightSwitch to validate specific characters or patterns. You might use regexes to validate the formats of social security numbers, bank sort codes, postal codes, or domain names.

This technique works by using the `Regex` class in the `System.Text.RegularExpressions` namespace. The `IsMatch` method allows you to pass in an expression and returns a Boolean result indicating whether a match is found.

The most difficult part of using regex validation is working out the correct expression to use. Fortunately, an internet search will reveal many web sites which show prebuilt expressions. Listing 5-5 shows the code that you would use to validate the format of a credit card number. Of course, the code checks only that the formatting is correct and cannot check that the card number is actually valid for the purpose of taking a payment.

Listing 5-5. Regex Validation to Check the Format of a Credit Card

VB:
File: ShipperCentral\Common\UserCode\PaymentType.vb

```
Imports System.Text.RegularExpressions

Private Sub CreditCardNum_Validate(results As EntityValidationResultsBuilder)
    Dim pattern As String =
        "(^(4|5)\d{3}-?\d{4}-?\d{4}-?\d{4}|(4|5)\d{15})|(^(6011)-?\d{4}-?\d{4}-?↵
\d{4}|(6011)-?\d{12})|(^((3\d{3}))-\d{6}-\d{5}|^((3\d{14})))"

    If Not Regex.IsMatch(Me.CreditCardNum, pattern) Then
        results.AddPropertyError("Credit Card Number is not valid")
    End If
```

```
End Sub
```

C#:
File: ShipperCentral\Common\UserCode\PaymentType.cs

```csharp
using System.Text.RegularExpressions;

partial void CreditCardNum_Validate(EntityValidationResultsBuilder results)
{
    string pattern =
        @"(^(4|5)\d{3}-?\d{4}-?\d{4}-?\d{4}|(4|5)\d{15})|(^(6011)-?\d{4}-?↩
\d{4}-?\d{4}|(6011)-?\d{12})|(^((3\d{3}))-\d{6}-\d{5}|^((3\d{14})))";

    if( !Regex.IsMatch(this.CreditCardNum, pattern) )
    {
        results.AddPropertyError( "Credit Card Number is not valid" );
    }
}
```

Validating File Sizes

When working with image or binary data, you might want to restrict the size of the files that are uploaded into your application. You can restrict file size by writing code that checks size of the image or file that's uploaded by the user.

Listing 5-6 shows an example. The Product table contains a field called ProductPhoto that is used to store an image of the product. The listing contains code to ensure that uploaded images cannot be larger than 512KB.

Listing 5-6. *Validating File Sizes*

VB:
File: ShipperCentral\Common\UserCode\Product.vb

```vb
Private Partial Sub ProductPhoto_Validate(results As EntityValidationResultsBuilder)
    If Me.ProductPhoto IsNot Nothing Then
        Dim sizeInKB = Me.ProductPhoto.Length / 1024
        If sizeInKB > 512 Then
            results.AddPropertyError("File Size cannot be > 512kb")
        End If
    End If
End Sub
```

C#:
File: ShipperCentral\Common\UserCode\Product.cs
```csharp
partial void ProductPhoto_Validate(EntityValidationResultsBuilder results)
{
    if (this.ProductPhoto!= null)
    {
        var sizeInKB = this.ProductPhoto.Length / 1024;
        if (sizeInKB > 512)
        {
```

```
        results.AddPropertyError("File Size cannot be > 512kb");
      }
    }
}
```

Binary and Image data types are exposed in code as *byte arrays*. In the preceding code, the file size in kilobytes is calculated by dividing the byte array length by 1,024. If you want to calculate the size in megabytes, you divide by 1,048,576. If you want to calculate in gigabytes, you divide by 1,073,741,824. Table 5-3 indicates these conversions.

Table 5-3. *Converting Byte Array Length*

Unit of Measurement	Divisor
Kilobyte (KB)	1,024
Megabyte (MB)	1,048,576 (1,024 × 1,024)
Gigabyte (GB)	1,073,741,824 (1,024 × 1,024 × 1,024)
Terabyte (TB)	1,099,511,627,776 (1,024 × 1,024 × 1,024 × 1,024)

Checking Against Child Collections

When using custom validation, you can write code to access child collections and records. For example, the ShipperCentral system stores the order details in an Order table. Each order can contain many order items, and the order items are stored in an OrderItem table.

You can write validation to ensure that each order contains a maximum of ten items, for example. This validation is carried out by counting the number of related child items for an order. Listing 5-7 shows the code that you can use to do this.

The earlier custom validation examples used the Validate method on the property being validated. You can't use the same method to validate child items because navigation properties do not have a validate method that you can use. Instead, you need to apply the validation at the entity level or data-service level. To do this, open your screen, click the Write Code button, and select the EntitySet_Validate option from the General Methods group, as shown in Figure 5-6. In this example, the name of the method is Orders_Validate.

Listing 5-7. *Validating the Counts of Child Items*

VB:
File: ShipperCentral\Server\UserCode\ApplicationDataService.vb

```
Private Sub Orders_Validate(entity As Order,
    results As EntitySetValidationResultsBuilder)
    If entity.OrderItems.Count() > 10 Then
        results.AddEntityError("Orders can only contain a maximum of 10 items")
    End If
End Sub
```

C#:

```
File: ShipperCentral\Server\UserCode\ApplicationDataService.cs
partial void Orders_Validate(Order entity,
    EntitySetValidationResultsBuilder results)
{
    if (entity.OrderItems.Count() > 10)
    {
        results.AddEntityError("Orders can only contain a maximum of 10 items");
    }
}
```

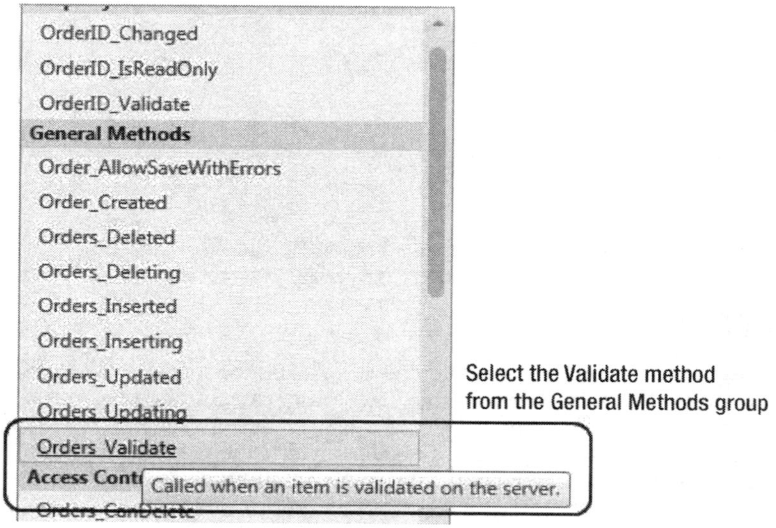

Figure 5-6. Creating entity or data-service validation

The code in Listing 5-7 shows how an aggregate function can be applied to a child collection. A point to bear in mind is that calling the Count function retrieves all related order records in order to produce the count.

As another example using child items, imagine that each product in an order could be a product on *special offer*. Each customer is allowed to purchase only one item on special offer per order. The product table contains a Boolean field called SpecialOffer that stores whether the item is on special offer. Listing 5-8 illustrates how a Where condition can be applied to a child collection.

Listing 5-8. Searching Related Child Items

VB:
```
File: ShipperCentral\Server\UserCode\ApplicationDataService.vb

Private Sub Orders_Validate(entity As Order,
    results As EntitySetValidationResultsBuilder)
```

```vb
    If entity.OrderItems.Where(
        Function(orderItem) orderItem.Product.SpecialOffer = True).Count() > 1 Then
            results.AddEntityError("Orders can only contain 1 item on special offer")
    End If
End Sub
```

C#:

```csharp
File: ShipperCentral\Server\UserCode\ApplicationDataService.cs
partial void Orders_Validate(Order entity,
    EntitySetValidationResultsBuilder results)
{
    if (entity.OrderItems.Where (
        orderItem => orderItem.Product.SpecialOffer == true).Count () > 1){
            results.AddEntityError("Orders can only contain 1 item on special offer");
    }
}
```

Performing Screen Validation

When applying validation on a property, entity, or data-service level, the rules apply whenever the entity is modified. This means that validation rules need to be written only once and are automatically applied (on both the client and the server) to every screen in your application.

However, you may want to perform validation that applies to only a single screen. In this scenario, using screen validation is the correct approach. To write custom screen validation, open a screen, click the Write Code button, and select the validate method from the Screen Property Methods group, as shown in Figure 5-7.

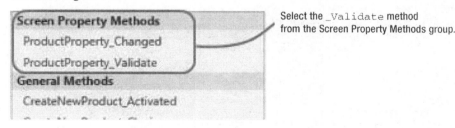

Select the _Validate method
from the Screen Property Methods group.

Figure 5-7. Creating screen validation

Listing 5-9 shows some sample code to make the RRP (Recommended Retail Price) field mandatory on a product screen. One of the differences here, compared to some of the earlier examples, is that the results object is of type ScreenValidationResultsBuilder. This object has two methods called AddScreenError and AddScreenMessage. Similar to the AddEntityError and AddEntityMessage methods that were described earlier, these methods accept a parameter that allows you to specify the property related to the error.

Listing 5-9. Performing Screen-Level Validation

VB:
File: ShipperCentral\Client\UserCode\CreateNewProduct.vb

```vb
Private Sub ProductProperty_Validate(results As ScreenValidationResultsBuilder)
    If Not Me.ProductProperty.RRP.HasValue Then
        results.AddPropertyError("RRP must be entered")
    End If
End Sub
```

C#:
File: ShipperCentral\Client\UserCode\CreateNewProduct.cs

```csharp
partial void ProductProperty_Validate(ScreenValidationResultsBuilder results)
{
    if (!this.ProductProperty.RRP.HasValue) {
        results.AddPropertyError("RRP must be entered");
    }
}
```

Validating Deletions

The previous examples have focused mainly on carrying out validation while inserting or updating records. You may also want to apply validation before a record is deleted. In the ShipperCentral system, a validation rule is required to prevent business customers from being deleted. The customer table includes a Boolean property called IsBusinessCust. If this is set to true, it indicates that the customer is a business or corporate customer, rather than a consumer.

One way to validate deletions in LightSwitch is to use screen-level validation. Listing 5-10 illustrates the screen code that you would use to enforce this validation rule.

Listing 5-10. Validating Deletions

VB:
File : ShipperCentral\Client\UserCode\CustomerDetail.vb

```vb
Private Sub Customers_Validate (results As ScreenValidationResultsBuilder)
    If Me.DataWorkspace.ApplicationData.Details.HasChanges Then
        Dim changeSet As EntityChangeSet = _
            Me.DataWorkspace.ApplicationData.Details.GetChanges()

        For Each cust In changeSet.DeletedEntities.OfType(Of Customer)()

            If cust.IsBusinessCust = True Then
                cust.Details.DiscardChanges()
                results.AddScreenResult("Unable to remove this customer.", & _
                    ValidationSeverity.Informational)
            End If

        Next
    End If
```

End Sub

C#:
File : ShipperCentral\Client\UserCode\CustomerDetail.cs

```csharp
partial void Customers_Validate(ScreenValidationResultsBuilder results)
{
    if (this.DataWorkspace.ApplicationData.Details.HasChanges)
    {
        EntityChangeSet changeSet =
        this.DataWorkspace.ApplicationData.Details.GetChanges();
        foreach (Customer cust in changeSet.DeletedEntities.OfType<Customer>())
        {
            if (cust.IsBusinessCust == true)
            {
                cust.Details.DiscardChanges();
                results.AddScreenResult("Unable to remove this customer. ", +
                ValidationSeverity.Informational);
            }
        }
    }
}
```

▪ **Note** Chapter 4 introduced the save pipeline and explained how save operations are performed inside a transaction. If a Cascade Delete rule is set up on the customer table and the deletion of a related order record fails because of validation, the entire transaction will be rolled back and your data will remain in a consistent state.

Validating Deletions on the Server

Validating deletions by using screen validation is relatively simple. The previous screen validation code was shown for its simplicity, but it's far from ideal. Relying on the client to perform validation isn't good practice. If you wanted to apply validation rules throughout your application, the code would have to be added to every single place where you could delete a customer. If you want to validate deletions on the server, the process can be quite complex.

This complexity arises because LightSwitch ignores validation errors on deleted entities during the save pipeline process. It does this for a good reason. If LightSwitch didn't behave like this, imagine how your users would react if they were forced to fill in all mandatory fields before deleting a record.

Because of this behavior, validating deletions on the server becomes a three-stage process:

1. In the entity set Validate method, check whether the EntityState is Deleted. If so, apply the validation rules that you want to enforce. If the entity fails validation, *add* the error by calling the AddEntityError method on the results object.

2. Any errors that you've added in step 1 can be detected in the entity set
   Deleting method. If any errors exist, throw an exception and prevent the
   deletion from being carried out.

3. In the client SaveError method, you can optionally undelete the deleted
   records that have failed validation.

If you want to perform validation against child records during a delete, another important point is to turn off Cascade Delete (that is, set it to Restricted). If not, any related child records are deleted prior to the validate method being called. You therefore won't be able to access related child records in the validate method of your parent entity. If you want to carry out Cascade Delete behavior, you can do this manually by deleting the child records in the validate method.

Listing 5-11 shows the code that you would use to prevent customers from being deleted if they still hold an active subscription. Each customer can have multiple subscriptions. These are stored in a table called Subscription, and active subscriptions are marked by using a Boolean property called IsActive.

Listing 5-11. Validating Deletions on the Server

VB:
File : ShipperCentral\Server\UserCode\ApplicationDataService.vb

```
Public Class ApplicationDataService

    Private Sub Customers_Validate(entity As Customer,
        results As Microsoft.LightSwitch.EntitySetValidationResultsBuilder)

        ' Check for validation errors for deletions
        If entity.Details.EntityState = EntityState.Deleted Then
            If entity.Subscriptions.Where(
                Function(s) s.IsActive.GetValueOrDefault()).Any() Then
                    results.AddEntityError("Cannot delete customers with active subscriptions.")
            End If
        End If

    End Sub

    Private Sub Customers_Deleting(entity As Customer)

        ' Check for validation errors for deletions
        If entity.Details.ValidationResults.Errors.Any Then
            Throw New ValidationException(Nothing,
                Nothing, entity.Details.ValidationResults)
        End If

        ' Cascade delete children because delete rule is Restricted
        For Each s In entity.Subscriptions
            s.Delete()
        Next

    End Sub

End Class
```

```vb
File: ShipperCentral\Client\UserCode\CustomersGrid.vb
' This is the screen code
Private Sub CustomersGrid_SaveError(exception As System.Exception,
    ByRef handled As Boolean)

    ' Un-delete deleted records that had server-side validation errors
    Dim validationExc =  TryCast(exception, ValidationException)

    If validationExc IsNot Nothing Then
          Dim entities = From v In validationExc.ValidationResults
                  Let e = TryCast(v.Target, IEntityObject)
                  Where e IsNot Nothing AndAlso
                      e.Details.EntityState = EntityState.Deleted
                        Select e
        For Each e In entities
            e.Details.DiscardChanges()
        Next
    End If

End Sub
```

C#:

```csharp
File : ShipperCentral\Server\UserCode\ShipperCentralDataService.cs

public class ApplicationDataService
{
    partial void Customers_Validate(Customer entity,
            Microsoft.LightSwitch.EntitySetValidationResultsBuilder results)
    {
        // Check for validation errors for deletions
        if (entity.Details.EntityState == EntityState.Deleted) {
            if (entity.Subscriptions.Where(s => s.IsActive).Any()) {
                results.AddEntityError(
                    "Cannot delete customers with active subscriptions.");
            }
        }
    }

    partial void Customers_Deleting(Customer entity)
    {
        // Check for validation errors for deletions
        if (entity.Details.ValidationResults.Errors.Any())
        {
            throw new ValidationException(null, null, entity.Details.ValidationResults);
        }

        // Cascade delete children because delete rule is Restricted
        foreach (var childSub in entity.Subscriptions)
```

143

```
        {
            childSub.Delete();
        }
    }
}

File: ShipperCentral\Client\UserCode\CustomersGrid.cs
' This is the screen code
partial void EditableCustomersGrid_SaveError(Exception exception, ref bool handled)
{
    ValidationException validationExc = (exception as ValidationException);
    if (validationExc != null)
    {

        var entities = from v in validationExc.ValidationResults
                       let e = (v.Target as IEntityObject)
                       where (e != null &&
                           e.Details.EntityState == EntityState.Deleted)
                       select e;

        foreach (IEntityObject e in entities)
        {
            e.Details.DiscardChanges();
        }
    }
}
```

Database Validation

You can create your own validation rules at the database when working with an external SQL Server database. For example, you could create SQL Server *check constraints* to validate the data against a T-SQL expression. If a user attempts to enter data that conflicts with the database rules that you have defined, LightSwitch will return the error to the user in the validation result summary.

Earlier in this chapter, we showed you how to prevent users from entering duplicate records. If you were using an attached SQL Server database, you could apply this validation using a SQL Server unique constraint. To create a unique constraint, open your table in SQL Server Management Studio. On the toolbar, click the Index button, and the Indexes/Keys dialog box opens, as shown in Figure 5-8.

In the General section of the dialog box, choose the column that you want to apply the index on, set the Is Unique option to Yes, and select the type Unique Key.

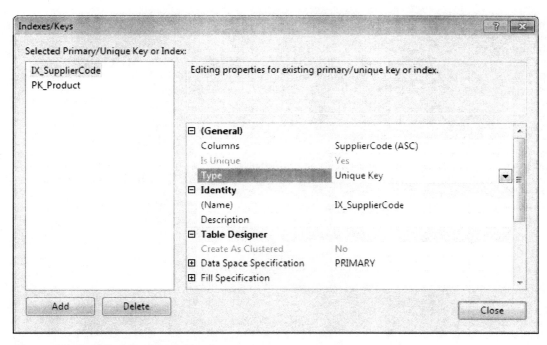

Figure 5-8. *Creating a unique index*

Figure 5-8 illustrates a unique constraint on the SupplierCode column in the product table. If you attempt to enter a product containing a duplicate supplier code, an error is returned after you attempt to save, as shown in Figure 5-9. This error message indicates the error that is returned from the server. Other server validation errors are grouped into the same block.

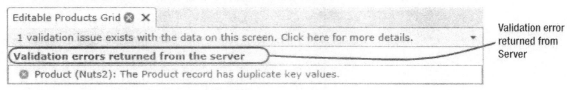

Figure 5-9. *Unique constraint violation error*

Summary

In this chapter, you have learned how to perform data validation in LightSwitch. The main topics that have been covered are as follows:

- Creating predefined validation rules

- Writing custom validation code

- Code examples of typical validation scenarios

Validation can be applied through entities, properties, and screens, and at the data-storage level. The actual validation itself is performed both on the client and on the server.

LightSwitch performs validation based on the predefined rules that are specified in properties. This enables data type, data length, and range validation to be carried out automatically.

For more-complex scenarios, custom validation can be performed at a property or entity level by using the validate method. To use this method, you would write your own conditional logic to check for any errors and then use the `EntityValidationResultsBuilder` object to specify the exact error message. If the `AddPropertyError` or `AddEntityError` methods of this object are called, the user cannot save their changes until the validation problems have been resolved. However, if the `AddPropertyMessage` or `AddEntityMessage` methods are used instead, the user will be warned of the validation issues and can save the changes afterward.

In this chapter, you have also seen various code samples that you can use. These include methods for preventing duplicates, comparing values against other properties, checking child collections, and using regular expressions.

Finally, you have seen how LightSwitch handles errors that are generated at the data-storage level.

CHAPTER 6

Querying Data

Along with creating tables and building screens, writing queries forms a key part of building a LightSwitch application. Queries enable you to filter data, and the results can be consumed by screens or other UI elements.

LightSwitch provides a designer that allows you to graphically build a query. For more-complex scenarios, you often need to extend queries by writing code. This chapter introduces you to the graphical designer, describes how you can extend queries by writing LINQ code, and shows you what happens inside the query pipeline.

Understanding Query Features

We'll start this chapter by describing some of the characteristics and features of queries in LightSwitch. The easiest way for you to create a query is to use the query designer, but there are several other ways that queries can be defined. The four main ways are shown in Table 6-1.

Table 6-1. *The Ways That Queries Can Be Defined in LightSwitch*

Query Type	Description
Default entity set queries	LightSwitch automatically creates All and Single queries for you.
User-defined data service queries	These refer to the queries that you write yourself. You can create and manage these queries by using the Queries folder in Solution Explorer.
Screen queries	When you design a screen, screen queries allow you to apply additional filtering and ordering.
LINQ queries	You can write your own queries in code by using LINQ. You've already seen some examples in Chapter 5 of how to validate data by using LINQ queries.

Of course, every query needs a data source. The data sources that queries can use are as follows:

- *Entity sets*: This type of data source could be, for example, a table such as Customers.

- *Other queries*: Queries in LightSwitch are composable. This means that you can create queries based on other queries.

- *Navigation properties:* When working on screens or in code, you can create queries based on navigation properties.

Now let's look at the way in which data is returned from the server to the client. In Chapter 1, you saw how each data source in your application has a corresponding data service that runs on the server. When you create a query in LightSwitch, a query operation is defined in the data service. This query operation is exposed as a RIA service endpoint. The LightSwitch client executes a query by calling the query operation method via RIA services. This returns a set of entities from an entity set in the data service. A very important thing to note is that every query returns entities from an entity set. This means that entities are the units of data that you'll actually work with. Single or multiple results can be returned, and the results can be optionally filtered or sorted. You can also define parameters, which allow you to pass in arguments that can then be used in your query.

Figure 6-1 shows an example of a user-defined query that returns customers filtered by surname. In this example, the actual filtering and sorting is applied at the server. In LightSwitch, the IDataServiceQueryable object allows you to create queries that are executed on the server. You'll discover more on how this works later in this chapter.

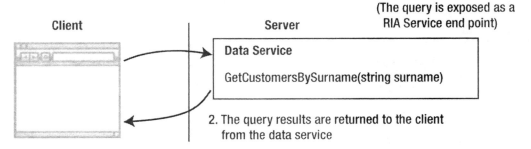

Figure 6-1. Calling a query that returns customers filtered by surname

You can also query against locally cached data. In this instance, the execution takes place locally, not on the server. You might need to do this if you want to carry out a filter operation that isn't supported by the data service. You'll see an example of how to execute a local query later in this chapter.

When you're using LINQ to write queries in code, it's also important to understand that deferred execution takes place. This means that your query isn't executed at the exact place where your query condition is specified in code. If you create a query based on an IDataServiceQueryable object, you'll find an Execute method that you can call. However, this method doesn't actually execute the query on the server. The query is executed only at the moment in time when you read the results. You might do this by enumerating over the results with a foreach loop, or by calling a method such as ToArray or ToList.

The Data Returned from a Query

Because query operations return entities from an entity set, the shape of the query results cannot be modified. For example, a query could return a single customer or a collection of customers. Alternatively, it could return a single order or a collection of orders. However, a query cannot be used to return just the firstname property from a set of customers, nor can it be used to return some sort of combined object that is created by joining customers and orders (you'd need a RIA service to be able do that). This behavior might seem strange at first, particularly for Access or SQL developers who are accustomed to using select clauses to specify whatever columns they choose, or to return results that are joined to other tables.

At this point, you might wonder how to retrieve additional data that isn't part of the underlying data set. As long as relationships have been defined between the entities, you can retrieve the related data later by using the navigation properties. Once you start thinking in the "LightSwitch way," you'll soon realize that it isn't necessary to return joined data from queries.

Default Queries Created by LightSwitch

For each table in your application, LightSwitch automatically generates two queries called Single and All. If you have a table called Customer, LightSwitch generates a query called Customers_All to return all customers, and a query called Customers_Single to return a single instance of a customer by ID value. Chapter 4 shows how these queries can be called in code.

By default, any user-defined entity-set query that you create is based on LightSwitch's autogenerated _All query. As mentioned earlier, LightSwitch queries are composable, meaning that you can create queries that are based on other queries. The root query for all user-defined queries is the _All query. When you base a query on another query, LightSwitch merges all of the underlying query expression operations into one. This expression is then applied at the server when the query is executed.

These default queries are also used when creating screens. If you create a screen based on a customer entity by using the Editable Grid Screen template, the screen uses the Customers_All query by default. Likewise, a customer screen based on the Details Screen template uses the Customers_Single query by default.

These queries are also shown when adding data items to a screen, as shown in Figure 6-2.

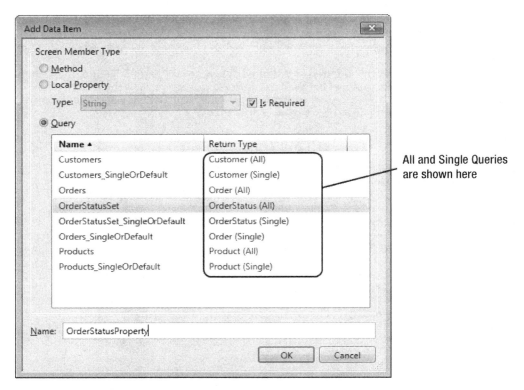

Figure 6-2. Default queries shown in the Add Data Item dialog box

Screen Queries

If you create a screen based on a collection of data (an editable grid screen or search screen, for example), you can define additional parameters, filtering, and ordering at the screen level. To do this, click the Edit Query link and use the options available through the graphical designer, as shown in Figure 6-3.

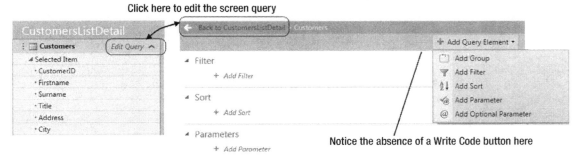

Figure 6-3. Editing a screen query

A disadvantage of this approach is that changes are applied only to the screen and cannot be reused on other screens. Furthermore, it is not possible to customize the query further by writing code.

Managing Included Data in Screen Queries

When you design a screen query, you'll find an option to manage the included data. This allows you to optimize the performance of your screen by choosing to exclude navigation properties.

Let's imagine that you've created a screen based on an Order entity. In the screen designer, click the Edit Query link (just as if you were about to apply some custom filtering or sorting). When the query designer appears, view the properties of the query. You'll see a link that is titled Manage Included Data. When you click this link, as shown in Figure 6-4, a dialog box appears that allows you to choose the child records that you want to return in your query.

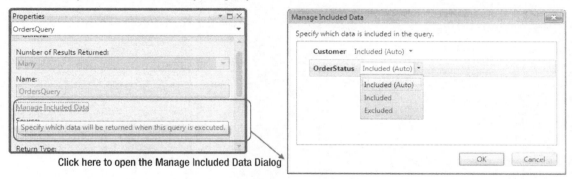

Click here to open the Manage Included Data Dialog

Figure 6-4. Managing the included data in a screen query

Entity Set Queries

Entity set queries can be used on multiple screens and can be further customized by using code. You can create these queries by right-clicking an entity in Solution Explorer and choosing the Add Query menu option, as shown in Figure 6-5.

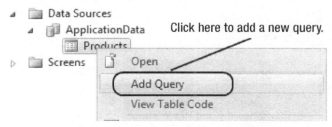

Figure 6-5. Creating a new entity set query

When you create a query in this way, LightSwitch uses the default All query as the data source. After creating your query, you can change the underlying data source. To do this, use the Source drop-down box in the title area of the query designer, shown in Figure 6-6. LightSwitch allows you to select only from other queries that return the same entity set.

Figure 6-6. *Use the Source drop-down box to change the data source for your query.*

After adding a query, you can set various settings by using the properties pane, shown in Figure 6-7.

Figure 6-7. *Query properties*

These settings are as follows:

- *Name*: The name is used to uniquely identify the query in Solution Explorer. When you create a new screen, the Add New Screen dialog shows the query name in the list of available data sources that you can base your screen on.

- *Number of Results Returned*: You can choose either One or Many from the list of available options in the drop-down box.

- *Description*: The description can be used to add a comment about the query at design time. It is not exposed elsewhere in LightSwitch during design time nor runtime.

- *Display Name*: On a screen, the display name is used to identify the query in the Query Source drop-down of an entity property, shown in Figure 6-8.

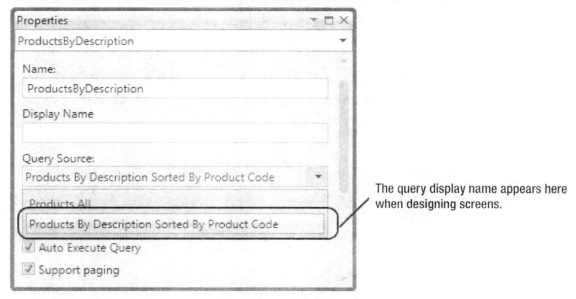

The query display name appears here when designing screens.

Figure 6-8. Query display name shown on a screen

The Number of Results Returned option is one of the main settings. By default, new queries are set to return many records.

Singleton queries can be created by selecting the One option. These queries return a single record or null. If you designate a query as a singleton query and write a query that returns more than one record, a compile-time error will not be generated. However, an exception will be thrown at runtime when you attempt to run the query. Singleton queries are not composable. This means that further queries cannot be based on a singleton query, and explains why only queries that return collections can be modified in the screen editor.

The Number of Results Returned option also specifies where the query is shown in the Add New Screen dialog box. Singleton queries can be used to create screens based on the New Data Screen and Details Screen templates. Queries that return multiple records can be used to create screens based on the Editable Grid Screen, List and Details Screen, and Search Data Screen templates, as shown in Figure 6-9.

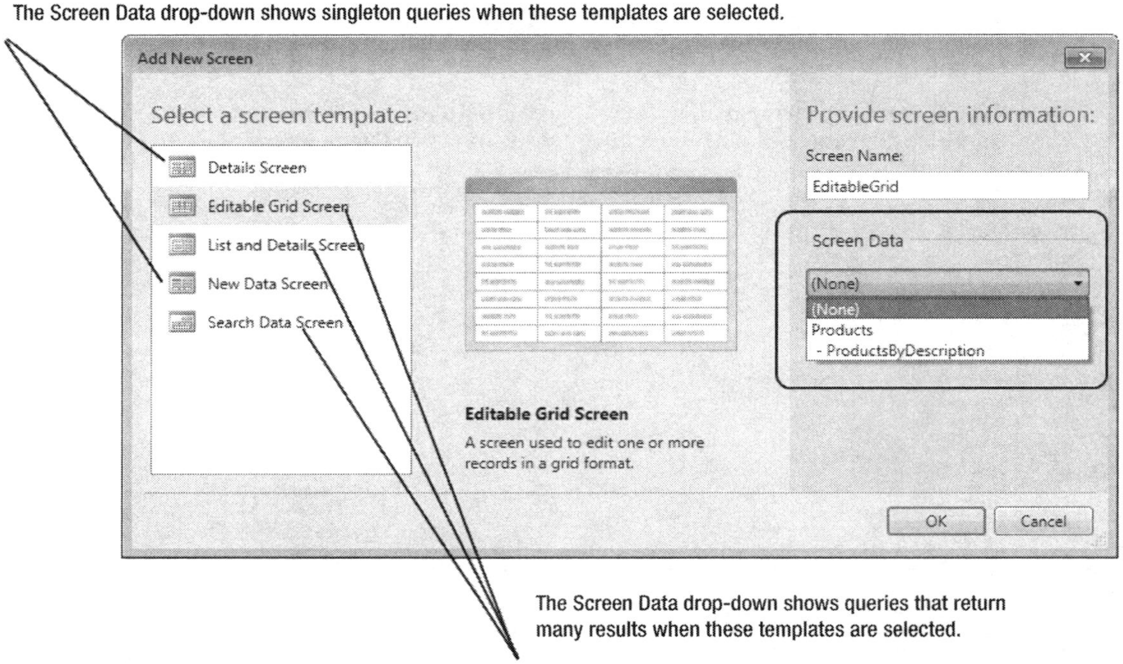

The Screen Data drop-down shows singleton queries when these templates are selected.

Figure 6-9. The contents of the Screen Data drop-down list depends on the screen template chosen.

Filtering and Sorting Data by Using the Designer

Now that you've added your entity set query, you can start to apply filter and sort conditions. You can do this either through code or by using the graphical designer. In this section, we'll show you how to use the graphical designer.

Filtering Query Data

You can use the graphical designer to create simple filters in your queries. Figure 6-10 illustrates the elements of the query designer that you would use to filter data.

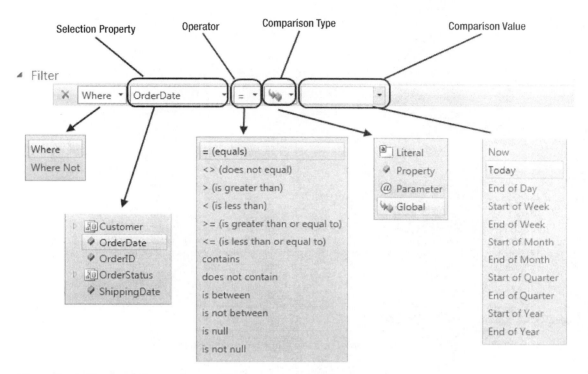

Figure 6-10. *The parts that make up a filter*

The first query drop-down allows you to select the type of query. Choosing the Where option creates a query that includes the records that match your query condition. The Where Not option excludes records that match your query condition.

If you've created multiple filters, you can organize your filters into groups. You can then apply operators between your filter groups, as shown in Figure 6-11. Applying the following operators between groups is similar to the way that you would parenthesize groups of conditions in a SQL WHERE clause:

- And

- Or

- And Not

- Or Not

Figure 6-11. Available operators between groups

For each specific filter, the query Operator drop-down list allows you to select from a list of operators that are shown in Table 6-2. Some of these operators will depend on the data type of the selected property, and whether the property is defined as a required property. For example, you can't filter for records with null customer surnames if a surname is required.

Table 6-2. Filter Operators

Operator	Description
= (Equals)	Available for all built-in LightSwitch data types
<>	Available for all built-in LightSwitch data types
>	Not available on Boolean, binary, or image types
<	Not available on Boolean, binary, or image types
>=	Not available on Boolean, binary, or image types
<=	Not available on Boolean, binary, or image types
Contains	Available on the String data type
Does Not Contain	Available on the String data type
Is Between	Not available on Boolean, binary, or image types
Is Not Between	Not available on Boolean, binary, or image types
Is Null	Available only on nonrequired fields
Is Not Null	Available only on nonrequired fields

The Comparison Type drop-down allows you to select the type of value that you want to filter against. You can choose from one the following four options (which are explained in the following section in more detail):

- Literal
- Property
- Parameter
- Global

Finally, the Comparison Value control allows you to enter the value that you want to use. The control shown to you varies, depending on the operator or comparison type chosen.

Comparing Values

The key part to creating a filter is to select a comparison type and to enter a value. In this section, we'll examine the four comparison types that you can choose from.

Using Literal Values

The Literal option allows you to filter by a hard-coded value. First, select the data property that you want to use by using the Selection Property drop-down. You can then type in the value that you want to compare against by using the Comparison Value text box. If you choose the Is Between operator, two text boxes are shown to allow you to enter To and From values.

When using the Selection Property drop-down list, you can choose to filter by related records. Figure 6-12 shows a query that filters the OrderStatusID property by using a literal value of 1.

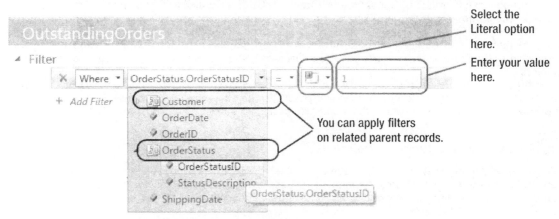

Figure 6-12. Creating filters by using literal values

157

Using Properties

The Comparison Type drop-down list allows you to compare by property. This enables you to compare two fields in the same record. After choosing the Property option, a second drop-down box appears that allows you to specify the comparison property.

Figure 6-13 shows an example of how you would use a property comparison. It illustrates a query on a Project table that returns records for which the target finish date exceeds the actual finish date.

***Figure 6-13.** Comparing against another property*

Using Parameters

Rather than using a hard-coded literal value, queries can be made more reusable by choosing the Parameter option from the Comparison Type drop-down list. After selecting the Parameter option, a second drop-down box appears that allows you to create a new parameter. If you choose to create a new parameter, the parameter appears in the Parameter section in the lower section of the query designer.

Parameters can be made optional by selecting the Is Optional check box, shown in the properties window of the parameter. If the value of the optional parameter is not set at runtime, the filter that uses the parameter is omitted. For example, an optional parameter might be used on a query that searches customers filtered by surname. If the parameter value is not set, all customer records are returned by the query because the filter clause is not applied. If a surname value is supplied, the filtering takes place as expected.

Optional parameters are most useful when designing search screens with one or more search filters. If the user doesn't specify a value, a null value is passed to the query parameter. This allows LightSwitch to optimize performance by omitting the associated WHERE condition in the SQL query that is generated.

Using Parameterized Queries on Screens

Having created a query that filters by a parameter value, it's important to know how to consume such a query. In this example, we'll create a screen with an AutoCompleteBox that displays a list of available order status values. When the user selects an order status, the orders that match the selected order status value are shown on a data grid.

First, create a query on the Order table and add a parameter called OrderStatusID. Now apply a filter on the OrderStatusID property that matches the data value against the OrderStatusID parameter, as shown in Figure 6-14.

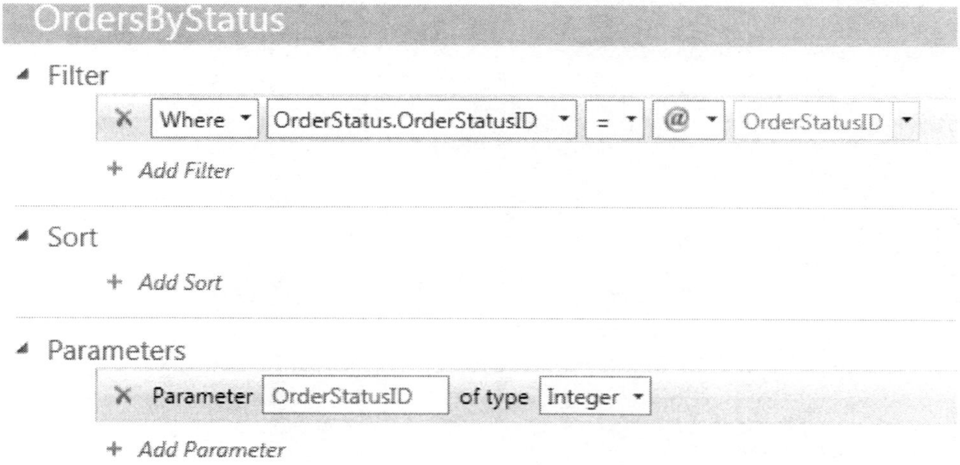

OrdersByStatus

◢ Filter

| ✕ | Where ▾ | OrderStatus.OrderStatusID ▾ | = ▾ | @ ▾ | OrderStatusID ▾ |

   ✛ *Add Filter*

◢ Sort

   ✛ *Add Sort*

◢ Parameters

| ✕ | Parameter | OrderStatusID | of type | Integer ▾ |

   ✛ *Add Parameter*

Figure 6-14. Creating a query that filters by an OrderStatusID parameter

Next, save the query as OrdersByStatus and create an editable grid screen based on this query. By default, LightSwitch creates a local property and a text box that binds to the query parameter. Because we want to replace this default text box with an AutoCompleteBox, delete the property and text box from the screen.

The next step is to create an autocomplete box that displays the order statuses. To do this, add a query onto your screen that returns a list of all order statuses. In the screen designer, click the Add Data Item button. In the dialog box that appears, select the Query radio button. Now choose the OrderStatusSet option, and name the query OrderStatusProperty, as shown in Figure 6-15.

Figure 6-15. *Adding a query to return order statuses*

After creating the query, the OrderStatusProperty appears on the left side of the screen designer. Drag this into the middle section to create an AutoCompleteBox. The steps that have been carried out so far are shown in Figure 6-16.

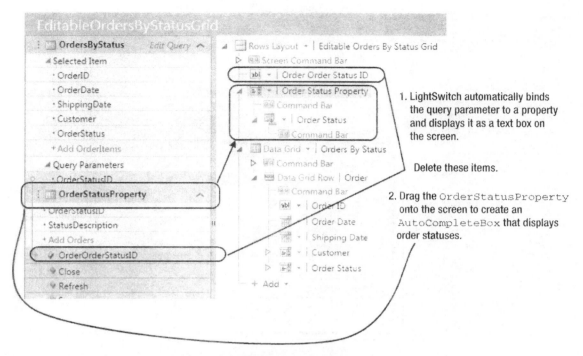

Figure 6-16. Steps to add a parameter-bound AutoCompleteBox

Having created an AutoCompleteBox, the value that the user selects must be bound to the query parameter. Bring up the properties of the OrderStatusID parameter and change the parameter binding text box to OrderStatusProperty.OrderStatusID , as shown in Figure 6-17.

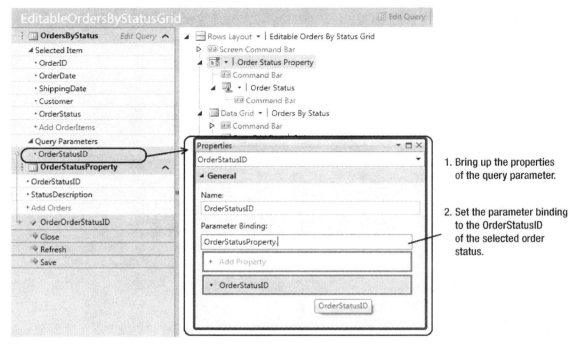

Figure 6-17. Changing the parameter binding

You can now run your project. When the screen is opened, you can use the AutoCompleteBox to control the items that are shown in the data grid (see Figure 6-18).

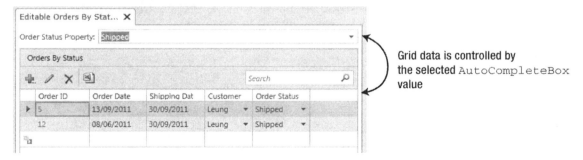

Figure 6-18. Using an AutoCompleteBox to control the screen data

Using Global Values

When you create filters on Date or DateTime properties, LightSwitch allows you to filter by global values. These are predefined values that are calculated by LightSwitch.

Figure 6-19 illustrates the global variables that are shown when a Date property is selected. You can choose from a set of values that include Today, Start of Week, End of Week, and several others.

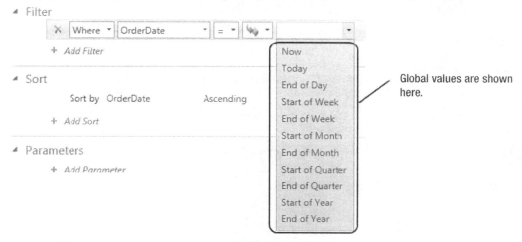

Figure 6-19. Global value options when filtering by Date or DateTime

Later, you will learn how to create your own custom global variables that you can use in queries.

When filtering on DateTime properties, you need to be careful when using the Equals operator with the Today global value. This is because DateTime properties also include a time element.

Let's suppose you have an Order table with an OrderDate property of data type DateTime. If you want to create a query to return all orders that were made today, creating a filter with the criteria OrderDate=Today would not work. This is because Today returns today's date with a time of 12:00:00 a.m. To return all orders that were made today, you would need to use the Is Between operator and filter for orders between Today and End of Day.

Therefore, Start of Day is perhaps a better description for the value that is returned by the Today global value.

Sorting Query Data

The graphical query designer also allows you to apply multiple sort orders to a query. Figure 6-20 illustrates a query called CustomersSorted, which is based on a table called Customer.

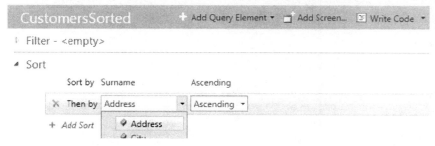

Figure 6-20. Creating sort expressions on a query

The first drop-down list allows you to select a property from the table. The second option allows you to select a sort order; the available options are Ascending and Descending. After specifying a sort order, you can sort on additional properties by clicking the Add Sort button.

Using LINQ

Language Integrated Query (LINQ) allows you to write more-complex queries in LightSwitch. By using LINQ, you can apply filtering that you otherwise couldn't achieve when using the graphical query designer. In LightSwitch, you can use LINQ in two main ways:

- After you create a query based on an entity set, you can use LINQ to apply further filtering before the results are returned.

- You can create your own queries in code, and use LINQ to retrieve the records that you need.

This section introduces you to LINQ, shows you how to construct a LINQ query, and explains how to use lambda expressions.

Why LINQ?

LINQ is a feature that was introduced in .NET 3.5. One of the goals of LINQ was to create a common query language to save you from having to learn multiple query languages. This is perfect for LightSwitch because it allows you to connect to many data sources, including SQL Server, SharePoint, or RIA data services.

LINQ allows you to use standard C# and VB syntax to describe query filter expressions and ordering. These query expressions can be translated into SQL (or whatever form the query provider supports) and executed remotely at the server.

LINQ also provides compile-time checking and IntelliSense support. For example, you could write a SELECT statement in SQL that attempts to retrieve a field that doesn't exist. If you attempted to do something similar in LINQ, your code would not compile. Furthermore, the IntelliSense in LINQ simplifies development by suggesting the field names that you can use. Therefore, there's no need for you to memorize the field names that you've used in your tables.

LINQ Syntax

To illustrate the syntax that makes up a LINQ query, Listing 6-1 shows an example. This code is attached to a screen button. When the button is clicked, a list of Order Status codes is shown to the user through a message box. The query contains a conditional statement so that only codes with an order status ID of less than 4 are returned.

Listing 6-1. Example of a Simple LINQ Query

VB:

```
File: ShipperCentral\Client\UserCode\OrderStatusCodeDetails.vb

Imports System.Text

Private Sub ShowOrderStatusCodes_Execute()
```

```
    Dim message = New StringBuilder

    Dim items = From dataItem In DataWorkspace.ApplicationData.OrderStatuses
            Where dataItem.OrderStatusID < 4
            Order By dataItem.StatusDescription
    Select dataItem

    For Each item As OrderStatus In items
        message.AppendLine(
            String.Format("{0} - {1}", item.OrderStatusID, item.StatusDescription))
    Next

    ShowMessageBox(message.ToString, "Order Status Codes", MessageBoxOption.Ok)

End Sub
```

C#:

File: ShipperCentral\Client\UserCode\OrderStatusCodeDetails.cs

```csharp
using System.Text;
using System.Windows.Controls;

partial void ShowOrderStatusCodes_Execute()
{

    StringBuilder message = new StringBuilder();

    var items = from dataItem in DataWorkspace.ApplicationData.OrderStatuses
                where dataItem.OrderStatusID < 4
                orderby dataItem.StatusDescription
                select dataItem;

    foreach (OrderStatus item in items)
    {
        message.AppendLine(
            String.Format("{0} - {1}", item.OrderStatusID, item.StatusDescription));
    }

    this.ShowMessageBox(message.ToString(), "Order Status Codes", MessageBoxOption.Ok);

}
```

Figure 6-21 shows the message box that appears when the code is run.

Figure 6-21. Results of string-matching code

The parts that make up a LINQ query are shown in Figure 6-22.

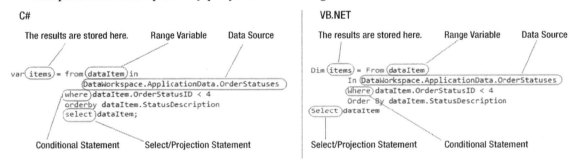

Figure 6-22. Parts of a LINQ query

Every LINQ query is based on a data source. In Listing 6-1 shown earlier, the data source used is the order status entity set. These data sources can be accessed by using the objects in the DataWorkspace object.

The dataItem variable is called the range variable. This behaves just like the iteration variable that is used in a foreach loop, but in LINQ, no actual iteration takes place in the query expression. When the query is executed, the range variable allows you to reference each element in the data source. This enables you to conditionally filter the results by using the Where method. If you don't specify the data type of dataItem, the compiler can infer it. However, C# won't allow query expression syntax over entity sets (described in the next section), so it's worth explicitly specifying the type of the range variable.

The Select clause at the end of the statement specifies the shape, or type, of each returned element. If you were writing a query that returns a collection of customers, for example, the Select clause allows you to return just the first name and surname of each customer. However, it's uncommon to do this in LightSwitch because most operations are designed to work around entities.

The results from a LINQ query can be a single object, multiple objects, or a subset of fields. These results are called a sequence and are of type IEnumerable<T> (or some other type that derives from this). This type is pronounced *I enumerable of T*, and *T* defines the data type. In this example, the items variable is of type IEnumerable<OrderStatus>. The data type of items is inferred by the compiler and is therefore not explicitly declared.

An important feature about LINQ is that query execution is deferred until the moment when you request the data. So in this example, the query is executed only when the foreach loop is run.

Two Types of Syntax

After you start learning LINQ, you'll soon discover that you can use two types of syntax to express queries. Query syntax is commonly found in documentation and is generally more readable. However, the .NET Framework cannot natively understand query syntax and converts it into a series of method calls. This type of syntax is called *method syntax*. Rather than using query syntax, you could write a query in method syntax in the first place.

Query syntax is generally easier to read and write, particularly when creating queries that involve joins. However, certain operations can be performed only when using method syntax. Retrieving the element with the maximum value in a source sequence is an example of this.

To illustrate the differences between the two types of syntax, Listing 6-2 presents a query that returns all customers with the surname of Smith, sorted in ascending order by first name.

Listing 6-2. Illustration of Query Syntax and Method Syntax

VB:

```
'Example of Query Syntax
Dim items = From dataItem In DataWorkspace.ApplicationData.Customers
            Where dataItem.Surname = "Smith"
            Order By dataItem.Firstname
Select dataItem

'Example of Method Syntax
Dim items2 =
    From dataItem In DataWorkspace.ApplicationData.Customers.Where(
        Function(cust) cust.Surname = "Smith").OrderBy(
            Function(cust) cust.Firstname)
Select dataItem
```

C#:

```
//Example of Query Syntax
var items =
from dataItem in DataWorkspace.ApplicationData.Customers
where dataItem.Surname == "Smith"
orderby dataItem.Firstname
select dataItem;

//Example of Method Syntax
var items2 =
from dataItem in DataWorkspace.ApplicationData.Customers
.Where(cust => cust.Surname == "Smith")
.OrderBy (cust => cust.Firstname )
select dataItem;
```

The data source for this query comes from a table called `Customers`. The actual output returned from both queries is identical. Don't worry too much about the method syntax that is shown; this is explained shortly in the "Lambda Expressions" section.

Your decision to use either query syntax or method syntax often boils down to personal preference. For now, the important point is to realize that the two syntax types exist.

Joining Data

Unlike SQL, you rarely need to create joins when using LINQ with LightSwitch. Provided that relationships have been set up, the navigation properties that are defined at the entity allow you to access related data without having to create explicit joins in LINQ, as shown in Figure 6-23.

```
var orders = from orderItem in DataWorkspace.ApplicationData.Orders
             where orderItem.Customer.Firstname == "Smith"
             select orderItem;
```

You don't need to create an explicit join between the `order` and `customer` tables because the `Customer` navigation property can be used to access the `Firstname` property.

Figure 6-23. Navigation properties

Furthermore, LightSwitch screens can consume only the entities that have been defined in your application. Therefore, there is little point in creating a query that returns a collection of customers joined with orders, because this is something that cannot be consumed by a LightSwitch screen.

Although you can write LINQ queries to explicitly create joins, we recommend that relationships are set up by using the table designer in the first place. This creates the navigation properties, which greatly simplifies the task of writing queries. If you haven't set up relationships because you're working across multiple data sources, or because you're working on an external data source in which relationships have not been explicitly defined, remember that you can set up virtual relationships between tables. Chapter 3 explains how to do this.

Lambda Expressions

In Chapter 5, you saw some examples of using lambda expressions during the validation of data. Lambda expressions are unnamed, inline functions that you can use with other parts of LINQ. They help you to filter and sort your data by using very few lines of code.

When using method-syntax LINQ, lambda expressions are often passed in as arguments to standard query operator methods such as `Where`. When IntelliSense prompts you to pass an expression tree into a method, as shown in Figure 6-24, you should think about using lambda expressions.

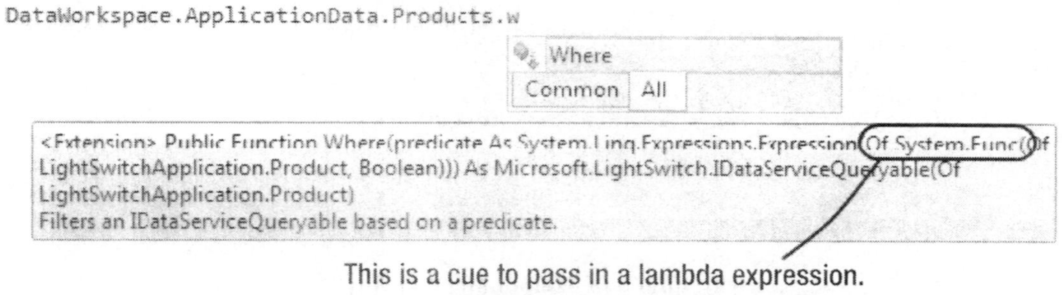

```
DataWorkspace.ApplicationData.Products.w
```

This is a cue to pass in a lambda expression.

Figure 6-24. IntelliSense for the Where method prompts you to pass in an expression tree.

Why Use Lambdas?

One of the great advantages of lambda expressions is that you can write terse expressions with very few lines of code. Another primary advantage is that query expressions can be sent to the server and executed remotely. This is all made possible by using the magic of LINQ expression trees. For example, let's say that you've written a LINQ query on a LightSwitch screen. LightSwitch can pass the query expression that you've expressed as a lambda expression to the middle tier via RIA services. This query expression can then be passed to SQL Server, and the query expression is executed at the server. When writing a LINQ query, the Where method allows you to pass in a function delegate, rather than a lambda expression. If you choose to do this, the query expressions that you specify will not be executed remotely.

To demonstrate the advantages of using lambda expressions, we'll write some code for searching out the first customer in a collection that matches the surname Smith.

An old-fashioned way of doing this is to write a foreach loop and to break when the customer is found. But that code can be improved by using query syntax LINQ, and improved even further by using lambda expressions, as shown in Listing 6-3.

Listing 6-3. Lambda Expression Sample

VB:

```vb
'1. For Each Loop Example - involves many lines of code
Dim foundCustomer As Customer = Nothing

For Each cust As Customer In DataWorkspace.ApplicationData.Customers
    If cust.Surname = "smith" Then
        foundCustomer = cust
        Exit For
    End If
Next

'2. Query Syntax LINQ
Dim foundCustomer =
    (From cust in DataWorkspace.ApplicationData.customers
     Where cust.Surname = "smith").FirstOrDefault()
```

```
'3.  Method Syntax LINQ & Lamda Expression
Dim foundCustomer2 As Customer =
     DataWorkspace.ApplicationData.Customers.Where(
          Function(cust) cust.Surname = "smith").FirstOrDefault()
```

C#:
```
//1. For Each Loop Example - involves many lines of code

Customer foundCustomer = null;

foreach (Customer cust in DataWorkspace.ApplicationData.Customers)
{
    if (cust.Surname == "smith")
    {
        foundCustomer = cust;
        break;
    }
}

//2. Query Syntax LINQ

Customer foundCustomer = (from cust in DataWorkspace.ApplicationData.Customers
            where cust.Surname == "smith"
            select cust).FirstOrDefault();


//3.  Method Syntax LINQ & Lamda Expression
Customer foundCustomer2 =
     DataWorkspace.ApplicationData.Customers.Where (
          cust => cust.Surname == "smith").FirstOrDefault ();
```

Let's take a look at the first example, which uses a foreach loop. The syntax is simple to understand. However, it requires many lines of code. More important, the code needs to retrieve all customers into the foreach loop in order to test each one locally. The query isn't efficient because there isn't any remote execution of the query expression.

The remaining LINQ examples are more efficient because the query expression is applied at SQL Server. Also, it's important to note that the LINQ queries are executed only when the data is needed. So in this example, the LINQ queries are executed when the FirstOrDefault method is called.

Lambda Syntax

Let's take a look at the lambda expression that has been used:

```
C#   cust => cust.Surname == "Smith"
VB    Function(cust)  cust.Surname = "Smith"
```

Cust represents the lambda parameter. This represents each customer in the collection of customers that you're working against. In this example, the implicit data-typing feature of .NET is used and saves you from having to explicitly define the data type of cust. The expression also could be written like this:

```
C#   (Customer cust )=> cust.Surname == "Smith"
VB     Function(cust as Customer)  cust.Surname = "Smith"
```

In the C# version, the lambda parameter must be enclosed in brackets if implicit typing is not used. Brackets must also be used if you want to specify more than one lambda parameter. In C#, the => operator is called the lambda or goes to operator. This is used to separate the lambda parameter(s) from the actual expression.

In VB, the Function keyword is used to specify the lambda expression, and the lambda parameters are specified inside brackets following the Function keyword. It may seem strange for the Function keyword to be used without a function name being specified. For example, a typical function in VB looks like this:

```
Public Function GetSurname (cust as Customer) As String
```

As you can see, the function name here is called GetSurname. In our lambda expression code, a function name can be omitted because the syntax uses a feature of .NET 3.5 called anonymous methods. Prior to .NET 3.5, methods had to be explicitly named, and separate named methods would have to be written to perform the same task. The beauty of using anonymous methods is that it saves you from having to write all of this extra code.

If you wanted to, you could still choose to use a named function rather than an anonymous method. However, the query expressions that are specified like this can't be executed remotely in the same way that a lambda expression can be. Therefore, the advantage of using lambda expressions with anonymous methods is that it allows queries to be executed more efficiently.

Finally, a conditional operation is applied by using the lambda parameter that returns true if the customer surname matches Smith. Because customer is a LightSwitch-generated entity, any navigation properties that you've defined on customer could also be used to construct a more complex query expression by referencing related records.

Standard Query Operators

The Where() function that is used in the preceding section is an example of an extension method. Extension methods allow you to add methods to an existing type without having to create a new derived type, or to modify and recompile the existing type.

Standard query operators in LINQ are extension methods on top of the IEnumerable<T> and IQueryable<T> types. There are about 50 of these standard operators. Appendix B provides a list.

Not of all of these query operators can be translated and executed remotely at SQL Server by LightSwitch. Therefore, LightSwitch uses IDataServiceQueryable to limit the set of extension methods to those that are known to be "remotable" through SQL Server and RIA services. These are shown in Table 6-3.

Table 6-3. IDataServiceQueryable Query Operators

Query Operator	Description
Include	This specifies which related entities should be included in the results when the query is executed
OrderBy	Orders the results in ascending order by the key value that you specify
OrderByDescending	Orders the results in descending order by the key value that you specify

Query Operator	Description
Search	Searches for entities whose string properties contain the search terms specified
Skip	Bypasses the specified number of entities and returns the remaining entities
Take	Returns the specified number of contiguous entities from the start of the collection
Where	Filters the IDataServiceQueryable based on a predicate

The Search operator is worth a mention. This lets you to pass in a search term, and finds matching records by searching across all string properties where the 'is searchable' setting has been set to true in the table designer. You'll recognize that any screens created using the Search Data Screen template performs the search in the same way.

If you want to access the remaining LINQ operators, you can do so by casting your object to IEnumerable<T>. You can use the Cast<T>() or OfType<T> methods to do this, as shown in Figure 6-25. However, you should be aware that not all query operators are guaranteed to work. When writing client or common code, you should stick to the operators that are available on IDataServicequeryable.

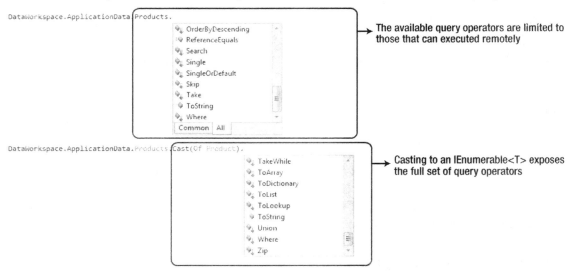

Figure 6-25. Accessing LINQ operators

Delegate Parameters

Several of the standard query operators expect a delegate parameter to be passed in (you would commonly pass in a lambda expression). The delegate parameter types that you'll encounter will be one of three types:

- Func

- Predicate

- Action

A *func delegate* defines a method that optionally takes a set of parameters and returns a value. Func delegate parameters are frequently encountered in LightSwitch. The argument passed to the Where extension method is an example of Func delegate argument.

A *predicate delegate* is a function that returns true or false. The All and Any query operators both accept a predicate delegate as an argument. The purpose of the All operator is to return a Boolean that indicates whether all elements of a sequence match a condition (just to clarify, the All query operator should not be confused with the default _All query that was mentioned earlier). The Any method returns whether any element satisfies a condition. Creating an exists type query (a query that returns records for which related child records exist) is an example of where you would use the Any operator. This is demonstrated later in this chapter.

Action delegates are used rarely in querying, but we'll mention them anyway to complete our discussion on arguments. Action delegates can include parameters but have no return value. If you use VB, think of an action delegate as a sub and a predicate delegate as a function that returns a Boolean. An example of a method that accepts an action delegate is the ForEach extension method on an object of type List<T>.

Listing 6-4 illustrates how this method can be used to build a string of customer surnames. Once done, the results are displayed to the user in a message box. This demonstration highlights how LINQ can be used to express foreach logic in just a single line of code.

Listing 6-4. *Example of Passing In an Action Delegate*

VB:
```
Dim customerSurnames As String = ""
Customers.ToList().ForEach(Function(item) customerSurnames += item.Surname)
ShowMessageBox(customerSurnames)
```

C#:
```
string customerSurnames = "";
Customers.ToList().ForEach(item => customerSurnames += item.Surname);
ShowMessageBox(customerSurnames);
```

This example is based on an editable grid screen of customers. The customer collection is of type VisualCollection<Customer>, and the ToList extension method coverts this to an object of type List<Customer>.

Outside of querying, the other common place you'll find action delegates are in threading code. For example, to execute some code on the main UI dispatcher, you would call the Application.Current.Details.Dispatcher.BeginInvoke method and pass in an action delegate.

Where Is the Query Executed?

Queries can be executed in two ways: either locally on the client, or remotely at the server. In the case of user-defined (entity set) queries, the choice is simple: user-defined queries are executed on the server. Queries that are executed at the server pass through a query pipeline. You can refine the results that are returned in your query by writing LINQ code in the PreprocessQuery method. The important point here is that the PreprocessQuery method runs on the server, as part of a server-side query.

When writing a query in code, you can choose where your query is executed. The syntax that you use determines where the query execution takes place. This is summarized in Table 6-4. In the sample code shown, `myOrder` and `myCustomer` represent local screen properties.

In most cases, it's preferable for queries to be executed remotely. However, it sometimes isn't possible to execute a query remotely, because the data service might not support a specific query operation. Alternatively, there might be some operation that you want to perform on locally cached data, rather than on the data on the server. The example shown later in this section provides an example of such a scenario.

Table 6-4. *Where the queries are executed*

Object Type	Example Code	Where It's Executed

EntitySet	`DataWorkspace.ApplicationData.Orders`
	or
	`myOrder.Details.EntitySet()`
		Remote

IDataServiceQueryable	`myCustomer.OrdersQuery`
	or
	`DataWorkspace.ApplicationData.Orders.GetQuery()`
		Remote

EntityCollection	`myCustomer.Orders`	Local

IEnumerable	`myCustomer.OrdersQuery.Execute()`
	or
	`DataWorkspace.ApplicationData.Orders.GetQuery().Execute()`
		Local

In general, queries performed against an `EntityCollection` (a navigation property, for example) are executed locally. Queries performed against an `EntitySet` are executed remotely. To work out where the data is filtered, you can hover the mouse over an object in order to establish the data type, as shown in Figure 6-26.

Figure 6-26. *The data type of an object tells you where the filtering takes place.*

The rest of this section examines the query pipeline, local execution, and remote execution in further detail. We'll also validate where the queries are actually executed by using SQL Profiler.

Query Pipeline

When you call a query in LightSwitch, the execution passes through the query pipeline. Just like the save pipeline (explained in Chapter 4), the query pipeline consists of phases that include points where you can inject your own custom server-side code. Figure 6-27 shows the phases in the query pipeline, and Table 6-5 describes the events that you can use to write custom code.

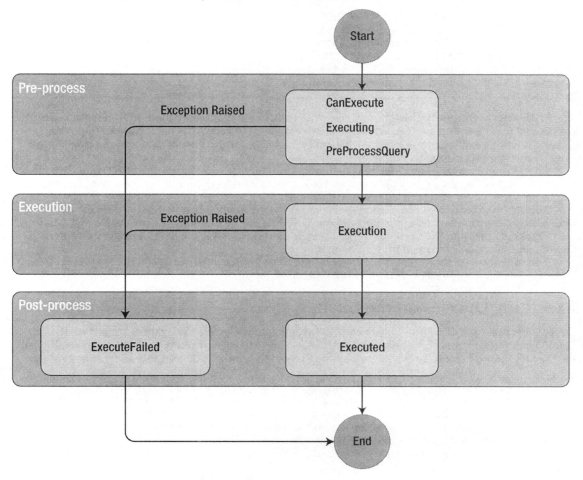

Figure 6-27. Query pipeline

Table 6-5. Events in the Query Pipeline

Event	Description
CanExecute	Determines whether the operation can be called.
Executing	Called before the query is processed.

Event	Description
PreprocessQuery	Allows you to override the query expression.
Executed	If the query succeeds, this event is called after the query is processed but before the results are returned to the client.
ExecuteFailed	Called if the query operation fails.

At the start of the query pipeline, you can write code in the CanExecute method to carry out security checks and to ensure that the user has sufficient permissions to access the data. You can find more details on writing authorization code in Chapter 14. LightSwitch also checks the CanRead status for the underlying entity set during this time.

At the Preprocessing phase, you can customize your query further by writing LINQ code. This allows you to append additional query operators, and to express more-complex query expressions beyond what can be achieved when using the LightSwitch designer.

During the Execution phase, LightSwitch transforms the query into one that the data provider understands. Examples of data providers are the ADO.NET Entity Framework provider for SQL Server, or the OData data provider for SharePoint. The query is then executed at the data store (for example, SQL Server), and the results returned to LightSwitch.

If the query succeeds, the Executed event is fired. If not, you can write code in the ExecuteFailed method to perform additional error handling if required.

Executing Queries on the Client

Entity collections and IEnumerables are used to execute queries locally. Navigation properties in LightSwitch return entity collections, and you can use these to execute queries locally. You can also call the Execute method on an IDataServiceQueryable object to return an IEnumerable. Here is an example:

```
DataWorkspace.ApplicationData.Orders.GetQuery().Execute()
```

This line returns an IEnumerable object that you can use to execute queries in code locally. This particular line returns all orders in the database and obviously has an impact on performance. Therefore, it's important to exercise some caution when running code like this.

When you create a query that uses an entity collection as a data source, LightSwitch first executes the query remotely (on the server) to return results. These results are exposed to you as an IEnumerable. Any additional filtering then gets carried out locally.

Let's examine a screen that contains a screen property called Customer. A navigation property called Orders allows you to see the related orders for the customer. The Customer property and navigation property in code are shown in Figure 6-28.

Screen Designer   Code View

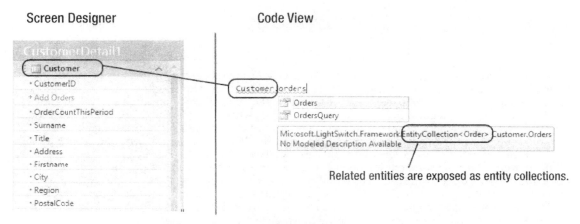

Figure 6-28. *Related entities are exposed as entity collections.*

To prove that all of the related data is pulled down and filtered locally, we'll create a button on a screen. This button executes the code shown in Listing 6-5 and returns orders with a shipped date of June 8, 2011.

Listing 6-5. *Querying an Entity Collection*

VB:

File: ShipperCentral\Client\UserCode\LocalQueryExample.vb

```
Private Sub GetEntityCollectionButton_Execute()

    Dim items = From ord In Customer.Orders
                Where ord.OrderDate = "2010-06-08"
                Select ord

    For Each ord In items
        'code to consume the data would be added here
    Next
End Sub
```

C#:

File: ShipperCentral\Client\UserCode\LocalQueryExample.cs

```
partial void GetEntityCollectionButton_Execute()
{
    var items = from ord in Customer.Orders
                where ord.OrderDate == DateTime.Parse("2010-06-08")
                select ord;

    foreach (Order ord in items)
```

```
  {
    //code to consume the data would be added here
  }
}
```

When you access a navigation property for the first time, LightSwitch fills the entity collection by fetching all related records from the server. This process is known as *eager loading*. These results are then cached on the client. This explains why local queries can be performed over locally cached entities.

However, note that LightSwitch doesn't fetch your data when you reference the Orders navigation property in your LINQ query. LINQ queries are deferred, and the data gets fetched and cached only when the code execution reaches the foreach loop. After the data has been retrieved, LightSwitch applies the filter locally to return only orders that match an OrderDate of June 8, 2011.

If you were to watch this operation being performed in SQL Profiler, you would see the results that are shown in Figure 6-29: LightSwitch selects all order records that are related to the customer shown onscreen. It does this by applying a WHERE clause that returns records that match a CustomerID of 1. The WHERE clause doesn't apply a filter on the OrderDate. This proves that the date filtering isn't carried out by SQL Server at the server, but is carried out by LightSwitch locally.

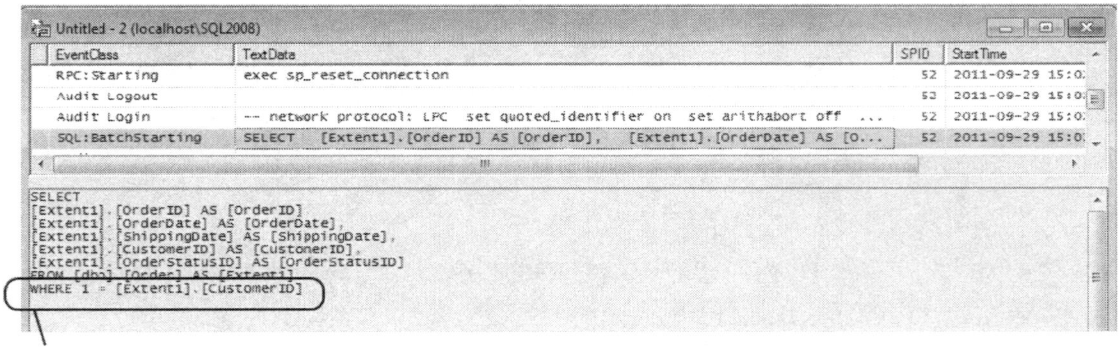

When querying an entity collection, all customers are returned from SQL Server even though the LINQ query specifies a date. The querying takes place locally.

Figure 6-29. SQL Profiler result when querying entity collections

This local caching isn't always ideal. For example, the size of the Customer.Orders can grow unbounded over time. If you want to work with a navigation property but don't want the results to be cached, LightSwitch provides a Query property for each navigation property. This returns the underlying IDataServiceQueryable object for the navigation property, and you can use this to construct a query that is executed remotely. Behind the scenes, LightSwitch screens use the underlying IDataServiceQueryable query to perform pagination over navigation properties.

Local Query Example

The following example demonstrates a query that is executed locally. It provides a perfect example of an operation that cannot be performed remotely.

In this demonstration, we'll create an order screen that allows line items to be entered. The order line items include a product name and quantity number. The example code combines any duplicate line items that are found and sums up the quantities. Figure 6-30 shows the screen that the user would see.

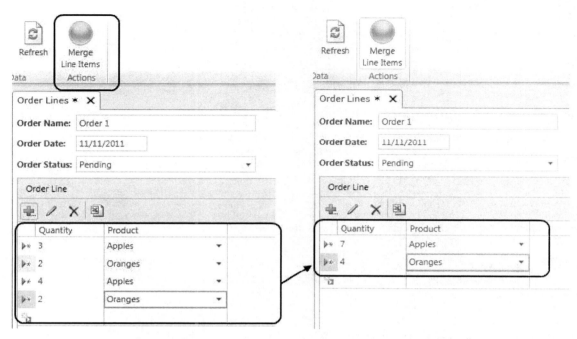

Figure 6-30. Local query example

In Listing 6-6, the OrderLine navigation property is used to return an entity collection. This allows you to locally apply the grouping logic that is needed to find the duplicates. After the duplicates have been found, the remaining code sums up the product quantities and deletes the duplicates.

Listing 6-6. Local Query Example

VB:

```
File: ShipperCentral\Client\UserCode\DuplicateOrders.vb

Private Sub MergeLineItems_Execute()

    Dim duplicates = From line In OrderProperty.OrderLine
        Group line By line.Product Into prodGroup = Group, Count()
        Where (prodGroup.Count > 1)
        Select prodGroup

    For Each dup In duplicates
        Dim totalQty = dup.Sum(Function(line) line.Quantity)
        Dim firstLine = dup.First()
        firstLine.Quantity = totalQty
        dup.Except(
            New OrderLine() {firstLine}).ToList().ForEach(Sub(line) line.Delete())
    Next
```

```
End Sub
```

C#:

File: ShipperCentral\Client\UserCode\DuplicateOrders.cs

```csharp
partial void MergeLineItems_Execute()
{
    var duplicates = from OrderLine line in this.Order.OrderLines
                     group line by line.Product into prodGroup
                     where prodGroup.Count() > 1
                     select prodGroup;

    foreach (var dup in duplicates)
    {
        var totalQuantity = dup.Sum(line => line.Quantity);
        var firstLine = dup.First();
        firstLine.Quantity = totalQuantity;
        dup.Except(
            new OrderLine[] { firstLine }).ToList().ForEach(line => line.Delete());
    }
}
```

Executing Queries on the Server

Entity sets and IDataServiceQueryable are used to build queries that run on the server. You can access entity sets through the DataWorkspace object, as shown here:

DataWorkspace.ApplicationData.Orders

If you want to query against a navigation property, LightSwitch exposes a Query method for each navigation property that is available. This returns an IDataServiceQueryable object that allows you to execute remote queries.

In Listing 6-7, we'll modify our earlier example so that the query is executed on the server. In this example, the query method that we'll use to return an IDataServiceQueryable is called OrdersQuery.

Listing 6-7. *Using an IDataServiceQueryable to Query a Navigation Property on the Server*

VB:

File: ShipperCentral\Client\UserCode\ServerQueryExample.vb

```vb
Private Sub GetIDataServiceQueryableButton_Execute()
    Dim items = From ord In Customer.OrdersQuery
    Where ord.OrderDate = "2010-06-08"
    Select ord

    For Each ord In items
        'code to consume the data would be added here
    Next
```

```
End Sub
```

C#:

```
File: ShipperCentral\Client\UserCode\ServerQueryExample.cs

partial void GetIDataServiceQueryableButton_Execute()
{
    var items = from ord in Customer.OrdersQuery
                where ord.OrderDate == DateTime.Parse("2010-06-08")
                select ord;

    foreach (Customer ord in items)
    {
        //code to consume the data would be added here

    }
}
```

Figure 6-31 illustrates what is shown in SQL Server Profiler when the query is executed. As before, the LINQ query includes a query condition to return only orders that were made on June 8, 2010.

The SQL Profiler trace shows a WHERE clause that filters the results by CustomerID and OrderDate. In the previous example, the results were filtered only by CustomerID. This proves that all of the query conditions that are applied against an IDataServiceQueryable are executed remotely at the server.

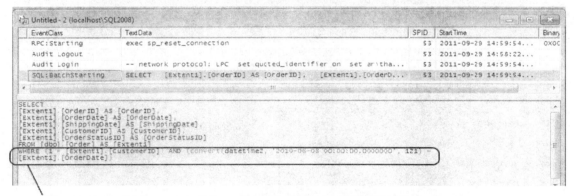

When querying an IDataServiceQueryable, the filtering is carried out by SQL Server.

Figure 6-31. SQL Profiler result when querying IDataServiceQueryable

Exploring Query Examples

This section presents some examples of queries. These examples are used to highlight typical problem scenarios that you might encounter.

Filtering by Related Child Items

If you create a query that is based on the Order table, the graphical designer allows you to filter your results by customer. In other words, you can very easily filter the results based on a parent record when using the graphical designer. Working in the other direction, however, a query based on the Customer table cannot be filtered by a property in the Order table. This is illustrated in Figure 6-32.

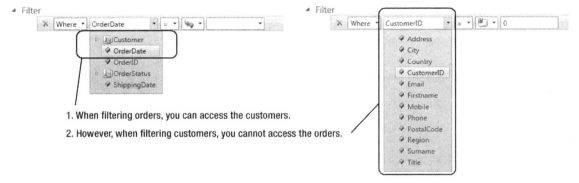

1. When filtering orders, you can access the customers.

2. However, when filtering customers, you cannot access the orders.

Figure 6-32. You cannot filter by child items in the graphical designer.

To filter by child items, create a query called CustomersWithOutstandingOrders. You'll now need to write some custom code in the PreprocessQuery method. To do this, click the Write Code button in the query designer and choose the PreProcessQuery method option, as shown in Figure 6-33. This opens the code editor window, where you can enter the code, shown in Listing 6-8. Running the query then returns all customers with orders that are outstanding. The outstanding orders are indicated by an OrderStatusID of 1.

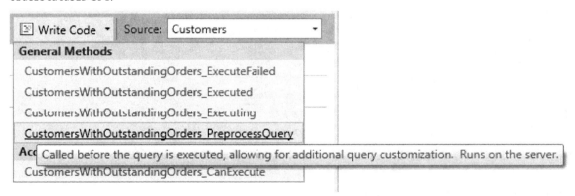

Figure 6-33. Accessing the preprocess query method

Listing 6-8. Filtering by Child Items

VB:
File : ShipperCentral\Server\UserCode\ApplicationDataService.vb

```
Private Sub CustomersWithOutstandingOrders_PreprocessQuery(
    ByRef query As IQueryable(Of Customer))
    query = query.Where(
        Function(custItem) custItem.Orders.Where(
            Function(orderItem) orderItem.OrderStatus.OrderStatusID = 1).Any())
End Sub
```

C#:
File : ShipperCentral\Server\UserCode\ApplicationDataService.cs

```
partial void CustomersWithOutstandingOrders_PreprocessQuery(
    ref IQueryable<Customer> query)
{
    query = query.Where
        (item => item.Orders.Where(
            orderItem => orderItem.OrderStatus.OrderStatusID == 1).Any());
}
```

Creating Exists/In Queries

This example demonstrates how to perform an exists or in query. This type of query returns records for which related child records exist. For example, this type of query can be used to return customers who have made an order. If you happen to be more conversant in SQL, Listing 6-9 provides a SQL translation to illustrate what this example strives to achieve.

Listing 6-9. SQL Equivilant of Example

```
SELECT  CustomerID, Surname, Firstname
FROM Customers
WHERE CustomerID IN (
    SELECT CustomerID FROM Orders)
```

This type of query is created in LightSwitch by writing code in the PreprocessQuery method. After creating a query called CustomersWithOrders, the code in Listing 6-10 returns all customers with orders.

Listing 6-10. Returning all Customers with Orders

VB:
File : ShipperCentral\Server\UserCode\ApplicationDataService.vb

```
Private Sub CustomersWithOrders_PreprocessQuery(
    ByRef query As IQueryable(Of Customer))

    query = query.Where(Function(custItem) custItem.Orders.Any())

End Sub
```

C#:
File : ShipperCentral\Server\UserCode\ApplicationDataService.cs

```
partial void CustomersWithOrders_PreprocessQuery(
    ref IQueryable<Customer> query)
{
    query = query.OrderBy(custItem => custItem.Orders.Any());
}
```

Creating Not Exists/Not In Queries

As a natural progression of the previous example, the next example shows how you would perform a not exists or not in query. This type of query returns records for which related child records do not exist.

Returning to the customer and orders example, this example illustrates a query for returning customers who have not made an order. Listing 6-11 shows the equivalent SQL that you would use to carry out this query.

Listing 6-11. SQL Equivalent of Not In Query

```
SELECT  CustomerID, Surname, Firstname
 FROM Customers
WHERE CustomerID NOT IN (
    SELECT CustomerID FROM Orders)
```

To carry out this example, create a query called CustomersWithNoOrders. The code in Listing 6-12 can now be added into the PreprocessQuery method to return all customers without orders.

Listing 6-12. Returning all Customers without Orders

VB:
File : ShipperCentral\Server\UserCode\ApplicationDataService.vb

```
Private Sub CustomersWithOrders_PreprocessQuery(
    ByRef query As IQueryable(Of Customer))

    query = query.Where(Function(custItem) Not custItem.Orders.Any())

End Sub
```

C#:
File : ShipperCentral\Server\UserCode\ApplicationDataService.cs

```
partial void CustomersWithOrders_PreprocessQuery(
    ref IQueryable<Customer> query)
{
    query = query.OrderBy(custItem => !custItem.Orders.Any());
}
```

Filtering by Date Elements

The ability to filter by date elements is a common scenario. For example, you might want to create a screen that shows birthdays by showing everyone born on a given day and month.

As an alternative example, you might want to create a screen that returns all orders that were made in a given month and year. The following example illustrates how you would do this.

To allow the end user to enter a month and year, we'll create a parameterized query called OrdersByMonthAndYear based on the Order table. Two parameters of data type Integer are created called OrderMonth and OrderYear, as shown in Figure 6-34.

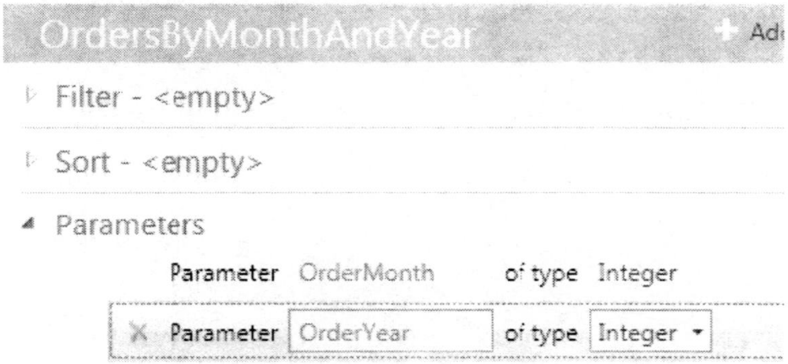

Figure 6-34. OrderMonth and OrderYear parameters

The code in Listing 6-13 can now be added to the PreprocessQuery to return all orders matching the month and year that has been passed in.

Listing 6-13. Filtering by Month and Year Parameter Values

C#:

```
File : ShipperCentral\Server\UserCode\ApplicationDataService.cs

partial void OrdersByMonthAndYear_PreprocessQuery(
    int? OrderMonth, int? OrderYear, ref IQueryable<Order> query)
{
    query = query.Where(
        order => order.OrderDate.Month == OrderMonth.GetValueOrDefault(-1)
            && order.OrderDate.Year == OrderYear.GetValueOrDefault(-1));
}
```

VB:
```
File : ShipperCentral\Server\UserCode\ApplicationDataService.vb

Private Sub OrdersByMonthAndYear_PreprocessQuery(
    OrderMonth As System.Nullable(Of Integer),
    OrderYear As System.Nullable(Of Integer),
    ByRef query As System.Linq.IQueryable(Of LightSwitchApplication.Order))
```

```
query = query.Where(
    Function(orderItem) orderItem.OrderDate.Month = OrderMonth.GetValueOrDefault(-1)
        AndAlso orderItem.OrderDate.Year = OrderYear.GetValueOrDefault(1))
```

End Sub

Because the `OrderMonth` and `OrderYear` parameters are nullable, the `GetValueOrDefault` method converts null values to -1 or 1, respectively. This causes the query to return no records, rather than throw an exception when null values are passed into the query. A screen based on the Editable Grid Screen template can now be created by using this query. As with all other parameterized queries, LightSwitch automatically creates text boxes that allow the parameter values to be entered. The final screen is shown in Figure 6-35.

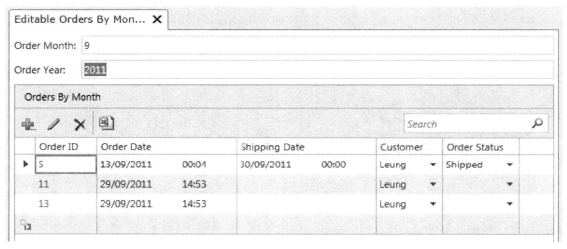

Figure 6-35. Screen to filter by month and year

Top *N* Records

This final example shows you how to return the top *n* records. This example consists of two parts. In the first part, a query is created to return the top 10 most expensive products from a `Product` table. In the second part, a query is created on a `Customer` table to return the details of customers who have made the most recent orders.

To create a query that shows the top 10 most expensive products, a query called `Top10ExpensiveProducts` is created based on the `Product` table. Listing 6-14 shows the code that is written in the `PreprocessQuery` method to return the top 10 records.

Listing 6-14. Query to Return the Top 10 Most Expensive Products

VB:

```
File : ShipperCentral\Server\UserCode\ApplicationDataService.vb

Private Sub Top10ExpensiveProducts_PreprocessQuery (
```

```
    ByRef query As System.Linq.IQueryable(Of LightSwitchApplication.Product))

    query = query.OrderByDescending(
        Function(productItem) productItem.ProductPrice).Take(10)

End Sub
```

C#:

File : ShipperCentral\Server\UserCode\ApplicationDataService.cs

```
partial void Top10ExpensiveProducts_PreprocessQuery  (
    ref IQueryable<Product> query)
{
    query = query.OrderByDescending(productItem=> productItem.ProductPrice).Take(10);
}
```

The second query illustrates how you can return the top *n* records based on data in a related table. In this example, the number of records to return is parameterized and enables the end user to specify the number of records to show. First, create a query called CustomersWithMostOrders based on the Customer table. Next, create a parameter called TopN of data type Integer.

In the PreprocessQuery method, enter the code as shown in Listing 6-15.

Listing 6-15. Query to Return the Top 10 Most Expensive Products

VB:

File : ShipperCentral\Server\UserCode\ApplicationDataService.vb

```
Private Sub CustomersWithMostOrders_PreprocessQuery(
    TopN As System.Nullable(Of Integer),
    ByRef query As System.Linq.IQueryable(Of LightSwitchApplication.Customer))

    query = query.OrderByDescending(
        Function(custItem) custItem.Orders.Count()).Take(TopN.GetValueOrDefault(1))

End Sub
```

C#:

File : ShipperCentral\Server\UserCode\ApplicationDataService.cs

```
partial void CustomersWithMostOrders_PreprocessQuery(
    int? TopN, ref IQueryable<Customer> query)
{
    query = query.OrderByDescending(
        custItem => custItem.Orders.Count()).Take(TopN.GetValueOrDefault(1));
}
```

This code orders the customer records by a count of related orders in descending order. Once again, the Take method is used, and this time around, the parameterized value is passed into this method rather than a hard-coded value.

Using Advanced Sorting Techniques

In this section, we'll discuss some of the issues that relate to sorting. First, we'll show you how users can sort data using the data grid control. We'll also describe how this control can remember the sort sequences that have been applied between sessions. Second, we'll show you how to sort your data by using related records.

Sorting the Data Shown in Grids

When data is displayed by using a LightSwitch grid, the end user can sort the columns by clicking the grid column headings. Clicking a column heading toggles the sort order between ascending and descending. An arrow in the column header indicates the sort order that is currently in use, as shown in Figure 6-36.

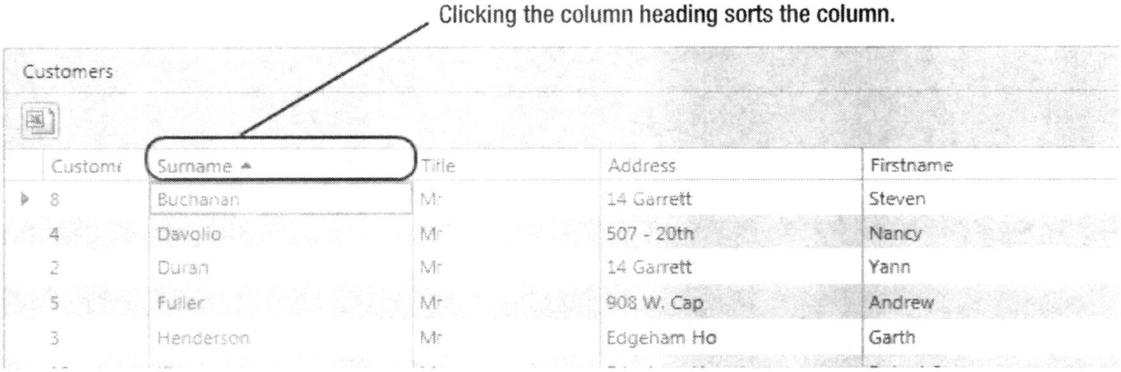

Figure 6-36. Sorting a query

If a user applies a sort order by using the column header, the selected sort sequence is remembered between sessions. If the user exits out of the application, starts the application again, and reopens the same screen, the previous sort order is retained.

There is no way that a user can clear the grid sort order, and this can present developers with a problem. Let's say that you want to show a grid of customers sorted by surname followed by first name. You've created an editable grid screen that is bound to a query that applies this sort order sequence.

When the user first opens the screen, the data is correctly sorted by surname followed by first name. If the user then applies a sort by clicking the Customer ID heading, there is no way for the user to return to the initial sort sequence of surname followed by first name. Because sort sequences are remembered between sessions, restarting the application does not fix the problem either.

The grid settings are saved on the file system along with other LightSwitch setting files. You can find these in the folder My Documents\Microsoft\LightSwitch\Settings\. This folder contains a subfolder for every LightSwitch application that has been run on your computer. Listing 6-16 shows the files that are found in this folder. For each screen in your application, you will find a file with a .SortSettings extension. This is an XML file that contains the grid sort sequences that are remembered across sessions. The only way for a user to clear the sort settings is to delete this file.

Listing 6-16. File Listing of C:\Users\Tim\Documents\Microsoft\LightSwitch\Settings
ShipperCentral.1.0.0.0

```
Application.OutOfBrowser.WindowSettings
EditableCustomersSortedGrid.CustomersSortedDesc.SortSettings
EditableCustomersSortedGrid1.grid.ColumnSettings
StandardShell.NavigationView.Settings
StandardShell.RibbonCommandBar.Settings
```

If a user resizes the widths of the grid columns, these are also persisted between sessions in the
.ColumnSettings file. The other files are used to retain the state of the application, navigation, and
ribbon settings. Listing 6-17 shows the contents of the Application.OutOfBrowser.WindowSettings file
and gives you a taste of what is contained in these various XML files. This file is used by LightSwitch to
reopen your application in the same screen position as your last session.

Listing 6-17. Contents of Application.OutOfBrowser.WindowSettings

```xml
<?xml version="1.0" encoding="utf-8"?>
<OutOfBrowserWindowSettings xmlns:xsi="http://www.w3.org/2001/XMLSchema-instance"
    xmlns:xsd="http://www.w3.org/2001/XMLSchema">
    <Top>10</Top>
    <Left>360</Left>
    <Width>1077</Width>
    <Height>604</Height>
    <WindowState>Normal</WindowState>
</OutOfBrowserWindowSettings>
```

Clearing a grid sort order by asking users to delete XML files is not a practical solution. If you need to
create a grid screen based on a sorted query, the best compromise is to prevent users from setting their
own sort orders by disabling sorting at a screen level. This is done by deselecting the Support Sorting
check box at the entity collection level, as shown in Figure 6-37.

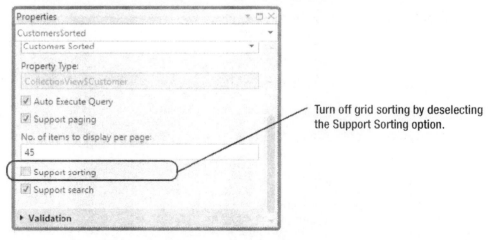

Turn off grid sorting by deselecting
the Support Sorting option.

Figure 6-37. Swiching off searching

189

Sorting by Related Parent Records

In a typical customer/order system, a relationship is set up so that one customer can have many orders. Let's imagine that you want to create a screen that displays order details ordered by customer name. It isn't possible to perform this type of sort by using the graphical designer, because the related customer is not shown in the drop-down list of available sort fields, as you can see in Figure 6-38.

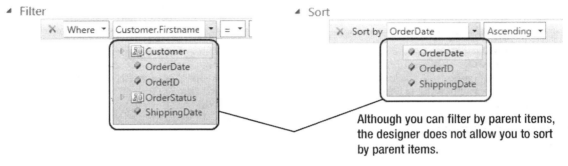

Figure 6-38. The Sort By drop-down list does not include related tables and fields.

To implement a sort by a parent record, you need to write code in the PreprocessQuery method. Listing 6-18 illustrates the code that is used to do this.

Listing 6-18. Sorting by a Related Parent Item

VB:
File: ShipperCentral\Server\UserCode\ApplicationDataService.vb

```
Private Sub OrdersSortedByCustomer_PreprocessQuery (
    ByRef query As IQueryable(Of Order))

    query = query.OrderBy(Function(order)order.Customer.Firstname)

End Sub
```

C#:
File: ShipperCentral\Server\UserCode\ApplicationDataService.cs

```
partial void OrdersSortedByCustomer_PreprocessQuery(ref IQueryable<Order> query)
{
    query = query.OrderBy(order => order.Customer.Firstname);
}
```

Sorting by Related Child Records

If you apply the previous example in the opposite direction, another scenario that you might want to perform is to sort by related child records. For example, you might want to display a grid of customers to highlight those who have recently made orders. The customer who has made the most recent order should appear at the top of the list.

Again, you would write code in the PreprocessQuery method to apply the sort sequence, as shown in Listing 6-19.

Listing 6-19. Sorting by Child Items

VB:
File: ShipperCentral\Server\UserCode\ApplicationDataService.vb

```
Private Sub CustomersSortedByOrder_PreprocessQuery(
    ByRef query As IQueryable(Of Customer))

    query = query.OrderBy(
        Function(custItem) custItem.Orders.Max(Function(ordItem) ordItem.OrderDate))

End Sub
```

C#:
File: ShipperCentral\Server\UserCode\ApplicationDataService.cs

```
partial void CustomersSortedByOrder_PreprocessQuery(ref IQueryable<Customer> query)
{
    query = query.OrderBy(
        custItem => custItem.Orders.Max(ordItem => ordItem.OrderDate));
}
```

This example uses the Max query operator. It's worth noting that the set of supported query operators are dependent on the back-end data source. For SQL Server, the Entity Framework can translate most (if not all) well-known operators. However, you may discover limitations when using other data sources such as SharePoint or a custom RIA data source. The only simple way to find out whether a query operator is supported is to try it and see if it succeeds.

Creating User-Defined Global Values

Earlier in this chapter, you saw some of the built-in global values that can be used when filtering on properties based on the Date and DateTime data types. It's possible for you to create your own global values, and this would be ideal when creating filters that need to reference some other calculated value. For example, you could extend the date/time global values to include values such as 30 days ago, 30 days from now, or some other calculated date value.

By default, a set of global values are available for the Date and DateTime types. However, there is nothing to prevent you from creating global values for other data types.

The task of creating a global value includes two parts:

- Editing the LSML

- Creating a class and writing the code to do the calculation

In the example that follows, a new global value is created that returns the name of the currently logged-on user. The name of the global value that we'll create will be called LoggedOnUser.

Editing the LSML

The `ApplicationData.lsml` file needs to be edited to include a definition for the global value that you're about to create. The file can be found in the Data folder for your project and can be edited by using a text editor such as Notepad. Chapter 2 includes a section on how to edit this file. As mentioned earlier, we highly recommend that you close out of Visual Studio and make a backup copy of the LSML file before editing.

After opening this file, find the XML root `ModelFragment` element and add the `GlobalValueContainerDefinition` element, as shown in Listing 6-20. The code in the listing can be added just before the `</ModelFragment>` tag, which generally appears at the very end of the file.

Listing 6-20. Global Value Definition to Add to the LSML

```
<?xml version="1.0" encoding="utf-8" ?>
<ModelFragment xmlns="http://schemas.microsoft.com/LightSwitch/2010/xaml/model"
               xmlns:x="http://schemas.microsoft.com/winfx/2006/xaml">
  <GlobalValueContainerDefinition Name="GlobalStrings">
    <GlobalValueDefinition Name="LoggedOnUser" ReturnType=":String">
      <GlobalValueDefinition.Attributes>
        <DisplayName Value=" Logged On User " />
        <Description Value ="Gets the currently logged on user." />
      </GlobalValueDefinition.Attributes>
    </GlobalValueDefinition>
  </GlobalValueContainerDefinition>
```

The `GlobalValueContainerDefinition` defines a container for `GlobalValueDefinition` elements. The `GlobalValueDefinition` element defines the global variable that we're about to create, and multiple `GlobalValueDefinition` elements can be specified in each `GlobalValueContainerDefinition`. The `ReturnType` element specifies that you're creating a global value for the data type string. The other data types that you could use are as follows:

- `:String`
- `:Binary`
- `:Boolean`
- `:Int32`
- `:Decimal`
- `:Double`

When editing the LSML, note that these values are case sensitive, so the LightSwitch IDE will not load the project if the case is incorrect.

Creating the Class

The next thing to do is to write the code that does the computation. In this example, the logged-on user is found by calling `Application.Current.User.Name`.

In Solution Explorer, switch to file view and create a new class in the common project. An ideal place to create this class is in the UserCode folder, if it exists. This folder is automatically created by LightSwitch if, for example, some custom validation code has been written for an entity.

The name of the class needs to match the name that is defined in the GlobalValueContainerDefinition element (GlobalStrings in this example). Now enter the code as shown in Listing 6-21.

Listing 6-21. *Code to Return Logged-On User*

VB:

```
File: ShipperCentral\Common\UserCode\GlobalStrings.vb

Namespace LightSwitchApplication

    Public Class GlobalStrings   ' The name of your GlobalValueContainerDefinition

        Public Shared Function LoggedOnUser() As String
            ' LoggedOnUser  matches the name of the GlobalValueDefinition
            Return Application.Current.User.Name
        End Function

    End Class
End Namespace
```

C#:

```
File: ShipperCentral\Common\UserCode\GlobalStrings.cs

using System;
namespace LightSwitchApplication
{
    public class GlobalStrings  // The name of your GlobalValueContainerDefinition
    {
        public static String LoggedOnUser ()
        // LoggedOnUser  matches the name of the GlobalValueDefinition
        {
            return Application.Current.User.Name;
        }
    }
}
```

The new class contains VB shared or C# static methods for each GlobalValueDefinition element defined in your LSML. The methods that you create cannot contain any parameters. Furthermore, the namespace of the class must be set to LightSwitchApplication.

As you can see in this example, the new class contains a string function called LoggedOnUser.

Having created this method, your new global value is ready for use. If you create a new query and filter on a string property, the Logged On User global value appears in the drop-down box, as shown in Figure 6-39.

Figure 6-39. Logged-On User global value shown in the designer

---

■ **Note** If you're curious as to how the default DateTime global values work, the equivalent logic for the built-in global values can be found in the Microsoft.LightSwitch.RelativeDates namespace.

Summary

In this chapter, you've learned about queries in LightSwitch. The main topics covered in this chapter are as follows:

- The ways that queries can be defined in LightSwitch and how queries always return entity sets

- How to create queries and filters by using the query designer

- An introduction to LINQ, lambda expressions, and writing queries in code

- Examples of some advanced query scenarios

- How to create your own global values for use in your queries

Every query in LightSwitch returns entities from an entity set. Single or multiple entities can be returned. Because entities are returned from queries, the shape of the results cannot be modified. For example, you cannot add or remove properties (for example, table columns) from the output of a query. If you want to work with related data, you would use the navigation properties that are defined by the relationships in your data.

By default, LightSwitch creates two queries for returning all entities or a single entity by ID value. Queries are composable, meaning that they can be built on other queries.

You can create your own user-defined queries by using the graphical query designer. These queries use entity sets as their data source and are executed on the server. After creating a query, you can change the data source by using a drop-down box in the title section of the query designer.

Queries can also be defined at a screen level. When designing screens, you can modify the filtering and sorting of the underlying data. However, screen query definitions cannot be shared on other screens. Also, any queries that are created in this way cannot be extended by using code.

When creating user-defined or screen queries, you can easily filter and sort your data by using the graphical query designer. You can apply filters on your data by using a comparison type. These comparison types include Literal, Parameter, and Property. A literal comparison allows you to filter against a hard-coded value, and a property comparison allows you to compare one property against another in an entity. Parameterized queries allow you to pass arguments into a query and are ideal for creating queries that are reusable across multiple screens.

When queries are executed at the server, execution passes through a query pipeline. This consists of several phases, and you can inject your own custom code at various points. The `PreprocessQuery` method allows you to append additional query operators by using LINQ.

Queries in code are written using LINQ. LINQ allows you to express query operators by using familiar VB.NET or C# syntax. There are two flavors of LINQ: query syntax and method syntax. Query syntax looks very similar to SQL code and is easy to read. When compiled, the query syntax is converted into a series of method calls (method syntax). LINQ queries can be written using either query syntax or method syntax. However, certain operations can be performed only by using method syntax.

You rarely need to create joins when creating LINQ queries, because the navigation properties that you define on your entities allow you to reference related data.

LINQ queries can be executed on the client or on the server. This is determined by the data source and syntax that you use to define your query. LINQ queries against entity collections and navigation properties are executed locally.

Queries against entity sets and `IDataServiceQueryable` objects are executed remotely on the server. The query expressions that you specify by using LINQ and lambda expressions can be passed to the middle tier and executed by SQL Server.

You've also seen code that demonstrates some of the typical problem scenarios that you might encounter. This includes Exists and Not Exists queries, and queries to filter results by date elements.

When choosing to filter by a date property, LightSwitch includes built-in global values. These are calculated values such as Today, Start of Week, and Start of Month. In the last part of this chapter, you've seen how to create your own global values that you can use in your own queries.

PART 3

Interacting With Data

CHAPTER 7

Creating and Using RIA Services

What is RIA Services? The full name is actually *Windows Communication Foundation (WCF) RIA Services*, which is a bit of a mouthful, so it's usually referred to as just *RIA Services* (pronounced *reeya*, not R-I-A, as some people tend to do). In essence, RIA Services provides a set of server components and ASP.NET extensions that simplify the *n*-tier application development process, making applications almost as easy to develop as if they were running on a single tier. This is a large part of how LightSwitch does its *magic*.

This chapter explains why you might need to create a RIA Service. You'll learn how to create a RIA service, and how to use it to carry out data aggregation. You'll then see how to update data, and finish the chapter by learning how to consume the RIA service in your LightSwitch application.

Why Would I Need a RIA Service?

If you need to do something that isn't currently built into LightSwitch, such as aggregating data, joining tables, or attaching to an external data source that doesn't have an Entity Framework data provider, you can probably do it with a custom RIA service.

In fact, LightSwitch already uses RIA Services when accessing data via the intrinsic, external SQL Server, or SharePoint data sources. Although this is largely transparent to you (the developer), RIA Services is the mechanism that allows the Silverlight client to communicate with the LightSwitch server.

To Aggregate Data

LightSwitch doesn't have any built-in ability to deal with anything other than an entity in its simplest form, other than including navigation properties in a grid or list. If you want to do any kind of aggregating of your data, such as grouping, counting, summing values, or totaling amounts, you'll usually need to create a RIA service to do that.

Sure, you can create calculated properties in your tables that will allow you to create and display totals and some calculations, but they can often result in quite poor performance, because LightSwitch has to make a trip to the database for each row in a grid or list. Using a RIA service that has already done these calculations on the server tier will result in much better performance.

To Simulate a SQL View

LightSwitch can work with only one (whole) entity at a time. As far as LightSwitch is concerned, an entity is a collection of its own properties, as well as related properties (from related entities). Other than for display purposes, in a list or grid, for example, you can't combine two or more entities to produce a third *made-up* entity (this is often called *entity projection*).

Sometimes you might want only certain properties from an entity, because some properties may not be needed all the time, and dragging the whole entity down to the client to do work on only a few properties isn't really efficient. Or you might not have been given sufficient permissions on an attached database to create a view, to either join tables, or reduce the amount of data coming from the server. Or you might have the necessary permissions, but a SQL view is always read-only in LightSwitch, so you'd be able to display the results of your SQL view, but you won't be able to update them.

And if you happen to be using the intrinsic database, and not an attached SQL database, you can't create any views anyway.

So you can't do any of these things out-of-the-box, but by creating a custom RIA service, you can simulate a SQL view, without any of the disadvantages we've just pointed out.

To Attach to an External Data Source

Out-of-the-box LightSwitch can connect to SQL database servers, SharePoint lists, and WCF RIA Services (see Figure 7-1). If you need to connect to a data source that doesn't have an Entity Framework 4 data provider, then creating a custom RIA service will allow you to get around this restriction.

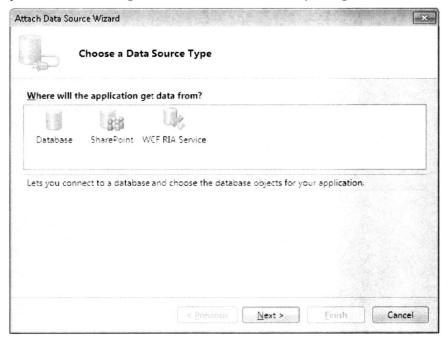

Figure 7-1. Attaching the data source wizard

WCF RIA Services are typically called as a remote service, so it's useful to clarify exactly how LightSwitch communicates with the RIA service. To retrieve or update data from a RIA Services data source, the Silverlight client doesn't access the RIA service directly. Instead, it communicates with the LightSwitch server (also known as the DomainService) in the same way as any other data source. The DomainService is the component that actually communicates with the RIA service, and this acts as an *in-process data adapter* for the Silverlight client.

Creating a RIA Service

The process of creating a custom RIA service to use in your LightSwitch project really isn't as hard as you might think. There are only a few, fairly simple, steps.

Step 1: Add a Class Library to the Solution

1. In Solution Explorer, right-click the solution name.

2. Choose Add ➤ New Project.

3. Click either the VB or the C# tab.

4. In the details pane, select Class Library.

5. Call the new class library Central.Data.Services (browse to the same folder where Central.Utilities was created).

6. Click OK.

■ **Note** Make sure that the project that you add targets the full .NET 4 Framework, not the .NET 4 Client Profile.

Step 2: Add Some References

In the code samples that we'll show you later, you'll need to add some assembly references that won't have been added to the class library:

- System.ComponentModel.DataAnnotations

- System.Configuration

- System.Data.Entity

- System.Runtime.Serialization

- System.ServiceModel.DomainServices.Server

    (browse to %ProgramFiles%\Microsoft SDKs\RIA Services\v1.0\Libraries\Server)

- System.Web

Of course, any references that you need to add will depend on what you want your RIA service to do.

Step 3: Add a Domain Service Class

A *domain service* is a WCF service that encapsulates the business logic part of a RIA service, which exposes a set of related operations as a service *layer*. When you define a domain service, you're actually specifying the data operations that are permitted in the RIA service. So, this class enables your application to do things such as CRUD database operations (create, read, update, and delete). In addition, and very important, it gives you a place to include your business logic. A domain service operates on the server or middle tier.

As you design a domain service, you should think of it as a set of *related* tasks that you expect users to be able to perform in your application. These tasks usually involve a small group of closely related entities. For example, in an expense-reporting application, you might expose entities for expense reports, line items, and details. You might also put entities for accounts and payments in a separate domain service.

There are two ways that you can add a domain service class:

1. Right-click the data project.

    a. Choose Add ➤ New Item ➤ Domain Service Class (see Figure 7-2).

    b. Call the class `ReportDataService`.

    c. Deselect the Enable Client Access check box.

    d. Click OK.

2. Rename the default `Class1` to `ReportDataService`.

    a. Make the class inherit from `DomainService`.

Using either of these methods, you now have a custom RIA service that LightSwitch can consume. Of course, it doesn't do anything yet, though.

In step 1, you might wonder why it's necessary to deselect the Enable Client Access check box. As we mentioned earlier, the RIA Service data source runs on the server and acts as an *in-process data adapter* for the Silverlight client. Because this works *in process*, you can disable the client access check box.

If you leave the Enable Client Access check box selected, the WCF service can be called by other external clients, which can cause a security risk. With the check box deselected, the WCF service gets exposed via the LightSwitch endpoint and is further guarded by the LightSwitch pipelines.

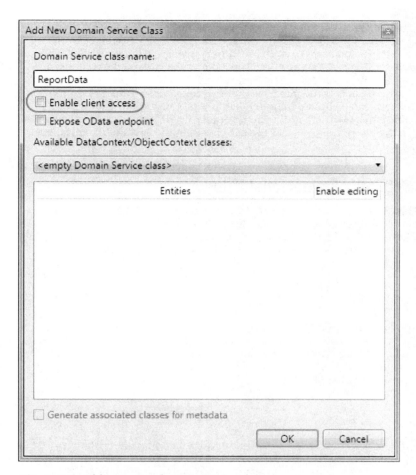

Figure 7-2. Adding a new domain service class

Step 4: Connect to the Data

In this step, you do the actual work, by connecting the RIA Service to an external database and querying the data. How do you do that? Well, there are several data access mechanisms that you can choose from. Some of these include the following:

- ADO.NET Entity Framework
- LINQ to SQL
- ADO.NET
- Reusing LightSwitch's Entity Framework model

If you're using a RIA service to work with data that you've already added as a data source to your LightSwitch application, reusing LightSwitch's Entity Framework model can save you a lot of work.

You can use the other data access mechanisms to wrap operations that you wouldn't natively be able to access through LightSwitch. Calling SQL Server stored procedures, user-defined functions, or returning views that don't contain a primary-key column are examples.

Of course, these are many more data access mechanisms that you can choose from. For example, if your company uses the NHibernate object-relational mapping (ORM) system, you can choose a data access technology that works around this. Alternatively, if you want to use a RIA service that exposes the contents of files that are stored on the file system, you can use the classes in the System.IO namespace.

We'll now describe the options that we've mentioned in more detail.

Option 1: Using an ADO.Net Entity Framework Model

The advantage of using the ADO.NET Entity Framework is that you can create more-complex models, beyond what LightSwitch could natively create. You'd use Entity Framework's EDMX designer to generate more-sophisticated object-relational (OR) mappings. This allows you to abstract the relational schema of the data that's stored in your database, and to present a cleaner conceptual model that LightSwitch can consume.

Option 2: Using LINQ to SQL

If we were attaching to a Microsoft SQL Server database, we could use *LINQ to SQL* to create a model that connects to the database. This could be useful if you have existing experience of using LINQ to SQL. But because LightSwitch uses the Entity Framework by default, a disadvantage is that you'll be using two data access technologies in your solution, instead of just one. This arrangement is not ideal because it would make your application more difficult to maintain.

Option 3: Using ADO.NET

To attach to a database that doesn't have a compatible Entity Framework data provider, you may need to go down a level further, and use plain old ADO.NET DataSets and DataReaders to access your data via OLEDB or ODBC. You might need to use this technique if you were connecting to something like an Access or FoxPro database.

Option 4: Reusing LightSwitch's Entity Framework Data Model

If you want to manipulate data that LightSwitch has already connected to, but in a way that LightSwitch is unable to do, it makes much more sense to just reuse the model that already exists in your LightSwitch project. Fortunately, there's a technique that allows us to do just that, by simply adding a link to the file that LightSwitch generates for the data source that you want to access, and then creating a Context property to access the data.

Writing the RIA Service Code

Now that you understand the steps involved in adding a class library, creating a domain service class, and choosing a data access mechanism, we'll show you a couple of RIA service examples.

First, we'll show you how to view aggregated data by using LightSwitch's Entity Framework model. Next, we'll show you an example of how to update and add data by using ADO.NET.

Creating a RIA Service to Aggregate Data

In this first example, we'll use a RIA service to create an aggregated view of data. To make life really simple, we'll reuse LightSwitch's Entity Framework data model.

We'll base our example on a person table. This table includes a relationship to a table called Gender. The Gender table contains a string property called GenderName. The Gender table contains two rows, with the GenderName set to male and female. In the person table, the name of the navigation property to the Gender table is called Person_Gender.

Our RIA service then returns a count of people grouped by gender.

Step 1: Add a Link to the Generated Model File

To make use of the data model that LightSwitch has already created, we simply add a link to the model file that LightSwitch generated for us. Here are the steps:

1. In Solution Explorer, right-click the Central.Data.Services project.

2. Choose Add ➤ Existing Item.

3. Browse to the LightSwitch project folder (the one with the lsproj file).

4. Browse to the ServerGenerated\GeneratedArtifacts folder (see the item marked *a* in Figure 7-3).

5. Select the ApplicationData.vb/cs file, but *don't* click the Add button yet (see the item marked *b* in Figure 7-3).

6. Click the drop-down button on the right-hand side of the button (see the item marked *c* in Figure 7-3).

7. Select Add As Link (see the item marked *d* in Figure 7-3).

Now the LightSwitch-created data model is being shared between the two projects, through the linked ApplicationData file. As changes are made in the LightSwitch project, those changes will be automatically made available to the Central.Data project as well, without needing to take any manual action.

How cool is that!

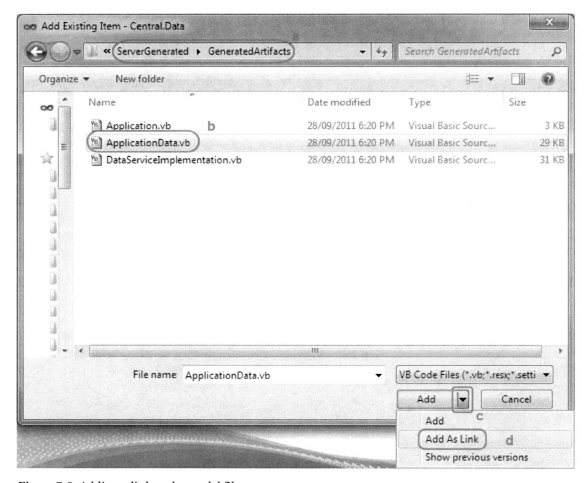

Figure 7-3. Adding a link to the model file

Step 2: Add Some Code to the *DomainService* Class

To be able to access the data, we'll need to create a Context property (see Listing 7-1) that's based on the ApplicationDataObjectContext that was created in the LightSwitch project's data model.

Listing 7-1. Creating an Object Context

VB:

File: Central.Data.Services\ReportDataService.vb

Imports System.ServiceModel.DomainServices.Server

```vbnet
Imports System.Data.EntityClient
Imports System.Web.Configuration
Imports System.ComponentModel.DataAnnotations
Imports System.Linq

'this might be named differently if you've set the namespace for your project
Imports Central.Data.Services.ApplicationData.Implementation

Public Class ReportDataService
    Inherits DomainService

    Const METADATA_NAME As String = "ApplicationData"

    'used to build the metatdata
    Const METADATA_FORMAT As String =
        "res://*/{0}.csdl|res://*/{0}.ssdl|res://*/{0}.msl"

    'LightSwitch uses a special name for its intrinsic database connection
    'instead of ApplicationData as you would normally expect
    Const CONNECTION_NAME As String = "_IntrinsicData"

    'the data provider name
    Const PROVIDER_NAME As String = "System.Data.SqlClient"

    Private _context As ApplicationDataObjectContext
    Public ReadOnly Property Context As ApplicationDataObjectContext
        Get
            If (_context Is Nothing) _
            Then
                Dim builder = New EntityConnectionStringBuilder

                builder.Metadata =
                    String.Format(METADATA_FORMAT, METADATA_NAME)
                builder.Provider = PROVIDER_NAME
                builder.ProviderConnectionString = WebConfigurationManager↵
                    .ConnectionStrings(CONNECTION_NAME)↵
                    .ConnectionString

                _context = NewApplicationDataObjectContext(
                    builder.ConnectionString)
            End If

            Return _context
        End Get
    End Property

End Class
```

C#:

File: Central.Data.Services\ReportDataService.vs

```
using System.ServiceModel.DomainServices.Server;
using System.Data.EntityClient;
using System.Web.Configuration;
using System.ComponentModel.DataAnnotations;
using System.Linq;

// this might be named differently if you've set the namespace for your project
using ApplicationData.Implementation;

public class ReportDataService : DomainService
{
    private const string METADATA_NAME = "ApplicationData";

    //used to build the metatdata
    const string METADATA_FORMAT =
        "res://*/{0}.csdl|res://*/{0}.ssdl|res://*/{0}.msl";

    //LightSwitch uses a special name for its intrinsic database connection
    //instead of ApplicationData as you would normally expect
    const string CONNECTION_NAME = "_IntrinsicData";

    //the data provider name
    const string PROVIDER_NAME = "System.Data.SqlClient";

    private ApplicationDataObjectContext _context;
    public ApplicationDataObjectContext Context
    {
        get
        {
            if (_context == null)
            {
                var builder = new EntityConnectionStringBuilder();

                builder.Metadata = string.Format(
                    METADATA_FORMAT, METADATA_NAME);
                builder.Provider = PROVIDER_NAME;
                builder.ProviderConnectionString = WebConfigurationManager↵
                    .ConnectionStrings[CONNECTION_NAME]↵
                    .ConnectionString;

                _context = new ApplicationDataObjectContext(
                    builder.ConnectionString);
            }

            return _context;
        }
    }
}
```

We'll also need to add a class to represent the entity we want to return to LightSwitch. We've called ours ReportDataClass (see Listing 7-2). This class can either be added to a separate class file, as we have, or it could be added to the service class itself, if you prefer.

Listing 7-2. Entity Class

VB:

File: Central.Data.Services\ReportDataClass.vb

Imports System.ComponentModel.DataAnnotations

```vb
Public Class ReportDataClass
    <Key()>
    Public Property Id As Integer

    Public Property Name As String
    Public Property Total As Decimal

    ' if you need to cast any values from one type to another,
    ' you'll need to do it here
    ' because casts aren't allowed in LINQ to Entity queries
    Friend WriteOnly Property TotalSingle As Single
        Set(value As Single)
            Me.Total = New Decimal(value)
        End Set
    End Property

End Class
```

C#:

File: Central.Data.Services\ReportDataClass.cs

using System.ComponentModel.DataAnnotations;

```csharp
public class ReportDataClass
{
    [Key]
    public int Id {get; set;}

    public string Name {get; set;}
    public decimal Total {get; set;}

    // if you need to cast any values from one type to another,
    // you'll need to do it here
    // because casts aren't allowed in LINQ to Entity queries
    internal float TotalSingle
    {
        set
        {
            this.Total = new decimal(value);
        }
    }
}
```

In the code shown, we've decorated the Id property with the Key attribute. This is important because it tells LightSwitch to treat this property as the primary key. You can decorate more than one property with the Key attribute, if you want to specify a combination key.

Finally, we'll need to add a couple of methods to allow us to query the data (see Listing 7-3).

Listing 7-3. Query Methods

VB:

File: Central.Data.Services\ReportDataService.vb

```vb
<Query(IsDefault:=True)>
Public Function GenderCount() As IQueryable(Of ReportDataClass)
    Dim result As IQueryable(Of ReportDataClass)

    result = From p In Me.Context.People
             Group By Gender = p.Gender
             Into g = Group
             Select New ReportDataClass With↵
               {
                   .Id = Gender.Id↵
                   , .Name = Gender.GenderName↵
                   , .Total = g.Count↵
               }

        Return result
End Function

Protected Overrides Function Count(Of T)(
        query As IQueryable(Of T)) As Integer
    Return query.Count()
End Function
```

C#:

File: Central.Data.Services\ReportDataService.cs

```csharp
[Query(IsDefault=true)]
public IQueryable<ReportDataClass> GenderCount()
{
    IQueryable<ReportDataClass> result = null;

    result =  from Person p in this.Context.People
              group p by p.Gender into g
              select new ReportDataClass
                {
                    Id = g.Key.Id
                    , Name = g.Key.GenderName
                    , Total = g.Count
                };
```

```
    return result;
}

protected override int Count<T>(IQueryable<T> query)
{
    return query.Count();
}
```

The GenderCount method is decorated with the Query attribute, and the IsDefault property of this is set to true. This tells LightSwitch to use the GenderCount method as the default method for returning a collection.

If you fail to decorate a method with the Query(IsDefault=true) attribute, and don't decorate any properties with the Key attribute, LightSwitch won't allow you to import the entity or entity set.

In addition to the Key and Query attributes, you can also define relationships and navigation properties by using similar attributes. If you do this, LightSwitch recognizes the relationships and navigation properties that you've specified when you attach to the RIA service.

Step 3: Attach the RIA Service as a Data Source

The process for attaching our custom RIA service as a data source is no different from attaching to any other RIA service. The steps required are explained in the section "Using a RIA Service" later in this chapter. Just make sure that you've built (or rebuilt) your solution, or else your custom service may not be available to select.

Creating a RIA Service to Update Data

We'll now move onto another example that shows you how to update, insert, and delete data by using a RIA Service. In this example, the data access is carried out using ADO.NET. We'll show you how to perform CRUD operations against a supplier table in an external SQL Server database. Although we're using SQL Server in this example, you're not limited to just SQL Server. Because we're using ADO.NET, you could just as easily connect to any other Database Management System (DBMS) provided that an ADO.NET data provider exists for that DBMS.

It's really easy to update data. To begin, you'll need to carry out the same two steps that we showed you earlier:

1. Create a class library project.

2. Add a domain service.

After that, you'll need to carry out the following steps:

3. Write a class that represents your entity.

4. Write the data access code.

Step 1: Write an Entity Class

Just as before, you'll need to create a class that represents your entity. Figure 7-4 shows the schema of our supplier table. Listing 7-4 shows the class that you'd use to represent the records in this table.

Column Name	Data Type	Allow Nulls
SupplierID	int	
CompanyName	nvarchar(60)	✓
ContactFirstname	nvarchar(25)	✓
ContactSurname	nvarchar(25)	✓
Title	nvarchar(30)	✓
Address	nvarchar(60)	✓
City	nvarchar(15)	✓
Region	nvarchar(15)	✓
PostalCode	nvarchar(10)	✓
Country	nvarchar(15)	✓
Phone	nvarchar(24)	✓
Mobile	nvarchar(24)	✓
Email	nvarchar(24)	✓

Figure 7-4. Schema of Supplier table

Your RIA service doesn't need to expose every single column in this table. You'd therefore design your class to suit the properties that you want to return. In fact, creating a RIA service that returns a subset of columns is an ideal way to optimize the performance of your LightSwitch application.

Listing 7-4. Supplier Entity Class

VB:

```
File: Central.Data.Services\SupplierRecord.vb

Imports System.ComponentModel.DataAnnotations

Public Class SupplierRecord
    <Key(), Editable(False)>
    Public Property SupplierID As Integer

    <Required(ErrorMessage:="Supplier Name must be entered"),
        StringLength(60)>
    Public Property SupplierName As String

    <StringLength(25)>
    Public Property FirstName As String

    <StringLength(25)>
    Public Property LastName As String
End Class
```

C#:

File: Central.Data.Services\SupplierRecord.cs

```csharp
using System.ComponentModel.DataAnnotations;

public class SupplierRecord
{
    [Key, Editable (false)]
    public int SupplierID { get; set; }

    [Required(ErrorMessage ="Supplier Name must be entered"),
        StringLength(60)]
    public string SupplierName { get; set; }

    [StringLength(25)]
    public string FirstName { get; set; }

    [StringLength(25)]
    public string LastName { get; set; }
}
```

We've decorated the primary-key property (SupplierID) with the key attribute. But unlike last time, we've also included the Editable attribute and have set this value to false. So LightSwitch won't allow users to edit this property on any screen that displays it.

We've also decorated several other properties with attributes, and we'll now explain what these do.

The SupplierName property is decorated with the Required attribute. This tells LightSwitch that the property can't be null or empty. If you create a screen that uses the Supplier entity and the user fails to enter a SupplierName, LightSwitch triggers its built-in validation and prevents the save operation from happening.

The StringLength attribute allows you to specify the maximum length of a property. This also hooks into LightSwitch's built-in validation and prevents users from entering text that exceeds the maximum length that you specify.

It's important to apply the StringLength and Required attributes to ensure that users enter valid data, and to prevent any exceptions that might occur if invalid data is entered.

Step 2: Write ADO.NET Code

Now that we've created our entity class, we'll need to write the code that performs the actual data access. This is shown in Listing 7-5.

The methods that we've used to add, update, and delete entities are called InsertSupplierData, UpdateSupplierData, and DeleteSupplierData, respectively. These methods must include a parameter that accepts an instance of your entity.

Prefixing the methods with the names Insert, Update, and Delete tells LightSwitch to use these methods for inserting, updating, and deleting entities. There isn't anything more that you need to do to specify that these methods should be used by LightSwitch to insert, update, or delete data.

We've used ADO.NET in our example to carry out the data access. The pattern that we've used is to create a SqlConnection object, and to specify the SQL command that we want to execute by using a SqlCommand object. If you want to use a non-SQL-Server data source, you can import the System.Data.OleDb namespace and use the OleDbConnection and OleDbCommand objects instead.

Any parameters that you need to supply are prefixed with the @ symbol in the SQL command text. We've used the `AddParameterWithValue` method to set the values of our parameters. It's important to supply parameters in this way, rather than build up the entire SQL command in code. This prevents rogue users from carrying out a SQL injection attack on your application.

The SQL command that's used in the `InsertSupplierData` method includes a command that selects `@@Identity`. This is a T-SQL command that retrieves the autogenerated identity value that's been assigned to the newly added entity, and sets the `SupplierID` property to this value. This allows the user to see the ID of the record onscreen immediately after a save.

We've also included some code that sets the connection string to the database, as well as some code that shows you how to call a SQL Server stored procedure. We'll now describe these in more detail.

Listing 7-5. Domain Service Code for Updating Records

VB:

```
File: Central.Data.Services\SupplierDataService.vb


Option Compare Binary
Option Infer On
Option Strict On
Option Explicit On

Imports System
Imports System.Collections.Generic
Imports System.ComponentModel
Imports System.ComponentModel.DataAnnotations
Imports System.Linq
Imports System.ServiceModel.DomainServices.Hosting
Imports System.ServiceModel.DomainServices.Server

Imports System.Configuration
Imports System.Data.SqlClient

<Description ("Enter the connection string to the Shipper Central DB")>
Public Class SupplierDataService
    Inherits DomainService

    Private ReadOnly _supplierRecordList As List(Of SupplierRecord)
    Public Sub New()
        _supplierRecordList = New List(Of SupplierRecord)()
    End Sub

    Private _connectionString As String

    Public Overrides Sub Initialize(context
        As  System.ServiceModel.DomainServices.Server.DomainServiceContext)

        _connectionString = ConfigurationManager.ConnectionStrings↵
            (Me.[GetType]().FullName).ConnectionString
        MyBase.Initialize(context)
```

```vb
End Sub

<Query(IsDefault:=True)>
Public Function GetSupplierData() As IQueryable(
    Of SupplierRecord)
    _supplierRecordList.Clear()
    Dim cnn As New SqlConnection(_connectionString)

    Dim cmd As New SqlCommand(
        "SELECT SupplierID, CompanyName,ContactFirstname, ContactSurname ↵
        FROM Supplier", cnn)

    Try
        cnn.Open()
        Using dr As SqlDataReader = cmd.ExecuteReader()
            While dr.Read()
                Dim supplier As New SupplierRecord()
                supplier.SupplierID = CInt(dr("SupplierID"))
                supplier.SupplierName = dr("CompanyName").ToString()
                supplier.FirstName = dr("ContactFirstname").ToString()
                supplier.LastName = dr("ContactSurname").ToString()
                _supplierRecordList.Add(supplier)
            End While
        End Using
    Finally
        cnn.Close()
    End Try

    Return _supplierRecordList.AsQueryable()
End Function


Public Sub UpdateSupplierData(Supplier As SupplierRecord)
    Dim cnn As New SqlConnection(_connectionString)
    Dim cmd As New SqlCommand(
        "UPDATE Supplier SET CompanyName = @CompanyName,  ↵
        ContactFirstname=@ContactFirstname, ↵
        ContactSurname=@ContactSurname ↵
        WHERE SupplierID = @SupplierID", cnn)

    cmd.Parameters.AddWithValue("CompanyName", Supplier.SupplierName)
    cmd.Parameters.AddWithValue("ContactFirstName", Supplier.FirstName)
    cmd.Parameters.AddWithValue("ContactSurname", Supplier.LastName)
    cmd.Parameters.AddWithValue("SupplierID", Supplier.SupplierID)

    Try
        cnn.Open()
        cmd.ExecuteNonQuery()
    Finally
        cnn.Close()
    End Try
```

```vb
    End Sub

    Public Sub InsertSupplierData(Supplier As SupplierRecord)

        Dim cnn As New SqlConnection(_connectionString)
        Dim cmd As New SqlCommand("INSERT INTO Supplier ↵
          (CompanyName,ContactFirstname, ContactSurname) ↵
           VALUES ↵
          (@CompanyName ,@ContactFirstname, @ContactSurname); ↵
           SELECT @@Identity ", cnn)

        cmd.Parameters.AddWithValue("CompanyName", Supplier.SupplierName)
        cmd.Parameters.AddWithValue("ContactFirstName", Supplier.FirstName)
        cmd.Parameters.AddWithValue("ContactSurname", Supplier.LastName)

        Try
            cnn.Open()
            Supplier.SupplierID = CInt(cmd.ExecuteScalar())
        Finally
            cnn.Close()
        End Try

    End Sub

    Public Sub DeleteSupplierData(Supplier As SupplierRecord)

        Dim cnn As New SqlConnection(_connectionString)
        Dim cmd As New SqlCommand("DeleteSupplier", cnn)
        cmd.Parameters.AddWithValue("@SupplierID", Supplier.SupplierID)
        cmd.CommandType = System.Data.CommandType.StoredProcedure
        Try
            cnn.Open()
            cmd.ExecuteNonQuery()
        Finally
            cnn.Close()
        End Try

    End Sub

End Class
```

C#:

File: Central.Data.Services\SupplierDataService.cs

```csharp
namespace Central.Data.Services
{
    using System;
    using System.Collections.Generic;
    using System.ComponentModel;
    using System.ComponentModel.DataAnnotations;
    using System.Linq;
```

```
using System.ServiceModel.DomainServices.Hosting;
using System.ServiceModel.DomainServices.Server;
using System.Data.SqlClient;
using System.Configuration;

[Description ("Enter the connection string to the Shipper Central DB")]
public class SupplierDataService : DomainService
{
    private readonly List<SupplierRecord> _supplierRecordList;
    public SupplierDataService ()
    {
        _supplierRecordList = new List<SupplierRecord>();
    }

    string _connectionString;
    public override void Initialize
        (System.ServiceModel.DomainServices.Server.DomainServiceContext
            context)
    {
        _connectionString = ConfigurationManager.ConnectionStrings ⏎
          [this.GetType().FullName].ConnectionString;
        base.Initialize(context);
    }


    [Query(IsDefault = true)]
    public IQueryable<SupplierRecord> GetSupplierData()
    {
        _supplierRecordList.Clear();
        SqlConnection cnn = new SqlConnection(_connectionString);

        SqlCommand cmd = new SqlCommand(
            "SELECT SupplierID, CompanyName,ContactFirstname, ⏎
                ContactSurname FROM Supplier", cnn);

        try
        {
            cnn.Open();

            using (SqlDataReader dr = cmd.ExecuteReader())
            {
                while (dr.Read())
                {
                    SupplierRecord supplier = new SupplierRecord();
                    supplier.SupplierID = (int)dr["SupplierID"];
                    supplier.SupplierName = dr["CompanyName"].ToString();
                    supplier.FirstName = ⏎
                            dr["ContactFirstname"].ToString();
                    supplier.LastName = dr["ContactSurname"].ToString();
                    _supplierRecordList.Add(supplier);
                }
            }
```

```
        }
        finally
        {
            cnn.Close();
        }

        return _supplierRecordList.AsQueryable();
    }

    public void UpdateSupplierData(SupplierRecord Supplier)
    {
        SqlConnection cnn = new SqlConnection(_connectionString);
        SqlCommand cmd = new SqlCommand(
            "UPDATE Supplier SET  ↵
                CompanyName = @CompanyName ,  ↵
                ContactFirstname=@ContactFirstname ,  ↵
            ContactSurname=@ContactSurname↵
            WHERE SupplierID = @SupplierID", cnn);
        cmd.Parameters.AddWithValue(
            "CompanyName", Supplier.SupplierName );
        cmd.Parameters.AddWithValue(
            "ContactFirstName", Supplier.FirstName );
        cmd.Parameters.AddWithValue(
            "ContactSurname", Supplier.LastName );
        cmd.Parameters.AddWithValue(
            "SupplierID", Supplier.SupplierID );

        try
        {
            cnn.Open();
            cmd.ExecuteNonQuery();
        }
        finally
        {
            cnn.Close();
        }

    }

    public void InsertSupplierData(SupplierRecord Supplier)
    {
        SqlConnection cnn = new SqlConnection(_connectionString);
        SqlCommand cmd = new SqlCommand(
            "INSERT INTO Supplier ↵
            (CompanyName,ContactFirstname, ContactSurname) ↵
                VALUES ( @CompanyName ,@ContactFirstname, @ContactSurname);↵
            SELECT @@Identity ", cnn);

        cmd.Parameters.AddWithValue(
            "CompanyName", Supplier.SupplierName);
        cmd.Parameters.AddWithValue(
```

```
                    "ContactFirstName", Supplier.FirstName);
            cmd.Parameters.AddWithValue(
                    "ContactSurname", Supplier.LastName);

            try
            {
                cnn.Open();
                Supplier.SupplierID = (int)cmd.ExecuteScalar();
            }
            finally
            {
                cnn.Close();
            }

        }

        public void DeleteSupplierData(SupplierRecord Supplier)
        {

            SqlConnection cnn = new SqlConnection(_connectionString);
            SqlConnection cnn = new SqlConnection(_connectionString);
            SqlCommand cmd = new SqlCommand(
                    "DeleteSupplier", cnn);
            cmd.Parameters.AddWithValue("@SupplierID", Supplier.SupplierID );
            cmd.CommandType = System.Data.CommandType.StoredProcedure;
            try
            {
                cnn.Open();
                cmd.ExecuteNonQuery();
            }
            finally
            {
                cnn.Close();
            }

        }

    }

}
```

Retrieving a Connection String from *web.config*

The RIA service uses an ADO.NET connection string to connect to the database. You'll want to save this connection string within the web.config file of your LightSwitch application, because this allows for easy modification after the deployment of your application.

When you connect to a RIA service at design time, LightSwitch prompts you to enter a connection string. We'll cover this later, in the "Using a RIA Service" section. LightSwitch saves this connection string into the ConnectionStrings section of your web.config file, and keys this entry using the fully qualified name of your class.

You can obtain the connection string value in your RIA service code by using the methods in the ConfigurationManager namespace, as shown here:

VB: ConfigurationManager.ConnectionStrings(Me.[GetType]().FullName).ConnectionString
C#: ConfigurationManager.ConnectionStrings[this.GetType().FullName].ConnectionString;

You'll need to add a reference to the System.Configuration assembly to access the ConfigurationManager object. In practice, you might also want to write some additional error-checking code to make sure that the connection string setting exists, and that it isn't null or empty.

You'll also notice that the name of our domain service class has been decorated with the description attribute. The value that you specify here is shown when you attach the RIA service from inside LightSwitch.

Calling Stored Procedures

Calling database stored procedures can be useful, particularly if you're connecting to an existing database that already contains stored procedures.

The DeleteSupplier method shown in Listing 7-5 shows the ADO.NET code that you'd use to call a stored procedure. The name of this stored procedure is DeleteSupplier, which is shown in Listing 7-6.

When you're calling a stored procedure using ADO.NET, you'll need to set the CommandType property of the SqlCommand object to StoredProcedure. If you don't do this, your SQL command will fail to execute.

Listing 7-6. T-SQL Definition of the DeleteSupplier Stored Procedure

```
CREATE PROCEDURE DeleteSupplier
    @SupplierID int
AS
BEGIN
    SET NOCOUNT ON;
    DELETE FROM Supplier
    WHERE SupplierID=@SupplierID
END
GO
```

Using a RIA Service

Now that you've created your RIA service, you'll need to attach it to your LightSwitch application. Using a RIA service in a LightSwitch application is as simple as adding it as a data source:

1. In Solution Explorer, right-click Data Sources.

2. Select Add Data Source.

3. Select WCF RIA Service (see Figure 7-5).

4. Click Next.

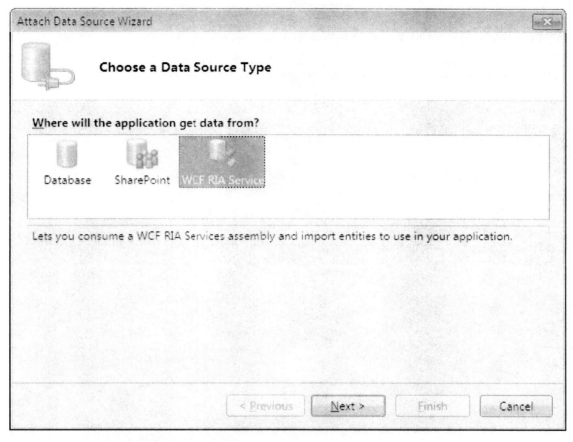

Figure 7-5. Attaching a WCF RIA Service

If this is the first time you're adding the RIA service, the list of available classes may be blank. If that's the case, follow these steps:

1. Click the Add Reference button.

2. Click the Browse tab (or the Projects tab if you're adding a custom RIA service in the current solution).

3. Locate the RIA service that you want to add as a data source.

4. Click OK.

If the service that you want to add is already listed (or you used Add Reference to get it in the list), follow these steps:

1. Select the service from the list, as shown in Figure 7-6.

2. Click the Next button.

3. Expand the Entities entry (see Figure 7-7).

4. Select the check boxes for any entities that you want to import.

5. Enter a suitable name for the data source. (This will appear in the list of Data Sources, so it's best to try to keep it consistent with ApplicationData, and so forth.)

6. Click Finish.

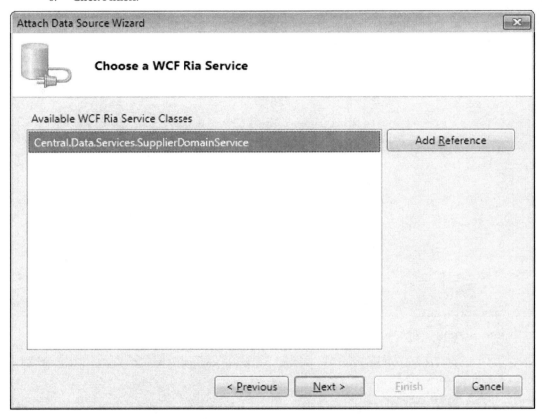

Figure 7-6. Choosing an available RIA service class

If your RIA service requires a connection string, you can enter it into the Connection String text box. In Figure 7-7, notice how the default Connection String text box indicates, *Enter the connection string to the Shipper Central DB*. This help text comes from the description attribute of the domain service class, which was shown in Listing 7-5.

You should now have a new table for each of the entities for which you selected a check box. You can leave the default name (which will be the name of the class that you created earlier), or you can change it to something else if you prefer.

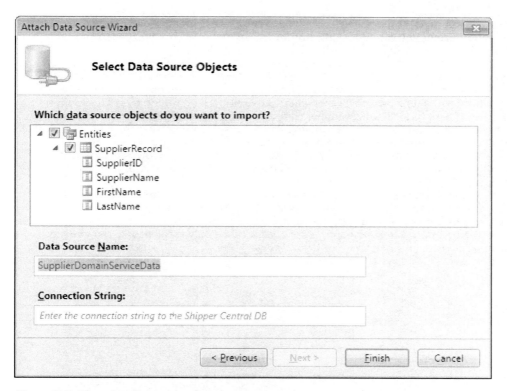

Figure 7-7. Choosing the entities that you want to use

Summary

In this chapter, you learned what a RIA service is, and why you might possibly need to create or use one. We showed you the following:

- How to create a RIA service by adding a class library project and creating a domain service class

- The data access methods that you can use in your RIA service, including a technique to reuse LightSwitch's data model

- How to perform data aggregation in your RIA service

- How to update data by using ADO.NET in your RIA service

- How to call a SQL stored procedure

RIA Services helps you perform data-related operations that you can't natively carry out in LightSwitch.

You can use RIA Services to aggregate your data. This allows you to group data and to apply arithmetic operations such as count, sum, average, and so on.

You can also use RIA Services to create views of your data. You can create views to join data from multiple tables. Alternatively, you can reduce the number of columns that are returned from a table, and you can use this technique to optimize the performance of your application.

RIA Services also allows you to access data sources that are not supported by LightSwitch. For example, you can write a RIA service that accesses data from a FoxPro or Microsoft Access database.

To create a RIA service, you'll need to create a class library project and then add a domain service class. Next, you'll need to create a class that represents your entity. If you want to return a supplier entity, for example, you'll need to create a supplier class and include properties that represent the supplier ID, supplier name, and so forth. The property that acts as the primary key must be decorated with the key attribute. If you don't specify a key property, LightSwitch won't import your entity.

Every RIA service needs a method that returns a collection of data. This method must return an IQueryable object and has to be decorated with the query attribute. The IsDefault property on the query attribute must be set to true.

To update data, you'll need to create methods that are prefixed with the name Insert, Update, or Delete. These methods have to include a parameter that accepts an instance of your entity.

The database connection string that your RIA service uses can be stored in your web.config file. This allows you to change the setting after you deploy your application. You've seen how to retrieve this setting in code, and how to set it when you attach your RIA service.

Finally, you've learned how easy it is to consume a RIA service by using the Attach Data Source Wizard.

CHAPTER 8

Creating and Using Screens

Once you've been using LightSwitch for even just a short time, you'll probably want to start designing screens that are a bit more advanced than those the wizards will produce for you. In this chapter we'll look at some techniques you can use to do exactly that. We'll begin by showing you:

- How to create screens, the screen template types you can use, and the parts that make up the screen designer.

- How to use the Add Data Item dialog to add properties, queries, and methods.

- The built-in controls that are available.

After explaining the screen designer, we'll show you how to perform screen-related actions using code. Some of the topics we'll cover will include:

- The screen events you can use.

- How to access controls using code.

- How to make your application respond to changes in data.

At the end of the screen code section, we'll show you how to extend and use the Modal window, and AutoCompleteBox controls using code.

To finish the chapter, we'll pull everything together and give some examples of how to create some customized screens. We'll show you:

- A home screen that includes static text, images, and links.

- A custom search screen that allows you to filter items using an AutoCompleteBox (this is a ComboBox control that filters the items shown as the user types into it).

- How to create a single screen that allows records to be added and edited.

- How to create screens to support many-to-many relationships in data.

- How to customize the data grid control to enable multiple selection of records.

We know this is a very long and detailed chapter, but we felt that completeness was important, especially on a topic as important as screen design. We've added plenty of reference detail, so you may prefer to skim through the chapter quickly first and then refer to it when you're actually writing your application.

Designing Screens

Screens are not just about "layout," they're also *business objects* in their own right that have properties, methods, and events, in addition to controls, that display data.

Each screen also represents what's called a *unit of work*, meaning that all changes that are made on the screen (including changes made to child records in any lists or grids) are saved or discarded, all as a single *unit*. This is made possible by each screen having its own data workspace, allowing it to maintain an independent set of data changes.

Adding a Screen

To add a screen to your application, right-click the Screens folder in Solution Explorer and choose the Add Screen … option. This opens the Add New Screen dialog, as shown in Figure 8-1.

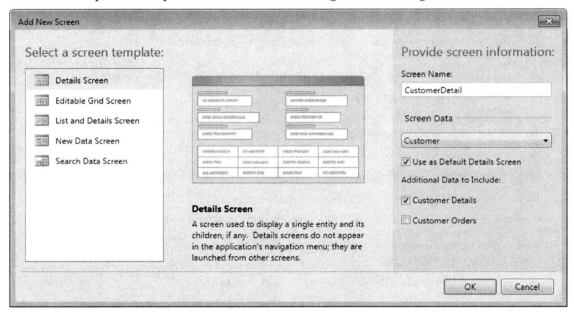

Figure 8-1. *Add new screen dialog box*

The first thing you'll need to do is to choose a screen template. The screen templates provide an *initial* layout of controls, but the screens they produce can be easily customized later. They each consist of a specific number of controls that are laid out in a particular way, according to the template's intended function, and some of them allow the inclusion of related data as well.

There are five screen templates that come with LightSwitch. Table 8-1 describes the purpose of each screen template.

Table 8-1. Screen Template Types

Name	Screen Template Overview
Search Data Screen	Search screens include a search text box. The search results are shown in a data grid.
Details Screen	Details screens are used to display a single entity.
New Data screen	Allows records to be added, one at a time.
Editable Grid Screen	Displays a grid that allows you to edit multiple records.
List and Details Screen	Displays records in a list. The properties of the selected item is shown on the right hand side of the grid.

After selecting a template, the next thing you'll need to do is to name your screen. When choosing your screen name, there are certain special characters you can't use. However, LightSwitch will warn you if you attempt to use characters that are not allowed.

In Solution Explorer, it isn't possible to organize your screens into subfolders. All of your screens appear beneath the Screens folder, and if you've created a sizable number of screens in you project, it can soon become unmanageable. To make life easier, you can invent a naming convention to help you organize your screens in Solution Explorer. For example, you can prefix the names of similar screens with similar characters so they appear grouped together in the Screens folder.

The Screen Data drop-down allows you to choose the underlying query for your screen. The queries shown in this drop-down will vary depending on the screen template you've chosen. If you've chosen the details or new data screen templates, a list of entities will appear in the drop-down. If you've chosen one of the other templates, the drop-down will be populated with queries that return multiple records (this was described in Chapter 6).

If you choose the Details Screen template, you'll need to select a value from the screen data drop-down—it's a mandatory option. If you choose one of the other screen template types, you can choose not to base your screen on a data item.

Not choosing a data item allows you to create an empty screen. This is useful for creating a home screen (or welcome screen), and we'll show you how to create one later in this chapter.

If you've selected a data item with related records, you can choose to include the related data in your screen. Check boxes beneath the screen data drop-down allow you to select any related data items.

All of the screens you create in LightSwitch will share some common items. We'll show you what these common items are, and then move on to describe each of the screen template types in more detail.

Common Screen Elements

Figure 8-2 presents the common screen elements that are shown when you run your application. These include Save and Refresh buttons, which we'll now discuss in more detail.

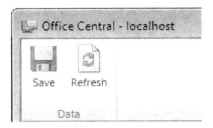

Figure 8-2. Common screen elements

Save Command Button

The Save button is found in the ribbon bar section of your application. Clicking it saves all the data in the underlying change set. The Save button saves any changes made to the properties on the screen, including any related records in any grids. LightSwitch performs the save inside a transaction. If you've made changes to multiple records and one record fails to save, LightSwitch won't commit the changes you've made to any other records.

If you create a screen using the Search Screen template, you'll find that the Save button still appears. Even though the default screen created with this template doesn't include any editable controls, the addition of a Save button can be useful. If you extend your Search screen to include some editable controls, the Save button will already be there for you.

If you don't want the Save button to appear, you can delete it by using the right-click context menu, as shown in Figure 8-3. If you change your mind afterward, you can always add it back in by using the Add drop-down box that you'll find beneath the Screen Command Bar node.

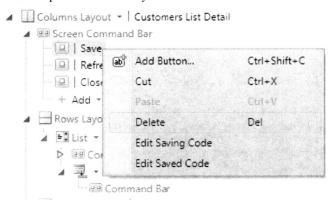

Figure 8-3. Deleting the Save Command button

Refresh Command Button

The Refresh button is also common to all screens. As the name suggests, it refreshes the screen data from the underlying data source and allows you to see the up-to date data.

If you have any unsaved changes and click the Refresh button, you'll be prompted to save your changes using the dialog shown in Figure 8-4.

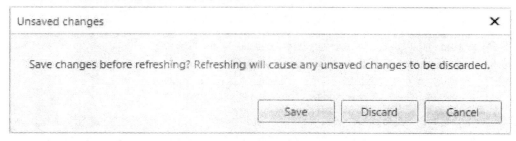

Figure 8-4. Refresh screen confirmation

This gives you the option to:

- *Save.* This will save your changes before attempting a refresh.

- *Discard.* This discards your changes before performing the refresh.

- *Cancel.* Nothing happens and you're returned to the screen.

If you've created a screen based on the New Data Screen template, it might not appear to make sense to have a Refresh button. Clicking the Refresh button effectively clears any values that have been entered and allows you to start over.

Because the word *refresh* might not seem appropriate in this scenario, you can change the button label by modifying the Display Name setting in the Properties pane (as shown in Figure 8-5). In this example, we've changed the display name from Refresh to Reset. The Refresh button will now be labeled Reset, rather than Refresh. You can change the labels of the other buttons in the same way.

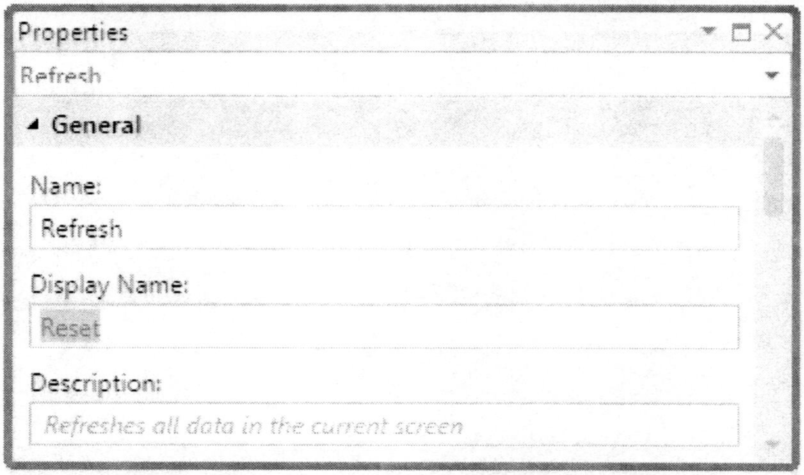

Figure 8-5. Changing the Refresh Command label

As with all other buttons that appear in the Screen Command Bar node, you can delete the Refresh button from your screen if you don't want it to appear.

■ **Note** The Refresh command actually destroys the current instance of the screen, creating a new one in its place. So any screen that has changes made to it will prompt for them to be saved before the "refresh" occurs.

Choosing a Screen Template Type

In this section we'll look at the five screen types you can choose from. You'll discover why you might want to use each particular type of template, or why each type might provide the basis for a more advanced screen you'd like to design.

Details Screen

Details screens are opened from other screens. For example, a details screen for an entity can be opened from the results of a search screen.

If you haven't created a details screen for an entity, LightSwitch automatically generates one for you. But the screen that LightSwitch autogenerates can't be modified in any way. So if you want to change any aspect of how it looks, or how it works, you'll need to create a custom details screen. Figure 8-6 illustrates a sample details screen.

Leung - Customer **X**	
Customer ID:	1
Firstname:	Tim
Surname:	Leung
Title:	Mr
Address:	722 High Street
City:	
Region:	
Postal Code:	

Figure 8-6. Details screen

When you add a new details screen, you'll be prompted to specify if the screen should be used as the *default* details screen. You can also specify any additional data you want to include, as shown in Figure 8-7.

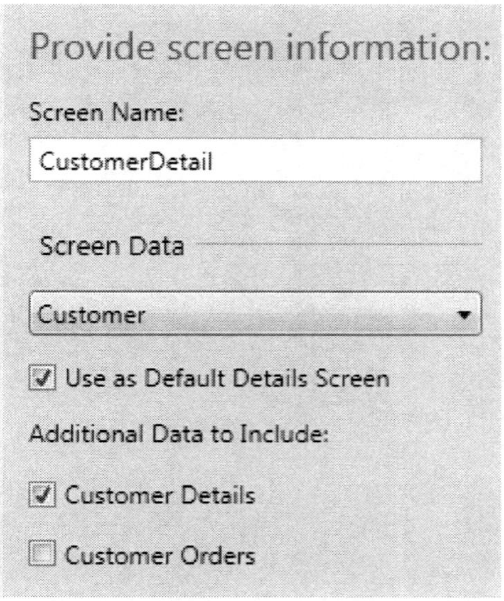

Provide screen information:

Screen Name:

CustomerDetail

Screen Data

Customer ▼

☑ Use as Default Details Screen

Additional Data to Include:

☑ Customer Details

☐ Customer Orders

Figure 8-7. Adding a details screen

So what exactly is a default screen? This is the screen that LightSwitch uses by default to display your data when you open a record from a summary control. You can only have one default screen per entity in your application. If you've already specified a default screen and create a new screen with the option Use as Default Details Screen check box selected, the new screen will be set as the default screen.

Details screens are based on a single entity, but you can also include related data by selecting the check boxes that appear in the Screen Data section.

You can uncheck the screen data check box that relates to the entity (in this example, the Customer Details check box). However, it doesn't seem to matter if this is checked or not. The entity's details are included anyway!

Editable Grid Screen

The Editable Grid Screen template creates a screen that allows users to view, add, and update multiple records at one time. Figure 8-8 shows an editable grid screen at runtime.

After creating an entity in the table designer, the Editable Grid Screen template is the fastest way to create a screen with full CRUD (Create, Read, Update, Delete) functionality.

The data contents are displayed using a data grid control. The command bar section of the grid includes buttons to add, edit, or delete records. Clicking the add or edit button opens an autogenerated modal dialog, rather than the default screen you've defined for your entity.

The command bar also includes a button that exports the results to Excel. The Export to Excel option is only available if your application is set up to run as a desktop application.

Figure 8-8. Editable grid screen

List Detail Screen

The List Detail screen displays a summary of your data in a list. When a user selects a record from the list, additional details about the selected item are shown in a **details section**. Figure 8-9 shows a List Detail screen in a running application.

Figure 8-9. Adding a List Detail screen

When you create a List Detail screen, LightSwitch adds a data list to the left-hand side of your screen. The data list also includes a search box, so that you can filter the items shown in the list.

An editable details panel is bound to the selected item in the list. This updates itself whenever the selected item changes.

New Data Screen

Another common thing you'll want to do in your application is to allow users to add new records. This is what the New Data Screen template was designed to do. It allows users to add new records, one at a time. Figure 8-10 shows a new data screen at runtime.

Notice how a * symbol appears in the tab title. This is LightSwitch's way of telling you that there are unsaved changes in the screen. All other screens in LightSwitch also show a * when there are unsaved changes.

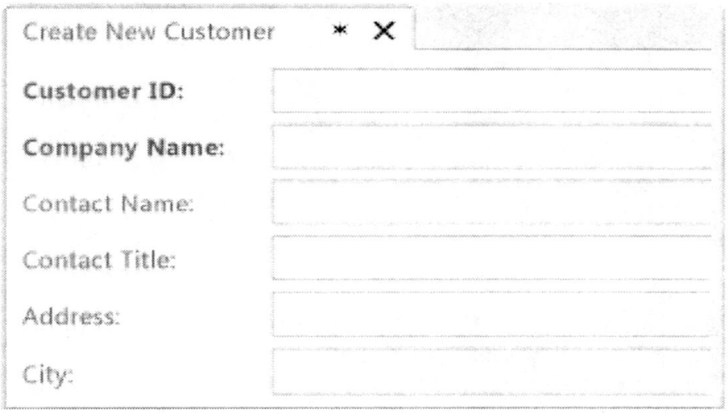

Figure 8-10. Adding a new data screen

When you save your record using the Save button, LightSwitch automatically closes the new data screen and opens the newly created record using the default details screen you've defined for your entity. If you don't have a default screen, LightSwitch displays the record using an autogenerated screen.

You might not want your application to behave like this. After saving a record, you might prefer to clear your screen and prepare it for the entry of another new record. You'll need to write some code to do this, and we'll show you how to do this later in this chapter.

■ **Note** In the current version of LightSwitch, you can't specify a default New Data screen, like you can for a default Details screen.

Search Screen

One of the most common things you'll want to do in any application is search for a specific entity or some group of entities. This is what the Search Screen template was designed to provide. Figure 8-11 shows a search screen at runtime.

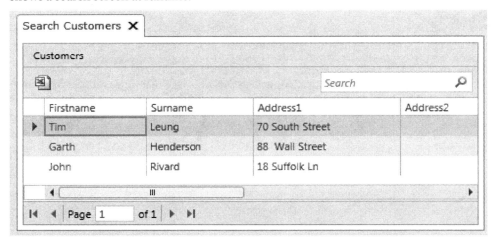

Figure 8-11. Search screen template

When you create a screen based on the Search Data template, LightSwitch creates a screen with a search text box. Users can enter a search string into this box, and the results are shown in a data grid. The data grid is paged, and, by default, 45 records are shown per page. The data grid also includes a clickable details link. Clicking the link opens the selected record using the default screen that's configured for your entity. If you prefer not to use the default screen, you can design your screen so that it uses a different details screen.

LightSwitch performs the equivalent of a "contains" search on the search criteria that's entered by the user. This means that the results will include any record that has a string property (where Is Searchable is set to true in the table designer) that *contains* the value you entered. Behind the scenes, LightSwitch uses the Search operator, which is exposed via the IDataServiceQueryable query property of your data source.

In the current version of LightSwitch, you can't change the way the search is performed to any other search method.

If you needed a search that returns records that have a string property that *begins with* the value that you entered, you'd have to turn off the built-in searching capabilities and create a custom search screen instead.

■ **Note** Only an entity's string properties will be included in the search. Numeric properties or navigation properties (even if you're displaying a string from it) are not included in the search. To perform a more advanced search, you'll need to create a search screen that uses a custom query.

Understanding the Screen Designer

After adding your screen, you can use the screen designer to customize your screen further. It's likely that you'll spend much of your time in the screen designer, so it's important to get to know this well.

Within the screen designer, there are three main parts you need to become familiar with (see Figure 8-12). These are:

- Screen Members list,
- Screen Designer Command bar,
- Screen Content Tree.

Screen designer command bar

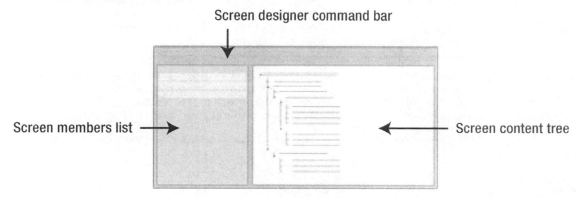

Screen members list ──▶   ◀── Screen content tree

Figure 8-12. Parts of the screen designer

We'll now describe each of these three parts in more detail and explain what each part does.

Screen Designer Command Bar

The Screen Designer Command bar is located at the top of the screen designer and has six buttons, some of which you'll find yourself using quite often as you design screens. These are shown in Figure 8-13.

The purpose of each button is explained in Table 8-2.

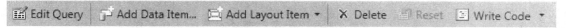

Figure 8-13. Screen Designer Command bar

Table 8-2. Screen Designer Command Bar Options

Button Name	Description
Edit Query	This opens the query editor and allows you to edit the underlying query.
Add Data Item	Clicking this button opens the Add Data Item dialog.

Button Name	Description
Add Layout Item	Clicking this button opens a drop-down box that shows a list of layout items. Selecting an item adds a layout item as a child of the currently selected node in the content tree. The options shown here are identical to those that are found when you use the add option in the content tree.
Delete Button	This deletes the control that's currently selected in the Screen Content Tree. You'll be prompted for a confirmation before LightSwitch deletes the selected object.
Reset Button	This resets all controls back to their default type and adds missing controls.
Write Code	This allows you to write screen code. We'll describe this further in the "Writing Screen Code" section.

The Reset button is a useful feature. Let's say you've created a screen. Later on, you add several extra properties to your table using the table designer. When you return to the screen designer, you can use the Reset button to reset the controls inside a container object back to their default state. This automatically adds the new properties you've added to your table and can save you from having to add each property one by one onto your screen.

The Edit Query and Add Data Item buttons are worth a special mention too. We'll now explain these in a bit more detail.

Edit Query Button

The Edit Query button opens the query editor and allows you to edit the underlying screen query. This button is only enabled on screens that are based on collections of data, such as the Editable Grid Screen or Search Screen template.

Editing the screen query allows you to apply additional filtering and sorting to your screen. Let's imagine you want to set up an editable grid screen that only shows customers from the United States. Editing the screen query allows you to do this.

For more details, you can refer to Chapter 6. This showed you how screen queries work and described how to use the query designer.

Instead of extending the query, you could even change the underlying query the screen uses. You'll find the option to do this in the Properties pane of your query.

Add Data Item Button

The Add Data Item button opens a dialog that allows you to add additional data items to your screen (shown in Figure 8-14).

The screen member types you can add are:

- Method,
- Local property,
- Query.

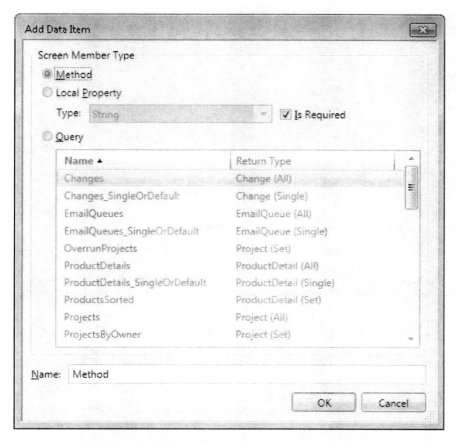

Figure 8-14. Add Data Item dialog

We'll now describe each of these screen member types in more detail.

Method

Methods allow you to add code to the screen, either for attaching to a button or for writing code that'll be used by other methods.

A common reason for adding a method is to create a button. After you add a method, it'll appear in the Screen Members list in the left-hand side of the screen designer. From there, you can create a button by dragging the method onto the Screen Content Tree (Figure 8-15).

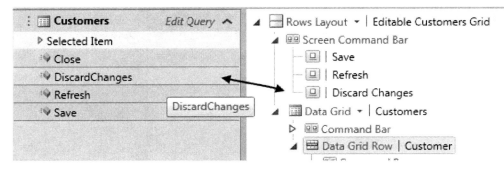

Figure 8-15. Adding a button onto the Screen Content Tree

This isn't the only way to add a button onto a screen however. You can also use the Add option that you'll find beneath the screen command bar nodes to add new methods.

Local Property

Local properties are a very important part of screen design. Imagine how difficult it would be to write a VB or C# program without using variables. Local properties are just as important to screen design, as variables are to writing code.

Local properties allow you to add entities that are independent of the underlying screen data. You can store data in local properties and use the properties during any intermediary processing you might want to carry out.

When you create a local property, you'll need to use the type drop-down box to specify a type. This drop-down contains all of the standard LightSwitch data types, in addition to the entities you've added to your application. Figure 8-16 shows the contents of the type drop-down. Notice how some of our user-defined entities (such as Change and EmailQueue) appear in the list.

Local properties are important because UI controls in LightSwitch can only be bound to entities or properties. Let's imagine you want to show a text box on your screen. You can't just declare a variable in C#/VB and set the text box value to the value of your variable. The text box must be data bound to a property or entity. This is why local properties are so important.

When you add a property, you'll also have the option to make it a required property. You would do this by checking the Is Required check box (also shown in Figure 8-16). Making a property required means that the user won't be able to save the screen unless the property contains a value. If the user attempts to save a screen with a required property that hasn't been set, LightSwitch shows a validation error to the user and prevents the save from happening.

Later in this chapter, we'll show you how to display a piece of static text (which isn't bound to a database record) on your screen. This illustrates a perfect example of where you might want to use a local property.

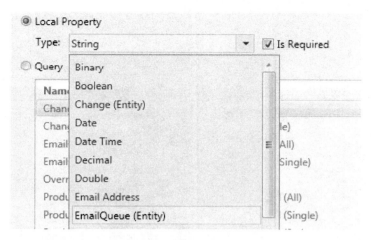

Figure 8-16. Screen property types

Query

The last option in the Add Data Item dialog allows you to add a query. Queries are important because they provide a data source for the controls you'll use on your screen.

After choosing the query radio button, you'll need to select a query from the query list that's shown. This list includes all of the default Single and All queries that are autogenerated by LightSwitch, as well as any user-defined queries you've created.

Here's an example of where you might want to add a query to your screen. Let's imagine you've created a new data screen for a customer entity. The customer entity includes a country of residence property, which stores where the customer lives. In the table structure of the customer table, country of residence is defined as a navigation property to the Country table.

The default screen that's created by LightSwitch displays the country of residence property as an AutoCompleteBox. By default, the AutoCompleteBox shows all of the countries in the country table. If you want to restrict the countries shown in the AutoCompleteBox to only those in the EMEA (Europe, Middle East, and Asia) region, you'd need to add a query that returns those countries in that region. You would then set the data source of your AutoCompleteBox to the query you've added to your screen using the Add Data Item dialog.

Screen Members List (Left-Hand Pane)

The Screen Members list is the screen designer section that appears down the left-hand side. For a long time, this panel was referred to by many people as the *View Model* pane. Even some in the LightSwitch team have trouble coming up with a definitive name they can all agree on. Consequently, it often just gets referred to as "that pane on the left of the screen designer."

Depending on the screen template you've chosen, it can contain the following elements, as shown in Figure 8-17:

- Screen query and selected item,

- Related collections,

- Screen properties,
- Query parameters,
- Methods.

Editable Grid Screen	New Data Screens	Details Screen
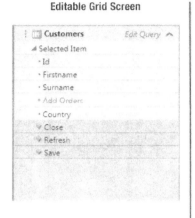	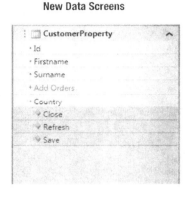	

Figure 8-17. Screen Members list

If you've chosen to create a screen based on a collection of data, the screen query appears as the first item in the Screen Members list. Because this represents a collection of data, this object includes a child object called *Selected Item*. This refers to the currently selected record in the collection of data.

If you create a screen using the new data screen template, LightSwitch creates a property that represents a single instance of your entity (rather than the screen query that we've just described). LightSwitch appends the word property after the object. So in this example, the data item has been named CustomerProperty.

If you create a screen using the Details Screen template, LightSwitch creates an object that represents a single entity. In Figure 8-17, this object is called Customer and represents a single customer. At first glance, the Customer object looks similar to the CustomerProperty object that was added using the new data screen template.

However, these two objects are not the same. The Customer object is a query that returns a single entity. If you look at the Properties pane, you'll find query-related attributes. You won't find these when you view the properties of the CustomerProperty object in a new data entry screen. This distinction is important when you begin referring to these objects in code.

We'll now move on to describe some of the other items you'll find in the Screen Member list in more detail.

Screen Query (Visual Collections)

When you create a screen based on a collection of data (e.g., using the editable grid screen template), the screen query represents the screen's data source. Initially this is what you specified in the Screen Data section of the Add Screen wizard.

The Screen Query item is an object of type VisualCollection<T>. This object contains the visible records that are bound to a control such as a data grid.

You'll find some *visual*-related settings when you view the Properties pane for a screen query (shown in Figure 8-18). These settings are reflected in the data grids and lists that are bound to the query, and it's useful to remember what they are. Otherwise, you could spend considerable time hunting around in the properties pane of a data grid trying to find a setting that actually belongs to the query (switching off pagination, for example).

Table 8-3 describes the purpose of the properties you'll find here.

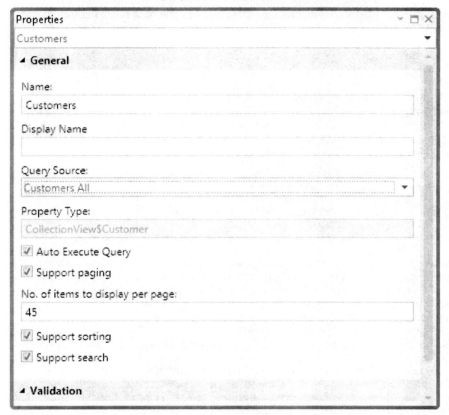

Figure 8-18. Screen query properties

Table 8-3. *Screen Query Properties*

Name	Notes
Query Source	Can be changed to any query that returns the same entity set as the current query.
Property Type	This shows the entity type that the visual collection contains. This setting can't be changed.

241

Name	Notes
Support Paging	When set to true, paging controls are shown in the footer of any data grids or list controls bound to the query. The paging control shows the page number, first, previous, next, and last buttons.
Number of items to display per page	This control is only shown when Support Paging is set to true. By default, this is set to 45.
Support Sorting	When set to true, data grids bound to the query can be sorted by clicking the header.
Support Search	When set to true, a search box is shown in the header of the data grid or list control.
Auto Execute Query	This indicates whether the query is run when the screen is opened.

If you want to change the data source of your visual collection, you can do so by using the Query Source drop-down box. LightSwitch only allows you to change to another query based on the same entity set, and the query drop-down is filtered as such.

The Auto Execute Query property indicates whether or not the query runs when the screen is first opened. In most cases, you'd leave this set to true. In general, you'd set this to false if you want to populate the visual collection manually in code (using the visual collection's Refresh method, for example).

To help improve performance, LightSwitch provides a paging mechanism that allows the client to only download a set number of records at a time. You would use the Support Paging check box to turn this option on or off. By default, the number of records downloaded is limited to 45. You can of course change this number to whatever suits you or you could disable the paging mechanism altogether if you know for certain you only have a reasonable number of records that will be returned.

You might also want to turn off paging if you have a desktop application and you have a fast local network connection. You wouldn't want to disable paging if your application was a web application, where the data were being retrieved over the Internet.

If support sorting is set to true, users can sort data grids that are bound to the query by clicking the column header. In desktop applications, LightSwitch remembers the selected sort sequence between sessions. If a user exits out of the application, starts up the application again, and reopens the same screen, the previous sort order is retained. If you've applied a sort condition on the underlying query, this makes it impossible for a user to return to the sort order that's defined in your query after clicking a column header. Switching off sorting is a way to avoid this problem. The "Sorting Grids" section in Chapter 6 describes this behavior in more detail.

Selected Item

When you're working with collections of data, LightSwitch keeps track of the currently selected data item. Let's say you've bound a data grid to your screen query. When a user selects a row in the data grid, LightSwitch sets the SelectedItem object to the record that's been selected by the user.

At design time, the SelectedItem is exposed as an entity property. This allows you to use or to bind the properties of the selected item to other UI controls.

Screens based on the List and Details Screen template provide a perfect illustration of how the Selected Item property is used on a screen.

Let's imagine that you've created a customer screen. You can use a list to display just the customer surname. When the user selects a customer, you can use the selected item object to display the address details in another part of your screen.

Related Collections

Let's imagine you've created an editable grid screen based on a collection of customers and you now want some way to display the orders that are related to the selected customer. If you've defined related items through the table designer, you can show these on your screen by adding related collections.

You'd do this by clicking a link that LightSwitch automatically generates for you. LightSwitch generates a link for all related child tables. Figure 8-19 shows how an Add Order link appears inside the customer collection. Clicking this link adds the order collection onto your screen (as a visual collection). You can then add the related orders onto your screen, and LightSwitch would render the collection as a data grid by default.

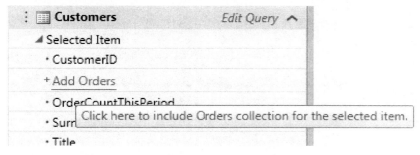

Figure 8-19. Adding related collections

Setting Query Parameters

If your underlying query expects parameters, you'll need some way to set these parameter values. We'll now show you a technique you'll need to use whenever you need to create any sort of custom search screen or whenever you need to apply any type of filtering on a screen. Filtering the items shown in an `AutoCompleteBox` is an example.

In this example, we'll create a screen that allows the user to filter order records by month and year. After creating a parameterized query, we've created an editable grid screen based on this query.

The query parameters are shown inside a Query Parameters group within your query. When you add a screen that's based on a parameterized query, LightSwitch makes life really easy for you. It automatically creates local screen properties to store your parameter values. It also adds UI controls onto your screen to allow your user to set the parameter values.

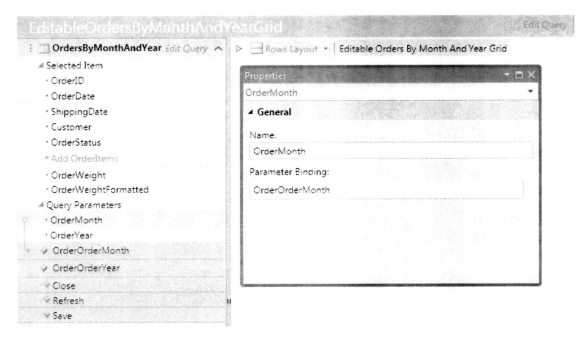

Figure 8-20. *Changing the parameter bindings*

The query we've created includes two parameters called OrderMonth and OrderYear. The OrderMonth query parameter is bound to a local screen property called OrderOrderMonth. Likewise, the OrderYear query parameter is bound to a local screen property called OrderOrderYear.

The OrderOrderMonth and OrderOrderYear screen properties are automatically created by LightSwitch. LightSwitch also renders these properties as text boxes on your screen.

The bindings themselves are specified in the properties pane of the query parameter. When you select a query parameter in the Screen Member list, LightSwitch uses an arrow to show you the property that's bound to the query parameter.

If you need to change a parameter binding, you can use the Parameter Binding text box to make this change (Figure 8-20). LightSwitch provides IntelliSense in the Parameter Binding text box, so you don't need to worry about knowing how to construct the correct syntax.

Screen Content Tree (Middle Pane)

We'll now discuss the final part of the screen designer—the Screen Content Tree. This represents the central part of the screen designer that allows you to design the layout of your screen and add or remove UI controls.

Unlike the WYSIWYG designers you may have seen in other development applications (such as Microsoft Access or Windows Forms), the screen designer shows the UI elements as a series of nodes. This is illustrated in Figure 8-21.

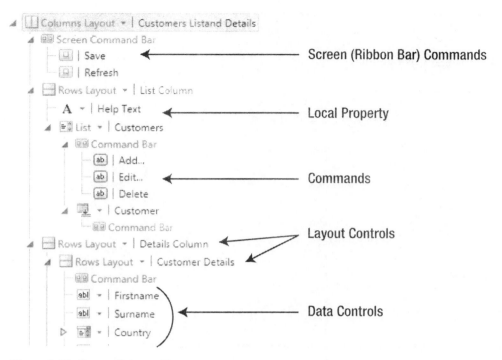

Figure 8-21. Screen Content Tree

Figure 8-21 shows a how a typical screen looks like within the content tree of the screen designer.
In general, the nodes you'll find will be one of two types:

- *Layout controls.* These allow you to layout your screen.

- *Data controls.* These are used to view or edit your data.

The columns layout and rows layout controls shown are examples of layout controls. The text box control is an example of a data control.

You can add controls by selecting a node and using the Add drop-down box. Alternatively, you can drag items from the Screen Member List onto the Screen Content Tree.

Beneath the root node, you'll find a Screen Command Bar node. This node contains the buttons that are shown in the ribbon bar of your application at runtime. By default, the Save and Refresh commands are shown here.

We'll now describe the root node, and then move on to describe the layout and data controls that you can use.

Root Node

The root node is the very first node that appears in the Screen Content Tree, and it allows you to set the main screen layout properties. When you select the root node and view the properties, you'll find a couple of useful properties you can set (Figure 8-22).

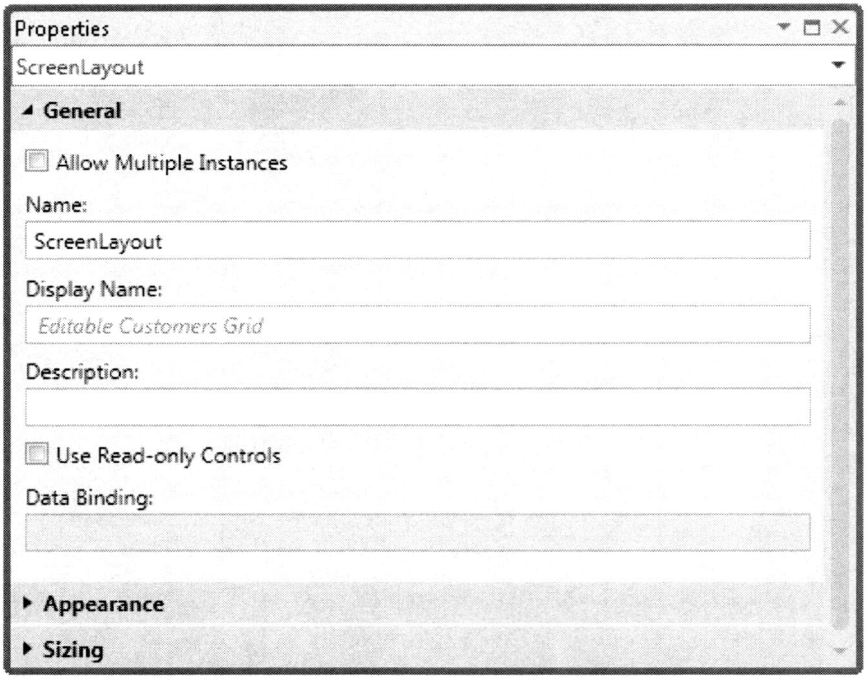

Figure 8-22. Screen Content Tree

The Display Name text box allows you to change the display name of your screen. This piece of text is shown in the screen's tab title and also in the screen navigation pane.

The Allow Multiple Instance check box specifies whether you want to allow the user to open multiple instances of your screen. If this is set to false, the user can only open a single instance of your screen. If your user attempts to open more than one instance, LightSwitch displays the screen that's already open.

Layout Controls

The layout container types that you can use fall into two different categories. These are:

- Presentational containers,
- Data item containers.

Presentational containers are used to layout your screen. You'd use presentation containers to position the data controls (e.g., text boxes, labels, check boxes) you want to show on your screen. These data controls are added as child items to a presentational container. Presentational containers can also be nested inside one another—you can create as many levels of nesting as you want.

The presentational containers you can use are shown in Table 8-4. Figure 8-23 illustrates how these layouts appear on screen.

Table 8-4. Presentational Containers

Name	Description
Rows Layout	This container displays child items in rows, one on top of another. Each item is added into a row in the order shown in the screen designer.
Columns Layout	This container displays child items in columns, spanning from left to right. Each item is added into its own column in the order shown in the screen designer.
Table Layout	This container displays child items inside a table-like structure, with cells organized into rows and columns.
Tabs Layout	This container creates a tabbed view. Each child item that you add to a Tabs Layout node is shown as a tab.

Rows Layout

Columns Layout

Tabs Layout

Table Layout

Figure 8-23. Presentational containers

Data item containers are used to display data. They contain placeholders you can bind to data items on your screen. Unlike presentational containers, data item containers cannot be nested. Table 8-5 shows the data item containers you can use.

Table 8-5. Data Item Containers

Name	Description
Address Editor	This container is used to render an address. The placeholders that you can set are: (STREET LINE 1), (STREET LINE 2), (CITY), (STATE),(ZIP CODE), and (COUNTRY).
Address Viewer	This is a read-only version of the address editor and includes the same placeholders.
Modal Window	This adds a button to the screen that opens a modal window when clicked.
Picture and Text	This container is divided into two vertical panels. The left-hand panel contains a picture placeholder. The right-hand panel contains the placeholders (TITLE), (SUBTITLE), and (DESCRIPTION). The picture placeholder needs to be bound to a data item of data-type picture. The remaining data items are bound to string data items.
Text and Picture	This container is almost similar to the Picture and Text container. It contains the same data items. However, the descriptive text is shown in the left-hand panel, and the picture is displayed in the right-hand panel.

Figure 8-24 shows how some of these data item containers appear at design time and runtime.

Address Editor

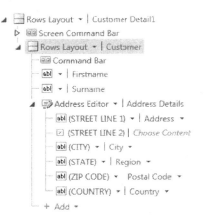

Modal Window

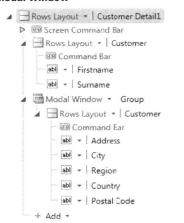

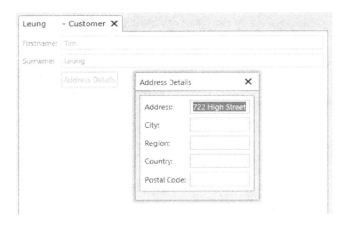

Picture and Text

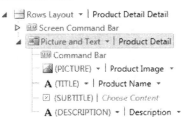

Figure 8-24. Data item containers

Data Controls

Data controls are the UI elements that allow users to view or edit your data. LightSwitch includes a host of controls you can use. We've split the available controls into three main categories:

- Editable controls,
- Read-only controls,
- Data controls.

If you can't find a control here that suits your needs, you can use custom controls. These are explained in Chapter 9.

Editable Controls

Table 8-6 shows the controls you can use to edit data. In many cases, you'll use the Text Box control. This is the default control that's used for editing string data. You can only use a control if it's supported by the underlying data type. For example, you can't use a check box to render string data.

Table 8-6. Editable Controls

Name	Description	Supported Data Types
Text Box	You can edit the data by typing into this control.	All LightSwitch data types
Check Box	Allows you to edit Boolean values.	Boolean
Date Picker	A control that can be used to type or select a date from a calendar view.	Date
Date Time Picker	Allows editing a date and time value using a calendar view and a time drop-down list.	Date, Date Time
Email Address Editor	Allows editing of an email address. Includes validation to ensure that only valid email addresses can be entered.	Email
Image Editor	Displays an image and allows you to upload an image using a file browser dialog.	Image
Phone Number Editor	Allows you to enter a phone number using predefined formats.	Phone Number
Money Editor	Allows editing a monetary value.	Money

Figure 8-25 shows the appearance of some of these editable controls. The Image Editor control allows you to upload an image. Clicking the control displays a Load Image button that opens a file browser dialog. This allows you to upload an image.

Figure 8-25. *Editable controls*

The Date Picker control displays a pop-up calendar that allows users to select a date.

The Email and Money controls will validate the data that is entered by users.

When users click the Phone Number control, a drop-down panel is displayed. This allows users to enter the parts that make up a phone number. The valid formats you want to allow are specified in the table designer.

Enabling Multiline Text Using the Text Box Control

By default, the Text Box control is shown as a single line text box. A common requirement is the ability to enter multiline text.

To allow multiline text, and to allow the entry of line breaks in your text, set the lines property that you'll find in the Properties pane to a value greater than one (as shown in Figure 8-26).

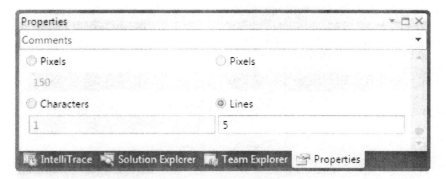

Figure 8-26. Enabling multiline text to be entered

Read-Only Controls

Table 8-7 shows the Read-Only controls you can use to allow users to view data. The Label control is the simplest control for displaying read-only data.

Some developers often overlook these controls when needing to make parts of their screen read-only. All of these controls provide a quick and simple way to make your data items read-only.

Table 8-7. Read-Only Controls

Name	Description	Supported Data Types
Label	This displays a read-only copy of the data value.	All LightSwitch data types
Date Viewer	Displays a date value.	Date
Date Time Viewer	Displays a date time value.	Date, Date Time
Email Address Viewer	Displays an email address.	Email
Image Viewer	Displays an image.	Image
Phone Number Viewer	Displays a phone number	Phone Number
Money Viewer	Displays a monetary value.	Money

In Table 8-7, notice how there isn't a read-only check box. If you want to display a read-only check box, you'll need to write some code to do this. We'll explain how to do this later in this chapter.

Changing Label Styles

In general, you can't change the fonts that are used by LightSwitch controls. This is because the font settings are designed to be configured using the theme you've defined for your application. The benefit is that it allows you to easily maintain a consistent look and feel throughout all screens in your application.

A nice feature about the Label control is that you can set the font style to one of six predefined styles. The font style is set in the Property pane for your label.

Figure 8-27 shows the drop-down that you can use to select the font style at design time. This figure also shows the appearance of these font styles at runtime.

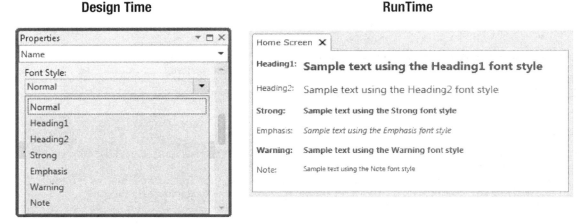

Figure 8-27. The available font label styles

Data Controls

The Editable and Read-Only controls are used to render scalar values. In other words, these controls can only display a single value (such as a surname).

LightSwitch includes *Details* controls to show related entities. These controls allow you to link a record with some other related data. If you created a customer screen, for example, you could use a Detail control to allow the user to select a country of residence.

The Detail controls you can use are described in Table 8-8. The AutoCompleteBox and Modal Window Picker controls are shown in Figure 8-28.

Table 8-8. Detail Controls

Name	Description
Modal Window Picker	This opens a modal window that you can use to find your related record
AutoCompleteBox	This control is similar to ComboBox control, in that it displays drop-down values. However, it also allows you to type into the control and filters the items shown when you type into it.
Summary	This control displays a summary of an entity and is shown in data grids and AutoComplete boxes.

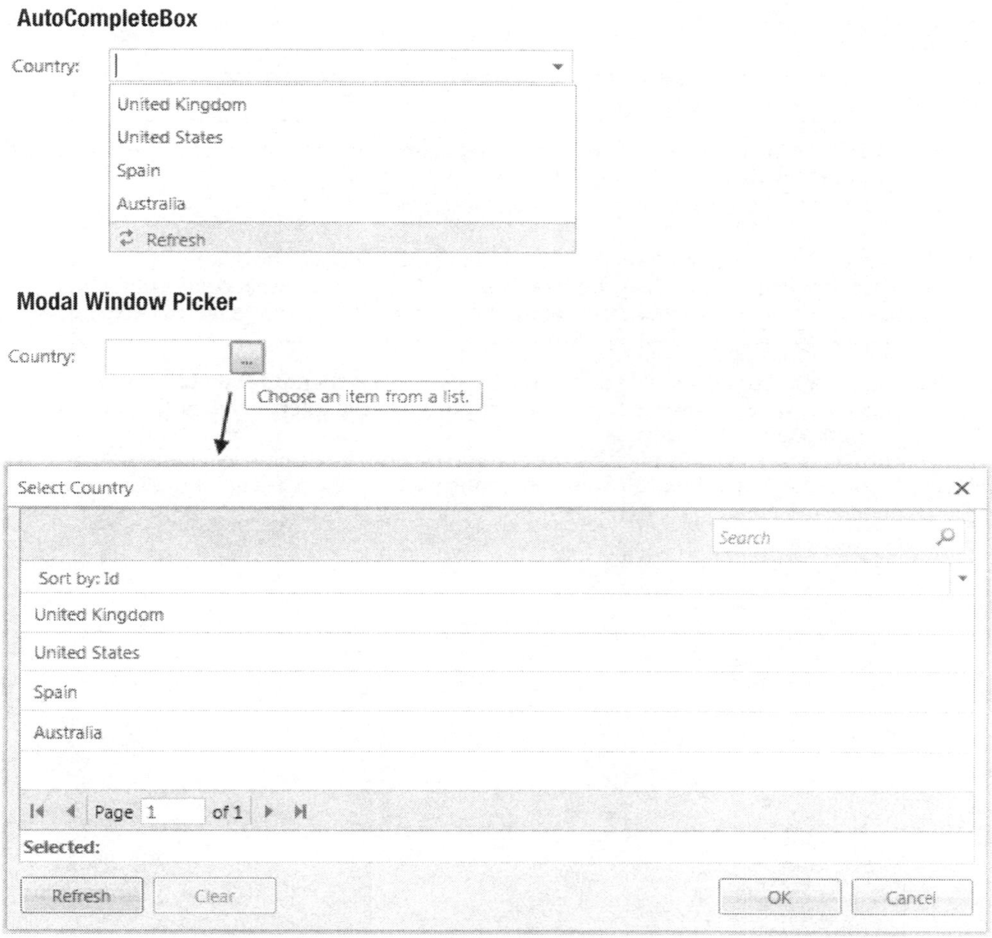

AutoCompleteBox

Country:

United Kingdom

United States

Spain

Australia

↻ Refresh

Modal Window Picker

Country:

Choose an item from a list.

Select Country   ×

                                                                    Search   🔎

Sort by: Id   ▾

United Kingdom

United States

Spain

Australia

⏮ ◀ Page 1   of 1 ▶ ⏭

Selected:

Refresh   Clear   OK   Cancel

Figure 8-28. AutoCompleteBox and Modal Window Picker controls

The AutoCompleteBox is a pretty complex control. We've devoted a section later in this chapter to describe some of the more advanced usage scenarios.

Finally, LightSwitch provides Collection controls that allow you to display related collections (Table 8-9). On a customer screen, for example, you'd use a Collection control to display the related orders for a customer.

Table 8-9. Collection Controls

Name	Description
Data Grid	The Data Grid control displays data in a grid. The properties are grouped into columns, and the user can sort the data by clicking the column headers (if sorting is enabled at the query level). Users can edit the data shown in the grid.
Data List	The Data List control displays a read-only list of data. By default, the summary control is used to display each entity in the list. If you want to display additional properties, you can change the summary control to a rows layout and add additional child data controls layout.

The main difference between the Data Grid and Data List controls is that the Data List control is used to display read-only data. If paging and searching is supported at the query level, both controls display a search text box and pagination controls.

The Data Grid control can be sorted by clicking the column header. The items in a data list are sorted by using a drop-down box in the header. These two controls are shown in Figure 8-29.

Data List Control

Data Grid Control

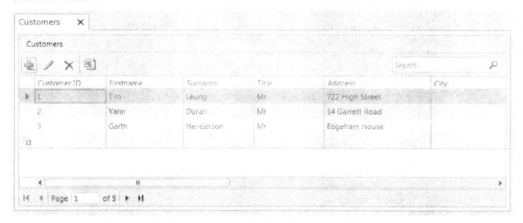

Figure 8-29. Collection controls

Data Grid Control

LightSwitch adds a Data Grid control onto any screens you create using the editable grid or search templates. In this section, we'll describe how the Data Grid control works in more detail.

You can add or remove the columns shown on your data grid by adding or deleting the child nodes that are shown beneath the Data Grid row.

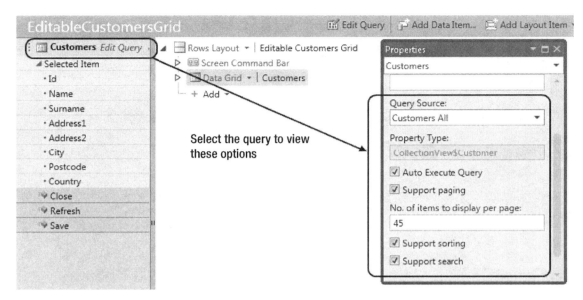

Figure 8-30. Data Grid paging, sorting, and searching options

As described earlier, the paging, sorting, and search options are attributes of the screen query. So to modify any of these settings, you'll need to refer to the Property pane that relates to the query, rather than the Property pane that relates to the Data Grid control (Figure 8-30).

Table 8-10 describes where you'll find the various options that relate to the data grid.

Table 8-10. Data Grid Properties

Element	Property
Screen Query	Auto Execute Query Support Paging Items Per Page Support Sorting Support Search
Data Grid	Disable Export to Excel Show Add New Row Is Visible
Data Grid Row	Use Read-Only Controls Is Visible

Data Grid Properties

There are a couple of useful properties you can set at the data grid level (Figure 8-31).

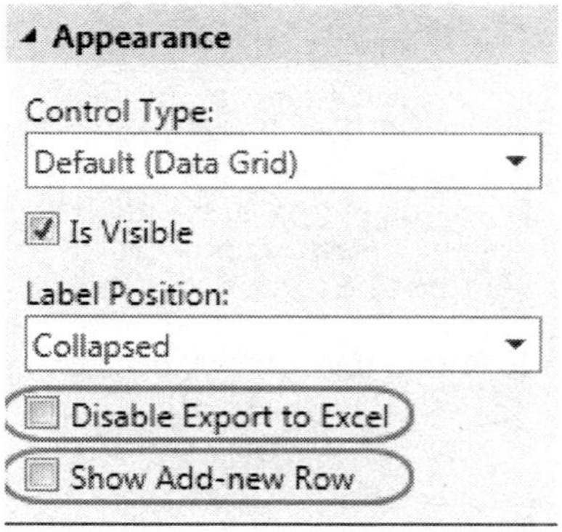

Figure 8-31. Data Grid properties

The first option disables Export to Excel. Checking this check box hides the Excel button, which is shown to the user on the toolbar of the data grid in a desktop application.

The second option is the Show Add-new Row check box. This refers to a feature that allows users to enter new records by typing directly into the data grid. Beneath any existing records that are shown, LightSwitch adds an empty row that acts as a new record placeholder. Users can type into this empty row to begin the entry of a new record (Figure 8-32).

Unchecking this check box disables this option. However, unchecking this option won't disable the option to add new records altogether. Users can still add records by clicking the Add button that appears in the command bar section of the data grid. We'll show you how to disable this button in the "Grid Commands" section that follows.

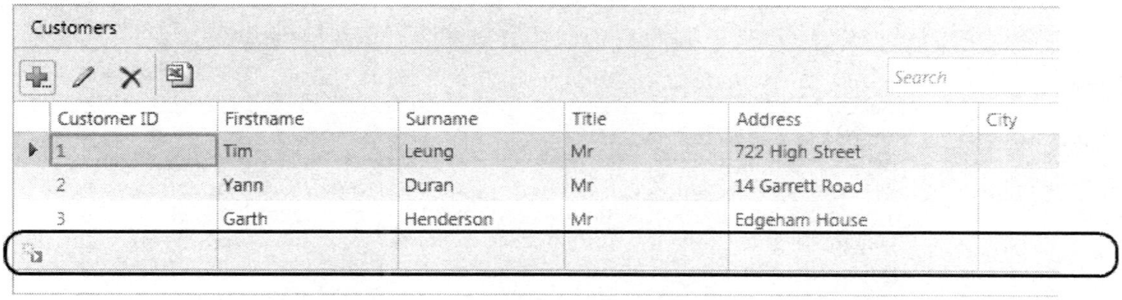

Figure 8-32. Show Add-new Row feature

■ **Note** When using an attached SQL Server data source, columns that use the text data type cannot be sorted. Use the varchar or nvarchar data types if you want users to be able to sort their data using the column headers.

Grid Commands

At runtime, the Data Grid Command bar is shown as a toolbar that sits above the contents of the data grid.

A point to remember is that the Data Grid Command bar is different from the Screen Command bar. Any item you add to the Screen Command bar is shown in the ribbon bar section of your application.

LightSwitch includes built-in commands that allow users to add, delete, or update records. You might want to disable some of these buttons or you might want to add a button that carries out some other custom action you want to perform on the selected row.

If you want to add a button to the command bar section, use the Add button that appears beneath the Command Bar node, as shown in Figure 8-33.

Figure 8-33. Data grid in command bar area

Table 8-11 describes the command types that are shown when you click this button.

Table 8-11. Commands You Can Add to a Data Grid (Actions)

Action	Purpose of Button
New Button	Adds a button that allows you to write some code to perform a custom task. Note that when using the search data screen template, the row can't be edited unless "Use Read-only Controls" is unchecked or some of the row's controls are manually changed to an editable control (e.g., TextBox).
AddNew	When the user clicks this button, it adds a new row to the grid.
AddAndEditNew	When the user clicks this button, it adds a new row to the grid and displays the new record in a modal window.
EditSelected	When the user clicks this button, it displays a modal window that allows the selected row to be edited.
DeleteSelected	When the user clicks this button, it marks the row as "deleted" and displays a red X icon to the left of the row.

Action	Purpose of Button
Refresh Button	This is used to refresh the data shown in the grid.

At runtime, clicking the Add or Edit button opens an autogenerated window (Figure 8-34) that allows the user to edit the data. There isn't any way for you to modify the appearance of this autogenerated form. However, a work around is to create your own custom modal window. We'll show you how to use this technique later in this chapter.

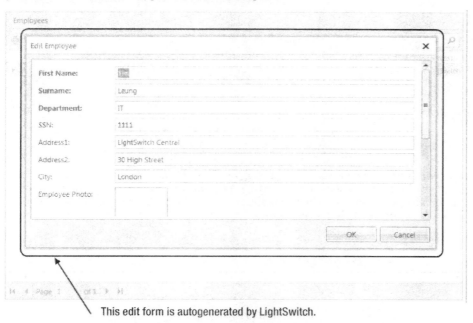

This edit form is autogenerated by LightSwitch.

Figure 8-34. Autogenerated screens

■ **Note** As with any grid, any data that are added, edited, or deleted are not saved to the database until the Save button is clicked. There's no way to "undo" a change to a single row via the grid, you'd have to do it by writing some code.

Setting Clickable Links

You can turn any label that's displayed in a data grid row into a clickable link. This allows the user to click the label and open the selected record in a details screen. You can even select the details screen you want to use to open your record.

If you've created a screen based on the Search Data Screen template, the first column shown will be set to show as a link. If you don't like this clickable link behavior, you can easily turn it off.

To customize the link behavior of a label, use the Show as Link and Target Screen drop-down, as shown in Figure 8-35.

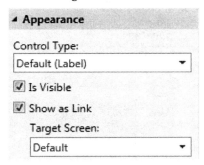

Figure 8-35. Setting a clickable link

Appearance Settings

The controls you add to your screen can be positioned using the controls you'll find in the sizing section of the Properties pane. Figure 8-36 shows the options that are available to you. Depending on the control you choose, additional sizing options may also be available. For example, you'll find an Is Resizable options in some of the layout controls. This allows your user to resize the contents using a splitter control.

Table 8-12 summarizes the sizing options you'll find for most controls.

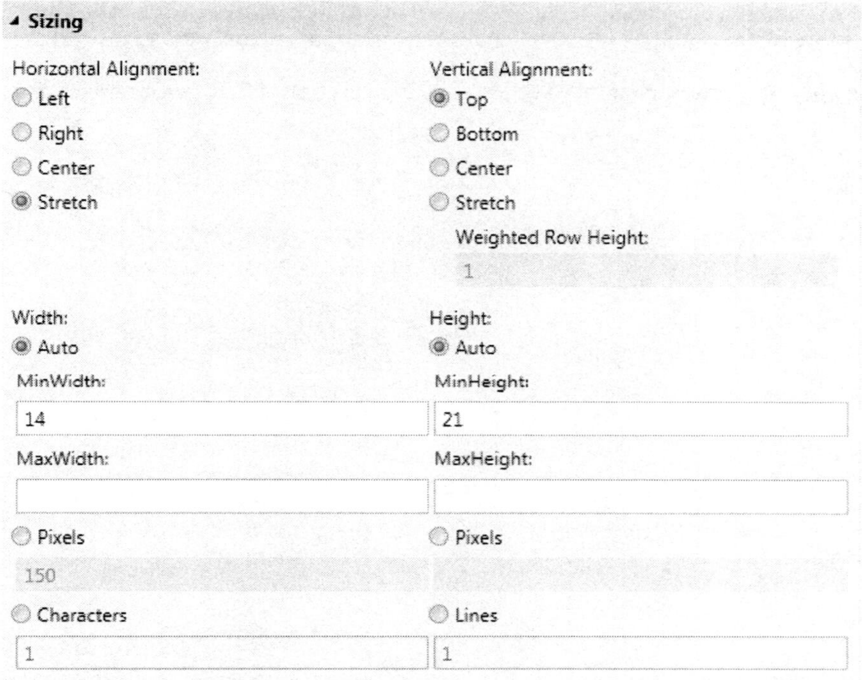

Figure 8-36. Sizing options

Table 8-12. Sizing Options

Size Setting	Description
Horizontal Alignment	This specifies the position of the control within the horizontal space that is allocated for the control. When alignment is set to stretch, *width* settings are ignored. However, you can still specify a maximum and minimum size.
Vertical Alignment	This specifies the position of the control within the vertical space that is allocated for the control. When alignment is set to stretch, *height* settings are ignored. However, you can still specify a maximum and minimum size.
Width	This specifies the width of the control in pixels or the number of characters. LightSwitch uses an optimal width if you choose the auto option. You can still provide a maximum and minimum size if you choose auto.
Height	This specifies the height of the control in pixels or the number of characters. LightSwitch uses an optimal height if you choose the auto option. You can still provide a maximum and minimum size if you choose auto.

For each data control you add to your screen, LightSwitch automatically displays a label. If you add a surname text box to your screen, for example, LightSwitch displays a surname label next to the text box.

Figure 8-37 shows the options in the appearance section for a typical control (in this example, a text box).

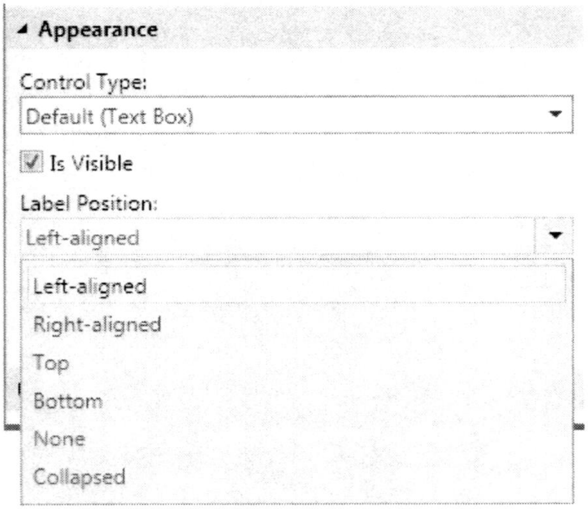

Figure 8-37. Label position dialog

Depending on the control you choose, additional appearance options may also be available.

If you view the appearance options for a rows layout control, for example, you can enable horizontal and vertical scrollbars and set a maximum label width. If you configure a label position (e.g., right-aligned or left-aligned), all child controls will inherit this setting. However, you can override this setting at the child level.

Table 8-13 describes the label positions you can use.

Table 8-13. Label Positioning Options

Label Position	Description
Left-aligned	The label appears to the left of the control.
Right-aligned	The label appears to the right of the control.
Top	The label appears above the control.
Bottom	The label appears below the control.
None	No label appears for the selected data field.
Collapsed	The label appears as collapsed.

If you want to hide a label, the options you can choose from are none or **collapsed**. If you set the label to none, the label still takes up space on the screen (even though it's not shown). If you choose the collapsed option, the label doesn't take up any space. This is illustrated in Figure 8-38.

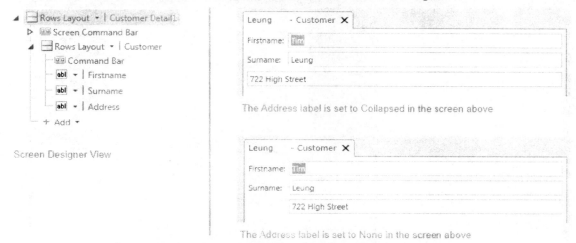

Figure 8-38. The difference between collapsed and none options

Designing Screens at Runtime

Due to the hierarchical manner that items are shown in the screen designer, you might find it difficult to visualize how your screen will appear at runtime.

The runtime designer is a really useful feature of LightSwitch. It allows you to design your screens during debug time. It's particularly useful for setting the sizing and appearance of controls because it allows you to see immediately the changes you're making.

To use the runtime designer, start up your application (press F5) and click the Design Screen button in the upper right-hand side of your application. This opens the runtime designer, as shown in Figure 8-39.

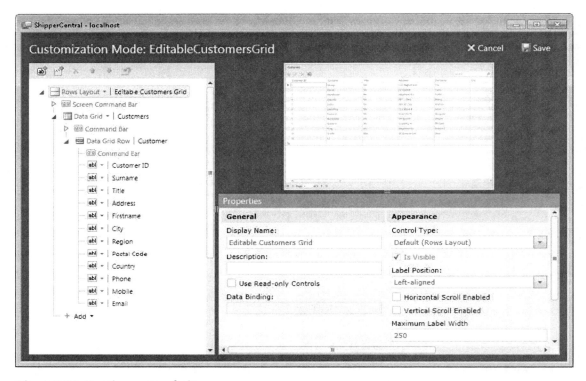

Figure 8-39. Runtime screen designer

The runtime designer lets you change the settings of the controls that are shown on your screen. You can even add and delete layout items. When you're happy with your changes, click the Save button. The changes you've made will be reflected in your Visual Studio project.

Although the runtime designer provides a great way to visually design your screens, it has some limitations. These are:

- You can't add new data items (such as local screen properties queries, or methods).

- You can't move items out of their layout containers.

- You can't edit the underlying VB or C# code. You can only change the way items appear visually on the screen.

User Interface Settings

So far in this chapter, we've only shown you how to modify the appearance of your screens. We'll now show you how to modify the appearance of other elements that are shown in your application. The majority of these settings are configured in the Properties pane of your application (Figure 8-40).

The Properties pane allows you to change the shell and theme of your application. As you learned in Chapter 1, changing the shell and theme allows you to quite radically change the look and feel of your application.

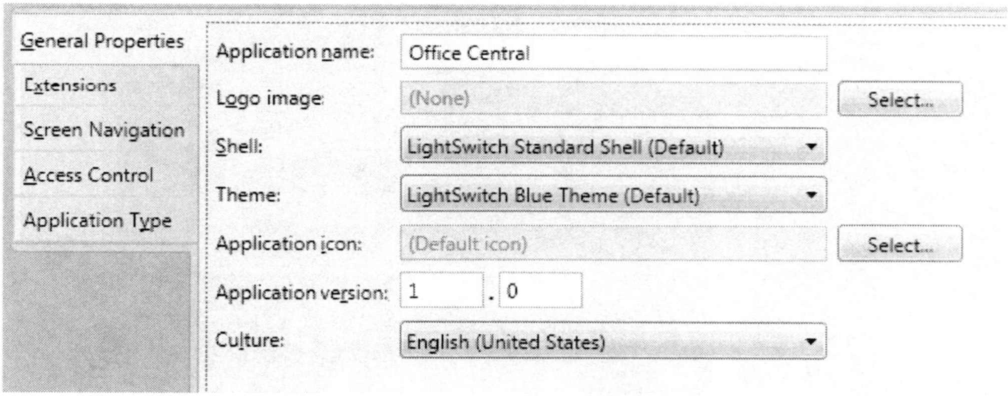

Figure 8-40. General Properties pane

The other properties you can set are shown in Table 8-14.

Table 8-14. General Property Settings

Property	Description
Application Name	The application name is shown in the title bar of your application.
Logo Image	When a desktop application is deployed, the logo image is used in the desktop icon.
Application Icon	In a desktop application, the application icon is shown in the title bar of your application.
Application Version	Use this to set the application version of your application.
Culture	Use this to change the culture of your application.

The application name is shown in the title bar of your application. In a desktop application, the server name is also shown in the title bar after the application name. This is a security feature that Silverlight imposes, and it isn't possible to hide the server name.

Each LightSwitch application uses a single language and culture. In the current version, LightSwitch applications cannot support multiple languages.

To change the culture, use the culture drop-down box to select one of the 42 available cultures.

Figure 8-41 shows a running application with the culture setting set to Spanish. As you'll see in the illustration, LightSwitch automatically localizes the built-in messages and menu items that are shown to the user. LightSwitch also provides support for right-to-left languages such as Arabic and Chinese.

Figure 8-41. *Localized application*

Screen Navigation

The screen navigation menu appears on the left-hand side of your running application. It allows users to open the screens you've defined in your application.

You can use the screen navigation tab in the properties of your project to order your menu items, set the display text, and organize your screens into groups. Figure 8-42 shows the screen navigation tab in the designer, alongside the screen navigation menu in the running application.

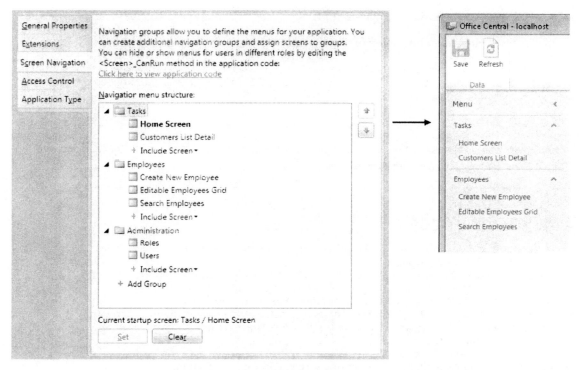

Figure 8-42. *Screen navigation at design time and runtime*

The Up and Down buttons are used to reorder the menu items. Any new screen you create automatically gets added into the navigation menu structure. This, however, excludes any screens that are based on the Details Screen template.

You can use the right-click context menu item to remove a menu item from the navigation menu. You would do this to hide screens from users.

The Add Group button allows you to add a group to the navigation menu. Within a group, you'd use the Include Screen drop-down to add menu items to the group.

You can add menu items that open the same screen multiple times. The Include Screen drop-down also includes the Users and Roles screens. These are built-in screens that allow you to manage the security of your application. By default, menu items for these screens are added to the Administration group. At debug time, the Administration group isn't shown. This group only appears in deployed applications and is only shown to application administrators.

LightSwitch recognizes the permissions of the logged-on user when it builds the navigation menu at runtime. If a user doesn't have sufficient permission to access a screen, LightSwitch doesn't show it in the navigation menu. You don't need to do any extra work in the Screen Navigation pane to configure menu-item permissions.

Chapter 14 describes authorization in more detail and how to restrict access to screens for specified users.

Finally, you can specify the startup screen by clicking the Set button. The startup screen is highlighted in bold—in Figure 8-42, this has been set to Home Screen. The startup screen is the first screen that's shown when your application starts. By default, the first screen you create is set to be the startup screen.

If you don't want your application to display a screen when it starts, you can use the Clear button to unset your startup screen.

Later in this chapter, we'll explain how to create a home screen. This type of screen might contain welcome text and a company logo. Such a screen can add a friendly image to your application and makes an ideal startup screen.

■ **Note** If you want to create a set of nested navigation groups, you can achieve this by manually editing your LSML file. This technique was described in Chapter 2.

Writing Screen Code

In this section, we'll describe some of the things you can do in code. Writing screen code is a key part of extending any LightSwitch application.

The screen code you write is executed on the client. The LightSwitch client uses Silverlight and, therefore, any C# or VB code that you write must target the Silverlight runtime.

There are various .NET classes that are not included or not supported through the Silverlight runtime. For example, the .NET SmtpClient class is not supported in Silverlight. This means that you can't send email directly from any screen code you write. However, we'll show you other techniques you can use to send email in Chapter 12.

The important point for now is to realize that there are certain classes or methods in the full .NET Framework that are not available when writing screen code in LightSwitch.

LightSwitch saves any screen code you write into your client project. If you want to find your code files in Windows Explorer, you can navigate to the client\usercode folder, which you'll find beneath your project folder. LightSwitch automatically creates the usercode folder when you write your first screen method.

Working with Screen Events

LightSwitch exposes various screen events you can handle. For example, you might want to perform some additional action in code when your user clicks the Save button. You can achieve this by writing code in the Saving method.

To handle the events you can use, you'll need to click the Write Code button. This produces a drop-down list of events, which can vary depending on the screen template type you've chosen (Figure 8-43). Clicking one of the events opens the code editor window.

New Data Screens	Details Screen	Editable Grid Screen

Figure 8-43. Screen events

The events you can use can be categorized into:

- General events,
- Access control events,
- Collection events,
- Screen property events.

We'll now describe these events in more detail.

General Events

General events are triggered throughout the lifecycle of your screen. You can handle these events and write code that runs when your data are loaded or saved or when your screen is closed. For example, you can use the `InitializeDataWorkspace` method to initialize some text you want to show on your screen. You'll see plenty of examples of how you would handle these events in the code samples that are shown later in this chapter.

Table 8-15 shows a full list of general events you can handle.

Table 8-15. General Events

General Events	Description
<ScreenName>_Activated	Called just after a screen is activated.
<ScreenName>_Closing	Called just before the screen closes.

General Events	Description
<ScreenName>_Created	Called just after the screen appears.
<ScreenName>_InitializeDataWorkspace	Called just before the screen data are retrieved.
<ScreenName>_Run	Called when a request is made to display the screen.
<ScreenName>_SaveError	Called when attempting to save the screen results in an error.
<ScreenName>_Saved	Called just after the screen is saved.
<ScreenName>_Saving	Called just before the screen is saved.

The Saving event includes a parameter called *handled*. If you set this to true in your code, the save operation that LightSwitch would normally carry out is canceled.

Likewise, the Closing event includes a parameter called *cancel*. Setting this to true cancels the close of a screen.

Access Control Events

Access control methods are called to verify whether a user has permission to perform a task.

Table 8-16 summarizes the access control events you can handle. The authorization chapter (Chapter 14) describes these events in more detail. Feel free to refer to that chapter if you want to see some code samples.

Although you'd normally write code in the CanExecute method to control access permissions, you can also write custom code here to guard your methods. For example, if you create a method that uses COM to automate Microsoft Word, you can write code in the CanExecute method to prevent the automation from happening if the application isn't running as a desktop application.

Table 8-16. Access Control Events

Access Control Events	Description
CanRun<ScreenName>	Called before a screen appears. LightSwitch calls this method to check permissions for the current user.
<MyMethodName>_CanExecute	Called before a method is run. LightSwitch calls this method to check permissions for the current user.

Collection Events

Collection methods are called when a collection is modified.

If you want to handle a collection event, a very important point is that the collection methods only appear in the Write Code drop-down list if the collection is selected in the screen member list. Many developers often struggle when they can't see the collection event they want to use and are left confused as to why the events are missing.

Table 8-17 summarizes the collection events you can handle.

Table 8-17. Collection Events

Collection Events	Description
<CollectionName>_Changed	Called just after the collection has changed.
<CollectionName>_SelectionChanged	Called just after the currently selected item in the collection is selected.

Screen Property Events

Screen property methods are called during the lifecycle of a property. Table 8-18 summarizes the events you can handle.

Table 8-18. Screen Property Events

Property Events	Description
<PropertyName>_Changed	Called just after the property value has changed.
<PropertyName>_Loaded	Called just after the property value has been loaded from the data source.
<PropertyName>_Validate	Called when an item is validated.

Displaying Messages

A common requirement in any application is to prompt your user for a confirmation, or to display a message in a pop-up dialog. LightSwitch includes a couple of built-in methods to help you. These methods are called ShowMessageBox and ShowImputBox.

Displaying Messages Using *ShowMessageBox*

You can use the ShowMessageBox method to display a message using a dialog box.

In the following example, we'll create a screen method called DiscardChanges. This method discards any changes that have been made on the screen. The code in Listing 8-1 demonstrates how to use the ShowMessageBox method.

Listing 8-1. Using the ShowMessageBox method

VB:

```
File: OfficeCentral\Client\UserCode\EmployeeDetail.vb

Private Sub DiscardChanges_Execute()
    If Me.ShowMessageBox(
        "Are you sure you want to discard your changes?",
        "Confirm", MessageBoxOption.YesNo) =
        System.Windows.MessageBoxResult.Yes Then
            Me.DataWorkspace.ApplicationData.Details.DiscardChanges()
            Me.ShowMessageBox("The changes have been discarded")
    End If
End Sub
```

C#:

```
File: OfficeCentral\Client\UserCode\EmployeeDetail.cs

partial void DiscardChanges_Execute()
{
    if (this.ShowMessageBox(
        "Are you sure you want to discard your changes?",
        "Confirm", MessageBoxOption.YesNo) ==
        System.Windows.MessageBoxResult.Yes)
    {
        this.DataWorkspace.ApplicationData.Details.DiscardChanges();
        this.ShowMessageBox("The changes have been discarded");
    }
}
```

The ShowMessageBox method lets you pass in a message, dialog caption, and an argument that specifies the buttons that are shown.

You can use the return value from the message box to control the logic flow in your application. In this example, the first call uses the return value to determine whether to carry out the operation. If the user chooses to discard the screen changes, the ShowMessageBox is called once again to display a confirmation.

Figure 8-44 shows what the first message box looks like.

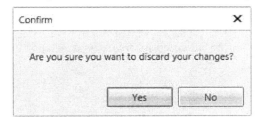

Figure 8-44. ShowMessageBox dialog

Displaying Messages Using *ShowInputBox*

The ShowInputBox method displays a dialog that contains a text box. The dialog allows you to carry out data entry, and the method returns the text the user enters.

Listing 8-2 shows how you would use the ShowInputBox method on a new customer screen. The code in the saving method prompts the user to enter any additional comments using an input box.

Listing 8-2. Using the ShowInputBox method

VB:

File: OfficeCentral\Client\UserCode\CreateNewCustomer.vb

```
Private Sub CreateNewCustomer_Saving(ByRef handled As Boolean)

    Dim comment = Me.ShowInputBox(
        "Do you want to include any additional comments?",
        "Confirm Save", "")

    If Not comment Is Nothing AndAlso comment.Length > 0 Then
        Me.CustomerProperty.Comment = comment
    End If
End Sub
```

C#:

File: OfficeCentral\Client\UserCode\CreateNewCustomer.cs

```
partial void CreateNewCustomer_Saving(ref bool handled)
{
    string comment = this.ShowInputBox(
        "Do you want to include any additional comments?",
        "Confirm Save", "");

    if ((comment != null) && comment.Length > 0) {
        this.CustomerProperty.Comment = comment;
    }
}
```

Just like the ShowMessageBox method, the ShowInputBox method allows you to specify a dialog caption. Figure 8-45 shows what the dialog looks like.

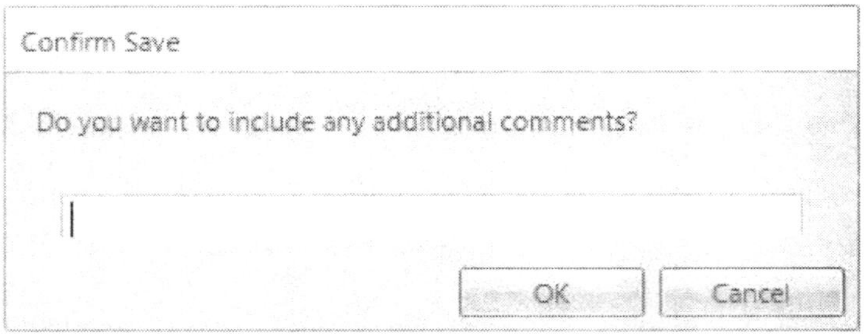

Figure 8-45. ShowInputBox dialog

Setting the Screen Title in Code

There are a couple of methods that you can use to set the screen title in code. These methods are called:

- `DisplayName`,

- `SetDisplayNameFromEntity`.

The simplest way to set the screen title in code is to use the `DisplayName` method and to pass in the screen title you want to display.

LightSwitch also includes a method called `SetDisplayNameFromEntity`. This requires you to pass in an entity, and LightSwitch sets the screen title using the summary property of the entity you've supplied.

Listing 8-3 shows the sample code you'd use to set the screen title using the `DisplayName` method. The commented out section of code shows how to use the `SetDisplayNameFromEntity` method. Figure 8-46 illustrates what the user would see at runtime.

Listing 8-3. Setting the screen title in code

VB:

```
File: OfficeCentral\Client\UserCode\CustomerDetail.vb

Private Sub Customer_Loaded(succeeded As Boolean)
    Me.DisplayName = "My title's been set in code"
    'Here's how you'd use SetDisplayNameFromEntity
    'Me.SetDisplayNameFromEntity(Me.Customer)
End Sub
```

C#:

```
File: OfficeCentral\Client\UserCode\CustomerDetail.cs

partial void Customer_Loaded(bool succeeded)
{
    this.DisplayName = "My title's been set in code";
    //Here's how you'd use SetDisplayNameFromEntity
    //this.SetDisplayNameFromEntity(this.Customer);
}
```

My title's been set in code ✕
Firstname: Tim
Surname: Leung

Figure 8-46. Setting the screen title in code

Changing the Save Behavior of New Data Screens

Earlier on we discussed the default behavior of screens that are created using the New Data Screen template. When a user clicks the Save button, LightSwitch automatically closes the new data screen and opens the newly created record using the details screen for your entity.

You might not want the new data screen to behave like this. After saving a record, you might prefer to clear the screen and prepare it for the entry of another new record. Now that you understand the screen events you can handle in LightSwitch, we'll show you the code you can write to change this behavior.

You'll find the code that closes the new data screen and opens the details screen in the Saved method. In the screen designer, click the Write Code button and select the Saved method.

Now modify the code as shown in Listing 8-4.

Listing 8-4. Reset the New Data Screen after a save

VB:

```
File: OfficeCentral\Client\UserCode\CreateNewEmployee.vb

Private Sub CreateNewEmployee_Saved()

    'The commented lines beneath are added by LightSwitch
    'Delete these lines
    'Me.Close(False)
    'Application.Current.ShowDefaultScreen(Me.EmployeeProperty)

    'Now add a line of code to reset the entity
    Me.EmployeeProperty = New Employee()

End Sub
```

C#:

```
File: OfficeCentral\Client\UserCode\CreateNewEmployee.cs

partial void CreateNewEmployee_Saved()
{
    //The commented lines beneath are added by LightSwitch
    //Delete these lines
    //this.Close(false);
    //Application.Current.ShowDefaultScreen(this.EmployeeProperty);
```

```
//Now add a line of code to reset the entity
this.EmployeeProperty = new Employee();
}
```

In the code shown, we've removed the line of code that closes the screen. We've added a new line that creates a new instance of the underlying entity. This effectively resets the screen and allows the user to immediately enter another record.

Opening Screens from Code

At times, you might want to open another screen using code. LightSwitch allows you to do this easily. It autogenerates a *show* method for every screen you've defined in your application. Calling the show method opens the screen. These show methods are exposed via the Application object.

Listing 8-5 shows a method that opens a customer search screen.

Listing 8-5. Opening screens from code

File: OfficeCentral\Client\UserCode\Home.vb

```
Private Sub OpenSearchScreen()
    Me.Application.ShowSearchCustomer()
End Sub
```

C#:

File: OfficeCentral\Client\UserCode\Home.cs

```
partial void OpenSearchScreen()
{
    this.Application.ShowSearchCustomer();
}
```

As you can see, LightSwitch creates a method called ShowSearchCustomer, where SearchCustomer is the name of the screen.

If you want to open a details screen, the show method that LightSwitch generates will require you to pass in the primary key of the record you want to display. This technique is particularly useful for opening details screens that are not set as the default screen.

Passing Argument Values into Screens

LightSwitch allows you to pass in arguments when you open a screen. You would do this by defining properties as parameters. Figure 8-47 shows the setting you'd use in the Properties pane.

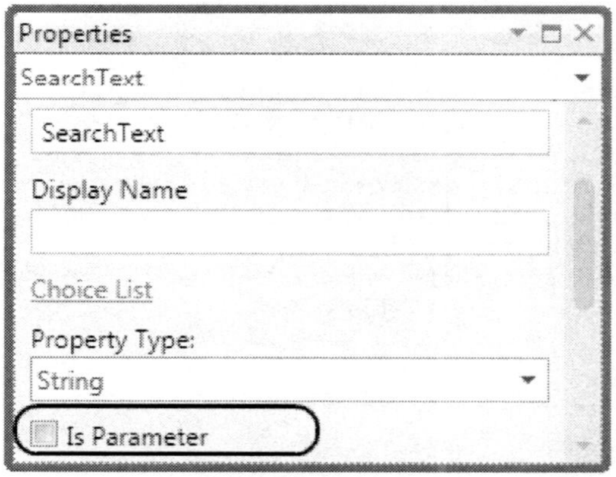

Figure 8-47. Defining screen parameters

This example illustrates a search screen with a SearchText property set as a parameter.

Using code you've defined on another screen, you can create a button that opens the search screen. This allows you to default the SearchText text to "Smith" by using the code shown in Listing 8-6.

Listing 8-6. Passing screen parameters

VB:
```
File: OfficeCentral\Client\UserCode\Home.vb

Private Sub OpenSearchScreen()
    Me.Application.ShowSearchCustomer("Smith")
End Sub
```

C#:
```
File: OfficeCentral\Client\UserCode\Home.cs

partial void OpenSearchScreen()
{
    this.Application.ShowSearchCustomer("Smith");
}
```

Setting Control Values in Code

An important point about LightSwitch is that all UI controls are bound to properties. If you want to change the text that's shown on a text box, for example, you'd change the value of the underlying property. Because the text box is data-bound to the property, the text displayed will be updated when you change the property value.

Many other development environments (Windows Forms or ASP.NET, for example) allow you to access text boxes and controls in code and expose a value or text property that allows you to set their values. In LightSwitch, you wouldn't work directly with controls to set their values. Instead, you always set control values by setting the value on the underlying property.

Finding Controls Using *FindControl*

The FindControl method allows you to reference a control in code. The method requires you to pass in the name of your control, which you can find in the Properties pane. Note that the control name doesn't always match the property name, since you could add multiple instances of a control onto your screen.

For example, imagine that you have a control called Surname on your screen. If you add Surname again onto your screen, LightSwitch names the new control Surname1. So if you want to reference the second Surname control using the FindControl method, you'll have to pass in the name Surname1.

The FindControl method returns an object of type IContentItemProxy, which is LightSwitch's View-Model object. The methods that are exposed by this object are shown in Table 8-19.

Table 8-19. IContentItemProxy Methods and Properties

Methods/Properties	Description
Focus	Sets the focus to the control.
DisplayName	Allows you to change the display name of your control. The display name is used for the label text.
IsEnabled	If set to false, the control is disabled. The control will still be visible, but is grayed out.
IsReadOnly	If set to true, the control becomes read-only and the user won't be able to edit the contents of the control.
IsVisible	The control will not be visible if this is set to false.
SetBinding	This method is used to perform data binding.

The SetBinding method becomes important when you start using custom controls. We'll show you how to use these in Chapter 9.

If want to refer to a control that belongs inside a data grid (or other collection control), you'll need to use the FindControlInCollection method, rather than the FindControl method. When you call the FindControlInCollection method, you'll need to supply an entity. This entity will refer to the data row you're searching within. Just like the FindControl method, FindControlInCollection also returns an IContentItemProxy object.

We'll now show you some examples of how you would use the FindControl method.

Setting the Focus to a Control

The IContentItemProxy object provides a method called *focus* that you can call to set the screen focus to a control.

Listing 8-7 shows how you would call this method in the screen-loaded method to set the focus to the surname control.

Listing 8-7. Setting the focus to a control

VB:

File: OfficeCentral\Client\UserCode\CustomerDetail.vb

```vb
Private Sub Customer_Loaded(succeeded As Boolean)
    Me.FindControl("Surname").Focus()
End Sub
```

C#:

File: OfficeCentral\Client\UserCode\CustomerDetail.cs

```csharp
partial void Customer_Loaded(bool succeeded)
{
    this.FindControl("Surname").Focus();
}
```

Hiding and Showing Controls

The IsVisible property allows you to hide controls or groups of controls.

In this example, we'll create a button that toggles the visibility of a row's layout on a customer detail screen. The name of the row's layout is AddressGroup and the name of the method is ToggleVisibility (Figure 8-48).

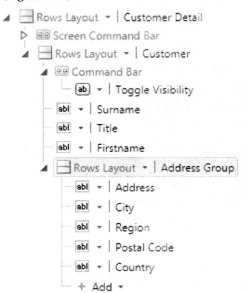

Figure 8-48. Hiding and showing controls

Calling this method shows or hides the address controls that relate to a customer. After creating the ToggleVisibility method, add the code shown in Listing 8-8.

Listing 8-8. *Hiding and showing controls*

VB:

File: OfficeCentral\Client\UserCode\CustomerDetail.vb

```
Private Sub ToggleVisibility_Execute()
    Dim rowLayout = Me.FindControl("AddressGroup")
    rowLayout.IsVisible = Not (rowLayout.IsVisible)
End Sub
```

C#:

File: OfficeCentral\Client\UserCode\CustomerDetail.cs

```
partial void ToggleVisibility_Execute()
{
    var rowLayout = this.FindControl("AddressGroup");
    rowLayout.IsVisible = !(rowLayout.IsVisible);
}
```

When you first open your screen and call the ToggleVisibility method, the rows layout and all associated child controls will be hidden. Calling the ToggleVisibility method again restores the visibility of the rows layout.

Making Check Boxes Read-Only

You can make a control read-only by setting the IsReadOnly property to true. This code works with all controls but is particularly useful when you're working with check boxes. This is because check boxes don't always behave quite as expected.

If you've checked the Use Read-Only Controls check box on the root node of your screen or on a data grid, LightSwitch renders your data using labels or other read-only controls. However, any check boxes you've added will still be enabled, despite the Use Read-Only Controls option being set to true. If you want to disable a check box, you'll have to write code to do this.

In this example, we'll show you how to disable a check box that's shown on an employee data grid. The name of our check box is SecurityVetted. This is a Boolean property that indicates whether the employee is security cleared. In the loaded method, we'll loop through the rows in the data grid. We'll then use the FindControlInCollection method to obtain a reference to the check box. We can then use the IsEnabled property on the IContentItemProxy that's returned to make the check box read-only.

The code to do this is shown in Listing 8-9.

Listing 8-9. *Making check boxes read-only*

VB:

File: OfficeCentral\Client\UserCode\Employees.vb

```
Private Sub Employees_Loaded(succeeded As Boolean)
```

```
    For Each emp In Employees
        Me.FindControlInCollection(
            "SecurityVetted", emp).IsEnabled = False
    Next

End Sub
```

C#:

File: OfficeCentral\Client\UserCode\Employees.cs

```
partial void Employees_Loaded(bool succeeded)
{
    foreach (Employee emp in Employees)
    {
        this.FindControlInCollection(
            "SecurityVetted", emp).IsEnabled  = false;
    }
}
```

When you run this screen, the check boxes in the grid are correctly disabled and the user won't be able to change any of the check box values in the grid.

Reference the Underlying Silverlight Control

Let's imagine you've created a screen that displays a text box. The actual control that LightSwitch displays is a Silverlight Text Box control. The IContentItemProxy object that we showed you allows you to control certain elements of the text box such as visibility and the enabled state. However, IContentItemProxy can only take you so far. To set text box specific properties, you'll need to reference the underlying Silverlight control.

To demonstrate how to do this, we'll show you some code that sets the background style of a text box.

Accessing the underlying Silverlight control still relies on you using the FindControl method to return an IContentItemProxy. This exposes two methods you can use to access the underlying control. These are:

- The SetBinding method,

- The ControlAvailable method.

You'd use the SetBinding method to data bind a screen property to a dependency property of your control. This technique is commonly used when working with custom controls. In the custom control chapter (Chapter 9), we'll show you how to use the SetBinding method and also explain exactly what a dependency property is.

In this example, we'll focus on how you would use the ControlAvailable method. For any given control, LightSwitch raises the ControlAvailable event when the control becomes available.

When you handle this event, the ControlAvailableEventArgs parameter gives you access to the underlying Silverlight control. As the name suggests, this event is fired when the control becomes available. When you write code that handles this event, you can be sure that you won't encounter the types of errors that might occur if you try accessing the control too early. Listing 8-10 specifies the code for ControlAvailable.

Listing 8-10. Referencing a control using ControlAvailable

VB:

File: OfficeCentral\Client\UserCode\CreateNewCustomer.vb

Imports System.Windows.Media

```vb
Private Sub CreateNewCustomer_InitializeDataWorkspace(
    ByVal saveChangesTo As System.Collections.Generic.List(
        Of Microsoft.LightSwitch.IDataService))

    Dim control = Me.FindControl("Surname")

    AddHandler control.ControlAvailable,
        Sub(sender As Object, e As ControlAvailableEventArgs)
            Dim textbox = CType(e.Control,
                System.Windows.Controls.TextBox)
            textbox.Background = New SolidColorBrush(Colors.Yellow)
        End Sub

End Sub
```

C#:

File: OfficeCentral\Client\UserCode\CreateNewCustomer.cs

using System.Windows.Media;

```csharp
partial void CreateNewCustomer_InitializeDataWorkspace(
   List<IDataService> saveChangesTo)
{
    var control = this.FindControl("Surname");

    control.ControlAvailable +=
      (object sender, ControlAvailableEventArgs e) =>
        {
            var textbox =
               (System.Windows.Controls.TextBox)e.Control;
               textbox.Background = new SolidColorBrush(Colors.Yellow);
        };

}
```

In the code shown, we've added inline event handlers to handle the ControlAvailable event. The e.control object gives you access to Silverlight control. Because we know that the surname control is rendered as a text box, we can simply declare a variable and cast it to System.Windows.Controls.TextBox.

This gives us access to all of the Silverlight text box properties and allows us to set the background color in code.

When you now run this screen, the background color of the surname text box is shown in yellow.

Handling Silverlight Control Events

When you obtain a reference to a Silverlight control using the `ControlAvailable` method, you can also add event handlers to handle the events that are raised by the Silverlight control.

To give you an example of the sort of events you can handle, Table 8-20 shows some of the events that are raised by the Silverlight text box control. There are many more events you can use. This table only shows a subset, but hopefully gives you a flavor of the sort of events you can handle.

Table 8-20. Events Raised by the Silverlight Text Box Control

Event	Description
GotFocus	Occurs when the TextBox receives the focus.
KeyDown	Occurs when a keyboard key is pressed while the TextBox has focus.
KeyUp	Occurs when a keyboard key is released while the TextBox has focus.
LostFocus	Occurs when the TextBox loses focus.
SelectionChanged	Occurs when the text selection has changed.
TextChanged	Occurs when content changes in the TextBox.

In the following example, we'll show you how to uppercase the characters that are entered into a text box by a user. We'll handle the `KeyUp` event so that characters are upper cased as soon as they're entered by the user.

Listing 8-11 extends our previous code sample. To show you a slightly different syntax, we've used named delegates rather than inline event handlers.

Listing 8-11. Handling the TextBox KeyUp event

VB:

```
File: OfficeCentral\Client\UserCode\CreateNewCustomer.vb

Private Sub CreateNewCustomer_InitializeDataWorkspace(
    ByVal saveChangesTo As System.Collections.Generic.List(
        Of Microsoft.LightSwitch.IDataService))
    Dim control = Me.FindControl("Surname")
    AddHandler control.ControlAvailable,
        AddressOf TextBoxAvailable
End Sub

Private Sub TextBoxAvailable(
    sender As Object, e As ControlAvailableEventArgs)
        AddHandler CType(e.Control,
            System.Windows.Controls.TextBox).KeyUp,
                AddressOf TextBoxKeyUp
```

```
End Sub

Private Sub TextBoxKeyUp(
    sender As Object, e As System.Windows.RoutedEventArgs)

    Dim textbox = CType(sender, System.Windows.Controls.TextBox)
    Dim textUppered As String = textbox.Text.ToUpper
    Dim selStart As Integer = textbox.SelectionStart
    textbox.Text = textUppered
    textbox.SelectionStart = selStart

End Sub
```

C#:

File: OfficeCentral\Client\UserCode\CreateNewCustomer.cs

```csharp
partial void CreateNewCustomer_InitializeDataWorkspace(
    List<IDataService> saveChangesTo)
{
  this.FindControl("Surname").ControlAvailable += TextBoxAvailable;
}

private void TextBoxAvailable(object sender, ControlAvailableEventArgs e)
{
    ((System.Windows.Controls.TextBox)e.Control).KeyUp += TextBoxKeyUp;
}

private void TextBoxKeyUp(object sender, System.Windows.RoutedEventArgs e)
{
    var textbox = (System.Windows.Controls.TextBox)sender;

    string textUppered = textbox.Text.ToUpper();
    int selStart = textbox.SelectionStart;
    textbox.Text = textUppered;
    textbox.SelectionStart = selStart;
}
```

In the code shown, we've saved the SelectionStart position prior to upper casing and replacing the text. After modifying the text, we've restored the SelectionStart property back to its original setting. If you don't do this, the control sets the cursor location to the end of the text box. This would make it impossible for a user to type into the middle of a text box, because every key press event would send the cursor position to the end of the string.

When you run this screen, the KeyUp event of the surname is handled and any text that you enter will be upper cased.

Reacting to Data Changes Using Property Changed

In any advanced application, you'll want some way to make your UI react to changes in your data.

The LightSwitch entities that represent your data (e.g., customer, order, etc.) implement the INotifyPropertyChanged interface. This causes an event called PropertyChanged to be raised whenever any property (e.g., surname, order status) changes. So to make your application react to data changes, you can handle this event and carry out any UI changes in the event handler.

In the earlier example, we showed you how to handle the events that are raised by the underlying Silverlight control. Handling these events provides an alternative to using PropertyChanged. So, for example, if you have an employee screen that contains an IsSecurityVetted check box, you can handle its LostFocus event and hide or show controls depending on the value.

However, the advantage of using PropertyChanged is that it aligns itself better with the way Silverlight works. If you want to use the LostFocus technique to monitor multiple properties, you would need to set up an event handler for each control. Using the PropertyChanged method, you only need to set up one event handler and you can use that to detect changes in any number of properties.

Furthermore, the LostFocus method assumes what the underlying Silverlight control will be. You could potentially break your application by changing the control type. Using the LostFocus technique is therefore more fragile than the PropertyChanged technique.

In the example that follows, we'll create a new data screen based on an employee table. In addition to the properties you would normally find such as name and contact details, the employee table also contains properties that relate to security clearance. These properties are:

- SecurityVetted. Required, Boolean field.

- SecurityClearanceRef. String field.

- VettingExpiryDate. Date field.

The details screen has a check box that indicates whether the employee is security vetted. If true, the text boxes that allow the user to enter a reference number and vetting expiry date are shown. If false, these controls are hidden.

The PropertyChanged method works differently on screens that are based on the new data and details screens. We'll begin by describing the technique on a new data screen.

Using *PropertyChanged* on a New Data Screen

To handle the PropertyChanged event for an entity on a new data screen, create a new screen based on an employee. By default, the screen template creates a local screen property called EmployeeProperty.

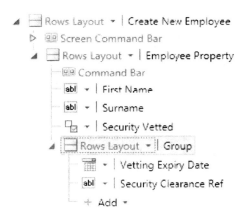
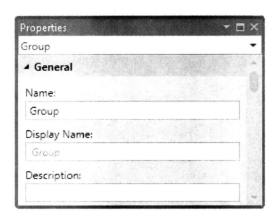

Figure 8-49. *Layout of the new data screen*

In the screen shown, we've created a rows layout called **Group**. This **group contains** the controls that we want to hide or show, depending on the value of the **SecurityVetted property** (Figure 8-49).

After creating the screen, enter the code as shown in Listing 8-12.

Listing 8-12. Using PropertyChanged on a new data screen

VB:

```
File: OfficeCentral\Client\UserCode\CreateNewEmployee.vb

Imports System.ComponentModel

Private Sub CreateNewEmployee_Created()
    Microsoft.LightSwitch.Threading.Dispatchers.Main.BeginInvoke(
        Sub()
            AddHandler DirectCast(
                Me.EmployeeProperty, INotifyPropertyChanged
                ).PropertyChanged, AddressOf EmployeeFieldChanged
        End Sub)

        'Set the initial visibility here
        Me.FindControl("group").IsVisible =
            EmployeeProperty.SecurityVetted.GetValueOrDefault(False)
End Sub

Private Sub EmployeeFieldChanged(
    sender As Object, e As PropertyChangedEventArgs)
    If e.PropertyName = "SecurityVetted" Then
        Me.FindControl("group").IsVisible =
            EmployeeProperty.SecurityVetted.GetValueOrDefault(False)
```

```
      End If
End Sub
```

C#:

File: OfficeCentral\Client\UserCode\CreateNewEmployee.cs

```csharp
using System.ComponentModel;

partial void CreateNewEmployee_Created()
{
    Microsoft.LightSwitch.Threading.Dispatchers.Main.BeginInvoke(() =>
        {
            ((INotifyPropertyChanged)this.EmployeeProperty).PropertyChanged +=
                EmployeeFieldChanged;
        });

    this.FindControl("group").IsVisible =
        EmployeeProperty.SecurityVetted.GetValueOrDefault(false);

}

private void EmployeeFieldChanged(object sender, PropertyChangedEventArgs e)
{
    if (e.PropertyName == "SecurityVetted") {
        this.FindControl("group").IsVisible =
            EmployeeProperty.SecurityVetted.GetValueOrDefault(false);
    }
}
```

In the created method of screen, we've added an event handler that handles the PropertyChanged event of EmployeeProperty. This event handler needs to be added using code that executes on the main UI thread. If you don't do this, you'll receive an error that says *It is not valid to execute the operation on the current thread.*

The EmployeeFieldChanged method includes a parameter of type PropertyChangedEventArgs. We can find out the name of the property that has changed by referring to the PropertyName property in PropertyChangedEventArgs.

If the SecurityVetted property has changed, we then call some code that uses the FindControl method to hide the group that contains the other controls related to security vetting.

The behavior of this screen at runtime is shown in Figure 8-50.

Figure 8-50. Checking SecurityVetted unhides the other controls

Using *PropertyChanged* on a Details Screen

The code you would use on a details screen is different from the code you would use on a new data screen.

The reason for this is because a detail screen uses a query that returns a single record filtered by the primary key value. A new data screen contains a local property, rather than a query. So in order to monitor PropertyChanged on a details screen, you'll need to create a local property you can monitor.

In this example, we'll create a details screen for an employee. The layout of this screen is identical to the layout shown in the new data screen example.

After creating the screen, we'll add the code that's shown in Listing 8-13. This code adds an event handler in the InitializeDataWorkspace method that handles the ExecuteCompleted event of the query loader. When the loader finishes executing the query, we save the results in a local property called monitoredEmployee. We can then handle the PropertyChanged event on the monitorEmployee property to detect any changes that have been made for the employee.

Just as before, we'll hide or show the group that contains the vetting details based on the value of the SecurityVetted property.

Listing 8-13. Using PropertyChanged on a details screen

VB:

```
File: OfficeCentral\Client\UserCode\EmployeeDetail.vb

Imports System.ComponentModel

Private monitoredEmployee As Employee

Private Sub EmployeeDetail_InitializeDataWorkspace(
    saveChangesTo As System.Collections.Generic.List(
        Of Microsoft.LightSwitch.IDataService))

    Microsoft.LightSwitch.Threading.Dispatchers.Main.BeginInvoke(
        Sub()
            AddHandler Me.Details.Properties.Employee.Loader.ExecuteCompleted,
                AddressOf Me.EmployeeLoaderExecuted
        End Sub)
End Sub

Private Sub EmployeeLoaderExecuted(
    sender As Object, e As Microsoft.LightSwitch.ExecuteCompletedEventArgs)

    If monitoredEmployee IsNot Me.Employee Then
        If monitoredEmployee IsNot Nothing Then
            RemoveHandler TryCast(monitoredEmployee,
                INotifyPropertyChanged).PropertyChanged,
                    AddressOf Me.EmployeeChanged
        End If

        monitoredEmployee = Me.Employee

        If monitoredEmployee IsNot Nothing Then
```

```
            AddHandler TryCast(
                monitoredEmployee, INotifyPropertyChanged).PropertyChanged,
                    AddressOf Me.EmployeeChanged

              'Set the initial visibility here
              Me.FindControl("group").IsVisible =
                    monitoredEmployee.SecurityVetted.GetValueOrDefault(False)

          End If
      End If
End Sub

Private Sub EmployeeChanged(sender As Object, e As PropertyChangedEventArgs)

      If e.PropertyName = "SecurityVetted" Then
          Me.FindControl("group").IsVisible =
                monitoredEmployee.SecurityVetted.GetValueOrDefault(False)
      End If

End Sub
```

C#:

File: OfficeCentral\Client\UserCode\EmployeeDetail.cs

```
using System.ComponentModel;

private Employee monitoredEmployee;

private void EmployeeDetail_InitializeDataWorkspace(
    System.Collections.Generic.List<Microsoft.LightSwitch.IDataService>
        saveChangesTo)
{
    Microsoft.LightSwitch.Threading.Dispatchers.Main.BeginInvoke(() =>
        {
            this.Details.Properties.Employee.Loader.ExecuteCompleted +=
                this.EmployeeLoaderExecuted;
        });
}


private void EmployeeLoaderExecuted(object sender,
Microsoft.LightSwitch.ExecuteCompletedEventArgs e)
{

    if (monitoredEmployee != this.Employee) {
        if (monitoredEmployee != null) {
            (monitoredEmployee as INotifyPropertyChanged).PropertyChanged -=
                this.EmployeeChanged;
        }
```

```
            monitoredEmployee = this.Employee;
            if (monitoredEmployee != null) {
                (monitoredEmployee as INotifyPropertyChanged).PropertyChanged +=
                    this.EmployeeChanged;

                //set the initial visibility here
                this.FindControl("group").IsVisible =
                    monitoredEmployee.SecurityVetted.GetValueOrDefault(false);
            }
        }
    }
}

private void EmployeeChanged(object sender, PropertyChangedEventArgs e)
{
    if (e.PropertyName == "SecurityVetted") {
        this.FindControl("group").IsVisible =
            monitoredEmployee.SecurityVetted.GetValueOrDefault(false);
    }
}
```

Working with Built-In Data Controls

Now that you know how to write screen code, we'll show you how to use some of the built-in data controls and how you can extend the functionality by using code. The controls we'll cover are:

- Modal window control,

- AutoCompleteBox.

Creating modal windows can be useful, particularly when designing screens that use the data grid control. The data grid includes buttons in the command bar area that allow users to add and edit records. You can't customize the screens that are shown when a user clicks one of these buttons. Therefore, designing your own modal window provides a work around.

The AutoCompleteBox is the default control that a user uses to select related records. In this section, we'll describe some of the more advanced things you can do with this control.

Introducing the Modal Window Control

Whenever you add or edit a record, LightSwitch will open it in a new screen tab. This will either be an autogenerated screen or a screen that you've designed yourself. Sometimes this is what you want, particularly if you have a lot of controls on the screen. But sometimes there may only be a few properties to display on the screen, which can look a bit odd if the application has been maximized.

To handle this situation, or if you just don't want to use a screen tab, you can create a *modal window* instead. A modal window appears as a pop-up on top of the screen that it was opened from, instead of opening in another screen tab (Figure 8-51).

In most applications, a modal window would prevent you from moving to other parts of the application until that modal window was closed. This is known as an *application modal*, meaning modal to the whole application. But LightSwitch is pretty clever with its modal windows that are *screen modal*, which allows each screen tab to have its own modal window open while still letting you move around to other screens in the application. When you come back to the screen that opened the modal window, it'll still be there.

This means, though, that you can only display one record for any particular screen at a time, whereas when you're using screen tabs you could be displaying multiple records, with each being displayed in its own tab (unless of course you had unchecked the Allow Multiple Instances option for the screen).

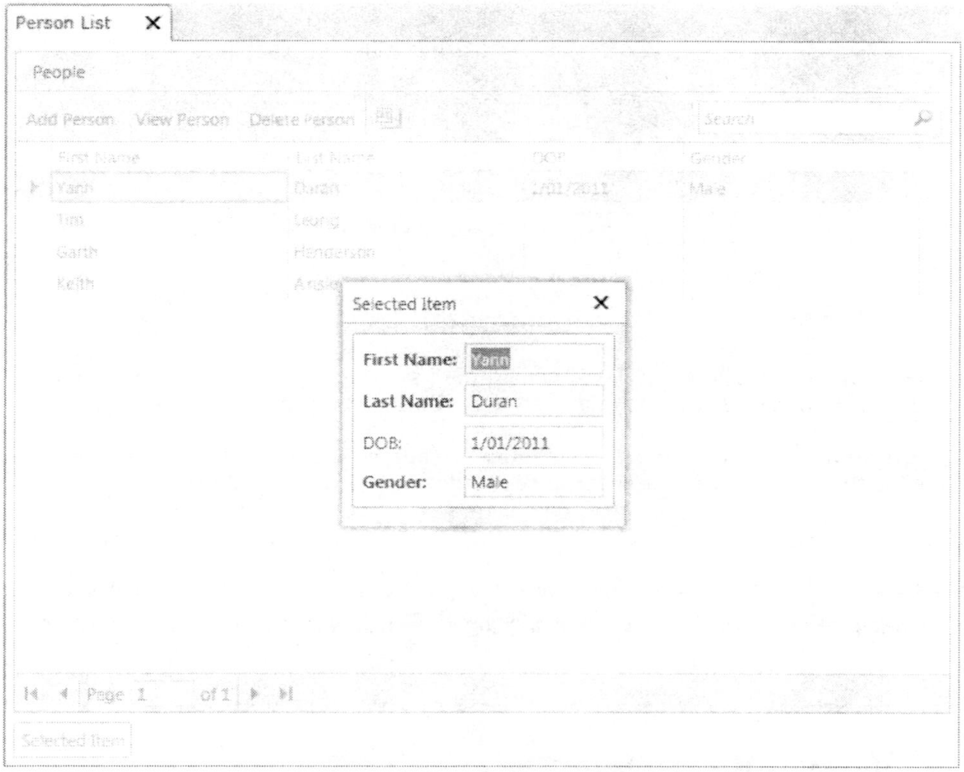

Figure 8-51. Displaying a modal window

You've got more control over the size of a modal window, but there's a little more work you have to do to set one up.

In any screen that has a list or grid on it that's bound to a collection, the easiest way to add a modal window is to drag the collection's SelectedItem to the bottom of the content tree (see Figure 8-52), then change the control type to ModalWindow. You could also use the root RowsLayout's Add drop-down button to add a ModalWindow control if you want, but you'd have to add each of the controls to it manually if you do it that way.

If you're going to have more than one modal window in your screen, it's a good idea to add something like a RowsLayout control to keep them all together. You might even want to get into the habit of doing this even if you only have one modal window, just in case. There are a couple of reasons why you might want to put your modal windows in a group control of their own.

The first reason is that it gives you the ability to collapse the group while you're designing the screen, so your design surface is less cluttered.

The second reason is that you then only have to uncheck the Is Visible setting for the group, and all the modal windows will inherit the visibility setting.

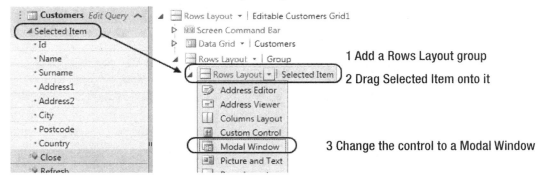

Figure 8-52. Dragging SelectedItem *to the screen's content tree*

Once you've added the ModalWindow control, you can lay out its controls the same way you would for any screen. By default LightSwitch will also automatically add a button you can use to open the modal window.

In many cases you're going to want to open the window via code, so you can hide the button by unchecking the Show Button check box in the ModalWindow control's properties window.

■ **Tip** Adding a *RowsLayout* or *ColumnsLayout* control (or any other group control) as the root control of your modal window, then moving the rest of your controls into that group, is the only way you can set the width of the window.

Creating a Modal Window Helper Class

In the example that follows, we'll add some buttons onto the toolbar of a data grid. When a user clicks one of the buttons, it'll open a customized modal window that allows a record to be added or edited.

But before we show you how to do this, we'll create a helper class that makes it easier for us to work with collections of data and modal windows.

Working on the basis that the modal window Show button will be hidden, our helper class includes methods to help show or hide the modal window. You'd initialize an instance of the modal window helper class with a collection of data, and Table 8-21 describes the methods that are exposed by this helper class.

Table 8-21. Modal Window Helper class methods

Method Name	Description
AddEntity	Adds an entity to the collection and opens the newly added record in a modal window.
ViewEntity	Opens the currently selected entity in a modal window.
DialogOk	This retains any changes that have been made in the modal window before closing it. This method will generally be called from an OK button that you'll add to the modal window.
DialogCancel	This discards any changes that have been made in the modal window and closes it.
CanAdd	This method examines the collection and determines if a record can be added, or not.
CanView	This method examines the collection and determines if a record can be viewed or not

We suggest that you add this class into a new project. This makes it possible to reuse the class in more than one LightSwitch project. Because this code is client related, you'll need to create a new Silverlight class library project.

If you don't have Visual Studio 2010 Professional or above, you can switch to File view and add the helper class to your client project.

If you decide to add the code to a Silverlight class library project, you'll need to add some assembly references:

- `System.Windows.Controls`
- `System.Windows.Controls.Data`
- `Microsoft.LightSwitch`
- `Microsoft.LightSwitch.Client`

You won't be able to choose the LightSwitch ones from the Assemblies list as you normally would. LightSwitch assemblies aren't stored in the GAC (Global Assembly Cache), so you'll have to use the Browse button to find them manually.

The two DLLs that you'll need are located on the drive where you installed Visual Studio 2010 (see Table 8-22). This will usually be the C drive, but if you've installed Visual Studio on a different drive, then you'll need to take that into account.

Table 8-22. LightSwitch Assembly Locations

Windows	Assembly Location (x = drive where Visual Studio 2010 was installed)
32-bit	x:\Program Files\Microsoft Visual Studio 10.0\Common7\IDE\LightSwitch\1.0\Client
64-bit	x:\Program Files (x86)\Microsoft Visual Studio 10.0\Common7\IDE↵ \LightSwitch\1.0\Client

After adding your assembly references, you can create the **modal window helper** class using the code shown in Listing 8-14.

Listing 8-14. Modal window helper class

VB:

```
File: Central.Utilities.Client\Windows\ModalWindow.vb

Imports System.ComponentModel
Imports System.Windows.Controls
Imports Microsoft.LightSwitch
Imports Microsoft.LightSwitch.Client
Imports Microsoft.LightSwitch.Presentation
Imports Microsoft.LightSwitch.Threading
Imports Microsoft.LightSwitch.Presentation.Extensions


Public Class ModalWindowHelper
    Public Delegate Function CanCloseFunction() As Boolean

    Private _collection As IVisualCollection
    Private _dialogName As String
    Private _entityName As String
    Private _screen As IScreenObject
    Private _window As IContentItemProxy
    Private _entity As IEntityObject
    Private _saveOnClose As Boolean

    Public Sub New( _
        ByVal visualCollection As IVisualCollection _
      , ByVal dialogName As String _
      , Optional entityName As String = "")

        _collection = visualCollection
        _dialogName = dialogName
        _entityName = If(entityName <> "",
                         entityName,
                         _collection.Details.GetModel.ElementType.Name)
        _screen = _collection.Screen
    End Sub
```

```vb
Public Sub Initialize( _
    Optional hasCloseButton As Boolean = True _
    , Optional saveOnClose As Boolean = False _
    )
    _window = _screen.FindControl(_dialogName)
    _saveOnClose = saveOnClose

    AddHandler _window.ControlAvailable, _
        Sub(s As Object, e As ControlAvailableEventArgs)
            Dim window = DirectCast(e.Control, ChildWindow)

            window.HasCloseButton = hasCloseButton

            AddHandler window.Closed, _
                Sub(s1 As Object, e1 As EventArgs)
                    DialogClosed(s1)
                End Sub
        End Sub
End Sub

Public Function CanAdd() As Boolean
    Return (_collection.CanAddNew = True)
End Function

Public Function CanView() As Boolean
    Return (_collection.SelectedItem IsNot Nothing)
End Function

Public Sub AddEntity()
    Dim result As IEntityObject = Nothing

    _window.DisplayName =
        String.Format("Add {0}", _entityName)
    _collection.AddNew()

    OpenModalWindow()
End Sub

Public Sub ViewEntity()
    _window.DisplayName = String.Format("View {0}", _entityName)

    OpenModalWindow()
End Sub

Private Sub OpenModalWindow()
    _entity = TryCast(_collection.SelectedItem, IEntityObject)
    _screen.OpenModalWindow(_dialogName)
End Sub

Public Sub DialogOk()
    If (_entity IsNot Nothing) Then
```

```vb
            _screen.CloseModalWindow(_dialogName)
        End If
    End Sub

    Public Sub DialogCancel()
        If (_entity IsNot Nothing) Then
            _screen.CloseModalWindow(_dialogName)
            DiscardChanges()
        End If
    End Sub

    Public Sub DialogClosed(sender As Object)
        Dim window = DirectCast(sender, ChildWindow)

        Select Case window.DialogResult.HasValue
            Case True
                If (_saveOnClose = True) Then
                    _screen.Details.Dispatcher.BeginInvoke( _
                        Sub()
                            _screen.Save()
                        End Sub)
                End If

            Case False
                DiscardChanges()
        End Select
    End Sub

    Private Sub DiscardChanges()
        If (_entity IsNot Nothing) Then
            _entity.Details.DiscardChanges()
        End If
    End Sub

End Class
```

C#:

File: Central.Utilities.Client\Windows\ModalWindow.cs

```csharp
using System;
using System.ComponentModel;
using System.Windows.Controls;
using Microsoft.LightSwitch;
using Microsoft.LightSwitch.Client;
using Microsoft.LightSwitch.Presentation;
using Microsoft.LightSwitch.Threading;
using Microsoft.LightSwitch.Presentation.Extensions;

namespace Central.Utilities.Client
{
    class ModalWindowHelper
```

```csharp
{
    public delegate bool CanCloseFunction();
    private IVisualCollection _collection;
    private string _dialogName;
    private string _entityName;
    private IScreenObject _screen;
    private IContentItemProxy _window;
    private IEntityObject _entity;
    private bool _saveOnClose;

    public ModalWindowHelper(
        IVisualCollection visualCollection,
        string dialogName, string entityName = "")
    {
        _collection = visualCollection;
        _dialogName = dialogName;
        _screen = _collection.Screen;
        if (entityName != "")
        {
            _entityName = entityName;
        }
        else
        {
            _entityName =
                _collection.Details.GetModel().ElementType.Name;
        }
    }

    public void Initialize(
        bool hasCloseButton = true, bool saveOnClose = false)
    {
        _window = _screen.FindControl(_dialogName);
        _saveOnClose = saveOnClose;

        _window.ControlAvailable +=
            delegate(object sender, ControlAvailableEventArgs e)
            {
                var window = (ChildWindow)e.Control;
                window.HasCloseButton = hasCloseButton;

                window.Closed +=
                    delegate(object sender1, EventArgs e1)
                    {
                        DialogClosed(sender1);
                    };
            };

    }

    public bool CanAdd()
    {
        return (_collection.CanAddNew == true);
```

```
    }

    public bool CanView()
    {
        return (_collection.SelectedItem != null);
    }

    public void AddEntity()
    {
        _window.DisplayName =
            string.Format("Add {0}", _entityName);
        _collection.AddNew();
        OpenModalWindow();
    }

    public void ViewEntity()
    {
        _window.DisplayName =
            string.Format("View {0}", _entityName);
        OpenModalWindow();
    }

    private void OpenModalWindow()
    {
        _entity =
            _collection.SelectedItem as IEntityObject;
        _screen.OpenModalWindow(_dialogName);
    }

    public void DialogOk()
    {
        if ((_entity != null))
        {
            _screen.CloseModalWindow(_dialogName);
        }
    }

    public void DialogCancel()
    {
        if ((_entity != null))
        {
            _screen.CloseModalWindow(_dialogName);
            DiscardChanges();
        }
    }

    public void DialogClosed(object sender)
    {
        var window = (ChildWindow)sender;

        if (window.DialogResult.HasValue && _saveOnClose == true)
        {
```

```
            _screen.Details.Dispatcher.BeginInvoke(
                delegate()
                {
                    _screen.Save();
                });
        }
        else
        {
            DiscardChanges();
        }

    }

    private void DiscardChanges()
    {
        if ((_entity != null))
        {
            _entity.Details.DiscardChanges();
        }
    }

    }
}
```

Using the Modal Window Helper Class

Now that you've created your modal window helper class, you can use this on any screen that uses a data grid.

First, create a new screen using the editable grid screen template. We've called our screen PersonList. As described earlier, create a new rows layout. Drag the Selected Item object from the screen member list into the rows layout. Change the control type to ModalWindow and hide the Show button by unchecking the Show Button check box using the ModalWindow control's properties window. While you're in the properties window, make a note of the name of the ModalWindow control. You'll need to know this when you initialize an instance of the ModalWindowHelper class.

Now carry out the steps that follow:

1. If you've created a Silverlight class library:

   a. Switch the LightSwitch project to File view.

   b. Add a reference to the new Central.Utilities.Client (or whatever you've called your Silverlight class library) project to your project.

2. Switch to File view and add a reference to the System.Windows.Controls.Data and System.Windows.Controls assemblies.

3. In the partial PersonList class (see Listing 8-15):

   a. Add a class level ModalWindowHelper variable.

b. In the `PersonList_InitializeDataWorkspace` method, initialize the variable to a new instance of `ModalWindowHelper`, passing it the collection it needs to works with, the name of the `ModalWindow` control, and an optional entity name (it'll use the name of the entity that the collection is based on if no entity name is supplied).

c. In the `PersonList_Created` method, call the helper's Initialize method, optionally passing a Boolean value that determines if the windows has a Close button or not, and whether any changes should be automatically saved when the window is closed.

d. Set the `LIST_CONTROL` constant to the name of your data grid or data list.

4. Delete the grid's Add, Edit, and Delete buttons (you could also override them if you prefer, instead of deleting and re-creating them).

5. Add a new Add button, a View button, and a Delete button (name these methods `AddItem`, `ViewItem`, and `DeleteItem`). Create their `CanExecute` and `Execute` methods.

6. In the Add button's `CanExecute` method, set the result to the helper's `CanAdd` method (the method examines the collection and determines if a record can be added, or not, in the case of a read-only collection—in a real scenario you'd probably want to combine this with a test for an add permission as well).

7. In the Add button's Execute method, simply call the helper's `AddEntity` method.

8. Follow the same procedure for the View button and the Delete button.

9. You'll need to add an OK button to your modal window (name this `SaveItem`), then set its Execute method to call the helper's `DialogOK` method (the method takes care of closing the window, and even saving the record in the collection if you specified `SaveOnClose` to be true in the Initialize method—you'd only do this in fairly rare circumstances, but the functionality is there for you if you need it).

10. You can optionally add a Cancel button (setting its Execute method the same way you set the OK button's Execute method), but if you click the X in the window's title bar, the changes will be discarded, and the window will close (you'd only need to add a Cancel button for cosmetic reasons).

That's it! Just by wiring up a few methods and buttons to the appropriate helper methods, you never have to worry about the complex workings of a modal window again.

▪ **Tip** After calling `AddEntity`, you can use the collection's `SelectedItem` property to initialize any of the newly added entity's properties, if you need to do that.

Listing 8-15. Using the ModalWindow helper class

VB:

File: OfficeCentral\Client\UserCode\PersonList.vb

Imports Central.Utilities.Client

Public Class PersonList

```vb
    'Set LIST_CONTROL to the name of your data grid or control
    'eg Grid or List
    Private Const LIST_CONTROL As String = "ListControl"
    Private Const ITEM_WINDOW As String = "ItemWindow"
    Private Const ITEM As String = "Item"
    Private itemsControl As DataGrid = Nothing
    Private itemWindow As ModalWindowHelper

    Private Sub PersonList_InitializeDataWorkspace(
        saveChangesTo As System.Collections.Generic.List(
            Of Microsoft.LightSwitch.IDataService))

        itemWindow =
            New ModalWindowHelper(Me.Items, ITEM_WINDOW, entityName:=ITEM)

            AddHandler Me.FindControl(LIST_CONTROL).ControlAvailable,
             Sub(send As Object, e As ControlAvailableEventArgs)
                 itemsControl = TryCast(
                     e.Control, System.Windows.Controls.DataGrid)
             End Sub

    End Sub

    Private Sub PersonList_Created()
        itemWindow.Initialize(hasCloseButton:=True, saveOnClose:=True)
    End Sub

    Private Sub AddItem_CanExecute(ByRef result As Boolean)
        result = (itemWindow.CanAdd = True)
    End Sub

    Private Sub AddItem_Execute()
        itemWindow.AddEntity()
    End Sub
    Private Sub ViewItem_CanExecute(ByRef result As Boolean)
        result = (itemWindow.CanView = True)
    End Sub

    Private Sub ViewItem_Execute()
        itemWindow.ViewEntity()
    End Sub
```

```
        Private Sub SaveItem_Execute()
            itemWindow.DialogOk()
        End Sub

        Private Sub CancelItem_Execute()
            itemWindow.DialogCancel()
        End Sub

End Class
```

C#:

File: OfficeCentral\Client\UserCode\PersonList.cs

```csharp
using System;
using System.Collections;
using System.Collections.Generic;
using System.Data;
using System.Windows.Controls;
using Central.Utilities.Client;

public class ListScreen
{

    //Set LIST_CONTROL to the name of your data grid or control
    //eg Grid or List
    private const string LIST_CONTROL = "ListControl";
    private const string ITEM_WINDOW = "ItemWindow";
    private const string ITEM = "Item";
    private DataGrid itemsControl = null;
    private ModalWindowHelper itemWindow;

    partial void ListScreen_InitializeDataWorkspace(
        System.Collections.Generic.List<Microsoft.LightSwitch.IDataService>
            saveChangesTo)
    {

        itemWindow = new ModalWindowHelper(
            this.Items, ITEM_WINDOW, entityName: ITEM);

        this.FindControl(LIST_CONTROL).ControlAvailable += (
                object send, ControlAvailableEventArgs e) => {
                    itemsControl = e.Control as System.Windows.Controls.DataGrid; };
    }

    partial void PersonList_Created()
    {
        itemWindow.Initialize(
            hasCloseButton: true, saveOnClose: true);
    }
```

```
partial void AddItem_CanExecute(ref bool result)
{
    result = (itemWindow.CanAdd() == true);
}

partial void AddItem_Execute()
{
    itemWindow.AddEntity();
}
partial void ViewItem_CanExecute(ref bool result)
{
    result = (itemWindow.CanView() == true);
}

partial void ViewItem_Execute()
{
    itemWindow.ViewEntity();
}

partial void SaveItem_Execute()
{
    itemWindow.DialogOk();
}

partial void CancelItem_Execute()
{
    itemWindow.DialogCancel();
}
```

}

Using the *AutoCompleteBox* Control

In this section, we'll show you how to use the AutoCompleteBox control. We'll begin by explaining what it does, before moving on to show you how to do the following:

- Add an *unbound* AutoCompleteBox that's unconnected to the main data on your screen.

- Set AutoCompleteBox values in code.

- Create sets of nested AutoCompleteBoxes.

The AutoCompleteBox control allows users to select an item from a list of drop-down values. It also allows the user to type into the control and filters the drop-down items based on the text that's entered.

You can set the filter mode by using the filter mode in the Properties pane of your AutoCompleteBox control (Figure 8-53).

Figure 8-53. AutoCompleteBox filter model

Setting the Items Shown on Each Row

By default, the AutoCompleteBox uses the summary control to display the summary property for each row that's shown in the AutoCompleteBox.

If you want to show additional properties in each row of the AutoCompleteBox, you can change the summary control to a columns layout and add the additional properties you want to show as child items (Figure 8-54).

Design Time

Runtime

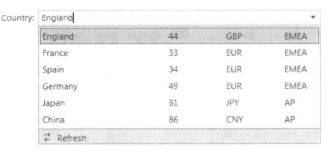

Figure 8-54. Setting the items shown on each AutoCompleteBox row

Creating an Unbound *AutoCompleteBox*

Sometimes you'll want to create an AutoCompleteBox that's unconnected with the main data that's shown in your screen.

Let's imagine you want to create a search screen that filters customers by country. The search results are shown in a data grid in the main area of the screen.

To allow a user to carry out the filtering, you'd like to add an AutoCompleteBox that returns a list of countries.

To do this, follow these steps:

1.   Create a new screen.

2.   Click the Add Data Item button and add a new local property. Using the Type drop-down, choose Country. Name your property CountryProperty.

3.   CountryProperty now appears in the screen member list. Drag this onto the Screen Content Tree. This will add CountryProperty as an AutoCompleteBox on your screen.

By default, the AutoCompleteBox returns all records in the country table. You might want to filter the items shown in the AutoCompleteBox. For example, you might only want to show countries that are in the EMEA region. To do this, you'd create a query that returns a filtered list of countries. Next, you'd add the query to your screen using the Add Data Item button. You can then set the data source of your AutoCompleteBox to the query you've added.

This concludes the process you would follow to add an AutoCompleteBox onto your screen. We'll come back to this example later when we describe how to complete our custom search screen.

Setting the Value of an *AutoCompleteBox* in Code

From time to time you'll want to set the value of your AutoCompleteBox in code. In the same way as you'd set the value of any other control on your screen, you'd do this by setting the value on your underlying data property.

Returning to the country example, let's imagine you want to set the AutoCompleteBox value to England when your screen loads.

To do this, you'll need to write a LINQ query that returns the England record from the database, and set the CountryProperty to the value that's returned. Listing 8-16 shows the code that you'd use.

Listing 8-16. Setting AutoCompleteBox values in code

VB:

```
File: OfficeCentral\Client\UserCode\CustomerSearch.vb

Me.CountryProperty =
    DataWorkspace.ApplicationData.Country.Where(
        Function(country) country.CountryName = "England"
            ).FirstOrDefault()
```

C#:

File: OfficeCentral\Client\UserCode\CustomerSearch.vb

```
this.CountryProperty =
    DataWorkspace.ApplicationData.Countries.Where(
        (country) => country.CountryName == " England"
    ).FirstOrDefault();
```

Nested *AutoCompleteBox* Example

Another common scenario you might encounter is the need to create sets of nested AutoCompleteBoxes.

In this example, we'll demonstrate a set of two AutoCompleteBoxes. The first AutoCompleteBox shows a list of international regions (such as EMEA, NCSA, AP). After a user selects a region, a second AutoCompleteBox will be filtered to show a list of countries that matches the region selected in the first AutoCompleteBox.

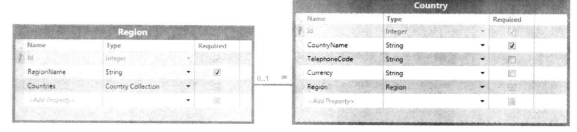

Figure 8-55. Country and region tables

To create this sample:

1.   Create a set of tables as shown in Figure 8-55.

2.   Create a new screen.

3.   Click the Add Data Item button and add a new local property. Using the Type drop-down, choose Region. Name your property RegionProperty.

4.   Click the Add Data Item button and add a new local property. Using the Type drop-down, choose Country. Name your property CountryProperty.

5.   Drag RegionProperty and CountryProperty onto the Screen Content Tree.

The data source of the CountryProperty needs to be set to a query that filters the countries based on region. You'll need to create a parameterized query that filters the country table by region. This query is shown in Figure 8-56. We've called this query CountriesByRegion and have named the parameter RegionIdParameter.

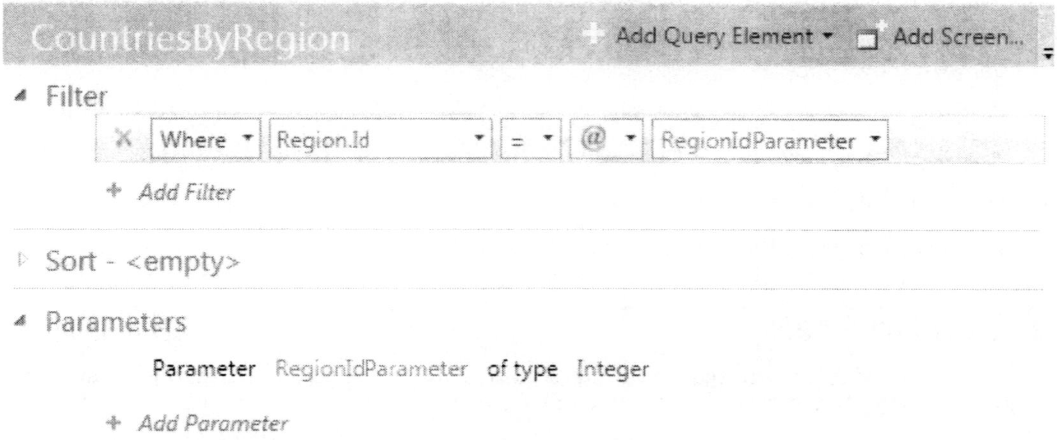

CountriesByRegion   + Add Query Element ▾   ☐ Add Screen... ⬝

◢ Filter

     ✕ | Where ▾ | Region.Id ▾ | = ▾ | @ ▾ | RegionIdParameter ▾

     + *Add Filter*

▷ Sort - <empty>

◢ Parameters

        Parameter RegionIdParameter of type Integer

     + *Add Parameter*

Figure 8-56. *CountryByRegion query*

After creating your query, you'll need to carry out the remaining steps in the screen designer:

6. Click the Add Data Item button and add a new query. Select the CountriesByRegion query that you've just created.

7. You'll need to set the Region parameter value of your CountriesByRegion query to the value that's selected in the Region AutoCompleteBox. To do this, select the RegionIdParameter parameter and set the parameter binding to RegionProperty.Id.

8. Select the Country AutoCompleteBox and go the properties window. Use the Choices drop-down to change the data source from Auto to the CountriesByRegion query.

This completes what you need to do to create a set of nested AutoCompleteBoxes. When you run your screen, the Country AutoCompleteBox will be filtered by the value selected in the Region AutoCompleteBox.

Custom Screens and Scenarios

The built-in screen templates allow you to quickly create screens that are functional. But these can only take you so far. If you want to create a rounded application to show off to an end user, you'll need to do some extra customization.

In this section, we'll describe some of the typical customization scenarios you'll encounter. We'll show you how to create a home page, a custom search screen, and describe how to create some customized data entry screens.

Adding a Home Page

Earlier in this chapter, we showed you how to specify a start-up screen. The start-up screen is the first screen that's shown to the user when your application starts. Your application won't look very attractive if the startup screen consists of a data grid or some bog standard data entry screen.

You can make your application more appealing by creating a custom home page. The home page might contain a company logo, welcome text, and links that open up other screens in your application. In this section, we'll show you:

- How to create a home page.

- How to add static text to a screen.

- How to add static images to your screen.

- How to add clickable links to a screen.

Creating an Empty Screen

The first thing you'll need to do is to create an empty screen. Unlike most other screens, the home screen doesn't require any data. All you really need is an empty screen that gives you a blank canvas to work from.

To create an empty screen, open the Add New Screen dialog (Figure 8-57). Select any screen template, apart from the Details Screen template. Leave the Screen Data drop-down as None and click the OK button to create your screen.

Figure 8-57. Creating an empty screen

The reason why you can't use the Details Screen template is because LightSwitch doesn't allow you to leave the Screen Data drop-down as None. If you try and do this, it disables the OK button, which prevents you from adding the screen.

In this example, we've named our home screen *Home*. You can set this as your startup screen by using the screen navigation tab in the properties of your project, as shown earlier in this chapter.

Adding Static Text to a Screen

A home screen is most likely to contain some static text. This could be a heading, welcome message, or some additional help text. Adding static text is a common task you'll want to do and not just limited to home screen design.

As you now know, any control you use in LightSwitch must be data bound to a data item. So in order to display a label, you'll need to first create a data item that represents the text you want to display. Only after you do this can you add a label to display the text.

In this example, we'll add a label that says *Welcome to the Office Central Application*. The steps that you'll need to follow in order to do this are:

1. In the screen designer, click the Add Data Item button.

2. When the Add Data Item dialog appears, select the Local Property radio option, and choose the type string. Name your property ScreenTitle.

3. The ScreenTitle property now appears in the Screen Members list. Drag this into your content tree and use the drop-down to change the control type from a text box to a label.

4. If you prefer, you can use the Font Style drop-down to change the display style to something different. For example, you can change the font style to Heading1 to display the label text in a larger and bolder font.

5. You'll now need to assign a value to the ScreenTitle property by adding some code to the Home_InitializeDataWorkspace method. This is shown in Listing 8-17.

If you now run your home screen, the screen title text appears as expected. You can now repeat the same process for any other labels you want to show on your screen.

Listing 8-17. Setting the label text in code

VB:

```
File: OfficeCentral\Client\UserCode\Home.vb

Private Sub Home_InitializeDataWorkspace(
    saveChangesTo As System.Collections.Generic.List(
        Of Microsoft.LightSwitch.IDataService))
    ScreenTitle = "Welcome to the Office Central Application"
End Sub
```

C#:

```
File: OfficeCentral\Client\UserCode\Home.cs

partial void Home_InitializeDataWorkspace(
    System.Collections.Generic.List<Microsoft.LightSwitch.IDataService>
```

```
          saveChangesTo)
{
    ScreenTitle = "Welcome to the Office Central Application";
}
```

Adding a Static Image to a Screen

When working with data in your application, it's pretty easy to add an image column to your table. This allows you to upload and display images.

In the home screen, however, we don't want to use an image that's stored in the database. Instead, we want to embed a static image within our client application and display that on our home screen.

Just like the static text example, you'll need to write some code that retrieves the embedded image and stores it into a local property.

To set up your screen, carry out the following steps:

1. In the screen designer, click the Add Data Item button.

2. When the Add Data Item dialog appears, choose the Local Property radio option, and select the type image. Name your property ScreenLogo.

3. The ScreenLogo property now appears in the Screen Members list. Drag this onto your content tree and use the drop-down to change the control type from an image editor to an image viewer. Because we don't want the users to modify the static image, changing the control to an image viewer makes the image read-only.

The most important part of this process is to embed your image file inside your Silverlight client. To do this, you'll need to switch your project into File view.

In Solution Explorer, right-click your client project and choose the Add ➤ Existing Item option. Using the file browser dialog that appears, select the image file you want to include. The image file must be in PNG or JPG format. This is because the image viewer control only supports these two formats.

In our example, we've embedded an image called ScreenLogo.png. After adding the image, you'll need to change the Build Action to Embedded Resource in the Properties pane (Figure 8-58).

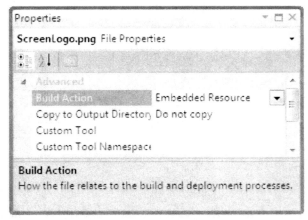

Figure 8-58. Embedding an image in the client project

The last thing that remains is to add the code that sets the ScreenLogo property. Click the Write Code button and select the Home_InitializeDataWorkspace method. Now add the code as shown in Listing 8-18.

Listing 8-18. Retrieving an embedded image

VB:

```
File: OfficeCentral\Client\UserCode\Home.vb

Private Sub Home_InitializeDataWorkspace(
    saveChangesTo As System.Collections.Generic.List(
        Of Microsoft.LightSwitch.IDataService))

    ScreenTitle = "Welcome to the Office Central Application"
    ScreenLogo = GetImageFromAssembly("ScreenLogo.png")
End Sub

Private Function GetImageFromAssembly(
    fileName As String) As Byte()

    Dim assembly As Reflection.Assembly =
        Reflection.Assembly.GetExecutingAssembly()

    Dim stream As Stream =
        assembly.GetManifestResourceStream(fileName)

    Dim streamLength As Integer = CInt(stream.Length)

    Dim fileData(streamLength - 1) As Byte
    stream.Read(fileData, 0, streamLength)
    stream.Close()
    Return fileData

End Function
```

C#:

```
File: OfficeCentral\Client\UserCode\Home.cs

partial void Home_InitializeDataWorkspace(
    System.Collections.Generic.List<Microsoft.LightSwitch.IDataService>
        saveChangesTo)
{
    ScreenTitle = "Welcome to the Office Central Application";
    ScreenLogo = GetImageFromAssembly("ScreenLogo.png");
}

private byte[] GetImageFromAssembly(string fileName)
{
    System.Reflection.Assembly assembly =
        System.Reflection.Assembly.GetExecutingAssembly();
```

313

```
Stream stream =
    assembly.GetManifestResourceStream(fileName);

int streamLength = Convert.ToInt32(stream.Length);
byte[] fileData = new byte[streamLength];
stream.Read(fileData, 0, streamLength);
stream.Close();
return fileData;
}
```

The code shown includes a helper method called GetImageFromAssembly. This is used to extract the image file from the client assembly. Note that in C#, the file name you pass to the GetManifestResourceStream method must be prefixed with the namespace (typically LightSwitchApplication). If you can't work out the correct file name to pass to this method, you can place a breakpoint in the GetImageFromAssembly method and interrogate the result of the assembly.GetManifestResourceNames method to show the names of the resources in the assembly.

Retrieving an Image from the Database

An embedded image is the ideal solution for the home page scenario. However, the disadvantage of this technique is that you can't easily change the image that's shown without redeploying your application. So if you want to allow your users to change the home screen image, it's better to use an image that's stored in the database, rather than a static image.

An easy way to store your home page image inside the database is to create a *control* table that contains a single row.

We'll now modify our code sample so that the image is retrieved from the database, rather than the client assembly.

First, you'll need to create a table to store the home page image. Figure 8-59 shows the schema of a table we've created called AppSettings. This table contains an image column called HomePageLogo.

AppSetting		
Name	Type	Required
Id	Integer	☑
HomePageLogo	Image	☑
<Add Property>		☐

Figure 8-59. AppSettings table

To upload your image into the AppSettings table, you'll need to create a simple data entry screen.

Listing 8-19 shows the change you'd make to the Home_InitializeDataWorkspace method to retrieve the image from the database.

Listing 8-19. Retrieving an image from the database

VB:

File: OfficeCentral\Client\UserCode\Home.vb

```vb
Private Sub Home_InitializeDataWorkspace(
    saveChangesTo As System.Collections.Generic.List(
        Of Microsoft.LightSwitch.IDataService))

    Dim appSetting = DataWorkspace.ApplicationData.AppSettings.FirstOrDefault()

    If Not appSetting Is Nothing Then
        ScreenLogo = appSetting.HomePageLogo
    End If

End Sub
```

C#:

File: OfficeCentral\Client\UserCode\Home.cs

```csharp
partial void Home_InitializeDataWorkspace(
    System.Collections.Generic.List<Microsoft.LightSwitch.IDataService>
        saveChangesTo)
{
    var appSetting =
        DataWorkspace.ApplicationData.AppSettings.FirstOrDefault();
    if (appSetting != null)
    {
        ScreenLogo = appSetting.HomePageLogo;
    }
}
```

In the code shown, we've created a query that retrieves the first record from the AppSettings table. The code then sets the ScreenLogo property to the HomePageLogo value of the first record.

The important point about this code is that it illustrates how to retrieve an image from a database table. In practice, you might want to write some validation code to ensure that the AppSettings table can contain only one record. You can also protect write access to your AppSettings table by setting permissions and only allowing administrators to update the contents of the table.

Adding Links to Open Other Screens

Another feature you'll typically find on a home screen is links. These allow users to open up other screens or perform other actions.

In this example, we'll add a link that opens up the customer search screen. A simple way of creating a layout that allows you to add links is to add a table layout.

After adding a table layout, add a child table column layout. Now add a rows layout beneath it, in order to create a table cell.

Right-click the Rows Layout and select the option to add a new button. The button appears in the command bar area after you've added it. You can then use the drop-down button to change the button into a link, as shown in Figure 8-60.

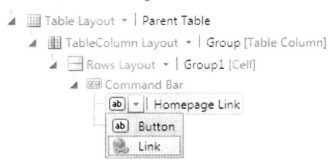

Figure 8-60. *Creating a link*

Once you've created your link, you can double-click it to open the code window. You can then use the code that was shown in Listing 8-5 to open the customer search screen. This code would open the customer search screen by calling the show method you'll find via the Application object.

Alternatively, you could write some other code that performs another custom action.

Creating a Custom Search Screen

The search screen that LightSwitch creates when you choose the Search Data Screen template is pretty basic.

By using the various techniques you've learned throughout this and the query design chapters, we'll show you how to create a more powerful search screen.

In this example, we'll create a search screen for finding customers. The screen contains an AutoCompleteBox that allows users to filter the customers by country. The screen contains a surname text box that allows the user to filter additionally by surname.

The first thing you'll need to do is to create a query that filters customers by country and surname. We've called this CustomerSearch, and it is shown in Figure 8-61. This query includes two optional parameters called CountryIdParameter and SurnameParameter.

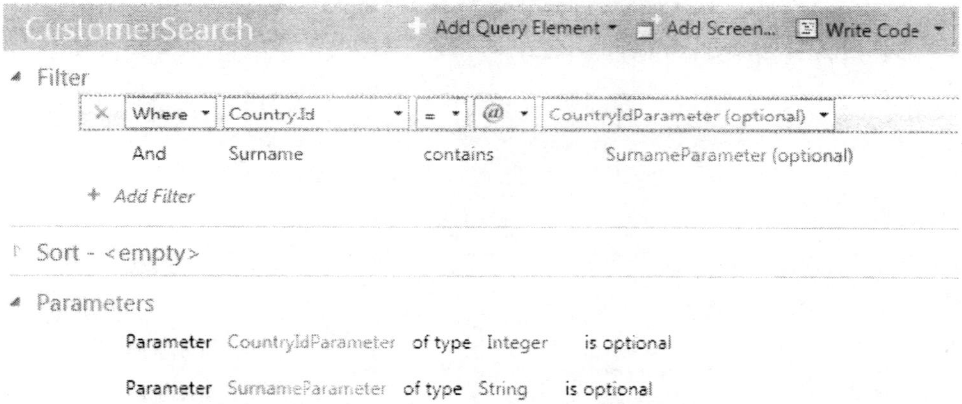

Figure 8-61. Custom search query

Having created your query, you'll need to create a screen that uses this query. Here are the steps you'll need to carry out:

1. Create a new screen based on the search data screen template. In the Screen Data drop-down of the Add New Screen dialog, select the CustomerSearch query that you've created.

2. You'll now need to create an AutoCompleteBox that shows a list of countries. Follow the instructions shown earlier in the "Creating an Unbound AutoCompleteBox" section. This involves creating a local property of type Country using the Add New Data dialog. Name this property CountryProperty.

3. After creating the CountryProperty property, drag this onto the Screen Content Tree to create your AutoCompleteBox.

4. By default, LightSwitch will bind the CountryIdParameter parameter of your query to a property that it automatically creates. Change the parameter binding so that it points to the CountryProperty property you created in step 2. The syntax you would use in the parameter binding text box would be CountryProperty.Id.

This completes the tasks you need to carry out in the screen designer. The screen you'll see when you run your application is shown in Figure 8-62.

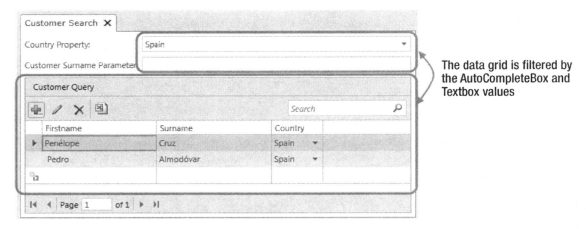

The data grid is filtered by the AutoCompleteBox and Textbox values

Figure 8-62. Custom search screen

Designing an Add/Edit Screen

As you now know, you can create screens to view data using the Details Screen template. For adding data, you can add a screen that uses the new data template. However, LightSwitch doesn't provide a screen template that allows you to both edit and view data using the same screen.

Let's suppose you want to create identical screens to carry out both tasks. If you use the default templates provided by LightSwitch, you'd first need to create a details screen and customize it as necessary. Afterward, you'd have to create a new data screen and carry out the same customization work you've already done before on the details screen.

In this example, we'll show you how to create a combined Add and Edit screen. If you need to create screens that look consistent for adding and viewing data, this technique will save you a lot of time. It'll also make your application more maintainable because you'll have fewer screens to manage in your application.

In the steps that follow, we'll build a combination screen that adds and edits a product entity.

1. Create a details screen for the product entity. In the Add New Data screen dialog, check the check box that sets this as the default screen for the entity.

2. By default, LightSwitch creates an ID property (called `ProductId` in our example). You'll need to make this optional by unchecking the Is Required check box.

3. Click the Add Data Item button and add a local property of data type product. Name this `ProductProperty`.

4. Delete the content on the screen that's bound to the product query.

5. Add the `ProductProperty` property onto the Screen Content Tree.

Now add the code, as shown in Listing 8-20.

Listing 8-20. Product add and edit code

VB:

File: OfficeCentral\Client\UserCode\ProductAddEdit.vb

```vb
Private Sub Product_Loaded(succeeded As Boolean)
    If Not Me.ProductId.HasValue Then
        Me.ProductProperty = New Product()
    Else
        Me.ProductProperty = Me.Product
    End If

    Me.SetDisplayNameFromEntity(Me.ProductProperty)
End Sub

Private Sub Product_Changed()
    Me.SetDisplayNameFromEntity(Me.ProductProperty)
End Sub

Private Sub ProductAddEdit_Saved()
    Me.SetDisplayNameFromEntity(Me.ProductProperty)
End Sub
```

C#:

File: OfficeCentral\Client\UserCode\ProductAddEdit.cs

```csharp
partial void Product_Loaded(bool succeeded)
{
    if (!this.ProductId.HasValue)
    {
        this.ProductProperty = new Product();
    }
    else
    {
        this.ProductProperty = this.Product;
    }

    this.SetDisplayNameFromEntity(this.ProductProperty);
}

partial void Product_Changed()
{
    this.SetDisplayNameFromEntity(this.ProductProperty);
}

partial void ProductAddEdit_Saved()
{
    this.SetDisplayNameFromEntity(this.ProductProperty);
}
```

When you create a screen that uses the details template, LightSwitch creates a query that returns a single product using the primary key value. It creates a screen parameter/property for you called ProductId.

We don't want the screen to be based on this query because it wouldn't work when the screen is in Add mode. We've therefore created a local product property called ProductProperty and have bound the UI controls on our screen to this property.

We've then made the ProductId screen parameter optional. If this parameter isn't set, ProductProperty is set to an instance of a new product and the screen opens in Add mode.

If the ProductId parameter is set, we simply set ProductProperty to the value that's returned by ProductQuery.

Because we've set this screen as the default screen, any product that's displayed using the summary control will navigate to this screen.

When you want to open this screen to enter a new product, you can simply create a method (CreateNewProduct in our example) and use the code as shown in Listing 8-21.

Listing 8-21. Opening the product screen to add a new record

VB:

File: OfficeCentral\Client\UserCode\Home.vb

```
Private Sub CreateNewProduct()
    Me.Application.ShowProductAddEdit(null);
End Sub
```

C#:

File: OfficeCentral\Client\UserCode\Home.cs

```
partial void CreateNewProduct()
{
    this.Application.ShowProductAddEdit(null);
}
```

Many-to-Many Screen

A common requirement is the ability to support many-to-many relationships. In this example, we'll show you how to create a screen that enables many-to-many details to be entered.

Our application includes a table of product attributes. Examples of product attributes could include *gluten-free* or *suitable for vegetarians*. Each product can be associated with many attributes. Each product attribute can be associated with many products.

In Chapter 3, we showed you how to set up tables to represent a many-to-many relationship. You'll need to set up a junction table as shown in Figure 8-63. This includes a one-to-many relationship between the ProductAttribute and Product tables and a one-to-many relationship between the ProductAttribute and Attribute tables.

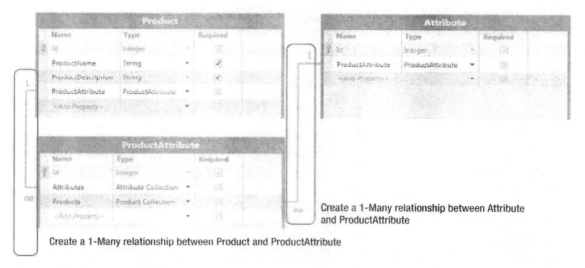

Figure 8-63. Structure of tables

After creating your tables, here are the steps you'll need to carry out in the screen designer:

1. Create a screen based on the product entity, using the new data screen template. In the additional data to include section, make sure the ProductDescription and ProductAttribute check boxes are selected

2. You'll need to add a query that returns all attributes. This allows the user to select an attribute and assign it to the product. Click the Add Data Item button and add a query that returns Attributes (All).

3. By default, LightSwitch creates a rows layout that contains a ProductAttribute data grid. Delete this and create a new group. Change it to a columns layout and call it ColumnGroup.

4. Add a new rows layout beneath ColumnGroup. Add the Attributes collection that you created in step 2 and change the control to a list.

5. Add another rows layout beneath ColumnGroup and call it ButtonGroup. Add two more row layouts beneath ButtonGroup and name them Button1 and Button2.

6. Right-click the Button1 group and choose the option to create a new button called AddAttribute. You won't find an option to add a new button using the Add drop-down box, so you'll need to use the right-click option.

7. Right-click the Button2 group and choose the option to create a new button called RemoveAttribute.

8. Add another rows layout beneath ColumnGroup and call it ProductAttributeGroup. Add the ProductAttribute collection to this group and change the control to a list. By default, a summary control is shown beneath

321

the data list, so change this to a rows layout. Delete the Products summary control so that only the Attributes summary control is shown.

9. Figure 8-64 shows how your screen looks after carrying out the above steps.

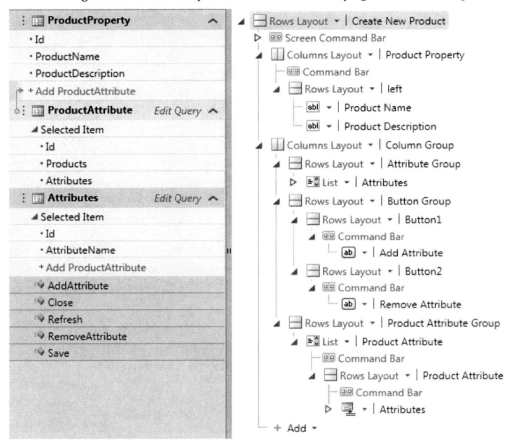

Figure 8-64. Screen layout of many-to-many screen

You'll now need to add the code that adds and removes attributes from a product. This is shown in Listing 8-22.

Listing 8-22. Code to Add/Remove product attributes

VB:

```
File: OfficeCentral\Client\UserCode\ProductAttributes.vb

Private Sub AddAttribute_Execute()
    ' Write your code here.
```

```
    If (Attributes.SelectedItem IsNot Nothing) Then
        Dim prodAtt As ProductAttribute = ProductAttribute.AddNew()
        prodAtt.Products = Me.ProductProperty
        prodAtt.Attributes = Attributes.SelectedItem
    End If
End Sub

Private Sub RemoveAttribute_Execute()
    ProductAttribute.DeleteSelected()
End Sub
```

C#:

File: OfficeCentral\Client\UserCode\ProductAttributes.cs

```
partial void AddAttribute_Execute()
{
    if (Attributes.SelectedItem != null) {
        ProductAttribute prodAtt = ProductAttribute.AddNew();
        prodAtt.Products = this.ProductProperty;
        prodAtt.Attributes = Attributes.SelectedItem;
    }
}

partial void RemoveAttribute_Execute()
{
    ProductAttribute.DeleteSelected();
}
```

This completes the design of our screen. Figure 8-65 shows how this screen looks when you run your application.

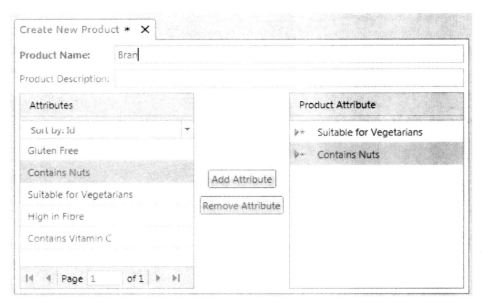

Figure 8-65. *Many-to-many list picker*

Creating a Multiselect Data Grid

One of the limitations of the built-in data is that you can't select **multiple records.**

To illustrate the use of a multiselect data grid, we'll create a **screen that displays orders.** We'll set up the data grid so that multiple orders can be selected. We'll then **create a button that allows** the user to set the order status to *shipped* on the records that are selected.

To begin, you'll need to add a reference to the `System.Windows.Controls.Data` assembly. To do this:

1. Switch your project to File view.

2. Right-click the client project.

3. Choose the Add Reference option and select `System.Windows.Controls.Data` from the .NET tab.

Now return to Logical view and carry out the following tasks:

4. Create an editable grid screen based on the Order entity. We've **called our** screen `UpdateOrders`.

5. Click the Add Data Item button and add a new **method called** `UpdateSelectedRecords`.

6. Create a button by dragging the `UpdateSelectedRecords` method from the Screen Member list to the screen command bar node.

7. Add the code as shown in Listing 8-23. In the Created method, **we use the** `FindControl` method to return a reference to the data grid. By default, **this is**

called grid, so you might need to change this line of code if you've named your data grid differently.

Listing 8-23. Opening the product screen to add a new record

VB:

File: OfficeCentral\Client\UserCode\UpdateOrders.vb

```vb
Imports System.Windows.Controls

Private WithEvents _datagridControl As DataGrid = Nothing

Private Sub UpdateOrders_Created()

    'Replace grid with the name of your data grid control
    AddHandler Me.FindControl("grid").ControlAvailable,
        Sub(send As Object, e As ControlAvailableEventArgs)

            _datagridControl = TryCast(e.Control, DataGrid)
            _datagridControl.SelectionMode =
                DataGridSelectionMode.Extended

        End Sub

End Sub

Private Sub UpdateStatuses_Execute()

    ' this query returns an OrderStatus entity
    ' in our data model, status id 3 means shipped

    Dim shippedStatus =
        DataWorkspace.ApplicationData.OrderStatusSet.Where(
            Function(item) item.OrderStatusID = 3).FirstOrDefault()

    For Each ord As Order In _datagridControl.SelectedItems
        ord.OrderStatus = shippedStatus
    Next

End Sub
```

C#:

File: OfficeCentral\Client\UserCode\UpdateOrders.cs

```csharp
using System.Windows.Controls;

private DataGrid _datagridControl = null;

partial void UpdateOrders_Created()
```

```
{
    //Replace grid with the name of your data grid control
    this.FindControl("grid").ControlAvailable +=
        (object sender, ControlAvailableEventArgs e) =>
        {
            _datagridControl = ((DataGrid)e.Control);
            _datagridControl.SelectionMode =
                DataGridSelectionMode.Extended;
        };
}

partial void UpdateStatuses_Execute()
{
    // this query returns an OrderStatus entity
    // in our data model, status id 3 means shipped

    var shippedStatus =
        DataWorkspace.ApplicationData.OrderStatusSet.Where(
            item => item.OrderStatusID == 3).FirstOrDefault();

    foreach (Order ord in _datagridControl.SelectedItems)
    {
        ord.OrderStatus = shippedStatus;
    }
}
```

In the Created method of the screen, we've added an event handler that handles the ControlAvailable event of the data grid. In the ControlAvailable method, we simply set the SelectionMode of the data grid to Extended.

The UpdateSelectedRecords method loops through the selected items on the grid and sets the OrderStatus as appropriate. To demonstrate the principle, we've hard coded the order status ID but in practice, it might be wise to avoid such magic numbers by using a constant.

When you run this screen, you'll be able to select multiple rows by using the Ctrl key. In Figure 8-66, notice how three rows have been selected in the grid. Clicking the update button updates all of the rows that have been selected.

Figure 8-66. Multiselect screen at runtime

Working with Files

The LightSwitch table designer allows you to define properties with a data type of binary. By using this data type, you can create applications that allow users to store and retrieve files. However, LightSwitch doesn't include a built in control for uploading and downloading files. Instead, you'll need to write your own code that uses the Silverlight file open dialog and save file dialog boxes.

In this section, we'll show you how to use these Silverlight file dialogs. We'll use a `ProductDocument` table as an example. This allows the user to upload and retrieve documents that relate to a product. Example documents might be product fact sheets in Word or Excel format. Figure 8-67 shows the schema of the `ProductDocument` table.

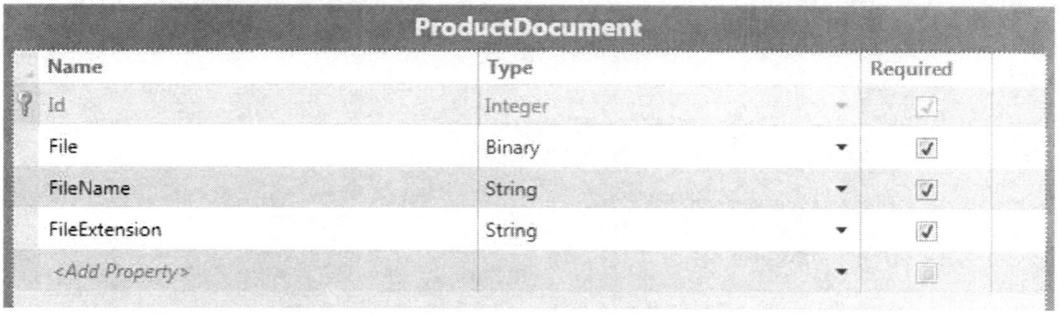

Figure 8-67. ProductDocument table schema

We'll now show you what you'll need to do to upload and retrieve a file.

The Silverlight file dialogs will only work in desktop applications—they won't work in browser applications. If you attempt to use these file dialogs in a browser application, you'll receive the error *Dialogs must be user-initiated*.

You'll see this error message in a browser application when you attach the file open dialog code to a button. This message doesn't make much sense, particularly given that a button click can only be user initiated.

The reason LightSwitch reports this error message is because it invokes all button logic asynchronously. Because of this, Silverlight doesn't consider the code you've written to be user initiated.

If you really need to use the Silverlight file dialogs in a browser application, a work around is to write your own custom control. You can then wrap the file dialog operations inside your custom control.

How to Upload a File

To upload a file, create a new data screen based on the ProductDocument table. Now carry out the following steps in the screen designer:

1. Click the Add Data Item button and add a new method called UploadFileToDatabase.

2. The UploadFileToDatabase method now appears in the Screen Members list. Create a button by dragging it onto the Screen Content Tree.

3. Now add the code as shown in Listing 8-24.

Listing 8-24. Uploading a file

VB:

File: OfficeCentral\Client\UserCode\ProductDocumentDetails.vb

```
Imports System.Windows.Controls
Imports Microsoft.LightSwitch.Threading

Private Sub UploadFileToDatabase_Execute()

    Dispatchers.Main.Invoke( Sub()

        Dim openDialog As New Controls.OpenFileDialog
        openDialog.Filter = "All files|*.*"

        'Use this syntax to only allow Word/Excel files
        'openDialog.Filter = "Word Files|*.doc|Excel Files |*.xls"

        If openDialog.ShowDialog = True Then
            Using fileData As System.IO.FileStream =
                openDialog.File.OpenRead

            Dim fileLen As Long = filedata.Length

            If (fileLen > 0) Then
                Dim fileBArray(fileLen - 1) As Byte
                filedata.Read(fileBArray, 0, fileLen)
                filedata.Close()

                Me.ProductDocumentProperty.File = fileBArray
```

```
                Me.ProductDocumentProperty.FileExtension =
                    openDialog.File.Extension.ToString()
                Me.ProductDocumentProperty.FileName =
                    openDialog.File.Name

            End If

        End Using
        End If

    End Sub)
End Sub
```

C#:

File: OfficeCentral\Client\UserCode\ProductDocumentDetails.cs

```csharp
using System.Windows.Controls;
using Microsoft.LightSwitch.Threading;

partial void UploadFileToDatabase_Execute()
{

    Dispatchers.Main.Invoke(() =>
    {
        OpenFileDialog openDialog = new OpenFileDialog();
        openDialog.Filter = "Supported files|*.*";
        //Use this syntax to only allow Word/Excel files
        //openDialog.Filter = "Word Files|*.doc|Excel Files |*.xls";

        if (openDialog.ShowDialog() == true)
        {
            using (System.IO.FileStream fileData =
                openDialog.File.OpenRead())
            {
                int fileLen = (int)fileData.Length;

                if ((fileLen > 0))
                {
                    byte[] fileBArray = new byte[fileLen];
                    fileData.Read(fileBArray, 0, fileLen);
                    fileData.Close();

                    this.ProductDocumentProperty.File = fileBArray;
                    this.ProductDocumentProperty.FileExtension =
                        openDialog.File.Extension.ToString();
                    this.ProductDocumentProperty.FileName = openDialog.File.Name;
                }
            }
        }
    }
```

```
        });
    }
```

Whenever you use the Silverlight file open or file save dialogs, the code that invokes the dialogs must be executed on the main UI thread. If you don't invoke the dialog on the main UI thread, you'll receive the error message *This operation can only occur on the UI Thread*.

The first line of code in the `UploadFileToDatabase` invokes the remaining code on the main dispatcher (UI thread). The file open dialog allows the user to choose a file. The file data are then read into a byte array using a `FileStream` object. Finally, the `ProductDocumentProperty` property is set to the byte array. We've also saved the file name and file extension of the uploaded document in the same section of code.

The file open dialog also allows you to restrict the files the user can select. You'd use the Filter property to do this. In our example, we've allowed all files to be selected by using the *.* filter.

The commented out line of code shows the syntax you would use if you only want to allow the user to select Word and Excel files.

How to Download a File

After uploading a file, you'll need some way of downloading the file that was uploaded. We'll now show you how to retrieve a file and save it locally using the file save dialog.

To demonstrate this feature, we'll create a screen based on the Details Screen template. Once again, we'll use the `ProductDocument` table as the data source. In the screen designer, you'll now need to carry out the following steps:

1. Click the Add Data Item button and add a new method called `SaveFileFromDatabase`.

2. The `SaveFileFromDatabase` method now appears in the Screen Members list. Create a button by dragging this onto your content tree.

3. Now write the code as shown in Listing 8-25.

Listing 8-25. Downloading a file

VB:

```
File: OfficeCentral\Client\UserCode\ProductDocumentDetails.vb

Imports System.Windows.Controls
Imports Microsoft.LightSwitch.Threading

Private Sub SaveFileFromDatabase_Execute()

    Dispatchers.Main.Invoke( Sub()

        'Replace ProductDocument with the name of your entity
        Dim ms As System.IO.MemoryStream = New
            System.IO.MemoryStream(ProductDocument.File)

        Dispatchers.Main.Invoke(Sub()
            Dim saveDialog As New Controls.SaveFileDialog
```

```
            If saveDialog.ShowDialog = True Then
                Using fileStream As Stream = saveDialog.OpenFile
                    ms.WriteTo(fileStream)
                End Using
            End If
        End Sub)
    End Sub)
End Sub
```

C#:

File: OfficeCentral\Client\UserCode\ProductDocumentDetails.cs

```csharp
using System.Windows.Controls ;
using Microsoft.LightSwitch.Threading;

partial void SaveFileFromDatabase_Execute()
{
    Dispatchers.Main.Invoke(() =>
    {
        //Replace ProductDocument with the name of your entity
        System.IO.MemoryStream ms = new System.IO.MemoryStream(ProductDocument.File );

        Dispatchers.Main.Invoke(() =>
        {
            SaveFileDialog saveDialog = new SaveFileDialog();

            if (saveDialog.ShowDialog() == true)
            {
                using (Stream fileStream = saveDialog.OpenFile())
                {
                    ms.WriteTo(fileStream);
                }

            }

        });
    });

}
```

Just as before, the code needs to be invoked on the main UI thread for the save file dialog to work.

After the user selects the desired file location, a MemoryStream object is used to write the data into the file.

Opening Files in Their Application

Instead of saving the file using the save file dialog, you can choose to download the file and open it using the default application.

Once again, we'll use the ProductDocument table as an example. Let's imagine that a user has uploaded a Word document. In this example, we'll create a button on a LightSwitch screen that starts

Microsoft Word and opens the document. Once again, this example will only work in a desktop application.

The process we'll carry out is as follows:

- Save the file to an interim file location.

- Use the shell execute method to start up Word and open the file that was saved above.

The first part of the process saves the file into a temporary location. There are some important points to consider when saving files using LightSwitch. The security restrictions applied by Silverlight mean that you can't save files wherever you want. The limitations that are applied depend on the method you've chosen to save your file. These are described in Table 8-23.

Table 8-23. Ways to Save a File Using LightSwitch

Method	Description
Use the classes in the System.IO namespace	Files can only be saved into special locations. These include the My Documents, My Music, My Pictures, and My Videos folders of the current user.
Use the Silverlight SaveFileDialog dialog	Files can be saved to any location that the user has permissions to read/write.
Use isolated storage	This is a virtual file system that's provided by Silverlight.

If you want to save a file to a temporary location without any user intervention, there are two options you can choose from. You can create the file in My Documents, or you can create the file in isolated storage.

Isolated storage is a virtual file system that's provided by Silverlight. The isolated storage location is a hidden folder that exists on the end user's machine. This makes it an ideal place to save temporary files.

However, the disadvantage of using isolated storage is that Silverlight imposes a default storage quota, and quotas can be additionally set by administrators. Therefore, there's no guarantee there'll be space for you to save your file.

In our example, we've chosen to save our temporary file in the My Documents folder. To run this example, you'll need to carry out the following steps:

1. Click the Add Data Item button and add a new method called OpenFileFromDatabase.

2. The OpenFileFromDatabase method now appears in the Screen Members list. Create a button by dragging this onto your content tree.

3. Now write the code as shown in Listing 8-26.

Listing 8-26. Opening files in their applications

VB:

File: OfficeCentral\Client\UserCode\ProductDocumentDetails.vb

```vb
Imports System.Windows.Controls
Imports Microsoft.LightSwitch.Threading
Imports System.Runtime.InteropServices.Automation

Private Sub OpenFileFromDatabase_Execute()

    Try
        If (AutomationFactory.IsAvailable) Then
            'here's where we'll save the file
            Dim fullFilePath As String =
                System.IO.Path.Combine(
                    Environment.GetFolderPath(
                        Environment.SpecialFolder.MyDocuments),
                            ProductDocument.FileName)

            'replace ProductDocument with the name of your file property
            Dim fileData As Byte() = ProductDocument.File.ToArray()

            If (fileData IsNot Nothing) Then
                Using fs As New FileStream(
                        fullFilePath, FileMode.OpenOrCreate, FileAccess.Write)
                    fs.Write(fileData, 0, fileData.Length)
                    fs.Close()
                End Using
            End If

            Dim shell = AutomationFactory.CreateObject("Shell.Application")
            shell.ShellExecute(fullFilePath)

        End If
    Catch ex As Exception
        Me.ShowMessageBox(ex.ToString())
    End Try

End Sub
```

C#:

File: OfficeCentral\Client\UserCode\ProductDocumentDetails.cs

```csharp
using System.Runtime.InteropServices.Automation;

partial void OpenFileFromDatabase_Execute()
{

    try
    {
        if ((AutomationFactory.IsAvailable))
        {
            //this is where we'll save the file
```

```
        string fullFilePath = System.IO.Path.Combine(
            Environment.GetFolderPath(Environment.SpecialFolder.MyDocuments),
            ProductDocument.FileName);

        //replace ProductDocument with the name of your file property
                byte[] fileData = ProductDocument.File.ToArray();

        if ((fileData != null))
        {
            using (FileStream fs =
                new FileStream(fullFilePath, FileMode.OpenOrCreate, FileAccess.Write))
            {
                fs.Write(fileData, 0, fileData.Length);
                fs.Close();
            }
        }

        dynamic shell = AutomationFactory.CreateObject("Shell.Application");
        shell.ShellExecute(fullFilePath );
    }

}
catch (Exception ex)
{
    this.ShowMessageBox(ex.ToString());
}

}
```

When you run your screen, you'll be able to open your document in the associated application by clicking the button you've assigned to the SaveFileFromDatabase method.

Summary

In this chapter, we've covered the following topics that relate to screen design:

- How to create screens and how to use the screen designer.

- How to write screen code.

- How to use the Modal Window and AutoCompleteBox controls.

- Examples of common screens.

- Techniques to upload and download files.

When you create a screen, you can use one of the five built-in template types. If you want to create an empty screen that's not based on any data, select a template type other than *details screen* and choose None using the screen data drop-down.

The Add Data Item dialog allows you to add local properties, queries, and methods. Local properties are particularly important because these are needed in order to add UI controls to your screen. For example, you can't just add a text box or label onto a LightSwitch screen. Any LightSwitch control that appears on a screen must be *backed* by a property or entity.

Local properties are also important because they can be made into screen parameters using the properties window. This allows you to pass in values when you open a screen in code.

The Screen Members list is the section that appears in the left-hand side of the screen designer. If your screen uses a query, it'll appear in this section. If there are any parameters defined in your query, they'll appear in the Screen Members list in a group beneath the query. You can use the Properties pane to set the value of any query parameters.

LightSwitch raises events that you can handle in code. To write code, you'd click the Write Code button that you'll find in the Screen Designer Command bar. This opens a drop-down that displays a list of events you can handle. If you want to handle an event that belongs to a collection (e.g., the SelectionChanged event), you have to make sure the collection is selected in the Screen Member list. If you don't do this, the collection events won't show up in the Write Code drop-down.

You can use the FindControl method to return an IContentItemProxy object for a control on your screen. This represents LightSwitch's view model for the control, and you can use this to set the visibility or enabled state of a control.

After finding a control, you can create an event handler that handles the ControlAvailable event. This event will allow you to reference the underlying Silverlight control.

To make your UI react to changes in data, you can handle the events that are raised by the Silverlight controls or you can handle the PropertyChanged event of the entity you've used.

In the final part of this chapter, we've described how to use the AutoCompleteBox and Modal Window controls. We demonstrated how to create various screens including a home screen, custom search screen, and combined add/edit screen. We've also shown techniques for entering data based on many-to-many relationships and have shown you a technique that allows users to select multiple records in a data grid.

Finally, you've learned how to upload and download files. You've also seen how you can create a method that opens a file using its associated application.

CHAPTER 9

Creating and Using Custom Controls

When building screens in LightSwitch, you can present your data by using built-in controls. These controls include labels, text boxes, autocomplete boxes, and data grids. When writing more-sophisticated applications, you might want to allow users to view and enter data by using nonstandard controls. For example, you might want to allow users to enter numbers by using a slider control or to display data by using charts or graphs.

Fortunately, you're not stuck with the default set of controls that LightSwitch provides. Because LightSwitch applications are based on Silverlight, you can choose to present your data by using any Silverlight custom control that you choose. This chapter shows you how to use Silverlight custom controls in your application, including how to perform the necessary data binding that makes everything work.

Using Custom Controls vs. Control Extensions

You may have encountered LightSwitch control extensions such as the Excel data importer control or search filter control. If so, you might wonder about the difference between a control extension and a custom control.

A *control extension* needs to be installed into the Visual Studio IDE and allows customized controls to be reused in multiple applications. You can create your own custom control extension, or download and install extensions that others have created.

Silverlight *custom controls*, on the other hand, can be used without having to install anything extra onto your machine. Creating a custom control therefore requires less work. However, you are more restricted in what you can do with a custom control. For example, group controls can be created only as an extension. RowsLayout and TableLayout are examples of group controls that you may have come across. This type of control represents a container for holding multiple child content items.

Directly Using Silverlight Controls

The easiest way to use custom controls is to set up the data items on your LightSwitch screen to directly use the UI controls in the Silverlight SDK. You can find these controls in the System.Windows.Controls namespace. Of course, you could choose to use any third-party or homegrown control. However, directly using the controls in the Silverlight SDK very quickly opens up a whole host of additional UI elements, including the following:

- PasswordBox

- WebBrowser

- TreeView

- RichTextBox

- MediaElement

- MultiScaleImage

- HyperLinkButton

- ComboBox

The biggest advantage of this technique is that you have to write only minimal code. For example, you don't have to create an additional project, or to install a higher level of Visual Studio 2010 onto your machine. The next section demonstrates this technique by using the PasswordBox control.

The *PasswordBox* Control

PasswordBox is a simple control that you can use to replace the default text box control. It provides a masked password input box and replaces any text characters that you type with a series of dots.

There are two parts to using a custom control. First, you must specify a custom control for the data item that you want to use. Second, you must write code that binds the control to your underlying data.

Specifying a Control from *System.Windows.Controls*

To demonstrate the PasswordBox control, we'll create a new data entry screen based on a table called users. This table contains a property called password, and the contents will be shown by using the PasswordBox control.

By default, LightSwitch displays the password value by using a text box control. In the screen designer, select the password data item and go to the properties pane (Figure 9-1). In the Appearance group, select the Custom Control option from the Control Type drop-down list.

In the General section, you'll see a Change hyperlink next to the Custom Control text box, as shown in Figure 9-2. Click this link, and in the dialog box that appears, expand the System.Windows node. Selecting the System.Windows.Controls namespace brings up a list of all the controls that you can use. In this example, we'll select the PasswordBox control. However, you would carry out the same process if you wanted to use one of the other controls instead.

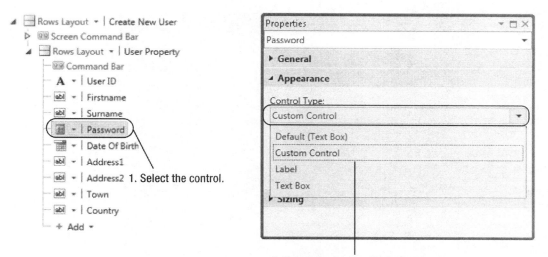

2. Select the Custom Control option.

Figure 9-1. Specifying a custom control

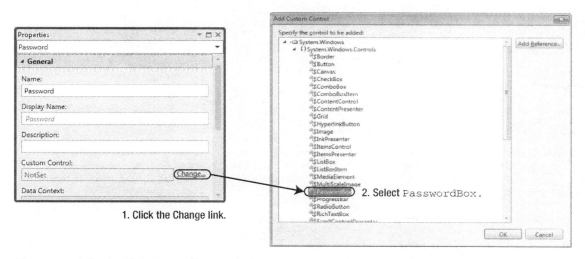

1. Click the Change link.
2. Select PasswordBox.

Figure 9-2. Selecting the PasswordBox control

If you can't see the PasswordBox control, make sure that you have chosen the System.Windows DLL, as shown in Figure 9-3, rather than one of the other DLLs in the Add Custom Control dialog box.

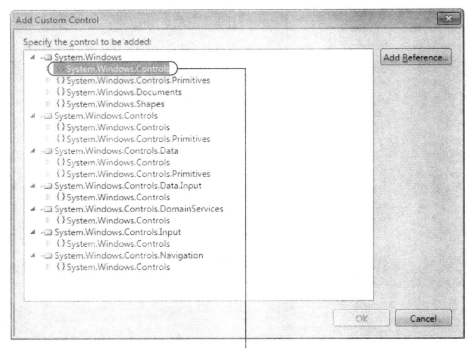

Expand this node rather than any of the others.

Figure 9-3. Make sure to choose the first node.

Data Binding by Using *SetBinding*

Now that you've specified a custom control, the next step is to bind it to the password property on your screen. You'll use the SetBinding method in the screen's activating event to do this.

In the screen designer, click the Write Code button and select the Activated event. Now enter the code as shown in Listing 9-1.

Listing 9-1. Calling the SetBinding Method

VB:

```
File : OfficeCentral\Client\UserCode\NewUser.vb

Private Sub CreateNewUser_Activated()
    Dim password As IContentItemProxy = Me.FindControl("Password")
    password.SetBinding(System.Windows.Controls.PasswordBox.PasswordProperty, "Value", ↵
        Windows.Data.BindingMode.TwoWay)
End Sub
```

C#:

File : OfficeCentral\Client\UserCode\NewUser.cs

```
partial void CreateNewUser_Activated()
{
    IContentItemProxy password = this.FindControl("Password");
    password.SetBinding(System.Windows.Controls.PasswordBox.PasswordProperty, "Value",↵
        System.Windows.Data.BindingMode.TwoWay);
}
```

The code obtains a reference to the PasswordBox control by using the FindControl method. This method requires the name of the control, which you can find in the properties window, shown in Figure 9-4. Note that the property name doesn't always match the control name, because you could add multiple instances of the password property onto your screen.

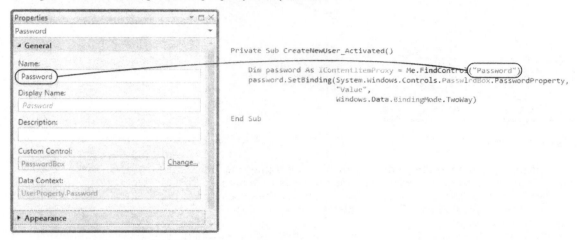

Figure 9-4. Using the FindControl method

The FindControl method returns an object of type IContentItemProxy, which is LightSwitch's view-model object. The object's SetBinding method performs the actual binding. This method accepts three arguments. The first argument is the dependency property that you want to bind to. In this example, the PasswordBox control exposes a dependency property called PasswordProperty. Don't worry too much if you don't understand what a dependency property is. This will be explained in more detail later in this chapter. For the time being, just think of this as a property that you can bind data to.

If you don't know which dependency property to use when working against a control, IntelliSense lists all the possible choices for you. For IntelliSense to show the correct choices, you'll need to specify the control type that you've used. In our example, the dependency property value is prefixed with the control type of System.Windows.Controls.PasswordBox.

The second argument is the binding path. This is the most difficult part to get right because a string value is expected, and Visual Studio provides very little guidance as to what you should enter. If you get this wrong, the data binding simply fails to work. Compile and runtime errors will not be generated, so tracing the exact cause of the error is often difficult.

The string property Value is commonly given as a binding path. This indicates that the dependency property will be bound to the object that is specified in the Data Context text box, shown in Figure 9-5. You could also choose to use the binding path StringValue rather than Value. StringValue reflects any specific formatting applied by the property, whereas Value simply returns the raw value. These property names (Value and StringValue) are public properties of Microsoft.LightSwitch.Presentation.Implementation.ContentItem.

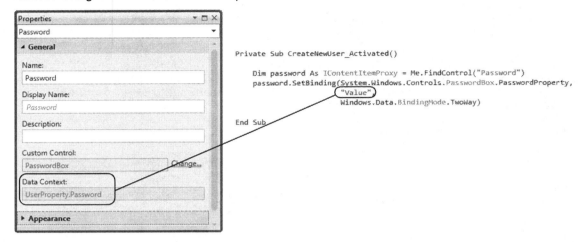

Figure 9-5. *The* Value *data binding path will reference the Data Context text box*

The final argument is the binding mode. You can supply one of three values: OneTime, OneWay, or TwoWay. OneTime updates the control from the source data when the data binding is created. OneWay updates the control from the source data when the data binding is created, and also whenever the source data changes afterward. TwoWay updates the control and source in both directions whenever either of them changes.

If you now run the application and open the screen, you'll see that the PasswordBox is bound to the password property. In Figure 9-6, you'll notice that the alignment doesn't quite match those of the other text boxes. You can set the Horizontal Alignment setting to stretch, and use the other appearance settings at your disposal to format your screen as desired.

Create New User ＊ ✕	
User ID:	0
Firstname:	Tim
Surname:	Leung
Password:	••••••••
Date Of Birth:	

The PasswordBox control is used to enter the password.

Figure 9-6. PasswordBox *control as it appears onscreen*

> ▪ **Tip** Rather than using hard-coded binding paths, you could create a helper library that exposes a set of constants. The C# class would look something like this:

```
public static class ContentItemProperty
{
    public const string Value = "Value";
    public const string StringValue = "StringValue";
    public const string DisplayName = "DisplayName";
    public const string Details = "Details";
    // etc.
}
```

The *ComboBox* Control

Another control that you can use from the `System.Windows.Controls` namespace is the Silverlight `ComboBox` control. This control is a useful alternative to the `AutoCompleteBox`. A disadvantage of the `AutoCompleteBox` is that items are not limited to the items that are shown in the list. Users can freely type in whatever text they choose, and if invalid data is entered, the user isn't notified until an attempt is made to save the screen. The `ComboBox` control resolves this problem by limiting item selections to only those shown in the list.

Designing the Screen

Setting up a screen collection to use a `ComboBox` control closely resembles the technique that was used to set up the `PasswordBox` control. To demonstrate this technique, we'll create a new data screen based on the orders table. A `ComboBox` control is added to enable a customer to be selected.

By default, LightSwitch renders the customer property as an `AutoCompleteBox` control. If you use the same technique as used earlier to change the `AutoCompleteBox` to a `ComboBox`, the control won't be automatically populated with data values. Instead, a collection must be added onto the screen to populate the `ComboBox` with data values.

To do this, click the Add Data Item button and create a new query to return all customers. Once again, you'll need some code in the screen activated event to perform the data binding (see Listing 9-2). Unlike the previous example, a second call to the `SetBinding` method has to be made to bind the `ComboBox` drop-down values. The binding path given is `Screen.Customers`. It may be interesting to know that the binding to `Screen.Customers` displays the `ToString()` value of the customer, which is governed by the Summary property on the customer entity. In the third part of the `SetBinding` syntax, `Customers` refers to the name given to the query.

Listing 9-2. Data binding a ComboBox control

VB:

```
File : ShipperCentral\Client\UserCode\NewOrder.vb
```

```
Private Sub CreateNewOrder_Activated()
```

```
Dim comboControl As IContentItemProxy = Me.FindControl("Customer")
comboControl.SetBinding(↵
    System.Windows.Controls.ComboBox.ItemsSourceProperty↵
    , "Screen.Customers"↵
    , Windows.Data.BindingMode.TwoWay↵
    )

comboControl.SetBinding(
System.Windows.Controls.ComboBox.SelectedItemProperty,
"Screen.OrderProperty.Customer",
Windows.Data.BindingMode.TwoWay)

End Sub
```

C#:

```
File : ShipperCentral\Client\UserCode\NewOrder.cs

partial void CreateNewOrder_Activated()
{
    IContentItemProxy comboControl = this.FindControl("Customer");
    comboControl.SetBinding(
        System.Windows.Controls.ComboBox.ItemsSourceProperty,
        "Screen.Customers",
        System.Windows.Data.BindingMode.TwoWay);

    comboControl.SetBinding(
        System.Windows.Controls.ComboBox.SelectedItemProperty,
        "Screen.OrderProperty.Customer",
        System.Windows.Data.BindingMode.TwoWay);
}
```

Now when you run the application and open the screen, the ComboBox appears as expected and allows you to select a customer.

The *HyperLinkButton* Control

The final control that we'll cover in the System.Windows.Controls namespace is the HyperLinkButton control. This example explores the SetBinding method further, and explains why and how you would use a ValueConverter.

As the name suggests, the HyperLinkButton control displays a clickable link that opens up a web page. The three important attributes that you can set are as follows:

- NavigateURL: The URL address that the hyperlink points to

- Content: The text that is displayed in the hyperlink

- TargetName: This is where the hyperlink will open

Value Converters

To show you how to use this control, we'll add a HyperLinkButton to a product screen. The text displayed on the hyperlink comes from a description field in a Product table. The hyperlink will point to a URL in the following format:

http://provslsdev.com/product.aspx?productId=8

In this URL, the number 8 serves as a placeholder and is replaced with the primary key ID of the product. A hyperlink URL needs to be constructed, and you would build this as a string. However, the HyperLinkButton control expects to be data bound to an object of type System.Uri. Something needs to convert your string URL into an object of type System.Uri, and this would be done by a value converter.

The code for a value converter called ProductID2UriConverter is shown in Listing 9-3. This class is best added into the UserCode folder in the common project. For simplicity, however, it could be added into the code file for your screen. A value converter class implements the IValueConverter interface. When writing a value converter, you need to implement the Convert and ConvertBack methods. In this example, the Convert method accepts a value argument, performs the conversion, and returns an object of type System.Uri. Because users cannot modify and update the URI the HyperLinkButton control, the ConvertBack method simply returns a null. (You could also throw a NotImplemented exception if you weren't going to provide an actual implementation, or if it doesn't make sense to convert back, or if the binding will always be one way.) In most other cases, you would write some code that performs the conversion in the opposite direction.

Listing 9-3. Value Converter Code

VB:

```
File : ShipperCentral\Client\UserCode\EditableProductsGrid.vb

Imports System.Windows.Data

Public Class ProductID2UriConverter
    Implements IValueConverter

    Public Function Convert(↵
        value As Object, targetType As System.Type↵
        , parameter As Object, culture As System.Globalization.CultureInfo↵
        ) As Object
    Implements System.Windows.Data.IValueConverter.Convert

        Return New Uri("http://provslsdev.com/product.aspx?productId=" & value.ToString())

    End Function

    Public Function ConvertBack(↵
    value As Object, targetType As System.Type↵
    , parameter As Object, culture As System.Globalization.CultureInfo↵
    ) As Object Implements System.Windows.Data.IValueConverter.ConvertBack

        Return Nothing
    End Function
```

```
End Class
```

C#:
File : ShipperCentral\Client\UserCode\EditableProductsGrid.cs

```csharp
using System.Windows.Data;

public class ProductID2UriConverter : IValueConverter
{
    public object Convert(object value, Type targetType, object parameter,↵
System.Globalization.CultureInfo culture)
    {
        return new Uri(@"http://provslsdev.com/product.aspx?productId=" + value.ToString());
    }

    public object ConvertBack(object value, Type targetType, object parameter,↵
System.Globalization.CultureInfo culture)
    {
        return null;
    }
}
```

To give another example of using a value converter, imagine that you have a slider control that expects to be bound to a decimal value. If you want to use this control with an integer value, you would need a value converter to perform the decimal-to-integer conversion, and vice versa.

As another example, you might want to bind the background color of a control to an integer value. Your data could include a priority field that stores numbers, say, from 1 to 5. If the priority is set to 1, the background color should be green. If the value is 5, the priority should be red. A value converter would allow you to convert an integer into an object of type System.Drawing.Color.

Data Binding Expressions

Now that you've written your value converter, you can build your screen. Create an editable grid screen based on the product table. In the same way as before, amend the Product Name content item to use a custom control. Set the custom control to be of type System.Windows.Controls.HyperlinkButton.

The HyperLinkButton control needs to have its TargetName property set. The values that you can use are identical to the standard HTML target values that you can set on a hyperlink. These values include _parent, _self, _top, and _blank. Because we want to open the link in a new window, the target value will be set to _blank. This value must be set by using a dependency property, and a local property is therefore needed to bind to this dependency property. Using the Add Data Item button, create a local string property called targetProperty.

Listing 9-4 shows the code that you would write in the Activated event to perform the data binding by using the SetBinding method.

Listing 9-4. Data Binding the HyperLinkButton Control

VB:
File : ShipperCentral\Client\UserCode\EditableProductsGrid.vb

```vb
Imports System.Windows.Controls
```

```
Private Sub EditableProductsGrid_Activated()
    Dim product As IContentItemProxy = Me.FindControl("ProductName")
    targetProperty = "_blank"
    Dim converter As New ProductID2UriConverter()
    product.SetBinding(HyperlinkButton.ContentProperty,
        "Value",
        BindingMode.OneWay)

    product.SetBinding(HyperlinkButton.NavigateUriProperty,
        "Details.Entity.ProductID",
        converter, BindingMode.OneWay)

    product.SetBinding(HyperlinkButton.TargetNameProperty,
        "Screen.targetProperty",
        BindingMode.OneWay)

End Sub
```

C#:

```
File : ShipperCentral\Client\UserCode\EditableProductsGrid.cs
using System.Windows.Controls;

partial void EditableProductsGrid_Activated()
{
    IContentItemProxy product = this.FindControl("ProductName");
    targetProperty = "_blank";
    ProductID2UriConverter converter = new ProductID2UriConverter();
    product.SetBinding(HyperlinkButton.ContentProperty,
        "Value",
        BindingMode.OneWay);

    product.SetBinding(HyperlinkButton.NavigateUriProperty,
        "Details.Entity.ProductID",
        converter,
        BindingMode.OneWay);

    product.SetBinding(HyperlinkButton.TargetNameProperty,
        "Screen.targetProperty",
        BindingMode.OneWay);

}
```

An important point about the preceding code is the binding path expressions that are used. Because the data context of the HyperLinkButton is set to the product name property, the ContentProperty dependency property is bound to the binding path expression Value. This means that the HyperLinkButton displays the product name.

The binding expression Details.Entity.ProductID is used for the NavigateUriProperty. The Details.Entity prefix is important because it allows you to reference the other fields in your property.

Because the ProductID needs to be converted to the string URL representation, an instance of the ProductID2UriConverter is passed into the SetBinding method.

Finally, the TargetNameProperty is bound to the local targetProperty property. The value of targetProperty is set to the string value of _blank prior to the SetBinding method being called. The binding expression Screen.targetProperty is used in the SetBinding method. The Screen prefix allows you to reference other screen properties that you've added on your screen.

Figure 9-7 shows how the binding expressions in code relate to the data items that you see in the screen designer.

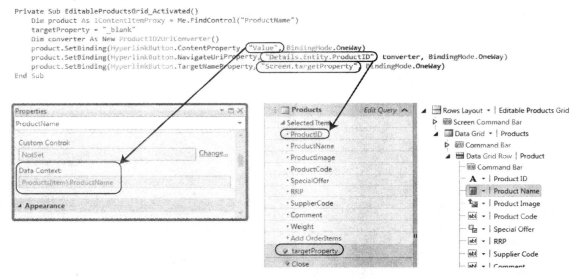

Figure 9-7. *Using* Details.Entity *and screen objects in data binding expressions*

░ **Tip** In all of the examples shown so far, the values of custom control properties are set by using the SetBinding method. This technique must be used when custom controls are contained within grids. If you're adding custom controls onto a details screen, you can use another technique, in which you obtain a reference to the control by using the FindControl method. You can then add an event handler to handle the ControlAvailable event. This allows you to access the custom control in code and lets you set any of the property values as required. Chapter 11 demonstrates this technique by showing you how to open a report via a custom HyperlinkButton.

Creating a Custom Silverlight Class

The examples that you've seen so far have used the controls straight from the System.Windows.Controls namespace. If you want to create something a bit more complex, you'll need to write your own custom control class. To do this, you'll need to create a Silverlight class library. You can do this only if you have

Visual Studio 2010 Professional or above installed. Therefore, you cannot create custom controls if you have only the stand-alone version of LightSwitch.

In the following example, you'll learn how to create a slider control. This example is based on a table called ProductFeedback. The table contains a field called Satisfaction and enables the user to enter a satisfaction rating. This would be an integer value ranging from 0 to 100. The example highlights how you would create a custom control and shows you how to perform the data binding in XAML.

Creating a New Class and Control

In Visual Studio, create a new project using the Silverlight Class library template. If a dialog box prompts you to choose a Silverlight version, select Silverlight 4. In this example, the project will be called CentralControls.

After creating the project, choose the option to add a new item from Solution Explorer. Add a new Silverlight user control and call the file SliderControl.xaml. Drag a slider control from the toolbox onto your control. Because you want to allow users to enter values in the range of 0 to 100, set the minimum attribute to 0 and the maximum attribute to 100.

Data Binding in XAML

You've already seen how to bind to data by using the SetBinding method. An even simpler method is to hard-code the data bindings into the control. The advantage of doing this is that you can bind the data without having to write a single line of VB.NET or C# code.

Let's suppose that you want to bind the contents of your control to the data context of a content item in LightSwitch. You can simply use the data binding path Value, just as before in the SetBinding example. If you use this technique to bind to specific properties on a screen, you'll end up with a custom control that isn't very reusable. We recommend not using anything other than Value when binding data in XAML.

Returning to the slider example, the XAML for this control is shown in Listing 9-5. This illustrates the minimum and maximum values mentioned earlier, and also the data binding syntax for the value.

Listing 9-5. *RichTextBoxInternal.XAML Contents*

```
<UserControl x:Class="CentralControls.Slider"
    xmlns="http://schemas.microsoft.com/winfx/2006/xaml/presentation"
    xmlns:x="http://schemas.microsoft.com/winfx/2006/xaml"
    xmlns:d="http://schemas.microsoft.com/expression/blend/2008"
    xmlns:mc="http://schemas.openxmlformats.org/markup-compatibility/2006"
    mc:Ignorable="d"
    d:DesignHeight="300" d:DesignWidth="400">

    <Slider Height="23" HorizontalAlignment="Left"
        Name="Slider1" VerticalAlignment="Top" Width="100"
        Value="{Binding Value, Mode=TwoWay }" Minimum="0" Maximum="100"/>

</UserControl>
```

Consuming the Control

Now that you've created your custom control, you can consume it in the same way as the earlier examples. First, you'll need to build your custom control project.

At this point, create a new data screen based on the ProductFeedback table. Amend the Satisfaction content item to use a custom control. When the Add Custom Control dialog box appears, click the Add Reference button and browse to the Silverlight class library that you've created. Now set the custom control to be of type CentralControls.Slider.

When you run the application and open the screen, the slider control appears and allows you to set the satisfaction level, as shown in Figure 9-8.

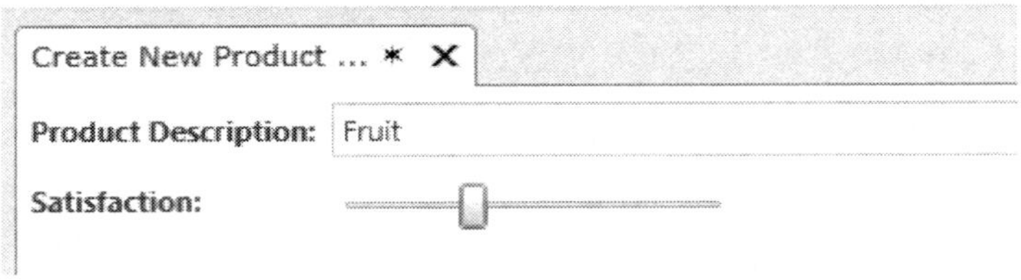

Figure 9-8. The slider control on a screen

Understanding Dependency Properties

In the first part of this chapter, you saw how to bind to a dependency property by using the SetBinding method. In this section, you'll find out more about dependency properties and learn how to create one for yourself. We'll create a rich text editor control to illustrate why you might want to create your own dependency property.

Introduction to Dependency Properties

Dependency properties are just like normal properties. Their values can be set and read in code just like normal properties. However, they are implemented differently by .NET and are optimized for performance in the scenarios where they are used. If you want to bind LightSwitch data to a property on a custom control, that property *must* be a dependency property.

Dependency properties are also used to support the use of styles and animations when writing custom Silverlight controls. They also provide change notifications, which alert your LightSwitch screen when a change is made to a custom control value.

Why Are They Called Dependency Properties?

The standard way of writing a property is to create setter and getter methods to set and retrieve the value of a private field. Additional logic can also be added to modify values during the set and get operations. In most coding scenarios, the value that you get from a property is the same as the value that is set. Dependency properties are different because private fields are not used for the underlying backing store. Instead, the value of a dependency property is determined by using a set of prioritized rules.

Let's imagine a dependency property that relates to the background color of a control. The background color could be dependent on various factors. It could be inherited from a parent control or could be set in styles and themes. Furthermore, the control could be involved in an animation that constantly changes the background color. Given that the color can be set in multiple places, what color would be returned when you read the background color dependency property?

To determine the current value, a process called *dynamic value resolution* is used. This process establishes the value that takes precedence by assigning priorities to the different types of settings. In order of high to low priority, the settings are as follows:

1. Animations

2. Local value

3. Styles

4. Property value inheritance

5. Default value

If the control is currently being used in an animation, the background color applied by the animation takes precedence. If the control is not used in an animation, the local value is used instead. *Local value* refers to settings that are explicitly set in code (for example, `MyCtrl.BackColor = Colors.Green`) or in XAML. If a local value is not set, processing carries on down the chain until a value is found.

You can hopefully see how dependency properties are efficient in terms of their memory usage. If the value of a property is not set locally, the value is retrieved from a template or style, therefore resulting in no additional memory usage.

So dependency properties don't hold a *concrete* value. Their value depends on how the property value has been set—hence the name *dependency property*.

Creating a Dependency Property

Having covered the theory behind dependency properties, what practical reason would you have for creating a dependency property in LightSwitch?

As you've seen, sharing data between LightSwitch and custom controls requires the use of a dependency property. If you want to use an existing Silverlight control and access a property that isn't exposed through a dependency property, you'll need to add one of your own.

As an example, let's say that you want to create a custom control for viewing and editing rich text. The `System.Windows.Controls` namespace contains a `RichTextBox` control that you can use. Although this control has a content property that allows you to get and set the rich text shown, there isn't a dependency property that you can bind to. You'll therefore need to add a dependency property that gets and sets the content property that is shown.

In the `CentralControls` class, create a new Silverlight User Control called `RichTextBoxInternal.xaml`. Add a `RichTextBox` into your control. Listing 9-6 shows the XAML for this control.

Listing 9-6. `RichTextBoxInternal.XAML` Contents

```
<UserControl x:Class=" CentralControls.RichTextEditorInternal"
    xmlns="http://schemas.microsoft.com/winfx/2006/xaml/presentation"
    xmlns:x="http://schemas.microsoft.com/winfx/2006/xaml"
    xmlns:d="http://schemas.microsoft.com/expression/blend/2008"
    xmlns:mc="http://schemas.openxmlformats.org/markup-compatibility/2006"
    mc:Ignorable="d"
    d:DesignHeight="300" d:DesignWidth="400" HorizontalAlignment="Stretch"↩
VerticalAlignment="Stretch">

    <Grid x:Name="LayoutRoot" HorizontalAlignment="Stretch" VerticalAlignment="Stretch" >
        <Grid.RowDefinitions >
            <RowDefinition Height="1*"></RowDefinition>
```

```
        </Grid.RowDefinitions>
        <Grid.ColumnDefinitions >
            <ColumnDefinition Width="1*"></ColumnDefinition>
        </Grid.ColumnDefinitions>
        <RichTextBox HorizontalAlignment="Stretch" Margin="0" Name="richTextBox"
        VerticalAlignment="Stretch" />
    </Grid>
</UserControl>
```

Now that you've created the XAML for your control, there are two extra things that you need to do in code:

- Create a regular CLR .NET property that exposes the DependencyProperty by using the GetValue and SetValue methods.

- Register a set of DependencyProperties by using the static DependencyPropertyClass.

In the code-behind for your control, enter the code as shown in Listing 9-7.

Listing 9-7. Code-Behind for RichTextBoxInternal Control

VB:

```
Partial Public Class RichTextEditorInternal
    Inherits UserControl
    Public Sub New()
        InitializeComponent()
    End Sub
    Public Property Text As String
        Get
            Return MyBase.GetValue(RichTextViewerInternal.TextProperty)
        End Get
        Set(value As String)
            MyBase.SetValue(RichTextViewerInternal.TextProperty, value)
        End Set
    End Property

    Public Shared ReadOnly TextProperty As DependencyProperty =
        DependencyProperty.Register(
            "Text",
            GetType(String),
            GetType(RichTextViewerInternal),
            New PropertyMetadata(Nothing, AddressOf OnTextPropertyChanged))

    Public Shared Sub OnTextPropertyChanged(
        re As DependencyObject, e As DependencyPropertyChangedEventArgs)

        Dim richEdit As RichTextViewerInternal = DirectCast(re, RichTextViewerInternal)

        If richEdit.richTextBox.Xaml <> DirectCast(e.NewValue, String) Then
            Try
                richEdit.richTextBox.Blocks.Clear()
```

```vbnet
            If String.IsNullOrEmpty(DirectCast(e.NewValue, String)) = False Then
                richEdit.richTextBox.Xaml = DirectCast(e.NewValue, String)
            End If
        Catch
            richEdit.richTextBox.Blocks.Clear()

            If String.IsNullOrEmpty(DirectCast(e.NewValue, String)) = False Then
                richEdit.richTextBox.Selection.Text = DirectCast(e.NewValue, String)
            End If
        End Try
    End If
End Sub

Private Sub richTextBox_ContentChanged(
    sender As Object,
    e As System.Windows.Controls.ContentChangedEventArgs
    ) Handles richTextBox.ContentChanged

    Text = richTextBox.Xaml

End Sub

End Class
```

C#:

```csharp
public partial class RichTextEditorInternal : UserControl
{
    public RichTextEditorInternal()
    {
        InitializeComponent();
    }
    public string Text {
        get { return base.GetValue(RichTextViewerInternal.TextProperty).ToString(); }
        set { base.SetValue(RichTextViewerInternal.TextProperty, value); }
    }


    public static readonly DependencyProperty TextProperty =
        DependencyProperty.Register(
            "Text",
            typeof(string),
            typeof(RichTextViewerInternal),
            new PropertyMetadata(null, OnTextPropertyChanged));

    public static void OnTextPropertyChanged(
        DependencyObject re, DependencyPropertyChangedEventArgs e)
    {
        RichTextViewerInternal richEdit = (RichTextViewerInternal)re;

        if (richEdit.richTextBox.Xaml != (string)e.NewValue) {
```

353

```
    try {
        richEdit.richTextBox.Blocks.Clear();

        if (string.IsNullOrEmpty((string)e.NewValue) == false) {
            richEdit.richTextBox.Xaml = (string)e.NewValue;
        }
    } catch {
        richEdit.richTextBox.Blocks.Clear();

        if (string.IsNullOrEmpty((string)e.NewValue) == false) {
            richEdit.richTextBox.Selection.Text = (string)e.NewValue;
        }
    }
    }
}

    private void richTextBox_ContentChanged(object sender, ↩
System.Windows.Controls.ContentChangedEventArgs e)
    {
        Text = richTextBox.Xaml;
    }

}
```

■ **Tip** If you're using C#, you can use code snippets in Visual Studio to help you write your dependency property. Type in `propdp` `<tab><tab>`. Visual Studio inserts the basic code that's needed for a dependency property. You can then extend this code as required.

Code for Registering a Dependency Property

As shown in Listing 9-7, the dependency property is registered by using the following code (because we're illustrating only the arguments to the Register method, only the C# code is shown for brevity):

```
public static readonly DependencyProperty TextProperty = DependencyProperty.Register(
    "Text"
    , typeof(string)
    , typeof(RichTextViewerInternal)
    , new PropertyMetadata(null, OnTextPropertyChanged)
    );
```

This code registers a dependency property called TextProperty. When you call the SetBinding method in your LightSwitch code, you can refer to this dependency property by using the name TextProperty. In keeping with standard .NET naming conventions, it is good practice to suffix any dependency properties that you create with the word *Property*.

The first argument to the Register method specifies the name of the underlying property that the dependency property exposes. In this example, we have created a standard .NET property called Text (shown in Listing 9-7). The second argument specifies the data type of the first argument (that is, the data type of the Text property).

For the third argument, you need to specify the owner type that is registering the dependency property. In the majority of cases, this will be name of the containing class (in this case, RichTextViewerInternal).

PropertyMetadata Argument

The final argument passed into the Register method is a PropertyMetadata object. This allows you to specify additional information about your dependency property. Referring back to Listing 9-7, a new PropertyMetadata object is created by using the following syntax:

```
new PropertyMetadata(null, OnTextPropertyChanged)
```

- The first argument to the PropertyMetadata constructor allows you to specify a default value. The default value is the final setting that is used when determining the value of a dependency property using dynamic value resolution. If you don't want to set a default value, you can pass in null (as shown in our example).

- The second argument that needs to be supplied is a *value changed callback method*. This is a method that gets called each time the dependency property value changes.

- In the example shown, OnTextPropertyChanged is specified as the callback method. This is a method that we have created to update the contents of the RichTextBox control.

- The PropertyMetadata constructor also accepts two additional optional parameters: the coerce value callback, and validation callback methods.

If you specify a coerce callback method, this method is executed first, whenever a value change is requested. You can use this to modify the specified value, and after this runs, the value changed callback method is called. As an example, you might use a coerce callback method if you wanted to create a maximum value dependency property to support the earlier slider control. The maximum value cannot be less than the minimum value. If an attempt is made to set the maximum value to less than the minimum value, the coerce callback method can be used to convert the value to be equal to the minimum value.

Finally, the validate callback method allows you to validate the value the user attempts to set. This method returns a Boolean. If you return false, an ArgumentException will be thrown.

Binding Dependency Properties to the Data Context

You've seen how to bind to the LightSwitch data context by specifying it in the XAML. The advantage of this is that you don't need to write any extra data binding code in your LightSwitch screen. Let's say that you wanted to bind the TextProperty that you've just created to the data context. The immediate problem is that the dependency properties that you write in code can't be accessed in the XAML.

To get around this problem, a trick that we can use is to wrap a parent control around our custom control. The parent control acts as a conduit and exposes the XAML that enables the necessary data binding. Returning to the rich text example, we'll create a custom control called RichTextEditor. The RichTextViewerInternal control is added onto this control. This exposes the underlying CLR Text property in the XAML. We can use this to set the data binding declaratively by specifying the binding path Value.

The XAML that is used for the `RichTextEditor` control is shown in Listing 9-8.

Listing 9-8. RichTextBox Parent Control

```
<UserControl xmlns:my="clr-namespace: CentralControls"  x:Class="↵
CentralControls.RichTextViewer"
    xmlns="http://schemas.microsoft.com/winfx/2006/xaml/presentation"
    xmlns:x="http://schemas.microsoft.com/winfx/2006/xaml"
    xmlns:d="http://schemas.microsoft.com/expression/blend/2008"
    xmlns:mc="http://schemas.openxmlformats.org/markup-compatibility/2006"
    mc:Ignorable="d"
    d:DesignHeight="300" d:DesignWidth="400" HorizontalAlignment="Stretch"↵
VerticalAlignment="Stretch">

    <Border BorderThickness="0" BorderBrush="Black"
        HorizontalAlignment="Stretch" VerticalAlignment="Stretch"   >
        <Grid x:Name="LayoutRoot" Background="White"
            HorizontalAlignment="Stretch" VerticalAlignment="Stretch">

            <my:RichTextViewerInternal HorizontalAlignment="Stretch" Margin="0"
                VerticalAlignment="Stretch"  Text="{Binding Value, Mode=TwoWay}"/>

        </Grid>
    </Border>
</UserControl>
```

Having created this new control, you can now use it in the same way as before. However, you no longer need to write any `SetBinding` code in the `Activated` method to do the binding. As you can see, this clearly makes it much easier to consume custom controls in your LightSwitch screens.

Using Dependency Properties to Call Methods

Another practical reason for creating dependency properties is to use them as a trigger for calling methods in existing Silverlight controls.

Let's take a look at the `WebBrowser` control as an example. This control is found in the `System.Windows.Controls` namespace. As the name suggests, the control allows you to display web pages or HTML content on a screen. Note that the control works only in LightSwitch desktop applications and won't work in a browser application.

The `WebBrowser` control contains a method called `Navigate`. When called, this method accepts a URL argument and navigates to the URL supplied. If you were to use this control on a LightSwitch screen, how exactly would you call this method? There isn't any easy way to reference the custom controls and to call their methods in the LightSwitch screen code. You could try using the `FindControl` method, which returns an `IContentItemProxy`, but there isn't any way to cast this to the underlying Silverlight control. (You could write code in the `ControlAvailable` event of the `IContentItemProxy` object, but this fires only once during the life cycle of the screen.)

To solve this problem, you can create a custom control for the `WebBrowser` control. You can then create a dependency property that allows LightSwitch to bind a URL value to the control. In the value changed callback method, you can then write the code to call the `Navigate` method. Listing 9-9 and Listing 9-10 shows the XAML and .NET code that would be used.

Listing 9-9. *WebBrowserControl Parent Control*

```
<UserControl x:Class="CentralControls.WebBrowserControl"
    xmlns="http://schemas.microsoft.com/winfx/2006/xaml/presentation"
    xmlns:x="http://schemas.microsoft.com/winfx/2006/xaml"
    xmlns:d="http://schemas.microsoft.com/expression/blend/2008"
    xmlns:mc="http://schemas.openxmlformats.org/markup-compatibility/2006"
    mc:Ignorable="d"
    d:DesignHeight="300" d:DesignWidth="400">

    <Grid x:Name="LayoutRoot" Background="White"
        HorizontalAlignment="Stretch" VerticalAlignment="Stretch" >
        <WebBrowser  Name="wb1" Source="" HorizontalAlignment="Stretch"
            VerticalAlignment="Stretch" ></WebBrowser>

    </Grid>
</UserControl>
```

Listing 9-10. *WebBrowserControl Code*

VB:

```
Imports System.Windows
Imports System.Windows.Controls

Namespace CentralControls
    Public Partial Class WebBrowserControl
        Inherits UserControl
        Public Sub New()
            InitializeComponent()
        End Sub

        Public Property uri() As Uri
            Get
                Return DirectCast(GetValue(URIProperty), Uri)
            End Get
            Set
                SetValue(URIProperty, value)
            End Set
        End Property

        Public Shared ReadOnly URIProperty As DependencyProperty =
            DependencyProperty.Register(
                "uri",
                GetType(Uri),
                GetType(WebBrowserControl),
                New PropertyMetadata(Nothing, AddressOf OnUriPropertyChanged))

        Private Shared Sub OnUriPropertyChanged(
            re As DependencyObject, e As DependencyPropertyChangedEventArgs)
```

357

```
            If e.NewValue IsNot Nothing Then
                Dim wb As WebBrowserControl = DirectCast(re, WebBrowserControl)
                wb.wb1.Navigate(DirectCast(e.NewValue, Uri))
            End If
        End Sub

    End Class
End Namespace
```

C#:

```
using System.Windows;
using System.Windows.Controls;

namespace CentralControls
{
    public partial class WebBrowserControl : UserControl
    {
        public WebBrowserControl()
        {
            InitializeComponent();
        }

        public  Uri uri
        {
            get { return (Uri)GetValue(URIProperty); }
            set { SetValue(URIProperty, value); }
        }

        public static readonly DependencyProperty URIProperty =
            DependencyProperty.Register(
                "uri",
                typeof(Uri ),
                typeof(WebBrowserControl),
                new PropertyMetadata(null, OnUriPropertyChanged));

        private static void OnUriPropertyChanged(
            DependencyObject re, DependencyPropertyChangedEventArgs e)
        {

            if (e.NewValue != null)
            {
                WebBrowserControl wb = (WebBrowserControl)re;
                wb.wb1.Navigate((Uri)e.NewValue);
            }

        }

    }
}
```

Calling Screen Code from a Custom Control

One of the things that you might want to do is to call methods on your LightSwitch screen from your custom control. This often makes a lot of sense. Custom controls are basically just views of the data and should be as *dumb* as possible. In other words, custom controls should contain minimal business logic.

As an example, let's imagine that you want to create a stylized button. Let's say that the end user wants a green button with white text. You'd create a custom control to apply the presentation style. However, clicking the custom button should call business logic on your LightSwitch screen, rather than logic on the control itself.

To demonstrate this example, create a new custom control called CustomButton and add a standard Silverlight button. Style the button as appropriate. Listing 9-11 shows how your XAML might look. For the purposes of this example, the button calls a screen method called SaveData, which saves the data on the screen.

Listing 9-11. CustomButton

```
<UserControl x:Class="CentralControls.CustomButton"
    xmlns="http://schemas.microsoft.com/winfx/2006/xaml/presentation"
    xmlns:x="http://schemas.microsoft.com/winfx/2006/xaml"
    xmlns:d="http://schemas.microsoft.com/expression/blend/2008"
    xmlns:mc="http://schemas.openxmlformats.org/markup-compatibility/2006"
    mc:Ignorable="d"
    d:DesignHeight="300" d:DesignWidth="400">

    <Grid x:Name="LayoutRoot" Background="White">
        <Button Content="Button Text" Height="125" HorizontalAlignment="Left"
            Margin="34,63,0,0"  Name="CustomButton1"
            VerticalAlignment="Top" Width="295" Background="#FF1FC453"
            Click= "CustomButton_Click" />
    </Grid>
</UserControl>
```

Listing 9-12 shows the code that you would write in the OnClick method of your custom code to call the screen method. A reference needs to be added to the Microsoft.LightSwitch.Client.dll and Microsoft.LightSwitch.dll files. By default, these can be found in the following directory:

```
C:\Program Files\Microsoft Visual Studio 10.0\Common7\IDE\LightSwitch\1.0\Client\
```

Listing 9-12. Code to Call a Screen Method Called SaveData

VB:

```
Imports Microsoft.LightSwitch.Presentation

Partial Public Class CustomButton
    Inherits UserControl

    Public Sub New()
        InitializeComponent()
    End Sub

    Private Sub CustomButton_Click(sender As System.Object, e As ↵
```

```vb
System.Windows.RoutedEventArgs)
        ' Get a reference to the LightSwitch Screen
        Dim objDataContext = DirectCast(Me.DataContext, IContentItem)
        Dim clientScreen = DirectCast(objDataContext.Screen,↵
Microsoft.LightSwitch.Client.IScreenObject)

        clientScreen.Details.Dispatcher.BeginInvoke(
            Sub()
                Try
                    SetEnabled(False)
                    ' Call the Method on the LightSwitch screen
                    clientScreen.Details.Commands.Item("SaveData").Execute()
                Finally
                    SetEnabled(True)
                End Try
            End Sub)

    End Sub

    Private Sub SetEnabled(value As Boolean)
        Me.Dispatcher.BeginInvoke(
            Sub()
                Me.CustomButton1.IsEnabled = value
            End Sub
        )
    End Sub

End Class
```

C#:

```csharp
using System;
using System.Windows.Controls;
using Microsoft.LightSwitch.Presentation;

namespace CentralControlsCS
{
    public partial class CustomButton : UserControl
    {
        public CustomButton()
        {
            InitializeComponent();
        }

        private void CustomButton_Click(System.Object sender,↵
System.Windows.RoutedEventArgs e)
        {
            // Get a reference to the LightSwitch Screen
            var objDataContext = (IContentItem)this.DataContext;

            var clientScreen = (Microsoft.LightSwitch.Client.IScreenObject)↵
objDataContext.Screen;
```

```
            // Call the Method on the LightSwitch screen
            clientScreen.Details.Dispatcher.BeginInvoke(
                () => {
                    try
                    {
                        this.SetEnabled(false);
                        clientScreen.Details.Commands["SaveData"].Execute();
                    }
                    finally
                    {
                        this.SetEnabled(true);
                    }
                });
        }

        private void SetEnabled(bool value)
        {
            this.Dispatcher.BeginInvoke(() =>
            {
                this.CustomButton1.IsEnabled = value;
            });
        }

    }
}
```

Listing 9-13 highlights the code that is used to obtain a reference to the data context. This allows you to reference the screen, and to execute your screen method via the screen dispatcher. The code that does this is in bold in Listing 9-12. Prior to executing the screen method, the custom button is disabled by using the SetEnabled method. Enabling or disabling the button must be performed on the UI thread, and the SetEnabled method contains the code to do this.

The screen method that you call must be added via the Add Data Item dialog box in the screen designer. If you directly create a method in your code file, this method will not work. In this example, we have called the screen method SaveData. Although the code in Listing 9-12 refers to a method called SaveData, notice how the name of the method is suffixed with the word _Execute (that is, SaveData_Execute). The screen method code is also shown in Listing 9-13.

Listing 9-13. Screen Code That Is Called by the Custom Button

VB:
```vb
Private Sub SaveData_Execute()
    Me.Save()
    ' You can call some some other logic here...
    ShowMessageBox("Data Saved")
End Sub
```

C#:
```csharp
partial void SaveData_Execute()
{
    this.Save();
    //Add additional screen logic here
    this.ShowMessageBox("Data Saved");
}
```

■ **Tip** In this example, we've hard-coded the name of the command (SaveData) into our custom control. This example can be made more reusable by passing the command name into the custom control, rather than hard-coding it. Using the techniques that you've learned in this chapter, you could do this by creating a dependency property. This would allow you to use the data binding mechanisms that you've seen to bind your custom control to the command objects in LightSwitch.

Summary

LightSwitch allows you to visualize your data by using Silverlight controls. This feature means that you're not just limited to using the standard set of controls that are provided by LightSwitch. For example, you could write your own controls to show data by using charts, slider controls, or other more-sophisticated input-entry controls. The main points covered in this chapter were as follows:

- The difference between custom controls and custom control extensions

- How to use Silverlight controls in the System.Windows.Controls namespace

- How to create your own custom control class

- How to data bind your custom controls

- How to create and use dependency properties

There is a difference between custom controls and custom control extensions. (Custom control extensions are covered in Chapter 10.) Custom control extensions are installed in Visual Studio and can be reused in multiple LightSwitch projects. Certain features can be implemented only by using custom control extensions, but they are more work to create. Custom controls allow you to easily use custom UI elements and are very suitable when you want to create UI controls for a specific project.

One of the simplest ways to extend the UI controls that are available to you is to directly use the controls in the System.Windows.Controls namespace.

To use a custom control, add a data item onto your screen and use the Control Type drop-down list in the properties window to select a custom control. After adding a control, you'll need to call the SetBinding method. The SetBinding method requires a dependency property and binding path. The binding path Value specifies that the control will be bound to the data context.

When creating binding path expressions, the screen object can be used to refer to other properties on your screen. Details.Entity can be used to refer to other properties in the selected entity.

Dependency properties are the glue that enables data binding to take place between LightSwitch and custom controls. Dependency properties are just like normal properties, but they don't hold a concrete value. The value of a dependency property could come from several sources, which are all prioritized. For example, if the value of a dependency property has been set in code, this will be used. If not, the value is inherited from a parent property. And if this doesn't exist, a default value will be used (if it has been set).

If you want to data bind to a property on a Silverlight control that hasn't been exposed through a dependency property, you can write your own. A dependency property also allows you to call other methods that are exposed by the underlying Silverlight control.

When performing data binding, data conversions will sometimes be necessary. For example, your table might contain an integer field that needs to be bound to a dependency property that expects a decimal. A value converter allows you to carry out this conversion. In this chapter, you have seen examples of how to create dependency properties and value converters.

The demonstrations of custom controls in this chapter have included slider, rich text editor, and web browser controls.

CHAPTER 10

Creating and Using Extensions

LightSwitch gives you a simpler and faster way to create high-quality business applications for the desktop and the cloud. When the team created LightSwitch, they also laid the groundwork for enterprise developers, IT departments, community contributors, ISV's (Independent Software Vendors), and even individual developers to extend it in various ways.

Out-of-the-box, LightSwitch is already a fairly compelling RAD (Rapid Application Development) experience, but there's room to add significant value to the product, by creating extensions. In essence, the team has tried to give you *what you need*, while allowing you to add *what you want*.

LightSwitch provides the following extension points: themes, shells, screen templates, controls, business types, and data sources. Each of these extension points involves different LightSwitch tiers, as shown in Figure 10-1.

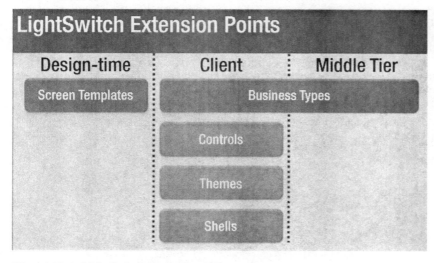

Figure 10-1. LightSwitch Extension Points

Understanding the Need for Extensions

Extensions can enable users to increase their productivity by providing extra functionality beyond LightSwitch's current capabilities. The six types of LightSwitch extensions fall into three broad categories:

- **Enhanced Look and Feel**
  - Theme extensions
  - Shell extensions
- **Advanced Data Entry**
  - Screen template extensions
  - Control extensions
  - Business Type extensions
- **External Data Access**
  - Data *Source* extensions

Enhanced Look and Feel

When you create a LightSwitch application, it looks the same as any other LightSwitch application. You can spot a standard LightSwitch application immediately. Microsoft has taken a pretty conservative approach with the program's default theme. Its internal name is *BlueGlossy*, even though it's far from, well, "glossy."

Actually, there are *two* built-in themes, but one of them isn't available for you to choose unless you happen to know it exists (which you now do) and you specifically make it available. It's a high-contrast theme that uses selected Windows system colors, and it's automatically used if your Windows theme is set to a high contrast theme. Its internal name is simply *Black*.

By the time you finish reading this chapter, you should be able to create your own theme. Later in the chapter, after we've showed you how to create a theme extension, we'll also show you how to activate this "hidden" theme (of course, it isn't really hidden) as one of the selectable theme choices.

So, if you'd like to ensure that your LightSwitch application doesn't look generic, you can add a bit of sophistication and polish to it by creating:

- A theme extension that uses *your* chosen color scheme (rather than someone else's idea of what looks good)
- A shell extension that might move various screen elements to a different place or change the look of them

A *theme* is the basically the *look* of the application (the colors, the fonts, the control styles), while a *shell* can be thought of as the *feel* of it (the position and functionality of, say, the menu system for example, whether screens are exposed as a series of tabs or in some other way). By using both a theme extension and a shell extension together, you can completely customize the look and feel of a LightSwitch application, compared to the default appearance.

Advanced Data Entry

Screen templates enable you to save time by not having to create the same type of screen from scratch, over and over. For example, for every application that you write, you will probably want some type of home page for it. Later in this chapter, we'll show you how you could create a standard home page by creating a screen template extension. The new template will then be displayed as another choice in the Add New Screen Wizard.

Chapter 9 showed you how to create custom controls. Using a custom control allows you to enter data in a way that isn't available in LightSwitch out-of-the-box. Creating a control extension allows you package custom controls for use in multiple projects, or to share them with the community, or even sell them.

Business type extensions enable you to create new data types based on the existing data types that LightSwitch already understands. When you choose Money as the type for a property, you're really storing a Decimal value. When you choose Phone Number, you're really dealing with a String value. Each business type extends the data type that it's based on, adding custom formatting and perhaps extra validation.

External Data Access

In Chapter 7, you learned how to create a custom RIA service, which enables you to access external data that LightSwitch doesn't natively know how to talk to. The downside is that you'd have to include that code in any application that needs access to that particular type of data.

If you need to access a particular type of external data in several LightSwitch applications, you can encapsulate the code in a data source extension, and by doing that make it available to those applications, without having to duplicate the code in each one.

Finding Extensions

While extensions can be developed in-house, they can also be created by third-party vendors, ISVs, and even members of the LightSwitch community. Some extensions are available at no charge, some are offered as trial versions (free to try, but must be purchased after a predetermined amount of time for them to continue to provide full functionality), and others are paid products that you'll have to buy before you can use them.

Installing a trial edition of an extension, if one's available, can be a good way to test it out first, to see whether it does what you need before you actually buy it. Colleagues and friends can share free extensions and trial extensions via email by simply sending the setup file. You can go to the Visual Studio Gallery web site or use Visual Studio's Extension Manager to search for, download, and then install any of the three extension types (free, trial, or paid).

Visual Studio Gallery

The Visual Studio Gallery web site (http://visualstudiogallery.msdn.microsoft.com/site/search) is a kind of marketplace for all types of Visual Studio extensions, including LightSwitch extensions. Being a website, you can access it with your favorite browser. On the site, you can either browse through the myriad of available extensions (there are thousands of them!), or use search criteria to narrow your search to the particular type of extension that you're interested in.

Figure 10-2 shows several free LightSwitch controls, made available to the LightSwitch community by one of the book's authors.

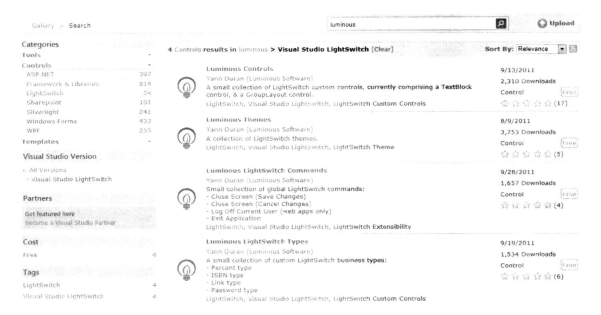

Figure 10-2. Visual Studio Gallery search

Visual Studio Extension Manager

The Extension Manager that's built into Visual Studio (see Figure 10-3) provides a more integrated way to access the gallery contents, without the need for a browser. You'll notice, though, that there are no criteria selections, as there are on the web site, apart from a text search. This is also the place (in fact, it's the only place) to select any extension that you've previously installed and either disable it or uninstall it altogether.

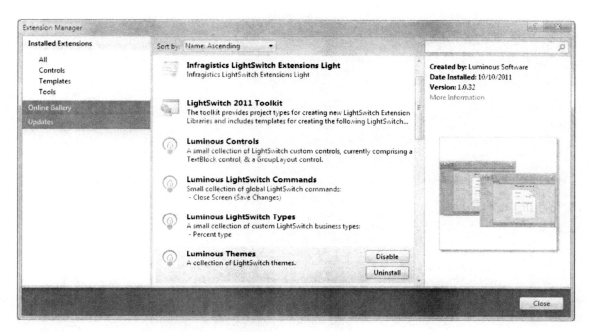

Figure 10-3. *Visual Studio Extension Manager*

Accessing the Extension Manager

There are two methods that you can use to access the Extension Manager.

Method 1 – LightSwitch Properties Screen

You can access the Extension Manager via the Extensions tab (see Figure 10-4) of the LightSwitch project's properties:

1. Double-click the LightSwitch project's `Properties` folder in Solution Explorer.

2. Click the Extensions tab.

3. Click the Browse for More Extensions Online link to browse the Visual Studio Gallery web site.

4. The Extension Manager window opens. By default, it shows the installed extensions, as you saw earlier in Figure 10-3.

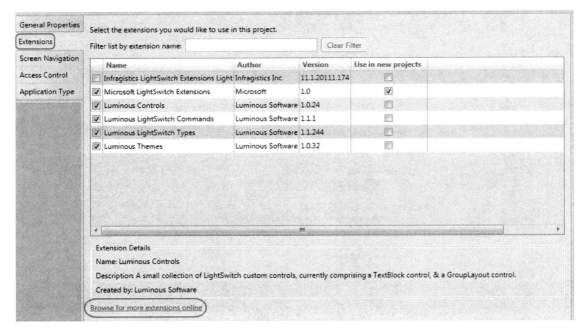

Figure 10-4. *Extensions tab's Browse for More Extensions Online link*

Method 2 – Visual Studio Tools Menu

You can also access the Extension Manager via the Tools menu in Visual Studio (see Figure 10-5):

1. Click the Tools menu.

2. Click the Extension Manager option.

3. The Extension Manager window opens. Again, by default it shows the *installed* extensions.

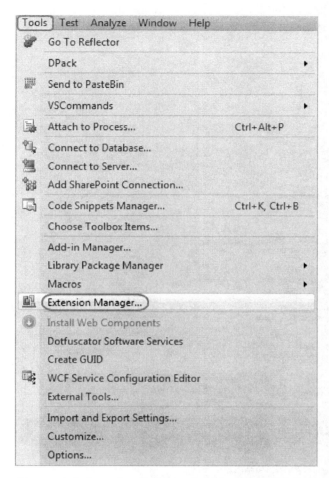

Figure 10-5. Accessing the Extension Manager through the Tools menu

Using the Extension Manager

After the Extension Manager is open, as shown in Figure 10-6:

    1.   Click the Online Gallery option.

    2.   A list of all available online extensions is displayed in the middle pane (not just LightSwitch extensions).

    3.   Type **lightswitch** in the search box.

    4.   A list of extensions that contain *lightswitch* is now displayed.

    5.   You can sort the list of extensions by:

- Highest Ranked

- Most Downloads

- Name: Ascending

- Name: Descending

- Author: Ascending

- Author: Descending

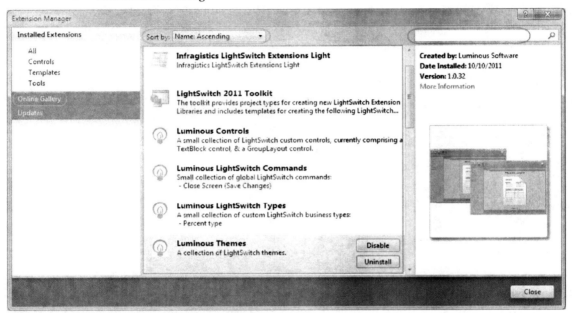

Figure 10-6. *Using the Extension Manager to search for extensions.*

LightSwitch Community Extensions

Several LightSwitch community members have made extensions available. These extensions fill gaps that exist in the current version or offer new functionality not provided by the team. In both cases, it's possible that the team just didn't have the time to include everything that they would have liked to include in the first version of the product.

Two of the first contributors, and the contents of their contributions, are listed below. Other community members have since followed their example.

Spursoft Solutions

Spursoft LightSwitch Extensions is the most polished of the currently available third-party commercial extensions. They started life humbly as a small suite of free controls, which has now grown into quite a professional offering. Although now a paid product, it's available at a very modest price.

- http://www.spursoft.com/Extensions.htm

- **Menu-Driven Shell** (menu can be docked by the user, at runtime, in 1 of 4 positions)

- **LightSwitch Themes**

  - Twilight Blue

  - Twilight Green

  - Hill Country (inspired by the colors in the Hill Country area in Texas)

- **Drop Down List** (simple list allowing for up and down arrow keys to navigate and select the items from the list)

- **Horizontal and Vertical Splitters** (allows the designer to split the UI into user resizable panes either vertically or horizontally)

- **SQL Server Reporting Server Viewer** (web browser based control, allowing for the display of SQL Server Reporting Services Reports)

- **Enhanced Selection DataGrid** (allows for the multiple selection of congruent or incongruent rows)

- **Web Browser Control** (allows displaying web content)

Luminous Software

Several extensions are currently available for free from Luminous Software, (although though donations are welcome to help cover development costs).

- http://lightswitchcentral.com.au/Extensions/LuminousSoftware.aspx

- **Luminous Themes** (a collection of two LightSwitch themes):

  - The first community-based themes to be released

  - Luminous Dark Purple

  - Luminous Dark Blue

- **Luminous Controls** (a collection of two LightSwitch controls:

  - TextBlock (allowing static text to be added to a screen, with no code)

  - GroupLayout (allowing controls to be grouped, with a title, a themed background, and a border, all with no code)

- **Luminous LightSwitch Types** (a collection of four LightSwitch business types):
  - Percent type (stores value as decimal, displays it as a percent)
  - ISBN type (validates ISBN-10, and ISBN-13 numbers)
  - Link type (clicking on the URL launches a web browser)
  - Password type (stores a string, displays a masked value)
- **Luminous LightSwitch Commands** (a collection of four *global* ribbon commands that appear on each screen automatically)
  - Close And Save (closes the current screen, saving any changes)
  - Close And Cancel (closes the current screen, cancelling any changes)
  - Log Off (logs off the current user, but only in web applications)
  - Exit (exits the application completely)

Third-Party Vendors

Several third-party vendors claim to support LightSwitch. As of this writing, only some have developed native LightSwitch controls, while others provide tutorials on how to use their Silverlight offerings as LightSwitch custom controls. We suspect that they may be waiting for version 2 of LightSwitch before making a full commitment.

Infragistics

- http://lightswitchcentral.net.au/Extensions/ThirdParty.aspx#infragistics
- **NetAdvantage for Visual Studio LightSwitch**
  - PAID product
  - Editor controls (mask, numeric)
  - Map controls (geo-spatial, and value-based)
  - Gauge controls (radial, linear, segmented display)
  - Chart controls (area series, column series, line series, spline series, spline area series, step area series, step line series, pie, bullet)
  - Themes (IG, Metro, Office 2010 Blue, Orange)
  - Shell (Outlook/TileView navigation)
  - Slider controls (DateTime, Numeric, DateTime range, Numeric range)
- **NetAdvantage for Visual Studio LightSwitch Light**
  - FREE product

- Editor Controls (mask, numeric)
- Themes (Metro, Office 2010 Theme)

First Floor Software

- `http://lightswitchcentral.net.au/Extensions/ThirdParty.aspx#firstfloor`
- **Document Toolkit for LightSwitch** (adds document-viewing capabilities to your LightSwitch application)
  - PAID product
  - XPS documents
  - PDF documents (At the time of this writing, PDF support is experimental and correct rendering is not guaranteed.)
  - Microsoft Office documents such as Word, Excel, and PowerPoint (This requires Microsoft Office 2007 and the Save As XPS add-in or Microsoft Office 2010. In addition, LightSwitch must be deployed as a desktop application.)

ComponentOne

- `http://lightswitchcentral.net.au/Extensions/ThirdParty.aspx#componentone`
- **OLAP for LightSwitch** (provides a pivoting data screen to get in-depth BI (Business Intelligence) functionality)
  - PAID product
  - Simply select a specific data entity or query for the component to use
  - Create a new screen using the accompanying screen template
  - The control is an example of both a custom control extension and a screen template extension being packaged together to make the control more usable for the LightSwitch developer.

RSSBus

- `http://lightswitchcentral.net.au/Extensions/ThirdParty.aspx#rssbus`
- **ADO.NET Data Providers**
  - PAID product
  - Google Data Provider
  - QuickBooks Data Provider
  - PowerShell Data Provider

- Salesforce Data Provider
- Twitter Data Provider
- Email Data Provider
- Facebook Data Provider
- Microsoft CRM Data Provider
- Excel Data Provider
- and more..

DevExpress

- http://lightswitchcentral.net.au/Extensions/ThirdParty.aspx#devexpress
- **DXEditors for LightSwitch**
    - FREE license (for a limited time)
    - Masked Text Edit (to enforce data format rules)
    - Accounting Editor (to present and store information using currency values)
    - Percentage Editor (to present and store information using percentage values)
    - Web Image (to display an image from a given URL or a database field)
    - Web Link Edit (to display URLs and launch them in a browser)
- **XtraReports for LightSwitch**
    - PAID product
    - Reporting tool

Telerik

- http://lightswitchcentral.net.au/Extensions/ThirdParty.aspx#telerik
- **RadControls For Silverlight**
    - PAID product
    - 60+ Silverlight controls

Installing Extensions

If you didn't install the extension from either the Visual Studio Gallery or Visual Studio Extension Manager (maybe you saved it instead, or received it in an email from a colleague), installation is as simple as clicking (or double-clicking) the extension's setup file (VSIX) and following the installation prompts.

But to actually use the extension in your current LightSwitch project, you need to *activate* it for the project by selecting the extension's check box in the column to the left of the Name column in the Extensions tab of the project's properties, as shown in Figure 10-7.

If you want to have an extension activated by default for all future projects, select its check box in the Use in New Projects column, also shown in Figure 10-7.

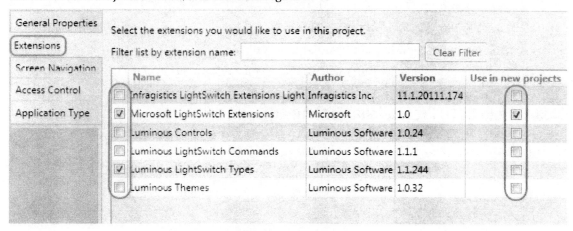

Figure 10-7. Activating extensions for a single project or for all future projects

If the extension that you've activated is a shell or a theme, you'll also need to make a selection on the General Properties tab (see Figure 10-8).

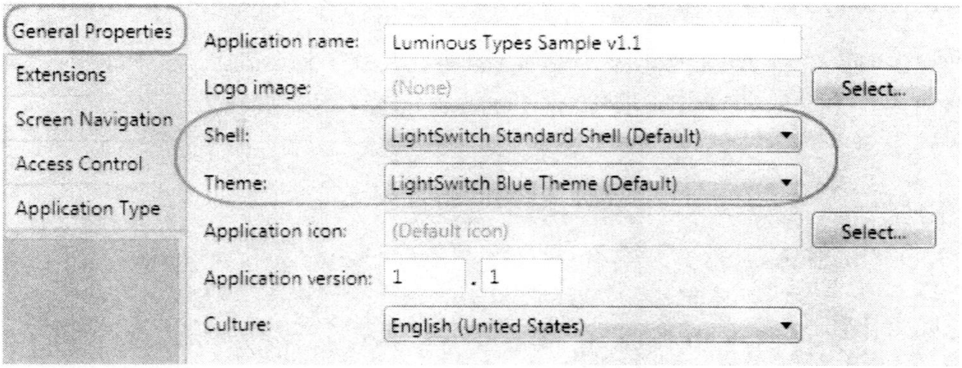

Figure 10-8. Selecting a shell and a theme

Creating Extensions

Advanced developers can extend the functionality of LightSwitch by creating their own extensions.

LightSwitch uses MEF (Managed Extensibility Framework) to enable extension elements to be defined by the developer at design-time (exported) and then consumed by LightSwitch at runtime (imported).

What You'll Need

You'll need three prerequisites before you can start creating extensions. The last item in the list is optional, but it will make your extension-creating life a *lot* easier.

- Visual Studio 2010 Professional (or higher)
- Visual Studio 2010 SP1 SDK (a free download)
- Visual Studio LightSwitch 2011 (90-day trial available)
- Visual Studio LightSwitch 2011 Extensibility Toolkit (also a free download)

Visual Studio 2010 Professional (or Higher)

The minimum version of Visual Studio that you can use to create extensions is *Visual Studio Professional*. You can use any of the higher versions (Premium or Ultimate), but you can't use any of the Express versions. If you have an MSDN (Microsoft Developer Network) subscription, you should be able to download LightSwitch as part of your subscription benefits.

Visual Studio 2010 SP1 SDK

The *Visual Studio 2010 SP1* (*SDK* (Software Development Kit)) provides tools and templates for building Visual Studio extensions. The SDK is available for free download from the Microsoft Download Center:

`www.microsoft.com/download/en/details.aspx?id=21835`.

■ **Note** Because Visual Studio SP1 has to be installed for you to be able to install LightSwitch, make sure you install the SP1 version of the SDK, not the earlier RTM version.

LightSwitch 2011

To test your extensions, you'll need either a trial version of LightSwitch or the retail version. You can obtain a copy of LightSwitch by:

- Downloading a trial version via the LightSwitch Home page:
  (`http://www.microsoft.com/visualstudio/en-us/lightswitch`)
- Purchasing the retail version from the Microsoft Store:
  (`http://www.microsoftstore.com/store/msstore/en_US/pd/productID.230090400`)
- Downloading LightSwitch as part of an existing Visual Studio + MSDN subscription

LightSwitch 2011 Extensibility Toolkit

Shortly after the release of the RTM (Release to Manufacturing) version of LightSwitch, the *LightSwitch 2011 Extensibility Toolkit* was made available as a free download. With the release of this toolkit, the creation of extensions became a reality for more developers than ever before. It's a *huge* improvement over the *Extensibility Cookbook* that was available in the Beta 2 time frame.

When you create an extension library (explained in an upcoming section), you can add any type of LightSwitch extension to it, or even different types of extensions. You might decide to create a separate extension library for each type of extension, or you might decide to create a suite of extensions, all contained in the one library. The choice is up to you.

The toolkit provides both VB and C# project types for creating LightSwitch extension libraries, as well as individual templates for creating themes, shells, screen templates, controls, business types, and data sources. The templates are really just an automated process to make adding an extension type to a library easier for you.

After a while, when you get used to what files make up a particular extension, you may find that it's just as easy to create a new extension by copying and pasting the various files, especially if you decide to make modifications to the automatically generated folders and/or code.

■ **Tip** A good example of a type of extension that you might want to put in its own project is a theme extension. A developer can choose only *one* theme at any particular time. The end user can't currently change that, so including several themes in one extension may not be the best way to distribute them.

Installing the Extensibility Toolkit

To install the Extensibility Toolkit, assuming that you already have Visual Studio Professional (or higher) installed on your machine (*make sure to follow the order listed below*):

1. Download and install the Visual Studio SP1 SDK from www.microsoft.com/download/en/details.aspx?id=21835.

2. Download the LightSwitch Extensibility Toolkit from http://visualstudiogallery.msdn.microsoft.com/0dfaa2eb-3951-49e7-ade7-b9343761e1d2.

3. Or use the Visual Studio Extension Manager to search for the toolkit and then install it.

4. Extract the LightSwitch Extensibility Toolkit.exe file to your local machine (be sure to remember where you extracted it).

5. Double-click the Microsoft.LightSwitch.Toolkit.vsix file.

6. Copy the Microsoft.LightSwitch.Toolkit.targets file into one of these folders:

   - \Program Files\MSBuild\Microsoft\VisualStudio\LightSwitch\v1.0 (if you're running a 32-bit machine)

- `\Program Files (x86)\MSBuild\Microsoft\VisualStudio\LightSwitch\v1.0`
  (if you're running a 64-bit machine)

7. Launch Visual Studio.

8. The LightSwitch Extension Library project templates will now be available
   under a LightSwitch/Extensibility node in the New Project dialog box.

■ **Caution** Failure to install the SP1 SDK or to copy the target files will mean that the toolkit will not perform as expected.

Creating the Extension Library Project

We'll be creating a single extension project to hold all of the examples in this chapter, but as mentioned earlier, you could just as easily create one project per extension type or even one project per individual extension if you really wanted to do it that way.

To create the project (see Figure 10-9):

1. In Visual Studio Professional (or higher), click on File ➤ New Project.

2. The *New Project* dialog opens

3. Select the LightSwitch node.

4. Select either the VB or C# version of LightSwitch Extension Library.

5. Enter the project's location and name. This example uses `Central.Extensions`.

6. Click OK.

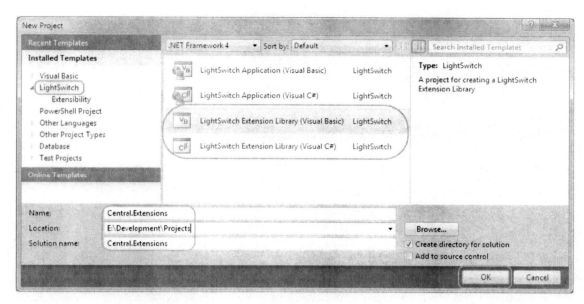

Figure 10-9. New Project dialog box

You should now have a Visual Studio solution that initially contains seven projects, as shown in Figure 10-10.

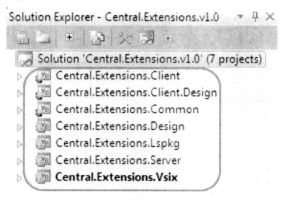

Figure 10-10. Solution Explorer showing the seven generated projects

---

■ **Caution** Be careful not to give your extension project a name that is too long. The extensibility toolkit project template can run into a character limit when the whole path is taken into consideration. Long names can result in an error message:

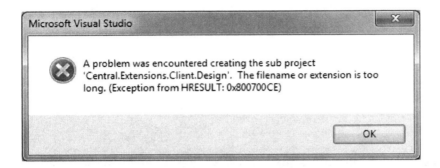

Microsoft Visual Studio

A problem was encountered creating the sub project 'Central.Extensions.Client.Design'. The filename or extension is too long. (Exception from HRESULT: 0x800700CE)

OK

Let's look at each of the projects in detail, so you know why they exist, as well as which parts of your extensions go into which projects, and why.

The *Client* Project

The Client project is a Silverlight project that contains client implementations that should be deployed with a LightSwitch application but are not found in the Common project (for example, controls, shells, and themes). The classes/files in this project are used to display the extension in the client application.

Client Folders

When the Client project is initially created by the template, it has no folders or files:

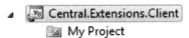

▲ Central.Extensions.Client
    My Project

Each extension type can create the Presentation folder if it hasn't already been created by another extension. However, no extension type adds files directly to the actual folder itself.

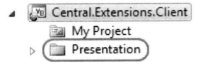

▲ Central.Extensions.Client
    My Project
  ▷ Presentation

Client Subfolders

Each extension type can add its own subfolder to the Presentation folder:

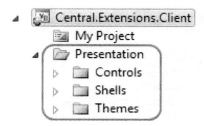

The *Client.Design* Project

The Client.Design project is a Silverlight project that contains the implementations necessary during the debugging of a LightSwitch application (for example, control images or custom property editors for the runtime screen designer). The classes/files in this project are used in the Design Screen experience.

Client.Design Folders

When the project is initially created, it has no folders:

As with the Presentation folder in the Client project, some extension types will add a Resources folder if it doesn't already exist, but no extension type adds files directly to the folder itself.

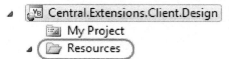

Client.Design Subfolders

A control extension or business type extension will add a ControlImages subfolder to the Resources folder. You can add further subfolders to it manually, as shown in Figure 10-11, in order to better organize the elements that get added to it by the extension templates (remember to manually move the files that the templates create, though).

For a single extension, this might not really be an improvement, but the more extensions that you add to an extension library, the more this will help. (Being able to collapse folders that you're not working on is a big advantage here.)

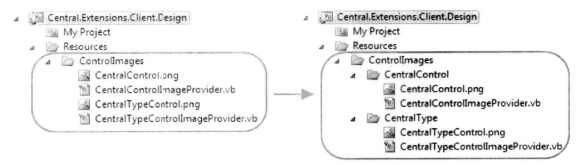

Figure 10-11. Organizing the ControlImages *files into subfolders*

The *Common* Project

The Common project is a Silverlight project that primarily contains the extension's metadata definitions, along with any code that runs on the middle tier (on both the client and on the server), such as metadata loaders and validators.

The metadata definitions are contained in LSML files, each of which represents a model *fragment* that is merged with all other model fragments at runtime.

When first created, the Common project has two folders, Metadata and Resources:

Metadata Folder and Files

The Metadata folder contains files that define and load metadata, both for the extension library itself and for any extension types that are added to it. The Metadata folder initially contains two files, Module.lsml and ModuleLoader.vb/cs:

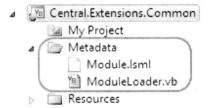

The Module.lsml file simply contains a small XML model fragment that declares a module name for the extension. There's only one of these files per extension library.

The purpose of the ModuleLoader class is to define the ResourceManager that'll be used by the extension to find its resources, and to define a ModuleLoader class to load any model fragments (LSML files) that have been added to the extension's assembly as a resource.

The ModuleLoader class has a Friend/Internal[1] modifier, meaning that it can be accessed by code that's in the same assembly, but not from code that's outside the assembly. There's only a single instance of this class per extension library.

The class is decorated with two attributes:

- Export attribute, to alert the LightSwitch application that this class exports an implementation of IModuleDefinitionLoader

- ModuleDefinitionLoader attribute, which provides the String value of the extension's name (Central.Extensions)

It implements a single interface, IModuleDefinitionLoader, which contains two methods:

- GetModelResourceManager sub (void function in C#), which returns the instance of a ResourceManager that the extension should use to find its resources

- LoadModelFragments function, which returns an IEnumerable(Of Stream) that gets populated with any file with an LSML file extension

The Metadata folder doesn't initially contain any subfolders, but each extension type can add its own subfolder:

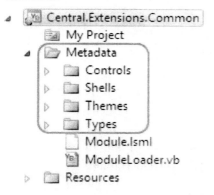

---

[1] Access modifiers are keywords used to specify the declared accessibility of a member, or a type:

- Public / public: access is not restricted

- Protected / protected: access is limited to the containing class, or types derived from the containing class

- Friend / internal: access is limited to the current assembly

- Protected Friend / protected internal: access is limited to the current assembly, or types derived from the containing class

- Private / private: access is limited to the containing type

Resources Folder and Files

The Resources folder contains resource files, both for the extension library and for any extension types that are added to it. The Resources folder is created with only a single file in it:

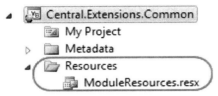

The ModuleResources.resx file contains any embedded resources, such as localized strings, which are added via the Resource Editor. Initially there aren't any resources in it.

The *Design* Project

The Design project is a WPF project, and contains elements such as design-time controls, images, and supporting code (for example, a screen template). The classes/files in this project are used for the design-time experience in the IDE (such as designing a screen).

At first, it may seem like the files in this project are redundant duplicates of the files in the Client.Design project, but the difference is that the Client.Design project is a Silverlight project, used for the display of the extension's UI elements in the Silverlight client, and the Design project is a WPF project, used for the display of the extension's elements in the Visual Studio IDE.

Design Folders

When the project is initially created, it has no folders:

As with the Resources folder in the Client.Design project, some extension types will add a Resources folder if it doesn't already exist, but no extension type adds files directly to the folder itself.

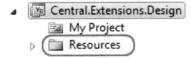

Design Subfolders

A control extension or business type extension will add a ControlImages subfolder. You can add further subfolders to it manually, as shown in Figure 10-12, to better organize the elements that are added to it by the extension templates (you'll have to manually move the files that the templates create, though).

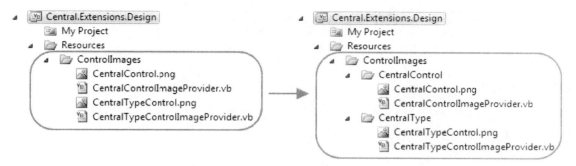

Figure 10-12. Organizing the ControlImages *files into subfolders*

The *Server* Project

The Server project is a .NET project that contains server implementations that should be deployed with a LightSwitch application but are not found in the Common project (for example, data sources). It has access to assemblies of the full .NET Framework.

Server Folders

When the project is initially created, it has no folders:

A data source extension item creates a DataSources folder if it hasn't already been created by another data source extension, but no files are added directly to the folder itself.

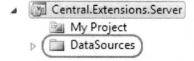

The *Lspkg* Project

This project exists only as a place to pull all of the other projects together, for packaging into the VSIX file. It packages the previous five projects so that LightSwitch can unpack and reference them when the package is installed.

If you watch carefully, you may notice that files and folders are created in this project, and then they're moved to one of the other projects. Interesting technique!

Occasionally you might also see errors displayed that tell you that you can't mix platform types. The error message states:

> *The project 'ExtensionName.ProjectName' cannot be referenced. The referenced project is targeted to a different framework family (Silverlight).*

These particular errors can safely be ignored, because the project doesn't generate any code. You'll also find that a project/solution *rebuild* will usually make them go away. But they can be a bit disconcerting when you see them for the first time.

Lspkg Folders

When the extension project is first created, the Lspkg project contains no folders or files:

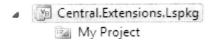

You add a template item by right-clicking the Lspkg project and then selecting Add ➤ New Item. The Add New Item dialog box opens, as shown in Figure 10-13.

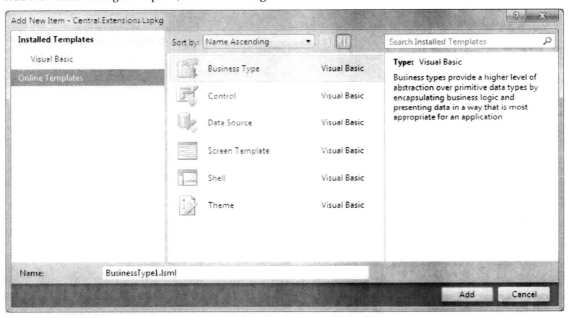

Figure 10-13. Adding a new extension template item

When you add a template item, one or more folders or files may be added to some of the other projects, depending on the type of item you're adding.

The *VSIX* Project

This project packages the generated LSPKG file into a VSIX package so that it can be added to LightSwitch through the Extension Manager. It initially contains only a single file:

◢ ⬚ **Central.Extensions.Vsix**

    ⬚ My Project

    ⬚ source.extension.vsixmanifest

Any VSIX-supported project template, including a LightSwitch extension library, generates a manifest file and calls it `source.extension.vsixmanifest`. When Visual Studio builds the project, it copies the content of this file into `Extension.VsixManifest` in the VSIX package. The package file is actually a simple ZIP file that uses the Open Packaging Conventions.

Exploring the VSIX Manifest Designer

There's usually no need to edit the manifest file manually. You can set the properties by using the *VSIX Manifest Designer* to modify the `source.extension.vsix` manifest file in the VSIX project. Simply double-click the file to open it in the editor (see Figure 10-14).

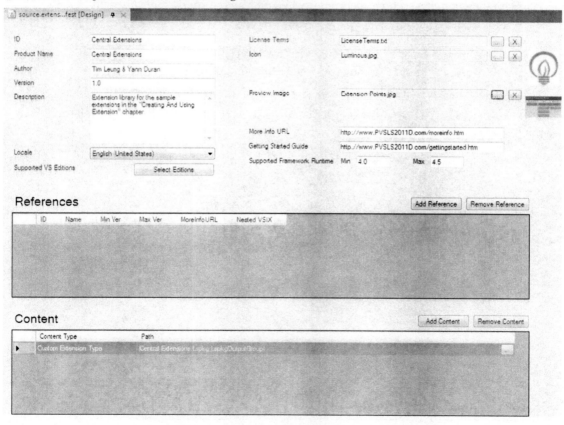

Figure 10-14. source.extension.vsix manifest open in the VSIX Manifest Designer

The VSIX Manifest Designer goes further than just providing an easy way to edit the VSIX manifest's XML contents. It integrates into Visual Studio to simplify the process of adding content to the VSIX file.

When the Icon setting, the Preview Image setting, or the License Terms setting is specified via the Manifest Editor, the corresponding files are added to the project if they are not already present. The Include in VSIX property for those files is also set to true, so they'll be copied into the VSIX file that's generated when the project is built (or rebuilt).

Let's look at each of the VSIX's manifest settings individually. We've sorted them into two categories:

- External settings, which are displayed externally

- Internal settings, which are used internally

External Settings

The values for these manifest settings determine what information appears for your extension in:

- Extension Manager (see Figure 10-15)

  - Installed Extensions tab (when an extension has been installed)

  - Online Gallery tab (when you're searching for extensions)

  - Updates tab (when an update is available for the extension)

- Visual Studio Gallery web site

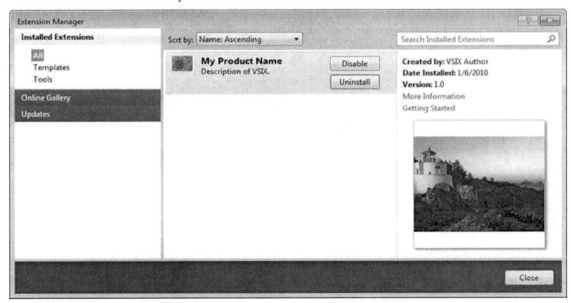

Figure 10-15. Extension Manager showing entered settings

The value for the License Terms setting is also displayed in the Visual Studio Extension Installer (see Figure 10-16), as the extension is being installed.

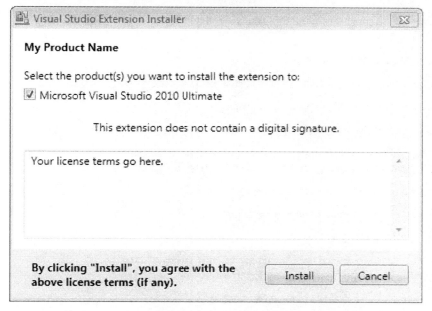

Figure 10-16. *Visual Studio Extension Installer showing license terms*

Product Name Setting

The value of this setting is displayed as the Name value in the Extensions tab of the LightSwitch project, and in the Extension Manager. The default is the name that you supplied for the extension library (solution name), but it can be changed at any time, to whatever you want to call your product.

The maximum length for this setting is 60 characters.

Author Setting

The value of this setting is displayed as the Created By value in the Extensions tab, and in the Extensions Manager. The default is the Company Name that was entered when you installed Visual Studio. You can change this property to anything you like, but it's a good idea to be consistent.

The maximum length is 50 characters.

Version Setting

The version number that you enter here will be used by the Extension Manager to determine whether there is a new version (update) of the extension. The Extension Manager won't allow the VSIX to be installed if there's already an extension installed with the same version number (or higher).

The maximum length is 23 characters.

SAMPLE VERSIONING SYSTEM

It's a good idea to have some sort of consistent system for your version numbering. A potential versioning system might use:

- The **first** digit as *major* product number
  - Changes only when there have been significant changes to the extension
  - May contain breaking changes to previous versions
- The **second** digit as a *minor* product number
  - Changes when there's been some small change made to the extension's functionality (and the new version of the extension has been published)
  - Doesn't contain breaking changes to previous versions
  - Reset to 0 each time the major number is incremented
- The **third** digit as a *build number*
  - Increment it to produce a unique version number for the Extension Manager (and the new version of the extension is not being published)
  - Doesn't contain breaking changes to previous versions
  - Reset to 0 each time the minor number is incremented

■ **Tip** If you have the Visual Studio Productivity Power Tools extension installed, you might find it helpful to pin the manifest file in Visual Studio, so it's always available for you during development and debugging of your extension. You can find yourself changing the build number often as you test or fix your extension's functionality.

Description Setting

The value of this setting is displayed as the Description value for the selected extension in the Extensions tab, as well as in the Extension Manager. The default is the solution name plus the word *description*.

It's best to keep the description fairly short, if possible, because although the gallery web page will display several lines, as will the Extensions tab, the Extension Manager will display only two lines. It may look odd if your description is cut off after two lines. You can change the Description setting at any time.

The maximum length is 1,024 characters.

Icon Setting

Here you can specify an ICO, BMP, JPG, GIF, JPG, PNG, or TIFF file that will be displayed beside the extension name. Specifying an icon file is optional but highly recommended. A default image will be used if you don't supply one.

Preview Image Setting

This optional setting allows you to specify a BMP, JPG, GIF, PNG, or TIFF file that shows a preview of what the extension looks like. The same image that was specified for the Icon setting will be used if you don't supply a value here.

Microsoft's documentation for this setting suggests that you should use an image that is 200×200 pixels, but you might want to find out for yourself what gives you the best result.

More Info URL Setting

Here you can enter an HTTP/HTTPS URL that points to a web page that has more information about your extension. A More Information link will be displayed in the Extension Manager and in the Visual Studio Gallery.

If you don't specify a URL, the hyperlink is disabled.

Getting Started Guide Setting

This setting allows you to enter an HTTP/HTTPS URL that points to a web page indicating how to get started with your extension. A Getting Started link will be displayed in the Extension Manager and in the Visual Studio Gallery.

If you don't specify a URL, the hyperlink is disabled.

Internal Settings

Internal settings aren't exposed to the consumer of the extension. They're used internally by the Extension Manager.

ID Setting

This setting is the extension's *unique identifier*. This value is used by the Extension Manager to identify when a new version of the extension is being deployed. You can't install two extensions that have the same ID in the same installed instance of Visual Studio.

Be careful what you use here, because if you change it later, any future versions of your extension won't be recognized as an update to the original extension. We learned this lesson the hard way, but now you know about it, so you can avoid this problem.

The value is initially set to the name that you supplied for the extension library (the solution name), but it can be changed to anything you like. You won't see it anywhere, though, because it is used only internally.

The maximum length is 100 characters.

Locale Setting

This setting determines the intended locale of your extension. The default value is the locale of the installed version of Visual Studio. Only a limited number of locales are currently available (see Figure 10-17).

Figure 10-17. *Available locales*

Supported VS Editions Setting

Figure 10-18 shows a hierarchy diagram of the various Visual Studio editions that an extension can normally support. The Express editions aren't supported for LightSwitch extensions, of course.
The default values for this setting are as follows:

- Visual Studio 2010

- VSLS (in Additional Visual Studio Products)

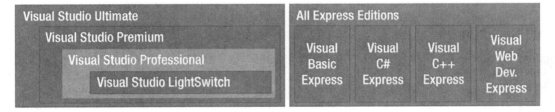

Figure 10-18. *Supported Visual Studio Versions*

■ **Caution** Don't change the values in this property. LightSwitch will recognize your extensions only if the default values haven't been changed.

The Extension Manager will allow the extension to be installed only if the version of Visual Studio that's currently installed on the machine (or a higher version) has been specified in this dialog box. The LightSwitch extension project template automatically selects Visual Studio 2010, as well as Additional Visual Studio Products. It also adds *VSLS* in the additional versions field, as you can see in Figure 10-19.

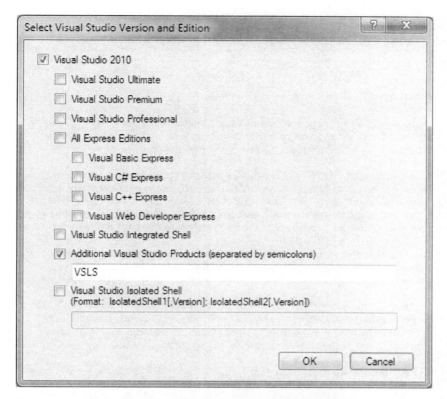

Figure 10-19. Select Visual Studio Version and Edition dialog box

License Terms Setting

This setting allows you to include a TXT or RTF file that describes the extension's terms of use or licensing agreement. This will be displayed in the Visual Studio Extension Installer's dialog box during installation.

It's an optional setting, and the default is empty. If you don't enter the name of a file, the installer will display *Your license terms go here*.

Supported Framework Runtime Setting

These two values are automatically set for you. In LightSwitch 2011:

- The Min value is set to 4.0 (the current version of the .NET Framework)

- The Max value is set to 4.5 (the next version of the .NET Framework)

■ **Caution** LightSwitch requires version 4.0. The extension may not install if you change these values.

Understanding Extensions

In the previous section, we explored the different projects that a LightSwitch extension is composed of. As you saw, not all projects are used by all extension types. However, each extension type has its own unique set of requirements. The most basic of these are certain attributes and interface implementations.

On the one hand, *attributes* enable LightSwitch to know what *features* your extension is offering, whether it's a theme extension or a shell extension, and so on. Attributes can also provide some basic information about the extension itself, such as an ID, a name, or even a version number. LightSwitch imports extensions, via MEF, that are made known to it through the use of the Export attribute and a *contract* value. This contract must match the contract that LightSwitch is expecting for a particular extension type.

On the other hand, *interfaces* give LightSwitch a way of consuming your extension by being able to make assumptions about their behavior in a consistent manner. The interfaces that LightSwitch provides determine *what* an extension can do, without having to have exact knowledge of *how* that's achieved.

Because of publishing deadlines, and to keep the chapter to a manageable length, we weren't able to include step-by-step instructions for each of the extension types, as much as we would have liked to. There's a huge amount of information to absorb regarding to how create extensions. Each extension type could easily be its own chapter. Each of the control type extensions could also fill a chapter of their own as well.

So although we could have written much, much more on actually *creating* extensions, we've chosen to concentrate on helping you understand them and hopefully provide the "missing" information that's hard to find anywhere else, or that's scattered all over the Internet. Microsoft and a few others have written articles that walk through creating various types of extensions, but without the background information, these articles can be hard to follow, or worse, hard to understand.

We hope that we'll able to follow up this book with more-specific extension-related articles. Be sure to visit LightSwitch Central (`www.lightswitchcentral.net.au`) for related blog posts, articles, or downloads.

Let's now have a look at understanding each of the extension types in a bit more detail.

Understanding Theme Extensions

As mentioned earlier in the chapter, a *theme extension* allows you to change your application's visual impact (the *look* part of *look and feel*). You do this by changing the font and color values, and by specifying alternative values for the various brushes that are used by your LightSwitch application's shell, screens, and controls. You could create a theme to make your application match your company's colors, for example.

A theme extension can contain two implementation types: a Theme and a somewhat unfortunately named ThemeExtension (not to be confused with an actual theme extension). It probably would have been a lot less confusing if it had been called something like a StyleExtension or a ControlStyleExtension, but its name comes from the fact that it's an *extension* to a theme, in the form of additional control styles.

Web sites often use what's called a *style sheet*, usually referred to as CSS (Cascading Style Sheets) to define the colors and fonts, as well as the control styles, for the entire site in one place. LightSwitch defines its color and font information in a Theme, which is stored in a ResourceDictionary in a XAML file. It can also define control styles in a ThemeExtension, which is also stored in ResourceDictionaries in one or more XAML files.

By using themes, it's easy to change the colors for the entire application in one place, just by selecting a different theme. By using control styles, it's easy to change the way various controls look in the application, again all defined in one place.

The attributes and interfaces that a theme extension requires are found in the Microsoft.LightSwitch.Theming namespace.

Creating a Theme Extension

There are a few simple steps required to create a theme extension:

1. Create an extension library, as described earlier in the chapter (or you can add to an existing extension library).

2. Right-click the LSPKG project (Central.Extensions.lspkg)

3. Select Add ➤ New Item.

4. Click the Theme option (see Figure 10-20).

5. Provide a name for the theme (we'll call it CentralTheme).

6. Click Add.

7. The template adds various folders and files (discussed later in this section).The code that's necessary to implement the required interfaces is provided by the template (we'll examine this next).

8. Modify the XAML that was provided by the template, to define the brush values and/or control styles for your theme.

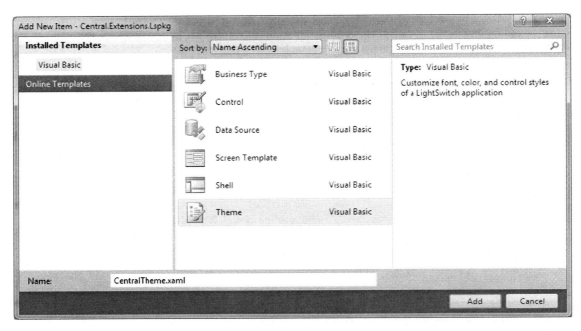

Figure 10-20. Adding a new theme extension template item

Using Theme Extension Attributes

Two attributes must be applied to any class that defines a theme, for it to be recognized by LightSwitch. Two attributes also need to be applied to any class that defines a ThemeExtension (not to be confused with a Theme extension), for it to be recognized by LightSwitch. Table 10-1 lists these four attributes.

Table 10-1. Attributes Used in a Theme Extension Class

Project	Attribute	Required Value	Description
Client	Export	ITheme type	Supplies a contract to LightSwitch indicating that the class represents a Theme
Client	Theme	ThemeId, ThemeVersion	Supplies both a string ID value and a string Version value for the Theme
Client	Export	IThemeExtension type	Supplies a contract to LightSwitch indicating that the class represents a ThemeExtension
Client	ThemeExtension	ThemeId	Supplies a string ID value for the ThemeExtension

Listing 10-1 shows these attributes being used in code, to decorate the class that defines a theme.

Listing 10-1. Theme-Related Attributes Being Used in Code

VB:

File: N/A

```
Friend Const ThemeId As String = "Central.Extensions:CentralTheme"
Friend Const ThemeVersion As String = "1.0"

<Export(GetType(ITheme))>
<Theme(CentralTheme.ThemeId, CentralTheme.ThemeVersion)>
Public Class CentralTheme
    Implements ITheme
    Implements IThemeExtension

    'implementation code goes here
End Class
```

C#:

File: N/A

```
internal const string ThemeId = "Central.Extensions:CentralTheme";
internal const string ThemeVersion = "1.0";

[Export(typeof(ITheme))]
[Theme(CentralTheme.ThemeId, CentralTheme.ThemeVersion)]
public class CentralTheme : ITheme, IThemeExtension
{

    //implementation code goes here
}
```

Using Theme Extension Interfaces

In addition to being decorated with the two attributes just described, a class that defines a *Theme* item must also implement the ITheme interface. You can also optionally implement IThemeExtension.

A theme extension can have one or more ITheme implementations, as well as one or more IThemeExtension implementations, though in practice you'd probably really want only one of either in a single theme extension. You can, of course, have multiple theme extensions in a single extension library.

ITheme Interface

The ITheme interface consists of three properties, shown in Table 10-2. The default values are based on the extension library name (CentralExtensions) and the theme extension pathname (Central/CentralTheme).

Table 10-2. ITheme Properties

Property	Type	Notes	Default Value
ColorAndFont Scheme	URI	Points to a ResourceDictionary (stored in a XAML file) that contains the brush definitions for the theme's colors and fonts	/Central.Extensions.Client; component/Presentation/Themes/ Central/CentralTheme.xaml
Id	String	Used internally, to identify the theme	Central.Extensions:CentralTheme
Version	String	Used internally	1.0

IThemeExtension Interface

The IThemeExtension interface has only one method to implement, GetControlStyleResources, which must return an IEnumerable(Of Uri). Its purpose is to expose one or more URI values that each point to a ResourceDictionary (stored in a XAML file) that contains *control style definitions*. The method has three parameters: themeId, themeVersion, and modules.

Theme Element Load Order

A LightSwitch application will load theme-related information in the following order:

1. The default ColorAndFontScheme

2. Your ITheme implementation's ColorAndFontScheme

3. The default ControlStyleResources

4. Your IThemeExtension's ControlStyleResources

Theme Extension Implementation

Let's look at what happens when you use the Extensibility Toolkit to add a theme. As we mentioned before, once you know what the template is doing for you, it can be almost as quick to copy/paste/edit an existing theme. This is especially true if you decide to change any of the locations of the various files, as we will in the example.

The following paragraphs assume that we've called our theme CentralTheme.

Client Project's Elements

When we add a theme, using the Extensibility Toolkit's Theme template, as we mentioned earlier in the chapter, a Themes folder is added to the Client project's Presentation folder for us (see Figure 10-21).

We recommend creating a separate folder for each theme in the Themes folder, and moving the files created by the template into it. You don't have to do this, but it helps keep the project more organized. For our example theme, we'll create a folder called Central and move the files into that folder.

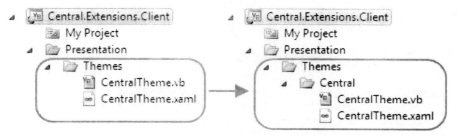

Figure 10-21. Client project's Themes folder

The Class File

The CentralTheme class contains the ITheme implementation (see Listing 10-2) that we discussed earlier. Because we moved the files for the theme into their own folder, we also have to make a small change to the ColorAndFontScheme property's value, changing /Themes/ to /Themes/Central/ in order to reflect the folder change.

You could also put the code for any IThemeExtension implementations in this file, or you could put them in a file of their own, or even a file per ThemeExtension.

■ **Caution** If you move the XAML file to a different folder than the one the template put it in, as we have, make sure that you edit the Theme class so that the ColorAndFontScheme property points to the correct location.

Listing 10-2. CentralTheme Class's Code

VB:

```
File: Central.Extensions\Central.Extensions.Client\Presentation\Themes\Central\CentralTheme.vb

Imports System
Imports System.ComponentModel.Composition
Imports System.Collections.Generic
Imports Microsoft.LightSwitch.Theming
Imports Microsoft.LightSwitch.Model

<Export(GetType(ITheme))>
<Theme(CentralTheme.ThemeId, CentralTheme.ThemeVersion)>
<Export(GetType(IThemeExtension))>
<ThemeExtension(CentralTheme.ThemeId)>
Public Class CentralTheme
    Implements ITheme
    Implements IThemeExtension

    'constants
    Friend Const ThemeId As String = "Central.Extensions:CentralTheme"
```

```vbnet
Friend Const ThemeVersion As String = "1.0"

'ITheme members
Public ReadOnly Property ColorAndFontScheme As Uri↵
Implements ITheme.ColorAndFontScheme↵
    Get
        'this is a modified version of what appears in the file created by the template
        Dim uriString = String.Format("{0}{1}{2}"↵
            , "/Central.Extensions.Client;"↵
            , "component/Presentation/Themes/Central/"↵
            , "CentralTheme.xaml"↵
            )
        Return New Uri(uriString, UriKind.Relative)
    End Get
End Property

Public ReadOnly Property Id As String↵
Implements ITheme.Id
    Get
        Return CentralTheme.ThemeId
    End Get
End Property

Public ReadOnly Property Version As String↵
Implements ITheme.Version
    Get
        Return CentralTheme.ThemeVersion
    End Get
End Property

'IThemeExtension members
Public Function GetControlStyleResources(↵
      ByVal themeId As String↵
    , ByVal themeVersion As String↵
    , ByVal modules As IEnumerable(Of IModuleDefinition)↵
    ) As IEnumerable(Of Uri)↵
Implements IThemeExtension.GetControlStyleResources
    'this is a modified version of what appears in the file created by the template
    Dim uriString =String.Format("{0}{1}{2}"↵
        , "/Central.Extensions.Client;"↵
        , "component/Presentation/Themes/"↵
        , "CentralTemplates.xaml"↵
        )
    Dim result as new List(Of Uri) From↵
        {
            New Uri(uriString, UriKind.Relative)
        }

    Return result
End Function
```

End Class

C#:

File: Central.Extensions\Central.Extensions.Client\Presentation\Themes\Central\CentralTheme.cs

```csharp
using System;
using System.ComponentModel.Composition;
using System.Collections.Generic;
using Microsoft.LightSwitch.Theming;
using Microsoft.LightSwitch.Model;

[Export(typeof(ITheme)), Theme(CentralTheme.ThemeId, CentralTheme.ThemeVersion)]
[Export(typeof(IThemeExtension)), ThemeExtension(CentralTheme.ThemeId)]
public class CentralTheme : ITheme, IThemeExtension
{
    //constants
    internal const string ThemeId = "Central.Extensions:CentralTheme";
    internal const string ThemeVersion = "1.0";

    //ITheme members
    public Uri ColorAndFontScheme
    {
        get
        {
            //this is a modified version of what appears in the file created by the template
            var uriString = string.Format("{0}{1}{2}"
                , "/Central.Extensions.Client;"
                , "component/Presentation/Themes/Central/"
                , "CentralTheme.xaml"
                );
            return new Uri(uriString, UriKind.Relative);
        }
    }

    public string Id
    {
        get
        {
            return CentralTheme.ThemeId;
        }
    }

    public string Version
    {
        get
        {
            return CentralTheme.ThemeVersion;
        }
    }

    //IThemeExtension members
```

403

```
public IEnumerable<Uri> GetControlStyleResources(↵
    string themeId↵
    , string themeVersion↵
    , IEnumerable<IModuleDefinition> modules↵
    )
{
    //this is a modified version of what appears in the file created by the template
    var uriString = string.Format("{0}{1}{2}"↵
        , "/Central.Extensions.Client;"↵
        , "component/Presentation/Themes/"↵
        , "CentralTemplates.xaml"↵
        );

    List<Uri> result = new List<Uri>()
        {
            new Uri(uriString, UriKind.Relative)
        };

    return result;
}
}
```

The XAML File

The XAML file contains a ResourceDictionary, which defines the colors and brushes for the theme, but is far too large to include here in its entirety. Instead, we'll examine the various categories of styles that are defined, along with any details that you'll need to know but that might not be so obvious.

Text Styles

There are 11 predefined text style definitions, as shown in Table 10-3.

Table 10-3. Text Styles

Name	Description
Normal	This style is used for standard text that has no other style defined for it.
Heading1, Heading2	This style is used for major headings and subheadings.
Strong	This style is usually just bold.
Emphasis	This style is usually just italic.
Warning	This style is usually colored red.
Note	This style is usually a smaller font.

Name	Description
Good	This style is usually colored green.
Bad	This style is usually colored red.
Neutral	This style is usually colored yellow/brown.
ToolTip	This style is used to display tooltips.

Each of these styles has a number of font substyles that can be also set for it, as shown in Table 10-4.

Table 10-4. Style Font Substyles

Name	Purpose	Values
FontFamily	Specifies a String value with a primary font family name, plus a secondary one to use if the primary font isn't available	Example (primary/secondary): Segoe UI, Arial Example (assembly path): /Central.Extensions.Client;↵ component/Presentation/Fonts↵ SegoeWP-Semibold.ttf↵ #Segoe WP Semibold
FontSize	Specifies a Double value for the size of the font	(default = px): Px – device-independent units (1/96th inch) in – inches (1in = 96px) cm – centimeters (1cm = 96/2.54 px) pt – points (1pt = 96/72 px)
FontWeight	Specifies a String value for the relative weight of a font (lightness or heaviness of the strokes)	(From lightest to darkest): Thin ExtraLight/UltraLight Light Normal/Regular Medium DemiBold/SemiBold Bold ExtraBold/UltraBold Black/Heavy ExtraBlack/UltraBlack

Name	Purpose	Values
FontStyle	Specifies a String value for the slant of a font	Normal (Characters are upright.) Italic (Characters are truly slanted, using an italic font.) Oblique (Characters are artificially slanted to simulate an italic font.)
FontBrush	Specifies a String value for the color of a SolidColorBrush for the text's foreground	Named colors (Blue, White, Red, etc.) Hexadecimal color values (#FF404040, etc.)
Font↵Background↵Brush	Specifies a String value for the color of a SolidColorBrush for the text's background	Named colors (Blue, White, Red, etc.) Hexadecimal color values (#FF404040, etc.)

Brush Definitions

The rest of the rather large XAML file consists of a series of brush definitions, grouped into style groups, as shown in Table 10-5. A color value is provided for every brush that's used in a theme by default. (Custom themes can add new style definitions, but it's not advisable to do so, because most of the themes that will be available won't be aware of your custom definitions.)

The hardest part of creating a theme extension is deciding and testing which colors to use for the various brush definitions, and then entering them into the XAML. A tool such as Microsoft Expression Blend can be useful here, but it's still a fairly tedious process.

Table 10-5 shows the groups of brushes that are found in the XAML file that defines a theme's colors. In most cases, you can derive the actual brush name by taking the value from the Group column, and then adding the value from the Brush column, plus one of the states mentioned in the Description column (except for Normal), and finally adding the word *Brush* on the end.

So, for the Screen group, you'd end up with three brushes called ScreenBackgroundBrush, ScreenLoadingBackgroundBrush, and ScreenControlBorderBrush. For the Button group, you'd have five brushes called ButtonBorderBrush, ButtonBorderFocusedBrush, ButtonBorderMouseOverBrush, ButtonBorderDisabledBrush, and ButtonBorderPressedBrush.

In the XAML file that the template produces for you, you'll see that some brushes are SolidColorBrushes, some are LinearGradientBrushes, and a few are RadialGradientBrushes. You don't have to keep the same type of brush that's defined in the template's XAML. You can change a SolidColorBrush into a LinearGradientBrush, or vice versa. As long as you provide some type of brush, you have complete freedom to create whatever effects that you want to achieve.

Table 10-5. Brush Definitions

Group	Brush	Description
Screen		
	Background	A brush that's used for the *background* of the screen

Group	Brush	Description
	LoadingBackground	A brush that's used for the *background* of a *control* that's currently loading
	ControlBorder	A brush that's used for the *border* of a *control* when the border hasn't already been defined by some other style
ScreenTab	*The tab at the top of each screen, that has the screen's name and indicates which screen is currently selected.*	
	Border	A brush that's used for the border around the entire screen tab
	Background	Two brushes that are used for the background of a screen tab (just the tab header) in one of two states (Normal, MouseOver)
	Text	A group of brushes that are used for the text of a screen tab in various states (Normal, MouseOver, Active[2])
ShellGlyphButton	*The small button used to expand the navigation menu or the ribbon, or to close a tab or modal window.*	
	Border	A group of brushes that are used for the *border* of the glyph button in various states (Normal, Focused, MouseOver, Disabled, Pressed)
	Background	A group of brushes that are used for the *background* of the glyph button in various states (Normal, Focused, MouseOver, Disabled, Pressed)
	ArrowGlyph	A brush that's used for the *color* of the expand/collapse arrow
	CloseGlyph	A brush that's used for the *color* glyph that is clicked to close a screen
Button		
	Border	A group of SolidColorBrushes that are used for the *border* of a button in various states (Normal, Focused, MouseOver, Disabled, Pressed)

---

[2] There's a bug in the screen tab control; the ScreenTabTextActiveBrush isn't actually used, even if you define it (it took some head scratching and lots of trial and error to work that out).

Group	Brush	Description
	InnerBorder	A group of SolidColorBrushes that are used for just *inside the border* of a button in various states (Normal, Focused, MouseOver, Disabled, Pressed)
	Background	A group of LinearGradientBrushes and a SolidColorBrush that are used for the *background* of a button in various states (Normal, Focused, MouseOver, Disabled, Pressed)
	Text	Two SolidColorBrushes that are used for the actual *text* displayed in a button in two states (Normal, MouseOver)
	Glyph	A brush that's used as the *foreground color* of a glyph (such as a down arrow in a combo box control)
	GlyphBorder	A brush that's used as the *border* around a glyph
	FocusBorder	A brush that's used by some themes to display a *rectangle* around the text (but inside the border) when the button has focus
	BackgroundOverlayEffect	A brush that's used for a *translucent overlay* over the button's background for a special effect (transparent by default)
	BackgroundWaveEffect	A brush that's used for a *translucent path* over the button's background for a special effect (transparent by default)
TextBox		
	Border	A group of brushes that are used for the *border* of a text box in various states (Normal, Focused, MouseOver, Disabled, ReadOnly)
	Background	A group of brushes that are used for the *background* of a text box in various states (Normal, Focused, MouseOver, Disabled, ReadOnly, Selected)
	Text	A group of brushes that are used for the *text* of a text box in various states (Normal, Disabled, ReadOnly, Selected)
	InfoText	A brush that's used for text that appears as a *hint* or *default value* (usually a lighter color and in italics)
	Caret	A brush that's used for the *text entry point* (the thing that blinks)

Group	Brush	Description
TextBoxButton		
	Background	A group of brushes that are used to display a *button* that appears inside the text box's boundary, and can get focus (such as a search button in a grid or list)
	Border	A group of brushes that are used for the *border* of a text box button in various states (Focused, MouseOver, Pressed)
	Glyph	A brush that's used for the color of a text box button's *text or glyph*
Link		
	Text	Two brushes that are used for a link's *text* in one of two states (Normal, Focused)
	FocusBorder	A brush that's used by some themes to display a *rectangle* around the text (but inside the border) when the link has focus
Label		
	Text	Two brushes that are used for a label's *text* in one of two states (Normal, Disabled)
CheckBox		
	Border	A group of brushes that are used for the *square* that contains the check glyph in various states (Normal, Focused, MouseOver, Disabled)
	Background	Two brushes that are used for the check box's *background* color in one of two states (Normal, Disabled)
	Glyph	Two brushes that are used for the check box's *glyph* one of two states (Normal, Disabled)
TabControl		
	Border	Two brushes that are used for the tab control's *border* (which goes around the entire control) in one of two states (Normal, Disabled)

Group	Brush	Description
	Background	A brush that's used for the *background* of the tab panel
	TabBackground	A group of brushes that are used for the *background* of a tab in various states (Normal, Active, MouseOver, Disabled)
	TabText	A group of brushes that are used for the *text* of a tab in various states (Normal, Active, Disabled)
	TabFocusBorder	A brush that some themes use to display a *rectangle* around the text (but inside the border) when the tab has focus
Toolbar	*A ToolBar can be used in any control that needs extra buttons or a header, such as a List, a Grid, or some future control.*	
	Background	A brush that's used for the color of a ToolBar's *background*
	Separator	A brush that's used for the color of any *separator lines* (such as between buttons or rows)
	ButtonBorder	A group of brushes that are used for the *border* of a toolbar's button, in various *states* (Normal, Focused, MouseOver, Disabled, Pressed)
	ButtonBackground	A group of brushes that are used for the *background* of a toolbar's button, in various *states* (Normal, Focused, MouseOver, Disabled, Pressed)
	ButtonText	A group of brushes that are used for the *text* of a toolbar's button, in various *states* (Normal, Focused, MouseOver, Disabled, Pressed)
ScrollBar	*A ScrollBar contains the buttons that are clicked to move up/down or left/right, as well as what's called the thumb control, which displays or sets the current scroll position.*	
	Background	Two brushes that are used for the *background* of a scrollbar in one of two states (Normal, Disabled)
	ButtonBorder	A group of brushes that are used for the *border* around a scrollbar button in various states (Normal, MouseOver, Disabled, Pressed)
	ButtonBackground	A group of brushes that are used for the *background* of a scrollbar button in various states (Normal, MouseOver, Disabled, Pressed)

Group	Brush	Description
	ButtonGlyph	A group of brushes that are used for the *border* around a scrollbar button in various states (Normal, MouseOver, Disabled, Pressed)
	ThumbBorder	A group of brushes that are used for the *border* around a scrollbar thumb control in various states (Normal, MouseOver, Disabled, Pressed)
	ThumbBackground	A group of brushes that are used for the *background* of a scrollbar's thumb control in various states (Normal, MouseOver, Disabled, Pressed)
	ThumbGlyph	A group of brushes that are used for the *glyph* of a scrollbar thumb control in various states (Normal, MouseOver, Disabled, Pressed)
List		
	HeaderBackground	A group of brushes used for the *header* at the top of a list or grid that displays the clickable column header (used to change the sort order) in various states (Normal, Focused, MouseOver, Pressed, Dragged[3])
	HeaderBorder	A group of brushes used for the *separator* between the columns of a list or grid (also used for grid lines in a grid) in various states (Normal, Focused, MouseOver, Pressed, Dragged)
	HeaderText	A brush that's used for the *text* in a list/grid header
	Border	A brush that's used for the *border* around the whole list/grid
Grid		
	RowBackground	A group of brushes that are used for the *background* of a grid row in various states (Normal, MouseOver, Selected, UnfocusedSelected, MouseOverSelected)
	AlternateRowBackground	A brush that's used for the *alternating background* of a grid row (only in the Normal state, as GridRowBackground is used for all other states)

---

[3] The Dragged state appears when the column is dragged (the border is used for the drop position color).

Group	Brush	Description
	`ActiveCellBorder`	A brush that's used for the *border* displayed around a *selected cell* (even if the grid doesn't have focus)
	`AddedBackground`	A brush that's used for the *background* of a record after the record has been *added*
	`EditedBackground`	A brush that's used for the *background* of a record after the record has been *edited*
	`DeletedBackground`	A brush that's used for the *background* of a record after the record has been *deleted*
List		
	`RowBackground`	A group of brushes that are used for the *background* of a list row in various *states* (`Normal`, `MouseOver`, `Selected`, `UnfocusedSelected`, `MouseOverSelected`)
	`RowBorder`[4]	A group of brushes that are used for the *background* of a list row in various states (`Normal`, `MouseOver`, `Selected`, `UnfocusedSelected`, `MouseOverSelected`)
	`RowSeparator`	A brush that's used to display the *horizontal line* between rows
Menu[5]		
	`Background`	A brush that's used for *background* of the entire pop-up
	`Border`	A brush that's used for the *border* around the entire pop-up
	`ItemBackground`	A group of brushes that are used for the *background* of a menu item in various states (`MouseOver`, `Selected`, `MouseOverSelected`, `Pressed`)
	`ItemBorder`	A group of brushes that are used for the *border* of a menu item in various states (`MouseOver`, `Selected`, `MouseOverSelected`, `Pressed`)
	`ItemText`	A brush that's used for the *text* of a menu item

[4] This set of brushes is not normally used but may be useful in a high-contrast theme.
[5] These brushes are used for either pop-ups (such as a combo box) or menus.

Group	Brush	Description
Ribbon		*The ribbon at the top of the screen that displays the available commands for the current screen.*
	Background	A brush that's used for the *background* of the ribbon menu
	Border	A brush that's used for the *border* between the ribbon and the screen
	Separator	A brush that's used for the *separator* between the ribbon groups
	Separator2	A brush that's used for the *padding* between the separator and the background
	GroupText	A brush that's used for the *label* text for a ribbon group
	ButtonBorder	A group of brushes that are used for the *border* of a ribbon button in various states (Normal, Focused, MouseOver, Pressed)
	ButtonInnerBorder	A group of brushes that are used for *just inside the border* of a ribbon button in various states (Normal, MouseOver, Pressed)
	ButtonBackground	A group of brushes that are used for the *background* of a ribbon button in various states (Normal, Focused, MouseOver, Pressed)
	ButtonText	A group of brushes that are used for the *text* of a ribbon button in various states (Normal, Focused, MouseOver, Pressed)
	ButtonDropShadow	A brush that's used as the *drop shadow* of a ribbon button
Nav		*The navigation menu, on the left side of the shell that contains the clickable navigation items (representing the application's screens) and expandable navigation groups.*
	ShellBackground	A brush that's used for the *color* that's *behind* the screen tabs, or when there are no open screens
	Background	A brush that's used for the *background* of the navigation menu

Group	Brush	Description
	GroupBackground	A group of brushes that are used for the *color* of the buttons that represent a navigation menu group in various states (Normal, Focused, MouseOver)
	GroupBorder	A group of brushes that are used for the *border* of a navigation menu group in various *states* (Normal, Focused, MouseOver)
	GroupInnerBorder	A group of brushes that are used to provide an *inner glow* for the selected navigation menu group in one of two states (Normal, Focused)
	GroupText	A group of brushes that are used for the *text* of a navigation menu group in one of two states (Normal, MouseOver)
	ItemBackground	A group of brushes that are used for the *background* of an item in a navigation menu group in various states (Normal, Focused, MouseOver, Pressed)
	ItemBorder	A group of brushes that are used for the *border* of an item in a navigation menu group in various states (Normal, Focused, MouseOver, Pressed)
	ItemText	A group of brushes that are used for the *text* of an item in a navigation menu group in various states (Normal, MouseOver, Pressed)
ValidationPopup		*The floating message that appears over a control when validation errors occur.*
	Background	A brush that's used for the *background* of the validation pop-up
	Text	A brush that's used for the *text* of the validation pop-up
	ErrorBorder	A brush that's used for the *border* of the validation pop-up when the message is an *error*
	MessageBorder	A brush that's used for the *border* of the validation pop-up when the message is *informative*

Group	Brush	Description
TabValidation	*The control that appears at the top of the screen when validation errors occur (it has a header and a pop-up list of errors that can be clicked).*	
	Background	A group of brushes that are used for the *background* of the *header* of the screen's tab validation control in various states (Normal, MouseOver, Pressed)
	Border	A group of brushes that are used for the *border* of the screen's tab validation control in various states (Normal, Focused, MouseOver, Pressed)
	Glyph	A brush that's used as the color of the *glyph* that expands the screen tab's validation control
	Text	A brush that's used as the *color* of the text of the screen tab's validation control
	ItemBackground	Two brushes that are used as the *background* of an individual validation error in one of two states (Focused, Pressed)
	ItemBorder	Two brushes that are used as the *border* of an individual validation error in one of two states (Focused, Pressed)
	ItemText	A brush that's used as the color the *text* of an individual validation error (be careful that the color of this brush is readable for both states of the ItemBackground brush)
Window	*A modal window control that pops up to provide messages.*	
	TitleBackground	A brush that's used for the *background* of the pop-up window's title bar
	TitleText	A brush that's used for the *text* of the pop-up window's title bar
	Border	A brush that's used for the *border* around the pop-up window
	Background	A brush that's used for the *background* of the body of the pop-up window
ContentItem	Border	A brush that's used for the *border* around the selected content item in the runtime screen designer

Common Project's Elements

When we add a theme, using the Extensibility Toolkit's Theme template, as described earlier in the chapter, a Themes folder is added to the Common project's Metadata folder for us (see Figure 10-22).

Because only one file is added per theme, there's not really any need to create a separate folder for each theme's LSML file, but of course you could if you wanted to. The file for our theme is called CentralTheme.lsml.

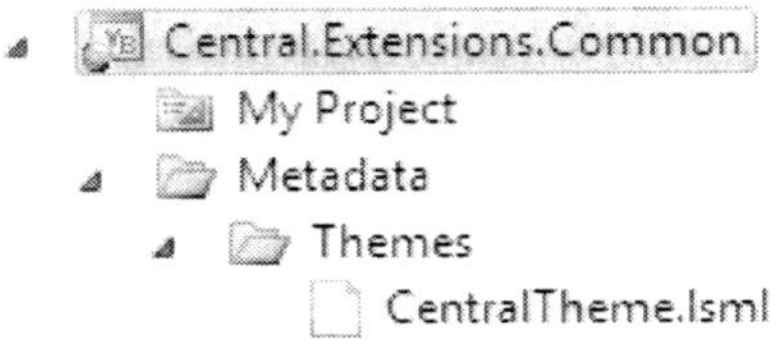

Figure 10-22. Common project's Themes folder

The LSML File

The CentralTheme.lsml file contains a model fragment that defines the theme's details, as shown in Listing 10-3. Two attributes are defined in it (see Table 10-6).

Table 10-6. Attributes Defined in the Theme's LSML File

Name	Description
DisplayName	Appears in the theme selection combo box in the General Properties tab of the LightSwitch project's properties
Description	(Not currently displayed anywhere)

Listing 10-3. CentralTheme's LSML file

XAML:

```
File: Central.Extensions.Common\Metadata\Themes\CentralTheme.lsml

<?xml version="1.0" encoding="utf-8" ?>
<ModelFragment
  xmlns="http://schemas.microsoft.com/LightSwitch/2010/xaml/model"
  xmlns:x="http://schemas.microsoft.com/winfx/2006/xaml">

  <Theme Name="CentralTheme">
    <Theme.Attributes>
      <DisplayName Value="Central Theme"/>
      <Description Value="Central Theme description"/>
    </Theme.Attributes>
  </Theme>
</ModelFragment>
```

Activating LightSwitch's "Hidden" Theme

Earlier, we mentioned the so-called *hidden* theme that uses Windows system colors to create a high-contrast theme. Now that we've explained the steps required to create a theme, for a bit of fun we can show you how to *activate* this theme:

1. Add a theme template item (by right-clicking the Lspkg project).

2. Call it HiddenTheme.

3. Modify the URI in ColorAndFontScheme (in the HiddenTheme.vb/cs file, located in the Client project) to match Listing 10-4.

4. Modify the attributes in HiddenTheme.lsml (located in the Common project) to put a space between *Hidden* and *Theme* (for display purposes).

5. Delete the HiddenTheme.xaml file that was created by the template (it's not needed).

We don't actually need the XAML file that the template created for us this time, because the brush definitions have already been defined in one of LightSwitch's assemblies, Microsoft.LightSwitch.Client.Internal. All we need to do is just point to that XAML resource in our code.

▪ **Caution** Be aware that the next version of LightSwitch might not contain that particular piece of XAML in that particular assembly, or even at all.

Listing 10-4. Code Required to Access the "Hidden" Theme

VB:

File: Central.Utilities\Presentation\Themes\Hidden\HiddenTheme.vb

```
<Export(GetType(ITheme))>
<Theme(HiddenTheme.ThemeId, HiddenTheme.ThemeVersion)>
Friend Class HiddenTheme
Implements ITheme
    'constants
    Friend Const ThemeId As String = "Central.Extensions:HiddenTheme"
    Friend Const ThemeVersion As String = "1.0"

    'ITheme members
    Public ReadOnly Property ColorAndFontScheme As Uri↵
    Implements ITheme.ColorAndFontScheme
        Get
            'this is a modified version of what appears in the file
            'created by the template
            Dim uriString = String.Format("{0}{1}{2}"↵
```

417

```
                    , "/Microsoft.LightSwitch.Client.Internal;"↵
                    , "component/Screens/ScreenPresentation/Implementations/Resources/Themes/"↵
                    , "Black/Black_VisualPalette.xaml"
                    )

                Return New Uri(uriString, UriKind.Relative)
            End Get
        End Property

        Public ReadOnly Property Id As String↵
        Implements ITheme.Id
            Get
                Return HiddenTheme.ThemeId
            End Get
        End Property

        Public ReadOnly Property Version As String↵
        Implements ITheme.Version
            Get
                Return HiddenTheme.ThemeVersion
            End Get
        End Property
    End Class
```

C#:

```
File: Central.Utilities\Presentation\Themes\Central.cs

[Export(typeof(ITheme)), Theme(HiddenTheme.ThemeId, HiddenTheme.ThemeVersion)]
internal class HiddenTheme : ITheme
{
    //constants
    internal const string ThemeId = "Central.Extensions:HiddenTheme";
    internal const string ThemeVersion = "1.0";

    //ITheme members
    public Uri ColorAndFontScheme
    {
        get
        {
            //this is a modified version of what appears in the file
            //created by the template
            var uriString = string.Format("{0}{1}{2}"↵
                , "/Microsoft.LightSwitch.Client.Internal;"↵
                , "component/Screens/ScreenPresentation/Implementations/Resources/Themes/"↵
                , "Black/Black_VisualPalette.xaml"↵
                );

            return new Uri(uriString, UriKind.Relative);
        }
    }
}
```

```
public string Id
{
    get
    {
        return HiddenTheme.ThemeId;
    }
}

public string Version
{
    get
    {
        return HiddenTheme.ThemeVersion;
    }
}
}
```

Renaming a Theme

Sometimes, after you've added a theme, you might need to rename it for some reason. Although you could just delete the original theme and add a new one, we'll show you the various places where the name needs to be changed. This will also be helpful if you decide to copy/paste/edit a theme, instead of using the template to create a new theme.

These instructions assume that you've followed our previous advice and have moved the theme to its own folder.

1. In the *Client* project

    •   rename the theme's folder from
        `Client\Presentation\Themes\OldFolderName` to
        `Client\Presentation\Themes\NewFolderName`

    •   rename the theme's class file from
        `Client\Presentation\Themes\NewFolderName\OldThemeName.vb/cs` to
        `Client\Presentation\Themes\NewFolderName\NewThemeName.vb/cs`

    •   change the Theme class's `ThemeId` from
        `"Central.Extensions:OldThemeName"` to
        `"Central.Extensions:NewThemeName"`

    •   change the Theme class's `ColorAndFontScheme` URI path from
        `"/Central.Extensions.Client;component/Presentation/Themes/⤸`
        `OldTemplatesName.xaml"` to
        `"/Central.Extensions.Client;component/Presentation/Themes/⤸`
        `NewTemplatesName.xaml"`

    •   rename the theme's XAML file from
        `Client\Presentation\Themes\NewFolderName\OldThemeName.xaml` to
        `Client\Presentation\Themes\NewFolderName\NewThemeName.xaml`

2. In the *Common* project

- rename the LSML file from
  Common\Metadata\Themes\OldThemeName.lsml to
  Common\Metadata\Themes\NewThemeName.lsml

Microsoft's Theme Extension Sample

Microsoft has made a sample theme available for download in the MSDN Samples Gallery: http://code.msdn.microsoft.com/LightSwitch-Metro-Theme-b1bfce24. It's quite a complex theme that not only defines fonts and colors, but also adds a number of ThemeExtensions, which define new appearances and behaviors for some of the built-in LightSwitch controls.

You might find that visually this theme is quite a jarring experience, with uppercase and lowercase fonts appearing in unusual places. However, it's actually based on the new Metro style that Windows 8 and Windows Phone 7 have introduced. Some people like it, others not so much.

Hidden away in the theme (well, not *really* hidden, but you do have to go looking) are an abundance of interesting and helpful techniques for anyone who wants to explore the theme in more depth.

Understanding Shell Extensions

In addition to theme extensions, *shell extensions* also allow you to change your application's visual impact (the *feel* part of *look and feel*), by creating an application shell with a potentially completely different layout, and even different capabilities than the standard application shell that comes with LightSwitch.

The attributes and interfaces required by the shell extension classes are found in the Microsoft.LightSwitch.Runtime.Shell namespace.

Creating a Shell Extension

There are a few simple steps required to create a shell extension:

1. Create an extension library, as described earlier in the chapter (or you can add to an existing extension library).

2. Right-click the LSPKG project (Central.Extensions.lspkg)

3. Select Add ➤ New Item.

4. Click the Shell option, shown in Figure 10-23.

5. Provide a name for the shell (we'll call it CentralShell).

6. Click Add.

7. The template adds various folders and files (discussed later in this section). The code that's necessary to implement the required interfaces is also provided by the template (we'll examine this next).

8. Modify the XAML provided by the template to define the layout and content of your shell.

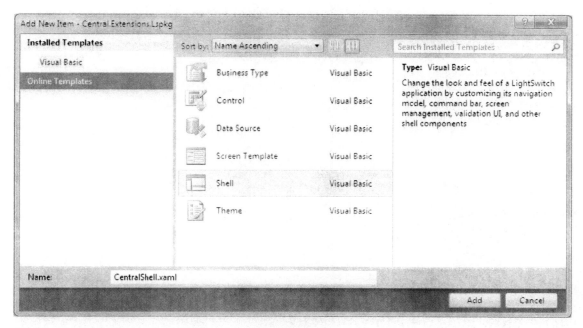

Figure 10-23. Adding a new shell extension template item

Using Shell Extension Attributes

Two attributes must be applied to any class that defines a Shell, for it to be recognized by LightSwitch (see Table 10-7).

Table 10-7. Attributes Used in a Shell Extension Class

Project	Attribute	Value	Description
Client	Export	IShell type	Supplies a contract to LightSwitch indicating that the class represents a shell
Client	Shell	ShellId	Supplies a String ID value for the shell

Listing 10-5 show the attributes being used in code, to decorate the class that defines a shell extension.

Listing 10-5. The Shell Attributes Being Used in Code

VB:

File: N/A

```
Friend Const ShellId As String = "Central.Extensions:CentralShell"
```

```
<Export(GetType(IShell))>
<Shell(CentralShell.ShellId)>
Public Class CentralShell
    Implements IShell

    'implementation code goes here
End Class
```

C#:

File: N/A

```
internal const string ShellId = "Central.Extensions:CentralShell";

[Export(typeof(IShell))]
[Shell(CentralShell.ShellId)]
public class CentralShell : IShell
{

    //implementation code goes here
}
```

Using the Shell Extension Interface

In addition to being decorated with the two attributes just described, a class that defines a shell must also implement the IShell interface.

The IShell interface consists of two properties, listed in Table 10-8.

Table 10-8. IShell Properties

Property	Type	Notes	Returned Value
Name	String	Used internally, to identify the theme	CentralShell.ShellID
ShellUri	URI	Points to a ResourceDictionary (stored in a XAML file) that contains the control definitions for the shell's layout	"/Central.Extensions.Client;↵ component/Presentation/Shells/↵ CentralShell.xaml"

Shell Extension Implementation

A shell enables users to interact with the application. It provides the navigation menu items and displays screens, associated commands, current user information, and other useful information. Let's look at how some of that is defined.

The following paragraphs assume that we've called our theme CentralShell.

Client Project's Elements

When we add a shell, using the Extensibility Toolkit's Shell item, as we mentioned earlier, a Shells folder and a Shells\Components folder are added to the Client project's Presentation folder for us, as shown in Figure 10-24.

We recommend creating a separate folder for each theme in the Shells folder and moving the files created by the template into it. Once again, you don't have to do this, but it helps keep the project more organized. For our example theme, we'll create a folder called Central and move the files into that folder (the Components folder seems unnecessary, so we've deleted it, but it's up to you what you do with it in your own projects).

Three files get added to the Shells folder.

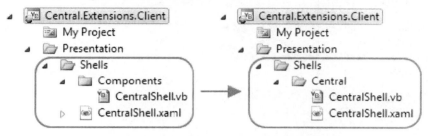

Figure 10-24. *Client project's* Presentation\Shells *folder*

The Class File

The CentralShell class contains the IShell implementation (see Listing 10-6) that we discussed earlier.

Because we moved the files for the shell into their own folder, we also had to make a small change to the ShellUri property's value, changing /Shells/ to /Shells/Central/ in order to reflect this folder change.

Listing 10-6. *CentralShell Class's Code*

VB:

```
File: Central.Extensions.Client\Presentation\Shells\Central\CentralShell.vb

Imports System
Imports System.ComponentModel.Composition

Imports Microsoft.LightSwitch.Runtime.Shell

Namespace Presentation.Shells.Components

    Friend Const ShellId As String = "Central.Extensions:CentralShell"

    <Export(GetType(IShell))>
    <Shell(CentralShell.ShellId)>
    Friend Class CentralShell
        Implements IShell
```

```vbnet
        Public ReadOnly Property Name As String⏎
        Implements IShell.Name
            Get
                Return CentralShell.ShellId
            End Get
        End Property

        Public ReadOnly Property ShellUri As Uri⏎
        Implements IShell.ShellUri
            Get
                'this is a modified version of what appears in the file
                'created by the template
                Dim uriString = String.Format("{0}{1}{2}"⏎
                    , "/Central.Extensions.Client;"⏎
                    , "component/Presentation/Shells/Central/"⏎
                    , "CentralShell.xaml"⏎
                    )
                Return New Uri(uriString, UriKind.Relative)
            End Get
        End Property

    End Class

End Namespace
```

C#:

File: Central.Extensions.Client\Presentation\Shells\Central\CentralShell.cs

```csharp
using System;
using System.ComponentModel.Composition;

using Microsoft.LightSwitch.Runtime.Shell;

namespace Presentation.Shells.Components
{
    internal const string ShellId = "Central.Extensions:CentralShell";

    [Export(typeof(IShell)), Shell(CentralShell.ShellId)]
    internal class CentralShell : IShell
    {
        public string Name
        {
            get
            {
                return CentralShell.ShellId;
            }
        }

        public Uri ShellUri
```

```
    {
        get
        {
            //this is a modified version of what appears in the file
            //created by the template
            var uriString = string.Format("{0}{1}{2}";↵
                , "/Central.Extensions.Client;"↵
                , "component/Presentation/Shells/Central/"↵
                , "CentralShell.xaml"↵
                );
            return new Uri(uriString, UriKind.Relative);
        }
    }
  }
}
```

Caution If you move the XAML file to a different folder than the one the template put it in, as we have, make sure that you edit the Shell class so that the ShellUri property points to the correct location.

The XAML File

The CentralShell.xaml file contains the XAML that represents the controls and the layout of the shell itself (see Listing 10-7). By default, the shell is based on a UserControl that simply contains an empty Grid. You can replace the grid with the XAML that's required to display your intended components.

The x:Class name has to match the name of the class in the code-behind file. The xmlns definitions are the XML namespaces that Silverlight requires, so they must be present in your XAML. They're always the same, and you won't have any need to change them.

As you can see, for various elements in your shell, you can refer to brushes that have been defined in the theme's resource dictionary, simply by specifying it as a static resource binding, using the syntax ElementName={StaticResource BrushName}.

Listing 10-7. CentralShell.xaml File's Initial Contents

XAML:

```
File:
Central.Extensions\Central.Extensions.Client\Presentation\Sehlls\Central\CentralShell.xaml

<UserControl x:Class="Central.Extensions.Presentation.Shells.CentralShell"
    xmlns="http://schemas.microsoft.com/winfx/2006/xaml/presentation"
    xmlns:x="http://schemas.microsoft.com/winfx/2006/xaml"
    >
    <Grid Background="{StaticResource NavShellBackgroundBrush}">

    </Grid>
</UserControl>
```

The Code-Behind File

The CentralShell class inherits from UserControl. The only method in the class is the constructor, which calls InitializeComponent. Most of the time, you won't need to add any code to this file.

Common Project's Elements

The Shell template also adds a Shells folder to the Common project's Metadata folder, as you can see in Figure 10-25. Only a single file gets added to the Shells folder for our shell. Based on the name we gave the shell, it's called CentralShell.lsml.

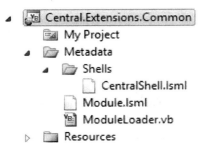

Figure 10-25. Common project's Metadata\Shells folder

The LSML File

The CentralShell.lsml file contains a model fragment that defines the shell's details (see Listing 10-8). Two attributes are defined in it (see Table 10-9).

Table 10-9. Attributes Defined in the Shell's LSML File

Name	Description
DisplayName	Appears in the shell selection combo box in the General Properties tab of the LightSwitch project's properties
Description	This setting doesn't seem to appear anywhere that we can see.

Listing 10-8. CentralShell.lsml File's XAML

LSML:

File: Central.Extensions.Common\Metadata\Shells\CentralShell.lsml

```xml
<?xml version="1.0" encoding="utf-8" ?>
<ModelFragment
  xmlns="http://schemas.microsoft.com/LightSwitch/2010/xaml/model"
  xmlns:x="http://schemas.microsoft.com/winfx/2006/xaml">

  <Shell Name="CentralShell">
    <Shell.Attributes>
      <DisplayName Value="CentralShell"/>
      <Description Value="CentralShell description"/>
    </Shell.Attributes>
  </Shell>

</ModelFragment>
```

Microsoft's Shell Extension Sample

Microsoft has made a simplified sample shell available for download in the MSDN Samples Gallery, at http://code.msdn.microsoft.com/LightSwitch-Shell-1869646f.

Understanding Screen Template Extensions

LightSwitch's built-in templates make it easy to implement various commonly required data display and maintenance screens, but in some situations, the built-in templates don't do quite what you need them to do. A *screen template* extension allows you to create (and share) templates that have common control layout patterns and are exactly suited to your particular needs.

The attributes and interfaces required by the screen template classes are found in the Microsoft.LightSwitch.Designers.ScreenTemplates.Model namespace.

Creating a Screen Template Extension

There are a few simple steps required to create a screen template extension:

1. Create an extension library, as described earlier in the chapter (or you can add to an existing extension library).

2. Right-click the LSPKG project (Central.Extensions.lspkg)

3. Select Add ➤ New Item.

4. Click the Screen Template option, shown in Figure 10-26.

5. Provide a name for the screen template (we'll call it CentralScreen).

6. Click Add.

7. The template adds various folders and files (discussed later in this section). The code that's necessary to implement the required interfaces is also provided by the template (we'll examine this next).

8. Replace the default images with images that are appropriate for your screen.

9. Modify the display name and description, along with any other property values that need to be changed.

10. Add the code required to the supplied Generate method, to add the screen template elements.

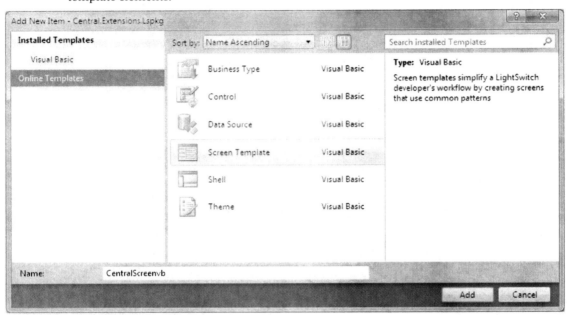

Figure 10-26. Adding a new screen template extension item

Using Screen Template Extension Attributes

Two attributes must be applied to any class that defines a screen template, for it to be recognized by LightSwitch: the Export attribute and the Template attribute (see Table 10-10).

Table 10-10. Attributes Used in a Screen Template Extension Class

Project	Attribute	Value	Description
Design	Export	IScreenTemplateFactory type	Supplies a contract to LightSwitch indicating that the class represents a screen template
Design	Template	TemplateId	Supplies a string ID value for the screen template

Listing 10-9 shows these attributes being used in code, to decorate the class that defines a screen template.

Listing 10-9. IScreenTemplate Attributes Being Used in Code

VB:

```
File: N/A

Friend Const TemplateId As String = "Central.Extensions:CentralScreen"

<Export(GetType(IScreenTemplateFactory))>
<Template(CentralScreen.TemplateId)>
Friend Class CentralScreenFactory
    Implements IScreenTemplateFactory

    'implementation code goes here
End Class
```

C#:

```
File: N/A

internal const string TemplateId = "Central.Extensions:CentralScreen";

[Export(typeof(IScreenTemplateFactory))]
[Template(CentralScreen.TemplateId)]
internal class CentralScreenFactory : IScreenTemplateFactory
{

    //implementation code goes here
}
```

Using Screen Template Interfaces

Two classes are required to define a screen template extension. One must implement the IScreenTemplate interface, and the other must implement the IScreenTemplateFactory interface.

IScreenTemplate Interface

The IScreenTemplate interface consists of eight properties and one method, listed in Table 10-11.

Table 10-11. IScreenTemplate Properties and Methods

Name	Type	Description	Returned Value
TemplateName	String	Used internally, to identify the screen template	"Central.Extensions:↵ CentralScreen"
DisplayName	String	Provides the name displayed in the Add New Screen wizard	"CentralScreen" (You'll want to add spaces when there's more than one word.)
Description	String	Provides the description displayed in the Add New Screen wizard	"CentralScreen description" (Replace this with something meaningful to the user.)
ScreenNameFormat	String	Used for determining the suggested name of the screen in the Create New Screen wizard	"{0}CentralScreen"
PreviewImage	URI	Points to a resource image that's used as the image displayed for the selected screen template in the Add New Screen wizard	"/Central.Extensions.Design;↵ component/Resources/↵ ScreenTemplateImages/↵ CentralScreenLarge.png"
SmallIcon	URI	Points to a resource image that's used as the image displayed for the screen template in the Select a Screen Template section of the Add New Screen wizard	"/Central.Extensions.Design;↵ component/Resources/↵ ScreenTemplateImages/↵ CentralScreenSmall.png"
RootDataSource↵ Type	Root↵ Data↵ Source↵ Type	Determines what types of data can be displayed by the screen template and will be available in the Screen Data option in the Add Screen dialog box	See Table 10-12 for available values.
SupportsChild↵ Collections	Boolean	Specifies whether the Additional Data to Include check boxes are displayed, so that the developer can decide whether to include related data collections	True

Name	Type	Description	Returned Value
Generate	Method	Contains most of the code written by the developer to actually *generate* the required controls for the screen	(Can be used to add data, code, or controls)

Table 10-12 shows the available values for RootDataSourceType, which are also found in the Microsoft.LightSwitch.Designers.ScreenTemplates.Model namespace.

Table 10-12. RootDataSourceType Values

Name	Description	Screens
Collection (default)	Enables the selection of collections or multiple result queries	Editable Grid screen List and Details screen Search Data screen
NewEntity	Used for screens that are intended to enable creating new entities	New Data screen
None	Used for screens in which no data is to be selected	Any screen type with *(none)* selected in Screen Data
ScalarEntity	Enables the selection of one entity type, or queries that return one item	Details screen

IScreenTemplateFactory Interface

The IScreenTemplateFactory interface consists of a single method, CreateScreenTemplate, which simply returns an instance of the screen template class (in our example, the CentralScreen class).

Screen Template Extension Implementation

A common requirement is to have a screen that you can use to both add and edit entities. With this, you would be able to replace the two separate screen templates that come with LightSwitch with just one. By doing this, you could encapsulate all of the code changes that you might need to write over and over, in just one screen template.

The following paragraphs assume that we've called our screen template CentralScreen.

Design Project's Elements

When we add a screen template, using the Extensibility Toolkit's Screen Template item, a ScreenTemplates folder is added to the Design project, and a ScreenTemplateImages folder is added to the project's Resources folder for us, as shown in Figure 10-27.

We recommend creating a separate folder for each screen template in the ScreenTemplateImages folder and moving the files created by the extension template into it. You don't have to do this, but it helps keep the project more organized. There's no need to create a subfolder for each screen template in the ScreenTemplates folder, because there's only one file added per screen template. But you could if you really wanted to.

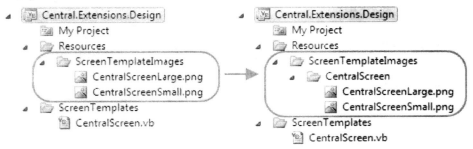

Figure 10-27. Design project's ScreenTemplateImages folder and ScreenTemplates folder

The Image Files

Two default image files, CentralScreenLarge.png (245×178) and CentralScreenSmall.png (24×24), are added to the project for you. These represent the images that will be displayed for the template in the Add New Screen Wizard.

The small image is used in Select a Screen Template section, shown at the left of Figure 10-28. The large image is displayed for the selected screen template, shown in the center of Figure 10-28.

You'll need to replace the default images with images that show the user what your screen template looks like.

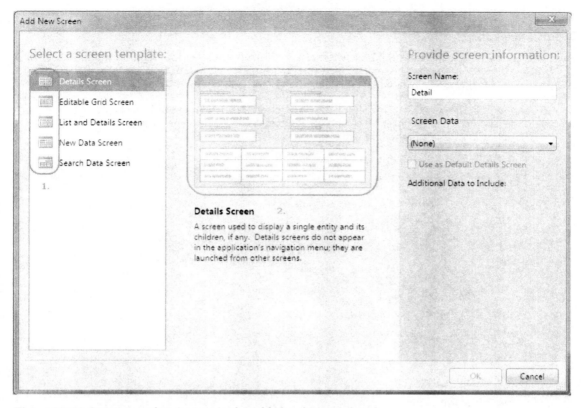

Figure 10-28. Screen template images in the Add New Screen Wizard

The Class File

When it's created by the template, the CentralScreen file will contain implementations for both the IScreenTemplate (CentralScreen class) and IScreenTemplateFactory (CentralScreenFactory class) that we discussed earlier (see Listing 10-10). Because we moved the files for the shell into their own folder, we also had to make a small change to the ShellUri property's value to reflect this folder change.

Imported Namespaces

Out of the nine namespaces that are listed in the Import/Using statements, only two (three for C#, if you include System) are required (the rest of them can safely be removed). The System.ComponentModel.Composition namespace is required for the Export attribute, and the Microsoft.LightSwitch.Designers.ScreenTemplates.Model namespace is required for the IScreenTemplate and IScreenTemplateFactory interfaces.

CentralScreen Class

The CentralScreen class contains the IScreenTemplate's implementation code that we discussed earlier (see Listing 10-10). Most of the actual code for a screen template is found in the Generate method. This method can be used to add any data, code, or controls required for screens that are based on the screen template.

You can modify the template's hierarchy of content items and create additional elements by using storage model classes such as ContentItem and all of its related classes. Generating a screen content tree can consist of any combination the following:

- Adding a content item for the root data of a screen
- Specifying a specific control to use for a content item
- Expanding the children of a content item
- Setting control property values
- Setting the display name for any content items or screen members
- Setting a screen's data member properties
- Adding screen members
- Displaying the selected item of a collection
- Adding group controls
- Accessing related collections
- Adding query parameters
- Adding an entity field
- Adding code to the screen

■ **Caution** Remember that if you've changed the folder structure, as we have, you also need to update the ImageProvider code that refers to the elements that have been moved.

CentralScreenFactory Class

The CentralScreen class contains the IScreenTemplateFactory's implementation code as well (see Listing 10-10). The only method in the class is the CreateScreenTemplate method, which simply returns a new instance of the CentralScreen class.

Listing 10-10. CentralScreen's Code

VB:

File: Central.Extensions.Design\ScreenTemplates\CentralScreen.vb

```vb
Imports System.ComponentModel.Composition

Imports Microsoft.LightSwitch.Designers.ScreenTemplates.Model

Namespace ScreenTemplates

    Friend Class CentralScreen
        Implements IScreenTemplate

        Friend Const TemplateId As String = "Central.Extensions:CentralScreen"

        Public ReadOnly Property TemplateName As String _
        Implements IScreenTemplateMetadata.TemplateName
            Get
                Return CentralScreen.TemplateId
            End Get
        End Property

        Public ReadOnly Property DisplayName As String _
        Implements IScreenTemplateMetadata.DisplayName
            Get
                Return "CentralScreen"
            End Get
        End Property

        Public ReadOnly Property Description As String _
        Implements IScreenTemplateMetadata.Description
            Get
                Return "CentralScreen description"
            End Get
        End Property

        Public ReadOnly Property ScreenNameFormat As String _
        Implements IScreenTemplateMetadata.ScreenNameFormat
            Get
                Return "{0}CentralScreen"
            End Get
        End Property

        Public ReadOnly Property PreviewImage As Uri _
        Implements IScreenTemplateMetadata.PreviewImage
            Get
                'this is a modified version of what appears in the file
                'created by the template
                Dim uriString = String.Format("{0}{1}{2}"↵
```

```vbnet
                       , "/Central.Extensions.Design;" ↵
                       , "component/Resources/ScreenTemplateImages/Central/" ↵
                       , "CentralScreenLarge.png" ↵
                       )
                Return New Uri(uriString, UriKind.Relative)
            End Get
        End Property

        Public ReadOnly Property SmallIcon As Uri _
        Implements IScreenTemplateMetadata.SmallIcon
            Get
                'this is a modified version of what appears in the file
                'created by the template
                Dim uriString = String.Format("{0}{1}{2}" ↵
                       , "/Central.Extensions.Design;" ↵
                       , "component/Resources/ScreenTemplateImages/Central/" ↵
                       , "CentralScreenSmall.png" ↵
                       )
                Return New Uri(uriString, UriKind.Relative)
            End Get
        End Property

        Public ReadOnly Property RootDataSource As RootDataSourceType _
        Implements IScreenTemplateMetadata.RootDataSource
            Get
                Return RootDataSourceType.Collection
            End Get
        End Property

        Public ReadOnly Property SupportsChildCollections As Boolean _
        Implements IScreenTemplateMetadata.SupportsChildCollections
            Get
                Return True
            End Get
        End Property

        Public Sub Generate(host As IScreenTemplateHost) _
        Implements IScreenTemplate.Generate

        End Sub

End Class

<Export(GetType(IScreenTemplateFactory))>
<Template(CentralScreen.TemplateId)>
Friend Class CentralScreenFactory
    Implements IScreenTemplateFactory

    Public Function CreateScreenTemplate() As IScreenTemplate _
    Implements IScreenTemplateFactory.CreateScreenTemplate
        Return New CentralScreen()
```

```
        End Function

    End Class

End Namespace
```

C#:

File: Central.Extensions.Design\ScreenTemplates\CentralScreen.cs

```csharp
using System.ComponentModel.Composition;

using Microsoft.LightSwitch.Designers.ScreenTemplates.Model;

namespace ScreenTemplates
{
    internal class CentralScreen : IScreenTemplate
    {
        internal const string TemplateId = "Central.Extensions:CentralScreen";

        public string TemplateName
        {
            get
            {
                return CentralScreen.TemplateId;
            }
        }

        public string DisplayName
        {
            get
            {
                return "CentralScreen";
            }
        }

        public string Description
        {
            get
            {
                return "CentralScreen description";
            }
        }

        public string ScreenNameFormat
        {
            get
            {
                return "{0}CentralScreen";
            }
        }
```

```csharp
public Uri PreviewImage
{
    get
    {
        //this is a modified version of what appears in the file
        //created by the template
        var uriString = string.Format("{0}{1}{2}";
            , "/Central.Extensions.Design;"
            , "component/Resources/ScreenTemplateImages/Central/";
            , "CentralScreenLarge.png"
            );
        return new Uri(uriString, UriKind.Relative);
    }
}

public Uri SmallIcon
{
    get
    {
        //this is a modified version of what appears in the file
        //created by the template
        var uriString = string.Format("{0}{1}{2}";
            , "/Central.Extensions.Design;";
            , "component/Resources/ScreenTemplateImages/Central/";
            , "CentralScreenSmall.png"
            );
        return new Uri(uriString, UriKind.Relative);
    }
}

public RootDataSourceType RootDataSource
{
    get
    {
        return RootDataSourceType.Collection;
    }
}

public bool SupportsChildCollections
{
    get
    {
        return true;
    }
}

public void Generate(IScreenTemplateHost host)
{

}
}
```

```
[Export(typeof(IScreenTemplateFactory)), Template(CentralScreen.TemplateId)]
internal class CentralScreenFactory : IScreenTemplateFactory
{
    public IScreenTemplate CreateScreenTemplate()
    {
        return new CentralScreen();
    }
}
}
```

■ **Tip** Remember that if you change the name of either of the image files, you need to change any code that references them as well.

Microsoft's Screen Template Sample

Microsoft's screen template sample can be found at http://code.msdn.microsoft.com/LightSwitch-Screen-1b414903.

Understanding Control Extensions

Control extensions are created by combining Silverlight user controls with additional attributes to allow them to be integrated into LightSwitch. So there's no need to manually select Custom Control as the control type, find the assembly that contains the custom control, and then select and bind it each time you want to use that particular custom control. Using control extensions make custom controls as easy to select as any of the controls that LightSwitch provides out-of-the-box.

Several types of control extensions can be created, as shown in Table 10-13.

Table 10-13. Control Extension Types

Name	Description
Value	Represents a content item for a specific simple data type; visualized by using a single control, such as a TextBox or a Label
Details	Represents a content item for an entity property; visualized by using a single control, such as a Summary control, an AutoCompleteBox, or a ModalWindowPicker
Command	Represents a content item for initiating an action, such as a Button or Hyperlink
Collection	Represents a collection content item, such as a Grid control or a ListBox
Group	Represents a group content item, such as a TableLayout, a ColumnsLayout, or a RowsLayout

From their name, *custom controls* may sound like they just deliver extra user interface/presentation layer capabilities. But they can provide packages of much broader functionality. Custom controls can be thought of as *little applications* within your bigger LightSwitch application. For example, a reporting control might not just *display* reports, it may also *generate* them. An analysis control might not just display a cross tab view of data, it might also provide filtering and aggregation capabilities.

The attributes and interfaces required by the control extension classes are found in the `Microsoft.LightSwitch.Presentation` namespace.

Creating a Control Extension

There are a few simple steps required to create a control extension:

1. Create an extension library, as described earlier in the chapter (or you can add to an existing extension library).

2. Right-click the LSPKG project (`Central.Extensions.lspkg`)

3. Select Add ➤ New Item.

4. Click the Control option, shown in Figure 10-29.

5. Provide a name for the control (we'll call it `CentralControl`).

6. Click Add

7. The various projects, folders, and files (discussed later in this section) are created

8. Provide whatever code is necessary for the required interface implementations, and the XAML for the visual representation.

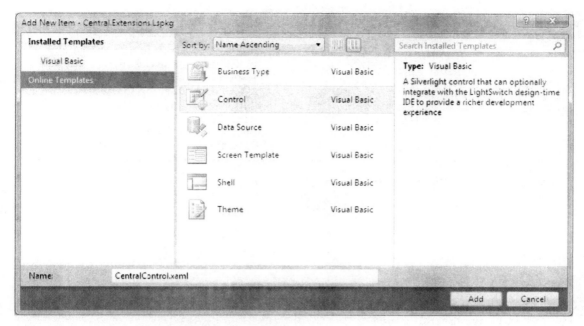

Figure 10-29. Adding a new control extension item

Using Control Extension Attributes

Several attributes must be applied to any class that defines a control, for it to be recognized by LightSwitch (see Table 10-14).

Table 10-14. Attributes Used in a Control Extension Class

Project	Attribute	Value	Description
Client	Export	IControlFactory type	Supplies a contract to LightSwitch indicating that the class represents a control
Client	ControlFactory	ControlId	Supplies a string ID value (in the form of ExtensionLibraryName:ControlName)
Client.Design	Export	IResourceProvider type	Supplies a contract to LightSwitch indicating that the class that provides resources for the control
Client.Design	ResourceProvider	Control Name	Supplies a string value that represents the name of the control that the resources are being provided for (in the form of ControlNamespace.Control)

Project	Attribute	Value	Description
Design	Export	IResourceProvider type	Supplies a contract to LightSwitch indicating that the class that provides resources for the control
Design	ResourceProvider	Control Name	Supplies a string value that represents the name of the control that the resources are being provided for (in the form of `ControlNamespace.Control`)

Listing 10-11 shows these attributes being used in code.

Listing 10-11. Control Attributes Being Used in Code

VB:

File: N/A

```vb
'in the Client project
<Export(GetType(IControlFactory))>
<ControlFactory("Central.Extensions:CentralControl")>
Friend Class CentralControlFactory
    Implements IControlFactory

    'implementation code goes here
End Class

'in the Client.Design and Design projects
<Export(GetType(IResourceProvider))>
<ResourceProvider("Central.Extensions.CentralControl")>
Friend Class CentralControlImageProvider
    Implements IResourceProvider

    'implementation code goes here
End Class
```

C#:

File: N/A

```csharp
//in the Client project
[Export(typeof(IControlFactory)), ControlFactory("Central.Extensions:CentralControl")]
internal class CentralControlFactory : IControlFactory
{

    //implementation code goes here
}

//in the Client.Design and Design projects
```

```
[Export(typeof(IResourceProvider)), ResourceProvider("Central.Extensions.CentralControl")]
internal class CentralControlImageProvider : IResourceProvider
{

    //implementation code goes here
}
```

Using Control Extension Interfaces

A class that defines a control item must implement two interfaces, the IControlFactory interface and the IResourceProvider interface.

IControlFactory Interface

The IControlFactory interface must be implemented in both the Client project and the Client.Design project. It consists of one property and one method (see Table 10-15).

Table 10-15. IControlFactory Interface Property and Method

Name	Description	Return Type
DataTemplate (property)	Returns a XAML fragment that represents the control's ControlTemplate	DataTemplate
GetDisplayModeDataTemplate (method)	Optionally returns another XAML fragment that represents a ControlTemplate that gets used if the control is in a grid, and you want to provide *display mode* functionality (usually a read-only representation that is less costly to display than the editable representation)	DataTemplate

IResourceProvider Interface

The IResourceProvider interface consists of just a single method, GetResource, which returns a BitmapImage from a URI that's constructed using the name of the image file path and the assembly that contains the image.

Control Extension Implementation

When you define a control extension, you use a Silverlight control to display the data. You can also include custom design-time properties that you can later refer to in code.

Client Project's Elements

Just as adding a theme extension added a Themes folder to the Client project's Presentation folder, adding a control extension will add a Controls folder to it as well. Three files get added to the Controls folder.

We recommend creating a separate folder for each control in the Controls folder and moving the files created by the template into it. You don't have to do this, but it helps keep the project more organized. For our example control, we'll create a folder called CentralControl and move the files into that folder, as shown in Figure 10-30.

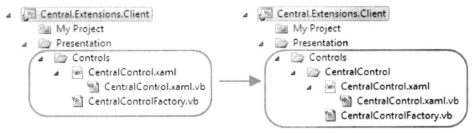

Figure 10-30. Client Project's ControlImages Folder

░ **Caution** Remember that if you've changed the folder structure, as we have, you also need to update any code that refers to the elements that have been moved.

The XAML File

The CentralControl.xaml file contains the XAML definitions that represent the control itself (see Listing 10-12). By default, it simply contains a TextBox, with a two-way binding to the StringValue control's property. You need to replace this with the XAML required to display your extension's control.

Listing 10-12. Default XAML Representation of the Control

XML:

File: Central.Extensions.Client\Presentation\Controls\CentralControl\CentralControl.xaml

```
<UserControl x:Class="Central.Extensions.Presentation.Controls.CentralControl"
    xmlns="http://schemas.microsoft.com/winfx/2006/xaml/presentation"
    xmlns:x="http://schemas.microsoft.com/winfx/2006/xaml"
    >
    <TextBox Text="{Binding StringValue, Mode=TwoWay}"/>
</UserControl>
```

The class declaration and the two namespace declarations will be added for you. There's no need to change either of the xmlns definitions, and in fact if you do change them in any way, your control will no longer work.

If you change the namespace where the control's code is found, or the name of the control itself, you'll have to change the class definition to match.

The Code-Behind File

There are three sections to take note of in the XAML's code-behind file.

Imported Namespaces

Out of the sixteen namespaces that are listed in the Import/Using statements, only three (four for C#, if you include System) are required; the rest of them can safely be removed. The System.ComponentModel.Composition namespace is required for the Export attribute, the System.Windows.Markup namespace is required for XamlReader, and Microsoft.LightSwitch.Presentation is required for IControlFactory and IContentItem.

CentralControl Class

The control's class inherits from UserControl. The only method in the class is the constructor, which calls InitializeComponent. As noted earlier, the name of this class must match the x:Class name in the XAML file.

CentralControlFactory Class

Curiously, the generated code in the XAML file's code-behind file contains not only the usual code that you'd find for a UserControl, but also the actual control's IControlFactory implementation (see Listing 10-13). This class contains the XAML definition for the control's DataTemplate, as well as an optional *display mode* DataTemplate.

We advise you to extract this class out into its own file, to give the class a bit more visibility, making it easier to find when you want to make changes to the data template definitions. This is especially helpful when using the copy/paste method of creating extensions.

Listing 10-13. CentralControl's Code

VB:

```
File: CentralExtensions.Client\Presentation\Controls\CentralControl\CentralControl.vb

Imports System.ComponentModel.Composition
Imports System.Windows.Markup

Imports Microsoft.LightSwitch.Presentation

Namespace Presentation.Controls

    Partial Public Class CentralControl
        Inherits UserControl

        Public Sub New()
            InitializeComponent()
        End Sub

    End Class

    'the template put this class in this file, but you can move it
```

```vbnet
    '(and the namespaces above) to a file of its own
    'as we discussed, it really doesn't belong in here
    <Export(GetType(IControlFactory))>
    <ControlFactory("Central.Extensions:CentralControl")>
    Friend Class CentralControlFactory
        Implements IControlFactory

        'Constants
        Private Const ControlTemplate As String =↵
            "<DataTemplate" &↵
            " xmlns=""http://schemas.microsoft.com/winfx/2006/xaml/presentation'" &↵
            " xmlns:x=""http://schemas.microsoft.com/winfx/2006/xaml'" &↵
            " xmlns:ctl=""clr-namespace:Central.Extensions.Presentation.Controls;" &↵
            "assembly=Central.Extensions.Client'>" &↵
            "<ctl:CentralControl/>" &↵
            "</DataTemplate>"

        'IControlFactory Members
        Private cachedDataTemplate As DataTemplate
        Public ReadOnly Property DataTemplate As DataTemplate↵
        Implements IControlFactory.DataTemplate
            Get
                If Me.cachedDataTemplate Is Nothing↵
                Then
                    Me.cachedDataTemplate = TryCast(↵
                        XamlReader.Load(CentralControlFactory.ControlTemplate)↵
                        , DataTemplate↵
                        )
                End If

                Return Me.cachedDataTemplate
            End Get
        End Property

        Public Function GetDisplayModeDataTemplate(↵
            ByVal contentItem As IContentItem↵
            ) As DataTemplate↵
        Implements IControlFactory.GetDisplayModeDataTemplate
            Return Nothing
        End Function

    End Class

End Namespace
```

C#:

File: CentralExtensions.Client\Presentation\Controls\CentralControl\CentralControl.cs

```csharp
using System;
using System.ComponentModel.Composition;
```

```csharp
using System.Windows.Markup;

using Microsoft.LightSwitch.Presentation;

namespace Presentation.Controls
{
    public partial class CentralControl : UserControl
    {
        public CentralControl()
        {
            InitializeComponent();
        }
    }

    //the template put this class in this file, but you can move it
    //(and the namespaces above) to a file of its own
    //as we discussed, it really doesn't belong in here
    [Export(typeof(IControlFactory)), ControlFactory("Central.Extensions:CentralControl")]
    internal class CentralControlFactory : IControlFactory
    {
        //Constants
        private const string ControlTemplate = "<DataTemplate" +⏎
            " xmlns=\"http://schemas.microsoft.com/winfx/2006/xaml/presentation\"" +⏎
            " xmlns:x=\"http://schemas.microsoft.com/winfx/2006/xaml\"" +⏎
            " xmlns:ctl=\"clr-namespace:Central.Extensions.Presentation.Controls;" +⏎
            "assembly=Central.Extensions.Client\">" + "<ctl:CentralControl/>" +⏎
            "</DataTemplate>";

        //IControlFactory Members
        private DataTemplate cachedDataTemplate;
        public DataTemplate DataTemplate
        {
            get
            {
                if (this.cachedDataTemplate == null)
                {
                    this.cachedDataTemplate =  XamlReader.Load(⏎
                        CentralControlFactory.ControlTemplate⏎
                        ) as DataTemplate;
                }
                return this.cachedDataTemplate;
            }
        }

        public DataTemplate GetDisplayModeDataTemplate(IContentItem contentItem)
        {
            return null;
        }
    }
}
```

Client.Design Project's Elements

A Resources\ControlImages folder, shown in Figure 10-31, also will have been added to the Client.Design project by the template. This is another case where we'd suggest adding a folder for each of the control extensions that you add, if there's more than one, or if you plan on adding more control extensions later.

Two files get added to the ControlImages folder.

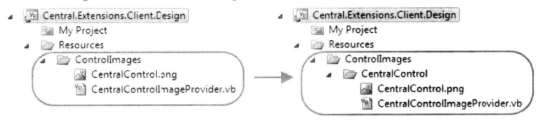

Figure 10-31. ControlImages folder added to Presentation folder

The Image File

By default, the CentralControl.png file will be a generic image (a 3D green sphere). You need to replace this with the image that you want to display for your control.

The file should be:

- A PNG, BMP, or JPG (but not a GIF, as Silverlight doesn't support GIF files)

- 32×32 pixels

The Image Provider Class

The CentralControlImageProvider file contains the IResourceProvider implementation, as shown in Listing 10-14.

Listing 10-14. Control Image Provider Code

VB:

```
File: Resources\ControlImages\CentralControl\CentralControlImageProvider.vb

Imports System
Imports System.ComponentModel.Composition
Imports System.Globalization
Imports System.Windows.Media.Imaging

Imports Microsoft.LightSwitch.BaseServices.ResourceService

Namespace Resources

    <Export(GetType(IResourceProvider))>
```

```vb
    <ResourceProvider("Blank.Extension.CentralControl")>
    Friend Class CentralControlImageProvider
        Implements IResourceProvider

        Public Function GetResource(↵
            ByVal resourceId As String↵
        , ByVal cultureInfo As CultureInfo↵
        ) As Object _
        Implements IResourceProvider.GetResource
            Return New BitmapImage(New Uri(↵
                "/Blank.Extension.Client.Design;component/Resources/ControlImages/↵
                    CentralControl.png"↵
                , UriKind.Relative)↵
                )
        End Function

    End Class

End Namespace
```

C#:

File: Resources\ControlImages\CentralControl\CentralControlImageProvider.cs

```csharp
using System;
using System.ComponentModel.Composition;
using System.Globalization;
using System.Windows.Media.Imaging;

using Microsoft.LightSwitch.BaseServices.ResourceService;

namespace Resources
{
    [Export(typeof(IResourceProvider)), ResourceProvider("Blank.Extension.CentralControl")]
    internal class CentralControlImageProvider : IResourceProvider
    {
        public object GetResource(string resourceId, CultureInfo cultureInfo)
        {
            return new BitmapImage(new Uri(↵
                "/Blank.Extension.Client.Design;component/Resources/ControlImages/↵
                    CentralControl.png"↵
                , UriKind.Relative)↵
                );
        }
    }
}
```

■ **Caution** Remember that if you've changed the folder structure, as we have, you also need to update any code that refers to the elements that have been moved.

Common Project's Elements

The template will have added a Controls folder to the Common project's Metadata folder, as shown in Figure 10-32. Only a single file is added to this folder for each control extension, so there's no need for separate folders.

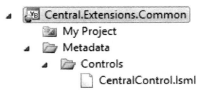

Figure 10-32. Common Project's Controls Folder

The LSML File

The CentralControl.lsml file contains a model fragment that defines the control's details, as shown in Listing 10-15. This includes several attributes and properties. By default there are four (see Table 10-16).

Table 10-16. Attributes Contained in Control's LSML File

Attribute Name	Description
Name	The name used to refer to the control programmatically
SupportedContentItemType	One of the control types (Value, Details, Command, Collection, Group)
DesignerImageResource	A string value that LightSwitch uses to locate the image for the control (in the form of ControlNamespace.ControlName::ControlImage note the double colon)
DisplayName	The name that appears in the control selection combo box in a screen's visual tree
SupportedDataType	One of the base data types that this control will be available for (Integer, String, etc.)

Listing 10-15. CentralControl.lsml File's XAML

LSML:

File: Central.Extensions.Common\Metadata\Controls\CentralControl.lsml

```xml
<?xml version="1.0" encoding="utf-8" ?>
<ModelFragment
  xmlns="http://schemas.microsoft.com/LightSwitch/2010/xaml/model"
  xmlns:x="http://schemas.microsoft.com/winfx/2006/xaml">

  <Control Name="CentralControl"
    SupportedContentItemKind="Value"
    DesignerImageResource="Central.Extensions.CentralControl::ControlImage">
    <Control.Attributes>
      <DisplayName Value="CentralControl" />
    </Control.Attributes>

    <Control.SupportedDataTypes>
      <SupportedDataType DataType=":String"/>
    </Control.SupportedDataTypes>
  </Control>

</ModelFragment>
```

Control Extension Element Mapping

The LightSwitch controls used in its shell and in its screens are all based on Silverlight controls. Table 10-17 contains the mappings of the LightSwitch control elements to their underlying Silverlight controls.

Table 10-17. LightSwitch Controls

Control Element	Inherits From
Button	Silverlight Button
TextBox	Silverlight TextBox
ComboBox/TextBox Button	Silverlight Button
Link	Silverlight HyperlinkButton
Label	Silverlight Label
CheckBox	Silverlight CheckBox
TabControl	Silverlight TabControl
Toolbar	Silverlight ContentControl

Control Element	Inherits From
ScrollBar	Silverlight ScrollBar
List/Grid	Silverlight DataGrid
Grid	Silverlight DataGrid
List	Silverlight ListBox
Popup/Menu	Silverlight Button

Microsoft's Control Extension Samples

Microsoft has provided the following control extension samples (usually with a link to a walk-through):

- LightSwitch Value Control Extension Sample:
  http://code.msdn.microsoft.com/LightSwitch-Value-Control-600cd408

- LightSwitch Detail Control Extension Sample:
  http://code.msdn.microsoft.com/LightSwitch-Detail-Control-a77ab62a

- LightSwitch Smart Layout Control Extension Sample:
  http://code.msdn.microsoft.com/LightSwitch-Smart-Layout-ed3bedae

- LightSwitch Stack Panel Control Extension Sample:
  http://code.msdn.microsoft.com/LightSwitch-Stack-Panel-530f630a

Understanding Business Type Extensions

Business types allow you wrap a base data type in what's called a *semantic type*. This enables you to present data in a way that's most appropriate for your application, adding extra validation and display capabilities in LightSwitch, while continuing to store the actual data as its underlying data type in the database.

The attributes and interfaces required for a business type extension are found in the Microsoft.LightSwitch.Presentation namespace.

Out-of-the-box, LightSwitch comes with several predefined business types, listed in Table 10-18. For those business types to be active, the *Microsoft LightSwitch Extensions* extension must be activated for the project (it's active by default).

Table 10-18. *LightSwitch's Predefined Business Types*

Business Type	Base Type	Description
Phone Number	String	Formats a string value to match the selected type. Eight built-in formats are available, and other developer-defined values can be added. Values can also be entered in four separate fields: • Country Code • Area Code • Number • Extension
Email Address	String	Attempts to validate a string value as a valid email address. Additional settings: • Default Email Domain • Require Email Domain • Display by Default
Money	Decimal	Formats a decimal value according to: • Currency Code • Decimal Places • Is Formatted • Is Grouped • Symbol Mode
Image	Binary	Provides a way to: • load an external image • clear a previously entered image

You can think of business types as an *extra layer* of validation and formatting that sits on top of a normal database type. This allows LightSwitch's data models to be even smarter than they would be if they could work with only the base data types.

Table 10-19 shows some examples of what a business type could be used for.

Table 10-19. *Ideas for Business Types*

Business Type	Base Type	Description
Percent	Decimal	Could: • calculate and display percent value • add a "%" after the value • ensure that the value is always greater than zero
Temperature	Integer	Could: • add °C or °F after the value • ensure that the value is never below −100°C • calculate the value in either Celsius or Fahrenheit

Business Type	Base Type	Description
Custom Product ID	String	Could: • format the value in a consistent way • ensure that the value has the right combination of characters
Country-specific Postcode	String	Could: • use a web service to obtain the postal codes for a selected country

Using a business type makes it easy to ensure that only valid data is entered, while enabling the work that went into creating the validation code, for example, to be done just once, rather than needing to be duplicated in any new application. So business types make it easy to share and reuse code that may have taken quite some time and effort to get working correctly, saving you both time and money. For example, an IT department could do all the hard work and then simply make the business type available to be installed and used by various other departments, knowing that the data will be handled correctly. They could even make its use compulsory.

Without a business type, each department could well end up creating their own implementations, wasting time *re-creating the wheel*, as they say, and possibly introducing bugs into the application that will also take time to track down and fix. So you can view business types as both a productivity tool and a data governance tool.

Creating a Business Type Extension

There are a few simple steps required to create a business type extension:

1. Create an extension library, as described earlier in the chapter (or you can add to an existing extension library).

2. Right-click the LSPKG project (Central.Extensions.lspkg)

3. Select Add ➤ New Item.

4. Click the Business Type option, shown in Figure 10-33.

5. Provide a name for the business type (we'll call it CentralType).

6. Click Add

7. Provide whatever code or XAML is necessary for the required interface implementations (also discussed in more detail, later in this section).

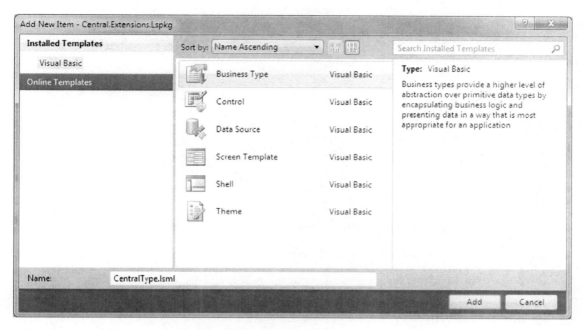

Figure 10-33. *Adding a new business type extension item*

Using Business Type Extension Attributes

Several attributes are used by classes that define a business type extension, in order for its elements to be recognized by LightSwitch. Two attributes are used in the Client project: Export and ControlFactory. Both the Client.Design project and the Design project also use two attributes: Export and ResourceProvider.

Export Attribute

The Export attribute supplies the contracts that LightSwitch requires for an extension to identify itself as a business type extension. These are IControlFactory and IResourceProvider (see Listing 10-16).

ControlFactory Attribute

The ControlFactory attribute then provides further information *about* the business type's control. The information required is a String Id value, in the form of ExtensionLibraryName:ControlName.

Listing 10-16. Business Type Attributes Being Used in Code

VB:

```
File: N/A

'in the Client project
<Export(GetType(IControlFactory))>
<ControlFactory("Central.Extensions:CentralTypeControl")>
Friend Class CentralTypeControlFactory
    Implements IControlFactory

    'implementation code goes here
End Class

'in the Client.Design and Design projects
<Export(GetType(IResourceProvider))>
<ResourceProvider("Central.Extensions.CentralTypeControl")>
Friend Class CentralTypeControlImageProvider
    Implements IResourceProvider

    'implementation code goes here
End Class
```

C#:

```
File: N/A

//in the Client project
[Export(typeof(IControlFactory))]
[ControlFactory("Central.Extensions:CentralTypeControl")]
internal class CentralTypeControlFactory : IControlFactory
{

    //implementation code goes here
}

//in the Client.Design and Design projects
[Export(typeof(IResourceProvider))]
internal class CentralTypeControlImageProvider : IResourceProvider
{

    //implementation code goes here
}
```

Using Business Type Extension Interfaces

A class that defines a business type extension must implement two interfaces: IControlFactory and
IResourceProvider.

IControlFactory Interface

The IControlFactory interface must be implemented in both the Client project and the Client.Design project. As we noted in the control extension section, it consists of one property and one method, listed in Table 10-20.

Table 10-20. IControlFactory Interface Property and Method

Name	Description
DataTemplate property (returns a DataTemplate)	Returns a XAML fragment that represents the control's ControlTemplate
GetDisplayModeDataTemplate method (returns a DataTemplate)	Optionally returns another XAML fragment that represents a ControlTemplate definition that gets used if the control is in a grid, and you want to provide *display mode* functionality (usually a read-only representation that is less costly to display than the editable representation)

IResourceProvider Interface

Also as noted in the control extensions section, the IResourceProvider interface consists of just a single method, GetResource, which returns a BitmapImage from a URI that's constructed using the name of the image file path, and the assembly that contains the image.

Business Type Extension Implementation

When you define a business type, you can add custom design-time properties that you can later refer to in code. A business type can also have a control associated with it (and in most cases, it does), so some of the implementation code is very similar to a control extension's implementation code. But we'll still include all of the implementation details in this section, so that each extension section is self-contained.

Client Project's Elements

Just as adding a control extension added a Controls folder to the Client project's Presentation folder, adding a business type extension will also add a Controls folder to it if it doesn't already exist, as shown in Figure 10-34. Three files get added to the Controls folder. Once again, we recommend creating a separate folder for each business type and moving the files that get created into it.

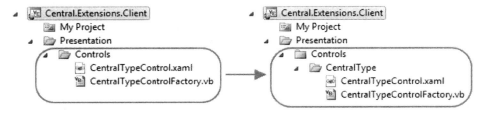

Figure 10-34. Client Project's Controls Folder

■ **Caution** Remember that if you've changed the folder structure, as we have, you also need to update any code that refers to the elements that have been moved.

The XAML File

The `CentralTypeControl.xaml` file contains the XAML that represents the business type's control itself, as you can see in Listing 10-17. By default, it simply contains a `TextBox`, with a two-way binding to the `StringValue` control's property. You need to replace this with the XAML required to display your intended control.

Listing 10-17. Initial XAML Representation of the Business Type's Control

XML:

File: Central.Extensions.Client\Presentation\Controls\CentralType\CentralTypeControl.xaml

```
<UserControl x:Class="Central.Extensions.Presentation.Controls.CentralTypeControl"
    xmlns="http://schemas.microsoft.com/winfx/2006/xaml/presentation"
    xmlns:x="http://schemas.microsoft.com/winfx/2006/xaml"
    >
    <TextBox Text="{Binding StringValue, Mode=TwoWay}"/>
</UserControl>
```

The class declaration and the two namespace declarations will be added for you. There's no need to change either of the `xmlns` definitions, and in fact if you do change them in any way, your control will no longer work.

The Code-Behind File

There are three sections to take note of in the XAML's code-behind file.

Imported Namespaces

Out of the sixteen namespaces that are listed in the `Import/Using` statements, only three (four for C#, if you include `System`) are required (the rest of them can safely be removed). The `System.ComponentModel.Composition` namespace is required for the `Export` attribute, the

System.Windows.Markup namespace is required for XamlReader, and the Microsoft.LightSwitch.Presentation namespace is required for IControlFactory and IContentItem.

CentralTypeControl Class

The control's class inherits from UserControl. The only method in the class is the constructor, which calls InitializeComponent.

CentralTypeControlFactory Class

As with the CentralControlFactory class in the control extension, the generated code in the XAML file's code-behind file contains not only the usual code that you'd find for a UserControl, but also the actual business type control's IControlFactory implementation (see Listing 10-18). This class contains the XAML definition for the control's DataTemplate, as well as an optional *display mode* DataTemplate.

We advise you to extract this class out into its own file, to give the class a bit more visibility, making it easier to find when you want to make changes to the data template definitions. This is especially helpful when using the copy/paste method of creating extensions.

Listing 10-18. CentralTypeControl's Code

VB:

File: CentralExtensions.Client\Presentation\Controls\CentralType\CentralTypeControl.vb

```vb
Imports System.ComponentModel.Composition
Imports System.Windows.Markup

Imports Microsoft.LightSwitch.Presentation

Namespace Presentation.Controls

    Partial Public Class CentralTypeControl
        Inherits UserControl

        Public Sub New()
            InitializeComponent()
        End Sub

    End Class


    'the template put this class in this file, but you can move it
    '(and the namespaces above) to a file of its own
    'as we discussed, it really doesn't belong in here

    <Export(GetType(IControlFactory))>
    <ControlFactory("Central.Extensions:CentralTypeControl")>
    Friend Class CentralTypeControlFactory
        Implements IControlFactory

        'Constants
```

```vb
        Private Const ControlTemplate As String =↵
            "<DataTemplate" &↵
            " xmlns=""'http://schemas.microsoft.com/winfx/2006/xaml/presentation'" &↵
            " xmlns:x=""'http://schemas.microsoft.com/winfx/2006/xaml'" &↵
            " xmlns:ctl=""'clr-namespace:Central.Extensions.Presentation.Controls;" &↵
            "assembly=Central.Extensions.Client'>" &↵
            "<ctl:CentralTypeControl/>" &↵
            "</DataTemplate>"

        'IControlFactory Members
        Private cachedDataTemplate As DataTemplate
        Public ReadOnly Property DataTemplate As DataTemplate↵
        Implements IControlFactory.DataTemplate
            Get
                If Me.cachedDataTemplate Is Nothing↵
                Then
                    Me.cachedDataTemplate = TryCast(↵
                        XamlReader.Load(CentralTypeControlFactory.ControlTemplate)↵
                        , DataTemplate↵
                        )
                End If

                Return Me.cachedDataTemplate
            End Get
        End Property

        Public Function GetDisplayModeDataTemplate(↵
            ByVal contentItem As IContentItem↵
            ) As DataTemplate↵
        Implements IControlFactory.GetDisplayModeDataTemplate
            Return Nothing
        End Function

    End Class

End Namespace
```

C#:

File: CentralExtensions.Client\Presentation\Controls\CentralControl**CentralTypeControl.cs**

```csharp
using System;
using System.ComponentModel.Composition;
using System.Windows.Markup;

using Microsoft.LightSwitch.Presentation;

namespace Presentation.Controls
{
    public partial class CentralTypeControl : UserControl
    {
```

```csharp
    public CentralTypeControl()
    {
        InitializeComponent();
    }
}

//the template put this class in this file, but you can move it
//(and the namespaces above) to a file of its own
//as we discussed, it really doesn't belong in here
[Export(typeof(IControlFactory)), ControlFactory("Central.Extensions:CentralTypeControl")]
internal class CentralTypeControlFactory : IControlFactory
{
    //Constants
    private const string ControlTemplate = "<DataTemplate" +⏎
        " xmlns='http://schemas.microsoft.com/winfx/2006/xaml/presentation'" +⏎
        " xmlns:x='http://schemas.microsoft.com/winfx/2006/xaml'" +⏎
        " xmlns:ctl='clr-namespace:Central.Extensions.Presentation.Controls;" +⏎
        "assembly=Central.Extensions.Client'>" +⏎
        "<ctl:CentralTypeControl/>" +⏎
        "</DataTemplate>";

    //IControlFactory Members
    private DataTemplate cachedDataTemplate;
    public DataTemplate DataTemplate
    {
        get
        {
            if (this.cachedDataTemplate == null)
            {
                this.cachedDataTemplate = XamlReader.Load(⏎
                    CentralTypeControlFactory.ControlTemplate⏎
                    ) as DataTemplate;
            }
            return this.cachedDataTemplate;
        }
    }

    public DataTemplate GetDisplayModeDataTemplate(IContentItem contentItem)
    {
        return null;
    }
}
}
```

Client.Design Project's Elements

A Resources\ControlImages folder (see Figure 10-35) will have been also added to the Client.Design project by the template. Two files get added to the ControlImages folder. This is another case where we'd suggest adding a folder for each of the control extension that you add, if there's more than one, or if you plan on adding more business type extensions later.

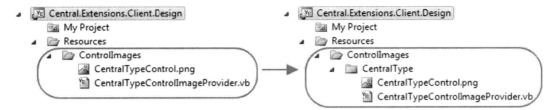

Figure 10-35. Client.Design project's ControlImages folder

The Image File

By default, the CentralTypeControl.png file will be a generic image (a 3D green sphere). You need to replace this with the image that you want to display for your control.

The file should be:

- a PNG, BMP, or JPG (but not a GIF, as Silverlight doesn't support GIF files)
- 32×32 pixels

The Image Provider Class

The CentralTypeControlImageProvider file contains the IResourceProvider implementation (see Listing 10-19).

Listing 10-19. Business Type Control's Image Provider Code

VB:

```
File: Resources\ControlImages\CentralType\CentralTypeControlImageProvider.vb

Imports System
Imports System.ComponentModel.Composition
Imports System.Globalization
Imports System.Windows.Media.Imaging

Imports Microsoft.LightSwitch.BaseServices.ResourceService

Namespace Resources

    <Export(GetType(IResourceProvider))>
    <ResourceProvider("Blank.Extension.CentralTypeControl")>
    Friend Class CentralTypeControlImageProvider
        Implements IResourceProvider

        Public Function GetResource(↵
            ByVal resourceId As String↵
            , ByVal cultureInfo As CultureInfo↵
            ) As Object _
        Implements IResourceProvider.GetResource
```

```vbnet
            Return New BitmapImage(New Uri(↵
                "/Blank.Extension.Client.Design;component/Resources/ControlImages/↵
                    CentralType/CentralType.png"↵
                , UriKind.Relative)↵
                )
        End Function

    End Class

End Namespace
```

C#:

File: Resources\ControlImages\CentralType\CentralTypeControlImageProvider.cs

```csharp
using System;
using System.ComponentModel.Composition;
using System.Globalization;
using System.Windows.Media.Imaging;

using Microsoft.LightSwitch.BaseServices.ResourceService;

namespace Resources
{
    [Export(typeof(IResourceProvider)),
ResourceProvider("Blank.Extension.CentralTypeControl")]
    internal class CentralTypeControlImageProvider : IResourceProvider
    {
        public object GetResource(string resourceId, CultureInfo cultureInfo)
        {
            return new BitmapImage(new Uri(↵
                "/Blank.Extension.Client.Design;component/Resources/ControlImages/↵
                    CentralType/CentralType.png"↵
                , UriKind.Relative)↵
                );
        }
    }
}
```

■ **Caution** Remember that if you've changed the folder structure, as we have, you also need to update any code that refers to the elements that have been moved.

Common Project's Elements

The Business Type template will have added a `Controls` folder and a `Types` folder to the `Common` project's `Metadata` folder, as shown in Figure 10-36. Only a single file is added to these folders for each business type extension, so there's no need for separate folders.

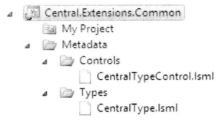

Figure 10-36. Common project's Controls and Types folders

The LSML File

The LSML file contains some XML, which defines a model fragment, shown in Listing 10-20. This model fragment specifies various attributes and properties for the business type. By default there are two (see Table 10-21).

Table 10-21. Attributes Contained in Control's LSML File

Attribute Name	Description
Name	The name used to refer to the control programmatically
SemanticType	Contains: • `UnderlyingType` (the type that's being stored in the database, in the form of `AssemblyName:DataType` • `DisplayName` that gets displayed when choosing a property in the table designer
DefaultViewMapping	Contains: • `ContentItemKind` • `DataType` • View

⬛ **Tip** A single colon (:) can often be used as a shortcut for `Microsoft.LightSwitch:`.

Listing 10-20. Default Business Type Model Fragment

LSML:

File: Central.Extensions.Common\Metadata\Types\CentralType.lsml

```xml
<?xml version="1.0" encoding="utf-8" ?>

<ModelFragment
  xmlns="http://schemas.microsoft.com/LightSwitch/2010/xaml/model"
  xmlns:x="http://schemas.microsoft.com/winfx/2006/xaml">

  <SemanticType Name="CentralType"
    UnderlyingType=":String">
    <SemanticType.Attributes>
      <DisplayName Value="CentralType" />
    </SemanticType.Attributes>
  </SemanticType>

  <DefaultViewMapping
    ContentItemKind="Value"
    DataType="CentralType"
    View="CentralTypeControl"/>

</ModelFragment>
```

Editor and Viewer Controls

You can create *multiple* controls for your business type. An Editor and a Viewer are the most common.

Understanding Data Source Extensions

LightSwitch applications can natively connect to SQL Server databases, SharePoint lists, and WCF RIA Services. If you need to connect to some other type of data source, that's where the extensibility features come in handy. A *data source extension* is essentially an adapter class (a domain service) that enables LightSwitch to work with data sources that it normally wouldn't understand.

By using RIA Services as service layer, you can write code that connects with just about any external data source. LightSwitch then interfaces with the service layer, allowing the data to appear as standard LightSwitch data entities. After the data source extension has been written, connecting with external services is transparent for LightSwitch application developers who are consuming the data source.

Data source extensions work particularly well for in-house use. An IT department can build a RIA service around data from a particular legacy application and wrap it in a data source extension. This enables it to be shared for use in other LightSwitch applications. Data source extensions can also be included as companions to other extension types in the same extension library. For example, the DevExpress XtraReports control provides its own data source extension to enable report preview screens to communicate with the report server.

The classes that are required for a data source extension come predominantly from:

- System.ServiceModel.DomainServices.Server
- System.ComponentModel.DataAnnotations

Creating a Data Source Extension

There are a few simple steps required to create a data source extension:

1. Create an extension library, as described earlier in the chapter (or you can add to an existing extension library).

2. Right-click the LSPKG project (Central.Extensions.lspkg).

3. Select Add ➤ New Item.

4. Click the Data Source option, shown in Figure 10-37.

5. Provide a name for the data source (we'll call it CentralSource).

6. Click Add.

7. The various projects, folders, and files (discussed later in this section) are created.

8. Provide whatever code or XAML is necessary for the required interface implementations (also discussed in more detail later in this section).

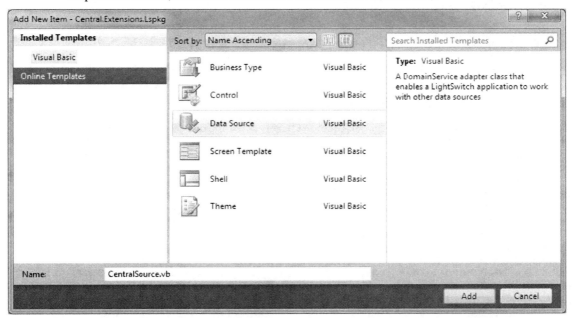

Figure 10-37. Adding a new data source extension item

Data Source Extension Implementation

From the point of view of writing extensions, a data source extension is the simplest of all the extension types. There are no special attributes that LightSwitch requires to advertise its presence as an extension. And there are no interfaces that are required to be implemented.

A data source extension is simply a custom RIA service (you learned about creating and using RIA services in Chapter 7). If you know how to create a RIA service, you know how to create a data source extension.

LightSwitch uses the custom DomainService class that you write as a kind of in-memory data adapter, calling the instance directly from its data service implementation to perform query and submit operations.

Using this mechanism, you can create a DomainService class that exposes entity types and implements query, insert, update, and delete methods. LightSwitch infers a LightSwitch entity model based on the exposed entity types and infers an entity set based on the presence of a query decorated with the Query attribute (with IsDefault set to true). A primary-key property also has to be defined by decorating it with the Key attribute.

Server Project's Elements

When we add a screen template, using the Extensibility Toolkit's Data Source item, a DataSources folder is added to the Server project for us, as shown in Figure 10-38. Unlike several of the other extension item types, there's no real need to create a subfolder for each data source in the DataSources folder, because only one file is added per data source. But again, you could if you really wanted to.

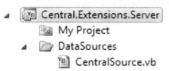

Figure 10-38. *Server project's DataSources folder*

The Class File

There are two sections to take note of in the CentralSource class file.

Imported Namespaces

Out of the five namespaces that are listed in the Import/Using statements, only one (two for C#, if you include System) is required, plus one that you'll need when you start writing the code for the data source (the rest of them can safely be removed). The System.ServiceModel.DomainServices.Server is required for DomainService, and System.ComponentModel.DataAnnotations is required for the Key attribute.

CentralSource Class

The data source's class inherits from DomainService. No other code is added to the class by the template, just a TODO comment that acts as a reminder that this is the place to create methods that contain the logic required for your data source.

Debugging Extensions

The Microsoft recommended way of debugging an extension is to use what's called the *experimental instance* of Visual Studio:

1. Set any breakpoints in your extension's code.

2. On the menu bar, select Debug ➤ Start Debugging (this opens the experimental instance.

3. On the menu bar of the experimental instance, select Add ➤ New Project (or, you could open an existing project instead).

4. In the New Project dialog box, select LightSwitch Application (either VB or C#).

5. Give the project a name and click OK.

6. In the Extensions tab of the project's properties, enable the extension for the project.

Distributing Extensions

There are two methods that you can use to distribute your extension, depending on whether you want to make it available to the general public or just to people you know personally.

When you're happy that your extension is behaving the way that you want it to, you should make sure that the solution configuration setting is set to Release, as shown in Figure 10-39. If you leave it set to Debug, you'll be publishing debug symbols with your extension, and the download time for your users may also be longer than necessary.

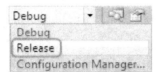

Figure 10-39. *Solution configuration*

If the solution configuration isn't available on your Visual Studio toolbar, you can access it by clicking Build ➤ Configuration Manager to access the dialog box shown in Figure 10-40.

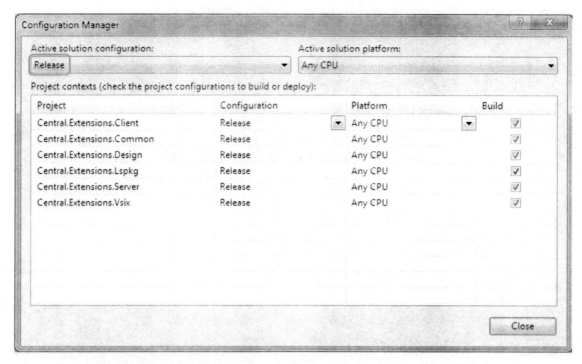

Figure 10-40. Configuration Manager

■ **Tip** Before distributing your extension, you should make sure that you've entered at least a name, description, and author in the VSIX project's settings, as described earlier in the VSIX project section.

Sharing the Setup File

To share the setup file, follow these steps (replacing Central.Extensions with the name you gave your extension):

1. In Windows Explorer, browse to the Central.Extensions.vsix\bin\Release folder.

2. Right-click Central.Extensions.vsix

3. Select Copy.

4. Browse to a network share or some form of removable media (flash drive or CD/DVD).

5. Select Paste.

6. On the machine where you want to install the extension, open the VSIX file (click or double-click, as required).

7. Select Install

8. Follow the Extension Installer prompts.

Publishing to the Visual Studio Gallery

To publish your extension so that everyone can access it:

1. In the Visual Studio Gallery web site, sign in (if you're not already signed in).

2. In Step 1: Extension Type, select Control and click Next. (You must select Control for a LightSwitch extension.)

3. In Step 2: Upload, select I Would Like to Upload My Control.

4. Browse to the `Central.Extensions.vsix\bin\Release` folder and select the VSIX file and click Next.

5. In Step 3: Basic Information, information from the manifest has been entered for you, and LightSwitch has been selected as the Category for you. Set the following options:

   - Add tags that will help categorize your extension.

   - Choose a Cost Category (Free, Trial, or Paid).

   - Set Allow Discussions for your extension to True/False.

   - Enter the description for your extension (either manually, or using one of the provided templates).

   - Read and accept the Contribution Agreement.

   - Select the Create Contribution option (the extension has not yet been published).

   - When you're happy with all of the information, click Publish.

Summary

There's been a lot to learn in this chapter. First we explored why you might need an extension:

- To enhance the look and feel of your applications

- To enable more-advanced data entry scenarios

- To get access to external sources data that LightSwitch doesn't know how to communicate with natively

Then you examined the two ways of finding extensions, through either the Visual Studio Gallery web site or with the built-in Extension Manager. You also learned how to install them.

You looked briefly at some extensions made available by community members as well as the offerings of some third-party commercial vendors.

Further on in the chapter, you learned about:

- How the LightSwitch 2011 Extensibility Toolkit makes creating extensions easier than ever before

- How to create an your own extension library

- The seven projects types that an extension is made up of (plus what extension type uses which project types)

- The setup file (and how to set the manifest's properties in the VSIX Manifest Designer)

We then gave you some background information to help you understand each of the six extension types:

- Theme extensions

- Shell extensions

- Screen template extensions

- Control extensions

- Business type extensions

- Data source extensions

Finally, we showed you how to debug your extensions, as well as how you can distribute them to other users.

PART 4

Getting Data Out

CHAPTER 11

Creating and Displaying Reports

Reports are perhaps the most important part of any IT system. Reports are often seen by decision makers or by those in a position of seniority who carry influence within an organization. Being responsible for good reports can therefore be politically good for any IT professional wanting to progress in their career. At a lower level, reports are used to create items that are seen by other stakeholders. Examples could include packing notes, remittance advice, and invoices. These pieces of output provide a public face to a company and are important in terms of creating the right impression.

Given the importance of reporting, it seems a shame that this feature could not make it into version 1 of LightSwitch. It's a particular surprise for those from an Access background, where reporting is firmly integrated into the product. Despite this limitation, there are still lots of methods for producing functional and good-looking reports in LightSwitch.

Microsoft SQL Server Reporting Services and Microsoft ASP.NET are two natural choices that developers can lean toward because both products belong inside the Microsoft technology stack. Both products share one thing in common: they are capable of producing output that can be accessed through a web address. This chapter shows you how to produce output by using both products and teaches you a common technique for hooking up your report with your LightSwitch application.

Programming Microsoft Word through COM automation is another option that can be used for out-of-browser applications. Finally, there are many third-party controls that you can purchase to produce reports. Table 11-1 summarizes the available options that are described in this chapter.

Table 11-1. Reporting Techniques

Technique	Desktop Application	Web Application
Use Reporting Services	✓	✓
Automate Microsoft Word	✓	
Create PDF on client	✓	
Use third-party controls	✓	✓

Using ASP.NET to Create Reports

A simple method of producing printable output is to create an ASP.NET web site that contains web pages populated with data. In this section, you'll learn how to create a simple ASP.NET web project and some simple data-driven web pages. This will be a fairly basic overview of ASP.NET. If you want to learn more, the official ASP.NET web site provides a great resource.

When deployed onto a web server, the reports will be accessible through a URL that you'll define during deployment. Later, you'll learn how to create reports by using SQL Reporting Services, which also exposes its output through a web URL. The technique of linking the web pages together with screens is described later, in the "Linking Reports to LightSwitch" section.

Creating an ASP.NET Project

The first step is to create an ASP.NET web site. You can either create this as a stand-alone project or you can create a new project in an existing LightSwitch solution. Adding a web site into an existing solution requires Visual Studio 2010 Professional or above. If this is not available, you can create a stand-alone web site by downloading a free copy of Microsoft Visual Studio Web Developer Express from the official Microsoft web site.

To add a web site into an existing solution, you have to first switch into file mode (see Chapter 2 for details). In Solution Explorer, right-click the solution and choose File ➤ New Project ➤ ASP.NET Web Application to create a new web site. For the purposes of this demonstration, the new web site will be named ReportingWebSite.

Figure 11-1 shows how the new project appears in Solution Explorer. When you press F5 or run your solution, the new web site project will appear and is hosted by default by using the ASP.NET Development Server.

By default, dynamic ports are used, which means that the URL used to access web pages during development may change, particularly after Visual Studio is restarted. To simplify development, you can specify a particular port through the properties of your project (as shown in Figure 11-2). This results in a more predictable URL and eases the task of development.

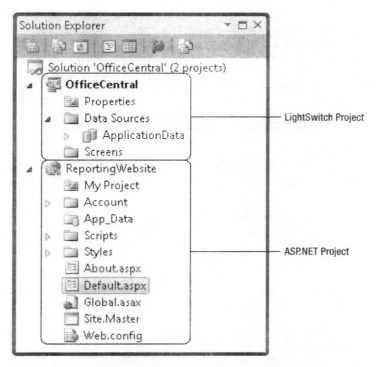

Figure 11-1. The web site as it appears in Solution Explorer

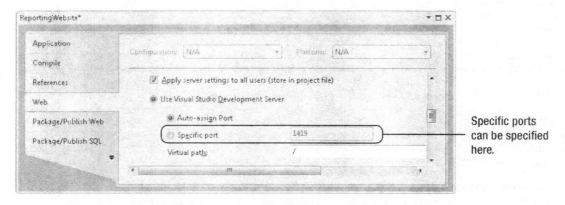

Figure 11-2. Choosing a static port

Creating a New Page

After creating a web project, you can produce new pages to display the desired output. In the following example, a time-sheet report is created to display the time-sheet entries relating to a given person. The page, named `TimesheetEntries.aspx`, accepts a `UserID` argument. The important point about this example is that it demonstrates how arguments can be passed into web pages.

To add a new page, right-click the `ReportingWebSite` project and select the option to add a new item. Select the Web Form option and rename the file `TimesheetEntries.aspx`.

To connect to a SQL database, use the buttons toward the lower part of the screen to place your page into either Split or Design view, as shown in Figure 11-3. Next, go the Data section of your toolbox and drag a `SqlDataSource` object onto your web form.

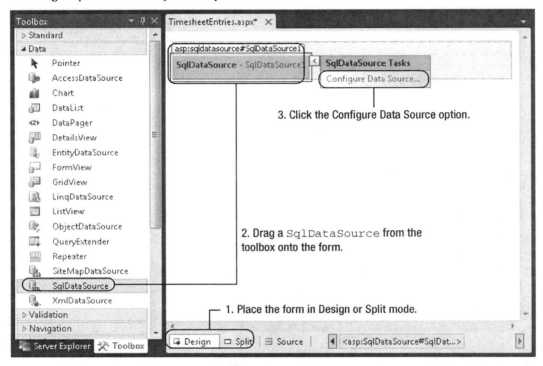

Figure 11-3. Adding a SQL Server data source

With `SqlDataSource` selected, click the Configure Data Source context menu item. The Configure Data Source Wizard appears. You can click the New Connection button to connect to your database. If you want to connect to your intrinsic database by using the LightSwitch intrinsic `ApplicationData.mdf` file, you can use the same technique that was described in Chapter 2. Make sure to set the User Instance option to True if you want to do this.

After entering your connection details, the wizard prompts you to save the changes into the `web.config` file. Choosing to do this is better than keeping the credentials hard-coded because it simplifies the process of deployment and allows the details to be shared across multiple web pages.

Continue through the wizard, and when you reach the Configure the Select Statement page, you can select the option to Specify a Custom SQL Statement or Stored Procedure. The next page in the wizard includes a Query Builder button that allows you to graphically build a `SELECT` query based on the `Timesheet` table. A `WHERE` clause can be added to the end of the statement by using the syntax `WHERE UserID=@UserID`.

@UserID defines a placeholder parameter. The data source wizard detects that this is a parameter and allows you to define additional details in the following wizard page, as shown in Figure 11-4.

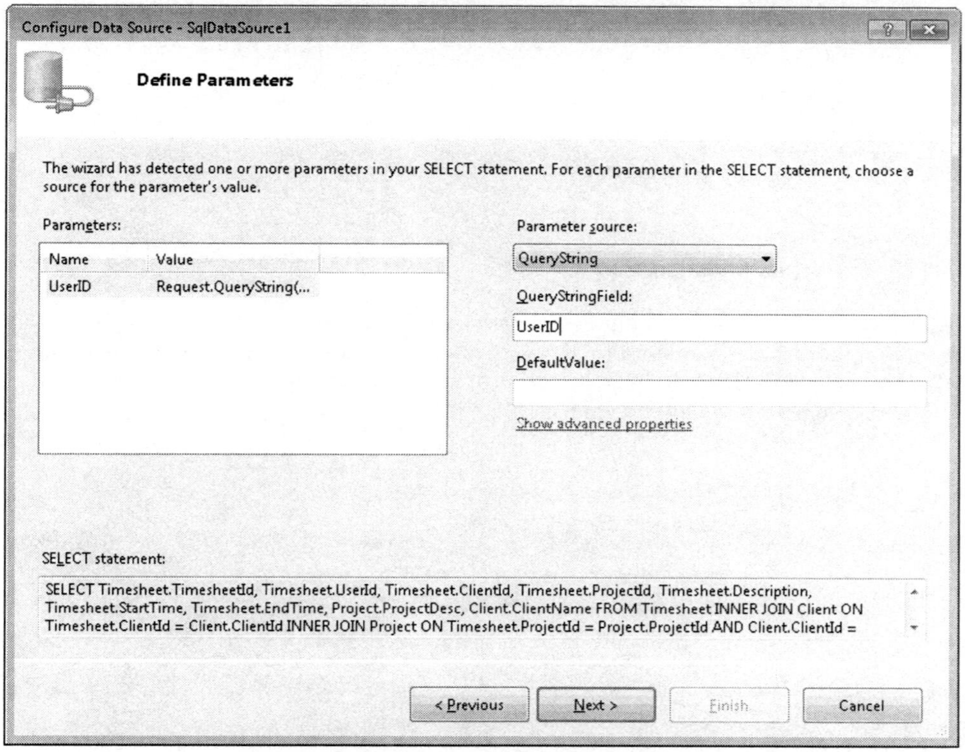

Figure 11-4. Defining the parameters that are used in a WHERE clause

In the Parameter Source drop-down box, select the QueryString option to enable the parameter to be passed through the URL. Finally, name the parameter by setting the QueryStringField text box to UserID.

Now that you've created a data source, you'll need to add a control to display the contents of the query. The ASP.NET GridView control allows you to bind to a SqlDataSource and creates a tabular view of the data. To add a GridView control onto the page, drag an instance of a GridView into your form from the Data section of the toolbox.

As shown in Figure 11-5, the DataSource of the GridView can now be set to the SqlDataSource that you've created. You can use the Auto Format link in the same dialog box to format your grid in a more attractive fashion.

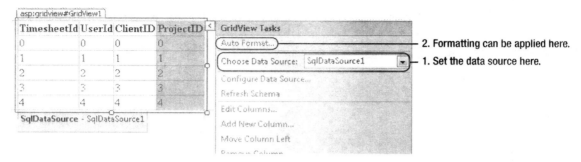

Figure 11-5. Setting the data source of the GridView

When you run your project, an instance of the ASP.NET Development Server is started. If you configured a static port earlier (shown in Figure 11-2), you'll already know the port number. If not, don't worry. Hovering the mouse over the icon in the notification area (shown in Figure 11-6) will show you the port number that is being used (for example, 1419).

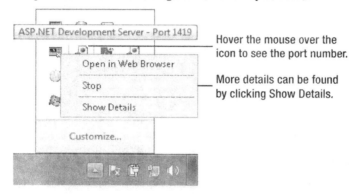

Figure 11-6. The Open in Web Browser option

Finally, you can construct a URL by appending a UserID argument to the address and then view the page in your browser. The format of the URL will look something like this: http://localhost:1419/TimesheetEntry.aspx?UserID=8. Figure 11-7 shows what the final report looks like. Make a note of the URL, because you'll need it to link your report with your LightSwitch application.

Figure 11-7. The final report

Creating Charts

ASP.NET 4 also contains a Chart control that you can use in your reports. All of the usual chart types are included, such as pie, area, range, point, circular, and accumulation. The following example shows you how to create a pie chart for displaying time-sheet hours, broken down by client code.

First, create a new web page and name it TimesheetHrsByProject.aspx. Just as in the earlier example, create a SqlDataSource (shown in Figure 11-8). When you reach the Configure the Select Statement page, select the option to Specify a Custom SQL Statement or Stored Procedure. In the following screen that appears, enter the SELECT statement shown in Listing 11-1.

Listing 11-1. T-SQL to Sum Time-Sheet Hours Grouped by Client

```
SELECT cl.ClientName , SUM(datediff(mi,StartTime,EndTime)) AS 'TotalMins'
FROM dbo.Timesheet ts JOIN dbo.Client cl
ON ts.ClientId = cl.ClientID
GROUP BY cl.ClientName
```

From the toolbox, drag a Chart control onto your form. Change the chart type to Pie, as shown in the Chart Tasks dialog box in Figure 11-8. Set the X Value Member and Y Value Members options as well.

481

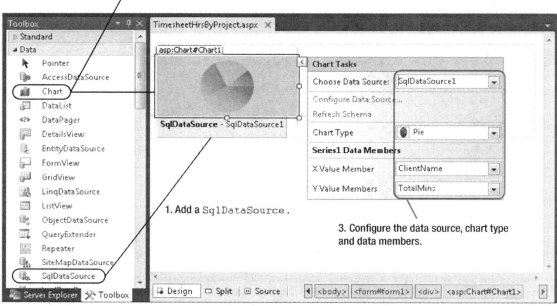

Figure 11-8. Creating a pie chart

When you run the page, the pie chart appears, as shown in Figure 11-9.

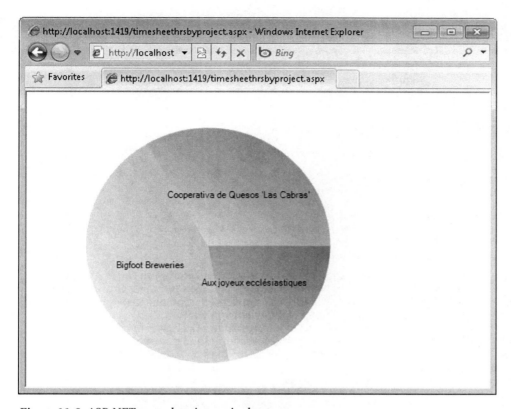

Figure 11-9. ASP.NET page showing a pie chart

Securing Reports

By allowing users to connect to your database outside of LightSwitch, you could be exposing data that should not be seen by certain individuals. If both the LightSwitch application and ASP.NET web site are set up to use Windows authentication, you can deny access to particular users. Listing 11-2 shows the example code that might be used to deny access to the user Tim, or to anyone belonging in the Active Directory Warehouse group.

Listing 11-2. Securing Access to Reports When Windows Authentication Is Used

VB:

```
File: ReportingWebsite\TimesheetHrsByProject.aspx.vb

Protected Sub Page_Load(ByVal sender As Object,
    ByVal e As System.EventArgs) Handles Me.Load

    If User.Identity.Name  = "DOMAIN\Tim" Then
        Throw New SecurityException("Access Denied to Tim")
```

```
    End If
    If User.IsInRole("DOMAIN\Warehouse")Then
        Throw New SecurityException("Access Denied to users the Warehouse group")
    End If
End Sub
```

C#:

File: ReportingWebsite\TimesheetHrsByProject.aspx.cs

```
protected void Page_Load(object sender, System.EventArgs e)
{
    if (User.Identity.Name == "DOMAIN\\Tim") {
        throw new SecurityException("Access Denied to Tim");
    }
    if (User.IsInRole("DOMAIN\\Warehouse")) {
        throw new SecurityException("Access Denied to users the Warehouse group");
    }
}
```

If you've set up your LightSwitch application to use forms authentication, you can configure your ASP.NET application to share the same authentication database. This means that logging into your LightSwitch application will also log you into your ASP.NET application. Chapter 13 describes the steps required to configure this in both your ASP.NET and LightSwitch applications.

Listing 11-3 shows the equivalent code that is used if forms authentication is in place. To illustrate the use of the ASP.NET membership class, we've used the GetUser method to return the current logged-on user (we could have used User.Identity again). Afterward, the User.IsInRole method is used to check whether the user belongs in the LightSwitch group Warehouse rather than an Active Directory group.

Listing 11-3. *Securing Access to Reports When Forms Authentication Is Used*

VB:

File: ReportingWebsite\TimesheetHrsByProject.aspx.vb

```
Protected Sub Page_Load(ByVal sender As Object,
    ByVal e As System.EventArgs) Handles Me.Load

    If Membership.GetUser().UserName = "Tim" Then
        Throw New Exception("Access Denied to Tim")
    End If
    If User.IsInRole("Warehouse")Then
        Throw New Exception("Access Denied to users the Warehouse group")
    End If
End Sub
```

C#:

File: ReportingWebsite\TimesheetHrsByProject.aspx.cs

```
protected void Page_Load(object sender, System.EventArgs e)
```

```
{
    if (User.Identity.Name == "Tim") {
        throw new Exception("Access Denied to Tim");
    }
    if (User.IsInRole("Warehouse")) {
        throw new Exception("Access Denied to users the Warehouse group");
    }
}
```

Instead of imperatively specifying the permissions in code on each page, another option for securing permissions is to specify the permissions declaratively in your web.config file. Listing 11-4 shows the snippet of code that would be added to the web.config file.

Listing 11-4. Securing Access via the web.config File

```
<system.web>
    <authorization>
        <deny role="Warehouse"/>
        <deny users="Tim"/>
        <deny users="?"/>
        <allow users="*"/>
    < /authorization>
…..
```

ASP.NET iterates through the entries in the authorization element and applies the first matching rule. In this example, users in the Warehouse role and the Tim user will be denied access. Next, all unauthenticated users will be denied access (indicated by the ? entry). Finally, all remaining users (indicated by the * entry) will reach the allow rule and will subsequently be granted access.

Using Microsoft Reporting Services

Microsoft SQL Server Reporting Services is a natural choice for creating reports because it is a product developed and supported by Microsoft. It allows more-powerful reports to be created beyond what you can achieve using simple ASP.NET pages. Other features in Reporting Services include subscription notifications and the ability to export data in formats such as Microsoft Word and Adobe PDF.

In this section, a Reporting Services report will be created in the ShipperCentral system. The report shows the number of subscription cancellations each month.

■ **Note** When deploying your Reporting Services solution into IIS (Internet Information Services), the Reporting Services Redistributable package must be installed on the server. This can be downloaded from the following URL: www.microsoft.com/downloads/en/details.aspx?FamilyID=a941c6b2-64dd-4d03-9ca7-4017a0d164fd&displaylang=en.

Installing Reporting Services

SQL Server Reporting Services comes as part of SQL Server. Although it's not included in the basic SQL Server Express version, it is available for free in the SQL Server Express with Advanced Services version. By default, SQL Server Express is installed during the LightSwitch installation. This basic instance can be upgraded to the Advanced Services version by installing the setup package that you can download from the official Microsoft SQL Server web site.

Creating Reports

Reporting Services reports are created, designed, and edited by using the Business Intelligence Development Studio (or BIDS, for short). When installing or upgrading SQL Server, an option will be available to install this component.

Reports are defined and saved in Reporting Definition Language (RDL) files. After starting BIDS, create a new Reporting Services project. Right-click the project menu and choose the Add New Item option. From here, you can either create a blank report or use a wizard. Because this is our first report, we will choose to go with the wizard. After specifying a name for your report, the first step in the wizard prompts you to select a data source. Similar to the ASP.NET example that was described earlier you can specify a connection to your intrinsic database if you choose to do so. The next step in the wizard prompts you to enter a query. In the Query String text box that appears, enter a query, as shown in Listing 11-5. The SQL shown here generates a count of cancellations, grouped by month and year.

Listing 11-5. SQL to Return Cancellation Counts Grouped by Date

```
SELECT
    MONTH(cancelDate) AS 'Month',
    YEAR(cancelDate) AS 'Year' ,
    COUNT(SubscriptionHeaderId) AS 'CancellationCount'
FROM dbo.SubscriptionHeader
GROUP BY MONTH(cancelDate), YEAR(cancelDate)
```

The next dialog box prompts you to select a report type. The available options include tabular, matrix, and tablix. We will create a simple tabular report . In the grouping section that appears, add Month, Year, and CancellationCount into the details section of the report. Complete the remaining steps of the wizard. At the end of the wizard, you can choose to preview the report.

Using the Report Designer

In this section, you'll take a look at the report that has been created in the designer and some of the features that are available. Along the top of the report designer are three tabs titled Design, Preview, and possibly Data (depending on the version of BIDS that you've installed). If you can't see the Data tab, you can open the Report Data window by choosing View ➤ Report Data from the top-level menu. This then appears in a tool window, as shown in Figure 11-10. Figure 11-10 also highlights some of the features that are available in the designer. In design mode, the toolbox appears on the left side and allows you to add additional components onto your report such as text boxes, lines, and subreports.

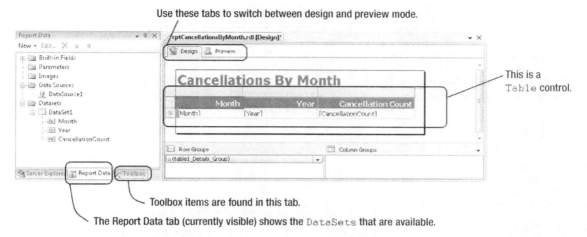

Use these tabs to switch between design and preview mode.

This is a Table control.

Toolbox items are found in this tab.

The Report Data tab (currently visible) shows the DataSets that are available.

Figure 11-10. The BIDS report design surface

Data Tab or Data Window

The Data tab allows you to select the data sources that are available in your report. The data that you bind to are stored in DataSets, although these are not the same as the ADO.NET DataSet objects that .NET developers might be familiar with.

If you look at the data window (or Data tab), you'll find a DataSet that contains the cancellation data shown in the body of the report. Additional DataSets can be added here if extra data needs to be shown on the report. For example, if you want to add a drop-down box that allows your report to be filtered, you'd add an additional DataSet here to populate the drop-down box.

Design Tab

Clicking the Design tab takes you into the designer, and this allows you to edit and design the report.

Looking at the cancellation report that we've designed (shown earlier in Figure 11-10), the body of the report contains a table. A table is a control that allows data to be shown in a tabular row and column format.

A table is an example of a data region. Other data regions include the list, matrix, and tablix controls. The list control displays individual data items by using text boxes. This provides more flexibility in terms of layout compared to tables. You can position the text boxes anywhere inside the row section, which is therefore much less rigid compared to the layout imposed by the table control.

The matrix control displays data grouped by row and column. This allows you to produce reports that are similar to cross tabs and pivot tables.

Writing Code

Although you can write simple reports without code, Reporting Services provides two options for writing custom code. Custom code can greatly assist with operations such as setting styles and formatting.

Option 1 is to write a .NET assembly and to reference it from the report. This option is ideal if you want to write code that is shared across multiple reports. It's also possible to reference classes from the .NET Framework, such as those from the System.Text namespace.

The second and simpler option is to embed the code into the report. If you view the properties of a report, a code section allows you to enter your own custom methods and functions.

A powerful technique is to set properties in your report by using expressions. For example, alternate row coloring can be applied in a report by entering the expression IIf(RowNumber(Nothing) Mod 2 = 0, "Silver", "Transparent") into the BackgroundColor property, as shown in Figure 11-11.

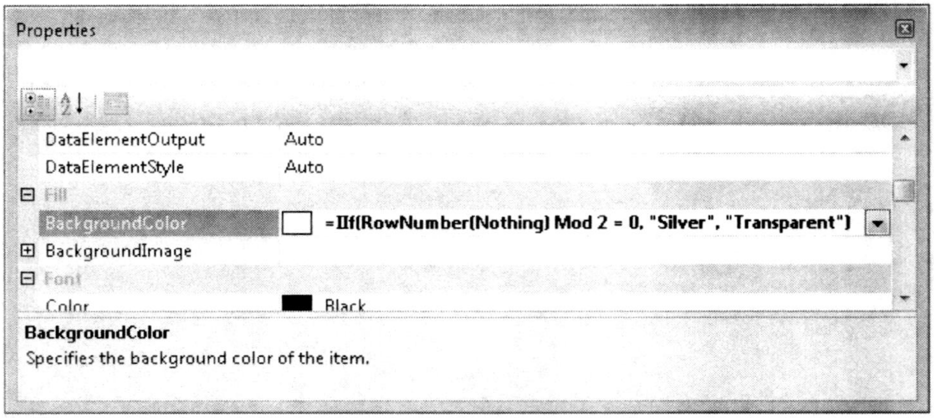

Figure 11-11. Setting property values by using expressions

In the properties pane, the default visualizer for BackgroundColor is a color picker. It might not be obvious that you can enter text expressions into this text box. This same behavior applies for many of the other properties that you see.

The example expression also illustrates the use of the IIf (conditional If) function. The first parameter accepts a test, the second parameter accepts the true condition, and the final parameter accepts the false condition. Combining expressions with the IIf function provides a powerful technique for authoring reports.

Drill-Through Reports

Drill-through reports allow a user to view additional details or other related data by clicking a link on the main report. For example, the cancellation report that was created earlier can be expanded to show a customer report when a link on a cancellation row is clicked.

Deploying Reports

Reporting Services uses a web-based report server. Any reports that you create will be finally deployed here. After deployment, the reports can be viewed through a URL on the server. You can directly deploy reports through an option in BIDs. Alternatively, you can use the web-based Report Manager to upload your RDL files.

If a report server is unavailable, the RDL report can be hosted through an ASP.NET page that contains a ReportViewer control. Using this method, the ReportViewer control can render the report by using *local processing*. This processing mode removes the dependency on the Report Server, and all of the report processing will be done by the control.

Deploying a Report from BIDS

The easiest way for you to deploy a report is to use the deploy option that is built into BIDS. Before you can deploy your reports, you'll need to configure some of the deployment options in your project. Right-click your project in Solution Explorer and open the property pane for your project, as shown in Figure 11-12.

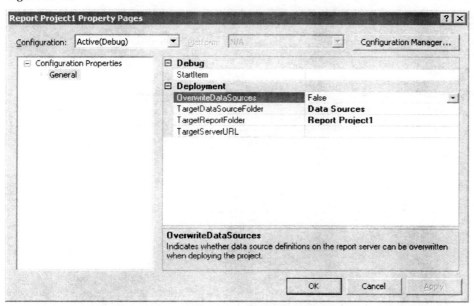

Figure 11-12. The properties of a Reporting Services project

You'll need to set up the following items:

- `TargetReportFolder`: Enter the folder on the Report Server where you want to publish your reports.

- `TargetDataSourceFolder`: If you leave this blank, the data sources will be saved in the `TargetReportFolder` specified in the preceding option.

- `TargerServerURL`: Enter the URL of your report server. Before you publish a report, this must be set to a valid report server URL. Type in the path to the virtual directory of your report server (for example, `http://server/reportserver` or `https://server/reportserver`), rather than the URL of the Report Manager.

After this is done, you can deploy your reports by using the right-click option in Solution Explorer.

Importing a Report from Report Manager

Another way to deploy a report is to import your RDL file by using Report Manager, shown in Figure 11-13. This option is ideal if you're unable to deploy from BIDS—for example, if you have developed a report on a computer that isn't connected to the same domain or network as the target report server.

To use this method, open a web browser and navigate to the Report Manager URL (for example, http://server/reportmanager). Navigate to the folder where you want to deploy your report. If you want to, you could create a new folder for your report.

Now click the Import link and upload your RDL file. After you've uploaded your report, you'll need to configure the data source by using the data option in Report Manager.

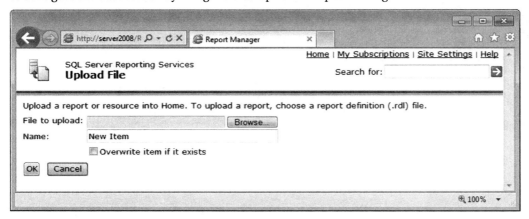

Figure 11-13. The Report Manager interface

Using the *ReportViewer* Control

If you don't have access to a report server, you can use a report viewer control instead. You'd add this control onto an ASP.NET web page. The processing mode on the control has to be set to local processing to remove the dependency on a report server.

The report viewer control is designed to render RDLC (Report Definition Language Client-side) files. These are cut-down versions of RDL files. You can create a new RDLC report in your ASP.NET project by using the File ➤ New menu option. If you've created an RDL report in BIDS and want to display it by using the report viewer control, you'll need to convert it into RDLC format before you can use it. Fortunately, this is quite an easy task. You can simply rename your RDL file with an .rdlc extension. If you now return to your ASP.NET project, you can import your report by choosing the Add Existing Item option from the project menu.

To populate your report with data, you'll need to create a new data source. On the web page that you want to display your report, drag a ReportViewer control from the data group in the toolbox. In the ReportViewer Tasks smart tags panel, select your RDLC file by using the Choose Report drop-down list, as shown in Figure 11-14. Next, select your data set by using the Choose Data Sources drop-down list. This completes the design of your web page.

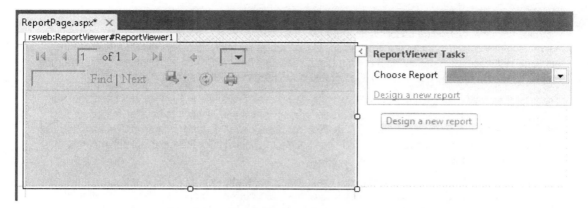

Figure 11-14. Adding the report viewer control onto a web page

REAL-LIFE LIGHTSWITCH

LightSwitch and SQL Server Reporting Services as Complementary Technologies

We spoke to Garth Henderson, who has carried out extensive work at Vanguard Business Technology using LightSwitch and SQL Server Reporting Services . Here is Garth's view on how these 2 products are complementary to one another.

Microsoft's SQL Server Report Services (SSRS) is a perfect complement for LightSwitch applications. One of the primary benefits of SSRS is that it can run as a separate integrated application that does not require any additional runtime functionality embedded and/or deployed in our LightSwitch applications. SSRS is the leanest possible reporting solution that can be integrated with LightSwitch applications. SSRS reports can be exported as PDF, Excel, and Word documents.

SSRS is included as part of SQL Server with no additional charges. Most .NET shared hosting providers offer SSRS IIS application hosting for a nominal charge of $5 per month as an added service. SSRS has its own database that can support multiple reporting for multiple application databases.

SSRS has a standalone Report Designer and reporting runtime that can work with any database available through the LAN (local area network) or Internet. The Report Designer has both a Desktop and web based version. SSRS is also integrated within Visual Studio.

The SSRS Report Designer provides Office users with the ability to create their own reports. Users can store and run their reports on their Desktop and/or use the SSRS IIS application to store and run their reports using a separate database to manage reports and data security access to application databases. The SSRS IIS application has a GUI interface that replicates a virtual Windows Desktop Explorer with options to use Active Directory or a standalone user security. It is possible to design LightSwitch applications so that SSRS reports and parameters created by users are setup by the users.

The advantage of running reports in the Browser is they can be viewed side-by-side with each other and side-by-side with LightSwitch applications Screens.

LightSwitch with SSRS is a perfect technology combination for integration solutions that extend and increase the value of existing applications that may be written in other platforms. LightSwitch supports fast server side processing that can use existing application tables for analysis whose results are stored in additional tables for user generated reporting that is managed by LightSwitch applications. SSRS reporting can be used as a runtime query tool that integrates with LightSwitch applications.

The advanced MVVM functionality of LightSwitch's RAD Screen Collection technology and LSML metadata can be stored as part of an LightSwitch application database that can be used to develop intelligent user reports. A good example is to use the MS "LightSwitch Filter Control" Extension to pass parameters to user defined SSRS reports. More commercial and open source LS Extensions will be available to integrate LightSwitch and SSRS.

Each year Microsoft continues to improve the functionality and features of SSRS as a scalable solution that meets the requirements for small applications as well as full enterprise reporting. The combination of LightSwitch and SSRS technologies provides developers with an incredible set of tools.

—Garth Henderson, Vanguard Business Technology

Linking Reports to LightSwitch

The earlier sections have shown you how to create reports by using ASP.NET or Reporting Services. Having created these web-based reports, the remaining step is to link them to LightSwitch. In this section, you'll learn how to do the following:

- Open a web report in a new browser window
- Display a web report inside a LightSwitch screen

Opening Reports in a New Browser Window

There are two methods for opening reports in a new browser window. The first technique opens a report by using a button on a screen. The second technique uses a hyperlink, and is particularly suitable for screens that contain grids.

Technique 1: Using a Button

The necessary code for opening a report in a browser differs based on whether you're running in a browser or out of a browser.

If you're writing desktop applications, you can use COM automation to *shell* an instance of your browser. In a browser application, you use the Silverlight HtmlPage class instead. In order to use the HtmlPage class, you have to add a reference to the System.Windows.Browser DLL in your client project. To do this, switch to File view, right-click the client project, and select the Add Reference option.

We'll now show you how to carry out this technique on a details screen, based on a user entity. This screen will contain a button that opens a time-sheet report for the selected user in a new browser window.

After you've added a reference to System.Windows.Browser, you'll need to add a helper class that launches the report. Switch to File view and add the VB ReportHelper module or C# ReportHelper class, as shown in Listing 11-6. We recommend adding this code into the UserCode folder (if it exists).

Now create a details screen based on the user entity. The steps that you'll need to carry out in the screen designer are as follows:

1. Click the Add Data Item button. When the Add Data Item dialog box appears, create a new method and call it ShowReport.

2. After adding the method, it'll appear in the screen member section of the screen designer. Create a button by dragging this method into the command bar area of your screen.

3. Right-click the ShowReport method in the screen member section and select the Edit Execute Code option. Add the code shown in Listing 11-7.

If you now run your application and open this screen, clicking the ShowReport button opens the time-sheet report in a new browser window.

Listing 11-6. The ReportHelper Class

VB:

File: OfficeCentral\Client\UserCode\ReportHelper.vb

```vb
Imports System.Runtime.InteropServices.Automation
Imports System.Windows.Browser

Namespace Central.Utilities

Public Module ReportHelper

    Const TimeSheetReportUrlFormat As String =
        "http://localhost:1419/TimeSheetEntry.aspx?UserId={0}"

    Public Sub LaunchUrl(ByVal userId As String)

        Dim urlPath = string.Format(TimeSheetReportUrlFormat, UserID)

        If AutomationFactory.IsAvailable Then
            Dim shell = AutomationFactory.CreateObject("Shell.Application")
            shell.ShellExecute(urlPath, "", "", "open", 1)
        Else
            HtmlPage.Window.Invoke(urlPath)
        End If

    End Sub

End Module

End Namespace
```

C#:

File: OfficeCentral\Client\UserCode\ReportHelper.cs

```
using System.Runtime.InteropServices.Automation;
using System.Windows.Browser;

namespace Central.Utilities
{

    public static class ReportHelper
    {
        const string urlPath = string.Format(TimeSheetReportUrlFormat, UserID);

        public static void LaunchUrl (string userId)
        {
            if (AutomationFactory.IsAvailable)
            {
                var shell = AutomationFactory.CreateObject("Shell.Application");
                shell.ShellExecute(urlPath, "", "", "open", 1);
            }
            else
            {
                HtmlPage.Window.Invoke(urlPath);
            }

        }
    }
}
```

Listing 11-7. The ShowReport Method Code for Opening a Report

VB:

```
Private Sub ShowReport_Execute()
    ReportHelper.LaunchUrl(User.UserID.ToString())
End Sub
```

C#:

```
partial void ShowReport_Execute()
{
    ReportHelper.LaunchUrl(User.UserID.ToString());
}
```

The code in the helper method stores the URL to the time-sheet report in a constant. To improve the code, you might want to consider storing this URL path in a configurable fashion to avoid hard-coding it.

The LaunchURL method performs a check to see whether you're running out of browser. If so, the method uses the ShellExecute command to open the URL in the default browser. If not, the HtmlPage object is used instead.

Technique 2: Using a Hyperlink

In this example, a Silverlight hyperlink is used to open the same ASP.NET time-sheet entry report. This HyperlinkButton control is used for displaying hyperlinks that users can use to navigate to other web pages.

One of the beauties of using a hyperlink is that you can easily control the text that is shown on the link. For example, you can data bind the text shown to some other data item on your screen. You might also choose to use a hyperlink as a matter of personal preference (for example, you might prefer to use hyperlinks over buttons in your application).

First, we'll apply this technique on a details screen in the same way as the earlier button example. We'll then extend the example so that it works in a grid.

Using a Hyperlink on a Details Screen

In this illustration, we'll create a details screen based on a user entity. We'll create a hyperlink that displays the surname of the user. Clicking this hyperlink opens the time-sheet report.

After you've created a details screen for your user entity, change the control type for the Surname field from a text box to a custom control, as shown in Figure 11-15. Set the Custom Control type to be of type System.Windows.Controls.HyperlinkButton.

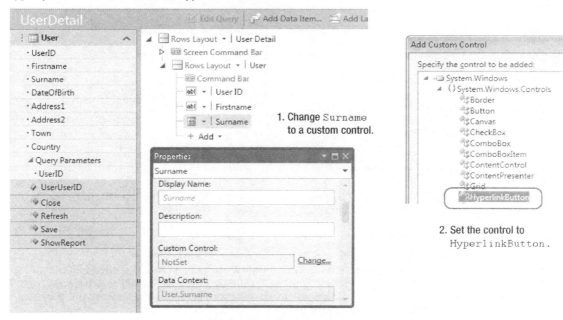

Figure 11-15. Creating a HyperlinkButton control on a screen

Now enter the code shown in Listing 11-8.

Listing 11-8. Hyperlink Control to Open Report

VB:

File: OfficeCentral\Client\UserCode\UserDetailHyperlinkReport.vb

```vb
Private Sub User_Loaded(succeeded As Boolean)
    Me.SetDisplayNameFromEntity(Me.User)
    Dim surnameControl = Me.FindControl("Surname")
    AddHandler surnameControl.ControlAvailable, AddressOf Me.OnSurnameAvailable
End Sub

Private Sub OnSurnameAvailable(sender As Object, e As ControlAvailableEventArgs)

    Dim url = "http://localhost:1419/TimesheetEntry.aspx?UserID=" & User.UserID.ToString()
    Dim control = DirectCast(e.Control, HyperlinkButton)
    control.NavigateUri = New Uri(url)
    control.Content = Me.User.Surname

End Sub
```

C#:

File: OfficeCentral\Client\UserCode\UserDetailHyperlinkReport.cs

```csharp
private void User_Loaded(bool succeeded)
{
    this.SetDisplayNameFromEntity(this.User);
    var surnameControl = this.FindControl("Surname");
    surnameControl.ControlAvailable += this.OnSurnameAvailable;
}

partial void OnSurnameAvailable(object sender, ControlAvailableEventArgs e)
{
    var url = "http://localhost:1419/TimesheetEntry.aspx?UserID=" + User.UserID.ToString();
    var control = (HyperlinkButton)e.Control;
    control.NavigateUri = new Uri(url);
    control.Content = this.User.Surname;
}
```

In this code sample, we've obtained a reference to the surname control by using the FindControl method. As you saw in Chapter 8 , the FindControl method returns an IContentItemProxy object. Because you might have added multiple surname controls onto your screen, you can work out the correct name to use by referring to the Name text box in the properties pane for the control.

When the control becomes available, the NavigateUri and Content properties are set in code. The NavigateUri property indicates the web address that the browser navigates to when the user clicks the link. The web address is constructed in code, and the UserID argument is appended by referencing the LightSwitch user property that we've added to the screen.

The Content property specifies the text that is shown on the hyperlink. The surname text is assigned to this property. When the screen is run, a surname hyperlink appears, which opens the time-sheet report when clicked.

Using a Hyperlink on a Grid Screen

We'll now extend the HyperlinkButton example so that it works on a grid of users. To begin, create a screen based on the Users table by using the Editable Grid Screen template. Using the same method as shown in the preceding example, change the Surname control from a text box to a custom control of type HyperLinkButton. Use the Add Data Item dialog to add a string property called blankTarget. Now enter the code shown in Listing 11-9.

Listing 11-9. Hyperlinkbutton in Grid

VB:

```
File: OfficeCentral\Client\UserCode\EditableUsersReportGrid.vb

Imports System.Windows.Data
Imports System.Windows.Controls
…..
Public Partial Class EditableUsersGrid
    Private Partial Sub EditableUsersGrid_Activated()
        Dim control = Me.FindControl("Surname")
        blankTarget = "_blank"
        Dim converter As New String2UriConverter()

        control.SetBinding(HyperlinkButton.ContentProperty,
            "Value", BindingMode.OneWay)
        control.SetBinding(HyperlinkButton.NavigateUriProperty,
            "Details.Entity.UserID", converter, BindingMode.OneWay)
        control.SetBinding(HyperlinkButton.TargetNameProperty,
            "Screen.blankTarget ", BindingMode.OneWay)

    End Sub
End Class

Public Class String2UriConverter
    Implements IValueConverter
    Public Function Convert(value As Object, targetType As Type,
        parameter As Object, culture As System.Globalization.CultureInfo) As Object

        If Not value Is Nothing Then
            Return New Uri("http://localhost:1419/TimesheetEntry.aspx?UserID=" &
                Convert.ToString(value))
        Else
            Return New Uri("")
        End If

    End Function

    Public Function ConvertBack(value As Object, targetType As Type,
        parameter As Object, culture As System.Globalization.CultureInfo) As Object
        Throw New NotImplementedException
    End Function
End Class
```

C#:

File: OfficeCentral\Client\UserCode\EditableUsersReportGrid.cs

```csharp
using System.Windows.Data;
using System.Windows.Controls;
…..
 public partial class EditableUsersGrid
    {
        partial void EditableUsersGrid_Activated()
        {
            var control = this.FindControl("Surname");
            blankTarget = "_blank";
            String2UriConverter converter = new String2UriConverter();
            control.SetBinding(HyperlinkButton.ContentProperty,
                "Value", BindingMode.OneWay);
            control.SetBinding(HyperlinkButton.NavigateUriProperty,
                "Details.Entity.UserID", converter, BindingMode.OneWay);
            control.SetBinding(HyperlinkButton.TargetNameProperty ,
                "Screen.blankTarget ",  BindingMode.OneWay);
        }
    }

    public class String2UriConverter : IValueConverter
    {
        public object Convert(object value, Type targetType, object parameter,
            System.Globalization.CultureInfo culture)
        {
            if (value != null)
            {
                return new Uri(@"http://localhost:1419/TimesheetEntry.aspx?UserID=" +
value.ToString());
            }
            else
            {
                return new Uri(@"");
            }
        }

        public object ConvertBack(object value, Type targetType, object parameter,
            System.Globalization.CultureInfo culture)
        {
            throw new NotImplementedException();
        }
    }
```

In the previous example, the NavigateUri and Content properties were set directly in code by using the ControlAvailable method. You can't use this technique on a grid. This is because the grid contains multiple surname controls, one for each row in the grid. Therefore, you have to set the NavigateUri and Content properties on the HyperLinkButton by using the SetBinding method instead.

The NavigateUri dependency property expects to be bound to an object of type *URI*. However, the web address that we've constructed is of type *string*. A *value converter* is therefore needed to convert the string URL representation into an object of type URI. The convert method in the String2UriConverter class generates the URL to the time-sheet web page and appends the UserID argument. Because we're binding one way and don't need to update the surname field, it's not necessary for us to implement the ConvertBack method. (Value converters were described in Chapter 9.)

In the Activated method of the screen, the SetBinding method is called three times to bind ContentProperty, NavigateUriProperty, and TargetNameProperty. Table 11-2 describes in more detail the binding paths that are used.

Table 11-2.Binding Paths Used to Bind the Hyperlink Button

Dependency Property	Binding Path Used	Description
Content	Value	This is used to show the surname text in the hyperlink. We can use the binding path Value because the data context of the control is set to Surname. The data context was set automatically when the control was originally added as a text box.
NavigateURI	Details.Entity.UserID	Notice that we've passed an instance of a String2UriCoverter value converter into the SetBinding method. The value converter converts a user ID into a time-sheet URL. The binding path used is therefore Details.Entity.UserID.
TargetName	Screen.blankTarget	TargetName needs to be set to a string value of _blank. This forces the time-sheet report to open in a new browser window. TargetName is bound to a local screen property called blankTarget. The value of this property is set in code.

Figure 11-16 shows the final result of this screen.

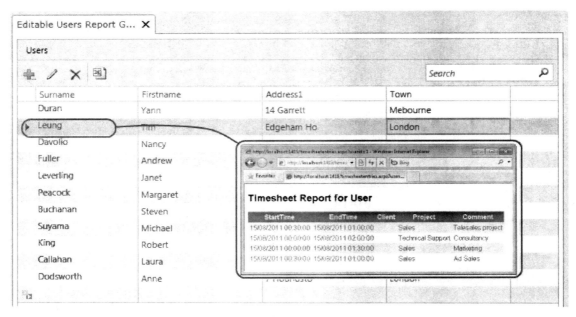

Figure 11-16. Clicking a link in the grid opens the report in a new window.

Displaying Reports Inside a LightSwitch Screen

Rather than opening pages in a new browser window, you might prefer to display the reports inside your LightSwitch screen. If you're writing a desktop application, you can use the Silverlight WebBrowser control to display web pages inside a LightSwitch screen. By setting the URL of this control to the URL of your report, the contents can be displayed without having to open other windows. This technique works only in desktop applications, because the WebBrowser control is not supported in LightSwitch browser applications.

We'll demonstrate this technique by using the time-sheet report shown earlier. We'll show you how to use this control on a screen that displays a single user, and a screen that shows a list of users.

■ **Caution** The WebBrowser control lives in a different windowing plane than Silverlight. Odd things can therefore happen when your resize or scroll your screens. The control also appears on top of all other controls on your screen. It won't honor any z-order values that you might try to apply. If you place an AutoCompleteBox control above the WebBrowser control, for example, the drop-down contents will appear behind the WebBrowser control. There isn't any easy way to fix this behavior. We recommend that you thoroughly test any screens that use the WebBrowser control.

Showing Reports in a Details Screen

First, create a screen based on the user table by using the Details Screen template.

In the screen designer, add a second instance of the UserID property. Change this control from a text box to a custom control, and set the control type to a System.Windows.Controls.WebBrowserControl control (refer to Chapter 9 for more details). Now enter the code shown in Listing 11-10. When you run the application, the screen appears as shown in Figure 11-17.

Listing 11-10. Showing a Web Page on a LightSwitch Details Screen

VB:

```
File: OfficeCentral\Client\UserCode\UserDetailReportInPage.vb

Imports System.Windows.Controls

Private Sub UserDetailReportInPage_Loaded(succeeded As Boolean)
    Me.SetDisplayNameFromEntity(Me.User)
    Dim control As = Me.FindControl("UserID1")
    AddHandler control.ControlAvailable, AddressOf Me.webControlAvailable
End Sub

Private Sub webControlAvailable(sender As Object, e As ControlAvailableEventArgs)
    DirectCast(e.Control, WebBrowser).Navigate(
        New Uri("http://localhost:1419/timesheetentries.aspx?userid=" &
User.UserID.ToString()))
End Sub
```

C#:

```
File: OfficeCentral\Client\UserCode\UserDetailReportInPage.cs

Using System.Windows.Controls;

partial void User_Loaded(bool succeeded)
{
    this.SetDisplayNameFromEntity(this.User);
    var control = this.FindControl("UserID1");
    control.ControlAvailable += this.webControlAvailable;
}

private void webControlAvailable (object sender, ControlAvailableEventArgs e)
{
    ((WebBrowser)e.Control).Navigate (
        New Uri(@"http://localhost:1419/timesheetentries.aspx?userid=" +
            User.UserID.ToString()));
}
```

Figure 11-17. Report shown inside a LightSwitch screen

▪ **Tip** If you're displaying web pages that you've created yourself by using the WebBrowser control, you can embed your own JavaScript into these pages. For example, you could add an HTML link onto your report that calls the JavaScript Window.Print() method. This would open the standard print dialog box and prompt the user to send the WebBrowser content to the printer. A useful C#/VB method that you can use is the WebBrowser.InvokeScript method. This allows you to call JavaScript methods on your web page from your C# or VB code.

Showing Reports in a List Screen

In this section, we'll use this technique on a list- or grid-type screen. In this example, we'll bind the contents of the WebBrowser control to the item that's selected on the list or grid. As we change the selected record, the page shown in the WebBrowser control automatically updates itself.

In the earlier example that uses a details screen, we've navigated to our web page by using code in the ControlAvailable method. The ControlAvailable event happens only once during the life cycle of a screen. Therefore, we can't use this technique to navigate to a different page when the selected record changes. We have to use the SetBinding method instead.

However, a limitation of the WebBrowser control is that the source property isn't exposed through a dependency property. This makes it impossible to for us to data bind to a source URL. To work around this limitation, we created our own custom web control in Chapter 9. This control includes a dependency property called URIProperty that you can use to set the source URL.

To create this example, you'll need to build the custom WebBrowserControl (as shown in Chapter 9). We've named this control Central.Controls.WebBrowserControl, and have built it into a DLL called CentralControls.dll.

To build this example, add a reference to the CentralControls.dll file that you've built. Now create a screen based on the user table by using the List and Details Screen template.

In the screen designer, add a second instance of the UserID property in the details section. By default, LightSwitch will name this UserID1. Change this control from a text box to a custom control, and set the control type to a Central.Controls.WebBrowserControl control. Now enter the code shown in Listing 11-11. When you run the application, the screen appears as shown in Figure 11-18.

Listing 11-11. Showing a Web Page on a LightSwitch List and Details Screen

VB:

File: OfficeCentral\Client\UserCode\UserListReportInPage.vb

```
Imports System.Windows.Controls

Private Sub UserListReportInPage_Activated()
        Dim control As = Me.FindControl("UserID1")
        Dim converter As New String2UriConverter()
        control.SetBinding(
            Central.Controls.WebBrowserControl.URIProperty,
            "Value", converter, BindingMode.OneWay)

End Sub
```

C#:

File: OfficeCentral\Client\UserCode\UserListReportInPage.cs

```
Using System.Windows.Controls;

partial void UserListReportInPage_Activated()
{
    String2UriConverter converter = new String2UriConverter();
    var control = this.FindControl("UserID1");
    control.SetBinding(Central.Controls.WebBrowserControl.URIProperty ,
        "Value", converter, BindingMode.OneWay);

}
```

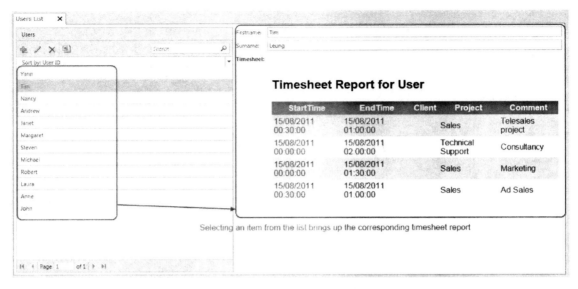

Figure 11-18. Report shown inside a screen based on the List and Details Screen template

Creating Reports with Microsoft Word

If you're writing an out-of-browser application, you can create reports by programming Microsoft Word using COM automation. A prerequisite is that you must install Microsoft Word on the end-user computer. In this section, you'll learn how to create simple reports based on a single record, and also how to create more-complex reports based on a collection of data. This is ideal for carrying out procedures such as mail merges.

▒ **Tip** Microsoft Excel is also a great tool for creating charts and reports. You can adapt the COM automation techniques that are described here to automate Excel rather than Word.

Performing Simple Automation

In the first example, we'll show you how to use Word automation to create a simple letter. We'll write code in a customer screen that opens an existing Microsoft Word template. Next, we'll retrieve the customer details from the LightSwitch screen and insert the contents into bookmarks that we've added to the Word template.

This method of automating Word is well established, and you might already be familiar with this technique. Unlike some other methods that rely on generating XML, for example, there's no requirement to have a modern version of Word.

Creating a Word Template

To create a Word template, first open Microsoft Word and type the body of your letter. In our example letter, the top section contains the recipient's address and name. These bits of data will be retrieved from the LightSwitch screen, and Word bookmarks will be added into these locations to allow a data substitution to take place.

To insert a bookmark, click the Insert menu and choose Bookmark, as shown in Figure 11-19. In the Bookmark dialog box that appears, enter a bookmark name and add the bookmark. For the purposes of this example, we've created a bookmark called *firstname*.

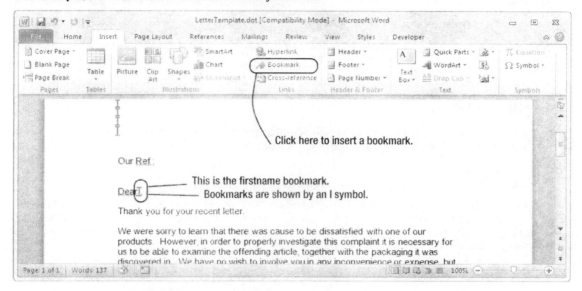

Figure 11-19. Inserting a bookmark in a template

Notice that the bookmarks are identified by an I symbol. By default, bookmarks are hidden in Word. However, you can make them visible by selecting the Show Bookmarks check box in the Word Options dialog box (shown in Figure 11-20).

After you've created your template, save the file as LetterTemplate.dot.

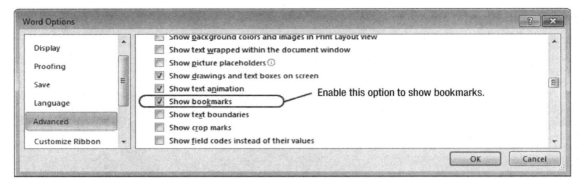

Figure 11-20. Enabling the option to show bookmarks in word.

Writing the Code

Having created your Word template, you can write code to show the results on screen, or you can send the results direct to a printer. We'll now describe both techniques.

Displaying Documents Onscreen

In your LightSwitch application, create a screen based on the Customer table by using the Details Screen template. Create a method called DoWordExport, add a button onto the screen, and enter the code shown in Listing 11-12. You'll need to add a reference to the System.Runtime.InteropServices.Automation namespace by using the imports or using statement.

Listing 11-12. Microsoft Word Automation Code

VB:

```
File: ShipperCentral\Client\UserCode\CustomerDetailWord.vb

Private Sub DoWordExport_Execute()
    If AutomationFactory.IsAvailable Then
        Try
            Using wordApp = AutomationFactory.CreateObject("Word.Application")
                Dim wordDoc = wordApp.Documents.Open(
                    "\\FileServer\Templates\LetterTemplate.dot")
                wordDoc.Bookmarks("firstname").Range.InsertAfter(
                    CustomerProperty.Firstname)
                wordApp.Visible = True
            End Using
        Catch ex As Exception
            Throw New InvalidOperationException("Failed to create customer letter.", ex)
        End Try
    End If
End Sub
```

C#:

File: ShipperCentral\Client\UserCode\CustomerDetailWord.cs

```csharp
partial void DoWordExport_Execute()
{
    if (AutomationFactory.IsAvailable) {
        try {
            using (wordApp == AutomationFactory.CreateObject("Word.Application")) {
                dynamic wordDoc = wordApp.Documents.Open(
                    @"\\FileServer\Templates\LetterTemplate.dot");
                wordDoc.Bookmarks("firstname").Range.InsertAfter(
                    CustomerProperty.Firstname);
                wordApp.Visible = true;
            }
        }
        catch (Exception ex) {
            throw new InvalidOperationException("Failed to create customer letter.", ex);
        }
    }
}
```

In Listing 11-12, we've created a COM reference to Word by calling the `CreateObject` method on the `AutomationFactory` class. The COM object is instantiated by supplying the string argument `Application.Word` (known as a `ProgID`). If you want to automate Excel instead, for example, you'd replace this with the string `Application.Excel`.

Creating a COM object by passing in a `ProgID` string illustrates the use of *late binding* in COM. By using late binding, there are no dependencies on any particular version of Word. As long as any version of Word is installed on the client computer, this code will work. A major disadvantage of this technique is that errors will not be caught at compile time, and IntelliSense is also not available in the code designer.

After carrying out the standard checks to make sure that the application is a desktop application, the Word template document is opened by calling the `Documents.Open` method (in the mail merge section, we'll show you how to disable the button if you're running inside a browser). In this call, a hard-coded path to the Word template document is supplied. To allow multiple users to access the Word template file, the location is specified in UNC (Universal Naming Convention) format (`\\FileServer\Templates\LetterTemplate.dot`). In practice, you'll want to save this file path in a configuration setting that you can modify afterward, rather than hard-coding it.

The data is then inserted into the document at a point immediately after the firstname bookmark by using the `Range.InsertAfter` method. `CustomerProperty.Firstname` refers to the LightSwitch `Customer` property on the screen. After generating the Word document, it is shown to the user by setting the `visibility` property of the Word application to `True`.

Sending Documents Directly to a Printer

Instead of showing the document to the user on the screen, you could send the Word document to a printer and discard it immediately afterward without saving changes. This would allow you to easily send reports to a printer without any additional user intervention.

Listing 11-13 shows the code that you would use to do this. The `Close` method expects you to pass in a `SaveChanges` argument. This argument forces Word to discard changes, to save changes, or to prompt the user to save their changes. We want Word to quit without saving changes, and this is done by passing 0 into the `Close` method.

Listing 11-13. Printing and Closing a Word Document

VB:

File: ShipperCentral\Client\UserCode\CustomerDetailWord.vb

```
wordApp.PrintOut()
wordDoc.Close(0)
```

C#:

File: ShipperCentral\Client\UserCode\CustomerDetailWord.cs

```
wordApp.PrintOut();
wordDoc.Close(0);
```

Distributing the Template with the LightSwitch Client

The preceding automation example relies on a Word template file being available via a UNC file path (alternatively, you could have chosen to use a mapped drive). The biggest disadvantages of this technique are that it works only on the internal network, and it won't work in environments where Windows file sharing is disallowed.

You can overcome this limitation by embedding your Word template in the XAP file. There are several other advantages and disadvantages of using this technique. These are summarized in Table 11-3.

Table 11-3. Template Distribution Techniques

Distribution via a File Share	Distribution via the XAP File
This technique works only within your local network.	This technique can be used in applications that are deployed over the Internet.
You can easily update your file template after deploying your application.	You'll need to rebuild and redeploy your LightSwitch application if you want to make changes to your template file.
There isn't any impact on the load time of your application.	Increasing the size of your XAP file makes your application slower to load.
This technique is more fragile because there's a dependency on a file outside of your application.	This technique is more robust because everything is self-contained.

To include the LetterTemplate.dot Word template in your XAP file, switch to File view and right-click the ClientGenerated project. Choose the Add Existing Item option, select the document, and set the Build Action property to Content, as shown in Figure 11-21.

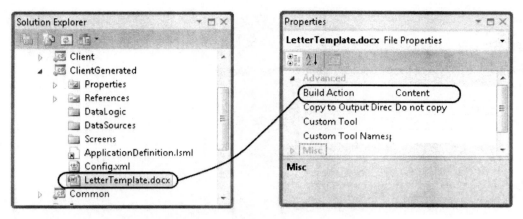

Figure 11-21. *Setting the Build Action to Content*

Listing 11-14 illustrates the code that extracts the file from the XAP package and saves it into the My Documents folder on the client computer. The template is saved into this location because security restrictions in Silverlight limit the places where you can save files on the local file system.

Listing 11-14. Saving the Word Template to My Documents\LetterTemplate.dot

VB:

```
File: ShipperCentral\Client\UserCode\CustomerDetailWord.vb

Dim resourceInfo = System.Windows.Application.GetResourceStream(↩
                            New Uri("LetterTemplate.dot", UriKind.Relative))

Dim path = Environment.GetFolderPath(
    Environment.SpecialFolder.MyDocuments) + "LetterTemplate.dot"

Dim file = System.IO.File.Create(path)
file.Close()

'Write the stream to the file
Dim stream As System.IO.Stream = resourceInfo.Stream

Using fileStream = System.IO.File.Open(path,
                                    System.IO.FileMode.OpenOrCreate,
                                    System.IO.FileAccess.Write,
                                    System.IO.FileShare.None)

    Dim buffer(0 To stream.Length - 1) As Byte
    stream.Read(buffer, 0, stream.Length)
    fileStream.Write(buffer, 0, buffer.Length)
End Using
```

C#:

File: ShipperCentral\Client\UserCode\CustomerDetailWord.cs

```csharp
var resourceInfo = System.Windows.Application.GetResourceStream(new ↵
Uri("LetterTemplate.dot", UriKind.Relative));

dynamic path = Environment.GetFolderPath(
    Environment.SpecialFolder.MyDocuments) + "LetterTemplate.dot";

dynamic file = System.IO.File.Create(path);
file.Close();

//Write the stream to the file
System.IO.Stream stream = resourceInfo.Stream;

using (fileStream == System.IO.File.Open ↵
(path, System.IO.FileMode.OpenOrCreate, System.IO.FileAccess.Write, System.IO.FileShare.None))
{
        byte[] buffer = new byte[stream.Length];
        stream.Read(buffer, 0, stream.Length);
        fileStream.Write(buffer, 0, buffer.Length);
}
```

This code uses the GetResourceStream method. This allows you to load resources that are embedded inside your application package. The URI identifies the resource to be loaded. This path is relative and doesn't require a leading slash.

After obtaining a resource stream, the Word template is extracted into the My Documents folder by using the methods in the System.IO.File namespace. In practice, you'll most likely want to save the template into a more specific location, and to perform some additional error checking to check whether the file exists.

Performing Mail Merges with Word

Another common scenario in many business applications is the ability to perform mail merges. In our example scenario, the marketing department wants to run a marketing campaign to encourage lapsed subscribers to resubscribe. The department uses the documents generated from a Word mail merge as a basis for a postal marketing campaign.

Creating a Mail Merge Word Template

The first step is to create a letter template in Word. This example uses Word 2010. The necessary steps might be slightly different if you have an earlier version of Word.

From the Word ribbon, click the Mailings tab, click the Start Mail Merge button, and select the Letters option. Next, click the Select Recipients button and choose the Type New List option. The New Address List window appears, as shown in Figure 11-22.

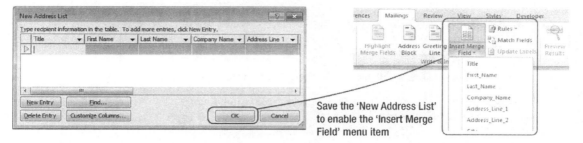

Figure 11-22. Creating the mail merge fields

The New Address List window displays the mail merge fields as columns in the grid. As you can see, some of the default mail merge fields include Title, FirstName, and LastName. You can add fields by clicking the Customize Columns button. Clicking the OK button prompts you to save the list as a new MDB file. Name this file `MailMergeData.mdb` and after saving, the Insert Merge Field buttons will become enabled on the ribbon. Although you'll no longer need to refer to this MDB file, these steps are required in order to create the mail merge fields. Save the file as `MailMergeTemplate.docx`.

Writing the Code

You can use the letter template that you've created as the basis for your mail merge. But if you're not sure what mail merge fields you'll need, or if you want to create a mail merge that's not based on a static template, you can create your mail merge fields in code instead. We'll explain both techniques in this section

Using the mail merge fields that are specified in the Word Template

We'll start by showing you how to carry out a mail merge by using the data from a grid screen. We'll create a button that mail merges the screen data with the Word template that was created earlier.

First, create a screen for the `Customer` table based on the Editable Grid Screen template. Next, create a method called `DoMailMerge`. By default, the customer collection shows only 45 records at time. Therefore, you might want to increase this by setting the No. of Items to Display per Page text box. If you want to mail merge all of the records in a table, you can adapt your code so that it uses a query rather than a screen collection.

Now enter the code as shown in Listing 11-15. Finally, create a button on your screen by dragging the `DoMailMerge` method onto the command bar area of your screen.

Listing 11-15. Mail Merge Code

VB:

```
File: ShipperCentral\Client\UserCode\CustomersWordMerge.vb

Imports System.Runtime.InteropServices.Automation
Imports System.Reflection

Namespace LightSwitchApplication
```

```
Partial Public Class CustomersWordMerge

    Private wordApp As Object
    Private wordDoc As Object
    Private missingValue As Object = System.Reflection.Missing.Value

    ' Here are the values of the WdMailMergeDestination Enum
    Const wdSendToNewDocument As Integer = 0
    Const wdSendToPrinter As Integer = 1
    Const wdSendToEmail As Integer = 2
    Const wdSendToFax As Integer = 3

    Private Sub CreateMailMergeDataFile()

        Dim wordDataDoc As Object

        Dim fileName As Object = "\\Fileserver\Documents\DataDoc.doc"
        Dim header As Object = "First_Name, Last_Name, Title, Address"

        wordDoc.MailMerge.CreateDataSource(fileName, missingValue, missingValue, header)

        ' Open the data document to insert data.
        wordDataDoc = wordApp.Documents.Open(fileName)

        ' Create the header items
        For count = 1 To 2
            wordDataDoc.Tables(1).Rows.Add(missingValue)
        Next

        ' Loop through the customer screen collection
        Dim rowCount As Integer = 2
        For Each c As Customer In Customers
            FillRow(wordDataDoc, rowCount, c.Firstname, c.Surname, c.Title, c.Address)
            rowCount += 1
        Next

        ' Save and close the file.
        wordDataDoc.Save()
        wordDataDoc.Close(False)

    End Sub

    Private Sub FillRow(WordDoc As Object, Row As Integer,
                        Text1 As String, Text2 As String, Text3 As String,
                        Text4 As String)

        If  Row > wordDoc.Tables[1].Rows.Count Then
            wordDoc.Tables[1].Rows.Add();
        End If

        ' Insert the data into the table.
```

```
        WordDoc.Tables(1).Cell(Row, 1).Range.InsertAfter(Text1)
        WordDoc.Tables(1).Cell(Row, 2).Range.InsertAfter(Text2)
        WordDoc.Tables(1).Cell(Row, 3).Range.InsertAfter(Text3)
        WordDoc.Tables(1).Cell(Row, 4).Range.InsertAfter(Text4)

    End Sub

    Private Sub DoMailMerge_CanExecute(ByRef result As Boolean)
        result = AutomationFactory.IsAvailable
    End Sub

    Private Sub DoMailMerge_Execute()

        Dim wordMailMerge As Object
        Dim wordMergeFields As Object

        ' Create an instance of Word  and make it visible.
        wordApp = AutomationFactory.CreateObject("Word.Application")
        wordApp.Visible = True

        ' Open the template file
        wordDoc = wordApp.Documents.Open("\\Fileserver\Documents\MailMergeTemplate.docx")
        wordDoc.Select()

        wordMailMerge = wordDoc.MailMerge

        ' Create a MailMerge Data file.
        CreateMailMergeDataFile()

        wordMergeFields = wordMailMerge.Fields
        wordMailMerge.Destination = wdSendToNewDocument
        wordMailMerge.Execute(False)

        ' Close the original form document.
        wordDoc.Saved = True
        wordDoc.Close(False, missingValue, missingValue)

        ' Release References.
        wordMailMerge = Nothing
        wordMergeFields = Nothing
        wordDoc = Nothing
        wordApp = Nothing

    End Sub

    End Class

End Namespace
```

C#:

File: ShipperCentral\Client\UserCode\CustomersWordMerge.cs

```
using System.Runtime.InteropServices.Automation;
using System.Reflection;

namespace LightSwitchApplication
{
    public partial class CustomersWordMerge
    {
        dynamic wordApp;
        dynamic wordDoc;
        Object missingValue = System.Reflection.Missing.Value;

        // Here are the values of the WdMailMergeDestination Enum
        const int wdSendToNewDocument = 0;
        const int wdSendToPrinter = 1;
        const int wdSendToEmail = 2;
        const int wdSendToFax = 3;

        private void CreateMailMergeDataFile()
        {
            dynamic wordDataDoc;
            Object fileName = @"\\Fileserver\Documents\DataDoc.doc";
            Object header = "First_Name, Last_Name, Title, Address";

            wordDoc.MailMerge.CreateDataSource(ref fileName, ref missingValue,
                ref missingValue, ref header);

            // Open the data document to insert data.
            wordDataDoc = wordApp.Documents.Open(ref fileName);

            // Create the header items
            for (int iCount = 1; iCount <= 2; iCount++)
            {
                wordDataDoc.Tables[1].Rows.Add(ref missingValue);
            }

            // Loop through the customer screen collection
            int rowCount = 2;
            foreach (Customer c in Customers)
            {
                FillRow(wordDataDoc, rowCount, c.Firstname, c.Surname, c.Title, c.Address);
                rowCount++;
            }

            // Save and close the file.
            wordDataDoc.Save();
            wordDataDoc.Close(false, ref missingValue, ref missingValue);

        }

        private void FillRow(dynamic wordDoc, int Row, string Text1,
            string Text2, string Text3, string Text4)
```

```csharp
{
    if (Row > wordDoc.Tables[1].Rows.Count)
    {
        wordDoc.Tables[1].Rows.Add();
    }

    // Insert the data into the table.
    wordDoc.Tables[1].Cell(Row, 1).Range.InsertAfter(Text1);
    wordDoc.Tables[1].Cell(Row, 2).Range.InsertAfter(Text2);
    wordDoc.Tables[1].Cell(Row, 3).Range.InsertAfter(Text3);
    wordDoc.Tables[1].Cell(Row, 4).Range.InsertAfter(Text4);
}

partial void DoMailMerge_CanExecute(ref bool result)
{
    result = AutomationFactory.IsAvailable;
}

partial void DoMailMerge_Execute()
{
    dynamic wordMailMerge;
    dynamic wordMergeFields;

    // Create an instance of Word  and make it visible.
    wordApp = AutomationFactory.CreateObject("Word.Application");
    wordApp.Visible = true;

    // Open the template file
    wordDoc =
        wordApp.Documents.Open(@"\\Fileserver\Documents\MailMergeTemplate.docx");
    wordDoc.Select();

    wordMailMerge = wordDoc.MailMerge;

    // Create a MailMerge Data file.
    CreateMailMergeDataFile();

    wordMergeFields = wordMailMerge.Fields;
    wordMailMerge.Destination = wdSendToNewDocument;

    wordMailMerge.Execute(false);

    // Close the original form document.
    wordDoc.Saved = true;
    wordDoc.Close(false, ref missingValue, ref missingValue);

    // Release References.
    wordMailMerge = null;
    wordMergeFields = null;
    wordDoc = null;
    wordApp = null;
}
```

```
    }
}
```

The mail merge works by saving the data from the `customers` screen collection into a new Word document called `DataDoc.doc`. This takes place in the method `CreateMailMergeDataFile`. This method creates a Word table in the `DataDoc.doc` file, and populates it with customer data by using the helper method `FillRow`. The first row in this table contains column headers that are defined in the variable `header`. The column names defined in `header` should correspond to the names of the mail merge fields that were specified in the template. This method also sets the mail merge data source of the Word template to the `DataDoc.doc` file that you've just created.

After creating the `DataDoc.doc` file, the remaining code in the `DoMailMerge` method performs the mail merge by calling the `Execute` method on the `wordMailMerge` object. At this point, the mail merge is complete, and the remaining code tidies up the objects that have been used. You can optionally add some code here to delete the `DataDoc.doc` file if you wish.

Prior to calling the `Execute` method, the `Destination` property of the `wordMailMerge` object is set to `wdSendToNewDocument`. This represents the numeric value of 0 and indicates that the results of the mail merge will be shown in the document. Other acceptable values are shown in Table 11-4.

Table 11-4. Constants That Are Used to Set the Mail Merge Destination

Name of Constant	Value	Description
wdSendToNewDocument	0	Mail merge will be shown in the document.
wdSendToPrinter	1	Mail merge will be sent to the printer.
wdSendToEmail	2	Mail merge will be sent to your default email client.
wdSendToFax	3	Mail merge will be sent to a fax.

This mail merge technique works only in desktop applications. Therefore, the code in the `DoMailMerge_CanExecute` method disables the button if automation isn't available.

Figure 11-23 shows the mail merge screen in action.

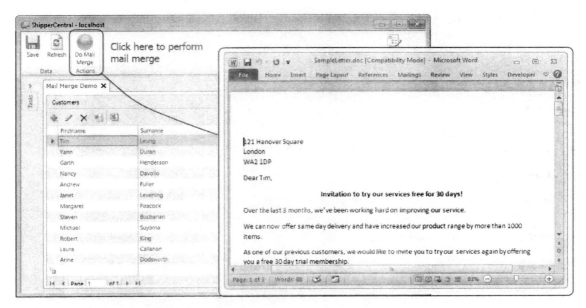

Figure 11-23. Word mail merge example

■ **Note** This scenario is an ideal example of where you might want to use a *multi select* piece of UI. This would allow you to select only those customers that you want to appear in your mail merge. Chapter 8 presents details on how to do this.

Creating Mail Merge Fields Programmatically

The preceding example relies on you creating a Word template in advance. If you prefer not to do this, you could use Word automation to create a blank Word document. You would then build up the content and merge fields of your document in code before performing the mail merge. Listing 11-16 demonstrates how you would modify the `DoMailMerge_Execute` method to create your template in code.

Listing 11-16. Creating the Mail Merge Fields Programmatically

VB:

```
File: ShipperCentral\Client\UserCode\CustomersWordMerge.vb

Dim wordMailMerge As Object
Dim wordMergeFields As Object

' Create an instance of Word  and make it visible.
wordApp = AutomationFactory.CreateObject("Word.Application")
```

```vb
wordApp.Visible = True

' Create a new file rather than open it from a template
wordDoc = wordApp.Documents.Add()

Dim wordSelection As Object
wordSelection = wordApp.Selection
wordMailMerge = wordDoc.MailMerge

' Create a MailMerge Data file.
CreateMailMergeDataFile()

wordMergeFields = wordMailMerge.Fields

' Type the text 'Dear' and add the 'First_Name' merge field
wordSelection.TypeText("Dear ")

Dim wordRange As Object = wordSelection.Range

wordMergeFields.Add(wordRange, "First_Name")
wordSelection.TypeText(",")
' programatically write the rest of the document here....

' Perform mail merge.
wordMailMerge.Destination = 0
wordMailMerge.Execute(False)

' Close the original form document.
wordDoc.Saved = True
wordDoc.Close(False, missingValue, missingValue)

' Release References.
wordMailMerge = Nothing
wordMergeFields = Nothing
wordDoc = Nothing
wordApp = Nothing
```

C#:

File: ShipperCentral\Client\UserCode\CustomersWordMerge.cs

```csharp
dynamic wordMailMerge;
dynamic wordMergeFields;
dynamic wordSelection;

// Create an instance of Word  and make it visible.
wordApp = AutomationFactory.CreateObject("Word.Application");
wordApp.Visible = true;

// Create a new file rather than open it from a template
wordDoc = wordApp.Documents.Add();
```

```
wordSelection = wordApp.Selection;
wordMailMerge = wordDoc.MailMerge;

// Create a MailMerge Data file.
CreateMailMergeDataFile();

wordMergeFields = wordMailMerge.Fields;

// Type the text 'Dear' and add the 'First_Name' merge field
wordSelection.TypeText("Dear ");
wordMergeFields.Add(wordSelection.Range, "First_Name");
wordSelection.TypeText(",");
// programatically write the rest of the document here....

// Perform mail merge.
wordMailMerge.Destination = 0;
wordMailMerge.Execute(false);

// Release References.
wordMailMerge = null;
wordMergeFields = null;
wordDoc = null;
wordApp = null;
```

Creating Adobe PDF Documents

In some cases, businesses may prefer to provide reports in PDF format. PDF documents are more difficult for the end user to edit (unlike Word files) and are better at preserving the positioning and layout of visual elements such as images.

In LightSwitch, PDF documents can either be generated on the server or within the Silverlight client. Microsoft Reporting Services includes an option for exporting reports in PDF format, and this provides a simple mechanism for generating PDFs on the server.

To demonstrate the creation of a PDF report on the client, we'll create a screen in the ShipperCentral application to create *dispatch* notices. Because there is no built-in function for generating PDFs in LightSwitch or Silverlight, writing your own procedures for doing this could be very time-consuming. Fortunately, various third-party libraries exist to help simplify the creation of PDF documents. The one that we'll use in this example is *silverPDF*, an open source library that's available on CodePlex. This is based on two other open source projects (iTextSharp and PDFsharp). If you've used either of these libraries before, the code shown here may be familiar to you.

To get started with silverPDF, download the silverPDF.dll file from the CodePlex web site (http://silverpdf.codeplex.com/). In your LightSwitch project, switch to File view and add a reference to the silverPDF.dll file in your client project.

Now create a screen for the Order table by using the Details Screen template. Create a method and add a button onto your screen (we've called this method DoPDF). Now insert the code shown in Listing 11-17 to trigger the creation of your PDF file.

Listing 11-17. Programming silverPDF

VB:

File: ShipperCentral\Client\UserCode\OrderDetailPDF.vb

```vb
Imports PdfSharp
Imports PdfSharp.Drawing
Imports PdfSharp.Pdf
…..

Private Sub DoPdf_Execute()
    ' Write your code here.
    Microsoft.LightSwitch.Threading.Dispatchers.Main.BeginInvoke(
    Sub()
        Dim document As New PdfDocument()
        document.Info.Title = "Dispatch Notice"

        ' Create an empty page
        Dim page As PdfPage = document.AddPage()

        ' Get an XGraphics object for drawing
        Dim gfx As XGraphics = XGraphics.FromPdfPage(page)

        ' Create a font
        Dim fontHeader1 As New XFont("Verdana", 18, XFontStyle.Bold)
        Dim fontHeader2 As New XFont("Verdana", 14, XFontStyle.Bold)
        Dim fontNormal As New XFont("Verdana", 12, XFontStyle.Regular)

        ' Create the report text
        gfx.DrawString ("ShipperCentral Dispatch" , fontHeader1, ⏎
        XBrushes.Black, new XRect(5, 5, 200, 18), XStringFormats.TopCenter )

        gfx.DrawString ("Thank you for shopping......" , fontNormal , ⏎
            XBrushes.Black, new XRect(5, 18, 200, 18), XStringFormats.TopLeft )

        gfx.DrawString ("Order Number: " + Order.OrderID.ToString(), fontHeader2, ⏎
        XBrushes.Black, new XRect(5, 32, 200, 18), XStringFormats.TopLeft )
        '.... create other Elements here

        ' Save the document here
        Dim myDocuments As String = Environment.GetFolderPath(
            Environment.SpecialFolder.MyDocuments)

        document.Save(myDocuments & "\DispatchNotice.pdf")

    End Sub
    )

End Sub
```

C#:

File: ShipperCentral\Client\UserCode\OrderDetailPDF.cs

```csharp
using PdfSharp;
using PdfSharp.Drawing;
using PdfSharp.Pdf;
…….

partial void DoPDF_Execute()
{
    Microsoft.LightSwitch.Threading.Dispatchers.Main.BeginInvoke(() =>
    {
        PdfDocument document = new PdfDocument();
        document.Info.Title = "Dispatch Notice";

        // Create an empty page
        PdfPage page = document.AddPage();

        // Get an XGraphics object for drawing
        XGraphics gfx = XGraphics.FromPdfPage(page);

        // Create a font
        XFont fontHeader1 = new XFont("Verdana", 18, XFontStyle.Bold);
        XFont fontHeader2 = new XFont("Verdana", 14, XFontStyle.Bold);
        XFont fontNormal = new XFont("Verdana", 12, XFontStyle.Regular );

        // Create the report text
        gfx.DrawString ("ShipperCentral Dispatch" , fontHeader1, ↵
        XBrushes.Black, new XRect(5, 5, 200, 18), XStringFormats.TopCenter );

        gfx.DrawString ("Thank you for shopping......" , fontNormal , ↵
            XBrushes.Black, new XRect(5, 18, 200, 18), XStringFormats.TopLeft );

        gfx.DrawString ("Order Number: " + Order.OrderID.ToString(), fontHeader2, ↵
        XBrushes.Black, new XRect(5, 32, 200, 18), XStringFormats.TopLeft );

        //.... create other Elements here

        // Save the document here
        string myDocuments = Environment.GetFolderPath(Environment.SpecialFolder.MyDocuments);
        document.Save(myDocuments + "\\DispatchNotice.pdf");

    });

}
```

The PDF creation code is invoked on the main dispatcher. If you don't do this, an *Invalid cross-thread access* exception will be thrown by LightSwitch. This is because many objects in the System.Windows namespace (and others) are internally guarded to be created and used on the main Silverlight dispatcher thread. The silverPDF library is likely to be using these objects internally.

The code creates a PDF document by using pdfDocument and pdfPage objects. Instances of XFonts objects are created to style the text that we'll add to our document.

The XGraphics object contains several Draw methods for creating graphical elements, and the code in Listing 11-17 demonstrates the use of the DrawString method to display text. Figure 11-24 illustrates some of the other Draw methods that are available for drawing shapes and lines.

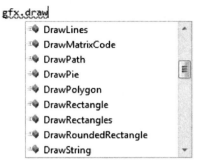

Figure 11-24. silverPDF Draw methods

Later in the code, the order number is drawn by using the DrawString method, and a reference is made to the LightSwitch order by using the code Order.OrderID.ToString(). Finally, the PDF file is saved into the My Documents folder by calling the Save method of PDFDocument. Figure 11-25 shows how the final report might look.

Figure 11-25. PDF output produced with silverPDF

■ **Tip** Microsoft Word 2010 allows you to natively save documents in PDF format. You can therefore create PDF files by using COM automation and the Word object model (in desktop applications). You'd create your PDF file by calling the `Save` method on your Word document, and by passing in the file format type of `17` (this relates to Word's `wdFormatPDF` enumeration value). The `C#` code would look something like this: `myWordDoc.Save(17);`

Using Other Third-Party Solutions

The final option for producing reports is to use a third-party reporting solution. Such products can simplify the report-writing process and offer an experience that's more integrated into the LightSwitch development environment.

Third-party reporting controls have sometimes been known for causing compilation problems during development and other issues during deployment. We therefore recommend that you research the controls that you want to use to beforehand. This will help you discover the types of problems that other developers may have encountered.

This section mentions a couple of third-party controls that are tailored for LightSwitch. Silverlight controls from other vendors could also be used, but this would require a custom control to be written around the control that you want to use.

DevExpress XtraReports

DevExpress offers LightSwitch support through their XtraReports reporting suite. This product will appeal to you if you've had some prior experience using DevExpress controls.

After installing XtraReports, you'll need to first enable it by using the extensions property pane in LightSwitch. To author a report, here are the steps that you would follow:

1. You can't directly base a report on any existing tables that you have. Instead, you'll need to add a new WCF RIA Service data source. Start the Attach Data Source Wizard and select the option to add a WCF RIA Service. In the next page that appears, you'll be able to select a WCF RIA Service Class called `XtraReportsService`. Choose this option, and you'll be prompted to select the entities from your LightSwitch application that you want to make available.

2. Now that you've added your data source, you can start to create your reports. Reports are created in the server project, so you'll need to switch into File view beforehand. Your reports are authored by using a graphical report designer, which is integrated into the Visual Studio IDE.

3. To display your reports, XtraReports adds a Report Preview Screen template to the list of templates that you'll find in the Add New Screen dialog box. You can create a new screen based on this template. Another option is to add the XtraReports `ReportViewer` control onto your screen.

Infragistics NetAdvantage

Infragistics has released a version of its NetAdvantage suite specifically designed for LightSwitch. Although there is no built-in reporting tool, it contains a set of gauge and data chart controls that you can incorporate into your LightSwitch application.

Summary

In this chapter, you've learned about reporting. Although built-in reporting is not available in LightSwitch, you have lots of options for building your own reports. The main topics covered in this chapter were as follows:

- Creating web-based reports using ASP.NET or SQL Reporting Services

- Linking and displaying these reports in LightSwitch

- Creating documents and mail merges by using Microsoft Word

- Creating PDF documents on the client

You can use ASP.NET to build web pages that display data or charts. You can add parameters to your pages, if you want to filter the data shown to the user.

If you need to produce richer output, you can use SQL Server Reporting Services. Reports are created in Business Intelligence Development Studio (BIDS) and saved in a format called Reporting Definition Language (RDL). The types of reports that you can create include matrix and tablix. The matrix option produces cross-tab and pivot-table reports. You can also create drill-through reports that allow users to click a link and to view additional details. Code can be added into reports to assist with operations such as styles and formatting. Visual Web Developer 2010 Express and SQL Server Reporting Services with Advanced Services are no-cost options but are more limited in functionality.

After creating your reports in ASP.NET or Reporting Services, you'll need a method to link them to your LightSwitch application. You can create a button or a hyperlink on your screen that opens the report in a new browser window. Alternatively, you can display your reports inside your LightSwitch screen by using the WebBrowser control, in the case of desktop applications.

If you want to open your report by using a hyperlink, you'd use the HyperlinkButton control. You'll need to point the HyperlinkButton to the URL of your report by setting the NavigateUri property. This can be done in the ControlAvailable event of the control or by using the SetBinding method. To convert a string representation of a URL into an object of type URI for the purposes of data binding, you'll need to use a value converter.

On desktop applications, you can create reports in Microsoft Word by using COM automation. You can also create mail merges based on Word templates that you've created in advance. Alternatively, the template document could be built entirely in code if you prefer. The mail merge works by creating a separate data document. Word automation methods are then called to merge the data document with the template document.

If it's important for you to create reports that look the same on most computers, you could create reports in PDF format. This chapter has shown you how to create PDF documents on the client by using the silverPDF library.

Finally, you could choose to purchase a third-party reporting tool, or you could build your own custom reporting control. To simplify the task of building your own reporting control, you could base your control on existing third-party Silverlight controls.

CHAPTER 12

Creating and Sending Emails

Email has become an indispensable part of our lives, and the modern world would struggle to function without it. This book, for example, could not have been written without the help of email. Most businesses rely on email and expect their applications to integrate with email systems too.

Typically, .NET developers have relied on the methods in the System.Net.Mail namespace to send email. However, LightSwitch applications are based on a Silverlight client, and this namespace is not available inside the Silverlight runtime. So how do you go about sending email when such an integral part of the .NET framework is missing from Silverlight?

Fortunately, you can use various techniques to send email, and in this chapter you will learn about the options that are available. Because the server portion of a LightSwitch application uses ASP.NET, the System.Net.Mail namespace can be used on the server tier to send email. In desktop applications, a second option is to automate Microsoft Outlook by using COM. However, this solution depends on Outlook being installed on the client. The final option is to construct HTML hyperlinks to open the default email client.

Table 12-1 summarizes the options that are available according to the application type that you have chosen to use.

Table 12-1. Emailing Techniques That You Can Use by Application Type

Technique	Desktop Application	Web Application
Send SMTP mail via server	✓	✓
Automate Microsoft Outlook	✓	
Use mailto links	✓	✓

Sending Email by Using Server-Side Code

Having established that the System.Net.Mail namespace can be used only on the server, the next step is to work out how to call these server methods from the LightSwitch client. However, there is no direct way of calling a server method from the LightSwitch client, which presents a challenge for us.

The way to work around this is to hook into the data source events that relate to an entity set. Table 12-2 summarizes the events within the save pipeline that you can use.

If you want to send an email when data changes in your application, this process is somewhat simplified. For example, if the status of a sales order changes from processed to shipped, the Updated method can be used to trigger an email.

If you want to send an email through a process that is disconnected from data, the procedure is more involved. For example, you might want to create a button on a screen that sends an email to the current customer shown onscreen, without saving any of that customer's details. To code around this problem, an *operation table* is created. This is used to temporarily store the details of the email that you want to send. Other names that you could choose for this table are *command table* or *conduit table*. This table gives you access to the data source events and allows you to call the server-side methods.

Figure 12-1 illustrates the techniques that are covered in this section.

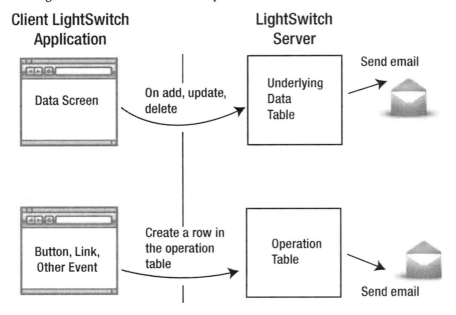

Figure 12-1. Sending an email by using server-side code

Table 12-2. Data Source Events in the Save Pipeline That We Can Use to Send E-mail

Event	Description
<Entity>_Deleting	Called before the item is deleted from the data store
<Entity>_Inserting	Called before the item is inserted into the data store
<Entity>_Updating	Called before the item is updated in the data store
<Entity>_Deleted	Called after the item has been deleted from the data store

Event	Description
`<Entity>_Inserted`	Called after the item has been inserted into the data store
`<Entity>_Updated`	Called after the item has been updated in the data store

Sending Email When Data Changes

In this section, you'll learn how to send an email when an element of an order changes. Code is written in the updated method of an Order entity to send the email.

To run this example, open the Order table in the table designer, click the Write Code button, and select the Updated method. Now write the code as shown in Listing 12-1.

Listing 12-1. Sending Email When Data Is Updated

VB:

File: ShipperCentral\Server\UserCode\ApplicationDataService.vb

```vb
Imports System.Net.Mail

Private Partial Sub Orders_Updated(entity As Order)
    Dim message As New MailMessage()

    message.From = New MailAddress("admin@lsfaq.com")
    message.To.Add(entity.Customer.Email)
    message.Subject = "Order Updated"
    message.Body = "The status of your order has changed. Order ID " & entity.Id
    Dim client As New SmtpClient("smtp.yourmailserver.net", 25)

    'Set the details below if you need to send credentials
    'client.Credentials = new System.Net.NetworkCredential("yourUsername", "yourPassword")
    'client.UseDefaultCredentials = false
    client.Send(message)

End Sub
```

C#:

File: ShipperCentral\Server\UserCode\ApplicationDataService.cs

```csharp
using System.Net.Mail;
partial void Orders_Updated(Order entity)
{
    MailMessage message = new MailMessage();
    message.From = new MailAddress("admin@lsfaq.com");
    message.To.Add(entity.Customer.Email);
    message.Subject = "Order Updated";
    message.Body = "The status of your order has changed";
    SmtpClient client = new SmtpClient("smtp.yourmailserver.net", 25);
```

```
    //Set the details below if you need to send credentials
    //client.Credentials = new System.Net.NetworkCredential("yourusername", "yourpassword");
    //client.UseDefaultCredentials = false;
    client.Send(message);
}
```

Listing 12-1 illustrates the use of the following objects in the System.Net.Mail namespace:

- SmtpClient: This class is used for sending email. It must be initialized with credentials such as the SMTP Server URL, port numbers, and authentication credentials. For the SMTP Server setting, you can supply either a server name or an IP address. The methods that you use to send the email message are called Send and SendAsync.

- MailMessage: This object represents an email message. It contains properties such as the recipient email address, email subject, and email body.

In order for the code to work, you'll first need to set the address of your SMTP server in the SmtpClient object. The SmtpClient constructor accepts the name of the mail server as the first parameter, and the port number as the second parameter (typically port 25). If a username and password are needed to log onto your mail server, these can be set using the Credentials property.

The Updated method gives you access to the underlying entity. In the code shown, we've incorporated the order ID and customer email address into the message that is sent.

Because you can access the entity in this method, you could modify the code to conditionally send the email. For example, you could write an if statement to send an email only if the order status changes. You can determine whether the order status has changed by calling the method entity.Details.OrderStatus.IsChanged.

⚫ **Tip** If your email fails to send, there are a few simple things that you can check. First, are there any firewalls or antivirus applications blocking the SMTP traffic? Some antivirus programs protect against mass-mailing worms and will block any outgoing SMTP traffic. Second, email servers such as Microsoft Exchange may need to have relay settings configured in order for it to be used in this way.

Writing an Email Helper Class

Because the code in Listing 12-1 can be used in several places, Listing 12-2 illustrates a helper method called SendMail to prevent you from having to write lots of lines of repetitive code.

This SendMail method allows you to send email by passing in details indicating the sender, recipient, subject, and email body. You will learn more about this method later in this chapter, when the server-side email example is extended further.

The SmtpMailHelper class can be added into the server project. Alternatively, you could compile the class into a separate DLL and add a reference to it in the server project.

If you choose to add the class directly into the server project, a good place to put it is in the User Code folder. This folder is automatically created when any server code is added into your project. If the folder doesn't exist, you can easily create it by using the designer to create a method for a data source event such as <entity>_inserted.

Listing 12-2. SMTP Mail Helper Class and Method

VB:

File: ShipperCentral\Server\UserCode\SMTPMailHelper.vb

```
Imports System.Net
Imports System.Net.Mail

Namespace Central.Utilities

Public Module SmtpMailHelper
    Const SMTPServer As String = "smtp.yourmailserver.net"
    Const SMTPUserId As String = "myUsername "
    Const SMTPPassword As String = "myPassword"
    Const SMTPPort As Integer = 25

    Public Sub SendMail(ByVal sendFrom As String,
                        ByVal sendTo As String,
                        ByVal subject As String,
                        ByVal body As String)
        Dim fromAddress = New MailAddress(sendFrom)
        Dim toAddress = New MailAddress(sendTo)
        Dim mail As New MailMessage

        With mail
            .From = fromAddress
            .To.Add(toAddress)
            .Subject = subject
            If body.ToLower().Contains("<html>") Then
                    .IsBodyHtml = true;
            End If
            .Body = body
        End With

        Dim smtp As New SmtpClient(SMTPServer, SMTPPort)
        'add credentials here if required
        'smtp.Credentials = New NetworkCredential(SMTPUserId, SMTPPassword)
        smtp.Send(mail)
    End Sub
End Module

End Namespace
```

C#:

File: ShipperCentral\Server\UserCode\SMTPMailHelper.cs

```
using System.Net;
using System.Net.Mail;
```

```
namespace Central.Utilities
{

    public static class SmtpMailHelper
    {
        const string SMTPServer = "smtp.yourmailserver.net";
        const string SMTPUserId = "myUsername";
        const string SMTPPassword = "myPassword";
        const int SMTPPort = 25;

        public static void SendMail(string sendFrom, string sendTo,
            string subject, string body)
        {
            MailAddress fromAddress = new MailAddress(sendFrom);
            MailAddress toAddress = new MailAddress(sendTo);
            MailMessage mail = new MailMessage();

            mail.From = fromAddress;
            mail.To.Add(toAddress);
            mail.Subject = subject;

            if (body.ToLower().Contains("<html>"))
            {
                mail.IsBodyHtml = true;
            }
            mail.Body = body;
            SmtpClient smtp = new SmtpClient(SMTPServer, SMTPPort);
            //add credentials here if required
            //smtp.Credentials = new NetworkCredential(SMTPUserId, SMTPPassword);
            smtp.Send(mail);
        }
    }
}
```

■ **Tip** If you choose to use the SMTP service provided by Google's Gmail, here are some tips to make the code work. First, the DeliveryMethod attribute of SmtpClient should be set to SmtpDeliveryMethod.Network. Second, make sure to set the SmtpClient Credentials property with the credentials of your Gmail account. At the time of this writing, the port number used by Google is 587, rather than the standard SMTP port of 25.

Using Configuration Settings to Save Credentials

The code in Listing 12-2 hard-codes configuration details such as the SMTP server, authentication credentials, and port number. Such details are subject to change, so it makes good sense to save these settings in a place where they can be easily modified. When writing code in the server project, *Application Settings* can be created to store such settings.

To create these settings, return to the server project and open the properties pane, as shown in Figure 12-2. Switch to the Settings tab and create a set of *application-scoped* settings to store your email credentials.

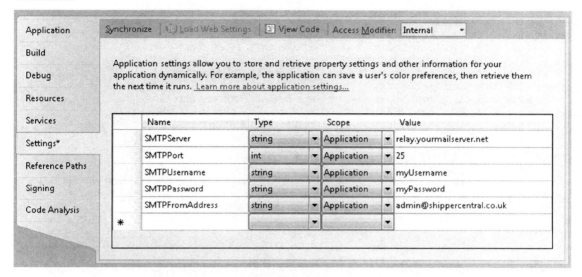

Figure 12-2. Creating configuration settings in the server project

You can then modify your code to use the configuration settings instead. Listing 12-3 highlights the change that you would make to the SmtpMailHelper method. In VB.NET, you can use the My.Settings object to easily refer to your configuration settings.

Listing 12-3. Configuration Settings Code

VB:

```
File: ShipperCentral\Server\UserCode\SMTPMailHelper.vb

Imports System.Configuration
Private Shared ReadOnly SMTPServer As String = My.Settings.SMTPServer
Private Shared ReadOnly SMTPUserId As String = My.Settings.SMTPUserId
Private Shared ReadOnly SMTPPassword As String = My.Settings.SMTPPassword
Private Shared ReadOnly SMTPPort As Integer = My.Settings.SMTPPort
```

C#:

File: ShipperCentral\Server\UserCode\SMTPMailHelper.cs

```
using System.Configuration;
private static readonly string SMTPServer =
    LightSwitchApplication.Properties.Settings.Default.SMTPServer;
private static readonly string SMTPUserId =
    LightSwitchApplication.Properties.Settings.Default.SMTPUsername;
private static readonly string SMTPPassword =
    LightSwitchApplication.Properties.Settings.Default.SMTPPassword;
private static readonly int SMTPPort =
    LightSwitchApplication.Properties.Settings.Default.SMTPPort;
```

Setting SMTP *MailMessage* Object Properties

In Listing 12-2, you saw how mail messages can be constructed by creating a `MailMessage` object and setting the `from`, `to`, `subject`, and `body` properties. In more-advanced scenarios, there are many more useful properties that you can use. These are summarized in Table 12-3.

Table 12-3. `MailMessage` *Object Properties*

Name	Description
Attachments	Gets the collection used for storing file attachments
Bcc	Gets a collection of blind carbon copy (BCC) recipients
CC	Gets a collection of carbon copy (CC) recipients
DeliveryNotificationOptions	Gets or sets the delivery notifications
From	Gets or sets the from address
IsBodyHtml	Gets or sets a value indicating whether the message body is in HTML
Priority	Gets or sets the message priority
ReplyToList	Gets or sets the list of reply to addresses
Sender	Gets or sets the sender's email address

Triggering Server Email from an Onscreen Button on the Client

If you want to send an email through a client method that is unrelated to data, an operation table can be created to mimic the steps that were carried out in the earlier examples. This would allow you to create a button or a link on your screen to trigger an email.

The first step is to create this table, which in this example we have named `EmailOperation`. Figure 12-3 shows the schema of this table.

Name	Type		Required
Id	Integer	▾	☑
SenderEmail	Email Address	▾	☑
RecipientEmail	Email Address	▾	☑
Subject	String	▾	☑
Body	String	▾	☑
Attachment	Binary	▾	☐
AttachmentFileName	String	▾	☐
<Add Property>		▾	☐

Figure 12-3. `EmailOperation` table

This table contains all of the fields that are required to send an email, such as the recipient email address, email body, and subject.

When a row is inserted into the table, code in the `Inserted` method is used to send out the email. We can therefore trigger the sending of emails just by inserting rows into this table.

Listing 12-4 shows the code that needs to be added into the `Inserted` method for the table. The code takes advantage of the `SmtpMailHelper` class that was created earlier to simplify the task of sending email.

Listing 12-4. Sending Email by Inserting Records into the `EmailOperation` Table

VB:

```
File: ShipperCentral\Server\UserCode\ApplicationDataService.vb

Imports Central.Utilities

Private Sub EmailOperations_Inserting(entity As EmailOperation)

    SmtpMailHelper.SendMail(
        entity.SenderEmail,
        entity.RecipientEmail,
        entity.Subject,
        entity.Body)

    'We've sent the email but don't actually want to save it in the database
    entity.Details.DiscardChanges()
)

End Sub
```

C#:

File: ShipperCentral\Server\UserCode\ApplicationDataService.cs

```csharp
using Central.Utilities;
partial void EmailOperations_Inserting(EmailOperation entity)
{

    SmtpMailHelper.SendMail(
        entity.SenderEmail,
        entity.RecipientEmail,
        entity.Subject,
        entity.Body);

    // We've sent the email but don't actually want to save it in the database
    entity.Details.DiscardChanges();
}
```

The only thing that remains is to create a button on your screen to send the email. Listing 12-5 presents the Execute code for your button. The email body, subject and address details are hard-coded in this example. To allow users to submit their own details, local properties could be added onto the screen, and the code in Listing 12-5 could refer to those properties instead.

Listing 12-5. Button Code for Sending Email

VB:

File: OfficeCentral\Client\UserCode\SendEmailScreen.vb

```vb
Private Sub SendEmail_Execute()

    Using tempWorkspace As  New DataWorkspace()
        Dim newEmail = tempWorkspace.ApplicationData.EmailOperation.AddNew()
        With newEmail
            .RecipientEmail = "tim.leung@hotmail.com"
            .SenderEmail = "admin@lsfaq.com"
            .Subject = "The email subject goes here"
            .Body  =  "The email body goes here"
        End With

        Try
            tempWorkspace.ApplicationData.SaveChanges()

            ' If you want, you can write some code here to create a record in an audit table
            newEmail.Delete()
            tempWorkspace.ApplicationData.SaveChanges()

        Catch ex As Exception
            ShowMessageBox(ex.Message)
        End Try

    End Using
```

```
End Sub
```

C#:

```
File: OfficeCentral\Client\UserCode\SendEmailScreen.cs

partial void SendEmail_Execute()
{

    Using (var tempWorkspace = new DataWorkspace() ){
        EmailOperation newEmail = tempWorkspace.ApplicationData.EmailOperation.AddNew();

        newEmail.RecipientEmail = "tim.leung@hotmail.com";
        newEmail.SenderEmail = "admin@lsfaq.com";
        newEmail.Subject = "The email subject goes here";
        newEmail.Body  =  "The email body goes here";

        try{
            tempWorkspace.ApplicationData.SaveChanges();

            //If you want, you can write some code here to create a record in an audit table
            newEmail.Delete();
            tempWorkspace.ApplicationData.SaveChanges();
        }
        catch (Exception ex) {
            this.ShowMessageBox(ex.Message);
        }
    }
}
```

In this code, we've added the `EmailOperation` record by using a temporary data workspace. We could have chosen to use the screen `DataWorkspace` instead (which would have been a simpler option). However, calling the `SaveChanges` method on the screen's data workspace would save all modified data. Performing the work in a temporary data workspace therefore provides greater isolation and is a safer option.

At the end of the procedure, the record is deleted from the `EmailOperation` table. If you want to maintain an audit of the emails sent, you could add some code to create a record in an audit table.

Including Email Attachments

You might want to include file attachments in the emails that you send. For example, you might want to attach a picture of a product in a marketing email.

In Table 12-3, you may have noticed that the `MailMessage` object includes a property called `Attachments`. This can be used to attach one or more files to your email.

The `EmailOperation` table shown in Figure 12-3 includes an `Attachment` field of data type `Binary`. Listing 12-6 illustrates a change to the SMTP `SendMail` helper method to enable a file attachment and file name to be passed in.

Listing 12-7 illustrates the code that opens a file browser dialog box and prompts the user to select a file from their file system. After this is done, the file is emailed by creating a row in the `EmailOperation` table.

Listing 12-6. Modified SendMail Method to Include Attachments

VB:
File: ShipperCentral\Server\UserCode\SMTPMailHelper.vb

```
Public Shared Sub SendMail(sendFrom As String,
    sendTo As String,
    subject As String,
    body As String,
    attachment As Byte(),
    filename As String)

    Dim fromAddress As New MailAddress(sendFrom)
    Dim toAddress As New MailAddress(sendTo)
    Dim mail As New MailMessage()

    mail.From = fromAddress
    mail.To.Add(toAddress)
    mail.Subject = subject
    mail.Body = body

    If attachment IsNot Nothing AndAlso Not String.IsNullOrEmpty(filename) Then
        Using ms As New MemoryStream(attachment)
            mail.Attachments.Add(New Attachment(ms, filename))
            Dim smtp As New SmtpClient(SMTPServer, SMTPPort)
            smtp.Send(mail)
        End Using
    End If

End Sub
```

C#:
File: ShipperCentral\Server\UserCode\SMTPMailHelper.cs

```
public static void SendMail(string sendFrom,
    string sendTo,
    string subject,
    string body,
    byte[] attachment,
    string filename)
{
    MailAddress fromAddress = new MailAddress(sendFrom);
    MailAddress toAddress = new MailAddress(sendTo);
    MailMessage mail = new MailMessage();

    mail.From = fromAddress;
    mail.To.Add(toAddress);
    mail.Subject = subject;
    mail.Body = body;

    if (attachment != null && !string.IsNullOrEmpty(filename))
```

```
    {
        using (MemoryStream ms = new MemoryStream(attachment))
        {
            mail.Attachments.Add(new Attachment(ms, filename));
            SmtpClient smtp = new SmtpClient(SMTPServer, SMTPPort);
            smtp.Send(mail);
        }

    }
}
```

Listing 12-7. Screen Code to Send Email Attachments

VB:

File: : ShipperCentral\Client\UserCode\EmailAttachment.vb

```
Imports Microsoft.LightSwitch.Threading
Imports System.Windows.Controls

Private Sub SendAttachment_Execute()
    Dispatchers.Main.Invoke(
        Sub()
            Dim dlg As New OpenFileDialog()
            If dlg.ShowDialog().GetValueOrDefault(False) = True Then
                Dim data As Byte()
                Using stream As FileStream = dlg.File.OpenRead()
                    data = New Byte(stream.Length - 1) {}
                    stream.Read(data, 0, data.Length)
                End Using

            Dim filename = dlg.File.Name

              'send the email here
              Me.Details.Dispatcher.BeginInvoke(
                  Sub()

                        Using dw As New DataWorkspace()

                            Dim newEmail = dw.ApplicationData.EmailOperations.AddNew()
                            newEmail.RecipientEmail = "tim.leung@hotmail.com"
                            newEmail.SenderEmail = "admin@lsfaq.com"
                            newEmail.Body = "The email body goes here"
                            newEmail.Subject = "The email subject goes here"
                            newEmail.Attachment = data
                            newEmail.AttachmentFileName = filename

                            Try
                                dw.ApplicationData.SaveChanges()
                                ' If you want, you can write some code here to
                                  ' create a record in an audit table
                                newEmail.Delete()
```

```
                            dw.ApplicationData.SaveChanges()
                        Catch ex As Exception
                            ShowMessageBox(ex.Message)
                        End Try
                    End Using

            End Sub)

        End If

    End Sub)
End Sub
```

C#:

File: ShipperCentral\Client\UserCode\EmailAttachment.cs

```csharp
using Microsoft.LightSwitch.Threading;
using System.Windows.Controls;

partial void SendAttachment_Execute()
{
    Dispatchers.Main.Invoke(() =>
        {
        OpenFileDialog dlg = new OpenFileDialog();
        if (dlg.ShowDialog().GetValueOrDefault(false)  == true)
        {
            byte[] data;
            using (FileStream stream = dlg.File.OpenRead())
            {
                data = new byte[stream.Length];
                stream.Read(data, 0, data.Length);
            }

            string filename = dlg.File.Name;
            //send the email here
            this.Details.Dispatcher.BeginInvoke(() =>
            {
                using (var dw = new DataWorkspace())
                {
                    EmailOperation newEmail = dw.ApplicationData.EmailOperations.AddNew();
                    newEmail.RecipientEmail = "tim.leung@hotmail.com";
                    newEmail.SenderEmail = "admin@lsfaq.com";
                    newEmail.Body  =  "The email body goes here";
                    newEmail.Subject  =  "The email subject goes here";
                    newEmail.Attachment  =  data;
                    newEmail.AttachmentFileName  =  filename;

                    try
                    {
                        dw.ApplicationData.SaveChanges();
                        //If you want, you can write some code here to
```

```
                //create a record in an audit table
            newEmail.Delete();
            dw.ApplicationData.SaveChanges();
        }
        catch (Exception ex)
        {
            this.ShowMessageBox(ex.Message);
        }
    }
  });
    }
  });
}
```

By default, the screen code that you write runs on the screen thread. Because the open file dialog box interacts with the user, the code must be run on the UI thread. The `Dispatchers.Main.Invoke()` method is used to execute this code on the UI thread.

After reading the file, the `Details.Dispatcher.BeginInvoke()` method is used to execute the remaining code on the screen thread. It isn't good practice to carry out data operations on the UI thread because a long-running operation could lock up your UI and leave your application unresponsive.

The record in the operation table is added by using a new data workspace. If we didn't do this, all other data changes made to the screen would be saved when the `SaveChange()` method is called.

This example won't work in a browser application because `ShowDialog` won't be on the same call stack as the UI button press. To work around this limitation, you could use a custom control (button) and handle its `Click` event directly.

Creating Mail in a Pickup Folder

If you cannot send email by using the preceding technique, a second option is to configure a *pickup folder*. Most SMTP servers including Microsoft Exchange can be configured with such a folder. Rather than sending the email, a plain-text message is saved into this folder. Any file placed into it will be processed as an outbound email. If the messages are in the correct format, they are sent to the recipient specified in the to line of the text file. The snippet in Listing 12-8 illustrates the format that should be used when creating files in this folder.

Listing 12-8. Mail Pickup Text File Format

```
to:tim.leung@hotmail.com
from: admin@lsfaq.com
subject:This is where you put the email subject.
this is a the body of the email.
```

Sending Mail via Outlook by Using COM Automation

If your company uses Microsoft Outlook and you're creating a desktop application, automating Outlook is another option that you can consider. This technique is entirely client based, and unlike the previous example, it requires no server-side coding.

The helper class defined in Listing 12-9 is created in the client project. Because this technique can be used only while in desktop mode, you'll need to first perform a check on

AutomationFactory.IsAvailable to make sure that COM automation is available. If this check succeeds, you can continue with your Outlook automation code.

Listing 12-9. Client-Side COM Code to Create an Outlook Message

VB:

File: ShipperCentral\Client\UserCode\OutlookMailHelper.vb

```vb
Option Strict Off

Imports System.Runtime.InteropServices.Automation

Namespace Central.Utilities

Public Module OutlookMailHelper
    Const olMailItem As Integer = 0
    Const olFormatPlain As Integer = 1
    Const olFormatHTML As Integer = 2

    Public Sub CreateEmail(toAddress As String, subject As String, body As String)
        Try
            Dim outlook As Object = Nothing

            If AutomationFactory.IsAvailable Then
                Try
                    'Get the reference to the open Outlook App
                    outlook = AutomationFactory.GetObject("Outlook.Application")
                Catch ex As Exception
                    'Outlook isn't open, therefore try and open it
                    outlook = AutomationFactory.CreateObject("Outlook.Application")
                End Try

                If outlook IsNot Nothing Then

                    Dim mail = outlook.CreateItem(olMailItem)
                    If body.ToLower().Contains("<html>") Then
                        mail.BodyFormat = olFormatHTML
                        mail.HTMLBody = body
                    Else
                        mail.BodyFormat = olFormatPlain
                        mail.Body = body
                    End If

                    mail.Recipients.Add(toAddress)
                    mail.Subject = subject

                    mail.Save()
                    'uncomment the code below if you prefer to send the email immediately
                    'mail.Send()
                    mail.Display()
                End If
```

```vb
            End If
         Catch ex As Exception
            Throw New InvalidOperationException("Failed to create email.", ex)
         End Try

      End Sub
   End Module

End Namespace
```

C#:

File: ShipperCentral\Client\UserCode\OutlookMailHelper.cs

```csharp
using System;
using System.Runtime.InteropServices.Automation;

namespace Central.Utilities
{

    public static class OutlookMailHelper
    {
        const int olMailItem = 0;
        const int olFormatPlain = 1;
        const int olFormatHTML = 2;

        public static void CreateEmail(string toAddress, string subject, string body)
        {
            try
            {
                dynamic outlook = null;

                if (AutomationFactory.IsAvailable)
                {
                    try
                    {
                        //Get the reference to the open Outlook App
                        outlook = AutomationFactory.GetObject("Outlook.Application");
                    }
                    catch (Exception ex)
                    {
                        //Outlook isn't open, therefore try and open it
                        outlook = AutomationFactory.CreateObject("Outlook.Application");
                    }

                    if (outlook != null)
                    {
                        //Create the email
                        dynamic mail = outlook.CreateItem(olMailItem);
                        if (body.ToLower().Contains("<html>"))
                        {
```

541

```
                        mail.BodyFormat = olFormatHTML;
                        mail.HTMLBody = body;
                    }
                    else
                    {
                        mail.BodyFormat = olFormatPlain;
                        mail.Body = body;
                    }
                    mail.Recipients.Add(toAddress);
                    mail.Subject = subject;

                    mail.Save();
                    mail.Display();
                    //uncomment the code below if you prefer to send the email immediately
                    //mail.Send()
                }
            }

        }
        catch (Exception ex)
        {
            throw new InvalidOperationException("Failed to create email.", ex);
        }
    }
}

}
```

After creating this class, you can add a button to your screen to call the CreateEmail function. Listing 12-10 illustrates the code that does this. The name of the method that we've added to the screen is SendToOutlook.

Listing 12-10. Screen Code to Create an Outlook Message

VB:

```
File: ShipperCentral\Client\UserCode\EmailOutlook.vb

Imports Central.Utilities

Private Sub SendToOutlook_Execute()
    Dim bodyText As String = "Dear " & CustomerProperty.Firstname &
        ", Thank you for your order etc…"

    OutlookMailHelper.CreateEmail (CustomerProperty.EmailAddress,
                                "Your Order Details -Email Subject", bodyText)
End Sub
```

C#:

```
File: ShipperCentral\Client\UserCode\EmailOutlook.cs
```

```
using Central.Utilities;

partial void SendToOutlook_Execute()
{
    string bodyText = "Dear " + CustomerProperty.Firstname +
        ", Thank you for your order etc…";

    OutlookMailHelper.CreateEmail(CustomerProperty.EmailAddress,
                                "Your Order Details (Email Subject)", bodyText);
}
```

When you run the application and click the button, Outlook opens and a new message is created containing the email message. The message can be manually sent by the end user when ready. If you prefer for the email to be sent without any user intervention, you can uncomment the code in Listing 12-9 to call the mail.Send method.

To disable the SendToOutlook button in a browser application, you can test for AutomationFactory.IsAvailable in the CanExecute method of the SendToOutlook command. The only way to test whether Outlook is available is to attempt to create an instance. Because this task is resource intensive, we don't recommend that you do this in the CanExecute method. Listing 12-11 shows the code that you would use to minimally check for Outlook. This type of authorization code is described in further detail in Chapter 14.

Listing 12-11. Code to Disable the SendToOutlook Button in a Browser Application

VB:

File: ShipperCentral\Server\UserCode\EmailOutlook.vb

```
Imports System.Runtime.InteropServices.Automation

Private Sub SendToOutlook_CanExecute(ByRef result As Boolean)
    result = AutomationFactory.IsAvailable
End Sub
```

C#:

File: ShipperCentral\Server\UserCode\EmailOutlook.cs

```
using System.Runtime.InteropServices.Automation;

partial void SendToOutlook_CanExecute(ref bool result)
{
    result = AutomationFactory.IsAvailable;
}
```

▪ **Tip** Although this chapter is primarily focused on sending email, Outlook can be automated in many other ways. Using similar code, you could create some powerful applications. For example, LightSwitch can be used to create Outlook appointments, contacts, or tasks.

Creating *mailto* Hyperlinks

The final method of generating an email is to use a `mailto` hyperlink. This technique can be used in desktop and browser applications. It works by opening the default email program on the client (if one exists). This could be Outlook, Outlook Express, Windows Live Mail, or any other email client. Arguments can be passed into the hyperlink to set the recipient email address, subject, and body. It's very likely that you've encountered such a link when browsing the Web, and web developers will be familiar with this technique.

The syntax of a simple `mailto` link is as follows:

```
mailto:tim.leung@hotmail.com
```

If you want to send an email to multiple recipients, the email addresses can be comma separated in the following manner:

```
mailto:tim.leung@hotmail.com,yann@live.com.au
```

After specifying the recipient(s), use a ? character if you want to pass in additional arguments. For example, the following syntax can be used to specify an email subject:

```
mailto:tim.leung@hotmail.com,yann@live.com.au?subject=Email Subject
```

If you want to pass in multiple arguments, separate the arguments by using the & symbol. Here's an example link that specifies both an email subject and body:

```
mailto:tim.leung@hotmail.com,yann@live.com.au? ↩
    subject=Email Subject&Body=Here is the body of the email.
```

Table 12-4 shows the list of available parameters.

*Table 12-4. *`mailto`* Parameters*

Function	*mailto* **Parameter**
Set the email subject	`subject`
CC a recipient (copy)	`cc`
BCC as recipient (blind carbon copy)	`bcc`
Set the body text	`body`

Using *mailto* in a Screen Button

Now that you know how to construct a `mailto` link, you can create a button on your screen to execute the `mailto` command. Listing 12-12 presents a method that constructs and executes the hyperlink.

If you're writing a desktop application, we'll use the shell command is used to open the default email client. Otherwise, we'll use the `HtmlPage` object from the `System.Windows.Browser` namespace instead. You will need to add a reference to the `System.Windows.Browser.dll` assembly in your client project. This code needs to be invoked on the main dispatcher. Otherwise, you will receive an error telling you that the operation can occur only on the UI thread.

In this example, we've created a button which is bound to a screen command called SendEmail. The code in the SendEmail command calls the SendEmailByHyperlink method, and passes in the recipient email address, subject, and body text.

Listing 12-12. Sending Email by Using a mailto Hyperlink

VB:

File: ShipperCentral\Client\UserCode\EmailByHyperlink.vb

```
Imports System.Runtime.InteropServices.Automation

Private Sub SendEmail_Execute()
    SendEmailByHyperlink("tim.leung@hotmail.co.uk",
        "Email subject", "Here's the body text")
End Sub

Public Sub SendEmailByHyperlink (
        ByVal toAddress As String,
        ByVal subject As String,
        ByVal body As String
    )

    subject = System.Uri.EscapeDataString(subject)
    body = System.Uri.EscapeDataString(body)

    Dim url As String = String.Format(
        "mailto:{0}?subject={1}&body={2}", toAddress, subject, body)
    Dim uri As Uri = New Uri(url)

    If AutomationFactory.IsAvailable Then
            Dim shell = AutomationFactory.CreateObject("Shell.Application")
            'shell.ShellExecute(url) if Option Strict is Off
            CompilerServices.Versioned.CallByName(shell, "ShellExecute", CallType.Method, url)
    Else
            Microsoft.LightSwitch.Threading.Dispatchers.Main.BeginInvoke(Sub()
                System.Windows.Browser.HtmlPage.Window.Navigate(uri, "_blank")
            End Sub)
    End If
End Sub
```

C#:

File: ShipperCentral\Client\UserCode\EmailByHyperlink.cs

```
using System.Runtime.InteropServices.Automation;

partial void SendEmail_Execute()
{
    SendEmailByHyperlink("tim.leung@hotmail.co.uk",
        "Email subject", "Here's the body text");
}
```

```
public static void SendEmailByHyperlink(string toAddress, string subject, string body)
{
    subject = Uri.EscapeDataString(subject);
    body = Uri.EscapeDataString(body);

    string url = string.Format("mailto:{0}?subject={1}&body={2}", toAddress, subject, body);
    Uri uri = new Uri(url);

    if (AutomationFactory.IsAvailable)
    {
        var shell = AutomationFactory.CreateObject("Shell.Application");
        shell.ShellExecute(url);
    }else{
        Microsoft.LightSwitch.Threading.Dispatchers.Main.BeginInvoke(() =>{
            System.Windows.Browser.HtmlPage.Window.Navigate(uri, "_blank");
        });
    }
}
```

When sending email by using this technique, special characters must be URI encoded. For example, the & symbol must be replaced with %25 because & is the character used for separating parameters in the mailto string. Therefore, you must call Uri.EscapeDataString on the subject and body values in order to encode special characters and punctuation that might appear in the query portion of the URL.

Summary

In this chapter, you've learned how to send email by using the following three techniques:

- Sending SMTP email via server-side code
- Automating Microsoft Outlook by using COM
- Generating mailto hyperlinks

Sending email on the server is possible for both web and desktop applications. This approach uses the methods that are available in the System.Net.Mail namespace. The server-side code that sends the email can be called from the client through data source events in the save pipeline. This makes it very easy to automatically send email when entities are created, updated, or deleted.

The SmtpClient and MailMessage objects are used to send SMTP mail. The MailMessage object represents an email and includes many properties that you can set. For example, you can add file attachments to a message by using the Attachments collection. The IsBodyHtml property allows you to create a richly formatted message by composing the body of your message in HTML format. To encourage code reusability, you've learned how to create an SMTP helper class and method to simplify the task of sending email.

The server can send an email in response to added, updated, or deleted entities. Or you can create an EmailOperation table to send email independent of other application data. This table would contain fields such as recipient address, subject, and body. Any row added to this table would trigger an email using the data that has been entered.

If your company uses Microsoft Outlook and you're creating a desktop application, automating Outlook is another option that you can choose. The sample code has shown you how to programmatically create an email based on data that is visible on a LightSwitch screen.

If Microsoft Outlook is not available, an alternative is to create a `mailto` hyperlink. This technique can be used on both desktop and browser applications. You can build your hyperlink so that it includes the email subject and body details. A button can then be added to your screen to call the hyperlink. On a desktop application, the hyperlink is called by using the shell command. On a browser application, the `HtmlPage` object from `System.Windows.Browser` is used instead.

PART 5

Securing Your Application

CHAPTER 13

Authenticating Your Users

In the next set of chapters, you'll look at some of the security-related aspects of LightSwitch. You'll start with *authentication*, the process that determines the identity of your user. This is perhaps the most important part of LightSwitch security. Unless you can correctly identify your user, you won't be able to restrict what users can do in your application. You also won't be able to apply any useful security auditing, because you'll be missing a key piece of information.

LightSwitch has three authentication options that you can choose from (one of which has two "flavors"):

- No authentication, which also means that no *authorization* is possible

- Windows Authentication, using the Windows identities of one of the following:

  - *All* Windows-authenticated users

  - *Specific* Windows-authenticated users

- Forms Authentication, using a set of application-defined identities

In the rest of this chapter, we'll show you when and why you should use each option. We'll also explain how to configure each authentication type. LightSwitch uses the ASP.NET membership provider behind the scenes, so we'll also describe how this works.

Note Many people confuse the terms *authentication* and *authorization*, and they're often used interchangeably. But they're not the same at all. *Authorization* is the process of determining *what your users can do* in your application, and is based on the roles that have been assigned to them. Roles and authorization are covered in Chapter 14.

Choosing an Authentication Method

We'll start off by showing you how to choose from among different types of authentication, and we'll also explain the pros and cons of each authentication type. Your application type will guide you toward the most appropriate choice of authentication. Table 13-1 summarizes the recommended options.

Table 13-1. Recommended Authentication Methods by Application Type

	None	Windows	Forms
Two-tier desktop app deployed on an internal network	✓	✓	
Three-tier desktop or web app deployed on an internal network		✓	✓
Three-tier desktop/web app deployed on the Internet or Windows Azure			✓

If you want to use authentication in a two-tier desktop application, the recommended choice is Windows Authentication. This is because Forms Authentication isn't secure in a two-tier application. In a two-tier application, the connection string to the membership database is saved in clear text inside the web.config file, which is stored on the client's machine. If a malicious user discovers the connection string to your membership database, that user could tamper with your membership data outside of LightSwitch.

If you want to make your application available via the Internet (or to deploy to Azure), Windows Authentication isn't really a viable solution. Forms Authentication is therefore the recommended choice in this scenario.

In a three-tier local network deployment (with the LightSwitch server components hosted in IIS), you have a choice of either Windows or Forms Authentication. Table 13-2 summarizes some of the features of these two authentication types and explains when you should use each type.

Table 13-2. When to Use Each Type of Authentication

Windows	Forms
Use Windows Authentication if all of your users belong in the same domain.	Use Forms Authentication if you don't have a Windows domain. For example, you may be using a workgroup or even a Novell network.
Use Windows Authentication if you don't want to have an extra login screen. Windows Authentication means that your users won't need to enter a username and password when they run your application.	Use Forms Authentication if you want your users to enter a username and password when they run your application. You might want to do this to enforce an extra layer of security.
	Forms Authentication is ideal if you want to share authentication details with other applications, perhaps with an existing ASP.NET web site.

We'll now explain each authentication type in more detail, beginning with the No Authentication option.

Using No Authentication

To manage the authentication settings for your application, open the properties pane by selecting the right-click option in Solution Explorer. You'll find the authentication settings inside the Access Control tab. On any new project that you create, authentication is disabled by default. If you view the Access Control tab, the Do Not Enable Authentication option is selected by default (see Figure 13-1).

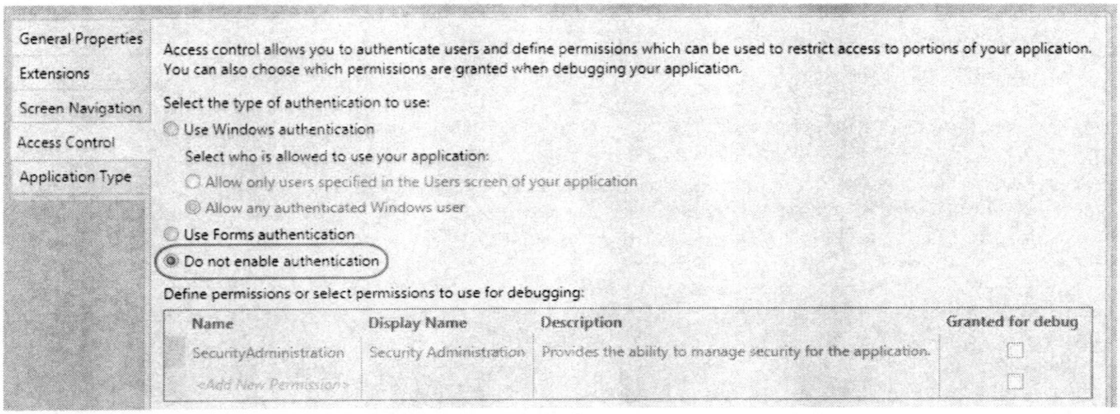

Figure 13-1. Default authentication option

This is the most basic of the available authentication options, because *no* authentication mechanism is used at all. Anybody who has physical access to your application can run it and will have full access to all of its features and data.

You would use this option if you have no need to know who is using your application. This isn't really a very wise practice. In some smaller companies, the need for security may not be a high priority, but at the very least, you want to be able to know who added an entry, or worse, who deleted one.

It's a much more likely scenario that you'll want to be able to restrict what your users can do, based on something such as membership of certain roles. But to be able to do this, you'll first need to enable authorization.

■ **Note** If you select Do Not Enable Authentication, the Define Permissions section (shown in the lower section of Figure 13-1) is automatically disabled, because it makes no sense to define permissions if you're not authenticating your users. Defining permissions is covered in the next chapter.

Using Windows Authentication—Allow Any Authenticated Windows User

Choosing this option in the Access Control tab of the LightSwitch project (see Figure 13-2) will allow any user who has been authenticated by Windows to run your application.

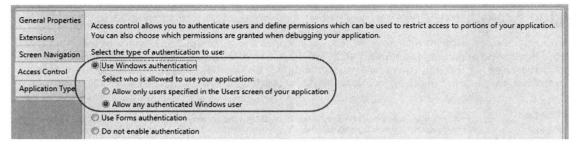

Figure 13-2. Allowing any authenticated Windows user

The Allow Any Authenticated User option is the less restrictive of the two Windows authentication types. When you select it, anybody who has been authenticated by Windows can run your application. You would use this option if you want *all* Windows users to be able to run the application, and not have to add each user individually.

However, the application administrator can still add specific users so that roles can be assigned to them. Roles can help you to secure your application by allowing only specific users to perform certain functions in your application. Chapter 14 covers this in greater depth.

The application administrator is a special user whom you specify at deployment. The application administrator can be designated by using the publish wizard or by using a command-line utility. Chapter 16 shows you the specific steps that you would follow to set up an application administrator.

The application administrator can add the specific users, and specify roles at runtime by using the screen shown in Figure 13-3.

Figure 13-3. Specifying users in the Users screen

■ **Caution** Allow Any Authenticated Windows User essentially means that anyone who can log onto your Windows domain can *run* your application.

Using Windows Authentication—Allow Specified Users

Choosing this option in the Access Control tab of the LightSwitch project (see Figure 13-4) allows *only* users who have been authenticated by Windows to run your application, provided they have *also* been added as a user in your application. This option is the more restrictive of the two Windows Authentication types.

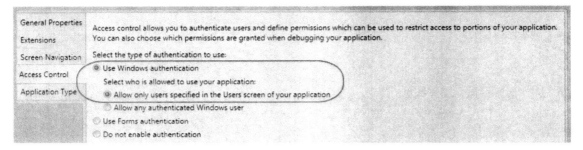

Figure 13-4. Allowing only users specified in the Users screen

You would use this option if you want only *specified* Windows users, as opposed to *all* Windows users, to be able to run the application. Just as before, the users whom you want to allow are added by your application administrator at runtime by using the Users screen.

Tip Instead of requiring the administrative user to enter Active Directory users into your application by hand, make their life easier and create a utility to import them automatically.

The Active Directory sample written by the LightSwitch team provides sample code that you can use to integrate with Active Directory: `http://code.msdn.microsoft.com/windowsdesktop/LightSwitch-Active-5092eaa8`.

Using Forms Authentication

When you choose Forms Authentication (see Figure 13-5), the user will be asked for a username and password when the application starts. Forms Authentication uses a set of application-defined identities. These identities are created by the application administrator.

There are a couple of security considerations that you should to be aware of. Forms Authentication can be regarded as a less-secure option, because your users' usernames and passwords are stored in a database table, rather than being securely maintained by Windows. Although LightSwitch stores the cryptographic hash of the passwords rather than the clear-text values, this might still be considered a security risk.

Second, the username and password details entered by the user are transmitted in clear text across the network. An attacker who snoops the network might discover the usernames and passwords that are being used. Enabling HTTPS on your server helps to mitigate this risk.

A properly secured server environment means that the overall security risk is low, but it's still good for you to be aware of these issues.

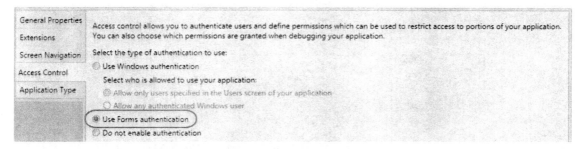

Figure 13-5. Forms Authentication

The identities and passwords that you want to add to your application are created at runtime. This is carried out by the application administrator using the Users administrator screen. This screen also allows the application administrator to delete users or to reset passwords.

When using Forms Authentication, your users can change their passwords after logging into your application. They would do this by clicking the Change Password link at the bottom-right side of the status bar. This opens a screen that prompts them to enter the new password (Figure 13-6).

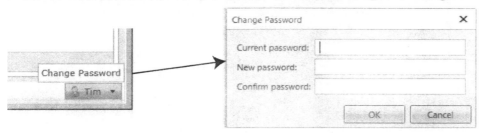

Figure 13-6. Changing a password

Membership Provider Settings

When you choose to enable authentication, LightSwitch uses the ASP.NET membership provider to manage your users. By default, the users that you create are added to a table called aspnet_Users in the intrinsic database. Figure 13-7 shows a screenshot of this table. The primary-key field is called UserId and is of data type GUID. The usernames that you specify are stored in a field called UserName.

	ApplicationId	UserId	UserName	LoweredUserName	MobileAlias	IsAnonymous	LastActivityDate
1	B9BE768D-141...	3027FEC8-B45B...	Garth	garth	NULL	0	2011-12-17 12:14:17.013
2	B9BE768D-141...	84BCF33A-E50...	Tim	tim	NULL	0	2011-12-17 12:14:17.017
3	B9BE768D-141...	80417E12-56C7...	Yann	yann	NULL	0	2011-12-17 12:14:17.017

Figure 13-7. aspnet_Users table

Any roles that you create are saved in a table called aspnet_Roles. This table is shown in Figure 13-8.

	ApplicationId	RoleId	RoleName	LoweredRoleName	Description
1	B9BE768D-1414-43...	4E4BC4DF-630B-481...	Admin Workers	admin workers	NULL
2	B9BE768D-1414-43...	974B373B-4409-450A...	Administrator	administrator	NULL
3	B9BE768D-1414-43...	F0E3E83E-4D87-4BB...	Managers	managers	NULL
4	B9BE768D-1414-43...	1CBF8CDE-470E-4CE...	Supervisors	supervisors	NULL

Figure 13-8. `aspnet_Roles` *table*

The user-to-role settings are saved in a table called `aspnet_UsersInRoles`. The user password details are stored in a table called `aspnet_Membership`, and details that relate to your application are stored in a table called `aspnet_Applications`.

These tables and the relationships between them are shown in Figure 13-9.

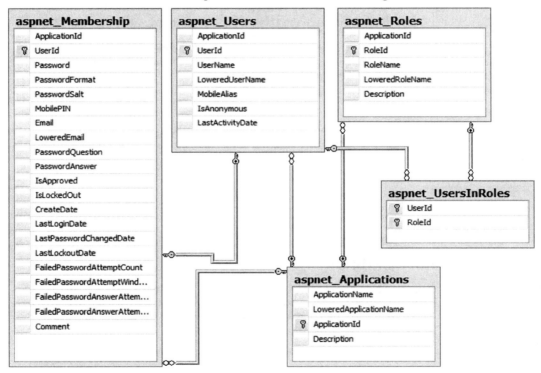

Figure 13-9. *Tables used by the membership provider and their relationships*

Changing Password-Complexity Rules

When using Forms Authentication, LightSwitch enforces a password-complexity rule to help keep your application secure. By default, any user password that's created must be eight characters in length and contain a non-alphanumeric character. An example of a valid password is `pass@word1`.

This default rule provides a good level of security, but some users might find this too restrictive, and you might want to weaken this rule. Alternatively, you might even want to strengthen the password-complexity setting to force users to use passwords that are even more complex.

 The password-complexity rules are managed by the ASP.NET membership provider. After deploying your application, you can change the password-complexity rule by modifying your web.config file. When you deploy your application in IIS, you'll find the web.config file in the root folder of your LightSwitch application. As mentioned earlier, we don't recommend Forms Authentication for two-tier applications. This section therefore focuses on the three-tier IIS setup.

 After you find your web.config file, open it in Notepad. Now search for the ASPNetSQLMembershipProvider element (shown in Listing 13-1). The password complexity is controlled by the attributes minRequiredPasswordLength and minRequiredNonalphanumericCharacters, which are highlighted in bold.

Listing 13-1. Changing the Password-Complexity Rules

```xml
<?xml version="1.0"?>
<configuration
    xmlns="http://schemas.microsoft.com/.NetConfiguration/v2.0">
  <connectionStrings>
    <remove name="LocalSqlServer"/>
    <add name="LocalSqlServer"
        connectionString="Data Source=.\SQLExpress;
        Integrated Security=True;UserInstance=True;
        AttachDBFilename=|DataDirectory|aspnetdb.mdf" />
  </connectionStrings>
  <system.web>
    <membership>
      <providers>
        <remove name="AspNetSqlMembershipProvider" />
        <add name="AspNetSqlMembershipProvider"
            type="System.Web.Security.SqlMembershipProvider,
                System.Web, Version=2.0.0.0, Culture=neutral,
                PublicKeyToken=b03f5f7f11d50a3a"
            connectionStringName="LocalSqlServer"
            enablePasswordRetrieval="false"
            enablePasswordReset="true"
            requiresQuestionAndAnswer="true"
            applicationName="/"
            requiresUniqueEmail="false"
            minRequiredPasswordLength="1"
            minRequiredNonalphanumericCharacters="0"
            passwordFormat="Hashed"
            maxInvalidPasswordAttempts="5"
            passwordAttemptWindow="10"
            passwordStrengthRegularExpression="" />
      </providers>
    </membership>
  </system.web>
</configuration>
```

Changing Password-Encryption Settings

By default, LightSwitch saves the hashes of the user passwords rather than the clear-text password. This is controlled by the passwordFormat attribute in the AspNetSqlMembershipProvider element of your web.config file (which you'll also see in Listing 13-1). There are three choices that you can enter here:

- Hashed
- Encrypted
- Clear

Hashed is the default value and is the most secure. When you choose this option, LightSwitch uses a one-way hash algorithm and a randomly generated salt value when storing passwords in the database. When a user enters a username and password at logon, LightSwitch hashes the password that's entered and compares it to the value that's stored in the database.

It's impossible for you to retrieve the plain-text password values when passwordFormat is set to Hashed. If you want your passwords to be stored in plain text inside your aspnet_users table, change the passwordFormat setting to Clear. This is obviously less secure, because anyone who can access the aspnet_users table will be able to see all of the passwords.

Although it is less secure, there are a couple of reasons why you might choose this option:

- You might want to build a mechanism outside of LightSwitch to remind users of their actual passwords.

- During the initial setup of your application, you might want to preload users and known passwords by manually populating the aspnet_users table. Maintaining clear-text passwords simplifies this process and means that you won't need to create an additional process to work out the hash or encrypted value.

Sharing Forms Authentication Data with ASP.NET

Let's imagine that you have an existing ASP.NET web site that uses Forms Authentication. Because your web site already contains a set of users, you might want to share these existing credentials with your LightSwitch application. You can set up your LightSwitch application to share Forms Authentication details with existing ASP.NET web sites by modifying your web.config file.

To do this, deploy your LightSwitch application to IIS and open the web.config file in Notepad (see Chapter 16 for more help on deployment). You'll need to make the following changes to this file:

- Create a new connection string that points to the authentication database that your existing ASP.NET application uses.

- Update the membership, role and profile provider strings to reference the connection string that you've created.

- Ensure that the same ApplicationName is specified in the provider strings in both your LightSwitch and ASP.NET application.

- Specify the same machine key setting for both of your applications.

To create a new connection string that references the authentication database that your existing ASP.NET application uses, search for the connectionStrings element. Beneath the _IntrinsicData connection string that's created by LightSwitch, create a new connection string that points to your existing authentication database (shown in bold in Listing 13-2). We've called this new connection string _AuthData.

***Listing 13-2.** Creating a New Connection String*

```
<connectionStrings>

    <add name="_IntrinsicData"
      connectionString="Data Source=myDBServer1;
      Initial Catalog=ShipperCentralDB; Integrated Security=False;
      User ID=Sqllogin1;Password=somepassword1;
      Pooling=True;Connect Timeout=30;User Instance=False" />

    <add name="_AuthData"
      connectionString="Data Source=MyDBServer2;
      Initial Catalog=MyAuthDB;Integrated Security=False;
      User ID=Sqllogin2;Password=somepassword2;
      Pooling=True;Connect Timeout=30;User Instance=False" />

</connectionStrings>
```

Now search for the AspNetMembershipProvider, AspNetRoleProvider, and AspNetProfileProvider entries in the web.config file for your LightSwitch application. By default, the connectionStringName setting for each entry is set to _IntrinsicData by default. Change this to _AuthData (as shown in Listing 13-3).

Open the web.config file for your *existing* ASP.NET application and search for the AspNetMembershipProvider entry. Find the applicationName that this uses. In this example, let's assume that the applicationName value is set to ExistingASPApp.

Make sure that the three provider strings in the web.config file for your LightSwitch application specify the applicationName of ExistingASPApp.

***Listing 13-3.** Changing the Settings in your LightSwitch web.config File*

```
<membership defaultProvider="AspNetMembershipProvider">
    <providers>
        <clear />

        <add name="AspNetMembershipProvider"
            type="System.Web.Security.SqlMembershipProvider"
            connectionStringName="_AuthData"
            applicationName="ExistingASPApp"
            requiresUniqueEmail="false"
            requiresQuestionAndAnswer="false" />

    </providers>
</membership>

<roleManager enabled="True"
    defaultProvider="AspNetRoleProvider">
    <providers>

        <clear />
```

```
      <add name="AspNetRoleProvider"
          type="System.Web.Security.SqlRoleProvider"
          connectionStringName="_AuthData"
          applicationName="ExistingASPApp" />

    </providers>
</roleManager>

<profile enabled="True"
    defaultProvider="AspNetProfileProvider">
    <providers>
      <clear />

      <add name="AspNetProfileProvider"
          type="System.Web.Profile.SqlProfileProvider"
          connectionStringName="_AuthData"
          applicationName="ExistingASPApp" />

    </providers>
</profile>
```

You'll need to have the same machine key defined in both of your applications. Because passwords are hashed (or encrypted), identical machine keys are needed to ensure that the encryption and decryption operate identically across both of your applications.

If a machine key isn't specified in the web.config file of your existing application, you'll need to generate a new key. IIS Manager includes a feature that generates machine keys for you (see Figure 13-10). Alternatively, a search on the Web will reveal some online web pages that can generate keys for you. After you've decided on a key, you'll need to add the machine key entry to the <system.web> section in both of your web.config files. Listing 13-4 shows how this looks.

Listing 13-4. Adding a Machine Config Key Section

```
<?xml version="1.0" encoding="utf-8"?>
<configuration>
    <system.web>
        <machineKey validationKey="C50B3C89CB21F4F1422FF158A5B42D0E8DB8CB5CDA↵
            1742572A487D9401E3400267682B202B746511891C1BAF47F8D25C07F6C39A104↵
            696DB51F17C529AD3CABE"
          decryptionKey="8A9BE8FD67AF6979E7D20198CFEA50DD3D3799C77AF2B72F"
          validation="ABC" />
    </system.web>
</configuration>
```

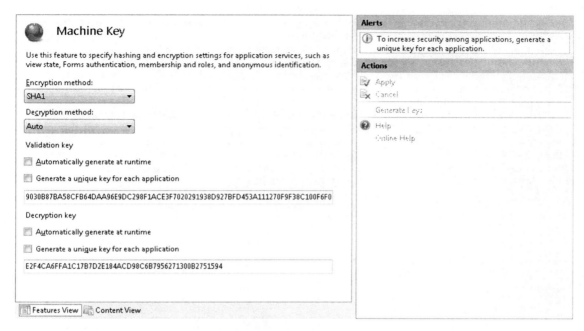

Figure 13-10. Generating a machine key in IIS 7 Manager

Summary

In this chapter, you've learned the difference between *authentication* and *authorization,* as well as the difference between *Windows* identities (Windows Authentication) and *application-defined* ones (Forms Authentication).

This chapter explained the following:

- The three authentication options that you can use in your application (No Authentication, Windows Authentication, and Forms Authentication) and *why* you would choose each of them.

- The default authentication option is in fact not to authenticate the user at all, therefore allowing everyone unrestricted access to your application and its data.

- LightSwitch uses the ASP.NET membership provider, and you can change authentication settings such as password-complexity rules and encryption settings by using the web.config file.

If you're creating a two-tier desktop application to run on your local network, Windows Authentication is the most secure choice. Three-tier desktop or web applications can use either Windows or Forms Authentication. Applications deployed over the Internet (or on Azure) should use Forms Authentication.

Forms Authentication is also a good choice if you don't have a Windows domain or if you want to share authentication details with other applications (such as ASP.NET applications). If you do have a

Windows domain, you can choose to use Forms Authentication if you want to force your users to enter an additional username and password when logging in.

When using Windows or Forms Authentication, you can explicitly define the users who can access your application. These users are specified by the application administrator at runtime.

By default, LightSwitch uses the ASP.NET membership provider to store and manage your users. The user details are stored in a table called aspnet_Users, and the password details are held in a table called aspnet_Membership (when using Forms Authentication).

Forms Authentication enforces a default password complexity rule of eight characters and a non-alphanumeric character. You can change this password rule by modifying the web.config file for your application. The web.config file also allows you to change the way that passwords are encrypted in your database. By default, passwords are hashed, but you can choose to store the encrypted or plain-text values instead. If you want to share your Forms Authentication credentials with other ASP.NET applications, you can do so by modifying your web.config file.

C H A P T E R 14

Authorization

Whereas *authentication* is all about users proving who they are, *authorization* is all about what they are allowed to do, within the context of your application. Of course, this whole chapter is applicable only if you're using Windows Authentication or Forms Authentication.

Understanding Authorization

Security can be extremely important in a business application. If you've chosen the Do Not Enable Authentication option, LightSwitch won't use any mechanism to authenticate your user, and you can skip this chapter. In other words, your application won't know who's using it, and you won't be able to restrict what the users of your application can do.

Here are just a few of the reasons that you might want to use authorization:

- Control access (for example, whether a user is allowed to run your application)

- Hide screens (to show users only certain screens, based on their job definition)

- Restrict data access (because maybe not everyone should be able to see all data)

- Prevent data changes (for example, allowing a user to view data but not change it)

Fortunately, LightSwitch has a number of "hooks" built into it—in entities, screens, and queries—where you can write code that represents your unique business requirements. This allows you to easily check that your users have the required permissions to do whatever it is that they're trying to do. LightSwitch implements authorization by allowing you to create permissions, roles, and users.

Setting Permissions

Permissions determine what your users can do in your application. As the developer, you define these permissions while you're developing your application. In your code, you then check that the current user has the required permission, either in your own code, or by using one of the various security points that LightSwitch provides out of the box.

Later in this chapter, you'll learn how permissions are assigned to roles, and then how those roles are assigned to users (see Figure 14-1).

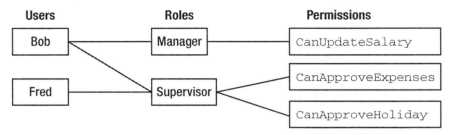

Figure 14-1. *Permissions get assigned to roles, and roles get assigned to users.*

In terms of the underlying implementation, permissions are claims that are defined by the application. Permissions are defined by your application in the same way that screens and entities are defined by your application. In fact, a permission definition is stored in the LSML file.

Roles and users are defined external to your application, so that an application administrator can manage them. LightSwitch lets the application administrator associate permissions with roles. But the application administrator cannot define permissions. Figure 14-2 illustrates where permissions, roles, and users are defined.

LightSwitch Application

LSML File

Permissions are defined here.

Database Tables

* `aspnet_Roles`
* `aspnet_Users`
* `aspnet_UsersInRoles`

Roles and users are defined here.

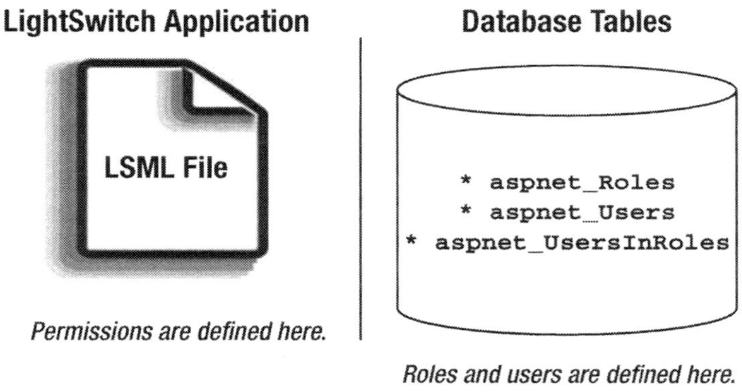

Figure 14-2. *This is where permissions, roles, and users are defined.*

Defining Permissions

Permissions are defined by adding them into the permissions grid in the Access Control tab of the LightSwitch project's properties (see Figure 14-3). You can add permissions to indicate, for example, whether a user can view a certain screen, to restrict access to individual controls on a screen, to determine whether an entity's properties are editable or read-only, and so on. You can be as general, or as granular, as your application requires.

For example, if you had an entity called Product, you might care only that a user is given a permission to *edit* a product, and not distinguish between the various ways that you can edit a product. You might call that permission EditProduct.

Or you might want to be able to provide a way that users can be given *different* permissions to add, edit, and delete that entity instead. In this case, you'd create individual AddProduct, EditProduct, and DeleteProduct permissions. It's a good idea to match your permission to the types of *actions* that your application's users are likely to need to perform, giving the administrative user the ability to assign the permissions required to perform those actions as they see fit.

More-granular permissions provide a much greater level of control, but it's also a bit of extra work for the administrative user who's setting up the roles and users. Adding a permission for every single possible action *might* be overkill. You really need to find the right balance between granularity and convenience.

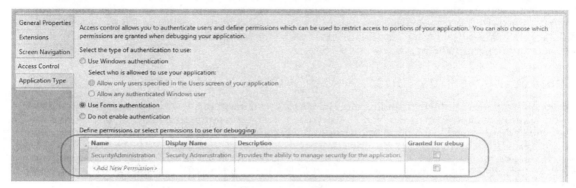

Figure 14-3. *Adding permissions in the Access Control tab*

You test whether the current user has a given permission within the code that you add for tables, screens, and queries. When you select a permission method name from the Write Code drop-down list, LightSwitch will create a method stub for you, where you can then write the code that provides the logic for the permission.

After you become more experienced, you can add these methods to the appropriate classes manually, without having to use the drop-down. If you decide not to use the drop-down, it's worth noting that the Partial modifier is optional in VB, but *must* be specified in your C# code (if that's the language you're using in your project). In fact, this is common to all partial methods including validation, and computed properties.

LightSwitch will also generate a Permissions class for you that contains a string constant for each of the permissions that you've defined in the grid, so you can refer to the permissions in a consistent way. The class is automatically kept up to date, when the project is built (or rebuilt), so you don't have to take any extra action if you add, change, or delete permissions in the grid.

The string constants have the following format:

```
"ApplicationName:PermissionName"
→ LightSwitchApplication:AddProduct
```

In your code, you refer to them like this:

```
"Permissions.PermissionName"
→ Permissions.AddProduct
```

▪ **Note** Either Windows Authentication or Forms Authentication must be selected. Otherwise, the Define Permissions grid will be disabled.

Setting the Security Administration Permission

Every LightSwitch application has a built-in permission called `SecurityAdministration`. Only users who have been granted this permission, through any of the roles that have been assigned to them, will be able to manage security for the application, through the Roles screen and the Users screen.

These two screens are visible only if the user has this permission, and will appear in a navigation menu group called Administration (although you can change the name of the navigation group if you prefer, just as with any other navigation group). Any other screens that you've added to the group will still be visible (if the user has permission to view them, of course), whether the user has the administration permission or not.

Debugging Permissions

When debugging a LightSwitch application, there's no mechanism to allow you to choose which user you're running the program as. But you'll want to be able to test your permissions, to make sure that they work as you expect. Each permission row in the grid has a column called `Granted for Debug`, which appears as a check box.

If you tick the check box, you'll be granted that permission while you're debugging (meaning the `Current.User.HasPermission` function will return `true` for that permission), so that any code that relies on it can be tested.

When debugging, actual users and roles don't matter. You're not tied to, nor do you have access to, any specific roles, so you can set any combination of permissions that you want to test, and you can change them for each debugging session.

Note If you enable the `SecurityAdministration` permission for use during debugging, you'll be able to add, view, and edit roles and users. However, any roles or users that you add while debugging *won't* be deployed with your application, and they have absolutely *no* effect on your debugging session permissions.

Setting Entity Set (Table) Permissions

The first area where you can set permissions is at the table/entity set level. These types of permissions apply to the whole entity set. You can control actions such as whether a user can add, view, edit, or delete any entity from the entire entity set. These permissions will be enforced by LightSwitch, whether the action is being performed in a screen on the client tier, or programmatically on the server tier (via any code that you've written to be executed there).

Checking permissions at the entity set level ensures that your data is protected, even if, for example, you forget to check for the appropriate permissions in a screen (on the client tier). The code that you write for a table runs on the server, so your application will check these permissions before it performs any action on your data, preventing anything unauthorized.

Although these permission checks are run and enforced on the server, the client queries and caches these values. In this way, the LightSwitch client can modify the screen functionality in accordance with the user's permissions.

The easiest way to access the code where you set the actual true/false value for these permission methods is to use the Write Code drop-down (see Figure 14-4), which is available when you're in the table designer. LightSwitch then adds a code stub for the chosen method for you, putting it in the data

service class. You'll find this class in the `Server\UserCode\ApplicationDataService.vb` (or
`ApplicationDataService.cs`) file when writing permissions for a table in the intrinsic database. You then
provide the code that represents the logic for the method.

We'll use the `Employee` entity/table to illustrate the various methods and how you'd use them.

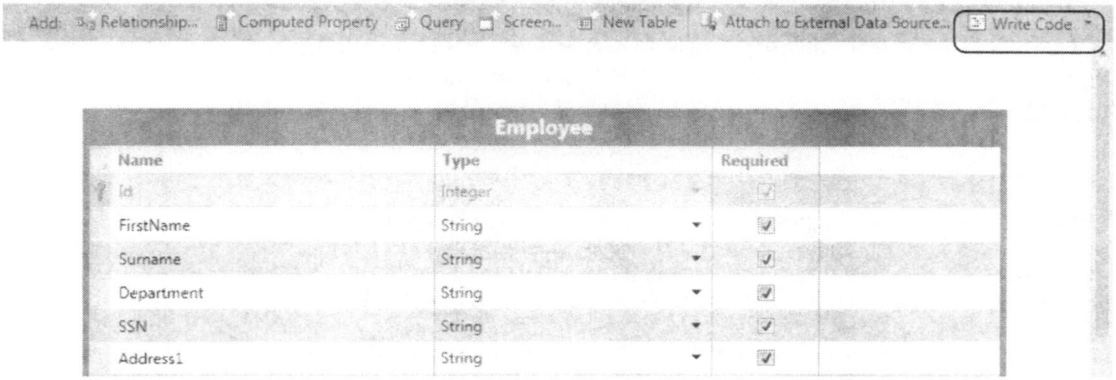

Figure 14-4. The Write Code drop-down menu

Entity Set Access Control Methods

These methods, as their names suggest, control the various levels of access that a user has to the entire
entity set or table (see Figure 14-5). If you restrict an operation by using these methods, LightSwitch will
make that operation unavailable to users who do not have unrestricted permissions. These methods run
on the server. The results of these methods are enforced both on the server and on the client.

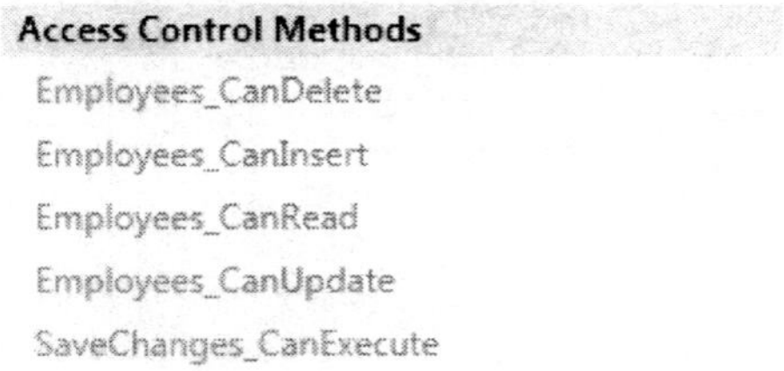

Figure 14-5. Access control methods

CanDelete Method

You can prevent a user from making any deletions from the entity set by setting the result of the
`CanDelete` method to `false` (see Listing 14-1). Any built-in Delete buttons on any screen will
automatically be disabled. If you create your own Delete buttons, or override the existing buttons, you'll
need to write code in their `CanExecute` methods to manually check for any delete permission you may
have defined in the permissions grid.

We've chosen to call the permission that we're using to determine whether a user can delete an
employee `DeleteEmployee`. In this case, the name of the permission that we've created (`DeleteEmployee`)
matches the name of the method's action (delete), but that won't always be the case, as you'll see next.

CanInsert Method

You can restrict a user from being able to insert any entity to the entity set by setting the result of the CanInsert method to false (see Listing 14-1). As with the built-in Delete buttons, built-in Add buttons will automatically be disabled, and any that you create yourself will also need to have its CanExecute method overridden as well.

This time, we chose to call the permission AddEmployee (rather than InsertEmployee), as that more correctly reflects the actual function that the user is performing, even though technically the record is being inserted into the table.

CanRead Method

This method is run before LightSwitch reads a record. This includes any queries that are based on the table (either the default queries, or any custom queries that you add). If you set the result of the CanRead method to false (see Listing 14-1), a user will not be able to read or load any entities from the table.

If you base a search screen, or an editable grid screen, on a table with CanRead set to false, the grid will not be able to display the records (you'll get a red X in the grid instead). Your end user won't find this behavior very attractive, so it'll be a good idea to also use the screen's CanRun method to restrict access to the actual screen.

Using the CanRead method is still very valuable, particularly if you have sensitive data in a table. If you deny access to a table by using the CanRead method, those records are also hidden in the server pipelines. This means that data cannot leak out in any way.

However, you could still use the *elevate permissions* technique to override the current user's restrictions, if your server-side business logic requires access. This technique grants permissions to the user by using the method Application.Current.User.AddPermissions.

CanUpdate Method

Similarly, by setting the result of the CanUpdate method to false (see Listing 14-1), you can prevent users from being able to update any entity in the entity set. The UI (on the client tier) will respond by automatically setting the controls displaying the entity's properties to be read-only. If a change is attempted outside of a screen, the check will still be run on the server tier to prevent any back-door type of data changes.

SaveChanges_CanExecute Method

SaveChanges_CanExecute determines whether the save operation can be executed in the current context.

This method is executed on the server, after a user attempts to save data. If the method returns false, the user won't be allowed to carry out the save. This extends to all tables in the data source. If SaveChanges_CanExecute returns false, the user won't be able to save any data in any table at all.

The logic that you write in SaveChanges_CanExecute can be based on permissions, and can also be based on other reasons for denying save operations. For example, you might want to prevent changes during certain business hours.

The code in Listing 14-1 shows how you can use this method to restrict access to your application between the hours of midnight and 3 a.m.

Listing 14-1. Setting Access Control Permissions

VB:

File : OfficeCentral\Server\UserCode\ApplicationDataService.vb

```vb
Namespace LightSwitchApplication

    Public Class ApplicationDataService

        Private Sub Employee_CanDelete(ByRef result As Boolean)
            result = Application.User.HasPermission(
                Permissions.DeleteEmployee)
        End Sub

        Private Sub Employee_CanInsert(ByRef result As Boolean)
            result = Application.User.HasPermission(
                Permissions.AddEmployee)
        End Sub

        Private Sub Employee_CanRead(ByRef result As Boolean)
            result = Application.User.HasPermission(
                Permissions.ReadEmployee)
        End Sub

        Private Sub Employee_CanUpdate(ByRef result As Boolean)
            result = Application.User.HasPermission(
                Permissions.EditEmployee)
        End Sub

        Private Sub SaveChanges_CanExecute(ByRef result As Boolean)
            'System is down for daily maintenance from midnight to 3am
            If Now.TimeOfDay.Hours >= 0 AndAlso
              Now.TimeOfDay.Hours <= 3 Then
                result = False
            Else
                result = True
            End If
        End Sub

    End Class

End Namespace
```

C#:

File : OfficeCentral\Server\UserCode\ApplicationDataService.cs

```csharp
namespace LightSwitchApplication
{
    public class ApplicationDataService
```

```
{
    private void Employee_CanDelete(ref bool result)
    {
        result = Application.User.HasPermission(
            Permissions.DeleteEmployee);
    }

    private void Employee_CanInsert(ref bool result)
    {
        result = Application.User.HasPermission(
            Permissions.AddEmployee);
    }

    private void Employee_CanRead(ref bool result)
    {
        result = Application.User.HasPermission(
            Permissions.ReadEmployee);
    }

    private void Employee_CanUpdate(ref bool result)
    {
        result = Application.User.HasPermission(
            Permissions.EditEmployee);
    }

    private void SaveChanges_CanExecute (ref bool result)
    {
        //System is down for daily maintenance from midnight to 3am
        if (Now.TimeOfDay.Hours >= 0 &&
            Now.TimeOfDay.Hours <= 3) {
            result = false;
        } else {
            result = true;
        }
    }
}
}
```

Property Permissions

In addition to being able to define table-wide permissions, you can have slightly more granular control over the ability to edit an entity by using a property-level IsReadOnly method (see Figure 14-6).

Property Methods

FirstName_Changed

FirstName_IsReadOnly

FirstName_Validate

Figure 14-6. IsReadOnly *method*

LightSwitch uses the IsReadOnly method only to manage the UI editable state. This method doesn't control read access from the entity set/table, so it can't be used for row-level security. This is in contrast to EntitySet_CanRead, which does prevent read access from the entity set.

To give an example, let's say that you've created an employee table that contains a salary property. You'd like to secure the salary property so that only managers are allowed to view and edit this property. It isn't possible to apply permissions at a property level. As a workaround, you'd need to create separate screens for managers and nonmanagers, and apply the permissions at a screen level.

Each property in an entity has its own IsReadOnly method (see Listing 14-2), so you can use custom (or shared) business logic to set individual properties to be read-only. For example, you might want a property's value to be able to be entered only if a value hasn't previously been entered, *unless* the current user has an override permission (which has been defined in the permissions grid, and assigned by the administrative user).

We've called our permission OverrideNames. By setting the result of a property's IsReadOnly method to false, *any* screen control that's bound to that property will automatically be displayed as a read-only value.

Listing 14-2. Setting a Property's IsReadOnly Method

VB:

File: OfficeCentral\Common\UserCode\Employee.vb

```
Namespace LightSwitchApplication

    Public Class Employee

        Private Sub FirstName_IsReadOnly(ByRef result As Boolean)
            result = (Not String.IsNullOrEmpty(Me.FirstName))↲
                OrElse↲
                (Current.User.HasPermission(Permissions.OverrideNames) = True)
        End Sub

    End Class

End Namespace
```

C#:

File: OfficeCentral\Common\UserCode\Employee.cs

```
namespace LightSwitchApplication
{
    partial void FirstName_IsReadOnly(ref bool result)
    {
        result = (!string.IsNullOrEmpty(this.FirstName))↲
            || (Current.User.HasPermission(Permissions.OverrideNames) == true);
    }
}
```

■ **Note** The IsReadOnly method is run on the tier where the method's result is being checked.

Setting Screen Permissions

Setting permissions in your screens for buttons, tabs, grids, and other controls is an effective way of restricting what your users can do. It's much better to visually inform your users (by way of a disabled button or a read-only control) that they can't perform a certain action, rather than rely on just the table permissions.

Imagine a user's frustration if he fills out a lengthy screen of information, only to be informed when he clicks the Save button that he's not allowed to save the data. Your application won't impress its users if you allow that to happen.

Screen Access Control Methods

There's only one permission-related method for a screen itself (see Figure 14-7). Setting the result of this method to false will prevent the user from being able to open the screen.

Access Control Methods

ProductList_CanRun

Figure 14-7. Access control methods

CanRun Method

If you want to prevent a user from being able to open a particular screen, you can check that the user has a permission that you've specifically defined for that purpose.

For example, in the ProductList screen, we're checking that the user has the EditProducts permission. If the user doesn't have the required permission, the result is simply set to false (see Listing 14-3), and the screen will not be allowed to run.

This method gets added to LightSwitch's Application class.

Listing 14-3. Setting a Screen's CanRun Method

VB:

```
File : OfficeCentral\Client\UserCode\Application.vb

Namespace LightSwitchApplication

    Public Class Application

        Private Sub ProductList_CanRun(ByRef result As Boolean)
            result = (Current.User.HasPermission(Permissions.EditProducts))
        End Sub
```

```
        End Class

End Namespace
```

C#:

```
File : OfficeCentral\Client\UserCode\Application.cs

namespace LightSwitchApplication
{

    public class Application
    {
        partial void ProductList_CanRun(ref bool result)
        {
            result = (Current.User.HasPermission(Permissions.EditProducts));
        }
    }

}
```

 Note If you've added a screen to a navigation menu group, but in its CanRun method your business logic sets the result to False, that screen won't be visible in the navigation menu. Using this method, you can hide screens that a user doesn't need (or doesn't have permission) to see.

Execute Methods

In Chapter 8, you saw how to add methods (or screen commands) to your screen by using the Add Data Item dialog box. You can then create buttons on your screen that are bound to the screen command. Screen commands provide two methods that allow you to write custom code: the CanExecute method and the Execute method (see Figure 14-8).

Because this chapter covers authorization, only the CanExecute method concerns us here.

Figure 14-8. Execute methods

CanExecute Method

Each screen command has its own CanExecute method (see Listing 14-4), where you can define the business logic that determines whether its associated control is enabled or disabled. In this example, the Add Product button (or associated control) is enabled only if the user has the AddProduct permission.

Listing 14-4. Editing a Command's CanExecute Method

VB:

File : OfficeCentral\Client\UserCode\ProductList.vb

```
Namespace LightSwitchApplication

    Public Class ProductList

        Private Sub AddProduct_CanExecute(ByRef result As Boolean)
            result = Me.User.HasPermission(Permissions.AddProduct)
        End Sub

    End Class

End Namespace
```

C#:

File : OfficeCentral\Client\UserCode\ProductList.cs

```
namespace LightSwitchApplication
{
    public class ProductList
    {
        partial void AddProduct_CanExecute (ref bool result)
        {
            result = this.User.HasPermission(Permissions.AddProduct);
        }
    }
}
```

■ **Tip** Although we've used the CanRun method to enforce permissions, you can also use this method to guard screen commands based on other conditions. Let's suppose you've created a method that generates Microsoft Word documents by using COM automation. If your application runs as a browser application (rather than a desktop application), you can hide the button that carries out the Word automation by writing code in the CanRun method that checks AutomationFactory.IsAvailable.

Setting Query Permissions

There's only one method that we need to concern ourselves with for queries related to access control: the CanExecute method (see Figure 14-9). This method is called prior to actually executing the query, so that the current user's permissions can be checked. It runs on the server.

Query Access Control Methods

Access Control Methods

HolidayRequests_ByPersonID_CanExecute

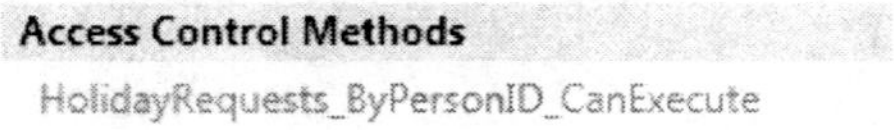

Figure 14-9. A query's CanExecute method

Let's imagine that you've created a query in the OfficeCentral system that returns holiday requests that are filtered by an employee parameter. Only managers should be able to run this query.

If you've created a permission called ViewHolidayRequests, the code shown in Listing 14-5 guards the query so that only those with this permission will be able to execute it.

Listing 14-5. Editing a Query's CanExecute Method

VB:

```
File : OfficeCentral\Server\UserCode\ApplicationDataService.vb

Namespace LightSwitchApplication

    Public Class ApplicationDataService

        Private Sub HolidayRequests_ByPersonID_CanExecute(
          ByRef result As Boolean)
            result = Application.User.HasPermission(
              Permissions.ViewHolidayRequests)
        End Sub

    End Class

End Namespace
```

C#:

```
File : OfficeCentral\Server\UserCode\ApplicationDataService.cs

namespace LightSwitchApplication
{
    public class ApplicationDataService
    {
        partial void HolidayRequests_ByPersonID_CanExecute(
          ref bool result)
        {
            result = Application.User.HasPermission(
```

```
                    Permissions.ViewHolidayRequests);
            }
        }
}
```

Specifying the Application Administrator

When you publish an application for the first time (see Chapter 16 for more details), you have to specify the details of a user who will be the *administrator* of the program. The administrator needs to run the application before anyone else does, because the administrator needs to add roles, and decide which permissions need to be added to those roles, and which roles are assigned to which users.

▪ **Note** If you've chosen Forms Authentication as your authentication method, the very first user that logs on needs to use the username and password that you entered into the publishing wizard when you published the application. If you didn't specify a username and password, you'll need to create these by using the Security Admin command line utility.

Creating Roles

Roles are a key part of the LightSwitch security model. Let's suppose you want to restrict the users who can delete employees. To do this, you've created a permission called DeleteEmployee. In LightSwitch, you wouldn't assign the DeleteEmployee permission directly to a user. Instead, you'd add the permission to a role. So to grant a user the DeleteEmployee permission, you'd assign the user to a role that contains this permission. Therefore, think of roles of as *containers* for users and permissions.

Permissions are created by you (the developer), and are defined in your application inside the LSML file. Roles are created by the application administrator, and it's also the application administrator who adds the permissions that you've defined into roles. This is done in the Roles screen (see Figure 14-10), in the Administration section of the navigation menu, *after* the application has been deployed.

In your code, you shouldn't be testing whether a user belongs to a particular role. You can't guarantee that the role that you're checking for will even exist. Stick with checking whether the user has the appropriate permission to perform a particular task or to access certain data, and leave the assigning of permissions to roles, and the assigning of roles to users, to the application's administrative user.

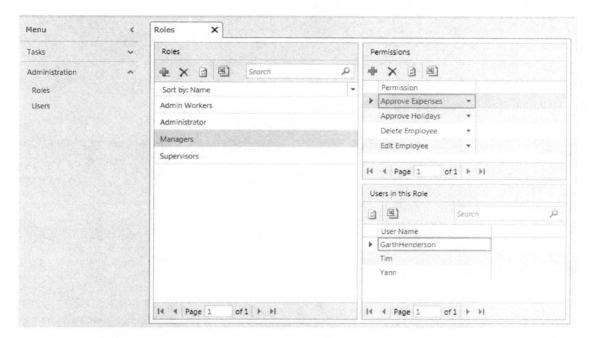

Figure 14-10. Roles screen

■ **Note** A role can have any number of permissions assigned to it, and any number of users assigned to it.

Adding Users

As with roles, *users* are also added by the application administrator, in the Users screen (see Figure 14-11), after the application has been deployed.

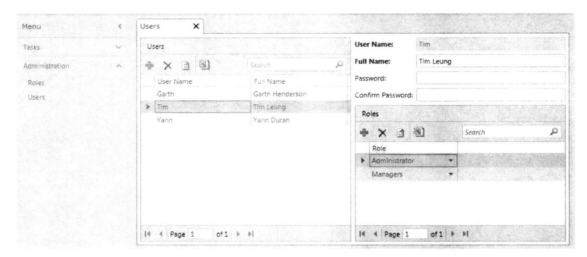

Figure 14-11. Users screen

■ **Note** A user's *effective* permissions are made up of the combination of permissions they have from each of the roles that they've been assigned.

Filtering Data Based on User

It's a common requirement to display only the data that is relevant to a particular user. You might want a data entry person to be able to view only his own entries, and not be able to see other people's entries, for example. In this section, we'll show you how to filter the data in a table based on the user. We'll demonstrate this functionality by showing you a holiday request system that is part of the OfficeCentral application.

The holiday requests are stored in a table. We'll show you how to create a query that returns holiday request records filtered by user. We'll then show you how to create a query that returns holiday requests automatically filtered by the currently logged-on user. You can then build a screen based on this query to display the records that relate to the user.

In this example, we'll show you the following techniques:

- We'll show you how to create a helper method that strips out the domain portion of the username (if you're using Windows Authentication).

- When a user creates a record, we'll show you how to store the username of the logged-on user into a field in the table. This allows you to mark the owner of a record.

- We'll show you how to query your table so that it returns records for only the currently logged-on user.

Helper Methods

We'll start off by describing some helper methods. If you're using Windows Authentication, you might prefer to store and work with only the username portion of a user's login name.

It's useful to have some methods to separate out the domain name, and username, from a user's logon name. We've created a couple of helper methods in our Security helper class to help you do this.

GetDomainName

The GetDomainName function (see Listing 14-6) will extract the domain out of the logon name that we pass to it.

Listing 14-6. GetDomainName Method

VB:

```
Namespace Security

    Public Function GetDomainName(logonName As String) As String
        Dim result = ""

        Try
            Dim parts() As String = Split(logonName, "\")

            result = parts(0)

        Catch ex As Exception
            result = ""
        End Try

        Return result
    End Function

End Namespace
```

C#:

```
Namespace Security
{
    public string GetDomainName(string logonName)
    {
        var result = "";

        try
        {
            string[] parts = logonName.Split('\\');

            result = parts[0];

        }
```

```
            catch (Exception ex)
            {
                result = "";
            }

            return result;
        }
}
```

GetUserName

The GetUserName function (see Listing 14-7) will return the username portion of the logon name that gets passed to it.

Listing 14-7. GetUserName Method

VB:

```
Namespace Security

    Public Function GetUserName(logonName As String) As String
        Dim result = ""

        Try

            If logonName.Contains("\") Then
                Dim parts() As String = Split(logonName, "\")
                result = parts(1)
            Else
                result = logonName
            End If


        Catch ex As Exception
            result = ""
        End Try

        Return result
    End Function

End Namespace
```

C#:

```
Namespace Security
{
{
    public string GetUserName(string logonName)
    {
        var result = "";
```

```
    try
    {
        if(logonName.Contains("\\")){
            string[] parts = logonName.Split('\\');
            result = parts[1];
        }
        else
        {
            result = logonName;
        }
    }
    catch (Exception ex)
    {
        result = "";
    }

    return result;
    }
}
```

The Table

To enable this type of filtering of data, the table that you're displaying must have a property that either stores the username of the person who it will be filtered by (which is the *easiest* to do but has disadvantages) or an Employee (which is a bit more work but is also more *reliable*).

In the HolidayRequest table, we've added a relationship to the Employee table (see Figure 14-12) so that when a HolidayRequest is submitted, we can track which employee submitted it. Another advantage of doing it this way, rather than just storing a username is that each Employee now has a collection of HolidayRequests associated with it. We can display them in a grid in the EmployeeDetail screen, with no extra work required.

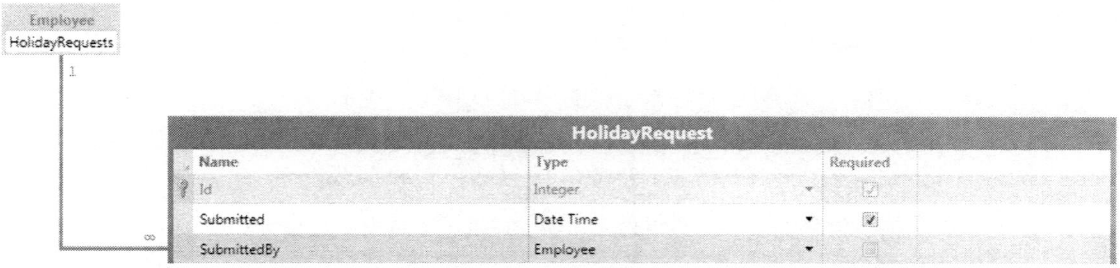

Figure 14-12. SubmittedBy property

The value that will be used to filter the records can be automatically stored when the entity is created, by adding a couple of lines of code to the HolidayRequest's Created method (see Listing 14-8).

Storing a username is fairly straightforward, so we'll show you how to store a related employee when creating a HolidayRequest, which is a slightly more advanced technique.

Listing 14-8. Saving the Current User

VB:

File : OfficeCentral\Common\UserCode\HolidayRequest.vb

```vb
Namespace LightSwitchApplication

    Public Class HolidayRequest

        Private Sub HolidayRequest_Created()
            Dim userName = GetUserName(Me.Application.User.Name)
            Dim submittedBy =
                Me.DataWorkspace.ApplicationData.Employees.Where(↵
                    Function(x) x.UserName = userName).FirstOrDefault

            Me.SubmittedBy = submittedBy
        End Sub

    End Class

End Namespace
```

C#:

File : OfficeCentral\Common\UserCode\HolidayRequest.cs

```csharp
namespace LightSwitchApplication
{
    public class HolidayRequest
    {
        partial void HolidayRequest_Created()
        {
            var userName = GetUserName(this.Application.User.Name);
            var submittedBy =
                this.DataWorkspace.ApplicationData.Employees.Where(↵
                    (x) => x.UserName == userName).FirstOrDefault();

            this.SubmittedBy = submittedBy;
        }
    }
}
```

The Query

Now that you've set up your table and have written the code that automatically populates the SubmittedBy property with the name of the user who created the record, we'll describe a couple of techniques that allow you to filter the records based on the SubmittedBy property.

First, we'll show you how to how to filter the holiday request table by user, using a parameterized query. Second, we'll show you how to automatically filter the table by the logged-on user.

Filtering Records by User

This first query example filters the holiday requests by employee. This would be ideal for someone in a manager role, who needs to be able to select any employee and to view that person's holiday requests.

To do this, you'd simply add a query with an `Integer` parameter, and pass the `Id` value of the current user to the query via the parameter (see Figure 14-13).

Figure 14-13. Query with a filter based on a parameter

After creating your query, you can create an editable grid screen based on this query. You can then add an `AutoCompleteBox` that shows a list of employees. The `PersonID` parameter would be bound to the value of the `AutoCompleteBox`. Whenever you change the selected employee by using the `AutoCompleteBox`, the holiday request data grid will refresh itself to show only those records that relate to the selected employee.

More details on building the UI to do this can be found in Chapter 8.

Filtering Records by Logged-on User

Let's say that a nonmanager logs into your application. You might want to provide nonmanagers with a screen that shows only that user's own holiday requests, and no one else's. To create a query that filters the results based on the logged-in user, you'll need to write some code in the `PreProcessQuery` method of your query.

In the example that follows, we've created a query called `HolidayRequestsByUser`. After creating the query, you'll need to add the code that's shown in Listing 14-9 to do the filtering. After you've created the `HolidayRequestsByUser` query, you can simply create a screen that's based on this query.

Listing 14-9. PreProcessQuery Method

VB:

```
File : OfficeCentral\Server\UserCode\ApplicationDataService.vb
```

```
Namespace LightSwitchApplication
```

```
    Public Class HolidayRequest

        Private Sub HolidayRequestsByUser_PreProcessQuery(↵
            ByRef query As IQueryable(Of
                LightSwitchApplication.HolidayRequest))
            Dim name = GetUserName(Me.Application.User.Name)

            query = From hr In query↵
                    Where (hr.SubmittedBy.UserName = name)
        End Sub

    End Class

End Namespace
```

C#:

File : OfficeCentral\Server\UserCode\ApplicationDataService.cs

```
namespace LightSwitchApplication
{
    public class HolidayRequest
    {
        partial void HolidayRequestsByUser_PreProcessQuery(↵
            ref IQueryable<LightSwitchApplication.HolidayRequest>)
        {
            var name = GetUserName(this.Application.User.Name);

            query = from hr in query
                    where (hr.SubmittedBy.UserName == name)
                    select hr;
        }
    }
}
```

If you want the holiday request data to be filtered by the logged-on user throughout your entire application, you could write code in the PreProcessQuery method of the All query that LightSwitch automatically creates. If you've named your table HolidayRequests, this default query would be called HolidayRequests_All.

However, this technique isn't guaranteed to always show holiday request data that's filtered by the logged-on user. Although any queries applied to the HolidayRequests entity set will be filtered correctly, the filter won't be applied if the user browses holiday requests through navigation properties (or related records). You therefore need to apply some caution if you're thinking about modifying the default All query.

■ **Caution** If you use the user's Windows logon (DOMAIN\user) to filter by, keep in mind that over time, either the domain name or the user's username could change and therefore affect which records are displayed. An organization's server hardware could be replaced or upgraded, and in the process could be given a new domain name. A spelling mistake in a user's name might be discovered and corrected, forcing a change in the username. A user could also get married or legally change her name for some other reason. So, wherever possible, use a numeric Id value (or a related property) to store identities that will be used for filtering.

Creating a Log Out Option

If you're using Forms Authentication in a LightSwitch *browser* application, you might like to add a Log Out button, so that the current user can log out, allowing another user to log in instead. In a desktop application, you'd simply close it, using the Windows-provided Close button. But even if you close a LightSwitch browser application, the session cookie for your application (also known as the *authentication cookie*) will still remain. When you open the application again, it won't prompt the user for a username and password, unless enough time has passed for the cookie to have expired.

To force the application to ask for new user credentials, we'll use a technique based on an article that was created by the LightSwitch team. This creates a special ASPX file that logs out the user and redirects the browser back to the default htm page. When the application reloads, the LightSwitch login screen will be displayed to the user.

Adding an ASPX Page

To add the LogOff.aspx page, follow these steps:

1. Switch your LightSwitch project to File view.

2. Click the Show All Files option.

3. Right-click the Server Generated project.

4. Choose Add ➤ New Item.

5. Select Web Form (to add an ASPX file), and call it LogOff.aspx.

6. Right-click the newly added Logoff.aspx file.

7. Select the View Code option.

8. Add the code (shown in bold) from Listing 14-10, and save the file.

Listing 14-10. Logoff.aspx Code-Behind

VB:

```
Imports System.Web.Security

Public Class LogOff
    Inherits System.Web.UI.Page

    Protected Sub Page_Load(ByVal sender As Object,
        ByVal e As System.EventArgs) Handles Me.Load

            FormsAuthentication.SignOut()
            Response.Redirect("default.htm")

    End Sub

End Class
```

C#:

```
using System.Web.Security;

public class LogOff : System.Web.UI.Page
{
    protected void Page_Load(object sender, System.EventArgs e)
    {
            FormsAuthentication.SignOut();
            Response.Redirect("default.htm");
    }
}
```

Including the ASPX Page in the Project's Build Output

By default, our added ASPX file won't be included in the project's build output, so to make sure it's included, we'll need to manually edit the project's lsproj file (be sure to make a backup of the file first):

1.   Right-click the LightSwitch project.

2.   Select the Unload Project option.

3.   Right-click the project again.

4.   Select the Edit Lsml option.

5.   Use Visual Studio's search function to find _BuildFile
     Include="default.htm".

6.   Immediately underneath the _BuildFile section for default.htm, add the XML
     fragment (shown in bold) that appears in Listing 14-11.

■ **Tip** If you have the PowerCommands for Visual Studio 2010 extension installed (which you can download and install via Visual Studio's Extension Manager), you can combine the unload/edit project steps into one with the Edit Project command.

Listing 14-11. Including LogOff.aspx in Build Output

XML:

```
<_BuildFile Include="default.htm">
  <SubFolder>
  </SubFolder>
  <PublishType>
  </PublishType>
</_BuildFile>
<_BuildFile Include="ServerGenerated\LogOff.aspx">
  <SubFolder>
  </SubFolder>
  <PublishType>
  </PublishType>
</_BuildFile>
```

Exposing the *LogOut* Functionality

Now that you have a method to trigger the logoff page, how you choose to expose that functionality to your application's users is really up to you. We'll show you two options. You can choose one of those, or you might come up with something entirely different.

Using a Screen Command

First, we'll show you how to add a button to your home page that logs out the user. In the screen designer, add a new screen command, as shown in Figure 14-14.

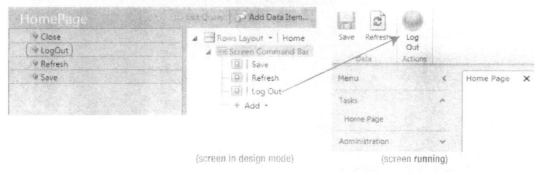

(screen in design mode)   (screen running)

Figure 14-14. Home page

You'll now need to do the following:

- Add a reference to the System.Windows.Browser assembly to your Client project (for HtmlPage).

- Add an Imports/Using statement to the Microsoft.LightSwitch.Threading namespace (for Dispatchers).

- Add an Imports/Using statement to the Microsoft.LightSwitch.Security namespace (for AuthenticationType).

Listing 14-12. Execution Code for the Log Out Button

VB:

File : OfficeCentral\Client\UserCode\HomeScreen.vb

```vb
Imports System.Windows.Browser
Imports System.Runtime.InteropServices.Automation
Imports Microsoft.LightSwitch.Threading
Imports Microsoft.LightSwitch.Security

Namespace LightSwitchApplication

    Public Class HomeScreen

        Private Sub LogOut_CanExecute(ByRef result As Boolean)
            result = (System.Windows.Application.Current.IsRunningOutOfBrowser = False)↵
                AndAlso↵
                (Application.Current.User.AuthenticationType =↵
                AuthenticationType.Forms)
        End Sub

        Private Sub LogOut_Execute()
            Dispatchers.Main.Invoke(↵
                Sub()
                    HtmlPage.Window.Navigate(
                        New Uri("LogOff.aspx", UriKind.Relative))
                End Sub)
        End Sub

    End Class

End Namespace
```

C#:

File : OfficeCentral\Client\UserCode\HomeScreen.cs

```csharp
using System.Windows.Browser;
using System.Runtime.InteropServices.Automation;
using Microsoft.LightSwitch.Threading;
```

```
using Microsoft.LightSwitch.Security;

namespace LightSwitchApplication
{
    public class Home
    {
        private void LogOut_CanExecute(ref bool result)
        {
            result = (System.Windows.Application.Current.IsRunningOutOfBrowser == false)
                && (Application.Current.User.AuthenticationType =↵
            AuthenticationType.Forms);
        }

    partial void LogOut_Execute()
        {
        Dispatchers.Main.Invoke(() =>
            {
                HtmlPage.Window.Navigate(
                    new Uri("LogOff.aspx", UriKind.Relative));
            });
        }
    }
}
```

Using a Navigation Menu Item

If you'd prefer to have a Log Out entry appear in the navigation menu, you can do this by adding a New Data Screen (see Figure 14-15), calling it LogOut, but leaving the Screen Data option set to (None).

Figure 14-15. Adding a new data screen

When you've added the LogOut screen, it'll appear in the navigation menu (see Figure 14-16).

Figure 14-16. Log Out navigation menu item

All that's left now is to do the following:

- Add some code to check whether the application is running in a browser, and also that Forms Authentication is being used.

- Add a reference to System.Windows.Browser (for HtmlPage).

- Add an Imports/Using statement to the Microsoft.LightSwitch.Threading namespace(for Dispatchers).

- Add an Imports/Using statement to the Microsoft.LightSwitch.Security namespace (for AuthenticationType).

- Set the result of the LogOut screen's CanRun method (see Listing 14-13), which will then show or hide the screen in the navigation menu. (There's no point having it visible in a nonbrowser application, or if Forms Authentication isn't being used.)

- Cancel the opening of the screen when the navigation item is clicked (by setting handled = true in the screen's Run method).

- Make the code to log the user out run instead.

Listing 14-13. Navigation Menu Logout Code

VB:

```
File : OfficeCentral\Client\UserCode\Application.vb

Imports System.Windows.Browser
Imports System.Runtime.InteropServices.Automation
Imports Microsoft.LightSwitch.Threading
Imports Microsoft.LightSwitch.Security

Namespace LightSwitchApplication
```

```vbnet
Public Class Application

    Private Sub LogOut_CanRun(ByRef result As Boolean)
        result = (System.Windows.Application.Current.IsRunningOutOfBrowser = False)↵
            AndAlso (Application.AuthenticationService.AuthenticationType↵
            = AuthenticationType.Forms)
    End Sub

    Private Sub LogOut_Run(ByRef handled as Boolean)
        Dispatchers.Main.Invoke( _
            Sub()
                HtmlPage.Window.Navigate(
                    New Uri("LogOff.aspx", UriKind.Relative))
            End Sub)

        handled = true
    End Sub
End Class

End Namespace
```

C#:

File : OfficeCentral\Client\UserCode\Application.cs

```csharp
using System.Windows.Browser;
using System.Runtime.InteropServices.Automation;
using Microsoft.LightSwitch.Threading;
using Microsoft.LightSwitch.Security;

namespace LightSwitchApplication
{
    public class Application
    {
        private void LogOut_CanRun(ref bool result)
        {
            result = (System.Windows.Application.Current.IsRunningOutOfBrowser ↵
                        == false)
                && (Application.AuthenticationService.AuthenticationType ==
                AuthenticationType.Forms);
        }

        partial void LogOut_Run(ref bool handled)
        {
            Dispatchers.Main.Invoke(() =>
                {
                    HtmlPage.Window.Navigate(
                        new Uri("LogOff.aspx", UriKind.Relative));
                });
```

```
            handled = true;
        }
    }
}
```

■ **Note** The LogOut screen's CanRun method and Run method are both located in the project's Client\UserCode\Application class, *not* in the Client\UserCode\LogOut class as you might expect.

Summary

In this chapter, you've learned what *authorization* is (as opposed to *authentication*), as well as when and how you'd use it in your LightSwitch application. Authorization is a pretty important part of your LightSwitch application.

We've shown you how, as a developer, you have several ways of controlling what a user can and can't do while using your program. This includes the following:

- Checking permissions at a table/entity set level
- Checking permissions at the entity property level

You also learned the following:

- How to secure various parts of your application by defining permissions
- That after deployment, an administrative user assigns permissions to roles
- That after deployment, an administrative user assign users to those roles
- That a user's *effective* permissions is the combination of permissions from each of the roles assigned to that user
- A handy technique (for developers of browser applications) to create a Log Out button, enabling the current user to log out of the application, and allowing a different user to log in

CHAPTER 15

Auditing What Your Users Do

Auditing is sometimes also called change tracking, but that's really only one part of the auditing process. Put simply, auditing is *who* did *what*, and *when* they did it. That can be adding, modifying, deleting, or even viewing data.

When you discover a problem with an entity's details, it's extremely helpful to be able to see who it was that added or edited the entity, and also when, in order to be able to ask questions about the information.

LightSwitch doesn't come with any out-of-the box way of tracking these details, so we need to create our own.

For some businesses it's just as important to know who's been *viewing* information as it is to know what changes have been made to it. Although a certain level of trust is involved when giving someone the permission required to add or modify data, keeping track of who's viewing that data can also be useful.

Audit logs can be used to catch those who use the system out of curiosity, rather than as part of their job, and those users could then be counseled, or disciplined, if necessary. It may even be required by law for a business to log who's accessing sensitive data.

We've seen several techniques for saving auditing information, some of which are fairly elaborate, but with a few clever techniques we've managed to reduce the complexity of the code to an absolute minimum by moving the majority of it to extension methods (see Listing 15-1), therefore reducing the amount of code needed to implement auditing in your project to just a few lines.

We've added the extension methods to the Utilities class library (in an Extensions namespace), so you'll be able to use this code in any LightSwitch project. Just remember to add a reference to it for any code that calls for it (as we explain later in the chapter, this will be LightSwitch's Server project) and to add an imports/using statement.

In this chapter, we'll describe two approaches for auditing the data that's inserted, or updated, in your application. We've called these the general and specific approaches. The main difference between the two approaches is where the audit data are saved:

- *General* (all audit details are stored in a single table).

- *Specific* (a separate audit table is used for each entity).

And, as with just about everything in life, there are pros and cons to each technique. It's pretty much a trade-off between convenience and functionality.

The advantage of the general approach is simplicity. This technique tracks changes to all of the tables in your application. You only need to add the auditing code into the save pipeline once. Any new table you add to your application will automatically be audited without you having to do anything more.

The specific technique allows you to choose the tables you want to audit. You can also create a relation between your actual table and the audit table. This allows you to easily create screens to view your audit data. However, this technique involves writing more code.

Figure 15-1 illustrates how these two techniques work. It shows what happens when the save button is clicked on a customer/order screen. We'll describe the methods that are illustrated in this diagram later in this chapter.

Of course, auditing is a wide subject area. If you're using attached SQL databases, auditing could also be implemented at the database level, using SQL triggers, so the methods we're describing here aren't the *only* ways to capture auditing information.

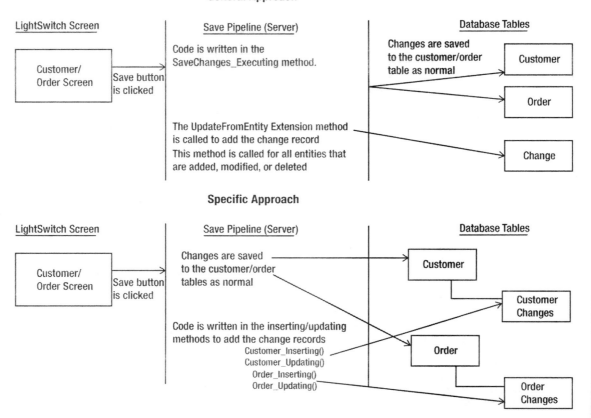

Figure 15-1. Auditing changes using the general and specific approaches.

▪ **Tip** While the code in this chapter intercepts the save pipeline to track changes that users make to the data, the query pipeline can also be intercepted to track who's viewing the data.

Basic Table Properties

You'll need to store your audit details in a table, and this is the most important part of both techniques. In the general approach, we'll create a table called change. When using the specific approach, we'll create separate change tables for each table you want to track.

The tables required for the two different approaches actually share quite a few basic properties (Table 15-1). We'll extend the schema of this table later when we describe the general and specific approaches in more detail.

Table 15-1. The Basic Schema of the Change Table

Property Name	Data Type	Description
Actioned	DateTime	The date and time that the change was recorded
Action	String	The type of change action—added, edited, deleted
ActionedBy	String	The person who saved the change
OldValues	String	The old values of any changed properties
NewValues	String	The new values of any changed properties

When you're auditing the creation of new records, OldValues will always be null. Therefore, make sure to uncheck the required checkbox for the OldValues property.

Figure 15-2 shows a screenshot of the final solution (using the general technique). It highlights the typical values that would be stored in the change table. In particular, you'll see how the OldValues and NewValues fields contain a concatenated list of all the properties that have changed for each entity.

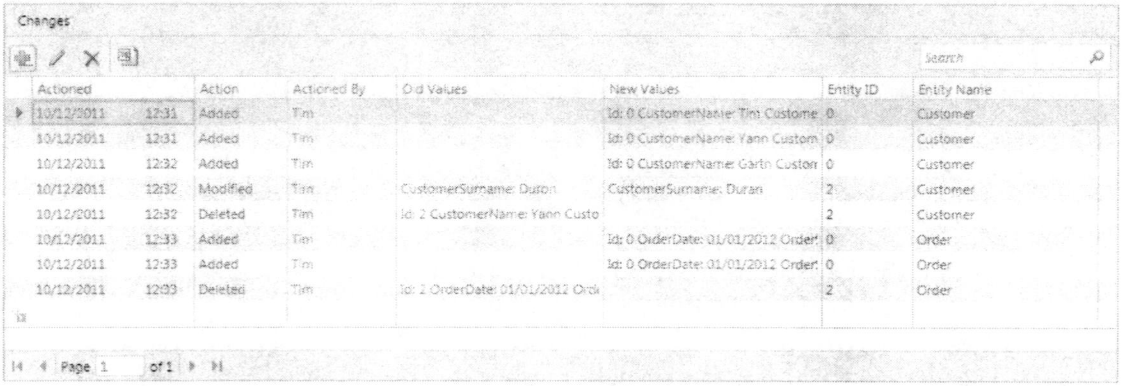

Figure 15-2. Screenshot based on the change table

The common code that you'll use for both techniques is shown in Listing 15-1. We've created the extension methods inside a new class library called Central.Utilities. Therefore, you'll need to have Visual Studio 2010 Professional or above installed (because the basic edition of LightSwitch doesn't support class libraries). If you only have the basic edition of LightSwitch, don't worry. You can add the IEntityObjectExtensions VB module or C# class directly into your server project. To work with the server project, you'll need to switch to File view using Solution Explorer.

Listing 15-1. Extension methods

VB:

```
File: Central.Utilities\Auditing\IEntityObjectExtensions.vb

Imports System.Runtime.CompilerServices
Imports System.Text
Imports Microsoft.LightSwitch
Imports Microsoft.LightSwitch.Details
Imports Microsoft.LightSwitch.Security

Namespace Extensions

    Public Module IEntityObjectExtensions

        <Extension()>
        Public Function StorageProperty(Of T As IEntityObject)(
            entityObject As T, name As String
                ) As IEntityStorageProperty

            'Here's how to check that entityObject isn't null
            If entityObject Is Nothing Then
                Throw New ArgumentNullException("entityObject")
            Else
                Return TryCast(
                    entityObject.Details.Properties(name),
                    IEntityStorageProperty)
            End If

        End Function

        <Extension()>
        Public Function TrackedProperties(Of T As IEntityObject)(
            entityObject As T) As IEnumerable(
                Of IEntityTrackedProperty)

            Return entityObject.Details.Properties.All.OfType(
                Of IEntityTrackedProperty)()

            'You can modify the results to exclude properties
            'Here's how you'd exclude the surname property
            'Return entityObject.Details.Properties.All.OfType(
            'Of IEntityTrackedProperty)().Where(
            'Function(x) x.Name.Contains("Surname") = False)

        End Function
```

```vbnet
<Extension()>
Public Sub GetChanges(entityObject As IEntityObject↵
    , ByRef oldValues As String↵
    , ByRef newValues As String↵
    , Optional valuesFormat As String = "{0}: {1}{2}"↵
    )

    Dim newResults = New StringBuilder
    Dim oldResults = New StringBuilder
    Dim properties =
        entityObject.TrackedProperties(excludedProperties)

    For Each p In properties
        Select Case entityObject.Details.EntityState
            Case EntityState.Added
                newResults.AppendFormat(valuesFormat↵
                    , p.Name, p.Value, Environment.NewLine)

            Case EntityState.Modified
                If (p.IsChanged = True) Then
                    oldResults.AppendFormat(valuesFormat↵
                        , p.Name, p.OriginalValue,↵
                        Environment.NewLine)
                    newResults.AppendFormat(valuesFormat↵
                        , p.Name, p.Value, Environment.NewLine)
                End If

            Case EntityState.Deleted
                oldResults.AppendFormat(valuesFormat↵
                    , p.Name, p.Value, Environment.NewLine)
        End Select
    Next

    'trim any trailing white space
    oldValues = oldResults.ToString.TrimEnd(Nothing)
    newValues = newResults.ToString.TrimEnd(Nothing)
End Sub

<Extension()>
Public Sub UpdateFromEntity(Of T As IEntityObject)(
        entityObject As T↵
    , changedEntity As IEntityObject↵
    , actioned As DateTime↵
    , user As String↵
    )
    Dim oldValues = ""
    Dim newValues = ""
    Dim action = changedEntity.Details.EntityState.ToString

    changedEntity.GetChanges(oldValues, newValues)
```

```
                With entityObject.Details
                    .Properties("Actioned").Value = actioned
                    .Properties("Action").Value = action
                    .Properties("ActionedBy").Value = user
                    .Properties("OldValues").Value = oldValues
                    .Properties("NewValues").Value = newValues
                End With
            End Sub

    End Module

End Namespace
```

C#:

File: Central.Utilities\Auditing\IEntityObjectExtensions.cs

```csharp
using System;
using System.Collections.Generic;
using System.Linq;
using System.Runtime.CompilerServices;
using System.Text;
using Microsoft.LightSwitch;
using Microsoft.LightSwitch.Details;
using Microsoft.LightSwitch.Security;

namespace Extensions
{
    public static class IEntityObjectExtensions
    {
        public static IEntityStorageProperty StorageProperty(
            this IEntityObject entityObject, string name)
        {
            //Here's how to check that entityObject isn't null
            if (entityObject == null)
            {
                throw new ArgumentNullException("entityObject");
            }
            else
            {
                return (entityObject.Details.Properties[name] as
                    IEntityStorageProperty);
            }
        }

        public static IEnumerable<IEntityTrackedProperty>
            TrackedProperties(
                this  IEntityObject entityObject)
        {
            return entityObject.Details.Properties.All()
                .OfType<IEntityTrackedProperty>();
```

```csharp
        //You can modify the results of this method to exclude properties
        //Here's how you would exclude the surname property
        //return entityObject.Details.Properties.All()
        //    .OfType<IEntityTrackedProperty>().Where (
        //     x=> x.Name.Contains ("Surname") == false );

    }

    public static void GetChanges(this IEntityObject entityObject↵
        , ref string oldValues↵
        , ref string newValues↵
        , string valuesFormat = "{0}: {1}{2}"↵
        )
    {
        var newResults = new StringBuilder();
        var oldResults = new StringBuilder();
        var properties =
            entityObject.TrackedProperties(excludedProperties);

        foreach (var p in properties)
        {
            switch (entityObject.Details.EntityState)
            {
                case EntityState.Added:
                    newResults.AppendFormat(valuesFormat↵
                        , p.Name, p.Value, Environment.NewLine);

                    break;
                case EntityState.Modified:
                    if (p.IsChanged == true)
                    {
                        oldResults.AppendFormat(valuesFormat↵
                            , p.Name, p.OriginalValue,↵
                                Environment.NewLine);
                        newResults.AppendFormat(valuesFormat↵
                            , p.Name, p.Value, Environment.NewLine);
                    }

                    break;

                case EntityState.Deleted:
                    oldResults.AppendFormat(valuesFormat↵
                        , p.Name, p.Value, Environment.NewLine);
                    break;
            }
        }

        //trim any trailing white space
        oldValues = oldResults.ToString().TrimEnd(null);
        newValues = newResults.ToString().TrimEnd(null);
    }
```

```
public static void UpdateFromEntity(
    this IEntityObject entityObject↵
    , IEntityObject changedEntity ↵
    , DateTime actioned↵
    , string user↵
    )
{
    var oldValues = "";
    var newValues = "";
    var action = changedEntity.Details.EntityState.ToString();

    changedEntity.GetChanges(ref oldValues, ref newValues);

    entityObject.Details.Properties["Actioned"].Value = actioned;
    entityObject.Details.Properties["Action"].Value = action;
    entityObject.Details.Properties["ActionedBy"].Value = user;
    entityObject.Details.Properties["OldValues"].Value = oldValues;
    entityObject.Details.Properties["NewValues"].Value = newValues;
}
}
}
```

The code shown includes four methods that we'll use in the general and specific approaches. These are summarized in Table 15-2.

Table 15-2. Description of Extension Methods

Method	Description
GetChanges	This method allows you to pass in an entity and two arguments called OldValues and NewValues (OldValues and NewValues are passed by reference). The OldValues parameter returns a concatenated list of the entity's old property values. The NewValues parameter returns a concatenated list of the entity's new property values.
UpdateFromEntity	This method contains the code that writes the audit information into the change (audit) table.
StorageProperty	This method takes in the string name of a property and returns the corresponding property (as an IEntityStorageProperty).
TrackedProperties	This helper method accepts an entity and returns its properties (as an IEntityStorageProperty).

When writing extension methods, it's good practice to check that the object that it extends isn't null. In the StorageProperty method, we perform a check on entityObject to make sure it isn't null. If it is, we'll throw an ArgumentNullException. It's a good idea to carry out the same checks on the remaining methods. However, we've left these out for the sake of brevity.

The TrackedProperties method returns all of the properties that belong to an entity. If you want to prevent certain properties from being audited, you can adapt this method as required. We've added a commented out section that shows you how to exclude properties named surname. We've hardcoded the value *surname*, but in practice you'll want to pass this value into the method to improve reusability. You could even create a string array, or IEnumerable<string>, to pass in a list of properties to exclude.

The General Approach

The general approach involves using a single table to hold the changes for *all* entities. Although it's quicker and easier to set up than using the specific approach, it has some downsides as well.

General Approach Pros

- You don't have to create a table for every entity for which you want to track changes.

- You can easily track deletions.

- You can view all changes to all entities in a single screen.

General Approach Cons

- No relations are possible between the entity table and the table that tracks its changes (depending on how you want to use the tracking data, it could result in more work to display it than if there were a relation between the two tables).

- The ID property value of an added entity is not available at the time of saving the entity. This means that it isn't possible to record the ID value that LightSwitch automatically generates for the added entity.

The General Changes Table

In addition to the shared basic properties listed earlier (Table 15-1), the general table will need two more properties. These are:

- EntityID (the ID of the entity that was changed).

- EntityName (the name of the entity type).

The table design is shown in Figure 15-3. Due to the fact that this table will be storing changes for more than one type of entity, it's not possible to create a relation between each entity and the change table. So instead, we'll store the entity's ID, along with the name of the entity's *type*.

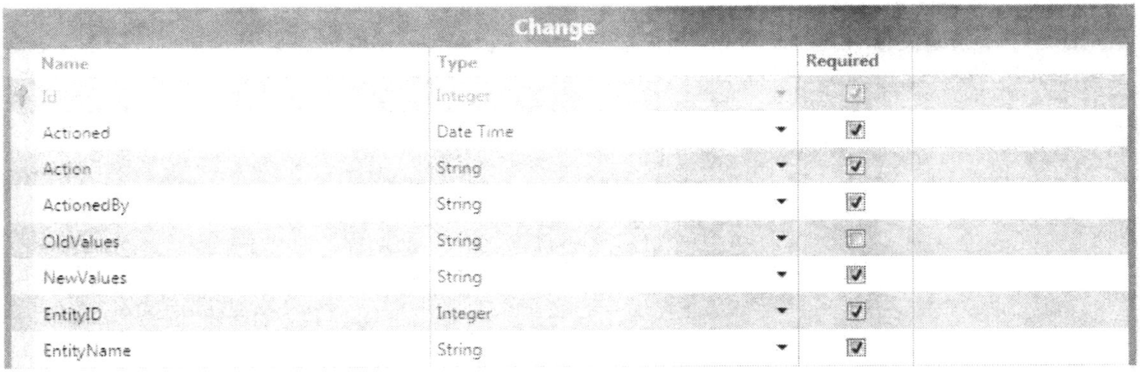

Figure 15-3. General changes table

■ **Note** We've added EntityID as an integer property because all intrinsic LightSwitch entities use integer IDs. An attached database could use another type, or even have a multikey. In this case, you might want to consider changing the data type of EntityID to string and adapt the general changes code as appropriate.

The General Changes Code

The code that we'll need to add to implement this approach will need to go in the ApplicationDataService class (see Listing 15-2).

The following example is designed to work with the tables you've created within LightSwitch. This is because the changes are tracked using the ID property of the table (LightSwitch automatically creates an ID property for every table so we know it always exists). If you're tracking the changes of entities in an attached SQL database, it's unlikely that all of your tables will contain a primary key field called ID. Therefore, you'll need to adapt the code shown as necessary. You'll also need to add the code to the data service class that relates to your external data source (rather than ApplicationDataService).

The ApplicationDataService class is located in the Server project. The easiest way to get there is by right-clicking the ApplicationData data source in Solution Explorer, then selecting View Code.

We'll be intercepting the save pipeline (also known as the *submit* pipeline), just before the changes are persisted to the data store. One of the down sides to tracking changes this way is that entities that are being added won't have an ID value at this point yet, so the ID will always be zero.

The first code method (SaveChanges_Executing):

- Saves the current date/time (so that all changes have the same timestamp).

- Saves the username of whomever is logged in to the application.

- Specifies the SaveEntityChanges method for each entity that has changed. Changed entities include added, modified, and deleted entities.

In order to retrieve the current date/time, we've used the DateTime.Now method. However, you could use the HttpRequest.Timestamp instead. This value will be consistent throughout any point in the request/pipeline processing. This might be helpful if you need to refer to a common date/time value within different methods inside your save pipeline code.

The second code method (SaveEntityChanges) is used by the first to:

- Add a new record to the changes table.

- Retrieve and store the entity's ID (if the entity's not being added, as discussed earlier).

- Retrieve and store the name of the entity's type (remember, there is no relation defined with the entity itself).

- Retrieve and store both the original values and the changed values of the changed properties.

Listing 15-2. General approach code

VB:

```
File: Server\UserCode\ApplicationDataService.vb

Imports System.Text
Imports Microsoft.LightSwitch
Imports Microsoft.LightSwitch.Details
Imports Central.Utilities.Extensions

Namespace LightSwitchApplication

    Public Class ApplicationDataService

        Private Sub SaveChanges_Executing()

            Dim actioned = Now
            Dim actionedBy = Me.Application.User.Name

            For Each entity In Me.Details.GetChanges
                SaveEntityChanges(entity, actioned, actionedBy)
            Next

        End Sub

        Private Sub SaveEntityChanges(↵
                entity As IEntityObject↵
            , actioned As DateTime↵
            , actionedBy As String↵
            )

            Dim changeRecord =
                Me.DataWorkspace.ApplicationData.Changes.AddNew

            With changeRecord
                Dim idProperty = entity.StorageProperty("Id")
```

```
                    .EntityID = CInt(idProperty.Value)
                    .EntityName = entity.Details.DisplayName

                    changeRecord.UpdateFromEntity(entity, actioned, actionedBy)
                End With
            End Sub

    End Class

End Namespace
```

C#:

File: Server\UserCode\ApplicationDataService.cs

```csharp
using System;
using System.Text;
using Microsoft.LightSwitch;
using Microsoft.LightSwitch.Details;
using Central.Utilities.Extensions;

namespace LightSwitchApplication
{
    public partial class ApplicationDataService
    {
        partial void SaveChanges_Executing()
        {

            var actioned = DateTime.Now;
            var actionedBy = this.Application.User.Name;

            foreach (var entity in this.Details.GetChanges())
            {
                SaveEntityChanges(entity, actioned, actionedBy);
            }

        }

        private void SaveEntityChanges(IEntityObject entity⏎
            , DateTime actioned⏎
            , string actionedBy⏎
            )
        {
            var changeRecord =
                this.DataWorkspace.ApplicationData.Changes.AddNew;

            var idProperty = entity.StorageProperty("Id");

            changeRecord.EntityID = (int) idProperty.Value;
            changeRecord.EntityName = entity.Details.DisplayName;
```

```
            changeRecord.UpdateFromEntity(entity, actioned, actionedBy);
        }
    }
}
```

This completes the code that you need to write to audit changes using the general approach. As a bonus, any new tables you create will be audited without you having to write any extra code. The only thing that remains is to build some screens based on the changes table. This will allow you to view the change records.

The Specific Approach

Although the more specific approach to tracking changes is a bit more work to set up than the general approach, it does have some advantages.

Specific Approach Pros

- There is no *single*, potentially monolithic, table that holds all of the change data (with a reasonable number of entities in your application, even a moderate amount of change activity can result in a large number of records in the tracking table).

- Having a single auditing table will become a bottleneck for all updates. Having separate auditing tables for each entity increases data independence and removes this bottleneck.

- Each entity can have its own *collection* of related changes.

Specific Approach Cons

- You have to add a separate table for each entity you want to track.

- You have to write code for each entity (a small amount of code, but it still has to be written).

- You can only view changes for one type of entity at a time (unless you use a custom RIA service to join the tables together).

In the example that follows, we'll create a relation between the table we want to track and the audit table. The advantage of doing this is that all change records are expressly related to the original entity. You can also easily create a screen that shows the entity and all related change records by using the built-in navigation properties—you wouldn't need to write any complicated queries to do this.

However, a disadvantage of creating a relation is that you can't track deletions. This is because there isn't an entity to associate the change record with. Also, you wouldn't be able to delete an entity without first deleting any associated change records. This wouldn't be very useful if you needed to retain all historical change records.

To overcome these disadvantages, you could choose not to create the relation. Instead, you could audit the ID and type names in the same way that was shown in the general approach.

The Specific Changes Table

If you want to create a relation between the table you want to track and the change table, you'll need to add one more property to the change table that was shown in Table 15-1. This extra property will be a navigation property to an actual related entity (instead of an ID and type name as in the general approach).

The example we'll show you is for the Person entity, but the process is the same for any other entity you might want to track changes for. Just create another change table and create the appropriate relation between it and the entity. The PersonChange table that we'll use is shown in Figure 15-4.

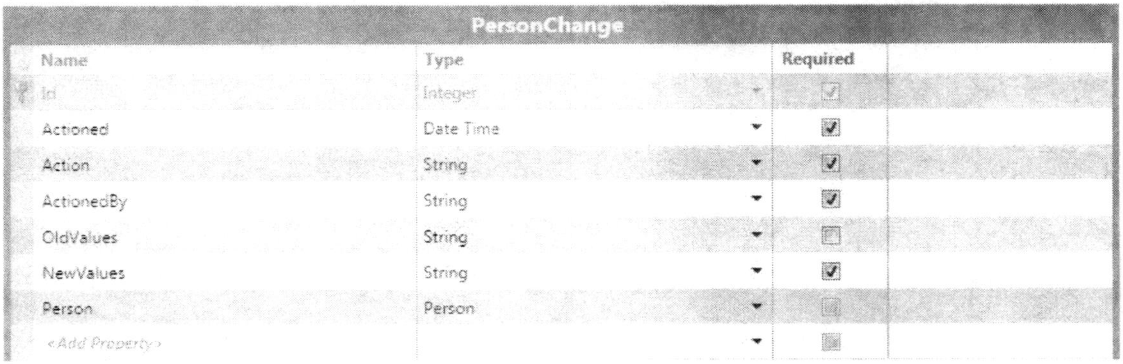

Name	Type		Required	
Id	Integer	▾	☑	
Actioned	Date Time	▾	☑	
Action	String	▾	☑	
ActionedBy	String	▾	☑	
OldValues	String	▾	☐	
NewValues	String	▾	☑	
Person	Person	▾	☐	
‹Add Property›		▾	☐	

Figure 15-4. Example of a specific change table

In our example, the change table will have a Many-1 relation defined between it and its related table. Although we've named our table PersonChange, you could choose a naming convention that prefixes all change tables with the word audit (e.g., audit_Person). The advantage of this is that all audit tables will be grouped together in the auto completion lists that you'll find in the code editor.

Each entity being tracked will have a navigation property (we've called it PersonChanges), which will be a collection of related changes (Figure 15-5).

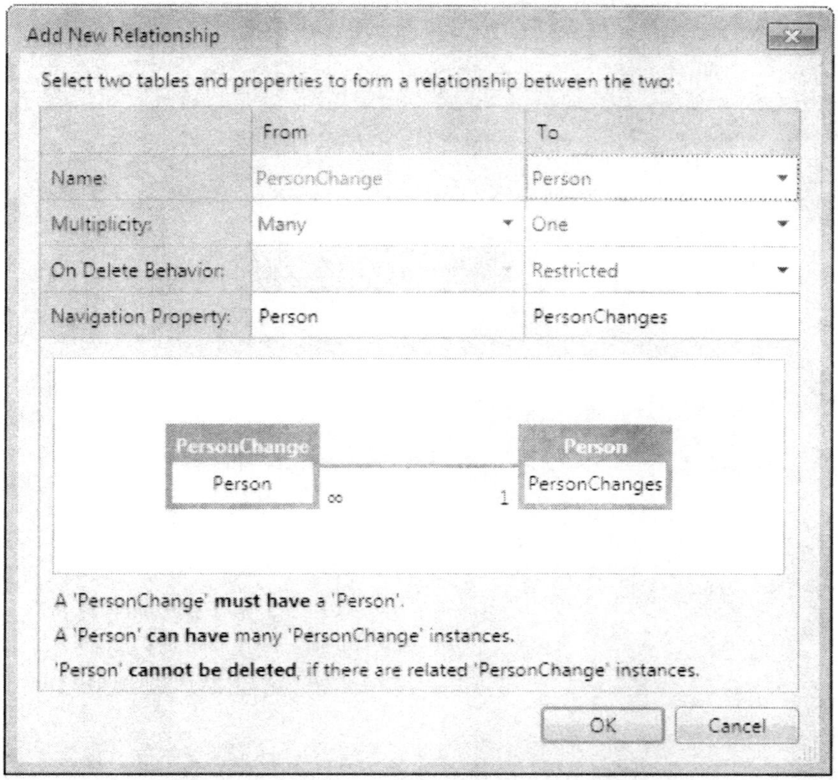

Figure 15-5. Person-PersonChange relation

After you've made your table changes, you'll also need to make a couple of adjustments to the code that implements the entity's tracking. We'll now show you what these are.

The Specific Changes Code

The code that we'll need to add to implement this approach will also go in the ApplicationDataService class (see Listing 15-3). Once again we'll be intercepting the save pipeline, just before the changes are persisted to the data store; whereas in the previous approach we added code to the data source's Saving_Executing method, this time we'll be adding code to the entity's inserting and updating methods. So, for this example, it'll be the People_Inserting and People_Updating methods.

The code for specific changes is actually even simpler than the code for the general changes was, thanks to the extension methods. Each of the two entity event methods:

- Adds a new record to the entity's change table.
- Retrieves and stores both the original values and the changed values of the changed properties.

Listing 15-3. Specific approach code

VB:

File: Server\UserCode\ApplicationDataService.vb

```vb
Imports System.Text
Imports Microsoft.LightSwitch
Imports Microsoft.LightSwitch.Details
Imports Central.Utilities.Extensions

Namespace LightSwitchApplication

    Public Class ApplicationDataService

        Private Sub People_Inserting(entity As Person)
            Dim changeRecord = entity.PersonChanges.AddNew()
            changeRecord.UpdateFromEntity(entity, Now, Me.Application.User)
        End Sub

        Private Sub People_Updating(entity As Person)
            Dim changeRecord = entity.PersonChanges.AddNew()
            changeRecord.UpdateFromEntity(entity, Now, Me.Application.User)
        End Sub

    End Class

End Namespace
```

C#:

File: Server\UserCode\ApplicationDataService.cs

```csharp
using System;
using System.Text;
using Microsoft.LightSwitch;
using Microsoft.LightSwitch.Details;
using Central.Utilities.Extensions;

namespace LightSwitchApplication
{
    public partial class ApplicationDataService
    {
        partial void People_Inserting(Person entity)
        {
            var changeRecord = entity.PersonChanges.AddNew();
            changeRecord.UpdateFromEntity(
                entity, DateTime.Now, this.Application.User.Name);
        }

        partial void People_Updating(Person entity)
```

```
        {
            var changeRecord = entity.PersonChanges.AddNew();
            changeRecord.UpdateFromEntity(
                entity, DateTime.Now, this.Application.User.Name);
        }
    }
}
```

The change record is added using the syntax `entity.PersonChanges.AddNew()`. In this example, `entity` refers to the person entity and `PersonChanges` refers to the navigation property. Creating the change record in this way automatically relates the change record with the person entity.

This completes the code you need to write to audit changes using the specific approach. As with the general approach, you can now build some screens to view your change records.

Summary

In this chapter we showed you why auditing data makes good business sense. Knowing who did what, and when, can help solve any data issues (such as who added a record, or who changed a property's value) and may even be required by law for sensitive information.

We explained:

- That auditing can be both tracking changes that users make as well as who's viewing the data.

- That SQL triggers can be used to capture audit information for attached databases.

- How to add audit records into a single table, or multiple tables, in a reusable fashion.

Auditing is carried out by writing code in the save or query pipeline. The methods in these pipelines are executed when data operations are carried out on the server. During this time, you can insert audit records into a change table.

You can store all audit records in a single table, or you can create separate audit tables for each table you want to track. In this chapter, the single table approach has been called the *general approach* and the multitable approach the *specific approach*.

We've showed you how to track changes when records are added, updated, or deleted in your application. If you want to track changes when data are read, you'd add similar code in the query pipeline. We've also highlighted how you can improve reusability by writing extension methods that are added to a separate class library. This is especially useful if you want to reuse the same auditing logic in more than one LightSwitch project.

This chapter has demonstrated the basis of how to carry out auditing. Depending on your application, you might need to adapt the code shown to better suit your needs. For example, you might want to audit attached tables that contain combination primary keys. The code shown in this chapter provides a good platform for you to customize, extend, and better fulfill your auditing requirements.

PART 6

Deployment

CHAPTER 16

Deploying Your Application

Now that you've built the perfect LightSwitch application, the only thing left to do is to make it available to your users. Following all the tips and tricks you've learned in this book, your users will surely be impressed.

As you already know, you can use LightSwitch to create desktop or browser applications. These can be deployed in either two-tier or three-tier mode. You can even deploy to Windows Azure. This results in several distinct deployment scenarios, each requiring a unique set of tasks to be carried out.

Table 16-1 gives you an overview of the various deployment options. It highlights the tasks that would have to be performed in each scenario.

Table 16-1. *Deployment Options and Tasks and the Tasks that Need to Be Performed*

(Application Type)	Web		Desktop		
(Hosted On…)	IIS	Azure	End User Machine	Azure	IIS
Client Tasks					
Install Silverlight	✓	✓	✓	✓	✓
Install Prerequisites			✓		
Server Tasks					
Configure IIS	✓				✓
Install ASP.NET 4	✓				✓
Install Prerequisites	✓				✓
Database Tasks					
Install SQL Server	✓		✓		✓
Create Database	✓	✓	✓	✓	✓
Create SQL User	✓	✓	✓	✓	✓

This chapter covers quite a bit of content, so we'll start by giving you a summary of what's to come.

The first decision you'll need to make is whether to choose a two-tier or a three-tier deployment. In simplistic terms, your application type will determine this choice.

Browser applications must be deployed as a three-tier application. Desktop applications can be deployed as either two-tier or three-tier applications.

If you choose to deploy a three-tier application, you'll need to configure a web server. Your web server needs to have IIS, ASP.NET 4, and the LightSwitch prerequisites installed. Later in this chapter we'll show you how to carry out the following IIS tasks:

- Set up IIS6 on Windows 2003 and IIS7 on Windows 2008.

- Install and configure ASP.NET 4

- Install the LightSwitch prerequisites using either the CD or Web Platform Installer tool.

- Add support for publishing and packaging using the Web Deploy tool.

- Set up Secure Sockets Layer (SSL) and application pools.

If you choose to deploy a two-tier desktop application, IIS isn't required and you can skip the entire section on "Setting Up Your Web Server."

Whatever route you choose, you'll need to perform some SQL Server tasks. At the very least, this involves creating a SQL Server database and a SQL Server login.

After you've carried out the server-related tasks, you can begin to focus on deploying the application you've written. LightSwitch includes a Deployment Wizard that guides you step by step through this process. In this chapter, we'll describe the pages that are shown by the wizard including the steps to:

- Configure database and authentication settings.

- Add application prerequisites (such as the .NET Framework) to a two-tier deployment package.

- Digitally sign your application with a certificate.

When the Deployment Wizard finishes, we'll show you the final steps that are needed to move the output onto your server. This includes:

- How to publish the output directly onto your IIS server.

- How to package your application into a zip file and install it manually.

- How to perform a manual XCOPY deployment.

Another way to avoid the complications of setting up IIS is to deploy your application onto Windows Azure. This makes your application available over the Internet and is particularly suitable if you don't want to limit the use of your application to your local intranet.

However, you'll be charged for bandwidth and compute time, so you'll need to weigh how much this might cost you—it could turn out to be quite expensive! You also might not want your data to be stored in the Cloud, perhaps for legal or security reasons. This is something you should take into consideration.

To end this chapter, we'll show you how to deploy your application into Windows Azure. We'll show you how to use the Azure web portal and also explain:

- What a hosted service is and how to create one.

- How to create a storage account and how to create an SQL Azure database.

- The steps you'll need to follow to publish your application onto Azure.

Note Deploying applications can sometimes be tricky. Chapter 17 on troubleshooting contains additional information that can help you if you encounter any deployment issues.

Deployment Fundamentals

The key feature that LightSwitch offers is the Deployment Wizard. This guides you step by step though the deployment process. At the end of the process, your application will either be published or a set of setup files will be produced.

Figure 16-1 illustrates a flow chart that shows the pages that are shown in the wizard. You'll need to carry out some prerequisite work if you want to follow certain routes through the wizard. We've indicated these on the chart by keying the stages with a *PR* (prerequisite) code.

We'll describe the wizard steps in more detail, but before we do so, we'll start by explaining some of the underlying concepts. This will help you to make informed choices when you reach the Deployment Wizard. In this initial section, we'll cover:

- Application and client topologies,

- The difference between publishing and packaging,

- Client installation requirements.

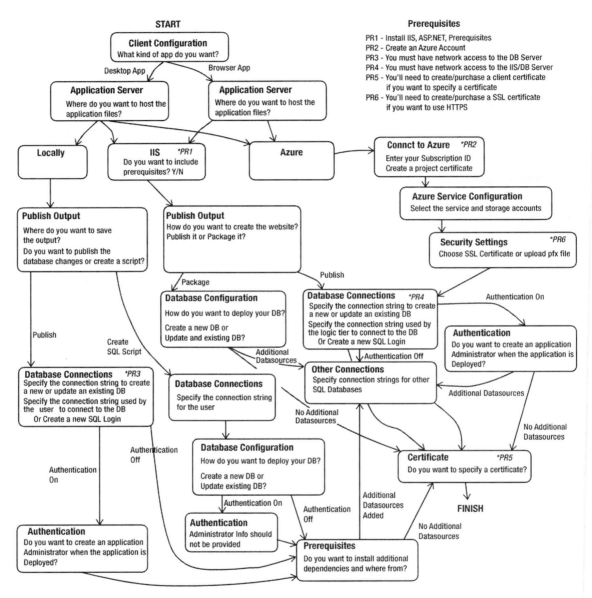

***Figure 16-1.** Deployment Wizard workflow*

Application Topologies

By now, you have learned that the LightSwitch application can run either inside a browser or outside a browser as a desktop application. The technical term for this is the *client topology*. Figure 16-2 shows how you would set this up in the properties pane of your application.

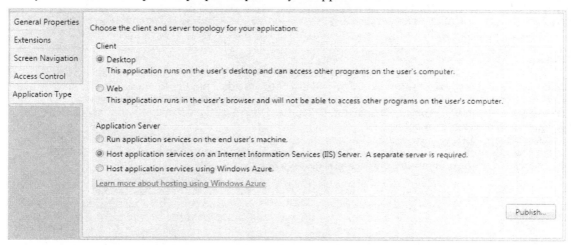

Figure 16-2. *The application type settings window*

Beneath the client settings (shown in Figure 16-2), you can find three more radio options that allow you to choose the *application topology*. These settings specify where the LightSwitch application services are installed and run.

Desktop Applications

When you deploy a desktop application, you can choose to install the LightSwitch application services on the end user's machine. Typically, the database is installed on a separate database server, and this type of deployment is known as a *two-tier deployment*. Running the application services on the end user machine simplifies deployment because it avoids having to set up IIS, and this is the place where some of the worst problems are often encountered.

The disadvantage of a two-tier deployment is that you'll need to install your application on every machine where you want to use it. This option is therefore more suitable for applications with a small number of users.

When you're performing a two-tier deployment, you can also choose to install the database on the end user machine using a local instance of SQL Server or SQL Server Express. This means that everything is installed and run from a single machine. This type of setup is ideal for a single-user application. If you need to install your application on multiple machines or have multiple users, it's best to install your database on a separate server rather than hosting it on an end user's machine.

At this point, you might wonder what *application services* are. As you've learned, LightSwitch applications rely on web-based technologies such as ASP.NET and RIA services. Since these services are traditionally hosted inside IIS, something needs to take their place if those services are not available.

Two-tier LightSwitch applications are therefore hosted using a process called VslsHost.exe. This executable is installed in your profile directory when you install your application using the setup.exe that you'll create. On a Windows XP machine, for example, VslsHost.exe would be installed into a subfolder of the folder C:\Documents and Settings\Tim\Local Settings\Apps\2.0\.

VslsHost.exe is essentially a web server that runs on the workstation. Just like IIS, VslsHost creates working files in the following temporary location:
C:\WINDOWS\Microsoft.NET\Framework\v4.0.30319\Temporary ASP.NET Files\root.

VslsHost is responsible for the *server* portion of your application. The client part is hosted using the Silverlight out of browser runtime. This process is called SLLauncher.exe and it is typically installed in the folder C:\Program Files\Microsoft Silverlight.

If you choose not to host the application services locally, you can host them on an IIS server or Windows Azure. This type of setup would be called a *three-tier* desktop deployment. The advantage of a three-tier application is that users can run your application by simply pointing a web browser to the URL where it's been installed. Apart from installing Silverlight, there isn't anything else that needs to be carried out on the client's machine.

Desktop applications are installed locally on the end user machine using Microsoft ClickOnce. Unlike browser applications, they can be uninstalled using the Programs and Features or Add and Remove Programs option in the Control Panel (shown in Figure 16-3).

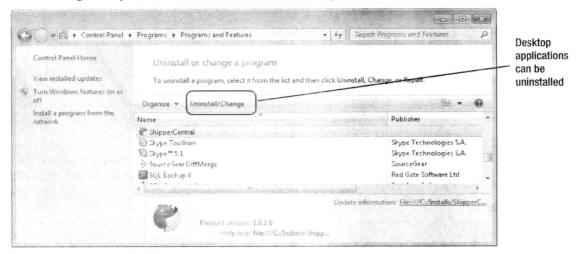

Figure 16-3. Uninstalling a desktop application

Browser Applications

Web applications must be deployed as three-tier applications and therefore must be hosted using IIS or Windows Azure. When you select the web client option from the Application Type settings window, the Run Application Services on the End User's Machine option is automatically grayed out.

Publishing vs. Packaging

In a three-tier setup, you can choose to either publish or to package your application (as shown in Figure 16-4).

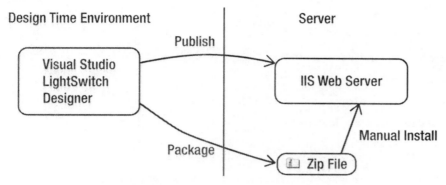

Figure 16-4. Publishing vs. packaging

If you choose to publish, your application is deployed directly from Visual Studio onto your IIS server. It's very easy to publish an application but more work is involved in preparing your IIS server beforehand. The supported platforms for publishing include Windows Server 2008, Windows Server 2008 R2, Windows Server 2003, or Windows 7.

The second option is to package your application. Packaging produces a set of install files that can be manually copied and installed on your server.

Packaging an application is a simpler option compared to the publishing. You don't have to carry out as much work in IIS or struggle to make Visual Studio talk to IIS. For example, publishing will fail if a firewall blocks the ports that are required for it to work (port 8172 by default). If you're developing your application on a machine that doesn't belong to the same domain as the server you want to deploy to, packaging is a better choice.

Client Requirements

The client deployment story is relatively straightforward. Since LightSwitch clients are Silverlight based, you'll only need to install the Silverlight 4.0 runtime on your client.

If a user attempts to run a LightSwitch browser application without the runtime installed, a page is displayed that prompts the user to download the Silverlight runtime from the official Microsoft web site.

For those in corporate environments, the Silverlight runtime can be installed using group policy, SMS (Microsoft Systems Management Server), or some other software distribution mechanism.

Some companies have policies in place that block Silverlight or Adobe Flash. If Silverlight has been blocked, your LightSwitch application simply will not work. Silverlight 4.0 must be installed on the client for your application to function.

Setting Up Your Web Server

In this section, we'll show you how to set up IIS and how to configure your web server. If you want to deploy a three-tier application and not use Windows Azure, this is a necessary requirement. If you're setting up a two-tier desktop application, you can skip this section and move straight to the "Deployment Wizard" section.

The version of IIS that you'll set up will depend on the server operating system you've installed. When you set up a web server, we recommend carrying out the following tasks in the sequence shown:

1. Install IIS

2. Install ASP.NET 4

3. Install LightSwitch prerequisites and the Web Deploy Tool

4. Configure Application Pools

5. Optionally set up SSL

We'll now describe each of these steps in more detail.

Setting Up IIS7

IIS7 is the web server you'll find in Windows 2008, Windows 7, or Windows Vista. The steps that you'll need to carry out are slightly different, depending on the operating system you've chosen. This section explains how to install and configure IIS7 on the above operating systems.

Setting Up IIS in Windows 2008

In Windows Server 2008, IIS7 is installed by adding the Web Server (IIS) role. To do this, open Server Manager by going to Administrative Tools Server Manager. In the Roles Summary group, open the Add Roles Wizard by clicking the Add Roles link (shown in Figure 16-5). The Add Roles Wizard includes a page that allows you to select the Web Server (IIS) role.

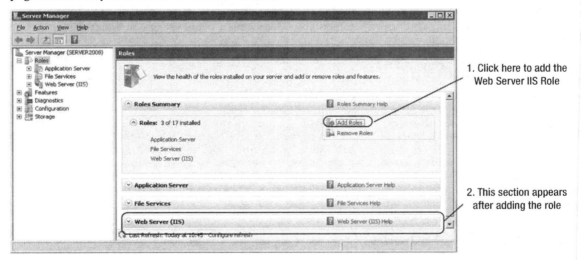

Figure 16-5. Adding the IIS server role

When you complete the Add Roles Wizard, the Web Server (IIS) link appears inside the Roles group that you'll find beneath the Roles Summary group. Clicking this link opens the IIS Summary page (shown in Figure 16-6).

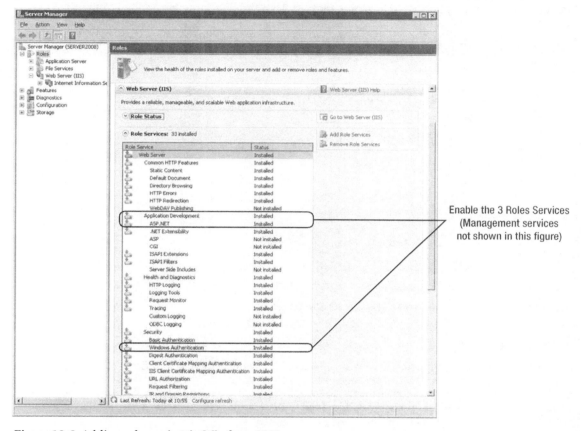

Enable the 3 Roles Services
(Management services
not shown in this figure)

Figure 16-6. *Adding role services in Windows 2008*

In the Role Services pane, enable the following role services:

- Management Service
- Application Development ➤ ASP.NET
- Security ➤ Windows Authentication

Setting Up IIS7 in Windows 7

When setting up IIS7 on Windows 7 (or Windows Vista), a slightly different process is used, compared to Windows Server 2008.

Instead of adding the Web Server role, IIS is installed using the Windows Control Panel. After opening the Control Panel, select Programs and Features and choose the option to Turn Windows features on or off. When the Windows Features dialog appears (shown in Figure 16-7), select the Management Service, Application Development ➤ ASP.NET, and Security ➤ Windows Authentication options.

Figure 16-7. Turning Windows features on or off in Windows 7

Setting Up IIS6

IIS6 is the web server that's included in Windows 2003. It's added by going into Control Panel Add/Remove Programs. In the Add/Remove Programs dialog that appears, click the Add/Remove Windows Components button that appears on the left-hand side. This opens the Windows Component Wizard. In the Windows Components section, select Application Server and click the Details button to open up the dialog shown in Figure 16-8.

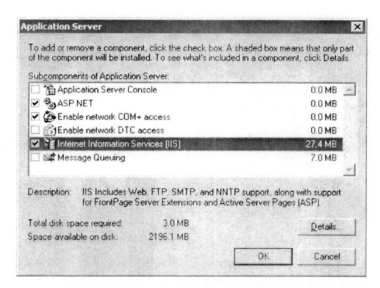

Figure 16-8. Enabling IIS6 on Windows 2003

After installing IIS6, make sure you've installed ASP.NET and the LightSwitch prerequisites (we'll explain how to do this shortly). Now open Internet Information Services (IIS) Manager and switch to the Web Service Extensions view. Make sure you've allowed the ASP.NET 4 Web Service Extension, as shown in Figure 16-9.

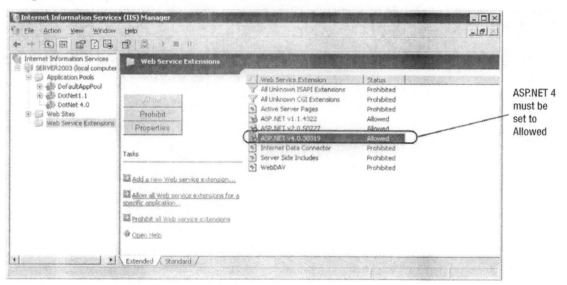

Figure 16-9. Enable the ASP.NET 4 Web Service Extension

Setting Up IIS Application Pools

When you create a web site in IIS, it gets added to the *default application pool*. Application pools improve reliability by isolating the applications that run within IIS. If a web site that belongs in an application pool crashes, it won't affect the other web sites that belong to other application pools. It therefore makes good sense to deploy each LightSwitch application into a separate application pool.

Each application pool also runs under a specific security context and this enables you to configure the logic tier of your application to connect to your SQL Server database using Windows authentication. This concept is illustrated in Figure 16-10.

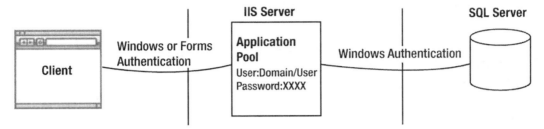

Figure 16-10. Set up an application pool to Windows authenticate to SQL Server

To create a new application pool, open Internet Information Services (IIS) Manager and right-click the Application Pools node on the left-hand navigation menu. A right-click context menu option allows you to create a new application pool, as shown in Figure 16-11. You must set up the Application Pool to use version 4 of the .NET Framework.

In IIS7, it is also preferable to choose the Integrated Managed Pipeline mode, as opposed to the Classic mode. Classic mode is primarily designed for legacy code, which may not run properly in integrated mode. Your LightSwitch server will run more efficiently and yield better performance if you set the IIS7 pipeline mode to integrated.

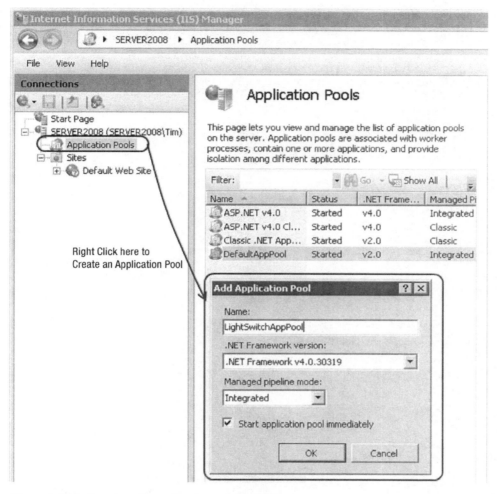

Figure 16-11. Creating an application pool in IIS7

After you've deployed your web site, you can configure it to use the new Application Pool that you've created by modifying the web site properties in IIS Manager.

Configuring SQL Server Windows Authentication

SQL Server can be set up to use two types of authentication: SQL Server authentication and Windows authentication. If you choose to use SQL Server authentication, you can create your own login and password in SQL Server and hard code these credentials into the database connection string. Some information technology departments regard Windows authentication as being more secure because credentials do not need to be persisted along with the application. If you want to learn more about the pros and cons of SQL Server authentication vs. Windows authentication, you can refer to the following TechNet article: http://technet.microsoft.com/en-us/library/ms144284.aspx.

To use Windows authentication, you'll first need to create a Windows domain user. If your IIS Server and SQL Server are on the same computer, you might find it easier to use a local Windows user, rather than a domain user (particularly if you don't have permission to create new domain users).

Now select the application pool you're using for your application. Bring up the Advanced Settings and choose the Custom Account radio button (Figure 16-12). Use the Set button to specify the Windows user you want to use.

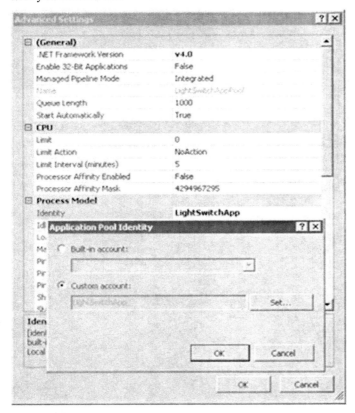

Figure 16-12. Changing the application pool identities

The Windows user you've specified must have read permissions on the folders where your LightSwitch application will be saved. You'll need to set the appropriate NTFS (New Technology File System) permissions. It's also a good idea to add the user to the local IIS_IUSRS group to avoid any problems with permissions. This grants access to web and ASP.NET resources that might be needed.

In the authentication section of your web site, you might also need to set up the NTLM provider or carry out a few additional steps to enable support for Kerberos authentication if you run into permission problems. The following TechNet article describes this in more detail: http://technet.microsoft.com/en-us/library/dd759186.aspx.

Finally, you'll need to create a SQL Server login for your Windows user using SQL Server Management Studio. You'll also need to configure object permissions to the tables in your application and any other tables that are used by the ASP.NET membership provider. The easiest way to get started is to add your user into the following roles:

- `aspnet_Membership*`
- `aspnet_Roles*`
- `db_datareader`
- `db_datawriter`
- `public`

Configuring Secure Sockets Layer

When application services are hosted in IIS, the LightSwitch client communicates with the web server (the logic tier) using the HTTP protocol. The data transfer between the client and logic tier takes place in clear text. Someone monitoring the local network traffic could eavesdrop on this communication and watch the data that are exchanged between the client and server. If forms authentication is used in your LightSwitch application, the username and password credentials of someone logging in could be exposed using this technique (we discussed why you want to use forms authentication in Chapter 13).

As with all web traffic, this vulnerability can be mitigated by encrypting your data using the HTTPS protocol, which uses an encrypted tunnel called Secure Sockets Layer.

To set up SSL, you need to install an SSL certificate for your web server. This certificate is used to verify the identity of the server, and it contains the keys that are used for encryption. You can either purchase a certificate from a third party company such as VeriSign or use an internal certificate server if your company has such an infrastructure in place. After receiving the server certificate, you can configure SSL using the Server Certificates and Site Binding options in IIS Manager.

The server certificate you install in IIS must be valid. The server name on the certificate must correctly match the server name, it must not be past its expiry date, and it must be signed by a trusted certificate authority.

If you use a LightSwitch browser application that is installed on a web server with an invalid certificate, the behavior depends on the browser you use, but it generally warns you of the error and then allows you to continue.

However, if you connect an out-of-browser desktop application to a web server with an invalid certificate, the security model in Silverlight prevents your application from working. The only solution in this instance is to resolve the certificate error.

If you want to be extra secure, you can force your application to use HTTPS and redirect any HTTP traffic to the HTTPS endpoint instead. You can configure this by modifying your `web.config` file as shown in Listing 16-1. When deployed, this file is found in the root folder of the ASP.NET web site, and during development, it can be found in the `ServerGenerated` folder.

Listing 16-1. Web.config setting to force SSL

```
<appSettings>
<add key="Microsoft.LightSwitch.RequireEncryption" value="true" />
```

■ **Note** You can find out more about setting up SSL on the official IIS7 and Microsoft TechNet web sites.

http://learn.iis.net/page.aspx/144/how-to-set-up-ssl-on-iis/

www.microsoft.com/technet/prodtechnol/WindowsServer2003/Library/IIS/56bdf977-14f8-4867-9c51-34c346d48b04.mspx

---

ASP.NET Configuration

ASP.NET needs to be installed on your IIS server for LightSwitch to work. This is done by installing the Microsoft .NET 4 Framework redistributable.

You can obtain the .NET 4 redistributable by using the Web Platform Installer (which we'll describe soon) or alternatively, you can download it separately from the Microsoft web site (www.microsoft.com/download/en/details.aspx?id=17718).

If .NET 4 is already installed on your server and you install IIS afterward, ASP.NET may not register itself correctly.

If you need to register ASP.NET in IIS, you can use the aspnet_regiis.exe command. To run this command, open a command prompt and change to the following directory:

- On a 32-bit server, change to:
  <WindowsDir>\Microsoft.NET\Framework\v4.0.30319\

- On a 64-bit server, change to:
  <WindowsDir>\Microsoft.NET\Framework64\v4.0.30319\

You can now run the command aspnet_regiis.exe –i to re-register ASP.NET. You can also follow the same process to reinstall or repair ASP.NET if necessary.

LightSwitch Prerequisites

LightSwitch includes a Prerequisites setup utility. You'll need to run this on your web server to install the necessary LightSwitch components. These components are needed by LightSwitch, and your application won't run correctly unless you install the prerequisites.

These prerequisites can be found on the LightSwitch installation CD. You can find them in the folder WCU\VSLSServerPrereqs. The two files in this folder are:

- vs_vslsserverprereqs_x86.exe (this is the 32-bit version)
- vs_vslsserverprereqs_x64.exe (this is the 64-bit version)

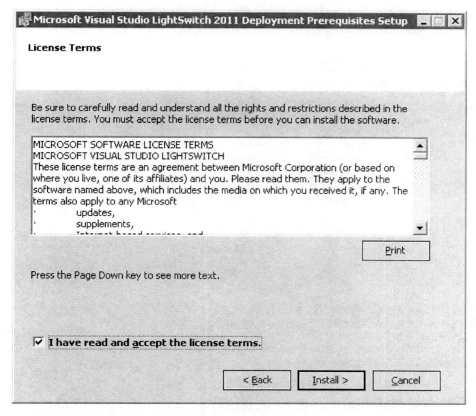

Figure 16-13. Running the prerequisites setup

After running the prerequisites (shown in Figure 16-13), the files are installed into the following folder: C:\Program Files\Microsoft Visual Studio 10.0\LightSwitch\1.0\Tools.

Listing 16-2 shows the files that are created by the prerequisites utility. Several subfolders are created that contain the localized DLLs (for example de, es, and fr). Listing 16-2 only shows the DLLs that are created in the German de folder. The other folders contain localized versions of the same files.

Listing 16-2. Files installed by prerequisites

```
Tools\Microsoft.LightSwitch.AppBridge.dll
Tools\Microsoft.LightSwitch.Base.Server.dll
Tools\Microsoft.LightSwitch.CodeMarker.dll
Tools\Microsoft.LightSwitch.dll
Tools\Microsoft.LightSwitch.ExportProvider.dll
Tools\Microsoft.LightSwitch.ManifestService.dll
Tools\Microsoft.LightSwitch.SecurityAdmin.exe
Tools\Microsoft.LightSwitch.Server.dll
Tools\System.ServiceModel.DomainServices.EntityFramework.dll
Tools\System.ServiceModel.DomainServices.Hosting.dll
Tools\System.ServiceModel.DomainServices.Server.dll
Tools\de
Tools\es
Tools\fr
Tools\it
Tools\ja
Tools\ko
Tools\ru
Tools\zh-Hans
Tools\zh-Hant
Tools\de\Microsoft.LightSwitch.ExportProvider.Resources.dll
Tools\de\Microsoft.LightSwitch.ManifestService.Resources.dll
Tools\de\Microsoft.LightSwitch.Resources.dll
Tools\de\Microsoft.LightSwitch.SecurityAdmin.Resources.dll
Tools\de\Microsoft.LightSwitch.Server.Resources.dll
```

Microsoft Web Platform Installer

If you don't have access to the LightSwitch installation CD, the prerequisites can be installed by downloading and running the free Web Platform Installer tool (or Web PI as it's known). You can find this through the official Microsoft web site (www.microsoft.com/web/downloads/platform.aspx). After running Web PI, select the Products group and choose Tools from the left-hand pane, as shown in Figure 16-14.

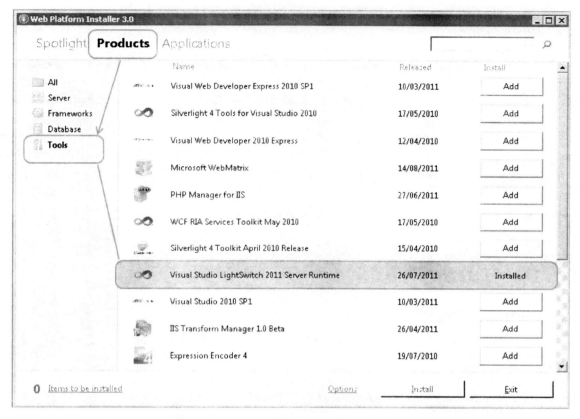

Figure 16-14. Installing the prerequisites using Web PI

Web PI provides a simple way for you to set up a server. If you want to install SQL Server Express on your server, Web PI can also do this for you.

Microsoft Web Deploy Tool

If you want to publish LightSwitch applications onto your server, you'll need to install the Microsoft Web Deploy tool. This also adds support for installing packages you've created using the Deployment Wizard from Visual Studio.

The Web Deploy tool is included as part of the LightSwitch prerequisites. It can also be obtained by downloading it from the IIS web site (www.iis.net/download/WebDeploy).

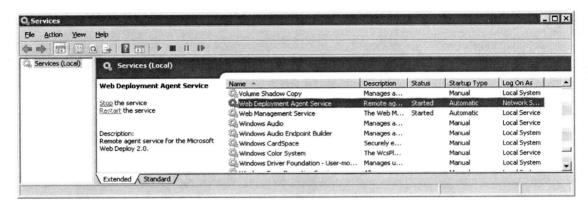

Figure 16-15. *The Web Deployment Agent Service must be started*

The Web Deploy tool installs a Web Deployment Agent Service. For publishing to work, it's important to ensure that this service is started (shown in Figure 16-15). The installer sets the startup type of this service to automatic. But if you experience problems publishing your application, you should manually check that the service is started.

Deployment Wizard

Now that you understand the principles and know how to set up a server, we'll show you how to use the LightSwitch Publish Application Wizard (or Deployment Wizard as we'll call it).

You can start the wizard by right-clicking your project in Solution Explorer and selecting the Publish menu option. At this point, the initial page prompts you to select the client topology (Figure 16-16).

This figure also shows the warning message that appears if the active configuration is set to Debug. When publishing an application for production, the active configuration should be set to Release using the dropdown that appears in the Visual Studio toolbox.

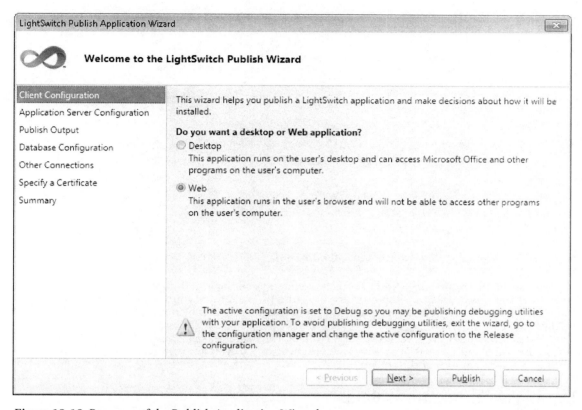

Figure 16-16. Page one of the Publish Application Wizard

After choosing whether or not you want to deploy a Desktop or Web application, you will need to specify where you want to host the server components. As mentioned earlier, there are two or three options you can choose from (shown in Figure 16-17).

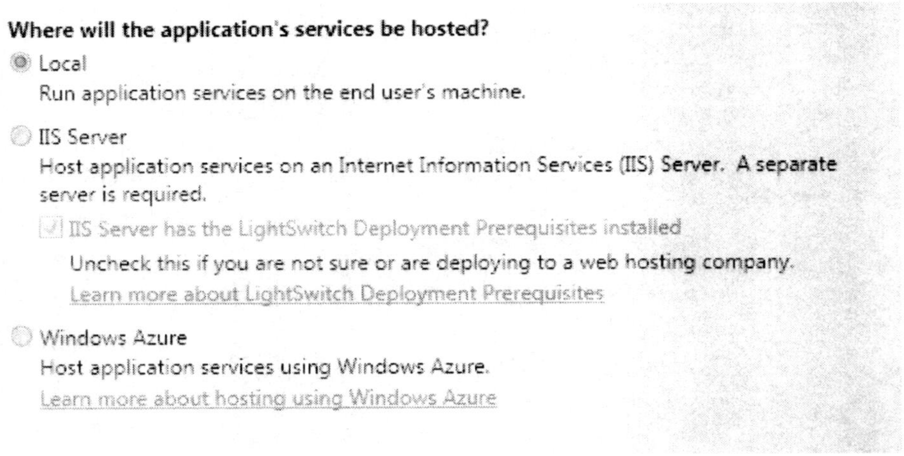

Where will the application's services be hosted?

⦿ Local
Run application services on the end user's machine.

◯ IIS Server
Host application services on an Internet Information Services (IIS) Server. A separate
server is required.

☑ IIS Server has the LightSwitch Deployment Prerequisites installed

Uncheck this if you are not sure or are deploying to a web hosting company.
Learn more about LightSwitch Deployment Prerequisites

◯ Windows Azure
Host application services using Windows Azure.
Learn more about hosting using Windows Azure

Figure 16-17. Page two of the Publish Application Wizard

The rest of the wizard allows you to enter the remaining settings. At this point, it might be worth
referring to the flow chart that we showed you in Figure 16-1 to remind yourself of the steps that are
shown in the wizard. At the end of process, your application will either be published or a set of setup files
will be produced.

Most of the screens you'll encounter are intuitive. The Azure publishing process will be covered
toward the end of this chapter. We'll now cover some of screens you'll encounter in the wizard and we'll
begin with the database-related screens.

Database Connections Page

If you choose to publish your application, you'll reach a Database Connections page as shown in Figure
16-18.

This page allows you to specify two connection strings. The first connection string is used by the
wizard at *publish time* to create and/or update your intrinsic database.

The user connection string is used by the application during runtime to connect to the intrinsic
database. In a three-tier application, the user connection string is used by the IIS to connect to the
database.

If you click the '…' buttons that you'll find to the right of the connection string textboxes, a
Connection Properties dialog opens up. This allows you to create a connection to your database, and the
dialog also includes a test button to check that your connection works. When you OK this dialog, the
connection string textbox is populated with the database connection you've specified.

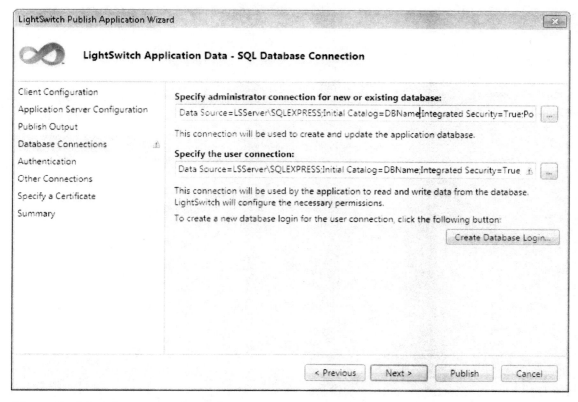

Figure 16-18. Database connection dialog

Figure 16-18 illustrates a warning against the user connection string. This is because you're not allowed to specify a user connection string that uses Windows authentication (i.e., Integrated Security). The connection string has to use SQL Server authentication, and the Create Database Login button can be used to create an SQL login. This button opens a dialog that allows you to specify a login name and password for your new login. When you OK this dialog, the login is created immediately using the administrator connection you've specified, rather than at the end of the publishing wizard.

If you choose a two-tier deployment and choose the option to create an SQL script, the administrator connection textbox will not be shown because the wizard does not need to connect to the database server.

Database Configuration Page

If you choose to package your application, the Database Configuration page is presented (Figure 16-19).

Using this dialog, you can choose the option to either create a new intrinsic database or update an existing database.

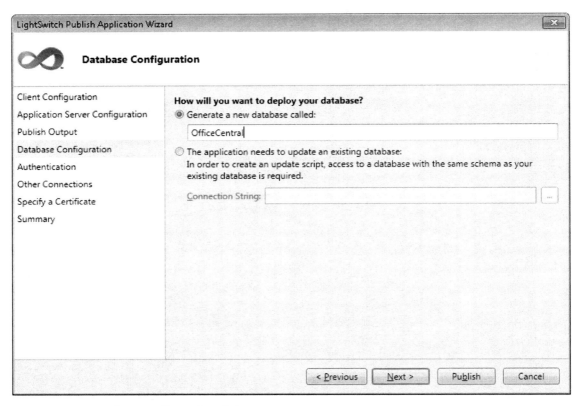

Figure 16-19. Database configuration dialog

You would typically choose the option to update an existing database when updating an application you have already deployed. When you choose this option, a connection string needs to be specified. The wizard uses this to compare your new schema to your existing schema and creates an update script.

You might wonder why the wizard doesn't prompt you for database security credentials at this point. The reason for this is because you are prompted for these credentials when you actually run the package.

Prerequisites Page

If you choose a two-tier deployment, you can add additional components into your setup package using the page shown in Figure 16-20. Adding prerequisites can improve the end user install experience because the installer won't fail if any required components are not found.

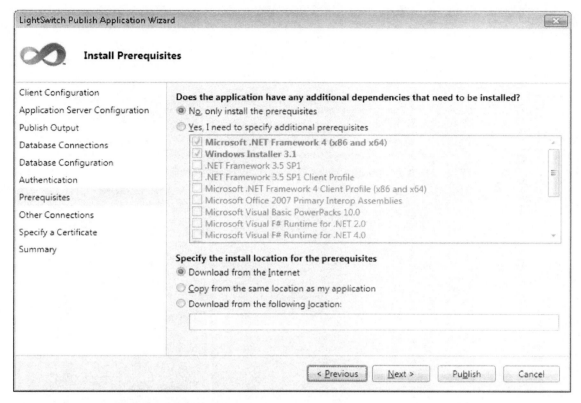

Figure 16-20. Install prerequisites dialog

You can specify additional prerequisites by choosing the "Yes" radio button. If you do this, the wizard automatically selects the .NET Framework 4 redistributable and Windows Installer 3.1 checkboxes. The .NET 4 Framework is required by LightSwitch, and Windows Installer is needed to install the .NET 4 Framework.

The final set of radio buttons allows you to specify the install location for your prerequisites. You can select the option to download from the Internet if you want to reduce the file size of your setup package.

The LightSwitch wizard doesn't allow you to include your own prerequisites. For example, Microsoft SQL Server Express 2008 is an option that is shown in the list. If you want to include the R2 version of SQL Server 2008 Express instead, there isn't an option for you to do this.

Authentication Page

If you've chosen to use authentication in your application, the Application Administrator page allows you to specify the LightSwitch administrator. As we showed you in Chapter 13, enabling authentication allows you to determine the identity of the logged in user and allows you to secure your application by specifying users, groups, and permissions.

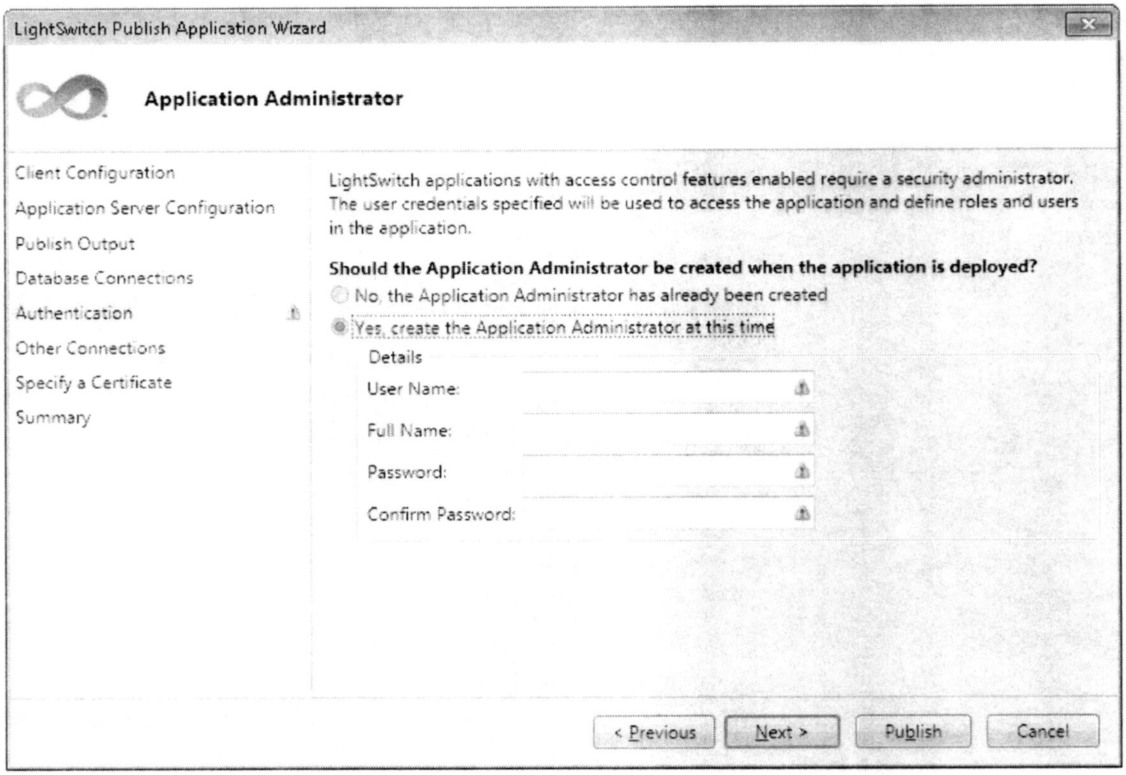

Figure 16-21. Application administrator dialog

Figure 16-21 shows the page that appears when forms authentication is chosen. If your application uses Windows authentication, the full name and password textboxes are not shown. You'll only be prompted to enter a domain username.

If you're updating an application you've already deployed, you would select the radio option that specifies an application administrator has already been created.

If you're deploying a two-tier application and choose the option to create an SQL script, the wizard prevents you from creating an administrator. You have to use the SecurityAdmin.exe utility instead during the actual installation.

Certificate Page

In all the deployment scenarios, you can optionally specify a certificate. But what's the purpose of a certificate and why would you want to add one?

The certificate page allows you to digitally sign the XAP file. The purpose of the XAP file was described in Chapter 2, but in essence, it's the Silverlight application that is downloaded to the end user.

When a user installs a two-tier desktop application you've created, signing the XAP file verifies that the setup package comes from you and that it hasn't been tampered with.

If you choose not to sign your application, a warning is shown to the user when your application is installed. This warning states that the publisher cannot be verified and that your application may be harmful (Figure 16-22). The only way to prevent this warning from appearing is to specify a certificate.

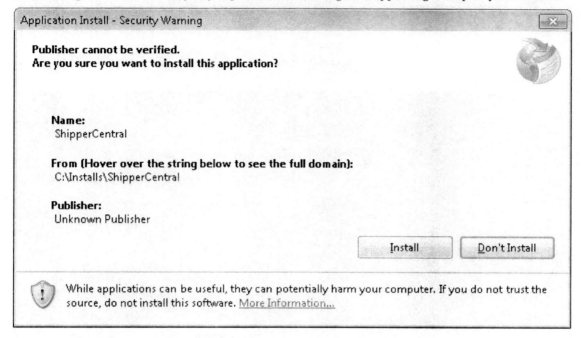

Figure 16-22. Dialog shown during installation

Figure 16-23 shows the page in the wizard that you would use to specify a certificate. Just like the SSL certificates, which were described earlier, you can purchase one from a third party company such as VeriSign or use an internal certificate server if your company has such an infrastructure in place.

When signing the XAP file, you can also choose to create your own self-signed test certificate. However, such a certificate should only really be used for testing purposes since the validity period will be short.

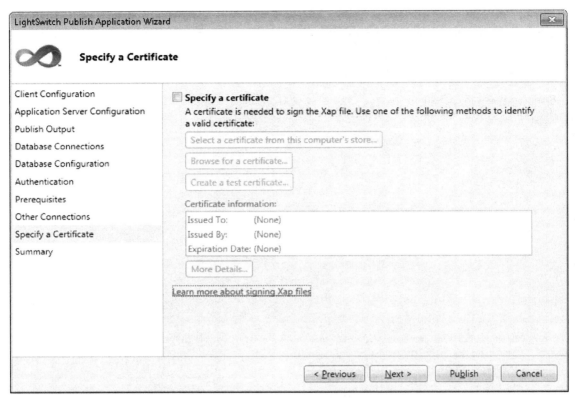

Figure 16-23. Dialog for specifying a certificate

You can use a command line tool called makecert to create a self-signed certificate. You can find out more about this command, and the command line switches you'll need to use, at the following Microsoft Developer Network page: http://msdn.microsoft.com/en-us/library/bfsktky3%28v=vs.80%29.aspx.

Installing the Packages

If you choose to produce a package or a two-tier application, a set of files are created. The following section describes how to install these files onto your server and/or client computers.

Two-Tier Desktop Installation

After completing the steps in the wizard, a set of files are generated (shown in Listing 16-3). A file called Install.htm contains a set of instructions you can read for additional information.

The steps that you need to follow are:

- Install the SQL database
- Change the database connection string

- Install your application

- Set up the initial user

Listing 16-3. *Files created by the wizard*

```
ShipperCentral\CreateUser.sql
ShipperCentral\files.txt
ShipperCentral\Install.htm
ShipperCentral\setup.exe
ShipperCentral\ShipperCentral.application
ShipperCentral\ShipperCentral.sql
ShipperCentral\ShipperCentral.zip
ShipperCentral\Application Files
ShipperCentral\Application Files\bin
ShipperCentral\Application Files\ClientAccessPolicy.xml
ShipperCentral\Application Files\default.htm
ShipperCentral\Application Files\ShipperCentral.exe.manifest
ShipperCentral\Application Files\Silverlight.js
ShipperCentral\Application Files\vslshost.exe
ShipperCentral\Application Files\vslshost.exe.config
ShipperCentral\Application Files\Web
ShipperCentral\Application Files\web.config
ShipperCentral\Application Files\Web\Manifests
ShipperCentral\Application Files\Web\ShipperCentral.Client.xap
ShipperCentral\Application Files\Web\Manifests\Microsoft.LightSwitch.Server.Manifest.dll
ShipperCentral\Application Files\bin\Application.Common.dll
ShipperCentral\Application Files\bin\Application.Server.dll
ShipperCentral\Application Files\bin\Application.ServerGenerated.dll
ShipperCentral\Application Files\bin\ApplicationDefinition.lsml
```

Database Tasks

The output produced by the wizard contains an SQL script called `<YourApplication>.sql`—in our example, this file is called `ShipperCentral.sql`. This script creates the database, tables, stored procedures, and all other objects that are needed to support your application. You'll need to run this script on your database server to install your database. The script can be executed using the `sqlcmd` command line tool or by using SQL Server Management Studio.

If you've installed a basic instance of SQL Server Express without the Management Tools, `sqlcmd` is the method you would choose. By default, this is installed in the folder `Program Files\Microsoft SQL Server\100\Tools\Binn`. On a 64-bit computer, this will be `Program Files(x86)` rather than `Program Files`.

To use `sqlcmd`, open a command prompt and navigate to the directory where it's installed. Now run the command shown in Listing 16-4. `ShipperCentral.sql` should be replaced with the name of your SQL file, and *.\SQLExpress* should be replaced with the name of your database server.

Listing 16-4. *Installing the script file using sqlcmd*

```
sqlcmd.exe -i ShipperCentral.sql -S .\SQLExpress
```

By default, sqlcmd connects to an SQL Server using Windows authentication. If you need to connect using SQL authentication, you can use the -U and -P switches to pass in your username and password.

If you choose to install the SQL script using SQL Server Management Studio, make sure to place your query window into SQLCMD Mode by using the option you will find under the Query menu. The script won't run correctly if you fail to do this.

Set the Database Connection String

Having installed the database, the application connection string needs to be modified to point to the database you've installed.

Locate the web.config file in the Application Files subdirectory (shown in Listing 16-3).

Open the file in Notepad and edit the connection string value in the <connectionStrings> section. Listing 16-5 illustrates the section you should look for in the web.config file. If you've defined additional data sources in your application, the connection strings for those databases can also be found in the same section of the web.config file.

Listing 16-5. Modifying the web.config file

```
<add name="_IntrinsicData" connectionString="Data Source=SERVERNAME\SQLEXPRESS;Initial
Catalog=MyApplication;Integrated Security=True;Pooling=True;Connect Timeout=30;User
Instance=False" />
```

Replace SERVERNAME with the name of your database server, and replace MyApplication with the name of your application.

Run Setup.exe

The wizard creates a file called setup.exe in the publish output location (shown in Listing 16-3). Run this program on the end user machine to install your application. If you've specified any prerequisites during the wizard, these will also be installed by setup.exe.

Setting Up Your Administrative User

If you choose to deploy a database script in the publish wizard (rather than publishing the database directly), you'll need to provide the default administrator login for your application using the Security Admin utility. Producing a database script in the wizard is handy when the computer you're publishing on doesn't have network access to the target SQL Server.

You can find this utility on your development machine in the following location: C:\Program Files\Microsoft Visual Studio 10.0\LightSwitch\1.0\Tools\Microsoft.LightSwitch .SecurityAdmin.exe.

The utility is also installed by the LightSwitch prerequisites, which was shown earlier.

To run the utility, open a command prompt and navigate to where the utility is installed. If your application is set to use Forms authentication, run the command as shown in Listing 16-6.

Listing 16-6. Running LightSwitch.SecurityAdmin—Forms authentication

```
Microsoft.LightSwitch.SecurityAdmin.exe /createadmin /user:username /password:password
/fullname:user'sfullname /config:pathtowebconfig
```

You'll need to point the utility to your web.config file using the config switch.
The username, password, and fullname arguments are also required.

If Windows authentication is used instead, run the listing as shown in Listing 16-7. The user switch needs to be specified in the format domainname\username, and unlike forms authentication, a password does not need to be supplied.

Listing 16-7. Running LightSwitch.SecurityAdmin—Windows authentication

```
Microsoft.LightSwitch.SecurityAdmin.exe /createadmin /user:domainname\username
/fullname:user'sfullname /config:pathtowebconfig
```

Three-Tier Desktop

If you select the option to create a three-tier desktop application, a single zip file is produced (shown in Listing 16-8).

Listing 16-8. Files created by the wizard

```
ShipperCentral\ShipperCentral.zip
```

After copying this file onto your server, you can install your application using IIS Manager. To do this, open IIS Manager, navigate to your web server using the left-hand pane, and select the Install option from the right-click context menu. The Install Application dialog appears, as shown in Figure 16-24. This initial page allows you to review the files that will be installed.

This includes an SQL script for deploying the intrinsic database, the option to create an IIS application, and the option to install the actual web files. You'll want to select all of these options.

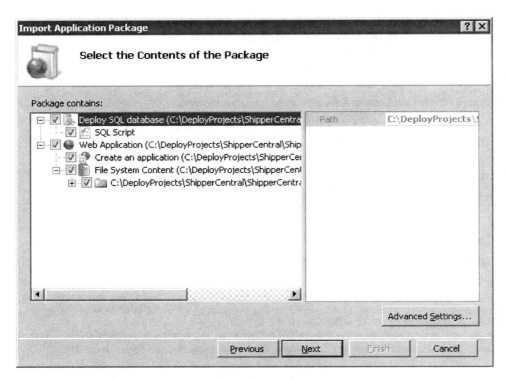

Figure 16-24. Import application package dialog—first page

The next page (shown in Figure 16-25) allows you to specify the database connection strings.

The initial Connection String textbox is used by the import tool to connect to a database server and to install or update the intrinsic database.

The next set of textboxes are used by IIS at runtime to connect to the intrinsic database. The import tool expects you to use SQL Server authentication and therefore, DatabaseUserName and DatabaseUserPassword textboxes are provided. If you want to use Windows authentication, you'll need to modify the web.config manually after the import tool finishes and set up an application pool in IIS, as described earlier.

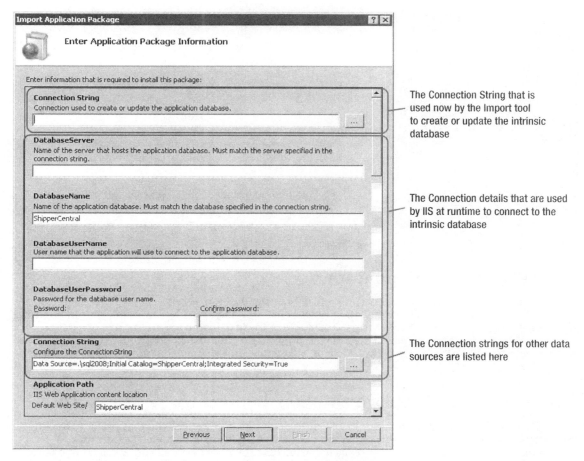

Figure 16-25. Import application package—database connection strings

After completing the steps in the import tool, your application will be installed into IIS. You may want to double check that the IIS settings have been set up correctly. For example, you might want to check that the application belongs in an application pool that is configured to use .NET 4.

If everything worked correctly, you can open a web browser and navigate to the web address where your application is installed. An installation page appears, similar to the one shown in Figure 16-26. Clicking the button installs the out-of-browser application and creates a desktop icon. Your three-tier desktop deployment is now complete.

Figure 16-26. Out-of-browser application install page

Three-Tier Browser Application

A three-tier browser installation is very similar to a three-tier desktop install.

Just like a desktop install, the installation wizard creates a single zip file. This is installed in IIS using the same process as above, and the dialogs shown during the installation are identical.

When you navigate to the web address of your application after installation, your actual application will be shown. Unlike the two-tier setup, you won't see a placeholder page that prompts you to install the application.

Three-Tier Manual Deployment

Although the wizard provides a rich graphical way to deploy an application, you may prefer to deploy your three-tier application manually, rather than creating a zip file using the Web Deploy tool.

Some corporate information technology departments prefer not to install additional components such as Web PI or the Web Deploy tool on production servers. Performing a manual deployment will suit such scenarios well.

Deploying ASP.Net Web Site

Fortunately, performing a manual deployment isn't difficult. A LightSwitch application is simply an ASP.NET web site that uses a Silverlight client. Therefore, deploying a LightSwitch application is no more difficult than deploying any other ASP.NET web site.

In Chapter 2, you learned about the various files that make up a LightSwitch application. The ServerGenerated project contains the ASP.NET web site, and when you do a "build" in LightSwitch, the ASP.NET project is built into the 'bin\debug' or 'bin\release' folder depending on your build type. The files from the bin folder can then be copied onto your IIS server. You would then set up the web site manually using IIS manager. This would involve creating an application and configuring it to use an application pool that targets the .NET 4 framework.

SQL Server Connection String

The database connection string for your database is specified in the web.config file, which is found in root folder of your web site.

As shown earlier in the two-tier deployment example (Listing 16.5), this file can be modified using Notepad. Search for the ConnectionStrings section and modify the connectionString value for the _IntrinsicData entry. If you've specified additional data sources in your application, you'll need to modify the connection string for those too.

IIS7 ZIP File Deployment

Rather than deploying straight to a server, some developers prefer to publish onto to their own development computer.

This allows you to test the install, and once you're ready, the LightSwitch application can be exported from IIS (shown in Figure 16-27) and imported into your server.

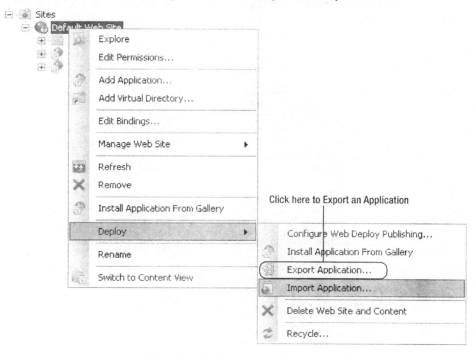

Figure 16-27. Exporting an application from IIS7

Before exporting, you can carry out additional tasks on your local copy such as setting permissions or adding extra files to your solution. The export includes the changes you make and generates a zip file.

You can then copy the zip file onto your production server and install the package using the import option, which you'll also find beneath the right-click Deploy menu item.

For this to work, you will need to install the Web Deploy tool onto both your development machine and your server.

Deploying Data

During development time, you might have entered data into tables that you've created in the intrinsic database. Although the publishing wizard deploys the schema of your database, it won't deploy any data you've added during debug time.

Earlier on, you saw how the publish wizard creates an SQL script that contains the schema of your database. The easiest way to deploy data during setup is to append SQL statements to the end of that file to insert your data.

If you want to recover the data that you've entered into your intrinsic database during design time, you can attach your MDF file using SQL Server Management Studio (as described in Chapter 2). Management Studio includes a feature that enables you to script out the data in your tables. To do this, right-click your database in object explorer. Start up the Script Wizard by selecting Tasks ➤ Generate Scripts. When you reach the options page, set the Script Data option to true. When the wizard completes its run, you can copy the SQL statements that have been generated when inserting the data and append them to the end of your deploy script.

Updating an Application

Updating an application is very simple. You can update an application you have already deployed by running the Deployment Wizard again. Each time you run the Deployment Wizard, LightSwitch automatically increments the version number of your application.

In a three-tier setup, you can simply deploy your updated application over the original installation. The new version will be automatically used by browser clients. If you've deployed a desktop application, the client will detect that an updated version is available and will install it.

If you've made any changes to your database schema, the wizard can create SQL change scripts for you using the Database Configuration page.

Deploying to Azure

A great feature about LightSwitch is that it allows you to easily deploy applications onto Windows Azure. Azure is a Cloud-based service that offers many benefits. It's ideal if you want to make your application available over the Internet and don't want to worry about the difficulties of setting up and maintaining a public facing web server.

To get started with Azure, you'll need to sign up for an Azure account. You can do this from the Windows Azure web site (www.microsoft.com/windowsazure/). You'll also find the pricing details on this web site.

After creating an account, you can configure and manage the Azure services via the Windows Azure Web Portal.

The tasks you'll need to carry out in the Azure portal are:

- Create a hosted service
- Create a storage account
- Set up a SQL Azure database

After that, you can publish your application from LightSwitch by using the Deployment Wizard. We'll now describe these steps in further detail.

Setting Up Azure in the Web Portal

Before you can publish your LightSwitch application, you'll need to carry out a few steps on the Azure web portal. First, you'll need to make a note of your *subscription ID*. Your subscription ID is a globally unique identifier (GUID) that is used to uniquely identify your Azure account. We'll now show you how to set up a hosted service and storage account and configure a database server.

Creating a Hosted Service

Hosted services are used in Azure to host your files and applications. If you're new to Azure, think of a hosted service as a web site. You'll need to create one to host your LightSwitch application.

Using the Azure web portal, you can create, run, suspend, and delete hosted services. Management certificates are also added to hosted services. These are used to secure client access to your Azure resources.

To get started, you'll need to create a hosted service from within the Azure web portal. On the homepage, you'll find a button on the toolbar that allows you to create a new hosted service. Click this button to open the dialog shown in Figure 16-28. Within this dialog, specify a name and URL. In the deployment options group, you can select the do not deploy option.

After you've created your hosted service, you can find your subscription ID by viewing the properties of service you've created.

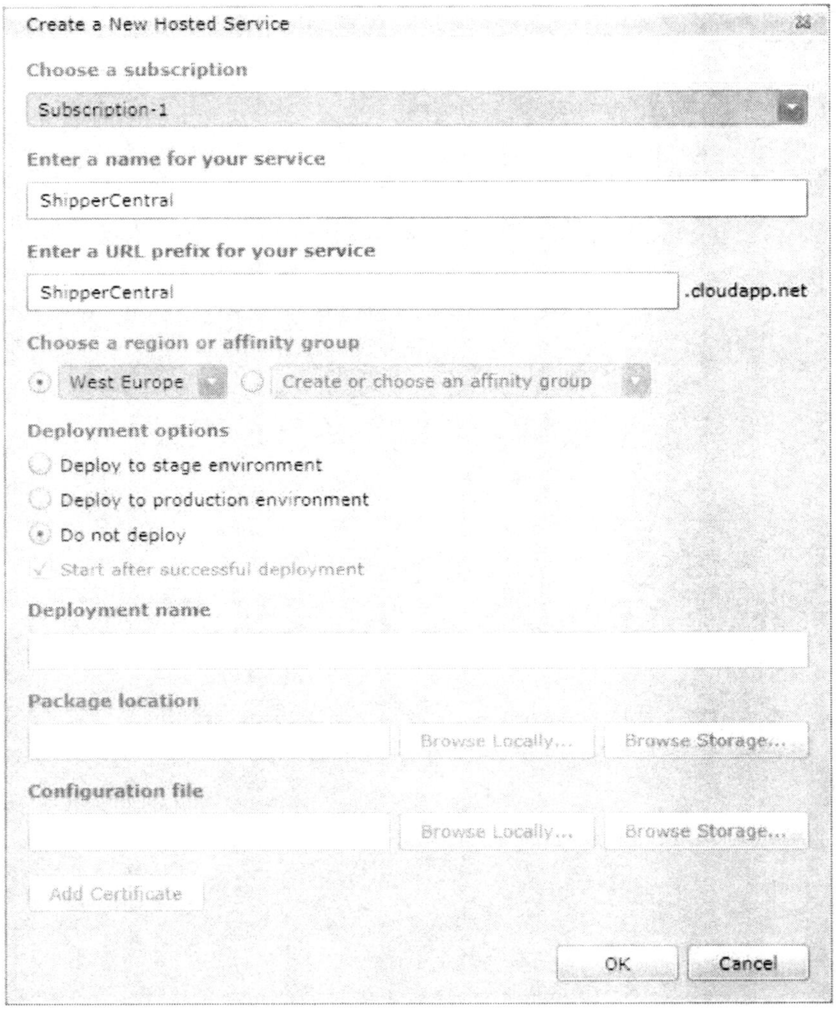

Figure 16-28. Creating a hosted service

An important point about Azure is that billing gets calculated by deployed hours (rather than the time your application is running). If you suspend a hosted service, your web site will be stopped. However, you'll still accrue compute hours and be charged accordingly. To stop being billed for compute hours, you have to delete your hosted service.

Note that if you deploy the same application to both the stage and production environments, you'll double your deploy hours and will be charged more.

Creating a Storage Account

In Azure, storage accounts provide access to services such as the blob, queue, and tables services. You'll need a storage account to store your LightSwitch binaries when you publish to Azure.

To create a new storage account, log into the Azure portal. Use the left-hand navigation panel to go to the Storage Accounts section. Now click the Toolbar button to create a New Storage Account. This opens the Create a New Storage Account dialog, shown in Figure 16-29.

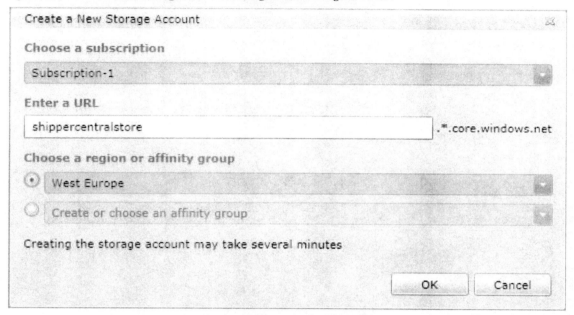

Figure 16-29. Creating a new storage account

After creating your storage account, you can view the properties of the account using the Properties window (shown in Figure 16-30). A couple of important attributes you'll find here are the access keys. These are the security credentials that allow you to access the storage account.

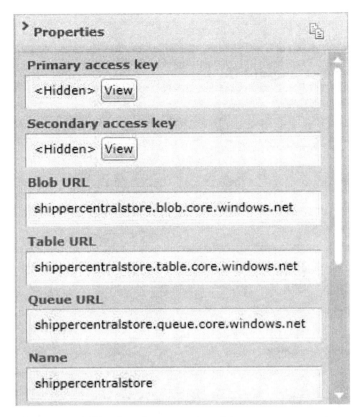

Figure 16-30. Viewing the properties of the storage account

Creating a Database

The final step you need to carry out in the web portal is to create a new database.

Each Azure subscription includes a single SQL Server Azure database. You can set this up in the databases section of the web portal. To create a new database, click the Toolbar button to create a new SQL Azure database. This opens a dialog and prompts you to choose the database size (1GB or 5GB). The next step prompts you to create an Administrator login. You'll therefore need to make up a username and password combination.

The final step prompts you to configure the firewall rules, as shown in Figure 16-31. SQL Azure includes a built in firewall to help secure your data. You'll need to check the Allow other Windows Azure services to access this server checkbox. You'll also need to click the Add button, and add a rule that enables your development machine to connect to the database. The screen for adding the rule shows you your current IP address. This saves you from having to find out what it is.

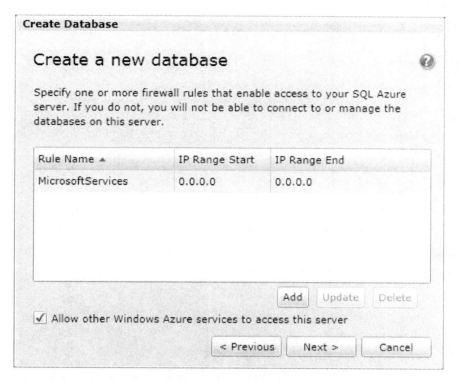

Figure 16-31. Setting firewall rules

Once you've created your server, the details are shown on the properties pane. You can use this to find out the Fully Qualified DNS Name of your server. This will look something like `ood8rdffa.database.windows.net` and you'll need to refer to this later on.

Publishing Steps

Now that you've set up your account in Azure, the difficult part is over and you can use the Publish Application Wizard to publish your application to Azure.

Connecting to Azure

After starting the wizard, select the client topology and select the Azure option in the Application Server Configuration page. When you reach the Connect to Windows Azure page (Figure 16-32), enter your subscription ID into the textbox.

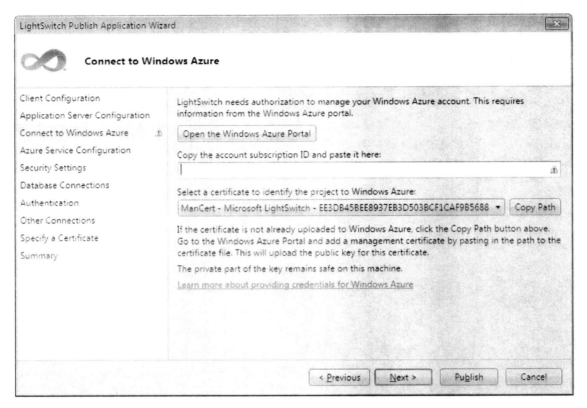

Figure 16-32. Connecting to Windows Azure

At this point, you'll need to specify a management certificate. You can select the option to create a new self-signed certificate using the dropdown box (shown in Figure 16-33). Management certificates are used to secure access to your Azure service. Once you've created a new self-signed certificate, you'll need to associate this certificate with your Azure account. This is done through the Azure portal.

When you create a new self-signed certificate, a certificate file is saved on your computer. The Copy Path button copies the file location onto the clipboard.

You'll now need to log into the Azure portal and upload your certificate file. Once logged into the portal, navigate to the Management Certificates section and click the Add Certificates button (Figure 16-32). This opens a file browser dialog. From here, you can paste the file path that you copied earlier on and upload your certificate.

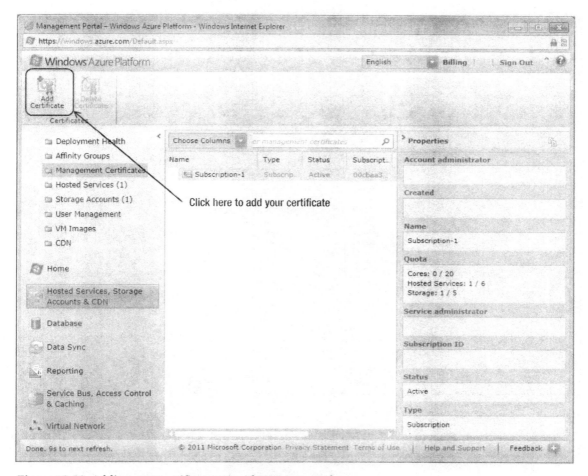

Figure 16-33. Adding your certificate using the Azure portal

Remaining Steps

During the next stage, you'll need to specify the hosting service and storage accounts you want to use. You can specify the ones you created earlier using drop-down boxes (shown in Figure 16-34). You'll also see an Environment drop-down box, which allows you to choose from the options of staging or production.

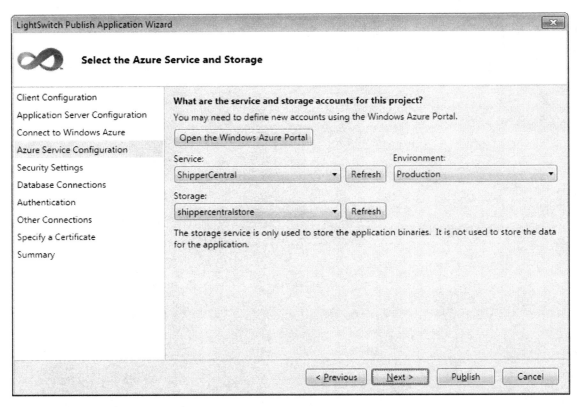

Figure 16-34. Azure service configuration page

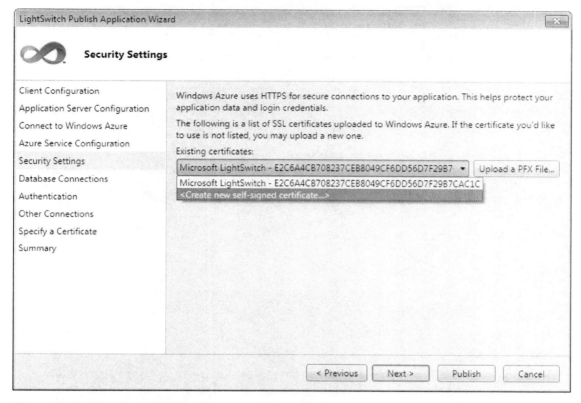

Figure 16-35. Selecting an SSL certificate

The next page (Figure 16-35) prompts you to select an SSL certificate. This is needed to support secure communications over the HTTPS protocol. Just like the management certificate you created earlier on, you can choose to generate your own self-signed certificate. As mentioned before, desktop LightSwitch applications deployed to Azure won't work if you haven't installed a valid SSL certificate. This is due to security restrictions that are imposed by Silverlight. You'll therefore need to purchase a certificate from a third party vendor if you want to use desktop applications that are hosted in Azure.

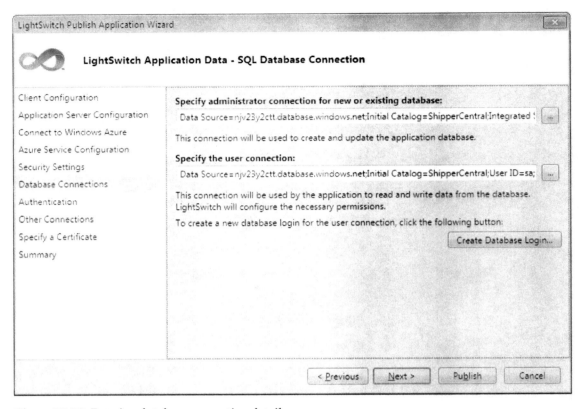

Figure 16-36. Entering database connection details

The next page (shown in Figure 16-36) prompts you to enter your database details. This screen is similar to the ones you've have seen previously. This time, however, you'll need to specify a connection string that points to your SQL Azure database. You'll need to know the fully qualified DNS name of your Azure database. This was displayed in the properties pane in the Azure portal when you created your database earlier on.

The final two pages allow you to specify an application administrator and to choose a certificate to sign your XAP files. These pages are identical to the ones you saw earlier.

Summary

In this chapter, you've learned how to deploy your LightSwitch application. The topics covered in this chapter include:

- Client and application topologies.

- The difference between publishing and packaging.

- Installing and configuring IIS and ASP.NET.

- The steps that are shown in the publishing wizard.

- Deploying an application into Windows Azure.

When you deploy an application, the application topology defines where the server components are run. These components could be hosted locally, in IIS, or in Azure.

The server components can be installed locally if you choose to deploy a desktop application. In a two-tier installation such as this, a local web server is installed called vslshost.

If you prefer to carry out a three-tier installation, this chapter has also shown you the steps you would need to carry out. In this scenario, the LightSwitch prerequisites must be installed for the server components to run properly. The Web Deploy tool is also needed to support publishing and packaging from within LightSwitch.

The difference between publishing and packaging is that publishing deploys an application immediately onto your IIS server, whereas packaging produces setup files that are manually installed afterward.

You can use the Microsoft Web Platform Installer to download and install the prerequisites, Web Deploy tool, and other necessary components onto your server.

Other tasks you might want to perform inside IIS include setting up SSL, or application pools. SSL enables secure communications to take place between the LightSwitch client and server. Application pools can make your application more reliable by isolating it from other web applications that are running on your server. They can also be configured to allow your web server to Windows authenticate to your SQL Server.

The LightSwitch publishing wizard allows you to publish or package your application. This wizard guides you step by step through the deployment process. It allows you to perform tasks such as add installation dependencies, set up the LightSwitch administrator, and digitally sign your XAP file.

If you don't sign your application, users receive a warning message if they attempt to install a desktop application. This message warns them that the application is potentially dangerous. A signed XAP file avoids this problem.

If you've created a deployment package, you've seen the steps that are needed to install the package. In a two-tier deployment, this includes setting up the intrinsic database using the sqlcmd command line tool. In this scenario, you would also need to create an application administrator using the SecurityAdmin.exe utility.

If you choose not to use the wizard, you can manually deploy your application. In a three-tier setup, you would deploy the output from the ServerGenerated project into IIS.

To update an application you have already deployed, you would simply update the application version number and rerun the wizard. The Database Configuration page can create SQL scripts to update the schema of your live database.

Finally, the wizard allows you to deploy your application into Windows Azure. Before using Azure, you'll need to set up an account using the Azure web portal. You'll need to create a hosted service, storage account, and database. You'll also need to create a management certificate. This enables you to authenticate to Azure. Once done, you can carry on through the steps in the wizard and complete the deployment of your application.

CHAPTER 17

When Things Don't Go Quite Right

We hope that your experience with LightSwitch turns out to be trouble free. However, if you do encounter problems, this chapter provides some tips and tricks to help you on your way. This chapter covers three areas:

- Problems that you can encounter during installations.

- Diagnosing SQL Server issues.

- Troubleshooting problems with deployed applications.

Troubleshooting Installations

LightSwitch 2011 is a complex product and has dependencies on many supporting components. The installer generally does a good job, but problems can sometimes occur during installation.

There are two ways you can install LightSwitch. The first method is to use the web installer. This method works by downloading a 3MB setup file called vs_vlsweb.exe. When you run the web installer, it checks to see what is already installed on your computer. It then downloads only the files that are needed on your computer.

The other method is to install LightSwitch from the installation CD. You can download an ISO image from the Microsoft web site. This can be burned onto a CD, or you can extract the files using a third party utility.

If you use the web installer and it fails, try using the setup files from the ISO instead. If the setup fails, the error message normally indicates where the failure has occurred. For example, an error may have been encountered during the installation of:

- SQL Server Compact Edition (needed for the LightSwitch data designer),

- SQL Server Express.

If such an error occurs, try manually installing the component that has failed. You can locate the individual installer files on the ISO image. Installing the components individually can sometimes reveal error messages that are hidden by the LightSwitch installer.

If that doesn't help, check the Windows event log. Also check the contents of your temp directory for any files that are prefixed with .dd. These .dd files contain a plain text log of the installation. Any errors that are encountered by the installer will be logged here. You can determine the location of your temp directory by clicking Start ➤ Run and typing %temp% into the open textbox. If your username is Tim and you've attempted to install LightSwitch on a Windows 7 computer, some of the files that you should check are:

- `C:\Users\Tim\AppData\Local\Temp\dd_depcheck_VS_SIM_100.txt`
- `C:\Users\Tim\AppData\Local\Temp\dd_error_vs_vslscore_100.txt`
- `C:\Users\Tim\AppData\Local\Temp\dd_install_vs_vslscore_100.txt`

If you're installing LightSwitch onto a machine with Visual Studio 2010 already installed, make sure to install Visual Studio 2010 Service Pack 1 before attempting to install LightSwitch 2011.

Troubleshooting the SQL Server

Most unexpected problems in LightSwitch 2011 are caused by the SQL Server. If your application reports an SQL Server Express problem at debug time, the first thing to check is that the SQL Server Express Service is showing the status "Started" (Figure 17-1).

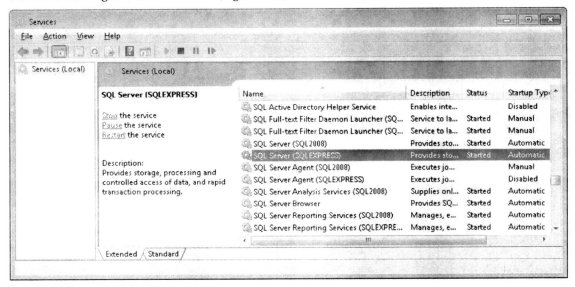

Figure 17-1. Make sure that SQL Express service is started

The Services Window can be found through Control Panel ➤ Administrative Tools ➤ Services. The following section describes some of the other SQL Server errors that you might encounter.

Failed to Generate a User Instance of SQL Server

You might see the error message "Failed to generate a user instance of SQL Server due to a failure in starting the process for the user instance." This problem can happen after applying an SQL Server update or by changing the language settings on your PC.

You can usually resolve this error by deleting the contents of the following folder:
`%AppData%\Local\Microsoft\Microsoft SQL Server Data\SQLEXPRESS`.

The SQL Server Express Service should be restarted for this fix to take effect. This can be done through the Services Window (shown in Figure 17-1).

SQL Express Instances That Are Not Named SQLEXPRESS

By default, LightSwitch expects to find a working instance of SQL Server Express called SQLEXPRESS. The SQLEXPRESS instance name is defined in Tools ➤ Options ➤ Database Tools ➤ Data Connections (Figure 17-2).

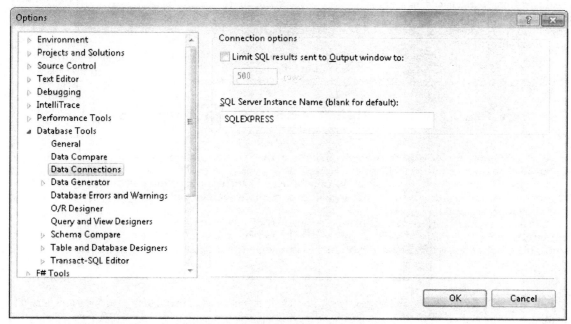

Figure 17-2. The SQLEXPRESS instance name is defined here

When a LightSwitch project is created, the SQLEXPRESS instance name is persisted in the MyApplication.lsproj file (substitute MyApplication with the name of your application).

If you share the project with someone who has changed their SQL Server Express instance name, your project will fail to run on his or her machine.

To resolve this problem, the LSPROJ file must be manually modified. Open the file in Notepad and search for the SqlExpressInstanceName element. The value of this setting can then be corrected as appropriate. Listing 17-1 shows the section in the file that you need to edit. If SQL Server Express is set to run as the default instance, this setting can be left blank.

Listing 17-1. Changing the SqlExpressInstanceName in the LSPROJ file

File: MyApplication\MyApplication.lsproj

```
<?xml version="1.0" encoding="utf-8"?>
<Project MSBuildVersion="4.0" ToolsVersion="4.0" DefaultTargets="Build"↵
 xmlns="http://schemas.microsoft.com/developer/msbuild/2003">
  <PropertyGroup>
    <-- Other elements here have been removed for brevity…-->
    <-- Modify the SqlExpressInstanceName  setting beneath…-->
    <SqlExpressInstanceName>SQLEXPRESS</SqlExpressInstanceName>
```

Errors Relating to Non-English Versions of SQL Express at Design Time

On your development machine, the default collation of the SQL Server Express Instance and collation of the intrinsic database should ideally match.

If a LightSwitch project is created on one machine and shared on a second machine with a different SQL Server collation, a mismatch will occur. This may result in search results being incorrect or data grids showing a red cross.

The easiest way to resolve this problem is to delete the intrinsic database file (found in bin\data\ApplicationDatabase.mdf). LightSwitch will re-create this database the next time you run your application. Note that any data previously entered into your application will be lost.

■ **Caution** The ApplicationDatabase.mdf file allows data to be persisted between debug sessions and should be treated as temporary (hence, the suggestion to delete this file). If it's important for you to retain the data that's entered at debug time, create your tables in an attached SQL Server database rather than the intrinsic database.

Errors Relating to User Instances

At debug time, you might receive the error "An attempt to attach an auto-named database failed" or some other error message that mentions SQL Server User instances.

If you see such an error, you should check that User Instances are enabled in SQL Server Express. You can turn on User Instances by running a piece of T-SQL. Open SQL Server Management Studio, connect to your SQL Server Express instance, and run the following command: EXEC sp_configure 'user instances enabled', 1

SQL Server Log File

If your LightSwitch has once worked but you now get red crosses against all of your controls at debug time, deleting the SQL Server log file for your intrinsic database may help.

Make sure that your application isn't running and search for the following file: bin\data\ApplicationDatabase.ldf.

If found, deleting this file may fix your problem. If not, use Fiddler and the ASP.NET `trace.axd` page to diagnose the problem further. We'll explain how to do this later in this chapter.

Tracing LightSwitch Applications

During design time, you can use the debugger to find and fix problems in your code. Once you deploy your application, what can you do to diagnose any problems you might encounter?

Fortunately, the tracing features built into LightSwitch can help you. You can use this to instrument and monitor the applications you have deployed. `Microsoft.LightSwitch.Trace` is the class that you would use to perform trace-related activities. This class contains three methods you can use to write out trace messages:

- TraceError,
- TraceInformation,
- TraceWarning.

The messages you create using these methods are sent to objects called *listeners*. During debug, a `DefaultTraceListener` displays any trace messages you have written into the Visual Studio output window. Other listeners that you can use include the `EventLogTraceListener` and `TextWriterTraceListener`. These listeners are used to write trace messages into the Windows event log or a text file. The `trace.axd` handler allows you to view trace messages through a web page, and we'll explain how to view this later on.

Creating Trace Messages

When writing your LightSwitch code, you can create trace messages using the three trace methods listed earlier. Listing 17-2 shows an example of a computed field. Prior to the calculation, the `TraceInformation` method is called to create a trace message containing the DateOfBirth value.

By using this technique, you can determine whether a method has been executed by searching for your message in your trace output. You can also append additional details into your trace message to help you further.

Listing 17-2. Calling Trace.TraceInformation in a computed field

VB:

File: ShipperCentral\Common\UserCode\Customer.vb

```
Private Sub Age_Compute(ByRef result As Integer)
    Trace.TraceInformation(
        "Calculating age - DateOfBirth=" & DateOfBirth.ToString)
    result = DateDiff(DateInterval.Year, Now, DateOfBirth)
End Sub
```

C#:

File: ShipperCentral\Common\UserCode\Customer.cs

```
partial void Age_Compute(ref string result)
{
    Trace.TraceInformation(
        "Calculating age - DateOfBirth=" + DateOfBirth.ToString());
    DateTime now = DateTime.Today;
    int age = now.Year - DateOfBirth.Year;
    if (DateOfBirth > now.AddYears(-age)) age--;
}
```

Viewing Trace Messages at Debug Time

To view the trace messages you've created at debug time, your application must be set up as a web application rather than a desktop application. Once your application starts, the address that's shown in the browser will be in the following format (the port number used by LightSwitch is set dynamically and can vary between sessions):

http://localhost:2142/default.htm?IsLaunchedByVS=True&AuthenticationType=None

You can turn on tracing by appending an argument to the end of your URL. Table 17-1 shows the arguments you would append. If you append the LC=Microsoft.LightSwitch,E argument, only messages created using the Trace.TraceError method are shown.

Table 17-1. Turning on Tracing

URL Argument to Append	Trace Items to Show
LC=Microsoft.LightSwitch,E	Show error-level trace
LC=Microsoft.LightSwitch,W	Show warning-level trace
LC=Microsoft.LightSwitch,I	Show information-level trace
LC=Microsoft.LightSwitch,V	Show verbose trace

The verbose option switches on tracing for all trace types. To illustrate how you would turn on verbose logging, type the following URL into your web browser:

http://localhost:2142/default.htm?IsLaunchedByVS=True&AuthenticationType=None& LC=Microsoft.LightSwitch,V.

This restarts your application and trace messages will begin to appear in the *output* window. If the output window isn't visible, you can enable it by clicking View ➤ Other Windows ➤ Output or by pressing Ctrl-Alt-O.

Figure 17-3 shows the trace message in the Output window when the age field is calculated.

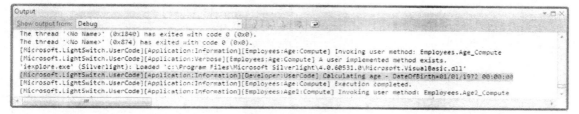

Figure 17-3. Information trace messages in the Output window

Tracing a Deployed Application

Tracing really becomes useful if you need to diagnose a problem after you deploy your application. LightSwitch includes a diagnostic subsystem that integrates with the built in ASP.NET tracing. The messages that are shown are ideal for analyzing configuration issues or working out why a query has failed. The details displayed in the trace message show you the server request, response, and any errors that are generated.

Tracing is turned off by default. This is done for performance and security reasons. To turn on tracing, you have to make a modification to your web.config file. In this file, you'll find five settings that relate to LightSwitch diagnostics system. These settings are shown in Table 17-2.

Table 17-2. Diagnostic Settings

Name	Values	Description
Microsoft.LightSwitch.Trace.Enabled	true, false	Set this to true to enables diagnostic tracing on the server.
Microsoft.LightSwitch.Trace.LocalOnly	true, false	When set to true (the default), the trace details can only be viewed on the IIS server and cannot be viewed on other machines.
Microsoft.LightSwitch.Trace.Level	None, Error, Warning, Information, Verbose	Defines the level of trace information to be logged. The values are in ascending order (i.e., Warning writes more log entries than Error). Default is Information.
Microsoft.LightSwitch.Trace.Sensitive	true, false	When set to true, it enables actual data (i.e., addresses, balances, prices) to be written to the diagnostic log. The default is false.

Name	Values	Description
Microsoft.LightSwitch.Trace.Categories	Microsoft.LightSwitch, unlimited other values	This specifies the categories that will be traced (in comma separated format). The default is Microsoft.LightSwitch. Extensions may declare more, or you can declare new ones in your own application.

To configure these diagnostic settings, open your web.config file in Notepad. The relevant contents are shown in Listing 17-3. The configuration options in Table 17-2 can be found beneath the appSettings element. To turn on tracing, modify the two elements that are shown in bold in Listing 17-3.

Listing 17-3. Trace settings in web.config

```
<?xml version="1.0" encoding="utf-8"?>
<configuration>
  <appSettings>
    <add key="UserCodeAssemblies" value="Application.Common.dll;Application.Server↵
.dll;Application.ServerGenerated.dll" />
    <!-- A value of true will enable diagnostic logging on the server -->
    <add key="Microsoft.LightSwitch.Trace.Enabled" value="true" />
    <!-- A value of true only lets local access to Trace.axd -->
    <add key="Microsoft.LightSwitch.Trace.LocalOnly" value="true" />
    <!-- The valid values for the trace level are: None, Error, Warning, Information,↵
  Verbose -->
    <add key="Microsoft.LightSwitch.Trace.Level" value="Information" />
    <!-- A value of true will indicate that logging sensitive
         information is okay -->
    <add key="Microsoft.LightSwitch.Trace.Sensitive" value="false" />
    <!-- The semi-colon separated list of categories that will be
         enabled at the specifed trace level -->
    <add key="Microsoft.LightSwitch.Trace.Categories" value="Microsoft.LightSwitch" />
    <!-- A value of true will indicate http requests should be
         re-directed to https -->
    <add key="Microsoft.LightSwitch.RequireEncryption" value="false" />
    <add key="AllowAllWindowsUsers" value="false" />
  </appSettings>
  <connectionStrings>
    <add name="_IntrinsicData" connectionString="Data Source=localhost;↵
Database=ApplicationData;uid=tim;Pwd=strongpassword;" />
  </connectionStrings>
  <system.web>
    <!-- LightSwitch trace.axd handler -->
    <trace enabled="true" localOnly="false" requestLimit="40"
        writeToDiagnosticsTrace="false" traceMode="SortByTime"
        mostRecent="true" />
    <httpHandlers>
      <add verb="GET" path="trace.axd" type="Microsoft.LightSwitch.WebHost.Implementation↵
```

```
.TraceHandler,Microsoft.LightSwitch.Server.Internal,Version=10.0.0.0, Culture=neutral,
PublicKeyToken=b03f5f7f11d50a3a" />
    </httpHandlers>
```

When you deploy an application to Azure, the tracing options are set in `ServiceConfiguration.cscfg` file rather than the `web.config` file.

After you make this change, you can view the trace messages by opening a browser and navigating to the `trace.axd` page. Using the previous example, our LightSwitch application ran on port 2142. The address you would use to view the trace details would therefore be `http://localhost:2142/trace.axd`.

When you navigate to this address, the trace messages are shown on the page (Figure 17-4). All HTTP requests are shown and you can view further details by clicking the View Details link.

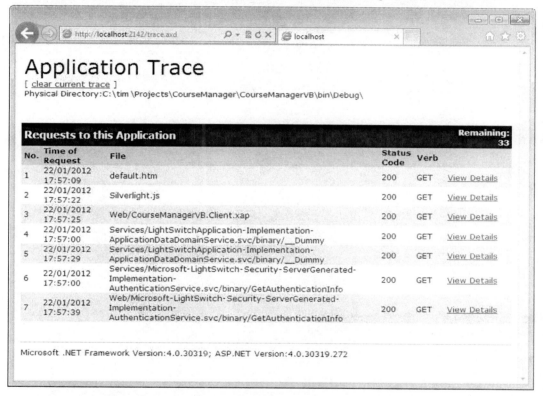

Figure 17-4. Details shown in the Trace.Axd page

The Application Trace page is the ideal place for diagnosing problems relating to database connectivity, or problems with queries.

Fiddler

Another tool that can help you is Fiddler. Fiddler is an HTTP debugging proxy that allows you to inspect the HTTP traffic that flows to and from the ASP.NET part of your LightSwitch application. It is ideal for diagnosing issues such as incorrectly configured IIS settings, problems with RIA services, or authentication issues.

To get started, download and install Fiddler from `www.fiddler2.com`. If you're diagnosing a deployed LightSwitch application, disable ASP.NET custom errors in the `web.config` file. You'll find this in an element called `customErrors`, which is found beneath `system.web`.

Now start up Fiddler and run your LightSwitch application. All HTTP traffic will be logged and displayed on the left-hand pane, as shown in Figure 17-5. Further details can be viewed on the right-hand pane.

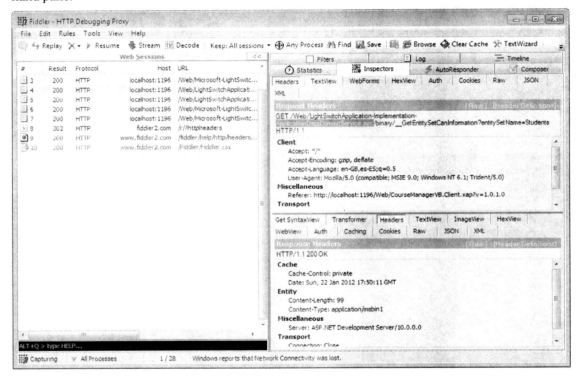

Figure 17-5. Fiddler results window

Note After deploying an application you may receive the error "Load operation failed for query 'GetAuthenticationInfo'. The remote server returned an error: Notfound."

GetAuthenticationInfo is the first call that the LightSwitch Silverlight client makes to the web server and can fail for many reasons, some of which may not be authentication related.

Fiddler is a great tool for diagnosing such issues. By viewing the data logged by Fiddler, you can hopefully find the details of HTTP or ASP.NET errors indicating what the error is. Such issues could include incorrect configurations of IIS, AppPool settings, or ASP.NET 4.

SQL Server Connection Problems

A failure to connect to your SQL Server database is the most common problem you'll encounter after deploying a LightSwitch application.

When starting your application, it might attempt to load for about 30 seconds before timing out. At this point, all the controls on your screens will appear with a red cross. The most likely culprit for this condition is a database connection problem. The 30 seconds corresponds with the default connection timeout period of 30 seconds.

Another common error message that you'll see when a database connection failure occurs is "Exception has been thrown by the target of an invocation" (Figure 17-6). We'll now show you how to diagnose such SQL problems.

Figure 17-6. Exception has been thrown by the target of an invocation

Resolving SQL Server Connection Issues

The first thing to do is to check that your SQL Server is up and running. Make sure the SQL Server service is running in Control Panel ➤ Administrative Tools ➤ Services. Check that you can establish a connection to the SQL Server using SQL Server Management Studio.

If you've just installed SQL Server, make sure you've enabled the TCP/IP (Transmission Control Protocol/Internet Protocol) protocol. By default, this is disabled as a security precaution. You can enable this in SQL 2008 by using the SQL Server Configuration Manager (Figure 17-7). In SQL 2005, use the Surface Area Configuration tool instead.

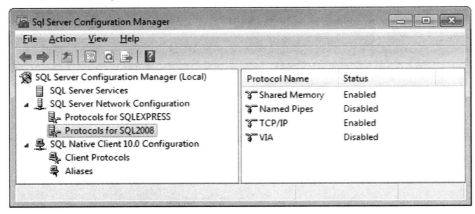

Figure 17-7. Enable TCP/IP

If SQL Server is installed on a server separate from your LightSwitch application server, you might receive the error "The specified SQL Server could not be found." This error can indicate an underlying network connectivity problem.

To diagnose this further, use the ping command to ping your SQL Server. Open a command prompt from your LightSwitch server. If your SQL Server is called SQL2008Srv, type in the following command: Ping SQL2008Srv.

You should see some replies from your SQL Server. If you can establish a connection to your database server but still can't connect to SQL Server, check that database traffic isn't blocked by firewalls or antivirus software. For example, the McAfee Virus Scan product blocks ports using an Access Protection task.

If you're using a named instance of SQL Server, make sure you've specified the instance name in your connection string. It's sometimes easy to forget this.

A simple way to check that you can connect to your SQL Server is to use a UDL file. Create an empty text file on your web server and rename the file extension from TXT to UDL. When you double-click this file, the Data Link Properties window opens (Figure 17-8).

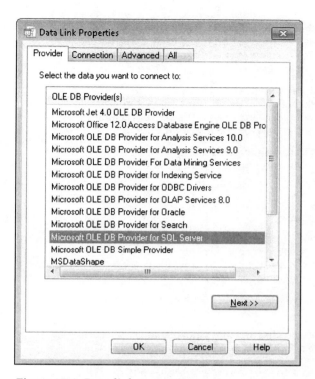

Figure 17-8. Data link properties window

Select "Microsoft OLE DB Provider for SQL Server," and then click Next. Enter your SQL Server details and click the Test button. If the test succeeds, you can change the file extension of this file back from UDL to TXT. If you open the text file in Notepad, the database connection string is shown in plain text.

This test proves that the connection string is correct and you can reuse this in your `web.config` file.

ASP.NET Settings (Three-Tier Setup)

Incorrect IIS or ASP.NET configuration settings are typical reasons as to why your LightSwitch application could fail to work. The Application Trace page (shown earlier) is the best method for diagnosing such problems.

Other tips that can help you are:

- Check the Windows event log. Many IIS errors are reported here.

- Make sure that the .NET 4 Framework is installed. Also ensure that your application pool is configured to use .NET 4.

- Check that ISAPI (Internet Server Application Programming Interface) restrictions have not been applied for ASP.NET. In IIS Manager, select the Server node and choose ISAPI and CGI Restrictions. Make sure that the ASP.NET v4.0 entry is set to allowed.

- If you installed the .NET 4 Framework before installing IIS, make sure that ASP.NET is properly installed in IIS. You can run the command `aspnet_regiis -i` to reinstall ASP.NET. The `aspnet_regiis` is usually found in the location `C:\Windows\Microsoft.NET\Framework\v4.0.30319\`.

- Ensure you have installed the LightSwitch prerequisites. If you've set up the IIS application pool to run under the context of a domain account, make sure that you've entered the correct username and password. Also, is the domain account valid? For example, has it been locked out or has the password expired?

- If you've set up an IIS application pool to run under the security context of a Windows user (to allow Windows authentication to take place between ASP.NET and SQL Server), make sure that a login has been created in the SQL Server.

Troubleshooting Publishing

Publishing an application from Visual Studio to IIS7 is an area that can cause much pain. After setting up your server, try packaging an application as a zip file (described in Chapter 16). Check that you can import the packaged application into IIS. If this works, the problem is more likely related to connectivity. The tips that you can follow to get publishing working are:

- Make sure that the Web Deployment Service is running correctly in Control Panel ➤ Services.

- Make sure that firewall settings are not blocking any of the ports that are needed for the deployment service. By default, port 8172 is used.

- Check the authentication settings in IIS. You can set these to anonymous to rule out any problems.

- Follow the tips shown in the ASP.NET settings section to rule out IIS- or ASP.NET-related issues.

- Try using HTTPS to publish your application. When you do this, make sure that a valid SSL certificate is installed in IIS. If you're using a self-certificate, make sure you've installed this into the trusted root authority on the computer from which you're publishing.

Summary

This chapter has shown you how to:

- Diagnose installation failures.

- Troubleshoot SQL Server connectivity issues.

- Use the diagnostic tracing that is built into LightSwitch.

- Diagnose issues related to IIS/ASP.NET configuration.

You can install LightSwitch by downloading all of the LightSwitch installation files in the form of an ISO image or by running a small web installer. If you encounter problems when using the web installer, you should try using the installer from the ISO image instead. If a failure occurs while installing one of the component parts (i.e., SQL Server Express), you can try manually installing the part that has failed. This will often reveal error messages that can help you diagnose the exact cause of the failure.

SQL Server is an area where you might encounter difficulties. SQL Express files are stored in the folder %AppData%\Local\Microsoft\Microsoft SQL Server Data\SQLEXPRESS. Deleting the contents of this folder can often resolve SQL Server problems.

LightSwitch includes built in tracing. After you deploy an application, you can turn on tracing by modifying some of the settings in the web.config file. This allows you to view trace messages in a web page called trace.axd. The information you'll find on this page will help you diagnose the majority of problems you might encounter.

Always check the Windows event log whenever things don't go to plan. The contents of the event log can often reveal much detail.

Culture Names

When defining the currency codes used in the Money business type, you can specify a culture name. The culture name is a combination of an ISO 639 two-letter culture code associated with language and an ISO 3166 two-letter uppercase subculture code associated with a country or region. For the name to be accepted, the culture part must be in lowercase, and the country/region part in uppercase.

Table A-1 shows the list of culture names that you can use.

Table A-1. Culture Names

Code	Description
af	Afrikaans
ar-AE	Arabic (U.A.E.)
ar-BH	Arabic (Bahrain)
ar-DZ	Arabic (Algeria)
ar-EG	Arabic (Egypt)
ar-IQ	Arabic (Iraq)
ar-JO	Arabic (Jordan)
ar-KW	Arabic (Kuwait)
ar-LB	Arabic (Lebanon)
ar-LY	Arabic (Libya)
ar-MA	Arabic (Morocco)
ar-OM	Arabic (Oman)
ar-QA	Arabic (Qatar)

Code	Description
ar-SA	Arabic (Saudi Arabia)
ar-SY	Arabic (Syria)
ar-TN	Arabic (Tunisia)
ar-YE	Arabic (Yemen)
be	Belarusian
bg	Bulgarian
ca	Catalan
cs	Czech
da	Danish
de	German (Standard)
de-AT	German (Austria)
de-CH	German (Switzerland)
de-LI	German (Liechtenstein)
de-LU	German (Luxembourg)
el	Greek
en	English
en	English (Caribbean)
en-AU	English (Australia)
en-BZ	English (Belize)
en-CA	English (Canada)
en-GB	English (United Kingdom)
en-IE	English (Ireland)

Code	Description
en-JM	English (Jamaica)
en-NZ	English (New Zealand)
en-TT	English (Trinidad)
en-US	English (United States)
en-ZA	English (South Africa)
es	Spanish (Spain)
es-AR	Spanish (Argentina)
es-BO	Spanish (Bolivia)
es-CL	Spanish (Chile)
es-CO	Spanish (Colombia)
es-CR	Spanish (Costa Rica)
es-DO	Spanish (Dominican Republic)
es-EC	Spanish (Ecuador)
es-GT	Spanish (Guatemala)
es-HN	Spanish (Honduras)
es-MX	Spanish (Mexico)
es-NI	Spanish (Nicaragua)
es-PA	Spanish (Panama)
es-PE	Spanish (Peru)
es-PR	Spanish (Puerto Rico)
es-PY	Spanish (Paraguay)
es-SV	Spanish (El Salvador)

Code	Description
es-UY	Spanish (Uruguay)
es-VI	Spanish (Venezuela)
et	Estonian
eu	Basque
fa	Farsi
fi	Finnish
fo	Faeroese
fr	French (Standard)
fr-BE	French (Belgium)
fr-CA	French (Canada)
fr-CH	French (Switzerland)
fr-LU	French (Luxembourg)
ga	Irish
gd	Gaelic (Scotland)
he	Hebrew
hi	Hindi
hr	Croatian
hu	Hungarian
id	Indonesian
is	Icelandic
it	Italian (Standard)
it-CH	Italian (Switzerland)

Code	Description
ja	Japanese
ji	Yiddish
ko	Korean
ko	Korean (Johab)
lt	Lithuanian
lv	Latvian
mk	Macedonian (FYROM)
ms	Malaysian
mt	Maltese
nl	Dutch (Standard)
nl-BE	Dutch (Belgium)
no	Norwegian (Bokmal)
no	Norwegian (Nynorsk)
pl	Polish
pt	Portuguese (Portugal)
pt-BR	Portuguese (Brazil)
rm	Rhaeto-Romanic
ro	Romanian
ro-MO	Romanian (Republic of Moldova)
ru	Russian
ru-MO	Russian (Republic of Moldova)
sb	Sorbian

Code	Description
sk	Slovak
sl	Slovenian
sq	Albanian
sr	Serbian
sr-Cyrl-CS	Serbian (Cyrillic, Serbia, and Montenegro)
sr-Latn-CS	Serbian (Latin, Serbia, and Montenegro)
sv	Swedish
sv-FI	Swedish (Finland)
sx	Sutu
sz	Sami (Lappish)
th	Thai
tn	Tswana
tr	Turkish
ts	Tsonga
uk	Ukrainian
ur	Urdu
ve	Venda
vi	Vietnamese
xh	Xhosa
zh-CN	Chinese (Simplified, PRC)
zh-HK	Chinese (Traditional, Hong Kong SAR)
zh-SG	Chinese (Simplified, Singapore)

Code	Description
zh-TW	Chinese (Traditional, Taiwan)
zu	Zulu

LINQ Query Operators

In Chapter 6, we showed you some of the common LINQ operators that you can use. Table B-1 provides a more complete list of operators, and an indication of the type of operation that each operator performs.

Table B-1. *LINQ Operators*

Standard Query Operator	Type of Operation
Aggregate	Aggregate
All	Quantifier
Any	Quantifier
AsEnumerable	Conversion
Average	Aggregate
Cast	Conversion
Concat	Concatenation
Contains	Quantifier
Count	Aggregate
DefaultIfEmpty	Element
Distinct	Set
ElementAt	Element
ElementAtOrDefault	Element
Except	Set

Standard Query Operator	Type of Operation
First	Element
FirstOrDefault	Element
GroupBy	Grouping
GroupJoin	Join
Intersect	Set
Join	Join
Last	Element
LastOrDefault	Element
LongCount	Aggregate
Max	Aggregate
Min	Aggregate
OfType	Conversion
OrderBy	Ordering
OrderByDescending	Ordering
Reverse	Ordering
Select	Projection
SelectMany	Projection
SequenceEqual	Equality

Index

B

Business type extensions, 452–454
  attributes, 455
    ControlFactory attributes, 455–456
    Export attributes, 455
  creation, 454
  implementation, 457
  interfaces, 456
    IControlFactory interfaces, 457
    IResourceProvider interfaces, 457

C

Change sets
  DataWorkspace.ApplicationData.Details, 102
  DiscardChanges method, 103
  GetChanges method, 104
  IsChanged property, 105
  methods and properties, 103
  OriginalValue property, 105
  orginal value retrieve method, 105
ChangePassword and IsValidPassword methods,
  121
Client design project, 383
  business type extensions
    Image file, 462
    ImageProvider class, 462–463
  control extensions, 448
    Image file, 448
    Image Provider class, 448–450
  folders, 383
  subfolders, 383
Client project, 382
  business type extensions
    CentralTypeControl class, 459
    CentralTypeControlFactory class, 459–461
    Code-Behind file, 458
    namespaces, 458
    XAML file, 458
  CentralTheme Class file, 401–404
  control extensions, 443
    CentralControl class, 445
    CentralControlFactory class, 445–47
    namespaces, 445
    XAML file, 444
  folders, 382
  shell extensions, 423
    CentralShell Class file, 423–425

    Code-Behind file, 426
    XAML file, 425
  subfolders, 382
  Themes folder, 400
  XAML file, 404
    brush definitions, 406–415
    Text Styles, 404–406
ComboBox control, 343–344
Command's CanExecute method, 575–576
Common project, 384, 416
  business type extensions
    Editor and Viewer controls, 465
    LSML file, 464–465
  control extensions, 450
    LSML file, 450–451
  LSML file, 416
  Metadata folder and files, 384–385
  Resources folder and files, 386
  shell extensions, 426–427
  Theme folder, 416
Comparison-Type drop-down
  global values, 162
  literal values, 157
  parameters
    optional parameters, 158
    on screens, 158–162
  properties, 158
Concurrency, 116
  conflict resolution, code, 119–120
  data conflict screen, 116, 118
Connection transactions, 111
Control extensions
  attributes, 441–443
  creation, 440–441
  element mapping, 451
  implementation, 443
  interfaces
    IControlFactory interface, 443
    IResourceProvider interface, 443
  Microsoft's sample, 452
  types, 439
Custom controls
  calling screen code
    code to call SaveData, 359
    CustomButton, 359
    reference to data context, 361
  vs. control extensions, 337
  Silverlight class library (*see* Silverlight class)
  Silverlight controls
    ComboBox control, 343–344

CPSIA information can be obtained at www.ICGtesting.com
Printed in the USA
LVOW130506230312

274436LV00004B/124/P

9 781430 240082